Intelligence for Multilateral Decision and Action

Perry L. Pickert

Edited by Russell G. Swenson

Joint Military Intelligence College
Washington, DC
June 1997

The Joint Military Intelligence College supports and encourages research on intelligence issues that distills lessons and improves support to policy-level and operational consumers.

This manuscript was prepared from student theses written in a DoD school environment at the Joint Military Intelligence College from 1992 through 1996. Therefore, the information may be dated in some instances due to the rapid development of Peacekeeping and Humanitarian Operations during the past few years. Additionally, the development of U.S. and UN policy regarding Operations Other Than War has changed substantially since the time some of these theses were written. However, the academic process remains valid and the papers provide insight, information, and a useful point of departure for the purposes of the "Intelligence in Partnership" conference held at the College in June 1997. These papers were based exclusively upon open sources available to the general public and the views expressed are those of the authors and do not necessarily reflect the official policy or position of the Department of Defense or the U.S. Government.

This document has been approved for unrestricted public release by the Office of the Secretary of Defense (Public Affairs).

Library of Congress Catalog Card Number **97-72395**
ISBN **0-9656195-0-8**

Intelligence for Multilateral Decision and Action

Preface

In early 1996, the Joint Military Intelligence College began planning for a conference on "Intelligence in Partnership" that would bring together U.S. and international experts in the fields of intelligence, operations, policy and planning to:

- Take stock of remarkable changes in the international scene,
- Examine lessons from international crises, peacekeeping, peacemaking and coalition warfare,
- Assess the role of intelligence in the evolving operations-intelligence partnership, and
- Weigh different options for improving the effectiveness of our contributions to national security and international stability.

As part of our preparations for the conference, Dr. Perry L. Pickert of the college's faculty undertook a review of relevant research performed by Joint Military Intelligence College graduate students in satisfaction of their thesis requirement for the Master of Science of Strategic Intelligence degree. Selecting from among these theses, Dr. Pickert arrayed subject headings spanning the spectrum of issues to be addressed by the conference. Working with the authors, he then distilled this research into essays that would complement one another and contribute to each of the conference's major areas of inquiry.

With the essays in draft, Dr. Russell G. Swenson of the College's Office of Applied Research collaborated with Dr. Pickert in editing the often-pathfinding research that contributes to *Intelligence for Multilateral Decision and Action.* The volume is fresh and it is instructive, addressing events, decisions and lessons to be learned from the viewpoints of prime participants, reaching into important new areas of inquiry such as:

- *Intelligence Support to Refugee Operations: Who's the Expert?*, by Captain James D. Edwards, U.S. Army,
- *Intelligence and the International Atomic Energy Agency*, by Captain Audrey D. Hudgins, U.S. Army, and
- *Driftnet Fishery Enforcement: A New Intelligence Problem*, by Lieutenant Commander William J. Quigley, U.S. Coast Guard.

Intelligence for Multilateral Decision and Action offers one reflection of the college's strong commitment to innovative curriculum development and research on intelligence issues, the results of which are published in journals, monographs, books, the college's Occasional Paper and Discussion Paper series, and otherwise professionally disseminated.

Beginning in 1994 the college responded to the new emphasis on intelligence in multilateral fora by introducing courses and assisting with intelligence training. Dr. Perry Pickert began a course at the college on "Intelligence in a UN Context," Majors Michael Kuszewski and Troy Bates, USMC, integrated a peace operations component into their course on "Intelligence in Other Than War Settings" and Douglas H. Dearth began conducting a workshop on "Intelligence and Peace Operations" at the Joint Military Intelligence Training Center. Dr. Pickert, using a grant from the College's Office of Applied Research, consulted faculty at the service academies and professional military schools and added primary UN documentation and academic publications to the Joint Chiefs of Staff's *Joint Electronic Library* "Peace Operations" CD-ROM for use in the classroom and for research throughout the Department of Defense.

Fifteen faculty members have chaired more than 60 student thesis research projects which relate to intelligence in a multilateral setting. The faculty also began research and publication on the subject. Jan Goldman published "A Changing World: A Changing UN," in *Military Review* in September 1994. Associate Dean, Lt. Col. Joseph C. Bebel published "Peacekeeping: Let's Get Back to Basics," in *Eueopaische Sicherheit* in October 1994. Dr. Royal Thomas Goodden contributed "Intelligence and Peace Operations" in the second edition of *Strategic Intelligence: Theory and Application,* published jointly by the United States Army War College Center for Strategic Leadership and the Joint Military Intelligence Training

Center in 1995. The Joint Military Intelligence College funded on-site research by Marine Corps University Professor Daniel W. Fitz-Simons and published as Discussion Paper Number Three, *Australian Intelligence Collection in Combined Peacekeeping Operations,* in February 1996.

Student research has been recognized. Captain Audrey D. Hudgins and Major Gary L. Crone received the Joint Military Intelligence College's annual award for outstanding master's thesis. George Mason University awarded Ms. Elizabeth N. Starr the Outstanding Bachelor of Individualized Study Project in the Public Interest Award in 1995 for her paper on UN humanitarian intervention, begun in the college's undergraduate degree-completion program. The College received an unsolicited letter from the Office of the Deputy Assistant Secretary of Defense for Peacekeeping and Humanitarian Assistance commending Second Lieutenant Steven E. Maceda for the integration of military and political analysis in his thesis on Japanese peacekeeping.

The work offered here provides a useful benchmark in our examination of intelligence in partnership in the 1990s. It signals priority research next to be done. It brings a useful new map to the journey into the 21st century.

A. DENIS CLIFT
President,
Joint Military Intelligence College

Intelligence for Multilateral Decision and Action

Contents

Contents (Continued)

Appendixes

Maps, Photos, Diagrams and Tables

Acronyms and Abbreviations Used in This Work

ACDA	Arms Control and Disarmament Agency (U.S.)
ACSA	Acquisition and Cross-Servicing Agreement (U.S.-Japan)
AFFOR	Air Force Forces
AOC	Army Operations Center (U.S.)
Art	Article
ASD/ISA	Assistant Secretary of Defense for International Security Affairs (U.S.)
ASDF	Air Self-Defense Force (Japan)
BLDP	Buddhist Liberal Democratic Party
CDR	Centre for Documentation and Research (UN)
CGDK	Coalition Government of Democratic Kampuchea
CGSC	U.S. Army Command and General Staff College, Ft. Leavenworth, KS
CIA	Central Intelligence Agency
CINC	Commander in Chief
CJCS	Chairman of the Joint Chiefs of Staff
CJTF	Combined Joint Task Force
Clog	Chief of logs
CMOC	Civil-Military Operations Center
COIP	Country Information Project (UN)
COMSEC	Communications Security
Cong	U.S. Congress
CONOP	Concept of Operations
CPAF	Cambodian People's Armed Forces
CR	Congressional Record
CRS	Congressional Research Service
CTF	Combined Task Force
DCI	Director of Central Intelligence

DCID	Director of Central Intelligence Directive
DHA	Department for Humanitarian Affairs (UN)
DIA	Defense Intelligence Agency
DMZ	Demilitarized Zone
DNA	Defense Nuclear Agency
Doc	Document
DoD	U.S. Department of Defense
DOMREP	Mission of the Representative of the Secretary-General in the Dominican Republic
DPA	Department for Political Affairs (UN)
DPKO	Department of Peacekeeping Operations (UN)
DPRK	Democratic People's Republic of Korea
ECOMOG	Economic Community of West African States Cease-Fire Monitoring Group
EEZ	Exclusive Economic Zone
EIU	Economist Intelligence Unit
EMIS	Electromagnetic Isotope Separation
FALD	Field Administration and Logistics Division (UN)
FBIS	Foreign Broadcast Information Service
FETZ	Free Economic and Trade Zone (North Korea)
FM	Field Manual
FOD	Field Operations Division (UN)
FUNCINPEC	United National Front for an Independent, Neutral, Peaceful and Cooperative Cambodia
GAO	U.S. General Accounting Office
GPO	U.S. Government Printing Office
GSDF	Ground Self-Defense Force (Japan)
H	House (U.S. Cong)
H.R.	House Report (U.S. Cong)
HEWS	Humanitarian Early Warning System (UN)
HJ	House Joint (U.S. Cong)
HPSCI	House Permanent Select Committee on Intelligence (U.S. Cong)
IAEA	International Atomic Energy Agency
IC	Information Center; Intelligence Community (U.S.)
I.L.M.	International Legal Materials
INFSUM	Information Summary
INR	Information and Research Branch (UN DPKO)

INREP	Information Report
INSUM	Intelligence Summary
INTREP	Intelligence Report
INTSUM	Intelligence Summary
IPA	International Peace Academy
IRDN	International Refugee Documentation Network
IRENE	International Refugee Electronic Network
ISA	International Studies Association
ISE	Intelligence Support Element
JDISS	Joint Deployable Intelligence Support System
JSO	Joint Staff Office (Japan)
JTF	Joint Task Force
JWICS	Joint Worldwide Intelligence Communications System
KPNLF	Khmer People's National Liberation Front
L	Law
LDP	Liberal Democratic Party (Japan)
MAC	Military Armistice Commission (Korea)
MCIA	U.S. Marine Corps Intelligence Activity
MDL	Military Demarcation Line (Korea)
MFO	Multinational Force and Observers
MINURSO	United Nations Mission for the Referendum in Western Sahara
MIO	Military Intelligence Officer (UN)
MMWG	Mixed Military Working Group
MNF	Multinational Force
MSC	Military Staff Committee (UN)
n.d.	No date
n.p.	No publisher
NADK	National Army of Democratic Kampuchea
NAG	North African Group
NAM	Non-Aligned Movement
NGO	Non-Government Organization
NIMA	National Imagery and Mapping Agency (U.S.)
NMOG	Neutral Military Observer Group
NPR	National Police Reserve (Japan)
NPT	Nuclear Non-Proliferation Treaty
NSC	National Security Council (U.S.)
NUB	National Unification Board (Korea)

OASD	Office of the Assistant Secretary of Defense (U.S.)
ONUC	United Nations Operation in the Congo
ONUCA	United Nations Observer Group in Central America
ONUMOZ	United Nations Operation in Mozambique
ONUSAL	United Nations Observer Mission in El Salvador
OPCON	Operational Control
ORCI	Office for Research and Collection of Information (UN)
OSD	Office of the Secretary of Defense (U.S.)
OSPA	Office of Special Political Affairs (UN)
PDK	Party of Democratic Kampuchea
PIOOM	Interdisciplinary Program of Research on Root Causes of Human Rights Violations (Netherlands)
PKO	Peacekeeping Operations
PRC	People's Republic of China
PSCA	Department of Security Council Affairs (UN)
Pt	Part
Pub	Public
REFWorld	Refugee World (UN)
Res	UN Resolution
ROK	Republic of Korea
S	Senate (U.S. Cong)
SDF	Self-Defense Forces (Japan)
Sec	Section
SITREPS	Situation Reports
SNC	Supreme National Council (Cambodia)
SOC	Phnom Penh Regime, Cambodia
SWAPO	Southwest Africa People's Organization
TOR	Terms of Reference
TRADP	Tumen River Area Development Program
TREDA	Tumen River Economic Development Area
UK	United Kingdom
UN	United Nations
UNAEC	United Nations Atomic Energy Commission
UNAMIC	United Nations Advance Mission in Cambodia
UNAMIR	United Nations Assistance Mission for Rwanda
UNASOG	United Nations Aouzou Strip Observer Group
UNAVEM	United Nations Angola Verification Mission
UNC	Unified Command, or United Nations Command (Korea)

UNCMAC	United Nations Command Military Armistice Commission
UNCRO	United Nations Confidence Restoration Operation in Croatia
UNCTAD	United Nations Conference on Trade and Development
UNCURK	United Nations Commission for the Unification and Rehabilitation of Korea
UNDOF	United Nations Disengagement Observer Force
UNDP	United Nations Development Program
UNEF	United Nations Emergency Force
UNFICYP	United Nations Peace Keeping Force in Cyprus
UNGA	United Nations General Assembly
UNGOMAP	United Nations Good Offices Mission in Afghanistan and Pakistan
UNHCR	Office of the United Nations High Commissioner for Refugees
UNIDO	United Nations Industrial Development Organization
UNIFIL	United Nations Interim Force in Lebanon
UNIIMOG	United Nations Iran-Iraq Military Observer Group
UNIKOM	United Nations Iraq-Kuwait Observation Mission
UNIPOM	United Nations India-Pakistan Observation Mission
UNITAF	Unified Task Force
UNMIBH	United Nations Mission in Bosnia and Herzegovina
UNMIH	United Nations Mission in Haiti
UNMOP	United Nations Mission of Observers in Prevlaka
UNMOGIP	United Nations Military Observer Group in India and Pakistan
UNMOT	United Nations Mission of Observers in Tajikistan
UNOGIL	United Nations Observer Group in Lebanon
UNOMIG	United Nations Observer Mission in Georgia
UNOMIL	United Nations Observer Mission in Liberia
UNOMOZ	United Nations Observer Mission in Mozambique
UNOMSA	United Nations Observer Mission to South Africa
UNOMUR	United Nations Observer Mission Uganda-Rwanda
UNOSOM	United Nations Operation In Somalia
UNPKO	United Nations Peacekeeping Office
UNPREDEP	United Nations Preventive Deployment Force
UNPROFOR	United Nations Protection Force

UNSC	United Nations Security Council
UNSCOM	United Nations Special Commission
UNSec	United Nations Secretariat
UNSF	United Nations Security Force in West New Guinea (West Irian)
UNSMIH	United Nations Support Mission in Haiti
UNSYG	United Nations Secretary-General
UNTAC	United Nations Transitional Authority in Cambodia
UNTAES	United Nations Transitional Administration for Eastern Slavonia, Baranja and Western Sirmium
UNTAG	United Nations Transition Assistance Group
UNTCOK	United Nations Temporary Commission on Korea
UNTSO	United Nations Truce Supervision Organization
UNYOM	United Nations Yemen Observation Mission
U.S.	United States
USA	U.S. Army
USAF	U.S. Air Force
USAICS	U.S. Army Intelligence Center and School, Ft. Huachuca, AZ
USAR	U.S. Army Reserve
USCENTCOM	U.S. Central Command
USCG	U.S. Coast Guard
USDAO	U.S. Defense Attache Office
USEUCOM	U.S. European Command
USGSPA	Under-Secretary-General for Special Political Affairs (UN)
USLO	U.S. Liaison Office
USMC	U.S. Marine Corps
USN	U.S. Navy
USNR	U.S. Naval Reserve
USSR	Union of Soviet Socialist Republics

We will need to develop planning, crisis management and intelligence capabilities for peacekeeping and humanitarian operations.

President George Bush
Address to the UN General Assembly, 21 September 1992

We support the creation of a genuine UN peacekeeping headquarters with a planning staff, with access to timely intelligence, with a logistics unit that can be deployed on a moment's notice, and a modern operations center with global communications.

President William Clinton
Address to the UN General Assembly, 27 September 1993

The U.S. is prepared to . . . share information, as appropriate, while ensuring full protection of sources and methods.

Presidential Decision Directive 25, 3 May 1994

Intelligence for Multilateral Decision and Action

INTRODUCTION

Perry L. Pickert

On 31 January 1992, the United Nations Security Council, meeting for the first time at the Heads of State level, recognized "favorable international circumstances" under which the Security Council could fulfill its responsibility for maintenance of international peace and security and invited the UN Secretary-General to recommend ways of strengthening the UN's capacity for preventive diplomacy, peacemaking and peacekeeping. In June, Boutros Boutros-Ghali issued *An Agenda for Peace* which outlined a set of wide-ranging proposals to enhance the UN. In his 21 September 1992 speech to the General Assembly, President George Bush welcomed the Secretary-General's new agenda and promised American support in key areas, including planning, crisis management and intelligence. As one of its first foreign policy initiatives, the Clinton Administration conducted a review of American policy toward the United Nations and adopted a new multilateral approach which included an unprecedented level of U.S. intelligence support.

Responding to the end of the Cold War and increased emphasis on multilateral institutions in U.S. foreign policy, the students of the Joint Military Intelligence College have made intelligence in a UN context a significant research agenda for the college by selecting master's thesis topics focused on:

- Analysis of the Enhanced UN Role in World Politics
- Intelligence in UN Decisionmaking

- Support to Peacekeeping Operations
- Nuclear Nonproliferation
- Congressional Oversight
- Future of U.S. Intelligence in Multilateral Environments

The direct American intelligence participation and support in the context of multilateral institutions required rethinking basic assumptions about the nature of the intelligence process in a Hobbesean world of state against state in preparation for the next war. The students recognized that intelligence and policy in this area are beset by unresolvable tensions and trade-offs. There has been a clear perception of the need for a professional intelligence infrastructure in the international organizations charged with the maintenance of international peace and security. Yet this need for intelligence is balanced against the inherent problems of a multilateral bureaucracy and decisionmaking structures which reflect the narrow interests of the member states. Intelligence support of public diplomacy risks compromise of intelligence sources. Intelligence sharing is always a two-way street with dim lighting and few road signs. Ambiguity and an imperative to move forward have generated opportunities for original research.

Intelligence is meaningless if it is not an integral part of decisionmaking for action. In a UN context, however, the policy process is multilateral and actions are authorized and taken by individuals who are nationals of any of the more than 190 member states and at the same time international civil servants. Thus, intelligence in the UN is inherently a multilateral political process. As both the Bush and Clinton Administrations have indicated, American leadership in the post-Cold War world requires participation in UN decisionmaking and effective intelligence support to UN decision and action. This is no easy task.

In 1993, as an interagency review helped formulate Presidential Decision Directive 25, Captains John M. Piskator and Gregory D. Lautner suggested a methodology to analyze U.S. military readiness to conduct UN peace operations. They offered a decision matrix for use by U.S. policymakers as they decided whether to commit U.S. forces to a particular UN operation. The students concluded that while U.S. military forces were the most capable in the world for global power projection and could be used to conduct peacekeeping operations, a lack of experience, training, doctrine and a joint staff planning mechanism left U.S. forces only marginally prepared to execute the administration's ambitious multilateral agenda.

In the early 1990s, the conventional wisdom of the intelligence, press, academic and policy communities was that the UN lacked any sort of intelligence capability. Captains Timothy M. Sebenick and James D. Edwards and Lieutenant Robert J. Allen took a hard look at the UN organizational structures and decisionmaking procedures and found competing centers of power which had developed intelligence functions without using the "I" word. UN Headquarters shares many of the problems of highly bureaucratic, national foreign policy decisionmaking apparatuses that rely on compartmentalized intelligence capabilities. The UN's lack of integration of tactical and strategic intelligence was reminiscent of the U.S. Intelligence Community's lessons learned from the Gulf War. Yet especially in the area of direct access to both sides of a potential conflict and in humanitarian and refugee operations, the UN has an "intelligence architecture" that has worked for 50 years.

Blending theory and practice, students have studied the impact of enhanced intelligence support to post-Cold War peace operations. Captain William S. Brei evaluated intelligence support to the humanitarian intervention to help the Kurds in northern Iraq. Captain William E. Whitney analyzed the complex UN transitional regime in Cambodia, highlighting the inherent intelligence functions that were critical to the success of the mission. Finally, Lt. Allen and Technical Sergeant Payton A. Flynn reviewed the intelligence successes and failures of the UN operation in Somalia and discovered a mismatch between the rigid, highly technical U.S. intelligence capability being applied to a primitive tribal conflict and the required intelligence flexibility to change from a humanitarian focus to combat support.

Several students have conducted research on other countries' participation in UN collective security and peace operations. Captain John W. Loffert Jr. reviewed the history of Sub-Saharan African military performance in UN peacekeeping and assessed the prospects for their contribution in the future. He concludes that on the whole African forces have performed well and in fact are a mainstay of UN peacekeeping in general. Second Lieutenant Fae M. Crissman analyzed Japan's quest for international status through a permanent seat on the UN Security Council. The competition between regional groups and other prospective permanent members will make it difficult in the near term for Japan to achieve the consensus necessary to amend the UN Charter. Second Lieutenant Steven E. Maceda analyzed the peacekeeping mission of the Japanese Self-Defense Forces and concludes that in spite of the initial political controversy, there is broad support for peacekeeping as a substitute for the anti-Soviet justification for maintaining a military.

Well before the development of political controversy over increased U.S. intelligence support to UN peace operations, the U.S. Intelligence Community had begun enhanced support to the joint UN Special Commission and the International Atomic Energy Agency (IAEA) inspections of the Iraqi nuclear program. In 1992 Captain Audrey D. Hudgins produced the first paper in the college's line of research on intelligence support to multilateral institutions by outlining cooperation with the IAEA as a model for intelligence relationships for the future. Senior Master Sergeant William E. Campbell and Theodore W. Wolff Jr. followed up with studies of intelligence support to inspections and the public diplomacy of the Korean nuclear crisis.

The prospect for a UN role in a peaceful settlement on the Korean peninsula was the subject of research by two students. Although the UN is known as the court of last resort in a crisis, it also has a role in preventive diplomacy and negotiations. Captain Jennifer M. Hoyle studied the UN's recent success in mediating the end of long-standing civil wars in Cambodia, El Salvador and Mozambique as potential models for a transitional regime to ease the reunification of Korea. Master Sergeant Bradley J. Curran reviewed the UN role in the Tumen River Development Project at the border between China, Russia and Korea. This project will use the incentive of economic development to build better relations between North and South as a bridge to eventual reunification.

The issue of the commitment of U.S. forces to UN operations and the Clinton administration's proposals for information support to the UN were also the subject of intense argument on Capitol Hill. Mr. William D. O'Hara monitored the debate as a classic case of constitutional separation of powers, and Mr. Joseph G. Hays III focused on specific congressional action on the issue of intelligence sharing with the UN. Not surprisingly, behind the political rhetoric there appears to be a bipartisan consensus that some U.S. participation in UN peace operations is necessary, and that intelligence sharing, if conducted professionally, is in the U.S. interest.

Finally, students have looked at basic issues in the future of the UN system of collective security. Major Gary L. Crone analyzed the legal basis in the UN Charter for increased UN intervention in the internal affairs of member states involved in civil war, humanitarian emergencies, or the massive violation of human rights. He notes that the rationale has been in the Charter since 1945, but superpower confrontation prevented action. He concludes that while on an abstract level the international community may wish to act in humanitarian crises, nationalism on a local level may be too powerful when set against an international force unwilling to sustain casualties. Ms. Margaret T. Mitchell reviewed the use of UN peacekeepers in recent humanitarian interventions and concludes that the internal logic of a traditional peacekeeping mission means it is bound to fail where humanitarian intervention is required. The prospects for the future of the intelligence mission in a UN context, with its attendant opportunities and risks, are considered by Captain Hudgins and Lieutenant Allen.

The student theses distilled for this volume have been modified as little as possible, and then only to preserve readability and continuity within the chapters. Inevitably, excerpts from some theses are lengthier than others. Any modifications of the original theses by the principal author or the editor are their responsibility alone.

Several papers on issues related to intelligence in the humanitarian or peacekeeping context were omitted from this volume. There is also considerable work in progress at the college on such topics as UN Safe Areas in Bosnia, the role of intelligence in UN Security Council-led destruction and monitoring of Iraq's weapons of mass destruction, peace in El Salvador, East European contributions to UN peacekeeping, China's participation in the Human Rights Commission, the UN/NATO relationship in Bosnia and the impact of peacekeeping training on U.S. readiness for combat. At a future date this work may also be published.

The Joint Military Intelligence College offers a unique opportunity for students to conduct original research on intelligence and policy issues. The student body comprises professional intelligence officers who are trained to acquire, interpret and report. They have excellent analytical and writing skills, which are the prerequisites for academic research. In the past few years typical career paths have brought them from the field to the college for a mid-career academic program designed to provide a strategic perspective for young intelligence officers as they leave the tactical level of intelligence work. This unique window of history has meant that many of the students, after service in the Gulf War, also participated in the wide spectrum of UN peace operations from PROVIDE COMFORT in Iraq to Somalia, Haiti, and Bosnia. Many members of the faculty also have direct experience in the conduct of peacekeeping missions.

The On-Site Research Support Program of the College's Office of Applied Research has funded visits to the UN in New York for students conducting research on UN issues. In addition, students have been supported to conduct interviews and to visit UN libraries in Vienna at the IAEA, Geneva at the offices of the UN High Commissioner on Refugees, Korea at the UN Command and the U.S. Forces Korea, and in Japan at the UN University and the Japanese foreign and defense ministries. High-level U.S. and UN officials and academics from around the world have generously taken time to provide their insights in support of our students' research.

Chapter 1
PROLOGUE

In the summer of 1993, well before the ambush of American peacekeepers on the streets of Mogadishu, Captains Lautner and Piskator anticipated the forthcoming extensive deployment of U.S. forces in UN peace operations throughout the world. Looking beyond the conventional wisdom that the United States was the only remaining superpower with a global power projection capability, they analyzed the readiness of the U.S. military to conduct peacekeeping in a UN context. They defined the peacekeeping mission, reviewed the history of U.S. participation in peace operations, utilized standard measures of military preparedness, and assessed the current ability of the Department of Defense to conduct peacekeeping operations. Their conclusion was that while the U.S. had a highly capable military force for the conduct of combat operations, the U.S. was only partially prepared for UN missions, lacking experience, doctrine, trained personnel and established procedures.

In addition to assessing the current capability of the U.S. military, they also developed a matrix for the use of U.S. policymakers in deciding whether to commit U.S. forces to a future peacekeeping operation. After establishing a set of key factors that would influence the success of a peacekeeping mission, they tested the model against past and current U.S. deployments in the Middle East and then assessed the prospects for a potential U.S. deployment to Bosnia.

The accuracy of the analysis and the validity of their decisionmaking matrix can be established by a review of subsequent actions undertaken by the U.S. Government and the Department of Defense. The key factors they suggested for deciding whether to support a UN mission in the UN Security Council or to commit U.S. forces closely anticipated the 1994

Clinton Administration Policy on Reforming Multilateral Peace Operations (PDD-25).

Meanwhile, all of the U.S. military professional schools were directed to add peace operations to their curricula. Basic doctrine was published in 1994 with FM 100-23, Peace Operations; Joint Pub 3-07.3, Joint Tactics, Techniques, and Procedures for Peacekeeping Operations; and Joint Pub 2-0, Joint Doctrine for Intelligence Support to Operations, which included a chapter entitled "Intelligence for Multinational Operations." A UN Division was established by the Joint Chiefs of Staff, and a UN desk was created in the National Military Joint Intelligence Center with links to the U.S. Mission to the UN, the UN Situation Room in New York and UN peace operations headquarters in the field. U.S. units that deployed to Haiti and Bosnia were given months of formal predeployment training for peace operations, a need highlighted by Captains Lautner and Piskator.

In short, these master's theses were right on the mark.

IS THE U.S. MILITARY PREPARED TO CONDUCT PEACEKEEPING IN A UN CONTEXT?

Greg Lautner
Captain, U.S. Army
June 1993

John M. Piskator
Captain, U.S. Army
August 1993

This paper will review recent U.S. participation in peacekeeping operations, analyze current U.S. capabilities, and develop a decision matrix to assist U.S. policymakers in deciding whether the U.S. should participate in a proposed peacekeeping operation.

As of 1993, there are three broad missions performed by the U.S. military: peacekeeping support, observer missions, and deployment of forces. Currently, U.S. forces are engaged in all three types of operations.

First, peacekeeping support consists primarily of logistical and financial assistance to international and UN-sponsored peacekeeping efforts, and is used to purchase equipment for other countries and their contingents as they perform peacekeeping missions. Additionally, the U.S. is the largest contributor to UN peacekeeping: the 1993 budget included $460.3 million for UN operations (Browne *b*: 2). Logistical support provided by the U.S. includes supplies and equipment in addition to air and sealift. U.S. air and sealift assets are used to ferry both U.S. and other countries' forces in and out of peacekeeping theaters of operation. The U.S. Air Force, for instance, has flown over 5,500 sorties for UNOSOM I/II and Operation PROVIDE PROMISE in the former Yugoslavia (Murry).

The second type of peacekeeping mission involves sending individuals to serve under UN command as observers. They can perform communications, logistics, medical, administration or general purpose functions such as:

- Observing;
- Reporting;
- Investigating cease-fire violations;
- Liaison;
- Maintaining current information;
- Conducting periodic visits to forward positions to observe and report on the disposition of forces;
- Supervising elections, administering civil functions;
- Verifying the destruction of military equipment.

WORLDWIDE PEACEKEEPING OPERATIONS-1993

UN MISSIONS	UN TOTAL	US DoD	USA	USAF	USMC	USN
HQ UN		1		1		
Angola (UNAVEM II)	105	0				
Cambodia (UNTAC)	19,085	47	23	8	8	8
Iraq-Kuwait (UNIKOM)	318	14	8	2	1	3
Israel-Egypt-Jordan-Syria (UNTSO)	239	17	9	2	3	3
W. Sahara (MINURSO)	334	29	17	4	5	3
Cyprus (UNFICYP)	1,151					
El Salvador (ONUSAL)	387					
India-Pakistan (UNMOGIP)	38					
Israel-Syria (UNDOF)	1,121					
Lebanon (UNIFIL)	5,216					
Yugoslavia (UNPROFOR)	23,549	312	297	15		
Mozambique (ONUMOZ)	1,215					
Somalia (UNOSOM II)	20,706	3,896	3,889	5	2	
TOTAL	**73,464**	**4,316**	**4,243**	**37**	**19**	**17**
OTHER MISSIONS						
Sinai (MFO)	2,100	829				
Rwanda Neutral Mil. Obs. Group (NMOG)	50					
Econ. Comm. of W. African States Cease- Fire Monitoring Group (ECOMOG)	9,000					
TOTAL	**11,150**					
COMBINED TOTAL	**84,614**	**5,145**	**4,243**	**37**	**19**	**17**

Source: Sauer, Fleitz.

The third peacekeeping mission involves the use of peacekeeping forces. These operations involve all four services working from the ground, in the air, or at sea. Peacekeeping forces also perform peace support operations and observation missions. In situations involving U.S. forces, peacekeepers can be expected to:

- Establish a buffer zone;
- Ensure free access and usage of international maritime routes or airways;
- Supervise cease-fire agreements;
- Supervise withdrawals and disengagements;
- Separate the belligerents;
- Verify the disposition of troops;
- Oversee prisoner of war exchanges;
- Oversee demilitarization and demobilization operations;
- Maintain law and order by defusing potential conflict;
- Administer elections;
- Perform civil administration duties for the Host Nation (Campbell).

ASSESSING THE READINESS OF THE U.S. MILITARY FOR UN PEACE OPERATIONS

READINESS FACTORS
Command, Control and Communications (C^3)
Intelligence
Force Structure
Training
Doctrine
Experience

With the fall of the Soviet Union, there is little question that the U.S. is the only military that has a worldwide power projection capability. The fact that the United States is prepared to deploy forces for combat does not mean that the U.S. military is prepared to contribute individuals or units to successful peacekeeping operations in a UN context. In order to measure the readiness of the U.S. military for the peacekeeping mission, we have selected key factors which commanders use to assess the readiness of an individual or a unit and applied the decision matrix program of the Military Application Program Package (MAPP) available at the U.S.

Army Combined Arms and Services Staff School, Ft. Leavenworth, Kansas (USA *a*). The following key factors are used to analyze the current U.S. military capability in peace operations.[1]

COMMAND, CONTROL, AND COMMUNICATIONS

The first key factor to consider is command, control and communications. To evaluate U.S. readiness to support a peace operation it is necessary to consider the actual organizational structure in place today to conduct peace operations, and the procedures that are followed to actually place an individual in a UN mission or deploy a unit to participate in a peace operation. The actual number of people in the U.S. military establishment who are prepared today to start work immediately on request for a new UN mission comes to a grand total of three.

UN Peacekeeping Office

The oldest, smallest, and most obscure office that supports U.S. peacekeeping is the UN Peacekeeping Office in the Pentagon. The U.S. Department of Defense has provided individual military observers to serve with the UN in peacekeeping operations since 1948 (USA *c*: 7). Although this support to the UN had been ongoing for over 25 years, the Department of Defense did not designate the Army as the executive agent for UN peacekeeping until 1973 (U.S. DoD OSD *a*). Executive agent status gives the Army tasking authority over other services to provide personnel and assets in support of various UN peacekeeping missions, when approved by the Secretary of Defense. The Army's role of executive agent for UN peacekeeping expanded in May 1991 with the establishment of the UN Iraq-Kuwait Observer Mission (UNIKOM). Army responsibilities continued to grow until, in May 1992, they included over 140 all-service personnel supporting five UN peacekeeping operations and a small liaison element to the UN Headquarters in New York (USA *c*: 7). The UN Peacekeeping Office (UNPKO) in the Army Operations Center (AOC) of the Pentagon is the

---

1 In their Master's theses, Captains Lautner and Piskator used a complex decision matrix program in which they assigned numerical values and employed a hierarchical scale to variables. Space constraints in the present work do not permit the inclusion of the methodological rationale for their analysis. Their evaluation of current U.S. capabilities and their reasoning for their assessments have been reduced here to a simple color-coding scheme to represent their judgments.

central point for coordination of all individual military observer support for UN missions.

The UNPKO office is currently authorized only two officers to manage and coordinate for over 5,000 personnel from five services serving in peacekeeping missions. This has led to an *ad hoc* approach. The office is new, growing in responsibilities and functions, and woefully understaffed.

Whenever a new UN mission is authorized, the UNPKO establishes how many observers are required, what skills are necessary to qualify for the mission, and how many slots will be allocated to each service. The UNPKO, through the AOC, then tasks each service to provide a number of officers who have the requisite skills. The Department of Defense recognizes that peacekeeping operations are predominantly a ground force mission, and the Army and the Marines usually fill a majority of positions. However, Air Force, Navy, and Coast Guard personnel are also used as UN peacekeepers (U.S. DoD *f*).

Once individual service members are designated to deploy as UN peacekeepers, they are trained in conducting peacekeeping operations. This training is usually a two-week course that emphasizes anti-terrorist techniques, mine recognition, field craft, and peacekeeping principles. The U.S. Army recognizes that Special Forces, Military Police, and Military Intelligence officers have been trained in certain areas and possess skills that are conducive to conducting successful peacekeeping operations. Because of this, a large number of Army officers deployed as UN peacekeepers are from these three branches.

It would be useful to maintain a pool of trained officers to deploy on short notice in support of the UN. However, this is not the policy of the Department of Defense. New personnel must be trained to support new missions and to relieve personnel on existing missions. The selection and training period limits how quickly the U.S. can respond to requests from the UN for support. Further, the Peacekeeping Office does not maintain a data base of all U.S. Army personnel who are trained in peacekeeping. Nor does the Army record additional skill identifiers to track personnel specially trained and experienced in peacekeeping. Skills such as language qualification, anti-terrorist training, area training, on-ground experience, specific branch and job qualifications, and even cultural heritage are all important to peacekeepers. If these specific skills and qualifications were effectively monitored by the Army, a data base of prepared and deployable personnel to support UN operations would be readily available.

Army Operations Center

The U.S. Army also maintains a point of contact in the Army Operations Center (AOC) responsible for coordinating all actions to support the U.S. Army elements participating in the Multinational Force and Observers (MFO) mission in the Sinai. This MFO constitutes the Army's only experience in conducting a large-unit peacekeeping mission. The MFO officer in the AOC monitors the U.S. support to MFO, tasks additional units to rotate to the Sinai to replace existing units, and coordinates with the civilian headquarters of the MFO in Italy. The AOC has no responsibility to provide extensive peacekeeping training to the soldiers that deploy for a six-month rotation to the Sinai. This training is strictly the responsibility of the individual units and their immediate headquarters. A briefing packet and additional instructions are given to MFO participants, but the principal training is conducted by deployed or deploying units.

Ad Hoc Support

There are several other ways in which U.S. forces support peacekeeping operations. U.S. military assets quite frequently provide communications, airlift, intelligence, and logistics support to various peacekeeping efforts, both with and without the UN. The majority of this support is conducted on an *ad hoc* basis, through various military commands, to provide one-time, unique support to peacekeeping operations.

When smaller, short-duration support missions are required, the U.S. Department of Defense may direct military operations using existing command structures. If the peacekeeping support or effort requires a larger, specifically designated headquarters, then either an existing unit will be tasked or a new unit formed to provide command and control, possibly under a Joint Task Force (JTF).

Within the Department of Defense there is no central peacekeeping office designated to act as the executive agent for all peacekeeping operations. The new Office of the Assistant Secretary of Defense (OASD) for Democratic Security and Peacekeeping should not be considered a solution to the problem, since the main function of the new office will primarily be the formulation of defense policy. A separate office at the Joint Staff level is needed to facilitate and coordinate all military support to peacekeeping operations. A coordinated effort at the Joint Staff level would smooth operations during joint and combined operations. It would also ensure that the designated DoD agencies and services understand and perform their assigned tasks. Nevertheless, until a joint peacekeeping office is created, the Army's UN peacekeeping office will continue to support all peacekeeping missions.

In general, all peacekeeping requests enter the U.S. Government informally through the Bureau of International Organizations in the Department of State, the lead government agency responsible for overall planning and execution of U.S. support to peacekeeping operations. The Secretary of State notifies the President and the National Security Council (NSC) of the request. Once staffed by the International Organizations Bureau in State, the request is passed to the Secretary of Defense, who forwards it to the Assistant Secretary of Defense for International Security Affairs (ASD/ISA), the primary staff section at the OSD/OASD level. ASD/ISA then staffs and sends the request to the Chairman of the Joint Chiefs of Staff (CJCS), who provides overall guidance prior to routing the request to the Joint Chiefs of Staff (JCS). The Chairman, at his discretion, may also direct the formation of a joint action cell to organize, coordinate, and monitor any support required. Once routed to the JCS, the request is studied and staffed to determine the military's position, and this process will continue until the new OASD for Democratic Security and Peacekeeping is prepared to take over for the ASD/ISA, to coordinate various service positions, and to work out the details of the mission. Today, a regional Commander in Chief (CINC) or service is selected to be the Executive Agent responsible for coordinating and/or providing the following support for committed U.S. forces:

- Administrative
- Personnel
- Operational
- Logistics
- Intelligence
- Command, Control & Communications

The Executive Agent also publishes the terms of reference (TOR) based on the tentative mandate provided by the requesting organization. The TOR outlines the mission, force structure, command relationships, logistics, accounting procedures, coordination and liaison procedures, and the responsibilities of U.S. military units and personnel involved in the peacekeeping mission.

If there is non-concurrence concerning the military's position, or if there is a lack of consensus among the services, the issue is resolved by the NSC and the President. This was the case, for example, with support to the UN Transitional Authority for Cambodia. The services did not want to get involved in Cambodia for fear of being drawn in militarily, thus risking the possibility of another quagmire like Vietnam. Nevertheless, President Bush ordered the Department of Defense to support UN peacekeeping efforts in Cambodia (Campbell).

There are four types of command structures the U.S. follows in peacekeeping operations: U.S. observer missions to the UN, U.S. forces (units) under UN command, non-UN command structures, and unique structures such as those in airlift operations.

First, U.S. military personnel serving as UN observers have one chain of command. These individuals serve under the command of the UN, or the organization responsible for overall observer operations. Furthermore, they are supervised by a "Chief of Staff," responsible for directing and employing the observers.

Second, in contrast to the single chain of command of individual observers, U.S. units under a UN command have a dual command structure. Once in the peacekeeping Area of Operations, the U.S. contingent is under the Operational Control (OPCON) of the UN contingency commander. For example, the U.S. contingent in Macedonia is OPCON to the Danish commander. That means the Danish commander is responsible for directing and employing the U.S. force. The U.S. theater commander relinquishes operational control and direction for all aspects of the peacekeeping operation and the military personnel in the U.S. peacekeeping unit. He may, however, have his staff monitor the operation and provide support to the U.S. peacekeeping force, but only if the support is in accordance with the terms of reference. The senior U.S. officer of the contingent serves two functions: as the U.S. contingent commander reporting to the Danish commander, and as the link between the U.S. peacekeeping force and the U.S. theater command.

Third, U.S. units under a non-UN command differ according to the situation. For example, a two-headquarters command structure is employed by the MFO in the Sinai. The political headquarters is located in Rome, Italy and the military headquarters is located in the operational region.

Fourth, U.S. sea/airlift assets remain under control of the supporting nation. For example, U.S. airlift assets used in Operation PROVIDE PROMISE in the former Yugoslavia remained under USEUCOM. Requests for airlift support are passed to the USEUCOM air component commander through UN liaison personnel who are in the operational country. The air component commander then assigns a mission number(s) to specific planes. The number represents the aircraft's flight mission. Once in the air, the aircraft is technically under UN control but only for the duration of the flight. After the mission is completed the plane reverts back to U.S. control (Murry).

As U.S. forces enter the peacekeeping arena subordinated to other national forces, U.S. commanders will experience a series of challenges, including language barriers, cultures and customs. The various military organizations have their own doctrine for organization, training, tactics, and staff operations which may differ from U.S. doctrine (Freeman: 6). Logistics will be a major challenge. The U.S. has one of the best logistical systems in the world. But as U.S. units participate in peacekeeping operations, the local area may limit the logistical support they receive (Pacific Armies: 192). As a result, U.S. commanders may find it difficult to carry out their mission. If it is perceived that U.S. forces receive superior support in comparison to other nations, animosity toward the U.S. may develop among the multinational forces, thus impacting on the overall morale and efficiency.

INTELLIGENCE

Intelligence activities in peacekeeping are multifaceted, and intelligence activities, especially collection, are extremely sensitive. In peacekeeping the term "intelligence" is replaced by the term "information gathering" due to the negative connotations associated with the word "intelligence" and the political nature of peacekeeping operations. Host countries and belligerent parties may perceive intelligence collection as a hostile act (USA *g*: 13). As a result, intelligence activities may erode trust and impartiality, placing the force at risk (Malone: 17).

Still, intelligence and information gathering, when performed in accordance with the terms of reference and the agreement of the parties, serve an important role in U.S. peacekeeping operations. Even though the term intelligence is avoided to emphasize impartiality, the bulk of staff work is performed with intelligence in mind. The intelligence principles and intelligence cycle — direction, collection, processing, and dissemination — are adhered to as much as possible to ensure that intelligence products are clear and unambiguous (Ayers: 55).

The guidance for the UN Truce Supervision Organization (UNTSO) in Lebanon provides an example of well-established procedures designed to restrict certain behavior that may be perceived as partial toward one of the belligerents. Individual observers, for example, are required to sign a document that outlines these restrictions, including both the observers' responsibilities when handling information and information obtained during their tour of duty:

> Military observers shall exercise the utmost discretion in regard to the handling of documents, cables, maps or other UNTSO papers, and they shall follow detailed instructions issued by UNTSO concerning such documentation. In particular, documents, cables, maps or other papers, copies thereof or notes of their contents may not be taken away from the mission, published or otherwise handled or communicated to others, except with the prior approval of the Chief of Staff in each case...Military observers, after UNTSO assignment, shall not divulge the contents of documents, cables, maps or other papers of UNTSO, except with the prior approval of the Secretary-General in each case (UNTSO: 28).

The U.S. has agreements with other nations concerning the collection, production and dissemination of intelligence information. Since a UN peacekeeping force is multinational, many participating countries will not have sharing arrangements. If it is perceived by other nations of the force that information is intentionally withheld, mistrust and suspicion may develop and undermine peacekeeping efforts. Maintaining a delicate balance is a critical aspect of an overall intelligence effort.

The mandate of a peacekeeping mission often contains restrictions on flying, specifically overflights and airspace control. Since parties to a peacekeeping agreement are often suspicious of espionage, certain restrictions may be included in the agreement with the parties. The most common restrictions associated with flying include:

- Prohibited areas of overflight
- Photography
- Night flying
- The carrying of non-peacekeeping force personnel

The battlefield in peacekeeping, in contrast to conventional conflict, is not linear. The key terrain comprises not just military objectives, but the people and military in the area. There are no separate Rear Area Operations Centers, Main Command, or Forward Command Posts. As a result, the intelligence staff officer(s) must coordinate widely and as far in advance as possible.

There are three general intelligence functions in peacekeeping: early warning, intelligence in support of the mandate, and force protection. Information for early warning provides decisionmakers the time needed to prevent the possible outbreak of conflict. Intelligence in support of the mandate is tactical in nature, and allows the force commander to employ peacekeeping forces to carry out the mandate. Information for U.S. commanders is also needed to protect U.S. peacekeeping forces from terrorists, assassination, sabotage, and full-scale military attack.

Five broad intelligence requirement categories apply across the peacekeeping spectrum. Each category will have a specific set of essential elements of information or priority intelligence requirements that are situational and time dependent. They include:

- **Political:** Requirements that involve detailed information on the political and military aspects of the conflict between the belligerents;
- **Economic/Social:** Requirements that focus on the factors of the conflict, resources, general conditions, cultural information, the ethnic situation, and religious taboos or sensitivities of the belligerents and Host Country;
- **Geographic/Environmental:** Requirements that are predicated upon the location and the type of conflict, or level of war;
- **Security:** Requirements that are designed to analyze the loyalties and intentions of the Host Country, and the capability of the force to provide security for U.S. forces;

- **Threat:** Requirements that examine the threat to U.S. forces. These include the military capabilities and intentions of the belligerents; their Order of Battle, and their combat history, as well as any other threats such as terrorism or civil unrest.

Secretary-General Boutros Boutros-Ghali visiting UNOSOM II operations in Somalia, October 1993.
UN photo by Fabrice Ribere

Experiences in Iraq and in Somalia illustrate the importance of possessing and comprehending this information. First, in Somalia information was required on various clans, political parties, feuds, and economic realities. The intelligence provided on the militia proved reliable. However, U.S. commanders realized that to be successful they needed continuous information about local civil conditions. Consequently, U.S. commanders were forced to shift their efforts to gather and process information in their "tactical" area (Abizaid and Wood: 19).

Second, Operation PROVIDE COMFORT further validates the need for cultural and political information:

> Besides the normal intelligence requirements, this type operation called for a strong and immediate provision of "cultural" intelligence. Information on the Kurds such as their political and tribal structure; life-style habits such as food, clothing, etc.; leaders and military organization; and history of their conflict with the Iraqis,

> became valuable Essential Elements of Information for Combined Task Force leaders. This information was extremely important in shaping certain decisions and in direct dealings with the Kurds. It also greatly affected our psychological operations and the way the themes were developed to influence events. This capability was eventually developed but should have been sought and provided earlier (USEUCOM *b*: 12).

Once deployed, U.S. units might not receive external intelligence support. Predeployment planning must take into account the ability of the unit to receive and properly store classified materials (Ayers: 19).

The most common methods and techniques for information gathering include:

- **Observation:** U.S. forces and personnel not only conduct their mandated mission, they also operate and interact in well-populated areas. Because of this they need to be aware of their surroundings to observe and report on activities around them;
- **Patrols (mounted and dismounted):** Squads and platoons, as in observation, must also be aware of all activity in their surroundings;
- **Contacts and conversations with the parties to the dispute:** Local officials, local inhabitants, soldiers on and off duty, often come in contact with these people;
- **Official reports** from the host government and other sources;
- **The media:** newspapers, radio, and television;
- The **interaction** between peacekeeping forces and observer groups: Since observer groups serve longer than the peacekeeping force, they can provide the peacekeeping force with valuable background information used to reduce ambiguities and preclude possible errors.

To ensure a steady and efficient exchange of information, observer groups working in the same area may attach an observer to each battalion headquarters to coordinate observation and patrol reports (Ayers: 22).

In the end, the ability of the U.S. to provide adequate intelligence support to peacekeeping rests with agreements established by the UN mandate and agreements with the parties. This is a result of the sensitive nature of intelligence activities in peacekeeping and the need to maintain impartiality.

FORCE STRUCTURE

Currently, the number of U.S. personnel authorized to participate in UN peacekeeping operations through the UN Participation Act of 1947 is not to exceed 1,000. That is, no more than 1,000 U.S. military personnel may participate in UN peacekeeping operations at any given time. On the other hand, there is no limit for U.S. military personnel participating in non-UN peacekeeping operations (Story *b*: 2).

In planning for the use of these forces, the regional commands use the "Adaptive Planning" approach. CINCs conduct operational planning in four broad categories: nuclear forces and strategic defense, regional conflict, the emergence of a global threat, and peacekeeping, all by maintaining normal high readiness levels.

Planning is decentralized. Regional commanders generally determine the assumptions, concept of operations, and forces to be deployed. However, their plans are approved by the Chairman of the Joint Chiefs of Staff, and are coordinated with the services and Department of Defense agencies. The CINCs also receive their policy guidance, mission assignment, and final plan review from the Secretary of Defense. Finally, UN peacekeeping mandates are negotiated by the Security Council in New York, and the force structure is put together on an *ad hoc* basis depending on the contributions of members. The U.S. process can only begin after the UN has defined the mandate—creating a planning environment that is the exact opposite of the usual U.S. staff procedures.

The basic force structure and support mechanisms are situationally dependent and based on the mandate. The battalion is the smallest fully staffed and self-contained unit, and is exemplified by the light infantry battalion, with staff, from the 82d Airborne Division currently supporting the MFO in the Sinai (Ayers: 8).

Currently there is no U.S. doctrine that specifies task organizations for peacekeeping missions. To ensure success, commanders need to task-organize their forces to meet the various challenges associated with multinational peacekeeping operations:

- Make sure the force is balanced so that no one national element dominates the others;

- Make sure the force is supplied with the proper mix and amount of qualified linguists;
- Ensure the force is prepared to support liaison operations;
- Structure the force to facilitate the logistics support needed to preserve its effectiveness (Bateman: 9).

As mentioned, light infantry battalions are the basic unit for peacekeeping. Even though light forces have great utility, they may not be suitable for all peacekeeping missions. They have less equipment and, lacking troop transport, must walk, carrying most of their equipment. This was a problem in UNOSOM I in Somalia, where units from the 10th Mountain Division were tasked to control between 50 and 100 square kilometers. Because they lacked organic transportation assets, light forces found it difficult to maintain control over their sectors of responsibility without augmentation by lift assets.

The U.S. military has other assets to augment existing force structures based on the mission. These include Military Intelligence assets, Engineer assets, Civil Affairs, Military Police, and mechanized forces.

Military Intelligence units consist of counterintelligence and interrogator teams. These teams are designed for force protection and information gathering. They are taught interpersonal skills enabling them to interact with various groups of people. Interrogators are qualified linguists. Military Intelligence units also train and maintain other linguists who can bridge the language barrier.

Military Intelligence units also possess Ground Surveillance Radars. These assets collect on walking and moving targets at distances up to 10 miles and fill the information-gathering gap on certain types of peacekeeping missions, such as truce supervision and observation missions. These assets do have limitations. They cannot identify friend or foe, and terrain dictates their employment. On the other hand, these radars could be used to cue other assets or observer teams to a specific location to observe and report.

Engineers are another valuable asset available to commanders. One of the three Engineer missions that apply to peacekeeping, for example, is sustainment operations. If, for some reason, the Host Government/Host Nation is unable to provide adequate support to U.S. units, engineers could assist in establishing facilities and other force protection measures such as bunkers, observation posts, and reinforcement to existing structures. Engineers could also improve trust through humanitarian operations such as digging wells and repairing damaged facilities and structures.

Next, Civil Affairs teams provide the critical link between the commander and the Host Nation agencies and departments. Commanders in UNOSOM I, for example, expressed the need for personnel with backgrounds in civil affairs and relief agencies to assist in solving daily civil problems (Abizaid and Wood: 23). Civil Affairs teams were critical in bringing needed assistance to the Kurds in Northern Iraq.

Military Police possess the skills required for peacekeeping, including:

- Basic soldiering skills
- A case-by-case approach to the use of force
- The use of discretion in the de-escalation of potential violence
- Handling and exchange of Prisoners of War (POW)
- Assisting the Host Nation law enforcement authorities
- Traffic control and checkpoints
- Force protection
- Investigative and reporting techniques.

Military Police are in demand for UN operations. Constitutional and procedural difficulties are associated with obtaining host country civilian law enforcement because many law enforcement agencies/departments are under city, state, or provincial control with different legal guidelines and operating procedures. Local law enforcement organizations often operate under full strength and are therefore unable to deploy as units to support peacekeeping operations (Campbell).

Mechanized forces, specifically armored cavalry units, possess the mobility to conduct numerous patrols over large areas. These forces are the eyes and ears for the commander on the ground. As a result, they are skilled in observation techniques and reporting. They are also equipped with armored protection against small arms, grenades, and other material used by possible protestors. Nevertheless, as in any tactical situation, terrain dictates movement. Consequently, certain environments, such as the mountainous terrain in the former Yugoslavia, may hinder the mobility of mechanized forces, but the threat still requires them.

TRAINING

Increased demands for U.S. military participation in peacekeeping operations and the reorientation of U.S. military personnel and units away from their warfighting mission toward a peacekeeping environment has raised an air of caution in the military community. The most common argument is that peacekeeping operations reduce combat readiness. As former Army Chief of Staff General Gordon Sullivan put it:

> Although the Army can execute a variety of non-combat missions well, we recognize that lowered combat readiness is the price if we mistakenly structure the force with these missions primarily in mind (G. Sullivan: 33).

In peacekeeping, the aggressive warrior mentality shifts to caution and restraint. Any overreaction in word or deed by an inexperienced troop may shatter any good will that may have taken weeks, months or years to develop.

Part of the indoctrination process in the military is the familiarization with the importance of flexibility, discipline, and professionalism. There are certain personal traits required in peacekeeping, however, that cannot be easily taught. They include patience, impartiality, tact and inquisitiveness (MacKinlay and Chopra: 113). Service members must avoid thoughtless comments and behavior, both on and off duty. Furthermore, individuals need to question everything that occurs in their area, not allowing themselves to be lulled into a false sense of security (Ayers: 67-76; Abizaid and Wood: 10-22; UNTSO: 7).

After selection, U.S. observers attend the 5- to 10-day Individual Terrorism Awareness Course given at the U.S. Army John F. Kennedy Special Warfare Center and School, Fort Bragg, North Carolina. The course teaches observers to minimize their vulnerability to terrorist identification, selection, and attack by learning how to detect terrorist surveillance. The course also includes instruction on terrorist operations, self-protective measures, and hostage survival techniques, including resistance to interrogation (Campbell). The Fort Bragg course is also used for administrative functions and additional training based on the location and situation of the mission. Observers receive Department of State and UN briefs, country and area briefs, intelligence briefs, and medical preparation for overseas requirements. Observers may also receive additional training in mines, booby traps and unexploded ordnance, as well as Global Positioning System instruction.

It is imperative that units conduct predeployment training to prepare and become familiarized with expected peacekeeping activities. During their peacekeeping tour, units need to conduct training to reinforce what they have learned. Upon completion of peacekeeping operations and redeployment, units need to train back up to warfighting standards to regain their aggressive warrior mentality. They accomplish this by conducting live-fire exercises and field training exercises.

Emphasis on particular skills is predicated upon the situation, mission, and environment. Somalia, for example, possesses virtually no infrastructure. As a result, field sanitation and first aid take on added importance to prevent the spread of local diseases and illness within military units. Moreover, basic skills such as patrolling and mine awareness are exercised more frequently among combat arms units in comparison to combat support units. As more combat support units become involved in peacekeeping, emphasis on these skills will be required.

In addition to basic soldier skills, soldiers need to learn the Rules of Engagement to know when to use force. There are degrees of coercive methods of persuasion such as warning blows and warning shots. This was illustrated when British forces in the UN Protection Forces in Yugoslavia (UNPROFOR) fired carefully aimed .50 caliber rounds in the vicinity of Serbian snipers. Rather than engaging the Serb snipers with deadly force, the British commander fired warning shots that proved to be successful in forcing the Serbian snipers to disengage (Hunter).

Another requirement is force protection. This not only applies to the unit, but to the individual soldier as well. Since peacekeepers are often the victims of violence, emphasis must be placed on wearing body armor, constructing proper fighting positions, and practicing dispersal and cover procedures.

Handling civilians and detainees, and negotiation skills, are extremely important. In the peacekeeping environment soldiers and junior leaders are often away from their command for duties such as operating checkpoints. As a result, many find themselves in stressful situations dealing with civilians and military personnel from both sides of the dispute. U.S. soldiers and junior leaders must exercise both good judgment and the ability to interact in an effective and fair manner with people. Peacekeepers must also know how to deal with the media. As mentioned earlier, soldiers need to exercise thought, judgment, and tact when dealing with people to prevent sending the wrong signal that may upset the disputants. Consequently, soldiers need to be aware of the media and the types of questions they may ask.

There are, in addition, particular tasks that require added emphasis in peacekeeping operations. Force protection shifts from personal protection to unit protection. It includes physical security measures such as barricades, properly placed guards, and an adequate dispersal of personnel, material and equipment to improve survivability in the event of an attack. Force protection includes counterintelligence training designed to teach units about other threats such as terrorism, espionage, and sabotage.

U.S. military units require intelligence training. This training occurs under the direction of the intelligence staff officer and usually consists of a series of familiarization briefs. These include intelligence requirements, the political situation in the field, the economic/social situation, geographic/environmental factors, and host government security and threats. Intelligence staff officers are also responsible for familiarizing units with the area and country. These briefs include the following information:

- Customs
- Traditions
- Religious issues
- The Multinational Forces, the disputants, and uniform and equipment identification
- Familiarization with the host country language and the most commonly used words.

Unit training for peacekeeping is not as simple as observer training. The foundation for success begins at the soldier level with basic soldiering skills, then integrating the soldiers into collective unit training beginning at the squad level. Commanders identify weaknesses and train in those areas while at the same time reinforcing what the unit already knows. During collective training the staff also conducts training and familiarization in areas that require additional attention.

Today unit training for peacekeeping today is fragmented and lacks doctrine and standardization. No designated schools or training packages are designed to assist commanders in preparing their units for peacekeeping operations. Even though training has occurred on an *ad hoc* basis, too few experienced U.S. personnel are available to provide a blueprint for what the U.S. military may expect in future operations and their experiences have not been incorporated the into new doctrine.

DOCTRINE

Department of Defense peacekeeping doctrine development for the operational or theater level is the responsibility of the Army-Air Force Center for Low Intensity Conflict. The U.S. Army Training and Doctrine Command holds this responsibility at the service level. Official U.S. doctrine for peacekeeping operations is found in only one chapter of a joint publication (U.S. DoD JCS Pub 3-07), one chapter of an Army field manual (USA FM 100-20), and in a draft version of another joint publication (U.S. DoD JCS Pub 3-07.3). Overall, there exists little pertinent U.S. doctrine. This is due, in part, to the lack of U.S. experience in peacekeeping, and in part to the failure of the Department of Defense to capture all lessons learned from U.S. participation in peacekeeping operations (USA *c*).

U.S. doctrine does stress nine general principles for peacekeeping missions: consent, neutrality, balance, single-manager management, concurrent action, unqualified sponsor support, force integrity, freedom of movement, and self-defense. Neutrality is a principle in both UN and U.S. doctrine. The U.S. principle of seeking concurrent action reflects the UN emphasis on seeking a diplomatic solution. The U.S. principles of balance, freedom of movement, and self-defense are closely related to the UN principle of minimizing the use of coercive force. The U.S. principles of single-manager management and force integrity deal with the military concept of maintaining a functional chain of command. These nine U.S. peacekeeping principles have application to the entire spectrum of possible peacekeeping missions.

EXPERIENCE

The overall experience of the U.S. military in conducting peacekeeping operations is unfortunately rather minimal. Of the twelve peacekeeping operations currently being undertaken by the UN, U.S. personnel are involved in only six: the UN Truce Supervisory Organization (UNTSO) in

Palestine, the UN Angola Verification Mission (UNAVEM II), the UN Iraq-Kuwait Observer Mission (UNIKOM), the UN Mission for the Referendum in Western Sahara (MINURSO), the UN Transition Authority in Cambodia (UNTAC), and the UN Protection Force (UNPROFOR) in the former Yugoslavia (UN *e*). On 15 August 1992, of the 33,548 peacekeepers that the UN deployed around the globe, only 143 or one-half of one percent were U.S. soldiers (USA *c*). The U.S. supports UN peacekeeping operations with money, transportation, equipment, supplies and other items, but U.S. troop contributions are minimal.

The U.S. has had little experience participating in peacekeeping operations outside UN control. The U.S. military has had only three such opportunities. These three missions are the peacekeeping mission of U.S. forces in the Dominican Republic under Organization of American States control in 1965, the use of U.S. Marines as peacekeepers in the Multinational Force in Beirut in 1983, and the ongoing use of 1,200 U.S. Army soldiers in the Sinai under the Multinational Force and Observers. These three examples provide experiences in the full spectrum of success for peacekeeping.

The U.S. military operation in the Dominican Republic can be classified as a military intervention that evolved into a peacekeeping mission as the level of violence subsided. Therefore, the U.S. experience in conducting peacekeeping operations outside of UN control is limited to just two cases of actual peacekeeping. Incidentally, both of these cases constitute the only experience that the U.S. has had in using large units (battalion-size or larger) for peacekeeping.

ARE WE READY?

A sufficient level of readiness is required for U.S. military forces to succeed in peacekeeping operations. The accompanying color-coded assessment reflects a subjective judgment of the authors on each readiness factor. The rating of each factor is based upon its importance and application to U.S. assets employed in recent peacekeeping operations. A "5" is the highest value (green). A "1" is the lowest. The numbers "1" and "2" are represented by red, and "3" and "4" are keyed to yellow.

Command and Control received a value of 3 (sufficient). The commands and commanders of Operation PROVIDE COMFORT and UNOSOM I exercised initiative and good judgment during their respective operations. Command structures and procedures currently exist.

Intelligence also received a value of 3 (sufficient). National and strategic assets are available prior to deployment and provide limited support after deployment. Tactical systems are designed to provide access to intelligence products and information. In the field, the main obstacle is the knowledge and experience of the intelligence staff officers, and the lack of specific intelligence on the peacekeeping environment.

Force structure, like intelligence, exists. The U.S. military possesses the assets required to function in a peacekeeping environment. However, during PROVIDE COMFORT and UNOSOM I, force structure was not suitable. Light infantry forces were tasked to control large areas better suited to mechanized forces. Consequently, force structure received a value of 2 (deficient). The U.S. also lacks the necessary organizational structures for pre-deployment planning.

Next, doctrine, training, and experience work together. Doctrine provides the organizational and instructional basis, and training tests and provides experience for the doctrine. Where doctrine does not exist, *ad hoc* training and experience are left to develop the doctrine in a reverse manner. Currently, there is little or no doctrine. As a result, units have been forced

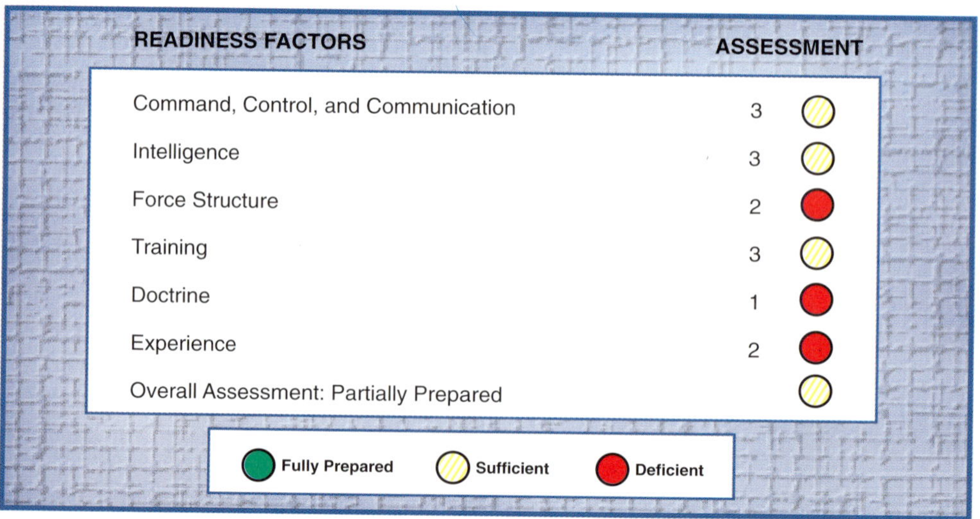

READINESS FACTORS	ASSESSMENT	
Command, Control, and Communication	3	Sufficient
Intelligence	3	Sufficient
Force Structure	2	Deficient
Training	3	Sufficient
Doctrine	1	Deficient
Experience	2	Deficient
Overall Assessment: Partially Prepared		Sufficient

Readiness Assessment.

source: compiled by author

to conduct limited and fragmented training in preparation for peacekeeping operations. Some peacekeeping units have had only one week to prepare for a mission. As a result, training and doctrine received a value of 3 (sufficient) and 1 (deficient), respectively.

Except for the MFO Sinai, U.S. military forces have limited experience in a peacekeeping environment. The two most current operations are PROVIDE COMFORT and UNOSOM I/II. UNOSOM I was actually a peace-enforcement mission. However, many of the functions performed during UNOSOM I overlap with peacekeeping and serve as a good analytical tool to evaluate the U.S. military. Consequently, experience received a value of 2 (deficient). The bottom-line assessment summarizes all of these factors.

Is the U.S. military prepared to conduct future peacekeeping operations? The U.S. has the tools to succeed in peacekeeping. However, the Department of Defense and the services lack clear doctrine and experience, resulting in the fragmented system that exists today. The U.S. military is partially prepared for future peacekeeping operations based on the limited successes of Operation PROVIDE COMFORT in Iraq and UNOSOM I in Somalia. However, there are still a number of command, control and communications, intelligence, force structure, and training issues that must be resolved before the U.S. military can say it is fully prepared for future peacekeeping operations.

TOWARD A PEACEKEEPING DECISION MATRIX

It is imperative that military leaders and policymakers weigh all the possible ramifications of employing U.S. troops on international peacekeeping missions. There are numerous factors that can cause a peacekeeping mission to either fail or succeed. Some of these factors are fairly static, while others, because of their dependence on world events, may be quite dynamic. The size and commitment level of a U.S. force will usually be quite stable, while the political consensus that originally fostered the deployment of the force may change considerably, depending upon world events.

While there exist many variables in the peacekeeping environment, three main principles consistently present themselves: 1) the requirement for host country support, 2) the maintenance of peacekeeper neutrality, and 3) the minimum use of coercive force. While many other conditions, factors, variables, and tenets are prescribed and written about, these three are the overwhelmingly basic common factors involved in the conduct of successful peacekeeping operations.

It is not easy to take the measure of the numerous variables that will contribute to the successful completion of any peacekeeping operation. Each mission is unique. It is risky to judge a dynamic situation in terms of unqualified yes or no answers. Because deploying peacekeeping forces is a political decision, it is subject to the vagaries and whims of any political process. However, some organized and objective decisionmaking process should be employed when trying to evaluate the viability of a given peacekeeping operation. By considering eight interdependent variables and applying relative weights to each variable, the three previous U.S. experiences can be systematically examined. The resulting peacekeeping assessment matrix can be used a tool for decisionmaking. The eight variables that will be individually assessed below for each case study are:

1. U.S. political controversy
2. World level of support
3. Complexity level of the operation
4. Host-country support
5. Neutrality
6. Use of force
7. U.S. troop participation
8. Level of force training.

ASSESSING PEACEKEEPING OPERATIONS

The three case studies evaluated in this paper are the UN Truce Supervisory Organization (UNTSO) in the Middle East, the Multinational Force (MNF) in Lebanon, and the Multinational Force and Observers (MFO) in the Sinai Peninsula. These three case studies span the spectrum of U.S. involvement in peacekeeping operations, from providing unarmed military observers to monitor a cease-fire (UNTSO) to providing a large conventional military unit that is interposed between two or more belligerents (MFO and MNF).

All of these cases involve peacekeeping operations in the Middle East, and there is some political overlap between them. The UNTSO operation provides support to the UN Interim Force in Lebanon (UNIFIL) and the UN Disengagement Observer Force (UNDOF) in the Golan Heights.

Observers from UNTSO, members of UNIFIL, and the MNF all coordinated their efforts from 1982 to 1983. The UNIFIL mandate attempted to ensure the withdrawal of Israeli forces from Southern Lebanon, and to restore control of that area to the Lebanese government.

These three examples provide a sampling of political diversity. UNTSO is a peacekeeping operation under UN auspices. Though the UN tried to establish peacekeeping forces in both the Sinai in 1980 and in Lebanon in 1983, for political reasons they were unable to do so. Therefore, the other two examples of U.S. peacekeeping missions were conducted outside of UN control. The MFO and the MNF were established under a political coalition. The MNF included peacekeepers from Italy, France, the U.S. and Great Britain. The MFO is a heterogeneous organization combining military and civilian members from Fiji, Colombia, France, Great Britain, Italy, the Netherlands, Australia, New Zealand, Uruguay, and the United States.

A great deal of political controversy may surround the deployment or even proposed deployment of a peacekeeping force. Internal U.S. political controversy can derive from many factors: the host country's attitude, U.S. public opinion, UN backing which can represent world opinion, the level of U.S. troop participation, and the current policies of both the executive branch and Congress. These three case studies include operations which generated very little political controversy (UNTSO), through operations that instigated some controversy (MFO), all the way to an operation that catalyzed a great debate on U.S. peacekeeping and foreign policy (MNF). They have succeeded, failed, or are inconclusive. The MFO has been lauded as one of the most successful peacekeeping operations ever undertaken (McDermott: 114). The MNF, on the other hand, has been called "America's Greatest Peacekeeping Disaster" (Shuger: 40). UNTSO, a supposedly temporary peacekeeping operation, has met with mixed success (UN *e*).

UNITED NATIONS TRUCE SUPERVISORY ORGANIZATION (UNTSO)

The UNTSO mission, beginning in 1948 and continuing to the present, did not create undue political controversy when it was initiated. As tensions grew in the Middle East, and UNTSO took on more diverse responsibilities, some criticism of its effectiveness arose. The greatest amount of internal U.S. controversy concerning UNTSO was sparked with the kidnapping of Marine Lieutenant Colonel William R. Higgins in 1988 (Watson: 33). Yet, the U.S. continued to support UNTSO with military observers.

Russian and U.S. UNTSO observers in Egypt, 1987. *photo used with permission*

UN and world support for UNTSO has been fairly high, but at the same time a larger, more ambitious mission has not been undertaken. In the UN there is some criticism of this longest running peacekeeping operation (UN e). Israel does not particularly welcome UNTSO (Horn: 128). For these reasons, UN, host-country and world support of UNTSO is considered neutral.

UNTSO is a fairly complicated peacekeeping mission. Some of its elements operate in an urban environment, cooperation is mixed, and a significant number of casualties have been incurred by UNTSO observers. Altogether, the level of complication of the entire UNTSO mission is high.

The Israeli government and many Arab factions do not really trust UNTSO. Further, there is widespread mistrust of the UN, which is sometimes perceived as an American political tool. The high number of UNTSO casualties is testament to the fact that the peacekeepers are not viewed with complete neutrality by either side (Wood: 14).

The UNTSO mission is only an unarmed observer mission. The mission itself, though working closely with UNDOF and UNIFIL, uses little coercive force. This is a very positive aspect of the UNTSO mission. While the UNTSO observers may not be able to enforce some of their mandate, by using only unarmed observers they can establish their neutrality in a better manner, and therefore gain more host country support.

The U.S. deploys only a handful of military personnel to UNTSO. Because of this, little political controversy has been raised in the U.S., and the overall UNTSO mission is not perceived to be dominated by any particular world power.

Joint Military Intelligence College faculty member on UNTSO assignment in Lebanon, 1986.

photo used with permission

U.S. military observers that participate in UNTSO are all commissioned officers. They have each received at least two weeks of specific training, in addition to their normal qualifications as U.S. military professionals (USA *c*: 13). Their training level is fairly high, even considering the many difficulties of the UNTSO mission.

MULTINATIONAL FORCE AND OBSERVERS (MFO)

The MFO, begun in 1981 and ongoing, shares many similarities with UNTSO, yet when examined using these eight variables produces different results. The MFO's employment did not cause a contentious political debate in the U.S., and Congress approved the mission, both as a treaty and under the War Powers Resolution (U.S. Cong *b*: 3). The majority of the international community supported the MFO's employment. The UN could not employ its own peacekeepers because of an anticipated Soviet veto, but widespread support did exist for this particular mission, even when considering that the UN Security Council (UNSC) had its hands tied (MacKinlay: 169).

The MFO has been very successful for many reasons. One of the most important reasons is the relative simplicity of the actual peacekeeping operation. The MFO's mandate is effective, a buffer zone exists, the MFO operates in desert terrain that is relatively unpopulated, and both host countries provide a great deal of support for the mission. Therefore, these factors have reduced the level of complication and have contributed to the successful conduct of the mission (MacKinlay: 5). Both Egypt and Israel support the mandate of the MFO. This is evidenced in their signing of the Camp David Accords. Further, both sides have continually demonstrated their support for the MFO by continuing to help fund the mission (U.S. Cong *b*: 29) and limiting the number of border infractions over the years.

The MFO organization is seen as neutral by both the Israelis and Egyptians. This could be due, in part, to the divestiture of the MFO from the UN. However, because both Israel and Egypt have some voice in choosing MFO leaders, and both provide funding for the MFO, they have seen this international organization as truly neutral.

The MFO does have the capability to use some coercive force in conducting its duties. The MFO employs a Civilian Observer Unit, but the majority of the peacekeepers are armed infantry soldiers. This policy has both helped and impaired the peacekeeping abilities of the MFO.

The U.S. provides an infantry battalion and a logistics support unit to the MFO. This level of support requires approximately 1,200 U.S. military personnel. This is one of the largest deployments of U.S. peacekeepers, and therefore has the potential to spark both internal U.S. controversy and world criticism of a superpower meddling in Middle Eastern affairs. Therefore, this is not a positive variable in the conduct of the MFO.

U.S. peacekeeping forces are trained before they deploy to the Sinai. However, soldiers who have served in the Sinai feel they did not receive sufficient predeployment training to succeed in their mission (Segal: 395). This perceived lack of sufficient training is not as detrimental as it could be in a more complicated peacekeeping scenario.

MULTINATIONAL FORCE (MNF)

A great deal of political controversy erupted when President Reagan deployed U.S. Marine peacekeeping forces to Beirut. This debate subsided somewhat when Congress passed a resolution authorizing the force's employment. Until the U.S. Marine barracks was bombed in October 1983, the U.S. political debate did not adversely affect the mission. Yet, because its status changed considerably as the mission progressed from 1982 through 1984, its outcome was controversial. The ratings for the MNF are tied to the beginning of the MNF mission, before the barracks bombing, and before the U.S. Marines conducted any major reprisal actions. After the Marine reprisals and the subsequent bombing a number of these variables changed drastically. This matrix is meant to be a predictive device. Therefore, these variables shall be assigned relative weights tied to the Beirut peacekeeping situation before it unraveled.

Similar to the U.S. political controversy, there was some international debate on the use of multilateral peacekeeping in Beirut outside of UN auspices. Because of the political intricacies involved in negotiating a peacekeeping force for Beirut and the threat of a Soviet veto if certain conditions were not met, the UN was precluded from taking additional action. This does not mean that the entire international community opposed some further peacekeeping effort, but just that there was a lack of consensus on what action to take.

The complexity of any peacekeeping force installed in Beirut was obviously very high. The Lebanese government did not exercise a great deal of control, and the multiple warring factions and internecine combat made the mission difficult. This was perhaps one of the most complicated peacekeeping operations ever conducted.

While the Lebanese government welcomed the employment of the MNF, it did not exercise authority over the entire operational area. Many of the other factions involved in the fighting in Beirut did not support the mission of the MNF. This would mean that the MNF did not have complete host country support. For the same reasons that the MNF did not have complete support from the international community or the various factions in Lebanon, they also were not perceived as truly neutral. Any sense of neutrality declined significantly after reprisals were taken.

The MNF comprised combat soldiers who employed armored cars, Marine amtracks, and various other military weaponry (MacKinlay: 78). They were not merely unarmed observers, but an interposed military force. They relied on some use of coercion to carry out their mandate, although initially blatant acts of violence did not occur. The U.S. employed over a battalion of Marines in the MNF. This high level of U.S. participation is equivalent to that of the MFO.

While the U.S. trained the infantry forces deployed to the MFO to conduct that specific type of peacekeeping mission, the Marines involved in the MNF received no peacekeeping training oriented to this coercive environment. Lack of training had a negative effect on the Marines' ability to conclude their mission successfully.

OVERALL ASSESSMENT

The MFO has been lauded as the most successful peacekeeping operation ever conducted. On the completed evaluation matrix, it receives a strong positive score (green). The MNF has been considered America's greatest peacekeeping disaster, and the MNF receives a strong negative rating (red). While UNTSO has been unable to meet its mandate completely, it has reduced the level of violence in its area of operation and provided some stabilizing effect. Therefore, UNTSO can be considered a peacekeeping operation with a mixed degree of success (yellow).

In order for the decision matrix to be more realistic and to reflect accurately the relationships among the eight variables, appropriate weights are assigned to each of the eight variables. This weighting technique produces a more responsive decision matrix, reflecting differing levels of significance for the variables in each case study. This weighting depends on the application of a hierarchical scale for the variables considered, in a procedure too detailed to be described here.

The overall assessment of these three case studies correlates very closely to the popularly perceived results of each of the three operations. As U.S. leaders consider any future opportunities to participate in peacekeeping operations, the combined or weighted assessment can guide the political decision required for participation.

FACTORS	ASSESSMENT UNTSO	MFO	MNF
United States Political Controversy	Neutral	Neutral	Neutral
United Nations/World Support	Neutral	Positive	Neutral
Complexity Level	Negative	Neutral	Negative
Host Country Support	Neutral	Positive	Neutral
Neutrality	Neutral	Positive	Neutral
Use of Force	Positive	Neutral	Neutral
United States Participation Level	Neutral	Negative	Negative
United States Force Training Level	Positive	Neutral	Negative
Overall Assessment	Mixed	Positive	Negative

Positive | Negative | Neutral | Mixed

Decision Matrix.

source: compiled by author

FURTHER APPLICATION OF THE PEACEKEEPING DECISION MATRIX

It is very difficult to predict the outcome of peacekeeping operations with any degree of accuracy. Peacekeeping operations not only fail or succeed, but they may also have an ambiguous or mixed outcome. Half of the peacekeeping operations undertaken by the UN have stagnated into a continuous presence of blue-helmeted soldiers with no clear resolution on the horizon. Committing U.S. soldiers and prestige to a peacekeeping operation is a major foreign policy decision. Therefore, it is necessary to reduce uncertainty in the decisionmaking process and to attempt to assess the outcome of any peacekeeping undertaking. While the national command authorities may seek a full settlement of a foreign conflict or crisis, it may not be realistic to expect a complete cessation of hostilities and a final solution. A status quo solution may be acceptable to many parties involved in the conflict, including the UN, particularly if the conflict experiences a decreased level of violence and garners a reduced level of world media attention.

The framework used to analyze the three previous case studies in U.S. peacekeeping can also be used as an assessment tool when considering future operations. The same decision matrix can be completed by using past peacekeeping experiences as a guide, thus gauging a possible future mission's chances of success or failure. A weighted decision matrix can provide a means to evaluate the risks involved when undertaking peacekeeping missions.

SHOULD THE U.S. COMMIT TO BOSNIA?

One can consider the potential for a larger contingent of NATO or UN peacekeeping troops to Bosnia-Herzegovina. This increased troop level could include up to 20,000 U.S. troops. An analysis of the Bosnian peacekeeping scenario using the methods illustrated above may illuminate the potential for either success or failure of the mission. This insight may then prove useful in the decisionmaking process involved in deploying U.S. peacekeepers.

We must first rate each of the eight variables in the matrix. Once each variable is assigned a relative value, corresponding weights will be multiplied by the values. This numerical total can then be compared against the scale of the three previous case studies. This will provide a general relationship or historically based comparison of the possible viability of the proposed peacekeeping operation.

While a great deal of political turmoil could be generated from the deployment of U.S. troops to Bosnia, President Clinton would most likely first secure a degree of political backing from both the Congress and the U.S. populace before authorizing further military action. This support could take the form of a congressional vote, similar to the approval given to the MNF in 1983. U.S. political controversy would then be considered neutral, if the President were able to generate enough political support to deploy troops. Most likely the President would not receive overwhelming support and there would be some controversy involved. Yet, if he were politically able to deploy additional troops, the controversy would not prevent deployment.

Before a larger contingent of peacekeepers would deploy to Bosnia under UN auspices, the UN Security Council would have to approve the expansion of the operation. The U.S. may participate under the NATO flag, but would first attempt to gain UN support to legitimize any actions. This UNSC approval would constitute world support.

FACTORS	ASSESSMENT
United States Political Controversy	Neutral
United Nations/World Support	Positive
Complexity Level	Negative
Host Country Support	Neutral
Neutrality	Positive
Use of Force	Neutral
United States Participation Level	Negative
United States Force Training Level	Neutral
Overall Assessment	Mixed

Positive | Negative | Neutral | Mixed

Decision Matrix: Proposed Peacekeeping Operations in Bosnia-Herzegovina.

source: compiled by author

The complexity level of extensive peacekeeping operations in Bosnia is high. This scenario could easily be compared to the internecine combat that occurred in Beirut in 1982-83. The Muslim, Croat and Serb feuds have the potential to embroil many combatants and inflame the situation. Therefore, this complex operational environment would appear to be a negative factor.

Similarly, the assessment of host-country support, neutrality, use of force, and U.S. participation and force training levels would likely follow historical trends, resulting in the matrix shown above.

THE BOTTOM LINE

The weighted decision matrix total when using these weights and values results in an overall assessment that is moderately negative. This rating is very close to the overall UNTSO rating (yellow). UNTSO's overall mission accomplishment has often come into question. Therefore, by historical comparison based upon these criteria, one can expect a peacekeeping operation in Bosnia under the present conditions to experience some difficulties and to meet with only a limited degree of success.

Peacekeeping operations are sometimes undertaken merely to reduce casualties and provide stability to a region as further solutions are sought. It is common for various peacekeeping missions to be only partially successful. These realistic limitations concerning certain peacekeeping missions have been acceptable to the world community in the past, and may therefore be seen as an acceptable alternative in Bosnia. Hence, peacekeeping forces may still be committed with the understanding that they may not be able to fully realize the international community's goals of ending the conflict.

Chapter 2

INTELLIGENCE IN A UN CONTEXT

The purpose of the United Nations as defined in Article 1 of the Charter is to "maintain international peace," to take effective collective measures for the removal of threats to the peace, and to suppress acts of aggression or other breaches of the peace. The Security Council, which consists of representatives of member states, decides what action should be taken. The Secretary-General is empowered by Article 99 of the Charter to bring to the attention of the Security Council "any matter which in his opinion may threaten" international peace. He is also charged with staff support and is chief administrative officer of the organization. Article 47 of the Charter establishes a Military Staff Committee to advise and assist the Security Council on all questions relating to the Council's military requirements for the maintenance of international peace and to be responsible for the "strategic direction" of any armed forces placed at the UN's disposal. Each of these crucial missions of the United Nations organization implies fact-finding, early warning, analysis, and assessment functions, which are performed by intelligence organizations of any of the UN's member states.

Superpower competition and internal bureaucratic posturing prevented the Military Staff Committee from assuming its proper role, and the Secretary-General gradually evolved support mechanisms replicating intelligence staff functions. The end of the Cold War allowed the Security Council to act in anticipation of threats to international peace posed by internal civil strife and humanitarian crisis. As the UN dispatched military forces all over the world for humanitarian assistance, peacekeeping, peace enforcing and preventive diplomacy, the need for an intelligence role in the strategic direction of UN resources became apparent. Thus, when the Security Council invited Secretary-General Boutros-Ghali to make recommendations for the improvement of the UN, he responded with an agenda for intelligence collection and analysis.

The explicit integration of intelligence into the UN decisionmaking process was evolutionary and not revolutionary. Captains Timothy M. Sebenick and James D. Edwards and Lieutenant Robert J. Allen analyzed the UN Secretariat and UN High Commissioner organizational structures and found an existing intelligence architecture performing the following functions:

- Fact-Finding
- Early Warning
- Assessment for Strategic Planning
- Operational Support

As intelligence support for the UN from member states increases and the UN develops more sophisticated intelligence organizations, the existing intelligence architecture provides the necessary context for understanding the future role of intelligence in the UN.

STRATEGIC INTELLIGENCE AND THE UNITED NATIONS

Timothy M. Sebenick
Captain, U.S. Army
August 1995

> [The General Assembly] welcomes the efforts of the Secretary-General to take appropriate steps through preventive diplomacy and, recognizing the need for those steps to be based on timely and accurate knowledge of relevant facts, encourages him to strengthen the capability of the Secretariat to secure and analyze all relevant information from as wide a variety of sources as possible (UNGA Res A/RES/48/42).

Since the end of the Cold War, there has been a dramatic increase in the number of UN resolutions responding to regional conflicts, ethnic strife, and mass human suffering. In 1990, the UN conducted five peacekeeping operations. In contrast, in 1993 the UN engaged in 24 peacekeeping operations comprising over 75,000 troops, 5,600 of whom were U.S. military personnel. The UN's ability to maintain this escalating trend of intervention is unclear, considering the current U.S. political shift toward limiting UN intervention. The shift may severely limit the UN's response because of its dependence on the U.S. for financial and military resources. But the U.S., as a permanent member of the Security Council and the leading military power in the world, will be under considerable pressure to undertake a principal role when the UN demands resources to address a threat to international peace.

In concert with this rise in UN activity is a rise in efforts to enhance the UN's ability to perform its function of maintaining peace and security. A common goal in this effort is to avoid large, costly, multinational operations by acting to alleviate the roots of conflict and intervene before the crisis develops into conflict. However, in order for this approach to be effective, the causes of conflict must be identified, a mechanism must be in place to discover where those causes are emerging, and resources must be available to execute the actions to alleviate them. Such a methodology, labeled preventive diplomacy, is dependent on the prediction of crisis far enough in advance to formulate and execute a policy to prevent it from occurring. It depends on intelligence.

A great deal of literature exists on the requirements for and development of intelligence support to UN multinational forces, regardless of whether those forces are controlled by the UN or a member-state. Accordingly, the term intelligence, when associated with the UN, is used almost exclusively to refer to operational-level decisions—those that directly affect the forces in the field.[1] Conspicuously absent from literature on intelligence and the UN is the recognition that a strategic-level decision is made before field operations begin—the decision to use military resources to execute UN policy.

The focus of this research is the development by the Secretary-General of a quasi-intelligence architecture that supports UN decisionmaking—specifically, intelligence support of his role as a strategic decisionmaker. This research will address the origin of the Secretary-General's role in creating UN strategy, his administrative and executive power, and the specific reforms he enacted during the Cold War and post-Cold War periods that have established an intelligence architecture. However, the reader should be forewarned that the UN's intelligence architecture is not a clearly defined structure that can be illustrated on a single organizational chart. Rather, it is intertwined within one of the most complex bureaucracies in the world.

The terms and concepts associated with strategic decisionmaking and strategic intelligence unnerve many of those intimately involved with the UN. These terms imply a level of secrecy and executive authority that is contrary to the openness and spirit of collective decisionmaking usually

---

[1] The Department of Defense, according to JCS Pub 2-0, *Joint Doctrine for Intelligence Support to Operations*, 5 May 1995, defines operational intelligence as: "Intelligence that is required for planning and conducting campaigns and major operations to accomplish strategic objectives."

associated with the UN. In most circumstances, the terms intelligence and information are considered almost interchangeable concepts.

STRATEGY AND THE UN

To gain a clear understanding of where strategic intelligence fits into the UN structure, one needs a sense of the type of strategic decisions being made and who makes them. I asked U.S. and UN officers: "Do you view a decision by the Security Council or the Secretary-General to use military resources to achieve a policy goal a strategic decision?" The answer was simply, "No, the UN doesn't create strategy." Officials mocked the idea that the UN deliberately attempts to create strategy in any form. I found their comments disturbing, because they dismissed the inherent tie between policy and strategy once military resources are employed.

Liddell Hart defines strategy as "the art of distributing and applying military means to fulfill the ends of policy" (Liddell Hart: 321). Liddell Hart expands his basic definition of strategy with the concept of "grand strategy," which seems almost tailor-made for the United Nations. For Liddell Hart, the role of grand strategy is to:

> coordinate and direct all the resources of a nation, or band of nations, towards the attainment of the political object of the war—the goal defined by fundamental policy. . . . Moreover, fighting power is but one of the instruments of grand strategy—which should take account of and apply the power of financial pressure, of diplomatic pressure, of commercial pressure, and, not least of ethical pressure, to weaken the opponent's will (Hart: 322).

The UN attempts to use the resources of the international community, bound by the Charter of the United Nations, to obtain a political objective—the maintenance of international peace and security. The UN's recognition of a crisis, the evaluation of its severity, the formulation of options to address the crisis, and the coordination and execution of a policy intended to end the crisis are elements of UN strategy. When a proposed option includes using military resources to address the crisis, it clearly implies the formation of military strategy. UN strategy, especially military strategy, may often be vague and seemingly ill-conceived, but it must exist. The idea that the UN must perform this function has a historical foundation that begins with the Charter of the United Nations itself. The drafters of the

Charter went so far as to create an organization to develop military strategy — the Military Staff Committee.

THE MILITARY STAFF COMMITTEE

The drafters of the UN Charter clearly intended to give the UN a set of teeth to address threats to peace if diplomatic or pacific measures failed. They unanimously accepted the concept of using force, as described in the Dumbarton Oaks Agreement (the founding document of the Charter of the United Nations) (Hilderbrand: 987). Section B, Chapter 8, of that agreement became Article 42 of the UN Charter. Article 42 authorizes the Security Council to "take action by air, sea, or land forces to maintain or restore international peace and security." It permits the creation of permanent UN military forces (which are described in Article 43), and subsequently, the creation of a body to provide strategic direction for those forces — the Military Staff Committee (MSC). Article 46 of the UN Charter is the first place the MSC is mentioned. It states: "Plans for the application of armed force shall be made by the Security Council with the assistance of the Military Staff Committee." Article 47 then formally establishes the MSC and outlines its basic responsibilities. The drafters of the UN Charter expected the MSC to be the cornerstone of a global Department of Defense, through which the security of all nations could be assured. It was to be a supranational military bureaucracy responsible for military planning, operations, and arms control (Rostow: 109).

The MSC, officially established on 4 February 1946, quickly drafted a statute and rules of procedure. On 16 February, the Security Council made three decisions that directly affected the MSC. First, it established a committee of experts to review the MSC's draft statute. Second, it instructed the MSC to operate under the provisions of the draft statute, pending its approval. Third, and most importantly, it issued the MSC its first task — to examine, from the military point of view, the provisions contained in Article 43 referring to the establishment of a UN armed force (R. Goldman: 27). The final draft of the statute and rules of procedure was submitted on 24 July 1946 and approved on 1 August 1946. The delay was a result of concern by Secretary-General Lie that the statute did not place enough importance on the role of the Secretariat. The exact details of the disagreement are not known, but supposedly a significant amount of correspondence was exchanged between the Secretary-General and the Chairman of the MSC prior to the submission of the final draft (U.S. DoD *l*: 2).

Ironically, the demise of the MSC began with its first official task. On 13 February 1946, the Security Council adopted a resolution on disarmament. In addition to the resolution, it issued a directive to the MSC to submit a recommendation (no later than 30 April 1947), regarding the basic principles that should govern the creation of permanent UN military forces (R. Goldman: 7). There was initial agreement among the permanent members of the MSC that such forces should not be autonomous and must be subject to Security Council veto. They also agreed with the spirit of the Charter that the preponderance of forces should be provided by the five permanent members of the Council. From that point forward agreements between the superpowers ceased. A consensus could not be reached on primary points of discussion. The most significant debate focused on the size of each member's contribution, the standby location of the contributed forces, and the source of supplies and funding to maintain the forces (Grove: 177).

On 30 April 1947, the MSC issued a report to the Security Council outlining both the agreements and disagreements between the permanent members of the MSC. On 10 August 1947, the MSC ceased debate about Article 43, and on 2 July 1948, a statement was issued to the Security Council indicating that no further agreement seemed likely (U.S. DoD *l*: 5). The MSC was deadlocked. It has not produced a significant report to the Security Council since 1947. The MSC continues to meet briefly (a matter of minutes) every other week, deciding only the time schedule and agenda for its next session.

The inability of the MSC to perform its role of providing strategic direction to military forces did not deter the use of military force by the UN. Consequently, the lack of a central body to create strategy led to numerous adaptations within the UN organizational structure. It ultimately empowered the UN Secretary-General to devise his own apparatus to organize and control the use of military resources contributed to the UN.

BIRTH OF STRATEGIC INTELLIGENCE

> At present, the UN lacks independent sources of information: its means of obtaining up-to-date information are primitive by comparison with those of states — indeed of most transnational corporations (UN *m*: 6).
>
> Secretary-General Perez de Cuellar

Secretary-General Boutros-Ghali, and all five of his predecessors, have written extensively about the need to improve the capacity of the UN to gather and analyze information for the purpose of decisionmaking. UN decisionmaking encompasses both the identification of a crisis (and responding to it) and the creation of policy to improve the relationship of member-states within the international community (Kaufmann: 16). If information presented to the UN indicates a threat to international peace, the UN may decide to address that threat directly — increasing the demand for information in order to assess the seriousness of the threat and to formulate a response to resolve it. Information, in the context of the UN, as with information associated with the U.S. political system, is an indispensable asset — it is literally the conduit for power and influence.

The control of information, and the quest to improve the ability of the UN to gather information, led to organizational changes — especially in the Secretariat and the Office of the Secretary-General.[2] These changes were made largely in response to the political climate of the Cold War and overt attempts by the Secretary-General to assert an executive role in international peacekeeping. The Secretary-General's reforms are an attempt to create a flow of strategic intelligence to support the concept of "early warning," simultaneously enhancing the power of the Secretary-General and the potential responsiveness of the Security Council.

Information about foreign countries, analyzed for the purpose of forming strategy, policy, or military plans, is the very definition of strategic intelligence in its basic form (U.S. DoD *a*: 8). Ironically, the term intelligence is nearly forbidden in context with UN operations. Many contend that the UN by design has no enemies and, therefore, has no need to collect intelligence against identified or potential adversaries. However, this narrow view of strategic intelligence is clouded in semantics. No one would claim, when the U.S. State Department's Bureau of Intelligence and Research provides assessments on foreign countries to the Secretary of State, that it is not providing strategic intelligence. The UN, in contrast,

2 In this context information control is the ability of the Secretary-General to hold back or emphasize information for political reasons. This control is afforded to the Secretary-General by nature of his position as head of the Secretariat. This is analogous to the control of information afforded Cabinet heads and senior members of the White House Staff. They inherently have the power to hold back or emphasize information going to the President of the United States.

does not have an organized intelligence agency or permanently stationed ambassadors with a reporting function. Yet the requirement for and use of strategic intelligence are clear (Rivlin and Gordenker: 90). Simply speaking, the terms information and intelligence are interchangeable with respect to how decisions are made in the UN. Even U.S. military commanders assigned to UN operations are advised by the *Joint Task Forces Commander's Handbook for Peace Operations* to use the term information synonymously with and in place of intelligence (U.S. DoD *m*: 29).

Information is arguably (in competition with funding) the most powerful single element in the political process in the UN. It is often the only tool available to a diplomat attempting to influence the actions of the UN or a member-state in crisis. It is also the element that brings the UN into action — the decision to actively address the crisis in Rwanda and not the crisis in Angola was largely a product of controlling (and emphasizing) information.

THE SECRETARY-GENERAL

The Secretary-General is charged with both administrative and political functions. The administrative role is specifically mentioned in the UN Charter. However, the political role of the Secretary-General depends largely on the incumbent's personality and the political climate of the international community. Although the Secretary-General is a member of the Secretariat, his office encompasses more than that organ. According to Article 97 of the Charter, the Secretary-General is the Chief Administrative Officer of the UN (encompassing all five organs) and not just the administrative head of the Secretariat (Simma: 1023). The role of the Secretary-General has been debated extensively since the creation of the UN in 1945. However, it is clear that the strength of the Secretary-General is based upon controlling (and reforming) the administrative functions of the Secretariat, including the management of information, and wielding political clout in the international community.

Article 98 of the UN Charter describes the duties of the Secretary-General in generic terms; it states that the organs of the UN may entrust him with "other functions." These unspecified functions are manifest in three categories: functions relating to the compilation of information and the creation of studies; functions in connection with solving procedural problems; and functions in connection with addressing legal questions (Simma: 1042). Of these, the one that warrants the most attention by the Secretary-General involves the creation of studies and the gathering of information. The other functions are most often left to the discretion of the Under-Secretaries-General and Assistant Secretaries-General. Since the Secretary-General is charged with administering the Secretariat, he therefore operationally controls the flow of information between the primary organs of the UN. The Secretary-General is the focal point for deciding when information must be sought and when and in what form it is released to the organs of the UN or the public.

UN Secretary-General-Elect Kofi Annan addresses press in New York, 18 December 1996. *UN photo by M. Grant*

Often the Security Council will "call upon" the "good offices" of the Secretary-General to gather facts and provide advice about a particular issue under consideration.[3] The Secretariat, however, is not officially vested as a gatherer of information. According to the UN Charter, its task is to manage and process information in an administrative sense (e.g., preparing documents and managing the distribution of documents). The power to gather information is implied when the Security Council issues a request for the Secretary-General to make judgments.

A Security Council request for information and advice from the Secretary-General demonstrates the importance of the perceived impartiality of the Secretary-General. But the impartiality of the office is a facade in these situations. When the Security Council asks the Secretary-General to gather information on a critical issue, the Secretary-General will likely rely on the powerful member-states and an informal set of personal contacts for the information — albeit in a confidential fashion. The lack of an "in house" information-gathering system, and the quest for more influence in the decisionmaking cycle of the Security Council, are historically the primary concerns of the Secretary-General.

---

[3] The term "call upon" is commonly used in UN Resolutions. It refers to a non-binding request for action. The term "good offices" is used to refer to the Office of the Secretary-General and includes individuals he appoints for a particular diplomatic mission.

The authority of the Secretary-General to intervene in the political process of maintaining peace and security is codified by Article 99 of the UN Charter. It is almost always cited when the executive authority of the Secretary-General is questioned. Article 99 of the Charter states: "The Secretary-General may bring to the attention of the Security Council any matter which in his opinion may threaten the maintenance of international peace and security." Although it has been used officially only twice (by Dag Hammarskjold in 1960 during the Congo crisis and by Kurt Waldheim in 1979 during the occupation of the American Embassy in Tehran), it is often cited by the Secretary-General to add emphasis to his role as the head of the organization when there is a threat to the peace (Simma: 1051-1055).

One of the most important concepts implied by Article 99 is that the Secretary-General is entitled to gather information for his own decisionmaking purposes versus responding to a request from the Security Council. The Article clearly implies that the Secretary-General has the right to conduct the necessary inquiries and investigations in order to decide whether there is a genuine threat to the peace and whether it should bc brought to the attention of the Security Council (Simma: 1047). The impact of Article 99 on the desire to create an information-gathering system is demonstrated by Secretary-General Perez de Cuellar:

> In order to avoid the [Security Council] becoming involved too late in critical situations, it may well be that the Secretary-General should play a more forthright role in bringing potentially dangerous situations to the attention of the Council within the general framework of Article 99 of the Charter. My predecessors have done this on a number of occasions, but I wonder if the time has come for a more systematic approach. Most potential conflict areas are well known. The Secretary-General has traditionally, if informally, tried to keep watch for problems likely to result in conflict and to do what he can to pre-empt them by quiet diplomacy. The Secretary-General's diplomatic means are, however, in themselves quite limited. In order to carry out effectively the preventive role foreseen for the Secretary-General under Article 99, I intend to develop a wider and more systematic capacity for fact-finding in potential conflict areas. Such efforts would naturally be undertaken in close coordination with the Council (UN *m*: 6).

The importance placed on increasing the capability to gather and analyze information has led to numerous reforms in the past 50 years. The Secretary-General has increasingly sought to enhance his political influence in the UN, using his role as an information manager and his authority to reform the structure of the Secretariat. Beginning with the second UN Secretary-General, Dag Hammarskjold, the reforms of the Secretariat structure reflect the concept that information is power for the Secretary-General. This power is vested in the ability to control the flow of valuable information, to insert emphasis in its content, and to distribute it among those who can approve action (Rivlin and Gordenker: 278). This power varies greatly among Secretaries-General, but there is no question that it exists.

COLD WAR REFORM

The Cold War greatly contributed to the growth and influence of the Secretariat and the office of the Secretary-General — especially in the realm of information gathering. The struggle between the superpowers unquestionably stifled the actions of the Security Council to collectively address threats to international peace. Between 1946 and 1970, the Soviet Union cast 103 vetoes to quell UN actions that it perceived as Western advances. Between 1970 and 1989, the United States cast 67 vetoes to stop actions that it perceived as supporting communist aggression (Rivlin and Gordenker: 8). This deadlock in the Security Council prompted numerous attempts by the Secretary-General to address international crises through the Secretariat and the General Assembly. These attempts required a mechanism to acquire, analyze, and manipulate information for the purpose of making (and promoting) decisions and creating operational plans. In these two decades, the Department of Political and Security Council Affairs and the Office for Research and the Collection of Information were established in response to the Secretary-General's quest for information and a desire to extend his influence in the Security Council and in peacekeeping operations in general.

Department of Political and Security Council Affairs

Secretary-General Dag Hammarskjold, responding to his involvement in UN peacekeeping operations in the Arab-Israeli conflict and what can be termed peace-enforcement operations during the Congo crisis, developed the Department of Political and Security Council Affairs (PSCA). One of the primary functions of PSCA was to: "[A]ssist the Secretary-General in

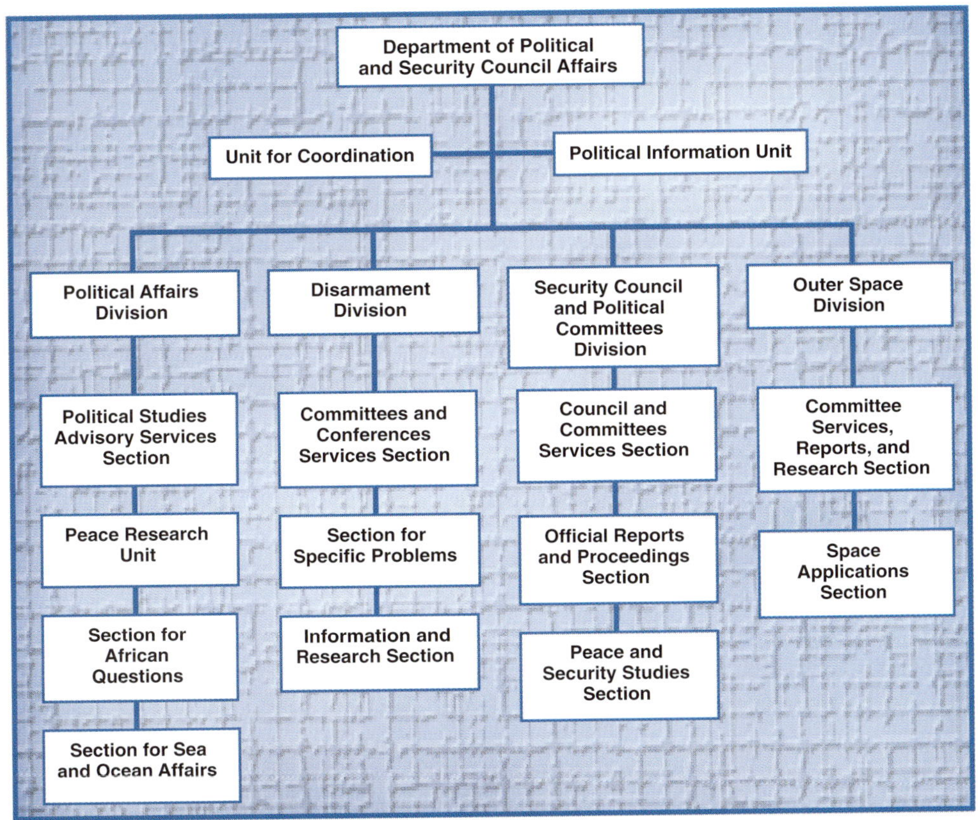

UN Department of Political and Security Council Affairs. *source: author*

the discharge of his political responsibilities under the Charter and in pursuance of resolutions of United Nations organs" (UNSec *c*: 1). Although it does not refer directly to Article 99 of the Charter, that is clearly the basis for the existence of the organization.

PSCA consisted of the Office of the Under-Secretary and four major subordinate divisions (see accompanying figure). Each subordinate department had three tasks in common: collect, analyze, and assess information; prepare reports; and provide secretariat services (i.e., administrative support) (UNSec *c*: 3-7). The organization was created to support the Secretary-General as well as the Security Council; however, it was the former who focused on the collection of information in order to better predict crises. Many of the Department's functions concerned the collection of information and provision of analysis (specifically, the Information and

Research Section of the Disarmament Division, the Space Applications Section of the Outer Space Division, one unit subordinate to the Political Affairs Division — the Peace Research Unit, and the Political Information Unit).

Information and Research Section

The functions of the Information and Research Section illustrate how pervasive the Secretary-General considered his political involvement in the actions of the Security Council.

> [C]ollects relevant information concerning disarmament . . . Prepares analytical notes and memoranda to advise the Secretary-General on current developments . . . Prepares the analyses and assessments concerning military technology and weapon effects, military strategy and tactics, national military developments and military alliances and the characteristics and consequences of the arms race (UNSec *c*: 4).

The Information and Research Section remained under the Director of the Political Affairs Division until 1974. On 1 August 1974, Secretary-General Kurt Waldheim moved it into the Office of the Under-Secretary-General and later, in 1975, merged it with the Unit for Coordination (UNSec *f*). Each successive reorganization brought the unit closer to the personal control of the Secretary-General's office.

The Space Applications Section of the Outer Space Division illustrates how concerned the UN Secretary-General was about the technical collection of information. The primary function of the section was to assess the use of space for peaceful means and to coordinate the activities of the growing U.S. and USSR space programs. However, the official description of the section's function specifically uses terms that refer to the gathering of information from space platforms. It states:

> [The Space Application Section] gathers information and compiles reports as required on the current state of space technology in the survey of earth resources by satellite, monitoring and control of the environment, space communications, education and training in the practical applications of space technology and possible future developments in space technology in general (UNSec *c*: 5).

Both the Information and Research Unit and the Space Applications Section were small, poorly staffed offices, but their development demonstrates how the Office of the Secretary-General—originating with Dag Hammarskjold—used its authority to reshape the Secretariat. They established organizational precedent for later reforms designated to eventually create an information network. Secretary-General Perez de Cuellar pushed this concept to its political limits with the creation of the Office for Research and the Collection of Information (ORCI).

Secretary-General Javier Perez de Cuellar, Windhoek, Namibia, July 1989, on a tour of UNTAG operations. *UN photo by M. Grant*

The Office for Research and the Collection of Information

On 1 March 1987, ORCI was established. It consisted of three major subordinate units: a Planning and Early Warning section, a News Distribution Section, and a Drafting Service (UNSec *h*: 1-2). The Assistant Secretary-General for ORCI, in contrast to the Department of Political and Security Council Affairs, reported directly to the UN Secretary-General with no formal relationship to the Security Council. Secretary-General Perez de Cuellar wanted a separation between the Security Council's role of addressing threats to the peace and the Secretary-General's role of predicting (or preventing) threats to peace (Rivlin and Gordenker: 274-275).

Additionally, he wanted to underscore the importance of early warning in the pursuit of preventive diplomacy (which he perceived as his primary function under the authority given to him by Article 99 of the Charter). This is clearly demonstrated within the official description of some of ORCI's primary functions:

- To assess global trends.
- To provide early warning of developing situations requiring the Secretary-General's attention.
- [To identify and coordinate] research on the issues on which long-range analysis and research are needed in connection with the

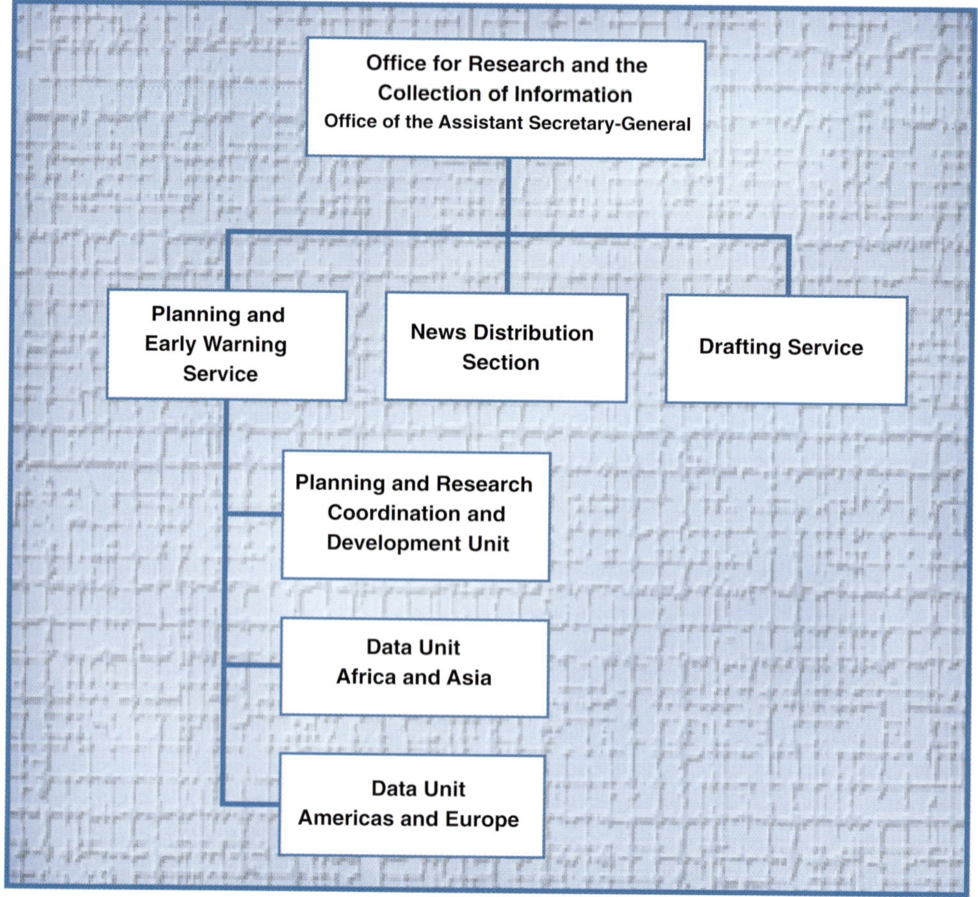

Office for Research and the Collection of Information. *source: author*

responsibilities of the Secretary-General under the Charter of the United Nations.

- [To provide] substantive advice, in conjunction with other departments dealing with political affairs, to the Secretary-General and senior staff on developments that may have a bearing on peace and security (UNSec *h*: 1-3).

The capability of ORCI to perform these functions was severely limited by the political realities associated with the UN. Secretary-General Perez de Cuellar was frustrated by the complexities of Cold War politics and the often strong opposition to his concept of executive authority over UN operations. He also was hindered by the bureaucratic difficulties associated with funding his proposals and organizational changes. The Secretary-General has the authority to make organizational changes, but if they require additional funding they must be approved by the General Assembly — a daunting task in light of the UN's poor financial condition. ORCI was not exempt from these realities. It was largely understaffed, had little automation support, and did not have the ability to "electronically connect" to outside information agencies as intended (Rivlin and Gordenker: 275).

The development of ORCI was an attempt at creating a "global watch" under the direct control of the Secretary-General. It was intended to be an organization that would systematically address the concept of early warning and solidify the role of the Secretary-General under Article 99 of the Charter (Simma: 1046). Although short-lived (five years), it did forge the infrastructure for later reforms by Boutros Boutros-Ghali. Both Secretary-General Perez de Cuellar and the incoming Boutros-Ghali, in light of the unexpected collapse of the Soviet Union, envisioned an "unchained" United Nations. With the vision and leadership of the Secretary-General, it would have the ability to address global issues in their infancy. Ironically, the post-Cold War world presented a host of complex problems that were exacerbated by the inability of the UN to implement its new-found freedom of action. Again, reform to enhance the capabilities of the Secretary-General was the first step taken to address the post-Cold War world and its challenges. And again, the focus of the reform was to create an information architecture to support strategic decisionmaking by the Secretary-General.

BOUTROS-GHALI'S REFORMS: AN AGENDA FOR COLLECTION AND ANALYSIS

Concurrent with the end of the Cold War was a rise in expectations that the United Nations would be the focal point for solving international disputes. This expectation was reinforced by President George Bush prior to the Persian Gulf War, and the term "New World Order" became synonymous with it (Bush *f*: 2). In light of the "New World Order," the UN Security Council, pressured by the superpowers, asked the Secretary-General to address the changes required to enhance the capability of the UN—especially the UN's role in conflict prevention. Secretary-General Boutros-Ghali responded by producing *An Agenda for Peace* (Boutros-Ghali *b*).

An Agenda for Peace outlines the concepts and reforms required to bring the capabilities of the UN in line with its expanded role. The reforms he suggests, along with subsequent documents on UN reform, encompass nearly every aspect of the UN. However, the importance placed on the early detection of international crises is frequently underscored. For example, the first "aim" listed in *An Agenda for Peace* is "To seek to identify at the earliest possible stage situations that could produce conflict, and to try through diplomacy to remove the sources of danger before violence results" (UNGA A/47/277: 4).

In 1945, the Secretariat had 2,450 employees. Today the Secretary-General has authority over approximately 10,000 employees dispersed around the world (Rivlin and Gordenker: 46). Secretary-General Boutros-Ghali, in March 1992, announced widespread organizational reform in the Secretariat. He reduced the number of Under-Secretaries-General from 16 to 8. He also decentralized the control of many functions that previously fell under the Office of the Secretary-General. His intent was to streamline the Secretariat by reducing redundancy. At the same time, he retained a large degree of control by assuming direct supervision over the Under-Secretaries-General—placing himself in a role similar to a Chief Executive Officer.

The most significant reforms relevant to this study are the creation of the Department of Political Affairs (DPA), the Department of Peacekeeping Operations (DPKO), and the Department for Humanitarian Affairs (DHA). DPA incorporated ORCI as well as other political bodies, including the Department for Disarmament Affairs. DPKO was created from the former Office of Special Political Affairs and then greatly expanded to facilitate the increased peacekeeping role of the UN. The offices throughout the UN, including those in Geneva which were focused on emergency relief, were incorporated into DHA. Other reforms, less significant to this study, occurred in 1992 and 1993 throughout the Secretariat (e.g., the creation of the Department of Economic and Social Information and Policy Analysis). However, DPA, DPKO, and DHA are more likely to be involved in crises requiring deployment of UN personnel.

THE INFORMATION ARCHITECTURE

> The Security Council strongly supports the Secretary-General's conclusion that peacekeeping operations need an effective information capacity, and his intention to address this requirement in future peacekeeping operations from the planning stage (UNSC S/PRST/1995/9).

By its very nature, the entire Secretariat is an information management organization. It is clearly understood that the Secretariat is responsible for administrative functions such as day-to-day word-processing, the creation of reports, and the distribution of those reports. What is not so clear is the role of the Secretariat in terms of collecting and analyzing information for the purpose of drawing conclusions and making recommendations. This role is not defined in the UN Charter but clearly exists according to the specified functions of the organizations that make up the Secretariat. Certain organizations within DPA, DPKO, and DHA are tasked with assisting the Secretary-General in his role as a UN decisionmaker. These components do not create a coherent intelligence infrastructure and often overlap the administrative functions of the Secretariat. However, they do form a loose information architecture, which produces products that far exceed simple administrative support to the UN. A direct link exists between the reforms in the Secretariat (and the creation of an information architecture) and the role of the Secretary-General under Article 99 of the UN Charter.[4]

Department for Political Affairs

DPA is the political arm of the Secretary-General in matters relating to the maintenance of international peace and the control of conflicts within

---

4 The outline of the intelligence architecture of the UN is based on the organizational structure provided by official UN documents and numerous interviews with U.S. delegates to the UN and members of the UN Secretariat.

member-states. It is responsible for political research and analysis in these areas, and it oversees the management of preventive diplomacy and peacemaking. DPA has three basic functions:

- Collect information about actual or potential disputes;
- Provide analysis of information to identify situations in which the UN could usefully take action;
- Advise the Secretary-General on what form that action should take (UNGA A/48/403: 9; UNGA A/49/336: 15).

The structure of DPA resembles the "regional desk" configuration used by many intelligence organizations (see accompanying figure). It encompasses six regional divisions (two for Africa, two for Asia, one for the Americas, and one for Europe). Each division is responsible for collecting regional information, analyzing that information, and preparing reports for the Secretary-General. Two Assistant Secretaries-General (one for the African divisions and one for the Americas, Europe, and Asia divisions) provide administrative

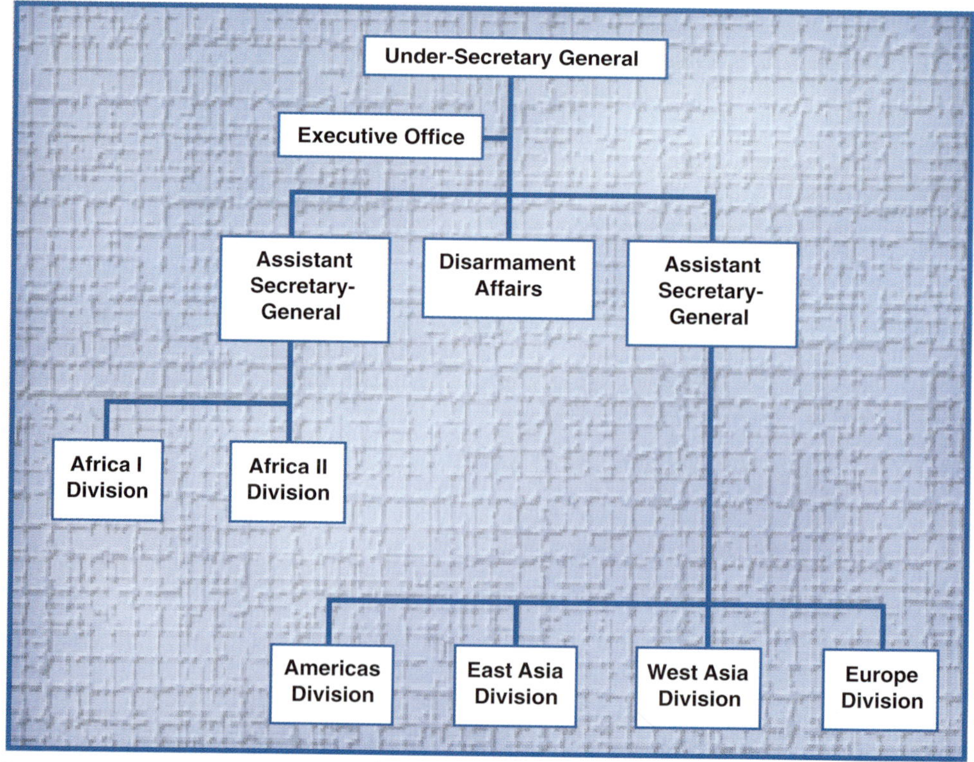

Department for Political Affairs.

source: author

guidance for the Directors in charge of each division. The Under-Secretary-General of DPA, Merrick Goulding of Great Britain, works very closely with the UN Secretary-General and is informally considered the "number two" man in the Secretariat (Kaufmann: 286).

Department of Peacekeeping Operations

The Department of Peacekeeping Operations (DPKO) is the operational arm of the Secretary-General. It has three major components: the Office of the Under-Secretary-General, the Office of Planning and Support, and the Office of Operations. The primary mission of DPKO is to plan peacekeeping operations authorized by the Security Council or to monitor peacekeeping operations currently in progress. Therefore, DPKO is much more

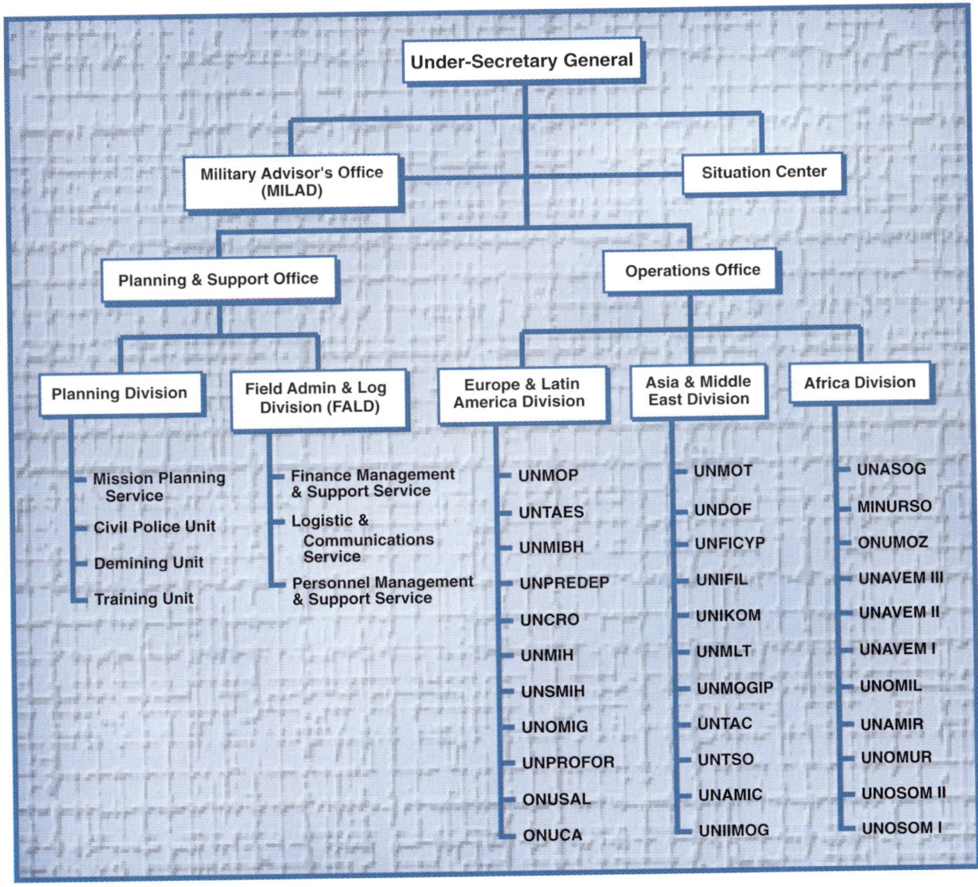

Department of Peacekeeping Operations. *source: author*

involved with operational information, which is beyond the scope of this paper. However, some of the sub-components of DPKO fall within the boundaries of strategic intelligence or strategic decisionmaking: the Policy and Analysis Unit, the Mission Planning Service, and the Information and Research Unit of the UN Situation Center. These sub-components are noteworthy because they address a little known function of DPKO—contingency planning (UNSec *e*: 1).

The concept of contingency planning relates directly to the continued expansion of the Secretary-General's power under Article 99 of the Charter. The Secretary-General's process for deciding which crisis warrants a peacekeeping contingency plan is not clearly defined. The Secretary-General may simply attempt to forecast the outcome of a Security Council session (knowing what crises are on the agenda) and provide DPKO with a list of countries where peacekeeping missions may emerge. This method provides DPKO with very little advance notice in order to formulate a contingency plan. However, the Secretary-General, through his own information architecture and decisionmaking cycle, may decide that a crisis is severe enough to warrant a peacekeeping mission (and subsequently the attention of the Security Council). In this case, he could order DPKO to start the planning process long before the crisis is addressed by the Security Council, which then may face a *fait accompli*. Because of international pressure to do something, the Security Council is much more likely to act if the Secretary-General can simultaneously emphasize the need for urgent action and present a contingency plan to execute that action (Burns: 199). Ultimately, the function of contingency planning greatly increases the Secretary-General's influence over the Security Council's actions.

Ironically, the mission of creating contingency plans is outlined in the mandate for DPKO but is not listed as a specified function of any subordinate unit. The responsibility for contingency planning rests with the Under-Secretary-General for DPKO and is encompassed in the following functions:

- Advises the Secretary-General on all matters related to the planning, establishment and conduct of United Nations Operations;
- Prepares the Secretary-General's reports to the Security Council on each Peacekeeping operation, with appropriate observations and recommendations (UNSec *e*: 2).

Both the Policy and Analysis Unit and the Mission Planning Service of DPKO are involved in the preparation of contingency plans. Their involvement is directly coordinated with and monitored by the Office of the Under-Secretary-General. This is evident in their close organizational ties to the Under-Secretary-General. The Policy and Analysis Unit and the Situation Center report directly to the Under-Secretary. Despite the fact that the Mission Planning Service is subordinate to the Planning Division of the Office of Planning and Support, the head of the Planning Division is the Military Advisor, who also reports directly to the Under-Secretary-General. In general, Boutros-Ghali decentralized the control of the Secretariat. However, in relation to these organizations, he established a more direct line of communication. It is likely that the direct link between these organizations and the Office of the Secretary-General demonstrates their relative importance.

Policy and Analysis Unit (DPKO)

The Policy and Analysis Unit (not on the official organizational chart) acts as the Under-Secretary's think-tank on issues concerning peacekeeping. Its broad mandate includes the development of peacekeeping doctrine as well as gathering information on the potential impact of peacekeeping operations on developing crises (UNSec *e*: 3-4). The Policy and Analysis Unit is more concerned with the information required to make the political decision to use peacekeeping operations (as a method to solve the crisis) than with the information required to create a contingency plan. The unit is focused on providing advice to the Secretary-General in reference to the feasibility of using military resources and not how and in what form those resources will be deployed.

Mission Planning Service (DPKO)

In contrast to the Policy and Analysis Unit's function, the Mission Planning Service drafts the peacekeeping operational plan. Its role in contingency planning is centered around the following tasks:

- Prepare guidelines (both generic and mission-specific) and procedures according to which the integrated planning for future missions is to be conducted, including directives for inter-and intra-departmental coordination and resource requirements;

- Prepare the detailed requirements of new peacekeeping operations encompassing timetables, troop contributions, civilian police, personnel and logistics in close cooperation with the Field Administrative and Logistic Division;
- Prepare comprehensive operational plans for new peacekeeping operations and other field missions and, as required, revise and modify plans for current operations and ensure effective implementation (UNSec *e*: 7).

The information and staff support required to perform these tasks for complex peacekeeping operations such as the United Nations Operation in Somalia (UNOSOM) far exceed the capacity of the Mission Planning Service. In these complex operations, the role of the Mission Planning Service is reduced to reviewing proposed operational plans (created by the U.S. in the case of UNOSOM) called "Option Papers." Often a member-state's option paper will be modified by the Mission Planning Service, briefed to the Under-Secretary-General, and eventually become a UN option paper for review and use by the UN Secretary-General. However, for less complex or less publicized UN peacekeeping contingency plans, the Mission Planning Service plays a greater role. For example, the Mission Planning Service created a contingency plan involving the deployment of UN personnel to Burundi to provide humanitarian relief. The contingency plan was created despite the fact that the Security Council did not issue a resolution addressing the crisis in Burundi. Members of the Mission Planning Service, in conjunction with other departments, deployed to Burundi on a "fact-finding" mission for the purpose of gathering relevant planning information. Assisting in fact-finding is a key responsibility of the Mission Planning Service and is an integral part of the information-gathering capability of the Secretary-General.

Information and Research Unit (DPKO)

The Information and Research Unit is not found on the official organizational charts produced by the Secretariat but is an essential component of DPKO operations. It is subordinate to the Situation Center and reports directly to the Under-Secretary-General. It serves as the focal point for information coming from the operational level (ongoing UN field operations) to the strategic decisionmaking level of the Secretariat.[5] The Information and Research Unit is staffed mainly by military personnel and is largely a product of U.S. recommendations and donations (including funding or providing personnel and equipment). The assigned functions of the unit illustrate the involvement of the Secretary-General in the planning and execution of peacekeeping operations. They also illustrate where and how operational-level information is transferred into UN strategic-level information. Some of these functions are listed below:

- Maintain background country files and mission area files to support information requirements of the DPKO Planning Staffs and other analysts. Maintain a basic map and reference library;
- Acquire background military, political and technical information to support the requirements of Field Missions and the DPKO Planning Teams;
- Produce the "Daily In-Brief," an executive summary of Peacekeeping missions, related world events and [monitor elections] . . . [T]he "In Brief" looks at indicators of potential security threats to UN personnel and likely developing DPKO operations;
- Put together the "Daily Information Digest." This is a combination of Joint Deployable Intelligence Support System (JDISS) material, Control Risks Assessments, Foreign Language Broadcasts (FBIS), Internet material, NATO open material, and analytical papers. This is circulated to Desk Officers in DPA, DPKO, DHA, and various planning teams;
- Write the "Secretary-General's Weekly Report on Peacekeeping." This is a series of key events in each peacekeeping mission and estimate of future intentions (UNSec *d*).

DPKO, more than any other department in the Secretariat, is concerned with the operational level of information collection, analysis, and dissemination. The operational information is transformed into numerous products used to evaluate past and current operations, plan future operations, create UN peacekeeping policy, and provide early warning to the Secretary-General for the purpose of decisionmaking. DPKO is the transition point between operational information and strategic information. It is also a conduit between UN decisionmakers and the UN operational command authority, if authorized by the Security Council.

---

[5] The strategic-level decisionmakers of the UN are the heads of the major departments, normally Under-Secretaries-Generals, and of course the UN Secretary-General.

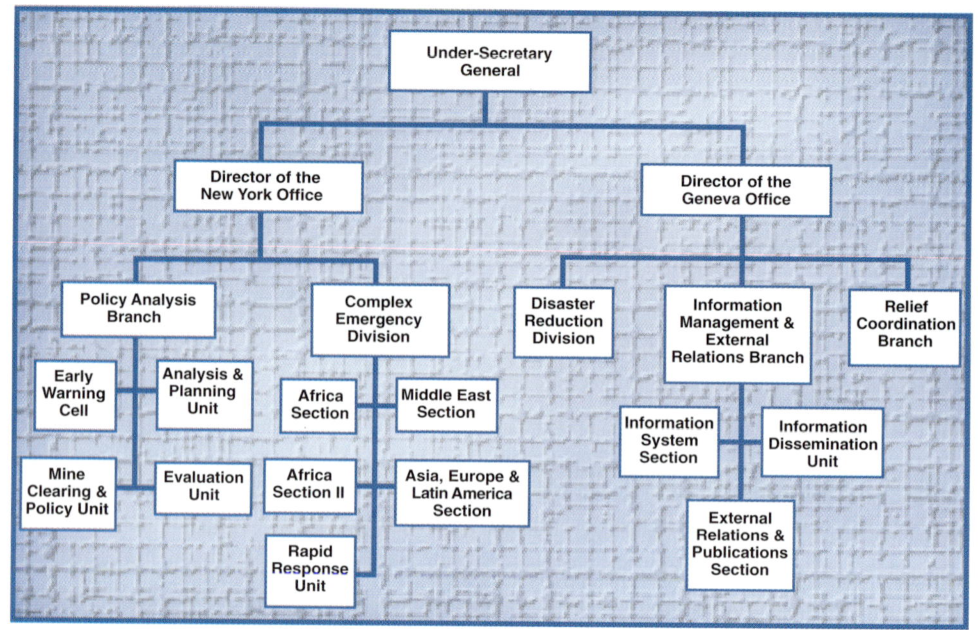

Department of Humanitarian Affairs. *source: author*

Department of Humanitarian Affairs

Boutros-Ghali's attempts at enhancing the UN's capability to conduct Preventive Diplomacy and Preventive Deployment were the catalyst for organizational reforms in the Department of Humanitarian Affairs (DHA). DHA was established in April 1991 and has continued to evolve and grow organizationally, technologically, and in status relative to the other departments. DHA is led by an Under-Secretary-General and further divided into two separate offices (located in New York and Geneva), each under the control of an Assistant Secretary-General (UNSec *e*). The role of DHA, according to the Secretary-General, is "to facilitate a coordinated and effective response by the United Nations, and the system as a whole, to emergencies, including complex emergencies involving political, military, humanitarian and other dimensions, as well as natural and man-made disasters" (UNGA A/49/336: 20). Historically, humanitarian relief functions were organized by the UN office in Geneva due to its proximity to the International Committee of the Red Cross and major European non-governmental organizations. But the increase in dynamic humanitarian operations, involving significant military resources for logistics and security, has heightened the scope and political sensitivity of humanitarian relief. In response, the Secretary-General expanded the New York office to manage the information requirements, political policy analysis and mission planning, and coordination of these sensitive and complex operations.

An important element of the DHA operation is information collection and analysis, especially for the purpose of early warning. The early warning concept grew out of the Secretary-General's desire to rapidly respond to humanitarian emergencies. Here again the organizational reforms are based upon the Secretary-General's desire to gain information for the purpose of exercising his implied power under Article 99 of the Charter. In fact, the majority of reforms in DHA, especially those enacted after the creation of UNOSOM, are associated with information gathering and analysis. A statement by the Secretary-General pertaining to UN reforms in 1995 highlights the major changes in this area:

> Recently, the internal structure of the Department of Humanitarian Affairs has been further reviewed in the light of experience, and its capability for responding to complex emergencies was consolidated into a single, unified desk structure under a Complex Emergency Branch in New York. That structure is intended to ensure clear lines of responsibility and accountability for addressing incipient and ongoing emergencies, on a country-by-country basis. It is also intended to enhance the Department's capacity to receive, analyze and act on early warning information, to advise the Under-Secretary-General and the Secretary-General on appropriate responses . . . [A] capacity in those areas will also be maintained in the United Nations Office at Geneva (UNGA A/49/336: 22).

The information required for the Secretary-General to promote, plan, and coordinate a rapid and dynamic response to humanitarian disasters led to the creation of the Complex Emergency Division and the Early Warning Cell of the Policy Analysis Branch.

Complex Emergency Division (DHA)

The Complex Emergency Branch configuration is similar to the "desk officer" concept found in the DHA. It consists of four regional desks or sections (two oriented on Africa; one for the Middle East; and one encompassing Asia, Europe, and Latin America). Each has the responsibility for monitoring and analyzing the humanitarian condition, preparing status reports, and providing advice about their respective regions through the Assistant Secretary-General to the Under-Secretary-General. In addition, the Division contains a Rapid Response Unit for conducting and coordinating the planning efforts of DHA, once a humanitarian crisis has been identified. The Rapid Response Unit is also incorporated into the Secretary-General's fact-finding deployments for the purpose of conducting on-site assessments. The Complex Emergency Division is an integral part of the UN Secretariat's information architecture. It is set up to monitor humanitarian concerns on a regional basis and provide information through the Under-Secretary-General to the UN Secretary-General.

Early Warning Cell (DHA)

Currently, DHA is the only department with a subordinate element whose sole function is early warning. The Early Warning Cell is subordinate to the Policy Analysis Branch and is located in the New York Office. The location and organizational subordination of the Early Warning Cell have been in a constant state of flux since it was created in 1994. The function of the Early Warning Cell indicates that it should be closely tied, if not subordinate to, the Rapid Response Unit in the Complex Emergency Division. However, because of unclear political circumstances, the cell falls under the control of the Policy Analysis Branch.

The Early Warning Cell and its functions will be discussed in detail because, more than any other component of the UN, it is associated with the tasks of a formal intelligence organization. Although the Early Warning Cell is a newly developing organization and is understaffed, it clearly represents the trend to create (through reforms in the Secretariat) an information collection system that is not subject to the control of a member state. The intent is to collect information specifically to provide advanced warning of developing crises and to make strategic-level decisions concerning those crises. The creation of the Early Warning Cell and its specified functions represent that intent. The primary tasks of the Early Warning Cell are summarized below:

- Manage the overall Humanitarian Early Warning System.
- Develop indicators of humanitarian crisis.
- Develop and manage a data base of information (both statistical and textual) oriented on the indicators of humanitarian crisis.

- Produce reports for the purpose of alerting the Secretary-General and to facilitate advanced planning (UNSec *b*).

The reports or products produced by the Early Warning Cell fall into three categories: monitoring, coordination, and warning. The reports are intended to provide the Secretary-General and the Under-Secretaries-General current information on humanitarian concerns and alert them of humanitarian crisis, triggering concurrent responses by other departments in the Secretariat. DHA is currently undergoing significant reforms in the information management arena. Both the New York Office and the office located in Geneva are concurrently developing their own information-gathering systems. Documentation outlining the specific developments taking place in the Geneva office was unavailable. However, references to a system known as Relief Web, a prototype Internet connection, give some indication that the Geneva office is attempting to enhance its ability to gain and disseminate information from a variety of sources. DHA is receiving a great deal of attention by the Secretary-General in relation to early warning and fact-finding. These reforms, as well as those in DPA and DPKO, are consistent with Boutros-Ghali's conviction that a rapid UN response, addressing the root causes of crisis, is the most efficient and effective method of maintaining peace and security (see Edwards, this volume, for a detailed analysis of early warning functions).

FACT FINDERS: THE EYES AND EARS OF THE SECRETARY-GENERAL

> An increased resort to fact finding is needed, in accordance with the Charter, initiated either by the Secretary-General, to enable him to meet his responsibilities under the Charter, including Article 99, or by the Security Council or the General Assembly. Various forms may be employed selectively as the situation requires (UNGA A/47/277: 7).

Fact finding is defined by the UN as "any activity designed to ascertain facts which the competent UN organs need to exercise effectively their functions" (Charter: 33). It received a large degree of emphasis in *An Agenda for Peace*, because of its connection with preventive diplomacy and peacemaking. Boutros-Ghali's concept of fact finding parallels a report issued from a UN committee designed to evaluate the mechanisms available to the UN to maintain international peace. This committee held a special session on fact finding and made the following recommendations.

- While fact-finding missions might be undertaken by the Security Council, the General Assembly or the Secretary-General, preference should be given to the Secretary-General, who could designate a special representative or a group of experts to report to him.
- The Secretary-General, on his own initiative or at the request of the States concerned, should consider undertaking such missions in areas where a situation exists which may threaten the maintenance of international peace and security.
- A world-wide survey of the state of international peace and security should be made to help prevent situations which might threaten international peace and security. Early warning of such situations should be enhanced. The Secretary-General should fully use and strengthen the Secretariat's information-gathering capabilities (Charter: 33).

The committee's report focused on limiting the risk of war and mass human suffering by creating a mechanism to identify and respond to growing crisis. This same theme is present in *An Agenda for Peace* and may have contributed to its development (Charter: 32).

This paper will now focus on the UN's capability to collect information in circumstances where it controls the collector. The official collection mechanism controlled by the UN falls under the direction of the Secretary-General and is divided into two categories, special representatives and fact-finding teams.

THE SECRETARY-GENERAL'S SPECIAL REPRESENTATIVE

The Secretary-General may, on his own initiative, appoint someone to represent him called a "personal representative," or he may appoint a "special representative," which denotes that an organ outside the Secretariat such as the Security Council requested the official (Rivlin and Gordenker: 82). In practice, both tend to be referred to as a "special representative." Regardless of who makes the decision that a special representative is required, clearly the Secretary-General controls all aspects of the special representative's mission. The Secretary-General, usually following consultations, decides who the special representative will be, what role he or she will assume, and most importantly what tasks are required.

Tasks of the Special Representative

The tasks of a special representative fall into three categories. First, he or she may be assigned the task of starting the peacemaking process between disputing parties. In this case, the special representative is a true diplomat assuming the role of a negotiator, mediator, or both. Second, the special representative may have the specific task of gathering information. Often the Security Council asks the Secretary-General for information concerning a dispute or regional conflict. Responding to this request, or to satisfy his own concerns, the Secretary-General dispatches a special representative for the purpose of collecting information. Third, the special representative may be dispatched as a surrogate for the Secretary-General to administer executive control of peacekeeping operations in the field (Rivlin and Gordenker: 84). This quasi-command-and-control function is not clearly defined and is often the subject of debate among the member-states and the UN organs.

Information Collection

Typically, the special representative is conducting all or combinations of these tasks simultaneously. However, the task of collecting information is probably the most common and, for the purposes of this study, will be discussed separately from the others. Collecting information has almost always been a primary mission for special representatives. As early as 1960, during a conflict between Great Britain and several Arab states, a special representative was sent to Oman for the purpose of gathering military information. The special representative, Swedish Ambassador de Ribbing, stated:

> [The] primary task of the mission would be a fact finding one. The mission would visit the area . . . and would report on such questions as the presence of foreign troops in Oman . . . [and] on the existence of any "rebel" forces actually in control of a particular area (Rivlin and Gordenker: 90).

A more recent example is included in a report from Boutros-Ghali's special representative to Angola. He clearly identified his assigned mission and reported the following information:

> As charged by the Secretary-General to report [what he sees] . . . [the government forces] entered the village and without provocation

> attacked the civilian inhabitants using small arms and a machine gun mounted on a truck. The commander of the force relayed to me a communique that identified the village as a supporting organization of the rebel forces (UNSC S/27954).

In both cases, it is clear that the special representative was tasked with the responsibility of collecting information and was placed in a position to be a direct observer of the events.

The information reported from the special representative normally flows through the Department for Political Affairs to the Secretary-General. In larger, more developed missions, such as the United Nations Protection Force in the Balkans, formal reporting by the special representative is conducted through the UN Situation Center in DPKO. However, regardless of the mission, it is very likely that a communications link is established between the special representative and DPA or directly to the Office of the Secretary-General.

FACT-FINDING TEAMS

Dispatching a special representative for the purpose of information collection is not the only option available to the UN. In fact, a special representative may be deployed in response to recommendations made by a previous information-gathering mission. The Secretary-General may send a fact-finding team into a region to ascertain if a crisis exists, to determine its severity, and to make recommendations about further UN involvement. Fact-finding teams, like the special representative, are controlled by the Secretary-General, and the decision to deploy them may originate with the Security Council, General Assembly, or the Secretary-General himself.

If the Secretary-General dispatches a fact-finding team without a request from the Security Council, he is likely using power implied under Article 99 of the Charter. For example, Secretary-General Boutros-Ghali deployed a fact-finding team to the Republic of Georgia in October 1993. That same month, the Security Council in Resolution 876 welcomed the decision by the Secretary-General, but it did not ask for or authorize a fact-finding mission. The wording used by the Secretary-General is revealing.

> Following reports of violations of human rights in Abkhazia, Republic of Georgia, and urgent requests to me to ascertain their nature and extent, in October I decided to dispatch a fact finding

> mission to investigate the situation of human rights violations in Abkhazia, including reports of "ethnic cleansing." The Security Council, in its resolution 876 welcomed that decision (UNSC S/26795: 17).

The Secretary-General is clear that he made the decision to send the fact-finding mission, but the origin of the reports of human rights abuses and the requests to verify those reports are unclear. This is in sharp contrast to the statements made in the Secretary-General's report concerning the fact-finding mission to Burundi in 1994.

> On 16 November 1993 the Security Council in a note from its President encouraged the Secretary-General "to continue using his good offices . . . and to consider dispatching in his support as soon as possible a small United Nations team, through existing resources, to Burundi a fact finding team . . ." In response to this request, the Secretary-General decided to send the Preparatory Fact finding Mission to Burundi (UNSC S/1995/157: 4).

The statement clarifies that the Security Council requested the Secretary-General's action. In this case, the Security Council used the position of the Secretary-General and the resources of the Secretariat to gain information about an issue the Council had already decided warranted its attention.

Varying Tasks and Ad Hoc Composition

There is no such thing as a standard fact-finding mission. The title, composition, and assigned tasks differ in almost every case. The only common element among the numerous missions deployed since 1991 is their connection to DPA. Historically, the teams are composed of any combination of Ambassadors from outside the formal UN structure, members from the Secretariat (commonly DPKO, DPA, and DHA), or appointed officials from interested member states. However, a member of DPA was included in all of the fact-finding missions reviewed for this study — which is consistent with its role as the leader in policy analysis. The titles and tasks assigned to fact-finding teams vary almost as greatly as their composition. UN documents use the terms fact-finding team (in a generic sense), Preparatory Fact-Finding Team, Initial Survey Team, Technical Survey Team, and Interagency Assessment Team. To date, there is no literature explaining what distinguishes these teams. However, by examining their mission statements and where the teams are located on a coordination flow chart, it is possible to speculate on distinguishing factors.

Fact-finding (and Preparatory Fact-Finding) Teams

Fact-finding is often the first active measure taken by the UN to verify reports of events that threaten peace and security. The initial reports of these events come from an almost unending list of sources. The most common are: public news media, Non-Governmental Organization reports, diplomatic reports from member-states, UN field offices, and member-states who are interested in the dispute. The information is processed through the many offices throughout the Secretariat that have a role in analysis and early warning. Subsequently, a decision is made to investigate the reports (by the Security Council, General Assembly, or the Secretary-General), and a fact-finding mission is deployed. The previously mentioned fact-finding mission to the Republic of Georgia in 1993 and to Burundi in 1994 had the following mission statements:

(Republic of Georgia)

- Investigate reports of human rights violations and ethnic cleansing.
- Make recommendations for the viability of future UN involvement to restore civil peace and security (UNSC S/26795: 2).

(Burundi)

- Investigate the coup d'etat and the massacres of October 1993.
- Consider, in concert with the Burundi Government, what activities future missions or an expanded United Nations political presence could undertake in order to encourage a return to civil peace (UNSC S/1995/157: 4).

In both cases, the information requirements are oriented toward the verifying incidents for the purpose of making decisions about possible UN action.

Assessment and Survey Teams

The Interagency Assessment Teams, Initial Survey Teams, and Technical Survey Teams are centered around collecting information for the purpose of planning UN field operations. Examining the mission requirements and composition of these teams is difficult because the documentation surrounding their mission preparation and findings is considered confidential in nature and classified UN Restricted. The survey teams, like the fact-finding teams, consist of both policy analysts and planning personnel. For example, a team might consist of a member of DPKO's mission planning service to gather information about airstrip conditions, a member of DPA's Policy Analysis Unit for the purpose of constructing profiles of key political figures, and a member of DHA's Rapid Response Team to conduct an assessment of food and supplies needed for life-sustaining relief. Again, like the fact-finding teams, there is no standard structure or information requirements. The mission and composition of the teams are tailored to the specific situation and the resources available to the UN.

Summary

Regardless of who initiates the fact-finding process or whether it is conducted by a special representative or a composite team, one of its primary purposes is to collect information. The Secretary-General, normally through DPA, controls the mission and the information it produces. The information collected is normally classified UN Restricted, but it is incorporated into the Secretary-General's reports to the Security Council. The fact-finding missions, in conjunction with special representatives, give the Secretary-General a comprehensive information collection capability. They are truly the eyes and ears of the Secretary-General and contribute greatly to the Secretary-General's overall efforts to conduct early warning.

EARLY WARNING

Former director of the U.S. Central Intelligence Agency Robert Gates stated that the U.S. Intelligence Community's most important role is to provide "warning." He defined warning as "a process of communicating judgments about threats to U.S. Security or policy interests to decision-makers." He elaborated by stating: "[the warning] must be received and understood in order for leaders to take action that can deter, defuse, or address the threat, and minimize the damage to U.S. interests" (McCarthy: 5). Comparing this description of "warning" with the following statement by Secretary-General Boutros-Ghali highlights the importance of understanding the UN's concept of early warning.

> [T]he United Nations system has been developing a valuable network of Early Warning Systems concerning environmental threats,

> the risk of nuclear accident, natural disasters, mass movement of populations, the threat of famine, and the spread of disease. There is a need, however, to strengthen arrangements in such a manner that information from these sources can be synthesized with political indicators to assess whether a threat to peace exists and to analyze what action might be taken by the United Nations to alleviate it (UNGA A/47/277: 8).

Clearly there are common themes present in the two descriptions. Both underscore that the collection and analysis of information must be coordinated with (or synthesized into) a decisionmaking process in order to be effective. Both are oriented toward strategic-level decisions and actions — one concerning threats to U.S. interests, and the other threats to international peace (which can be considered a UN interest). The primary difference between the descriptions is that one addresses the intelligence community of a sovereign state and the other, the UN, repudiates the concept of intelligence collection.

THE EARLY WARNING CELL

The UN's concept of early warning, and its link to successful preventive diplomacy, has a long historical development. Secretary-General Dag Hammarskjold promoted the concept in the early 1950s; Secretary-General Perez de Cuellar continued its advancement and, in 1987, created ORCI to conduct early warning. Secretary-General Boutros-Ghali champions the cause by reforming the Secretariat in accordance with *An Agenda for Peace*.

Boutros-Ghali has recently improved early warning. In 1992, he designated DHA as the focal point of the collection, analysis, and dissemination of early warning information. Specifically, he assigned the DHA's New York office to closely monitor crisis developments and "act on early warning information" (UNGA A/47/594: 18). In 1994 Boutros-Ghali, in *Strengthening of the Coordination of Emergency Humanitarian Assistance of the United Nations,* declared the existence of the Early Warning Cell in DHA (UNGA A/49/177: 6). The Early Warning Cell's mission is to manage the Humanitarian Early Warning System (HEWS) and to integrate it into an overall UN Early Warning System. The intended role and functions of the Early Warning Cell are nearly indistinguishable from those of some U.S. intelligence organizations. HEWS is a system that involves collecting information, managing that information in a database, analyzing information (trend evaluation), and creating products for planning and decisionmaking.

SUMMARY

Within the United Nations Secretariat there is a quasi-intelligence architecture supporting the UN Secretary-General's role as a strategic decisionmaker. The intelligence architecture supports the decisionmaking cycle of the Secretary-General, who subsequently influences UN policy and the decisions made in the Security Council. The conceptual foundation of the intelligence architecture dates back to the origin of the UN Charter and has evolved continuously over the past 50 years. The primary factors influencing this development fall into four categories: the UN's organizational requirement for grand strategy; the failure of the Military Staff Committee to provide strategic direction to the Security Council; the expansion of the Secretary-General's implied executive authority under Article 99 of the UN Charter; and the concept of (and emphasis placed on) preventive diplomacy.

The drafters of the UN Charter created the Military Staff Committee to provide strategic direction to the Security Council. However, the MSC failed to produce strategy because it could not overcome the inhibiting effects of the Cold War on its collective decisionmaking methodology. The lack of a dedicated strategic decisionmaking body enabled the Secretary-General to use his authority to create *ad hoc* organizations to influence the creation of UN policies and strategic decisions.

Cold War gridlock in the Security Council and the lack of strategic direction from the Military Staff Committee compelled the Secretary-General to seek to enhance powers implied in Article 99 of the UN Charter, in order to fill the strategic void. Article 99 simply allows the Secretary-General to personally inform the Security Council that there is a threat to the peace. However, by historical precedent, the Secretary-General's authority to address the Security Council has evolved into an implied power to monitor the international community, seek out the indications of potential crisis, and alert the Security Council that UN intervention is warranted. This implied power is closely linked to the Secretary-General's role of creating UN strategy and the concept of preventive diplomacy.

Preventive diplomacy has recently received renewed emphasis by the UN and many of its member-states (including the U.S.). However, it is not a new concept and has long been considered the ideal and most cost-effective method of addressing international crises. Preventive diplomacy is dependent on forward-looking strategy, early warning of crisis, and rapid UN pre-crisis intervention. These elements directly involve the expanded role of the Secretary-General. The Secretary-General has used his implied power under Article 99 of the Charter and his authority to reform the Secretariat to create an intelligence architecture to support strategic decisionmaking, early warning, and operational planning.

The intelligence architecture is intertwined in the bureaucracy of the UN Secretariat and consists of an analytical component and a collection component. The analytical component is located in the primary departments of the Secretariat structure. The Department for Political Affairs, the Department of Peacekeeping Operations, and the Department of Humanitarian Affairs all contain elements whose sole mission is analyzing information and producing assessments. The assessments are normally classified UN Restricted and are not disseminated for public use. The assessments are used for internal decisionmaking, and for operational and contingency planning.

The collection component of the intelligence architecture is housed in the concept of fact finding and early warning. The Secretary-General's Special Representatives and *ad hoc* fact-finding teams are assigned the mission of collecting information for the Secretary-General. The reports generated by these missions are initially classified UN Restricted and are used for internal coordination and decisionmaking. Eventually they are summarized and presented to the Security Council as official UN documents.

The intelligence architecture of the UN has developed over a long period and is not a formal organizational body. It is an *ad hoc* structure that is evolving in conjunction with the political climate of the international community, the personality of the Secretary-General, and the impact of the organizational inertia of the Secretariat. Further research is required to fully understand the structure of the intelligence architecture and its relationship to the decisionmaking cycle of the Secretary-General and the Security Council.

INTELLIGENCE SUPPORT TO REFUGEE OPERATIONS: WHO'S THE EXPERT?

James D. Edwards
Captain, U.S. Army
August 1996

INTRODUCTION

Increased U.S. military participation in refugee operations highlights the need for a better understanding of intelligence in these nontraditional missions. While skeptics assert that the Office of the UN High Commissioner for Refugees (UNHCR) does not produce intelligence, it does collect, analyze, and disseminate "information"—a term which has become a euphemism for intelligence within the United Nations. Because the UNHCR is a professional refugee protection and assistance organization with a worldwide presence in the field, its operational elements typically have better intelligence than an *ad hoc,* U.S. military joint task force. Consequently, the U.S. military can improve its intelligence in refugee operations by studying the UNHCR.

The UNHCR's intelligence-gathering system is specifically designed for refugee crises, while U.S. military intelligence organizations focus on an enemy or threat. As a result, operational elements within the UNHCR have more warning that they will be involved in an impending refugee crisis than their counterparts in the U.S. military, and the UNHCR has better intelligence to plan its response. Because of its technical collection capabilities and its emphasis on threats, however, the U.S. military is better at force protection during an ongoing refugee operation.

The lessons the military should draw from the UNHCR include: (1) Non-Governmental Organizations, and other organizations with a presence in the crisis area, are usually the best sources of information in a refugee emergency; (2) an infatuation with "threats" to the relief force should not inhibit the intelligence staff's ability to assess the political, economic, and social aspects of the situation; (3) clandestine human intelligence will probably not be effective; and (4) unclassified intelligence products are essential.

REFUGEES IN THE POST-COLD WAR WORLD

> Massive flows of refugees and displaced persons have become the central feature of most humanitarian emergencies (Eliasson: 185).
>
> Jan Eliasson
> former Under Secretary-General for Humanitarian Affairs

This essay compares intelligence in U.S. military "refugee operations" with a similar function in the world's leading refugee organization, the Office of the United Nations High Commissioner for Refugees (UNHCR).[1] After establishing the context for the study, the paper addresses the issues of intelligence in the United Nations (UN) and how intelligence differs from information. Then, it analyzes the intelligence functions of the U.S. military and the UNHCR by comparing strategic warning and the planning and conduct of refugee relief operations in each organization.

The end of the Cold War brought profound changes to the international security environment. Today, there is a paradox that while there is less threat of global war, there is also less peace in the world. Armed conflicts have increased dramatically since 1989, but the fighting is not between states; it is within them.[2] The result has been a proliferation of complex humanitarian emergencies which "combine internal conflicts with large-scale displacements of people, mass famine, and fragile or failing economic, political, and social institutions" (U.S. Mission to the UN *a*: 1). The accompanying map depicts areas in which the U.S. Government assesses there is an ongoing complex humanitarian emergency.

---

[1] In keeping with common practice, the term UNHCR refers to the institution known as the Office of the UNHCR. The term High Commissioner refers to the individual occupying this office.

[2] According to the UN, "of the 82 armed conflicts in the world between 1989 and 1992, only three flared up between countries. The rest occurred internally..." See Hal Kane, *The Hour of Departure: Forces That Create Refugees and Migrants* (Washington, DC: Worldwatch Institute, 1995), 21.

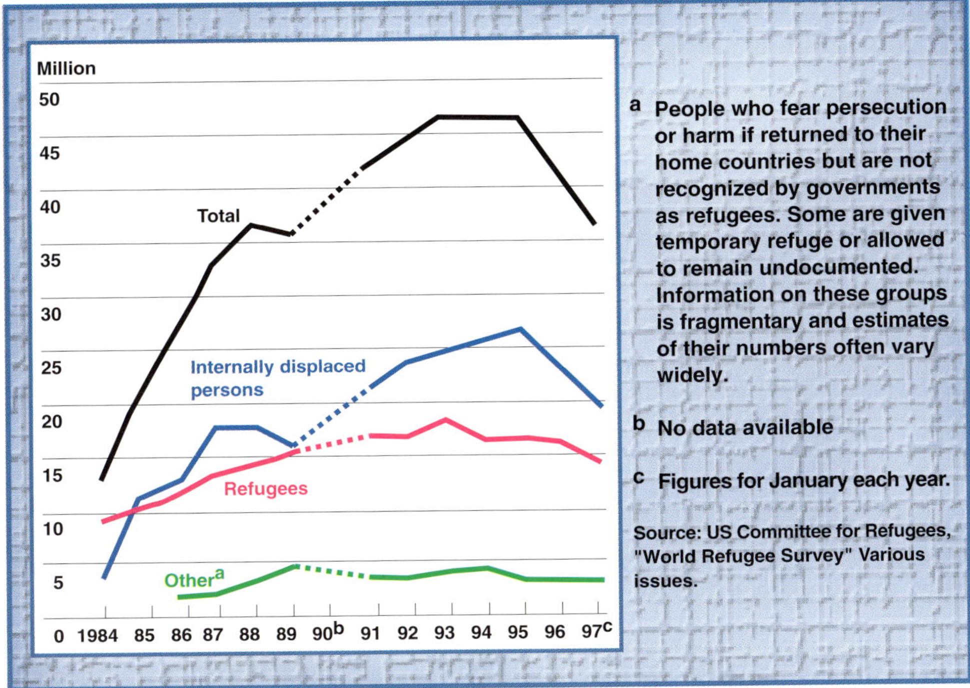

Estimated Number of the World's People in Need of Humanitarian Assistance, 1984-1997.

source: Central Intelligence Agency

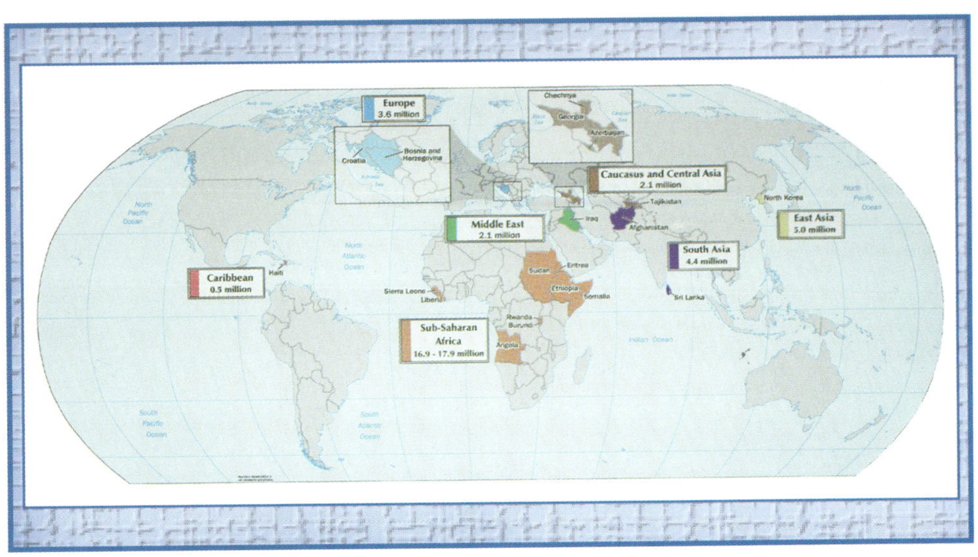

Estimated Number of People in Need by Region

source: Central Intelligence Agency

International organizations are poorly equipped to handle the victims of these intrastate problems. Their assistance, or intervention, causes the state to assert the prerogatives of sovereignty, limiting the international organizations' capacity to act under international law (Loescher *b*: 141). Taken collectively, the rapid growth of complex humanitarian emergencies has overwhelmed the international community's capability to respond.[3]

While refugee statistics are often a contentious political issue, there is a consensus that the world's refugee population grew rapidly following the end of the Cold War. According to the UNHCR, the number of "persons of concern" to its organization almost doubled during this period.[4]

Who Is a Refugee?

The difficulty of determining just who is a refugee—and is therefore entitled to protection and assistance under international law—contributes to the international community's dilemma in responding to complex humanitarian emergencies. The most widely accepted definition of a refugee is any person

> who is outside the country of his nationality . . . because . . . [of a] well-founded fear of persecution by reason of his race, religion, nationality or political opinion (UNHCR *c*: 6, 11).

As a result of intrastate conflict, however, millions of internally displaced persons (IDPs) now find themselves in refugee-like situations without ever having crossed a border. In many cases, the UN has responded by

---

3 In commenting on the 17 operations the UN was involved in during mid-1994, UN Secretary-General Boutros-Ghali noted the UN was at "system overload." See Hans Binnendijk and Patrick Clawson, eds., *Strategic Assessment 1995: U.S. Security Challenges in Transition* (Washington, DC: Institute for National Strategic Studies, National Defense University, 1995), 164.

4 While most governments and Non-Governmental Organizations (NGOs) accept the UNHCR's refugee statistics as authoritative, UNHCR estimates do not include the vast majority of the internally displaced persons (IDPs) in the world. In 1995, for example, the UNHCR acknowledged there were some 20 million additional IDPs not included in its numbers, placing the total number of people who had fled their homes at almost 50 million. (UNHCR, Brochure, *UNHCR by Numbers,* January 1995, 2.) A 1996 U.S. Government study reached similar conclusions, noting there were some 16 million refugees and an additional 22-24 million IDPs in the world. U.S. Mission to the UN, *Global Humanitarian Emergencies,* 1996 (New York: U.S. Mission to the UN, February 1996), 3-4.

authorizing the UNHCR to assist these IDPs as if they were actually refugees (Boutros-Ghali *c*: 268).

In practice, the lines between refugees, IDPs, and migrants have become increasingly blurred and subject to political manipulation. During the Cold War, Western governments encouraged refugees to flee from repressive regimes because their flight undermined the legitimacy of communist governments. Now, Western governments are tightening their immigration policies and strictly interpreting their obligations to provide asylum to refugees under international law (UNHCR *g*: 35-37).

This study takes a traditional view of the term refugee (Gorman: 15-20). It considers a **refugee to be any person who has fled persecution or is the victim of forced migration.** This determination facilitates a comparison of UNHCR and U.S. military operations in the field without cluttering the issue with the subtleties of international law. It also recognizes that the distinction between a refugee and an IDP is largely insignificant to an ongoing relief effort because the humanitarian support requirements are the same in either case. Thus, this study uses the term refugee in a much broader sense than most legal definitions of the word.

Refugees, U.S. National Interests, and the Military

Large population movements are inherently destabilizing influences on global and regional security structures. When the populations on the move are refugees, they are also symptomatic of an underlying political crisis that frequently involves U.S. national interests. The U.S. national security strategy implicitly recognizes this connection by stating, "transnational problems . . . like . . . refugee flows . . . have security implications for both present and long term American policy" (U.S. President *b*: 1). While many people view refugee assistance as a humanitarian obligation, the U.S. often has political, economic, or security concerns in a refugee emergency.

Of course population movements have always been a part of the "strategic landscape" (Sarkesian: 549). But the refugee crises of recent years have increasingly involved militaries for two major reasons. First, the suddenness, severity, and frequency of refugee emergencies have strained the international relief community's capability to provide emergency assistance. Militaries have been the only organizations capable of mustering viable relief efforts on short notice. Second, because most refugees are victims of ongoing internal conflicts, there has been a tremendous need for militaries to protect the relief workers laboring in the middle of these wars (Loescher *a*: 363 and McHugh: 10).

U.S. military participation in refugee relief efforts has been widespread. All five of the U.S. unified combatant commands have activated joint task forces (JTFs) to conduct refugee operations in recent years.

U.S. military doctrine classifies these activities as humanitarian assistance operations (U.S. DoD *d*: III-4). Unfortunately, humanitarian assistance implies tasks as diverse as disaster relief, support to police forces, and fighting forest fires (Siegel: 3-6). In order to compare a group of U.S. military operations with UNHCR activities, it is necessary to define a subcategory of humanitarian assistance as "refugee operations." The distinguishing feature is that a refugee operation has the primary mission of providing assistance to refugees, while other humanitarian assistance operations may treat this objective as an ancillary task.

Procedures for Comparing Intelligence Effectiveness

Having established a common vocabulary for refugees and refugee operations, it is now necessary to describe the nature of the comparison between intelligence in the U.S. military and the UNHCR. This study begins by establishing the context of intelligence in each organization. It then compares how the UNHCR and the U.S. military conduct the intelligence functions of strategic warning and support to planning and conducting refugee operations.

In making this comparison, this paper examines how each organization intends to conduct intelligence as well as how effectively they have actually conducted intelligence during refugee operations. For the U.S. military, joint doctrine defines the intent, and after-action reviews and press accounts describe what actually happened. Within the UNHCR, the *UNHCR Manual* and an assortment of the organization's internal documents provide the intent, while interviews with UNHCR officials provide a candid assessment of the effectiveness of UNHCR intelligence.

No two refugee operations are the same for the U.S. military or the UNHCR, but general trends are apparent. Each institution has similar intelligence requirements, but organizational culture, intelligence collection methods, and the degree to which intelligence is integrated with operations are among a host of dissimilar features.

INTELLIGENCE IN CONTEXT

> We don't call it intelligence, but it's the same thing. We both have a need for accurate and timely information (Ogata 1996).
>
> Sadako Ogata
> High Commissioner for Refugees

Author with UN High Commissioner for Refugees, Sadako Ogata, 1996. *photo used with permission*

People use an intelligence process to analyze information, but many organizations have bureaucratized this concept by assigning intelligence functions to individuals or elements of their organization. The U.S. military has thoroughly bureaucratized the concept of military intelligence by designating personnel, staffs, and even units responsible for collecting and producing intelligence. However, the UNHCR has never really separated its intelligence function from its operational elements. In the UNHCR, even the idea of intelligence is controversial because it connotes activities which an impartial, non-political organization would like to avoid. Nevertheless, the UNHCR needs intelligence for many of the same reasons militaries require intelligence in refugee operations. As Mrs. Ogata indicates, UN organizations frequently cloak their intelligence functions under the euphemism of information.

Information Is Not Intelligence: A U.S. Military View

In joint and service doctrine, the U.S. military considers intelligence to be something much more than just information. Information is raw, uninterpreted data, whereas intelligence is information that has been refined into meaningful knowledge about an area or an adversary. The distinction may not always be clear in practice, but the theoretical separation of intelligence from information is significant because of the value added by analysis.

For example, a story in *Pravda* may contain information of interest to the military. In order for it to become intelligence, however, an analyst must evaluate the story considering a variety of factors, including:

- the paper's editorial bias;
- the motivations and reputation of the author;
- the accuracy of previous stories;
- the possibility of deception (that the author has been duped or deliberately intends to deceive); and
- whether or not the information in the story is consistent with other information available to the analyst.

Based upon this evaluation, the analyst then fuses the information from the story with other available information to form a "product" that meets his consumer's needs.

In comparing these organizations, it is useful to think of intelligence products as the outcome of a process which converts information into intelligence. U.S. military doctrine calls this process the "intelligence cycle," and its most basic functions include collection, analysis, and dissemination. As the next section demonstrates, the UN follows a similar process in its "information" activities.

INTELLIGENCE IN THE UN

According to an authoritative peacekeeper handbook (International Peace Academy *a*: paragraph 140), in UN operations "the use of the word 'intelligence' is avoided and 'information' used instead." The reason for this semantic distinction is that the UN's fundamental principles clash with the popular notion of what constitutes intelligence. To most people, intelligence is not just the conversion of "information" into a useful product; rather, intelligence implies clandestine collection techniques, covert operations, and spying on an "enemy" (Hugh Smith: 174). All of these activities are anathema to the UN because it has no enemies and its Charter requires it to respect the sovereignty of member states.

Despite the stigma attached to intelligence, UN leaders have recognized a need for intelligence for decades. Their repeated efforts to create early warning systems to support preventive diplomacy demonstrate this desire. The argument is basically that the UN cannot be effective in maintaining international peace and security—its purpose as stated in the UN Charter—if it does not know when a conflict, famine, or massive refugee flow is likely to occur (Boutros-Ghali *a*: 46-49). The Department of Humanitarian Affairs (DHA) is particularly important to refugee operations because it is responsible for early warning of humanitarian emergencies.

As a semiautonomous UN agency,[5] the UNHCR maintains its own intelligence capability separate from the UN Secretariat. While the bulk of the intelligence work in the UNHCR occurs within the organization's operational elements, the Centre for Documentation and Research (CDR) fulfills a bureaucratic intelligence role. It collects, analyzes, and disseminates "information" on countries where refugees originate (Druke: 186), and it serves as the focal point for UNHCR early warning efforts.

Created in 1986, the CDR originally belonged to the UNHCR's Division of International Protection. The division promotes the UNHCR's traditional mission of "protecting" refugees by promoting international recognition of their legal rights. Consequently, initial CDR databases contained extensive information on refugee law. As the UNHCR has become more heavily involved in international relief efforts, however, the CDR's holdings have expanded to support operational requirements.

A reorganization in January 1996 highlighted the CDR's expanded role by removing the CDR from the Division of International Protection and placing it under the Assistant High Commissioner. This official is the number three position in the UNHCR, and he has responsibility for policy, planning, and operations. As such, he coordinates the activities of the UNHCR's five regional bureaus and its special operations.

INTELLIGENCE IN REFUGEE OPERATIONS

Intelligence requirements vary with each refugee operation, but they generally fall into one of three distinct, chronological groupings. First, intelligence provides the general, background knowledge necessary to interpret a refugee emergency. Then, intelligence performs a warning

---

[5] Technically, the UNHCR is a subsidiary organ of the General Assembly. See UN General Assembly *Resolution 428(V)*, 14 December 1950. The UNHCR's autonomy comes from its largely independent sources of funding and from its mandate to be "entirely non-political [in] character." See Yves Beigbeder, *The Role and Status of International Humanitarian Volunteers and Organizations: The Right and Duty to Humanitarian Assistance* (Dordrecht, Netherlands: Martinus Nijhoff Publishers, 1991), 27.

function, notifying policymakers that a crisis is likely to occur and their organization may need to act. Once a policymaker decides to act, intelligence supports planning processes and field operations. Although these activities frequently overlap in practice, they are conceptually separate.

General Knowledge

General knowledge of an area or situation relevant to a refugee operation includes intelligence on a tremendous variety of topics, including political, societal, economic, environmental, and even military issues. The UNHCR and the U.S. military often have similar requirements in these areas, and thus, they create many similar intelligence products.

Within the UNHCR, the CDR maintains the organization's general knowledge base. The CDR's databases, known collectively as "REFWORLD," (for Refugee World) include comprehensive information on a variety of topics related to refugees and countries that are likely to generate them. CDR products turn this information into intelligence by analyzing specific countries, areas, or topics.[6] Detailed analyses are the result of the CDR's Country Information Project (COIP). Begun in 1992, the COIP now includes information on "political, economic, social and legal structures, human rights, cultural and religious norms, minorities, . . . maps and chronologies of relevant events" (Rusu *b*: 2).

Within the U.S. military, a complex array of intelligence organizations have institutional responsibility for providing a similar "base" of knowledge necessary to support refugee operations. The U.S. Army's venerable *Area Handbook* series and the Defense Intelligence Agency's (DIA) Contingency Support Studies are two prime examples of this type of general intelligence (Constantine: 11). The content of these products is somewhat similar to UNHCR products.

General knowledge of an area or situation is the foundation of all intelligence analysis. In the context of refugee operations, it provides the requisite background on a broad variety of topics necessary to warn of an impending crisis and to plan and conduct assistance activities.

---

[6] Many CDR background papers are available on the Internet. Please consult Appendix B of this volume.

Strategic Warning of Refugee Flows

> When Rwanda exploded, frankly, we were focused on Bosnia and northern Iraq (Hayden: 18).
>
> Brigadier General Michael V. Hayden
> Intelligence Officer, U.S. European Command

> We always have warning of refugee emergencies . . . Early warning comes from the field (Ogata *c*).
>
> Sadako Ogata
> High Commissioner for Refugee

These quotes underline the basic differences between U.S. military and UNHCR concepts of warning in refugee emergencies. The military, with its abundant intelligence resources, is often surprised by refugee crises because of its understandable preoccupation with other issues — namely "enemy" forces. On the other hand, the UNHCR is completely focused on predicting future refugee flows, but it suffers from limited resources, constraints arising from its impartial nature, and an inability to act on the warning in most cases.

Strategic warning is an intelligence function in both the U.S. military and the UNHCR. Each organization conducts warning activities intended to enable proactive responses to impending refugee crises. However, there are significant differences in the concept of warning and the warning systems found in the U.S. military and the UNHCR. These differences arise from the divergent purposes of each organization. The military exists to fight wars, while the UNHCR is a refugee protection and assistance organization. This section compares the warning systems in the UNHCR and the U.S. military. After first considering the different concepts of warning in each organization, I conclude that the UNHCR's strategic warning is more effective than belated warnings of refugee flows in the U.S. military.

WARNING IS PRIOR KNOWLEDGE OF AN EVENT

There is no universally recognized concept of what constitutes warning of an impending crisis or disaster, but a common definition might be: Warning is knowledge of a future event early enough to allow action to influence events. Within a military context, several respected scholars share a fundamental assumption that the goal of warning is to prevent surprise (Betts: 5; Kam: 22). Within the UN, however, early warning is linked to concepts as diverse as "early notification, urgent action, the good offices of the Secretary-General, crisis control and preventive diplomacy" (Ramcharan: 7-8). In both the U.S. Government and the UN, however, the concepts of warning are inextricably linked to a desire to act to preempt or mitigate a crisis (McCarthy: 5; Dmitrichev: 264).

Warning in the U.S. Military

During most recent refugee operations, the U.S. military has had little warning prior to commencement of its relief efforts.[7] Certainly, the amount of warnings issued to policymakers and the reluctance of the U.S. to act preventively has varied in each instance, but Rwanda represents the worst possible warning failure on the part of the military. The senior military intelligence officer responsible for warning of the crisis admitted his attention was focused on other areas when the crisis erupted (Hayden: 18-19). Furthermore, the commander of the U.S. relief effort noted the difficulty his intelligence staff had "because there was no 'enemy' on which to focus, but rather a 'situation'" (USEUCOM *a*: 5). Thus, the military often experiences problems in applying wartime warning techniques to peacetime warning situations.

Warning in the UNHCR

The UNHCR's warning efforts have the sole purpose of detecting and warning of impending refugee flows, and the UNHCR's recent emphasis on preventive solutions has highlighted the need for more extensive efforts in these areas (UNHCR *g*: 43). Unfortunately, the UNHCR's mandate poses substantial problems for early warning—problems to which the UNHCR has developed several compromise solutions.

Three characteristics of the UNHCR's mandate reduce the utility of early warning and the UNHCR's capability to provide this warning. First, the UNHCR was originally mandated to act on behalf of refugees already

---

[7] For instance, the U.S. European Command mounted Operation PROVIDE COMFORT—the 1991 mission to assist the Kurds in northern Iraq—less than 24 hours after notification! See U.S. European Command (USEUCOM), Operation *PROVIDE COMFORT* After Action Report (USEUCOM *b*), 1-4. More recently, in Operation SAFE HAVEN, the commander of the JTF had about 96 hours notice until he was expected to receive and care for 10,000 Haitians. Ultimately, political considerations delayed the JTF's activation and changed the mission from assisting Haitians to Cubans, but there was very little initial warning. James L. Wilson, BG, USA, former commander, JTF SAFE HAVEN, interview by author, 3 April 1996.

in existence — not potential refugees. Thus, UNHCR warning efforts have little practical effect since the organization is not authorized to take action to avert new refugee flows. Second, all UNHCR actions must have the consent of the government concerned. Because this same government either intends to create the refugee flow or usually does not want to acknowledge its existence, the government generally resents UNHCR warnings (Gordenker: 360). Finally, the UNHCR is limited to "non-political," "humanitarian and social" activities. Strictly interpreted, this constraint restricts explicit warning because the warning itself almost certainly has political implications for the host state (Druke: 181).

Recent changes in the international security environment have demonstrated the inability of traditional solutions to resolve the world's refugee problems (UNHCR *g*: 19-40). By its very nature, prevention requires early warning, and this imperative has caused the UNHCR to intensify its warning efforts during the last five years. There are actually two distinct forms of so-called early warning now used within the UNHCR. The first is a systemic, bureaucratized form of early warning, while the latter involves early notification and emergency preparedness. Each represents a compromise solution to the constraints of the UNHCR's mandate.

The CDR is the focal point for **systemic early warning**, and its early warning systems are intended to identify crises before they occur so that the UNHCR, in cooperation with other UN entities (with appropriate mandates), can take preventive action to avert potential refugee flows. Toward this end, the CDR oversees two "warning systems" — the Country Information Project and the International Refugee Electronic Network (IRENE) (Ruiz: 155) — and it represents the UNHCR at DHA's interagency working group on warning (Dedring: 99).

These warning systems do not produce formal warning products, however, and the High Commissioner relies on early warning from the UNHCR's field offices. Privately, UNHCR officials comment they never receive early warning from DHA because it has no field presence. In fact, DHA relies on UNHCR reports for warning of refugee movements. Mrs. Ogata's comment that early warning comes from the field indicates a second type of UNHCR warning activity which is similar to **early notification.** Early notification does not predict a potential refugee flow; rather, it provides the earliest possible report that a refugee flow has already begun and is likely to escalate into a crisis.

Early notification allows the operational elements of the UNHCR to prepare for a potential emergency. One senior UNHCR official indicated that operational elements of the UNHCR develop their own, informal "early warnings" of impending crises using a variety of information sources that they monitor themselves. In this case, the purpose of early warning is to ensure the UNHCR's emergency response capability is prepared to meet the eventuality of a refugee emergency. Mr. Bernard Doyle of UNHCR likened the UNHCR's mission to that of an ambulance driver. The ambulance driver cannot prevent an accident from occurring, but he can anticipate the conditions (such as a snowstorm) under which accidents are likely to occur and plan accordingly.

Thus, early warning within the UNHCR means different things to different people. There is considerable institutional skepticism over the value of early warning, in its purest form, because of the UNHCR's inability to take preventive action in most situations. Operational elements of the UNHCR consider early warning to be linked to emergency preparedness, and Mrs. Ogata considers most early warning to be early notification. The CDR has institutional responsibility for coordinating early warning efforts with DHA and for overseeing the UNHCR's warning systems, and it is these warning systems which will be considered next.

The UNHCR's warning "systems" do not produce warning messages per se. Rather, they share information and intelligence that can be useful throughout the UNHCR and the international relief community (Ruiz: 155). While the UNHCR considers IRENE and the COIP to be warning systems, they really represent a communications system and a database that can support other early warning efforts.

IRENE. IRENE is a system of electronic bulletin boards that allows refugee agencies around the world to exchange information using electronic mail. It evolved from a project known as the International Refugee Documentation Network (IRDN) which originated following a 1986 conference attended by 25 different relief agencies. Conference participants recommended the UNHCR administer the IRDN, and in June 1987, the High Commissioner agreed to assume a "coordinating function" for the project (IRDN *b*: 10). Unfortunately, IRENE "suffers considerably from lack of participation by other IRDN members" (IRDN *a*: 6).

COIP. The COIP is really just a database with a modicum of intelligence analysis. According to the CDR, the COIP acts

> as the principal resource within the UNHCR for the provision of "relevant, credible, reliable, and current" information, including political, economic, social and legal structures, and human rights, in likely refugee producing or receiving countries (Ruiz: 155).

The COIP supports early warning efforts solely by making information and intelligence available to a wide variety of users throughout the UNHCR and the international relief community. Neither IRENE nor the COIP routinely produce warning products that are publicly available. However, the intent is eventually to produce warning reports for UN and UNHCR decisionmakers.

HEWS. The UN Department of Humanitarian Affairs does operate a Humanitarian Early Warning System (HEWS) which issues warning messages derived from an indicator-based methodology, but it is still not effective at forecasting future refugee flows. HEWS has never provided the High Commissioner with early warning (Ogata *c*), and HEWS actually relies on the UNHCR to provide most of its data on population movements through interagency coordination meetings. The fact that this working group has not met since May 1995 is symptomatic of how poorly this coordination process actually works.

Other problems which hinder UNHCR warning efforts — such as collecting, transmitting, and analyzing warning information — are related to the UNHCR's need to maintain its impartiality. For example, the UNHCR relies on its field offices in over 100 countries to report information on the situation in these areas, but it has traditionally discouraged its field personnel from attaching analytical comments to these reports. Lack of secure communications channels makes these reports subject to compromise, and any public disclosure of "confidential" information reported by UNHCR field offices could subject the UNHCR to criticism by the local government (Druke: 181).

Thus, although the CDR does receive "confidential" information from the field, the bulk of the useable data assembled under the COIP comes from public sources. Hans Thoolen, a former CDR director, explained the problem this way.

> A UNHCR protection officer in Sri Lanka sends in a report on the latest human rights and protection issues in Jaffna. The same day, both the Sri Lanka Monitor and the International Herald Tribune carry a story with precisely the same information. What to do? One is private, the other public. The former, if made public, could be mistaken for UNHCR's own assessment and could provoke immediate diplomatic, if not substantive, challenge. The latter, originating from the public domain, is immediately useable and can withstand challenge due, not so much because of what it is, but how it has been classified. So it is that public information takes on greater weight and authority simply because it can be verified, while the private report, though in the public domain, can be used solely in a controlled context, "for your eyes only" (Rusu *a*: 6).

For these reasons, the CDR's COIP relies almost exclusively on publicly available information obtained from a variety of NGOs, the media, governmental agencies, academics, and other sources. Unfortunately, the necessity of using public information creates its own analytical problems of bias and information overload (Thoolen: 170-175).

INTELLIGENCE SUPPORT TO PLANNING AND CONDUCTING REFUGEE OPERATIONS

> Information is not the problem; the problem is analysis.
>
> Senior Emergency Preparedness and
> Response Officer, UNHCR

The information required to produce intelligence for planning refugee operations is readily available to anyone who has access to a refugee crisis area. Because of its limited access and organizational culture, however, the U.S. military tends to use its traditional, "high-tech" collection assets to gather this information, while the UNHCR often assembles similar data through less costly and more effective use of its field offices.

This section examines the intelligence requirements common to both UNHCR and U.S. military planning and execution of refugee operations.

Both the U.S. military and the UNHCR plan and conduct refugee operations using a form of management by objective (U.S. DoD *c*; UNHCR *j*: 4/

3.2). Intelligence contributes to these efforts by providing the "situational awareness" necessary for planning. The U.S. military product containing this awareness is an intelligence estimate, while the UNHCR dubs it a needs and resources assessment (UNHCR *e*: 16).

Once a refugee operation is underway, intelligence supports the operation by monitoring the general situation in the crisis area and by assessing potential threats to relief providers. The U.S. military calls this latter intelligence function "force protection," (U.S. DoD *a*: III-5) while the UNHCR dubs it "safety and security."

Because intelligence supports similar planning and operational efforts in each organization, the UNHCR and the U.S. military share many similar intelligence requirements. Typical requirements found in both U.S. military and UNHCR publications include:

- political, economic, and social data
- details about the refugees themselves
    - specific needs (food, water, shelter, medical)
    - cultural and demographic considerations
    - future intentions
- maps and physical characteristics of the crisis area
- infrastructure and resources in the host country
- major relief organizations in the crisis area
- threats to relief personnel from
    - hostile armed forces
    - criminals
    - land mines
    - civic violence
    - health risks (USMC: 159-164; UNHCR *e*:16-19; UNHCR *i*: 4/3-4).

Although they have many similar intelligence requirements, the UNHCR and the U.S. military collect, analyze, and disseminate this intelligence in decidedly different fashions.

UNHCR INTELLIGENCE IN REFUGEE OPERATIONS

While the CDR serves as the UNHCR's institutional intelligence shop, its support to planning and operations is minimal. Executives in the UNHCR's "operational" sections—such as the regional bureaus, its special operations/units, and the emergency preparedness and response section — each produce their own intelligence. To do so, they rely heavily on reports which originate from UNHCR field offices, the media, and other UN organizations and NGOs with a presence in the crisis area. Field offices have the primary responsibility for collecting, analyzing, and reporting intelligence to UNHCR headquarters. Then, personnel in the regional bureaus further analyze the intelligence, passing it on to the policy level within the UNHCR as they deem appropriate.

Needs Assessments and Intelligence Reporting

In responding to a refugee crisis, the UNHCR immediately conducts a needs and resources assessment. The country overview is of particular interest from an intelligence perspective. Intelligence topics include summaries of:

> information on the general political, economic and social situation in the country . . . [and] major changes reflected in [refugee statistics], with any additional information, as relevant, on gender breakdown, vulnerable cases, sources of information, variances between UNHCR and official figures, group, or individual determination (UNHCR *k*: 1993).

Unsettled scene in Srebrenica, Yugoslavia, 1993. *photo used with permission*

Principal sources of information are:

- Refugees themselves
- NGOs in the crisis area
- Host Nation governments
- Regional and international organizations
- Other UN organizations with a field presence
- Local media (UNHCR *f*: 215, 225).

NGOs are often the most critical source of information because they generally have broad access to the crisis area. Unfortunately, the NGOs' need to negotiate for access may influence their ability to speak frankly about conditions (DeMars: 395).

Security and Safety

Security has become a major issue for UNHCR field personnel as the world's refugee crises increasingly occur in the midst of violent ethnic and civil conflicts. In 1993 and 1994, 11 UNHCR and other humanitarian staff lost their lives in the field, and although this number represents a smaller fatality rate than that for peacekeeping forces overall, it underscores the need for better tactical intelligence (Ogata *b*: 124; Boutros-Ghali *c*: 161; Browne *b*: 8). In response, the UNHCR has increased security training, added security specialists to UNHCR field missions, and formalized the security responsibility of its relief team leaders (UNHCR *d*: 7-8). However, the UNHCR is still not particularly efficient at assessing threats to its personnel in the field.

Because of its humanitarian nature, the UNHCR finds collection and interpretation of tactical intelligence very difficult. This has led the UNHCR to rely — to some extent — on UN peacekeeping forces in a crisis area. A recent UNHCR training document noted:

> Equally important is the use of military information [intelligence]. Commanders and heads of humanitarian missions alike require military information for the purpose of executing tasks in the conflict environment. The collection, collation and dissemination of military information is a skill that UNHCR staff members will most certainly lack . . . The collection and use of military information is obviously a matter of great sensitivity. The parties to the conflict will doubt the neutrality of any party which is in contact

with their opponents, especially where the neutral party shows an interest in military matters (UNHCR *h*: 29; UNHCR *a*:36).

Thus, the UNHCR excels at assessing the situation in a refugee crisis based largely on open sources of information, but it has great difficulty in assessing military-style threats which often require secretive methods of intelligence collection. The U.S. military, not surprisingly, has exactly the opposite problem.

INTELLIGENCE IN U.S. MILITARY REFUGEE OPERATIONS

U.S. military intelligence personnel excel at determining traditional "threats" to military forces, but their collection systems are not designed to capture the types of "situational" information necessary to support relief operations. This limitation is greatest during the planning phase of an operation because the military often lacks access to first-hand information on the crisis area, but it continues throughout the operation as the military struggles to assess a refugee situation in which there is no enemy. In cases where there is a hostile threat, however, intelligence personnel can provide useful information for force protection.

These themes were abundantly clear in the 1994 U.S. relief effort in support of Rwandan refugees. In his after-action review, the commander of JTF SUPPORT HOPE noted:

> Our intelligence systems initially had some difficulty readjusting from high-tech to low-tech requirements. Their task was made all the more difficult because there was no "enemy" on which to focus, but rather a "situation" with many low-tech angles that had to be developed. My contacts with the UN/NGO community, subordinate commanders, UNAMIR [UN Assistance Mission for Rwanda] and my ability to move around the widely-dispersed RCA [Rwanda Crisis Area] gave me a wide cross-perspective on the true nature of the situation in our area of responsibility that was unavailable to anyone else (USEUCOM *a*: 5).

Similar problems have occurred in other U.S. refugee operations even when there was an extremely permissive environment for intelligence collection. During Operation SAFE HAVEN, for instance, the intelligence staff focused overwhelmingly on its human intelligence collectors while paying minimal attention to other individuals in regular contact with the refugees (Wilson).

Reconnaissance and Planning

Most refugee operations require the military to activate a JTF, which rapidly deploys into a crisis area. JTF activation and deployment are usually concurrent with operational or contingency planning. This leaves little time for reconnaissance, and the intelligence staff frequently lacks the detailed knowledge of the situation required to support deliberate planning. In the case of Rwanda, the senior intelligence officer in USEUCOM noted: "By the time it had become clear that we were to deploy forces to central Africa, we were forced to run very hard to build the needed database" (Hayden: 19).

Imagery and signals intelligence collectors were designed to detect Cold War military forces. They are not well suited to many subtle intelligence requirements. For example, the after-action report for Operation PROVIDE COMFORT noted, "HUMINT [human source intelligence] collection used with tactical reconnaissance produced the key intelligence necessary for operations and security" (USEUCOM *b*: 12).

While human intelligence is ideally suited to collect on non-traditional intelligence requirements, the military's initial lack of access to the crisis area makes collection very difficult. The Defense Attache system offers a limited capability for overt collection, but any new human collection requires extensive amounts of time—to develop sources—that simply does not exist in a crisis scenario (Pelletiere: 11-12).

Force Protection and Intelligence Reporting

Unlike the UNHCR—where a capability to report intelligence information already exists in the crisis area—the U.S. military builds an intelligence architecture to support a new refugee operation. Thus, intelligence reporting from the crisis area tends to begin later and be less incisive than similar reporting by the UNHCR. Analytical reporting is typically called an intelligence summary (INTSUM) or an intelligence report (INTREP), but the formats of these reports vary widely in practice.

Because of the natural inclination for military intelligence personnel to focus on enemy "threats," INTSUMs and INTREPs are dominated by force protection—rather than situational awareness—reporting. In an environment where there is an ongoing or latent conflict, this is certainly appropriate, but these reports do not provide the JTF commander the intelligence necessary to assess the effectiveness of his relief operations (Wilson). In Rwanda, the JTF commander partially remedied this shortcoming by visiting UN organizations and NGOs (USEUCOM *a*: 5).

In most recent refugee operations, U.S. military commanders have used Civil Military Operations Centers (CMOC) to facilitate information exchange and unity of effort with UN organizations and NGOs. The CMOC holds tremendous potential to provide this situational awareness—or intelligence—to the JTF through a free and frank exchange of "information" with non-military organizations (Wallace: 36-41; U.S. DoD *g*: IV-4 to IV-7).

SUMMARY

As complex humanitarian emergencies proliferate around the world, the global refugee population will probably continue to increase. Simultaneously, traditional countries of asylum, like the U.S., will continue to tighten their immigration policies, interpreting the status of refugees more narrowly. These trends will make strategic warning of refugee flows more important, and they will require intelligence to plan and conduct refugee operations.

Both the UNHCR and the U.S. military collect, analyze, and disseminate intelligence, but the UNHCR has not bureaucratized intelligence to the extent the U.S. military has. In some ways, the comparison of intelligence in the UNHCR and the U.S. military is artificial because neither organization operates in a vacuum and because each organization has different objectives. Nevertheless, the U.S. military and the UNHCR each have a need for strategic warning of refugee emergencies and a need for intelligence to plan and conduct operations.

In the case of strategic warning, the UNHCR is clearly more effective. The UNHCR lacks the capacity to act unilaterally to prevent refugee flows, but it does use early warning to prepare its emergency response personnel and field offices for impending crises. Thus, while there can never be a warning "success" in the sense that U.S. government agencies define the term, early warning allows the UNHCR to respond rapidly to a crisis. Conversely, the U.S. military is often surprised by refugee crises, creating JTFs to conduct refugee operations in a purely reactive manner.

In planning and conducting refugee operations, the effectiveness of intelligence in the U.S. military and the UNHCR is mixed. Because of its earlier warning and access to the crisis area, the UNHCR typically is more effective at planning refugee assistance. However, the UNHCR lacks the capability to conduct military style "force protection" intelligence during a refugee operation, sometimes even relying on militaries to fill this void.

INTELLIGENCE LESSONS FOR FUTURE REFUGEE OPERATIONS

While the UNHCR is not perfect in conducting intelligence activities, the U.S. military can draw some important lessons from the UNHCR's wealth of experience. These include:

1) The best sources of information on an emerging refugee crisis will be the NGOs and other organizations with a presence on the ground. From an economic perspective, these sources are also much more effective than using expensive technical collection assets to obtain information that is already publicly available. Honest and open communication is the key to tapping this resource. Immediately after receiving warning of a refugee emergency, JTF intelligence personnel should conduct liaison with NGOs either using commercial telecommunications equipment or through on-line services. Once the relief force enters the crisis area, the Civil Military Operations Center may prove an excellent place for this liaison to continue to occur.

2) Information is abundant, but analysis (the conversion of relevant information into intelligence) is the problem. Determining the accuracy and biases of major NGOs involved in reporting information on refugees is essential.

3) Force protection will remain an issue, particularly in unstable security environments, but an infatuation with "threats" should not inhibit the intelligence staff's capability to monitor other aspects of the situation. These include political, economic, demographic, and societal factors which affect the overall success of the refugee operation.

4) Clandestine human intelligence is unlikely to be useful because there will be insufficient time to make it operational and because it undermines the humanitarian nature of the operation.

5) Unclassified intelligence products are imperative. In a complex humanitarian emergency, the U.S. military must coordinate with an

extensive array of international actors who will need access to U.S. intelligence. Sensitive information should be handled with discretion instead of classification.

6) Military leaders must understand the culture and objectives of other organizations involved in the relief effort. Many NGOs are as suspicious of the UNHCR — and each other — as they are of militaries. It is unrealistic to expect the UNHCR, or any other single organization, to be able to thoroughly coordinate all efforts of the entire range of actors in a refugee operation.

EVOLUTION OF THE UN DEPARTMENT OF PEACEKEEPING OPERATIONS

Robert J. Allen
Lieutenant, U.S. Navy
July 1994

When peacekeeping missions go awry, the world peers scornfully at the UN and wonders why it does not work better. A look inside the Peacekeeping Department—understaffed, starved for funds, beset by blizzards of changing instructions from the Security Council—raises a different question: how the system works at all (Brooks: A1).

INTRODUCTION

The United Nations system that has evolved over the last 30 years to manage peace operations is handicapped by bureaucracy and chronic understaffing. With the end of the Cold War and the explosion of the number of UN peace operations since 1988, this system has shown significant strain as it copes with the rigors of increasingly complex and dangerous new "peacekeeping" missions. The UN Department of Peacekeeping Operations (DPKO) has undergone a series of reorganizations in an attempt to rectify the shortcomings and limitations the UN inherited from its Cold War peacekeeping management system. Most observers agree, however, the structural changes implemented by the UN and focused on the DPKO are insufficient to deal with long-standing deficiencies in planning, command and control, and logistics of peacekeeping operations. A division of responsibilities and diffusion of power among the competitive bureaucracies within the UN Secretariat remains, threatening the viability of future peace operations.

Fielding a Peacekeeping Operation

A review of organizational roles and responsibilities in fielding a traditional peacekeeping operation is helpful to appreciate some of the shortcomings of UN peace operations management. When a dispute which may threaten international peace and security is brought before the UN Security Council (UNSC) (by UN member states, the UN Secretary-General, the UN General Assembly, or through the Council's own response to UN Charter responsibilities), the Council may elect to establish a peacekeeping mission. Nine members of the Council must approve the operation, but any one of the five permanent members can veto it.

UN survey teams with political, civil and military components conduct a fact-finding mission and develop the mission concept for presentation to the UNSC. The Council will subsequently request the Secretary-General to develop an implementation plan detailing force size, structure, duties and mission duration. This responsibility falls upon the planners in several UN Secretariat departments. This would include the Department of Peacekeeping Operations and the logisticians in what was, until September 1993, the Field Operations Division of the Department of Administration and Management. Security Council approval of the detailed mission concept is followed by development of its budget by the Field Operations Division for ultimate approval by the General Assembly (U.S. Congress *e*: 84).

Evolution of a Management Agency: The Office of Special Political Affairs

The management structure adopted for peacekeeping operations was a product of the Cold War. The UN Military Staff Committee, envisioned to direct UN military forces under Article 47 of the Charter, was rendered ineffectual by the U.S.-Soviet standoff. Thus, even when the UN could agree to authorize a peacekeeping mission, no infrastructure for its direction existed. Secretariat-level orchestration of the operations therefore initially fell upon the personal staffs of two "Under-Secretaries General Without Portfolio" created by Secretary-General Dag Hammarskjold in the 1950s. These offices were renamed Under-Secretaries General for Special Political Affairs when the Office of Special Political Affairs was created in 1961 (Durch *b*: 59).

The Office of Special Political Affairs (OSPA) was the locus of Secretariat peacekeeping management until replaced by the Department of Peacekeeping Operations in 1992. One Under-Secretary-General for Special Political Affairs (UNSGSPA) oversaw UN Middle East affairs, a region which included over half of the UN peacekeeping operations conducted through 1985. This office was initially held by the American Ralph Bunche, who was succeeded by Britons

Brian Urquhart in 1971, and Marrack Goulding in 1985. The other USGSPA post was traditionally held by Latin Americans. They served as the Secretary-General's mediators and trouble-shooters until their office was abolished in 1988 and its functions absorbed by the Executive Office of the Secretary-General (Durch *b*: 60). That action effectively divorced the diplomatic aspects (mediation and negotiation) of peace operations from its operational aspects resident in OSPA. Subsequent reorganizations have not rectified this problem.

Military Advisor's Office and Field Operations Division

The main actors in the operational management of peacekeeping therefore became the Office of Special Political Affairs (OSPA), primarily the Secretary-General's Military Advisor's Office, and the Field Operations Division (FOD) of the Department of Administration and Management. The Military Advisor post was created in 1960 as a result of the UN Congo operation and remained attached to both the UN Secretary-General (UNSYG) and the OSPA, but in fact provided little military advice to the UNSYG. Through 1992 the main function of the office of the Military Advisor and its small staff of five to six seconded officers was to serve as the operations staff for peacekeeping operations. It took the lead role in formulating the implementation plan for presentation to the Security Council by the UNSYG, recruited military contingents, and coordinated military operations in the field (Berdal *b*: 53). The latter task was not difficult while the peacekeeping operations remained essentially observer missions and small in number, because the FOD handled most daily mission support tasks. FOD administered communications, logistics, budget and transport with a staff of approximately 90 in New York (one-half UN civil servants, 10 seconded military officers and the balance temporary personnel from elsewhere in the Secretariat) and 100 in the field (Durch *b*: 73). This resulted in a bifurcated chain of command for peacekeeping missions.

Department of Peacekeeping Operations (DPKO)

The growth in number of peacekeeping operations during the late 1980s was not matched with a commensurate increase in the Secretariat staff to manage them. While the UN fielded just five peacekeeping operations with 10,000 troops in 1987, this burden grew to 15 operations and 40,000 troops by mid-1991 (Lewis *a*: A22), while the staff available to handle all mission planning and support remained at less than 24. Concurrent with the expansion of UN peacekeeping responsibilities, incoming UN Secretary-General Boutros Boutros-Ghali conducted a restructuring of the UN Secretariat in

February 1992 in an attempt to rationalize the bureaucracy. The Department of Peacekeeping Operations was created from the Office of Special Political Affairs as one of seven departments reporting to the UNSYG.

The reorganization exacerbated both the decentralization of authority and the segregation of peace operation responsibilities by moving the "peacemaking" functions (mediation and negotiation) from the Secretary-General's Executive Office to the new Department of Political Affairs while maintaining the Field Operations Division within the Department of Administration and Management. This disconnect of operational, political, and logistical planning responsibility for peace operations was supposed to be addressed by the establishment of the Senior Planning and Monitoring Group which, however, has failed to provide sufficient liaison between operators, negotiators and logisticians (Durch *b*: 60).

Personnel recruitment is a divided responsibility. The DPKO and the Secretary-General's Executive Office are responsible for troops and Human Resource Management for specialists and civilians. Once the required military capabilities for a mission are identified by the Military Advisor's Office, countries are individually solicited for troop contributions by the SYG's Executive Office. Troop training, quality, and competence often have a lower priority than willingness to participate and the "geographic distribution" of the contingents (Berdal *b*: 53).

Reorganization and Expansion

A reorganization of the DPKO was undertaken by Ghanaian Kofi Annan when he assumed the post of Under-Secretary-General for Peacekeeping Operations from Marrack Goulding in March 1993. Annan's key goal was to address the chronic under-manning which thwarted effective Secretariat pre-deployment planning, operational oversight, and liaison with the field. Through 1992 fewer than 150 people, including those in the Field Operations Division, were responsible for planning, recruitment and management of some 40,000 troops and a budget larger than that of all the rest of the UN (Durch *a*: 2).

Goulding had already begun to work toward the creation of a large staff on long-term contract. Annan set out to immediately double his small staff to 50 using long-term contract personnel and seconded military professionals toward an eventual goal of 100 personnel (Lewis *b*: A10). Under Annan, the DPKO staff was expanded by April 1993 to 18 civilian political officers,

8 military officers in the Military Advisor's Office, and 17 short-term personnel. Continuous expansion and absorption of the Field Operations Division into DPKO raised total personnel to 300 by May 1994. Despite increased manning, Military Advisor Canadian Major General Maurice Baril claims his enlarged staff of 62 in DPKO is expected to do "what in my army would require a staff of 1,000 (Brooks: A4).

UN Situation Center

A somewhat controversial element of the DPKO reorganization was the establishment of the UN Situation Center. Marrack Goulding was opposed to creation of a UN "war room" during his tenure as Under-Secretary-General for Peacekeeping Operations. He argued "[t]he management of peacekeeping forces is essentially political. You're trying to prevent wars not make them" (Lewis *c*: A12). Kofi Annan, however, saw a 24-hour UN operations center as a necessity to cope with the UN's large and complex peace operations (Lewis *b*: A10).

Initially conceived as an interface with NATO to coordinate enforcement of an expected Bosnian peace plan, the establishment of the Situation Center was hastened by the UN's scheduled May 1993 assumption of command of operation RESTORE HOPE, the humanitarian relief mission in Somalia. At the time the U.S. assessed that "[t]he UN was not organized or equipped to disseminate information critical to its expanding proactive peace enforcement/peacemaking operations" (U.S. DoD *k*). In accordance with U.S. government policy, the Joint Chiefs of Staff obtained UN permission and cooperation in organizing an around-the-clock watch center.

When the Situation Center was opened in April 1993, it provided the first capability for UN field commanders — known as "Force Commanders" — to communicate with UN Headquarters on a 24-hour basis (MacKenzie: 330-331). The facility also serves as an after-hours communications link with UN agencies and offices worldwide. The role of the Center is purely to monitor field operations. It is clearly not intended to be a command center (U.S. DoD *k*). In some respects the Situation Center serves an analogous role to that of the White House Situation Room — providing senior policymakers with information. Consequently, the Situation Center has fallen short of the desires of some to see a full-fledged command and control center developed to direct UN military operations (Saracino: 370; Friedman: A1).

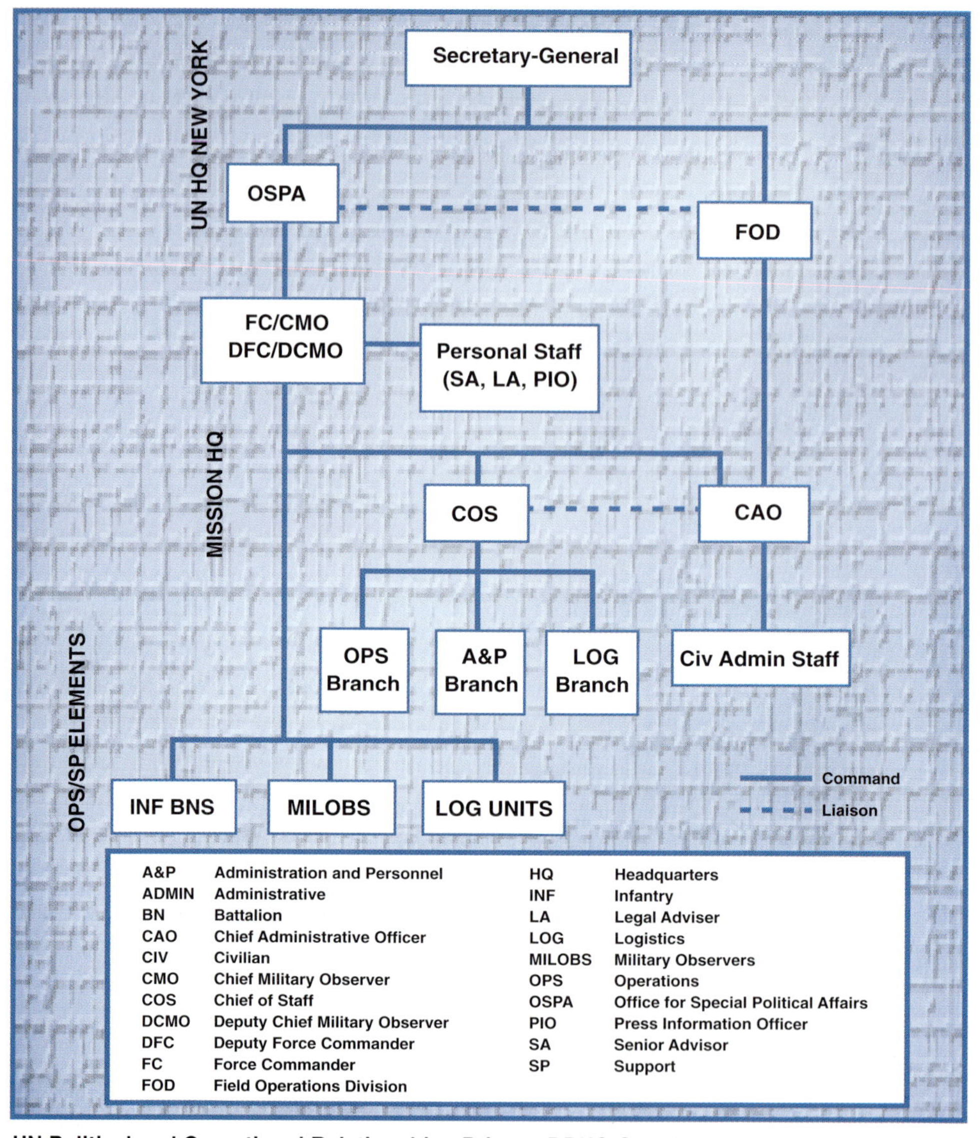

UN Political and Operational Relationships Prior to DPKO Creation. *source: author*

The UN peace operations in Somalia, former Yugoslavia, and Cambodia were the initial focus of the Situation Center's monitoring responsibilities, which today include all peacekeeping operations. Twenty-four hour watches are maintained by two duty officers drawn from the Center's staff of 26 personnel. A total of 25 seconded officers from 18 countries serve in the Center under a Canadian civilian director. Their equipment is limited to maps, secure phones, facsimile, commercial television, on-line data bases, and a U.S.-developed intelligence dissemination system. A small Information and Research Branch of four military intelligence personnel, known as "INR," provides intelligence support to UN peace operations in the field and at the Secretariat (U.S. DoD *k*).

Not all elements of the UN Secretariat support the concept of the Situation Center, but Major General Baril and Under-Secretary-General Annan are strong proponents (Best: 12). Even within the DPKO, the Center has met resistance. The civilian political officers in the Operations Office who are responsible for specific peace missions feel threatened that they will be "left out of the loop" by the Situation Center. Integration of political officers into the Center may diminish this prevailing "us and them" attitude, as well as broaden the exclusively military expertise at the Center to include diplomatic and humanitarian perspectives. Moving the Situation Center into the UN Secretariat Building (from its leased office space across the street) with other elements of the DPKO is also expected to mitigate the bureaucratic infighting.

Logistics & Administration

A persistent stumbling block in the management of peace operations, that of logistics, was addressed in the latest changes to the DPKO. The Field Administration and Logistics Division, formerly the Field Operations Division (FOD) of the Department of Administration and Management, was integrated into the DPKO during September 1993. The FOD had operated in a completely separate chain of command from its military counterparts in the field. It was a dual chain of command under which a Force Commander did not have control over his own logistics.[1] Within the Secretariat, the FOD enjoyed a great deal of autonomy, being merely required to "consult" with the DPKO.

Such an arrangement was the outgrowth of many factors peculiar to the UN: It views peacekeepers as temporary "employees" and career civil servants as therefore necessary to ensure continuity in a mission; personnel who understand the byzantine UN procurement and finance system are essential to get even a modicum of logistics support; and the presence of a Chief Administrative Officer in the field is thought to demonstrate civil

1 Major General Lewis MacKenzie claims the Field Operations Division's Chief Administrative Officer in the field had the ability to thwart the Force Commander's direction if he so desired.

over military authority in the Third World. Lastly, and probably most importantly, the bureaucratic infighting which pervades the UN dissuaded the Department of Administration and Management from surrendering its powers represented in the Field Operations Division.

The Field Administration and Logistics Division (FALD) of the DPKO is now responsible for all budget, civil personnel and procurement aspects of peace operations. In mid-1993, a New York staff of 106 civilians and a small number of seconded military personnel provided support to all UN overseas offices, agencies and operations which then numbered 13,000 civilians and 75,000 troops and expended $3.3 billion (U.S. Cong *e*: 44). The FALD is divided into three services: The Finance Management and Support Service determines a mission's cost and produces the budget that is presented to the General Assembly for approval and financing by member states. The Personnel Management and Support Service is responsible for recruiting all civilian personnel who must also be approved by the Office of Human Resources Management. Human Resources Management often ignores suggested candidates and promotes its own based on political, geographic, or gender considerations. Prior peacekeeping experience is not a prerequisite for these positions, nor are they perceived as career-enhancing by UN civil servants; better personnel tend to remain in New York (U.S. Cong *e*: 45). Yasushi Akashi, commenting on his experience as UN Special Representative in Cambodia, summed up the results. "The quality of personnel was not uniformly outstanding" (Michaels: 66).

While Field Administration and Logistics Division (FALD) financing and staffing practices may be major sources of criticism, actual supply of forces in the field is its greatest shortcoming. A UN logistic network requires two to three months to establish and must contend with a UN procurement system that needs four months to obtain items that can be routinely supplied in the U.S. military in three to four weeks (Michaels: 66). The long lead times mean that troops who often arrive ill-equipped for their peacekeeping duties must beg, borrow, steal or go without. (Lack of flak vests is said to have contributed to the Pakistani death toll in the 5 June 1993 Mogadishu ambush) (Richburg *b*: A36). The General Assembly has rejected a proposal to establish a $15 million equipment stockpile at the UN depot in Pisa, Italy, to deal with such contingencies. Logistic management capability is so meager that the UN had to resort to Western contractors to provide services upon the departure of American logisticians from

Mogadishu in March 1993. Denis Beissel, Acting FALD Director in November 1993, recounted his problems: "When we start in a new place everything is wrong. I don't have enough of anything to respond quickly. No staff, no stock, no money" (Michaels: 66).

PERSISTENT PROBLEMS

The restructuring of the UN Secretariat, and the Department of Peacekeeping Operations (DPKO) in particular, has failed to address persistent problems of fielding peace operations in the 1990s. The organizational disconnect between "peacemakers" in the Department of Political Affairs and "peacekeepers" in DPKO remains. Despite the existence of interdepartmental task forces for planning, peace operations have a potential for failure due to a lack of management coordination among competing Secretariat bureaucracies.

The basic problem of command and control of military forces in peace operations remains unresolved. No organization within the DPKO provides strong direction; operational control of the force rests with the commander in the field. The services of the nascent Situation Center provide monitoring, information and 24-hour communications capability, but little else. Harsh criticism describing it as a joke — "officers sitting around watching CNN" ("General Boutros": 36) or a "dump — Bucharest Town Hall circa 1950" (Brooks: A4) — is unwarranted as it was never intended to be a command center. However, without a robust command and control capability, major powers will be understandably reluctant to place their troops under UN command for large-scale or dangerous peace operations.

The logistics problems endemic to UN peace operations are unlikely to be completely solved by the integration of the Field Operations Division into DPKO. UN financing, personnel and contractual practices will not be overcome by a simple structural reorganization. The Field Administration and Logistics Division may at least prove more accountable to the field and in DPKO than its predecessor. The ambitious agenda envisioned for peace operations in early 1993 had foundered upon UN management deficiencies by the end of the year. Secretary-General Boutros-Ghali was forced to admit:

> The United Nations is not able to do a huge peace-enforcement operation. . . . If it is a traditional peacekeeping [operation) or something in between . . . we can do it. But if you move to a peace-enforcement operation-of tens of thousands, we don't have the capacity (Preston *b*: A24).

Under-Secretary-General for Peacekeeping Operations Kofi Annan promised "[t]he days of gifted amateurism are over" in March 1993 as he outlined his goals for a 24-hour UN "war room," stand-by armed forces and an intelligence system to conduct peace operations (Lewis *b*: A10). But a frustrating year in Bosnia, Haiti, and especially Somalia proved this boast was premature. Somalia highlighted the critical shortcoming which prevents the world body from successfully conducting anything but a traditional peacekeeping operation: the lack of any kind of a military command structure at its headquarters in New York that could devise military plans and strategies and quickly approve proposed military operations (Richburg *b*: A36).

Chapter 3
PEACE OPERATIONS

At the very moment President Bush was promising augmented U.S. intelligence support to the General Assembly in New York, British, French and U.S. forces were assisting Kurds in Northern Iraq. At the same time, political disintegration in Yugoslavia and Somalia was increasing pressure for multilateral action. Within months the United States had over 20,000 troops on the ground in Somalia and had committed a similar number to enforce a peace settlement in the Balkans if it could be achieved. In Cambodia the UN had more than 20,000 personnel conducting the most comprehensive transitional regime in history to end the civil war. With U.S. soldiers involved in UN peace operations, it was time to deliver on the promises and turn theory into practice.

Lieutenant Robert J. Allen sets the stage by describing the evolution of intelligence procedures at UN Headquarters in New York to support peace operations in the field. He analyzes the requirements for intelligence and then outlines the procedures and organization that evolved to meet the need. Captains William S. Brei and William E. Whitney, Lieutenant Allen and Technical Sergeant Payton A. Flynn review the first attempts by the U.S. to provide intelligence support to coalition or UN-sponsored peace operations in the field. The case studies include:

- PROVIDE COMFORT in Iraq
- UNTAC in Cambodia
- UNITAF and UNOSOM II in Somalia

The results were mixed. Military intelligence was not prepared to provide the kind of information most needed in the initial stages of a humanitarian assistance operation. The organizational cultures and bureaucratic imperatives of multinational parties or UN headquarters and military field operations do not make an easy match. Once the requirements of the

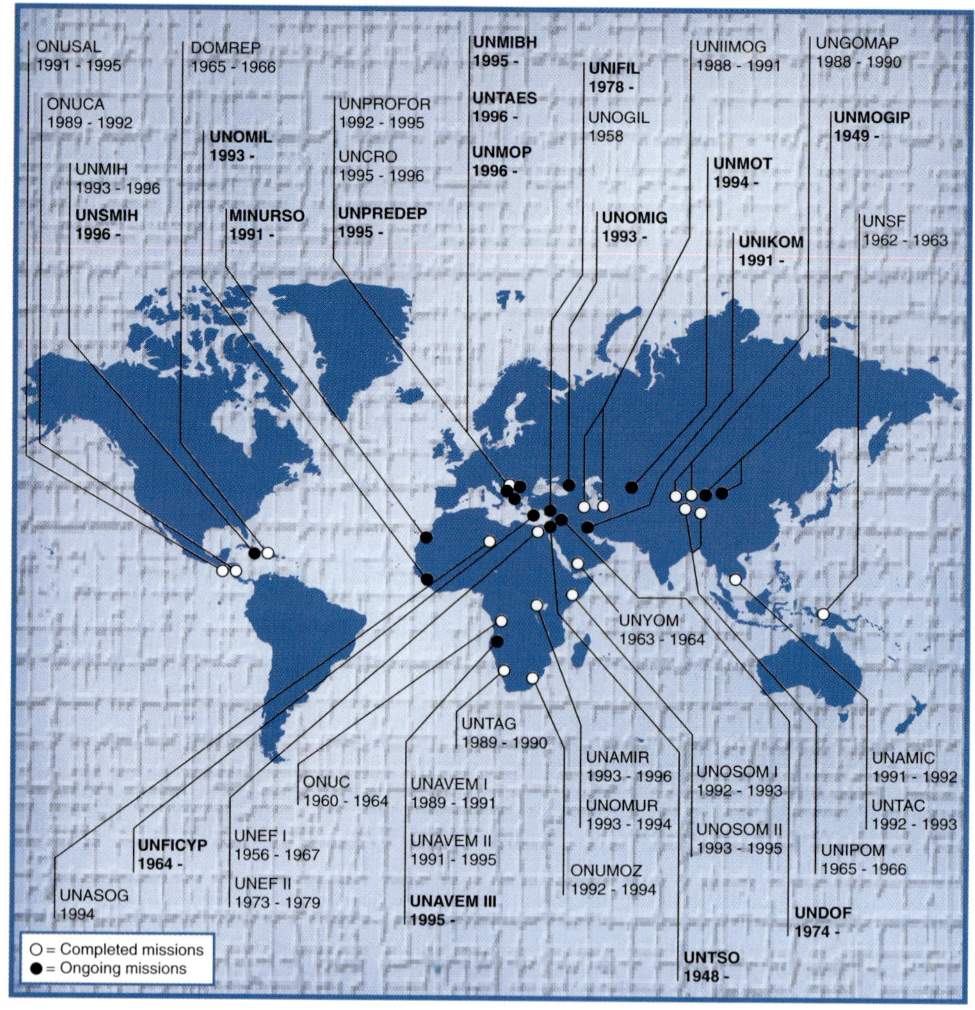

UN Peacekeeping Operations as of January 1997. *source: author*

operations were understood, the military intelligence task-organized its collection, analysis and production to respond. The U.S. or the UN developed the mechanisms to process the information. However, more serious problems have emerged, related to the sometimes obscure missions defined by Security Council mandates. The inherent contradiction between humanitarian assistance and intervention is reflected in the need to define the intelligence mission as overt and impartial fact finding, whereas obtaining intelligence on the intentions of hostile parties whose interests are threatened by a coalition or by a UN mission call for more traditional intelligence methods.

INTELLIGENCE SUPPORT FOR PEACE OPERATIONS

Robert J. Allen
Lieutenant, USN
July 1994

> [A]ny form of covert intelligence is liable to create prejudice and suspicion. . . . The UN has therefore resolutely refused to countenance intelligence systems as a part of its peacekeeping operations; intelligence, having covert connections, is a dirty word (IPA *b*: 39).

> I was also upset that I had to get my intelligence from the BBC. The UN was still following its outdated rules that precluded our even saying the word "intelligence," let alone producing it. Here we were, almost 300 kilometers from the nearest semi-secure border, and we scarcely had the foggiest notion what was going on around us (MacKenzie: 284-285).

INTRODUCTION

Overt intelligence collection operations that peacekeepers conduct have been cloaked in the guise of "public information" efforts, "civil affairs," and "military observer" duties (Berdal *b*: 44). "Military information gathering" and "military information officers" (MIOs) have served as non-provocative labels for collection and collectors of overt intelligence. MIOs in traditional peacekeeping operations have relied upon reports from non-threatening sources such as observation posts, patrols, visual sightings, UN Military Observers, conversations with local parties, host governments, the media, and, in some cases, aerial reconnaissance for intelligence reporting. Observer duties include investigating cease-fire violations, conducting liaison visits to military formations, monitoring military forces, maintaining an accurate order of battle, and visiting forward positions to report on the disposition of forces.

Reporting

Peacekeeping forces in the field and UN Military Observers are regarded as the best source of tactical intelligence reporting by the Department of Peacekeeping Operations (DPKO). It is viewed as the MIO's responsibility to compile information summaries to support UN Headquarters (IPA *b*: 60). MIOs in the field produce two types of reports: Information Reports (INREPs) and Information Summaries (INFSUMs). INREPs contain operational information that requires immediate attention while INFSUMs support trend analysis and are produced on a weekly basis. Intelligence contained in the INREP is included in the Force Commander's daily Situation Report which is seen along with the weekly INFSUMs by subordinate units and UN Headquarters.

Expanding Support Requirements

A change in the operational environment of post-Cold War peace operations is prompting recognition within the UN that an intelligence collection and analysis capability in the field and at the Secretariat (at least within the DPKO) is a necessity (Best: 12). Peace missions within the context of civil wars — where "peacekeepers" do not enjoy the consent of all the concerned parties or are outgunned by belligerents, at a minimum demand an intelligence collection and processing capability for the safety and security of troops. The wide scope of activities conducted in peace operations produces a number of requirements for information critical to mission success. At the Secretariat, information is required to implement the *Agenda for Peace*, monitor and assess current peace operations, provide a strategic outlook for deployed peacekeepers, and predict and plan future operations.

Field Collection Requirements

Traditional peacekeeping operations between states required information concerning adjustment to belligerent deployments, changes in belligerent military strength, preparation of defensive positions, location and types of minefields, changes in order of battle and equipment, changes in civilian behavior, changes in attitudes of the belligerent parties, and imposition of restrictions upon force movement ("Army-Air Force": 56). Multi-component operations and those in peace enforcement or quasi-combat situations have added further to these intelligence requirements. Verification of combatant demobilization and disarmament was necessary in Nicaragua

(ONUCA), El Salvador (ONUSAL), Angola (UNAVEM II), and Mozambique (UNOMOZ). Location, inventory, and tracking of heavy weapons were intelligence taskings in Croatia, Bosnia (UNPROFOR and NATO artillery exclusion zones around Sarajevo and Gorazde in 1994) and Somalia (UNOSOM II). UNPROFOR Sarajevo Sector Commander Major General Lewis MacKenzie felt "Sarajevo cried out for things like satellite imagery and counter-battery radar" to monitor cease-fire violations (Saracino: 370). Detection of arms caches and the cross-border movements of insurgents were intelligence problems confronted by UN peacekeepers in Cambodia (UNTAC). UN troops taking part in the preventive deployment to Macedonia have sanctions monitoring as one of their duties.

Indications and Warning: The Human Factor

Early warning of hostile action has become a paramount concern to forces deployed in *de facto* peace enforcement situations such as Bosnia (UNPROFOR) or Somalia (UNOSOM II). Discerning intentions is the key to avoiding casualties in civil war scenarios where conventional military forces and their attendant indicators of impending action are absent. The importance of human intelligence (HUMINT) in meeting this requirement cannot be over-emphasized. Richard Best, a national defense analyst with the Congressional Research Service, explains why human resources intelligence plays such a critical role in peace operations:

> Peacekeeping depends upon at least tacit support from the local population; perceiving shifts in local public opinion from support to disinterest or outright hostility can be a matter of fundamental importance to a peacekeeping mission . . . [T]here may also be armed elements determined to frustrate the peacekeeping effort and foreknowledge of their capabilities and intentions can save lives. Intelligence officers assessing subtle changes in public opinion and the goals of dissident groups will probably depend as much upon human agents as . . . sophisticated technological capabilities (Best: 1).

Non-military Intelligence Requirements

UN peacekeeping officials point out that many intelligence requirements of peace operations, like the operations themselves, are not military in nature. The military intelligence requirements derive from the need for a military component to facilitate and coordinate the other processes in the peace missions, such as political, diplomatic, humanitarian and economic elements. The breakdown of the Angolan (UNAVEM II) peace process illustrates the value (by its absence) of this military intelligence mission of coordination. In Angola, the UN proceeded with elections before confirming that insurgents were completely disarmed and demobilized. In contrast, the UN waited to administer elections in Mozambique until verifying the disarmament of insurgents. "A knowledge of local geography and economic infrastructure, the politics of the region, social and economic factors, and religious traditions will often be more important than the order of battle" for peace operations (Best: 3). Field operations therefore may require information on topics as diverse as political parties, belligerent negotiating positions, terrain, refugees, prices, roads, health, and customs for their success.

SECRETARIAT FUNCTIONS

Assessment and Analysis

Intelligence requirements of the Secretariat to support policy are generally much less detailed than those in the field. The Secretariat's peace support activities are primarily concerned with mediation, anticipation and resolution of conflicts. *An Agenda for Peace* outlines some of the requirements associated with these tasks: Preventive diplomacy necessitates "timely and accurate knowledge of the facts" and "an understanding of developments and global trends, based on sound analysis." Early warning of threats to peace is expected to be gained by a synthesis of political indicators with information supplied by the UN's existing network of early warning resources. This network warns of environmental threats, nuclear accidents, natural disasters, mass human migrations, famine and disease. This will permit preventive diplomacy and peacemaking to be applied to the disputes (Boutros-Ghali *a*: 7).

An independent intelligence assessment and analysis capability is required at the Secretariat if it is to fulfill its preventive diplomacy and peacemaking roles. Currently, the UN can be forced to action by media coverage of a crisis or through manipulation by belligerent parties. Media attention can precipitate UN action where more sober analysis would argue for non-intervention — Somalia and Rwanda are examples. Media attention can place a situation in global context: otherwise conflicts as vicious as Bosnia and Somalia might not have qualified for UN intervention. An especially effective disinformation effort waged by the Bosnian Muslims during the April 1994 siege of Gorazde (which is credited with securing UN authorization for NATO air strikes) is illustrative of the dangers of manipulation (Cohen: A3 and Pomfret: A18).

Supporting the Field: Indications and Warning

The intelligence needs of preventive diplomacy and preventive deployment illustrate how field requirements can only be met by the Secretariat or the Department of Peacekeeping Operations. All peacekeeping operations deployments require a strategic overview of the environment in which they are operating—information on the situation in neighboring countries and their attitudes toward the mission. Actions or events in surrounding states can decisively influence the success or safety of a peace operation. For example, Croatian incursions into the UN Protected Areas during January 1993 took the lives of UN peacekeepers and ultimately derailed ongoing peace negotiations. Major General MacKenzie recounts how the UNPROFOR Headquarters in Sarajevo, responsible for the peacekeeping mission in Croatia, was adversely affected by the eruption of the Bosnian civil war. With no ability to assess the likely results of Bosnian independence, the UN "assigned a couple of local employees to listen to the radio and watch television and keep [them] briefed" (MacKenzie: 135-136). A UN indications and warning capability would have minimized casualties and perhaps permitted diplomatic pressure to forestall the offensive (Bair: 12). In the case of a preventive deployment like Macedonia, intelligence on events within potentially unstable (Kosovo) or hostile (Serbia) neighboring regions is crucial to the security of the lightly-armed force.

Planning

Mission planning by the Department of Peacekeeping Operations (DPKO) is the one area where detailed intelligence is required by the Secretariat. Background information on a conflict, military capabilities of the belligerent, the population, politics, and culture of the area of operations would better prepare national contingent commanders for the challenges of their mission than the cursory briefs they now receive from the DPKO. Extensive information on infrastructure, available host-nation support, geography, economic, and health factors could aid DPKO planners in alleviating many of the deployment difficulties that peacekeeping missions experience. For example, Matts Berdal asserts that proper integration of intelligence in predeployment planning would have alleviated the logistics difficulties encountered by UNTAC in Cambodia (Berdal *b*: 45). At present, the necessary information is available only from the small technical survey team which is dispatched to the area of operations to formulate the mission concept for the Security Council. The pitfalls of relying on this source in Cambodia were noted in a General Accounting Office report:

> [M]uch of that information [collected by the survey team in 1989-90] was outdated by the time UNTAC began operations in 1992. Several UNTAC officials said the condition of roads and bridges had deteriorated in the 2 years between the survey and the beginning of UNTAC operations, and some roads initially thought usable were barely passable when UNTAC deployed (U.S. GAO: 34).

Despite an increasing need for intelligence in support of peace operations, the UN organization is still not committed to providing it. An aversion to intelligence collection is still present within some quarters of the UN (Best: 12). The U.S. has been instrumental in prodding the UN toward adoption of a more robust intelligence infrastructure to support the organization both in the field and at the Secretariat. The U.S. is the only nation yet to establish a formal intelligence-sharing relationship with the UN. Support to the UN's highly visible peace operations is a primary focus of U.S. intelligence sharing with the world body. Policy has been established, hardware procured and organizations put in place by both the U.S. and the UN to support this endeavor. Problems encountered by the intelligence system that presently supports the Department of Peacekeeping Operations (DPKO) and the obstacles it faces as its functions expand in accordance with U.S. policy and UN desires will now be considered.

U.S. INTELLIGENCE SUPPORT

During the Cold War, U.S. intelligence support to UN peace operations was provided on an *ad hoc* basis, as exemplified by the occasional U-2 flights which commenced in 1973 to support the UN Disengagement Observer Force (UNDOF) on the Golan Heights (Durch *b*: 69). The end of superpower competition and the expanded use of the UN to promote U.S. national security interests during the Gulf War led to an increased U.S. willingness to share information with the organization. U.S. U-2 reconnaissance aircraft have been dedicated to the UN since August 1991 to aid the UN Special Commission (UNSCOM) in monitoring the elimination of Iraq's weapons of mass destruction. The International Atomic Energy Agency (IAEA), the UN special agency charged with dismantling Iraq's nuclear weapons program and policing the Nuclear Non-Proliferation Treaty, also received U.S. intelligence support. IAEA Director Hans Blix has acknowledged "the satellite pictures that we get from the United States" are used by the North Korean government to question the agency's impartiality ("IAEA Director": 2; R. Smith *d*: A1).

The growing intelligence relationship between the U.S. and the UN was extended to include the organization's expanding peace responsibilities during 1992. Accordingly, then-Director of Central Intelligence Robert M. Gates designated the Defense Intelligence Agency (DIA) as the Executive Agent for U.S. intelligence support to UN peace operations. Within the DIA, the Joint Staff J2 (Intelligence Directorate) was assigned the task of providing the intelligence support approved on a case-by-case basis by the U.S. Intelligence Community for specific UN peace operations (U.S. DoD *l*). The UN peacekeeping mission in Cambodia (UNTAC) was the first to receive support under this arrangement beginning in May 1992. During his September 1992 address to the UN General Assembly, President Bush pledged to further "broaden American support for monitoring, verification, reconnaissance and other requirements of UN peacekeeping or humanitarian assistance operations" (Bush *c*: 1699). The policy was codified in National Security Directive 74 (November 1992) which sought to strengthen all aspects of UN management and operations (U.S. DoD *k*).

Arrival of the Clinton administration brought further impetus to efforts to enhance intelligence sharing with the UN. A Senate Foreign Relations Committee report evaluated UN operations underway in early 1993 and found:

> [T]here was little systematic recovery and dissemination of order of battle information between units in the field and [their] headquarters. There [was] also limited sharing of information between UN Headquarters in New York and the field. Although many believed that Western intelligence agencies were monitoring closely crisis areas through a variety of electronic and imagery intelligence methods, there appeared to be no system for disseminating this information to operational field commanders and unit commanders (U.S. Cong *e*: 39-40).

Clinton's policy of assertive multilateralism — relying upon the UN to deal with regional conflicts — clearly demanded a more effective intelligence capability for peace operations. A key element in rectifying the identified deficiencies was seen in the development of a watch center or situation room at UN Headquarters with dedicated U.S. intelligence support. With the UN set to assume control of the humanitarian relief operation in Somalia, the Joint Staff J2 obtained UN approval and cooperation in March 1992 to establish a communications network and watch center to support peace operations. The UN Situation Center began operations in April 1993, with an initial mandate to serve as a 24-hour monitoring and communications center for UN field operations.

Procedures and Organization

Deployed JDISS Workstation. *photo used with permission*

The U.S. provides intelligence to UN operations according to U.S. Intelligence Community concepts of operation (CONOPs) which delineate sanitization and release procedures for each approved peace mission. The CONOPs permit two levels of intelligence sharing with the UN. Level I information is sensitive and must remain under U.S. control, but can be shown to key UN officials. Level II information encompasses all other intelligence sanitized for release to the UN. Level II information can be given directly to the UN and is labeled "UN RESTRICTED" (U.S. DoD *b*: VIII-2). The U.S. uses the term "information" rather than "intelligence" to conform to UN practices.

The Joint Staff intelligence staff has provided the UN Department of Peacekeeping Operations (DPKO) with an intelligence dissemination network designed to be compatible with, and to emulate that of the Department of Defense. The thrust of the U.S. system, known as the Joint

JDISS consists of a transportable computer workstation and satellite communications suite based upon standard commercial hardware. Utilizing specialized software, JDISS permits worldwide exchange of data, messages, and images among nodes of the Joint Intelligence Architecture. The National Military Joint Intelligence Center is the focal point of this network which links the Unified Commanders and deployed tactical commanders (U.S. DoD *b*: GL-12).

Intelligence Architecture, is to transmit intelligence available from national collection assets and Washington-area elements of the Intelligence Community down to tactical commanders in the field while permitting the tactical commanders to communicate information upward through the chain of command (Best: 4). The Joint Deployable Intelligence Support System (JDISS) is the primary conduit for U.S. intelligence dissemination to the UN. The system was demonstrated at UN Headquarters in March 1993 and two suites were subsequently purchased by the DPKO.

JDISS links the DPKO Situation Center with the U.S. National Military Joint

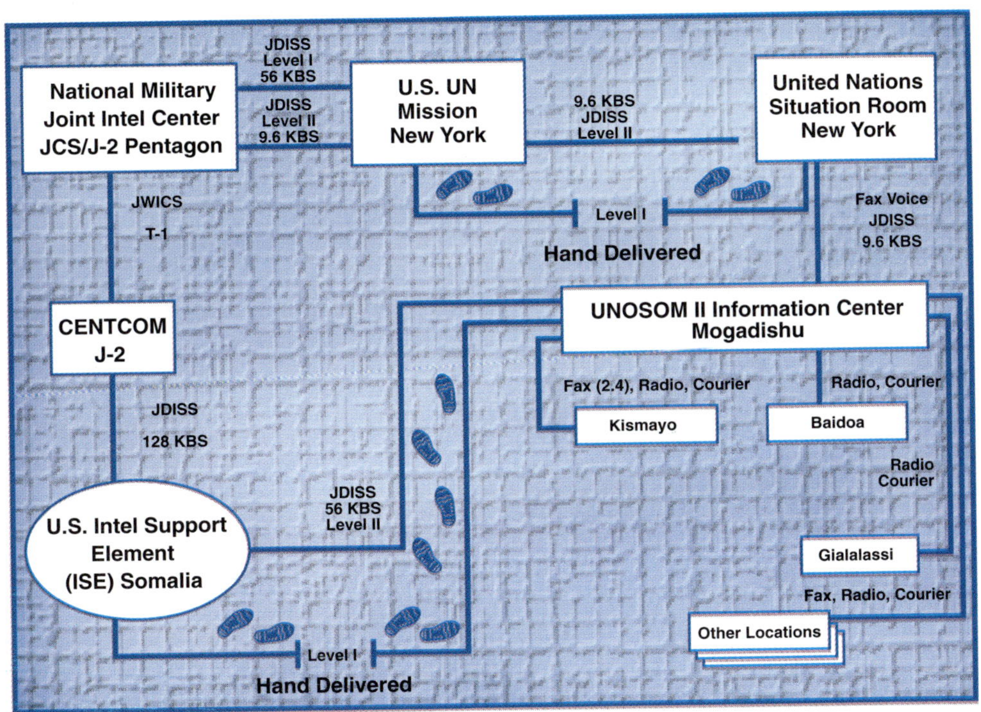

US/UN Intelligence Flow Chart.

source: U.S. DoD b

Intelligence Center (NMJIC) in the Pentagon via the U.S. Mission to the UN. The NMJIC is the hub of the U.S. intelligence support network for UN peace operations. A UN Support Desk was established in August 1993 to perform the Joint Staff intelligence role of providing Intelligence Community products to the UN Situation Center.

One U.S. officer serves on the 26-person staff of the Situation Center in the four-person Information and Research Branch. The Joint Staff J2 maintains its intelligence liaison with the UN through the Military Advisor assigned to the U.S. Mission to the UN.

All cleared Level I and II information is transmitted from the NMJIC via JDISS to the U.S. Mission to the UN. From there, Level I information may be disseminated to the Information and Research Branch at the Situation Center or to principal UN officials as appropriate. Level II information is transmitted directly to the Situation Center via JDISS. That information can be passed on to field missions by phone, facsimile, UN secure communications or JDISS.

A parallel path exists for sharing intelligence with the deployed peacekeeping operations through the U.S. Unified Commands or theater Commanders in Chief, if U.S. troops are involved. Intelligence is passed from the NMJIC through the Joint Worldwide Intelligence Communications System (JWICS) to a Unified Command J2 for relay to a JDISS-equipped Joint Task Force (JTF) tasked with supporting a UN peace operation. The J2 cell of a collocated JTF can hand-carry Level I information to a peace mission information (intelligence) center and forward Level II information on JDISS if the mission is so equipped. One UN JDISS suite can be located in the Situation Center and the other deployed to the field. Otherwise, a CINC intelligence liaison officer can disseminate the information. The overall U.S. intelligence organizational structure that supported the UN Operation in Somalia (UNOSOM II) through March 1994 is depicted in the accompanying figure.

All U.S. military support for UN peace operations is provided through proper U.S. diplomatic channels. This requires the parallel participation by both the U.S. Mission to the UN and the appropriate CINC in the UN intelligence support process. The dual dissemination network has supported UNPROFOR in Bosnia and UNOSOM II in Somalia.

Utilization of this organizational structure has the added advantage of avoiding direct interaction between the U.S. Intelligence Community and the UN. In this way, the desires of UN officials — who wish to maintain the world body's credibility and impartiality by avoiding relationships with national intelligence entities — and U.S. intelligence professionals — who seek to protect intelligence collection sources and methods in an organization staffed with personnel from countries hostile to the U.S. — are fulfilled (Best: 12). Further protection for sensitive U.S. intelligence information is achieved through isolation of the UN dissemination network from that of the U.S.

What Does the System Deliver in New York?

The quantity and quality of intelligence support delivered by the established U.S. support network through the U.S. Mission to the UN varies by consumer. Overall, the UN, especially the Secretariat, is a consumer, not a producer, of intelligence information. UN policymakers in the Department of Peacekeeping Operations and within the Secretariat are the users of most information provided to and by the Situation Center. U.S. intelligence support furnished through the U.S. Mission to the UN is directed to meet the needs of those policymakers. Field missions do not yet, however, derive substantial benefit from intelligence support at the Situation Center. The network the U.S. has helped the UN develop cannot yet respond to the needs of the tactical commander in the field as its U.S. counterpart can. Many obstacles will have to be overcome at the Secretariat if more effective intelligence support is to be provided in New York and in the field by the UN Situation Center.

Operational Perspective. The mission of the Situation Center is providing operational and significant intelligencc information to DPKO officials. Primary sources of information presently available to the Center — member states' intelligence products (almost exclusively from the U.S.), the media and data bases — however, restrict the intelligence content of its products. Heavy reliance is placed upon the media for information by the Center's Information and Research (INR) Branch. Foreign Broadcast Information Service translations furnished by the U.S. on JDISS are noted to be particularly useful resources. The Internet yields access to Reuters and Associated Press and other on-line data bases. Threat estimates from an independent risk-assessment corporation, data from Jane's, and general background information from a NATO unclassified data base are also available.

Current Information Products. The Situation Center uses these information sources and daily reports from the field to produce between 9 and 15 reports daily. These products, which are basically situation reports (SITREPs) rather than intelligence summaries (INSUMs), receive wide distribution within the UN organization to some 130 addressees, including all troop contributor nations. Daily distribution can require up to six hours with current communications systems.

Among the reports produced are a daily, two-page, executive highlights "in brief" aimed at senior DPKO officials, which covers significant developments in the peace missions. Daily mission summaries for each of the peace operations are produced overnight by the Situation Center duty officers and updated by DPKO political officers before distribution. An analogous mission weekly is also prepared — now limited only to UNOSOM II. INR is encouraging the Military Information Officers in the various peacekeeping missions to provide assessments in their reporting for inclusion in these products.

U.S. Intelligence Support to the DPKO. Understaffing at the U.S. Mission to the UN impedes more effective U.S. intelligence support to peace operations at the DPKO. The Military Advisor's Office, in the person of the Deputy Military Advisor, is the primary conduit through which U.S. intelligence passes to the DPKO in New York. With a staff of only five, the Military Advisor's Office is responsible for coordinating all U.S. military support to the UN (Sewall: 30-31). Intelligence support is but one of its many responsibilities.

The range of U.S. intelligence products shared with the Department of Peacekeeping Operations is still quite limited. Their value to DPKO policymakers is a matter of some contention. Most products that are passed by the U.S. Mission can be characterized as summary reports or SITREPs, covering previous activity. A UN official criticized them as "dated," mostly a report of what happened — taken from UN sources — not the predictive analysis desired to support UN policymakers. Although some estimative intelligence on the peacekeeping operations is shared, it is at the Level II/ "UN RESTRICTED" level, where it is essentially unclassified. These estimates, when included in a synthesized intelligence report with field and media reports, are held by some U.S. officials as valuable to the political officers within DPKO who deal with the peace missions on a day-to-day basis (Best: 9).

Intelligence to facilitate mission planning and preparation is a requirement of DPKO planners. In past cases where U.S. intelligence support has been provided to UN peace missions—UNTAC, UNOSOM II and UNPROFOR—it commenced following deployment of the mission. "[D]ata on ports and harbors, highways and transport systems, as well as the politics and culture of the area [could] be easily sanitized and forwarded in an unclassified version to the UN" (Best: 9). The U.S. responded on a one-time basis to a UN request for such mission planning information on Angola during 1994, but has established no procedure for other potential operations.

The Situation Center does not often require detailed tactical intelligence to fulfill its mandated mission of keeping DPKO policymakers informed and consequently treats tactical intelligence collection and reporting as a field-level concern. A lack of routine access to relevant tactical information prevents the Situation Center from channeling information down to field commanders as the U.S.-designed intelligence structure intends. However, the Situation Center recognizes it cannot assume the field is aware of all information and therefore must be prepared to disseminate such information to the field when available and necessary. Such situations may occur when peacekeepers' or observers' movements or access are restricted or weapons are declared and must be inventoried. The U.S. did furnish tactical intelligence through New York to help verify Bosnian-Serb compliance with the establishment of the artillery exclusion zone around Sarajevo in February 1994, but tactical information is most expeditiously communicated to peace operations by the intelligence elements of the responsible theater CINC. Tactical intelligence was conveyed to UN forces in Somalia by this route (Best: 14).

PERSISTENT PROBLEMS

Technical Issues

Lack of a capability to rapidly exchange intelligence between the DPKO and the field remains a major deficiency of UN peace operations, despite the establishment of the Situation Center. No JDISS equivalent exists to disseminate intelligence to UN field missions other than in Somalia. Intelligence information must compete with operational issues on limited UN telephone, facsimile, and secure communications circuits. Even the U.S.-supplied JDISS workstation in the Situation Center is usually unable to interface with its UN counterpart in Mogadishu due to persistent communications problems. Sufficient technical expertise resides within the Field Administration and Logistics Division's Logistics and Communications Service to address the communications shortfalls between the Situation Center and peace missions, but rectifying the situation does not appear to take priority within DPKO because of the cost and bureaucratic resistance.

Institutional Inertia

The neglect of the capability inherent in JDISS may be indicative of an aversion to change in peacekeeping practices present within the DPKO and in the field missions. The UN has only reluctantly acknowledged its need for intelligence to support peace operations. JDISS offers the capability to short-circuit traditional methods of conducting the business of peacekeeping, which relied upon personal contacts between and among UN officials in New York and their deployed counterparts. Like the perceived threat the Situation Center poses to long-entrenched political officers in DPKO, JDISS or like technologies challenge an "old boy network" where knowledge is power.

Nor may all the capabilities inherent in a rapid intelligence dissemination system be appreciated or even desired in the field. As with most military operations, peace missions do not wish to report all information to headquarters and chafe under requirements to keep New York abreast of developments. The potential for New York to interfere with the conduct of field operations if a real-time communications system were to be developed was noted to be a genuine concern by UN peacekeeping officials. Major General Lewis MacKenzie was critical of New York's appetite for information and proclivity for micro-management during the outbreak of fighting in Sarajevo in April 1992. He noted: "Keeping UN New York up-to-date was taking most of our time. Officials there were concerned we were getting involved in the conflict" (MacKenzie: 158).

National Participation

The whole concept of intelligence sharing with the UN is meeting resistance from outside the organization as well. Only the U.S. shares intelligence, case-by-case, in support of peace operations. Other UN member states participate in meeting the organization's needs on an *ad hoc* basis —if at all. Some nations and international organizations are, however, considering a position closer to that of the U.S. Britain has shared some low-level analysis and is looking toward establishing a more formal relationship. NATO is considering the establishment of an intelligence relationship with the UN modeled upon what it has with other international organizations. The Russian Federation extended an offer to begin intelligence sharing with the UN during the 1993 General Assembly session.

Security of Information

The lack of a security system at the UN for the protection of sensitive information has so far dissuaded other nations from developing formal intelligence relationships with the UN. Even for the U.S., protection of the sources and methods by which the U.S. Intelligence Community collects and analyzes intelligence data is a paramount concern (Best: 1). The risk of compromise of both sensitive information and the sources and methods by which it was gathered is present if the intelligence is not carefully reviewed before release (Best: 9; Di Rita: 42). Confidentiality of information at UN Headquarters is not well respected. The concept of security is very much anathema to the world body. Any intelligence provided in New York is essentially shared with the world, especially when written. The Secretariat can basically be described as a leaky organization where people feeding the rumor mill are part of the political process (Lancaster A1; Richburg *e*: A22).

Understandably, there is a lack of confidence among member states that sensitive information will be protected. Despite the risks, the U.S., as noted, shares Level I information with the Situation Center's Information and Research Branch or provides it to DPKO officials directly. This material usually involves threats to the lives of U.S. personnel or other urgent intelligence needed by UN peacekeepers (Best: 10). The concern over leaks of this information is assessed as minimal because most is force-protection oriented and is not politically controversial, unlike intelligence estimates.

The UN lacks adequate procedures to control sensitive material. Development of such a system to protect sensitive material would serve a secondary purpose at the UN of making its intelligence consumers confident of the information's value. Unfortunately, a security system is difficult to establish in a UN context because there is no perceived interest to protect as exists in a national setting. A classification system is under study, and is to be evaluated by NATO. NATO also is set to advise the Situation Center on development of methodology to share intelligence among many nations based on its experience.

THE FUTURE

U.S. Policy

Despite the obstacles to effective intelligence support the U.S. and UN have encountered through mid-1994, both are pressing ahead with more ambitious plans. A capability for the UN Situation Center to forecast global trouble spots and provide intelligence to all consumers in the Secretariat is a shared objective of both U.S. policy and UN peacekeeping officials. Even the earliest publicized drafts (August 1993) of the U.S. *Presidential Decision Directive* (PDD) on "Multilateral Peacekeeping Operations," known as PRD-13, included provisions for a "research staff" as an integral part of an enhanced UN peace management structure (Gellman *b*: A22). The final policy that emerged in May 1994 as PDD-25, "Reforming Multilateral Peace Operations," called for an

> Information and Research Division linked to field operations to obtain and provide current information, manage a 24-hour watch center and monitor open source material and non-sensitive information submitted by governments (U.S. President *d*: 806).

The intent of this U.S. policy is to see the UN Situation Center enhanced to perform an information and research function for the entire UN Secretariat. Under this arrangement the DPKO Situation Center will distribute information across all UN Departments while maintaining more sensitive material in channels for accountability (Lewis *b*: A10). The information disseminated would not be limited to peacekeeping data, but could include information for humanitarian relief and natural disaster response as well.

UN Aspirations

Under-Secretary-General for Peacekeeping operations Kofi Annan envisions the DPK0 Situation Center one day expanding to fill a conflict indications and warning role for the Secretary-General and the Secretariat as a whole (Lewis *b*: A10). Toward this end, the Situation Center is currently marketing its products to other elements of the UN bureaucracy and has established a billet for a liaison officer to interact with other UN Secretariat

Departments. Present sources of information available (U.S.-supplied intelligence, the media, and on-line data bases) restrict the Situation Center's ability to conduct the requisite predictive analysis. The U.S. is limiting its intelligence support to the specific peace operations approved by the Intelligence Community on a case-by-case basis (Best: 16).

Future Information Services. In line with the planned expansion of responsibilities for the Situation Center, the Information and Research Branch (INR) is planning new information products with greater intelligence content (and thus requirements) than the situation reports now produced. A daily information digest will supplement the daily "in brief" with topics of relevance to a wider UN audience than that concerned only with peacekeeping. A weekly digest will forecast short-term trends for each peace operation with contributions from the Force Commander, Secretary-General's Special Representative, and Military Intelligence Officer. Most ambitiously, an "INR World Review" will survey potential UN peace missions, examine non-UN peacekeeping missions, and serve as an indications and warning document predicting global flash points.

The ultimate goal for the Situation Center is for it to improve the quality of information available to UN policymakers. An ability to conduct assessments and trend analysis is thus viewed as imperative. In the analysis process, it is envisioned that public information can be created from a synthesis of sensitive material. The exact sources of the information will then not need to be stipulated because the fusion of multiple sources will provide an assessment in a non-sensitive product. Sensitive information may not even be necessary to provide the required intelligence analysis. According to the Congressional Research Service, "a careful review of publicly available information such as newspapers, journals, books, reports by international organizations . . ., radio, and television can provide essential intelligence (Best: 4).

In order to disseminate its information products, the Situation Center is developing an informal UN information network. The Center is now establishing relationships with other UN Secretariat departments and agencies to exchange information. The objective is to develop a common computer-based information system. The envisioned network would permit searches among numerous data bases by UN entities worldwide, while offering differing levels of access to maintain security. Development of this infrastructure will permit a virtual Situation Center to exist within the UN Secretariat without the present Situation Center necessarily becoming independent of the Department of Peacekeeping Operations.

Obstacles Ahead: Sovereignty and Impartiality

Increased cooperation from UN member governments will clearly be necessary if the Situation Center is to fulfill its perceived potential. The difficulty in achieving this cooperation without adequate security safeguards for sensitive information has already been noted. Further complications arise over the issues of sovereignty and impartiality. Article 2(7) of the UN Charter prohibits the organization from intervention "in matters which are essentially within the domestic jurisdiction of any state." Many activities necessary for global indications and warning, such as information gathering and political analysis, can be claimed to impinge on a nation's sovereignty and may be challenged by UN members. Some of those activities will surely not be conducted with a member state's consent.

Any perception of bias in UN information threatens the organization's credibility. With the U.S. as the only UN member state regularly contributing information to the UN and actively promoting an intelligence analysis capability for the organization, the UN's neutrality is vulnerable. Ironically, Perez de Cuellar's abortive attempt to establish the Office of Research and Collection of Information to provide political news and information was challenged and ultimately scuttled amid U.S. charges of "manipulation and illegal penetration" of the Secretariat by the Soviets (Gertz *b*: 1A).

U.S. and UN peacekeeping officials argue that the best way to assure impartiality and objectivity is to obtain information from as many countries as possible, refrain from uncritical acceptance of information from sources with a vested interest in a conflict (for example, the U.S. on Haiti, Russia on Tajikistan, Belgium on Rwanda, or the Bosnian-Serbs on Srebrenica), and avoid staffing the Situation Center with personnel with a perceived bias (from the U.S., Russia or China, for example). As Under-Secretary-General for Peacekeeping Operations Kofi Annan commented, "We have to be careful because the big powers only give us what they want us to know" (Lewis *b*: A10). Unfortunately, these proposed solutions pose a paradox: Were member states to contribute the necessary information to the UN, it would be met by a Secretariat wary of acceptance of possibly self-serving information and analysis from its member states (Evans: 162). A judgment on information validity will therefore rest upon personnel in the Situation

Center, whose staff, although international, is still predominantly Western and European — hardly reassuring to the Third World nations where the majority of UN peace operations are conducted.

CONCLUSION

The U.S. has committed itself to an expanding intelligence relationship with the UN. Dedicated intelligence support to specific peace operations figures prominently in this arrangement. Despite the creation of procedures and organizations to provide information to the DPKO in New York and to commanders in the field, obstacles have been or will be encountered in orchestrating intelligence support at the UN Secretariat: technical issues, institutional inertia, lack of national participation, inadequate security for information, and concerns over sovereignty and impartiality. Those obstacles handicap current informational support provided by the Situation Center and plans for an indications and warning role in its future. These are not problems unique to the New York Secretariat. UN operations in the field experience similar difficulties.

OPERATION PROVIDE COMFORT

William S. Brei
Captain U.S. Air Force
July 1993

THE GENESIS OF U.S. INVOLVEMENT

Four days before President Bush told a special 6 March 1991 joint session of Congress that "The war is over," another war in Iraq began (Bush *d*: 149). This new war consisted of Shi'a and Kurdish uprisings in response to Bush's repeated calls over the Voice of Free Iraq "for the people of Iraq to force Saddam Hussein to step aside" (Mortimer: 3). The Shi'a engaged Republican Guard forces and fought street-by-street in Basra and other southern Iraqi cities. Along Iraq's northern frontier, the Kurds rose up against 60,000 government troops and seized control of several cities and the northern oil production center of Kirkuk.

The Bush administration reacted to the sudden rebellion with ambivalence. Although Bush clearly wanted to see Saddam Hussein overthrown, he "was banking on the military or Baath leaders to pull [Saddam] out of power," according to an unidentified National Security Council (NSC) official (Robbins and others: 19). Indeed, another NSC official declared that "Our policy is to get rid of Saddam, not his regime" (Mylroie: 15).

President Bush was openly unsure of the manner in which to proceed. He waited until 13 March, two weeks after the start of the rebellion, to warn Saddam against using helicopters to deliver chemical weapons against the rebels. His next signals, moreover, were mixed. On 14 and 24 March, U.S. "heavy-armor units reoccupied positions deep in southern Iraq in what the U.S. press viewed as an effort to increase pressure on Saddam Hussein" (Mylroie: 17). Once in place, these soldiers witnessed Iraqi helicopters firing on Shi'a civilians with phosphorous rockets and napalm bombs, and pleaded for permission to shoot down the helicopters — yet were ordered to hold their fire (Waller: 25). On 20 and 22 March, however, U.S. Air Force F-15C fighters shot down two Iraqi SU-22 fighters. U.S. military officials justified this action by declaring that Iraq's use of fixed-wing military planes posed a threat to coalition forces in the region and violated the provisional cease-fire. The Iraqi jets, however, were intercepted in the vicinity of the Kurdish city of Kirkuk, over 250 miles from the nearest U.S. or coalition forces (Robbins and others: 18).

On 26 March President Bush declared the U.S. would not act to support or protect rebels seeking to overthrow the government of Iraq. Two days after this announcement, the Iraqi Army launched a "major attack" against the Kurds and indiscriminately used armored and helicopter forces to destroy Kurdish cities, block-by-block (Budiansky: 27). The rebellion ended as millions of terrified Kurds fled before the onslaught.

On 26 March, President Bush called a meeting of his top advisors to formulate policy options. With the President as the chair, this group consisted of Vice President Dan Quayle, Secretary of Defense Dick Cheney, Secretary of State Jim Baker, White House Chief Of Staff John Sununu, National Security Advisor Brent Scowcroft, Deputy National Security Advisor Robert Gates, and General Colin Powell, the Chairman of the Joint Chiefs of Staff (Waller: 16). General Norman Schwarzkopf, according to one press report, also contributed to this forum (Budiansky: 28). The participants discussed U.S. options regarding the rebellion in context of the two main objectives of the Operation DESERT STORM cease-fire: the preservation of an Iraq that would not threaten its neighbors, yet could defend itself from Iran; and Iraq's compliance with the United Nations cease-fire resolutions, especially those concerning the destruction of their weapons of mass destruction (Budiansky: 30).

President Bush debated the option of placing a ban on Iraq's use of helicopters, finally making the decision for non-intervention fully anticipating what would happen to the Kurds.

> Ambiguity existed over whether the U.S. would shoot down Iraqi helicopters, as it had shot down fixed-wing aircraft that were flying in violation of the provisional cease-fire. When the administration announced on 26 March that the helicopters would not be touched,

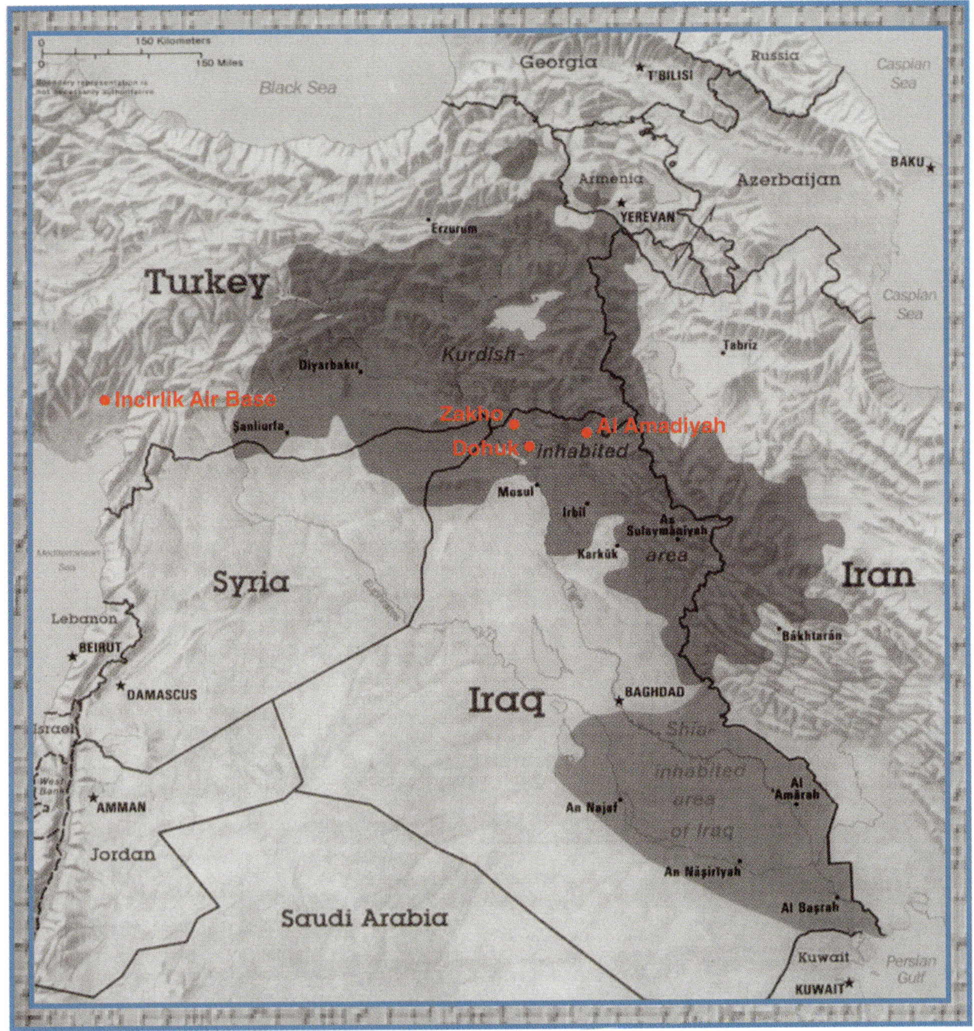

Dissident Areas. *source: modified by author from Central Intelligence Agency base map*

> the Kurds became the first victims of Saddam's retaliation. Turkish President Turgut Ozal called the clarification a "big help to Saddam." And it was. With Iraqi gunships bearing down, firing phosphorous and napalm, the Kurds fled (Mylroie: 11).

As an unidentified administration official said after Bush's announcement to not interfere, "It is a somewhat painful acceptance of a certain reality. You manage it in as low-key a way as possible and hope you get through"

(Mylroie: 17). President Bush probably knew that doing nothing was going to raise a storm of protest. He also knew that the rebels did not have a hope of beating Saddam Hussein's Army. Bush wanted to see a military coup, and he believed, perhaps, that the rebellion was actually strengthening Saddam by forcing his defeated forces to reunite (Mylroie: 17).

As the televised images of dying Kurds drew increasing media focus toward and criticism of his non-intervention policy, President Bush reiterated his conviction that military intervention was beyond the United Nations mandate and that he did "not want to . . . get sucked into the internal civil war" (Bush *e*: 382). When asked why the U.S. permitted Iraq to use attack helicopters against the rebels in violation of the informal cease-fire, Bush replied:

> I don't know whether technically, . . . it's in violation or not. It is in the fixed-wing planes to fly, but if it is a violation, that doesn't necessarily mean that we are going to commit our young men and our young women into further combat [sic] (Bush *e*: 382).

This statement came five days after the 26 March policy meeting, and Bush's response indicates that this issue had not been clarified before, during, or after that forum. Since Bush was in the position to dictate cease-fire terms, his statement indicates the political decision not to intervene, regardless of cease-fire violations.

The U.S. administration was unprepared for the outcome of the Persian Gulf War. It did not comprehend the depth of popular anger inside Iraq at Saddam Hussein and therefore did not anticipate the popular uprisings. In misjudging the rebels, the U.S. possibly lost an opportunity to overthrow Saddam Hussein in mid-March 1991. The administration was surprised by the rebellion it had called for, it did not anticipate the brutal nature of the Iraqi response, and it was unprepared to cope with the subsequent humanitarian crisis. These surprises could be directly traced to an outdated no-contact policy with the Iraqi opposition (U.S. Cong *d*: 13).

Partly due to the lack of intelligence information on the situation, and partly due to misperceptions and biases, President Bush and his senior advisors made significant tactical and strategic mistakes in formulating the policy of non-interference. Bush called for an uprising and then decided it was the wrong uprising. Finally, Bush and his advisors failed to foresee the tremendous impact that televised genocide would have on world and U.S. opinion.

Bowing to heavy television-inspired domestic pressure and a one-day blitzkrieg of personal calls from Prime Minister Major of Great Britain, President Mitterrand of France, President Ozal of Turkey, and Chancellor Kohl of West Germany, Bush acquiesced and committed the U.S. to an air-drop emergency aid operation (Bush *j*: 273). This international pressure may have been a coordinated campaign, as each of the European leaders called President Bush on 4 April with essentially the same message. Only six days after Bush declared the U.S. would not intervene in the Iraqi civil war, he committed U.S. forces to stop the slaughter.

IMMEDIATE RELIEF EFFORTS

Operation PROVIDE COMFORT began on 5 April 1991, after President Bush assigned the Department of Defense the mission of providing humanitarian relief to the Kurdish civilians who had fled into the mountains of northern Iraq and southern Turkey. Within 24 hours of the order to the U.S. European Command, the first military units arrived at Incirlik Air Base, Turkey. Within 36 hours, the U.S. Air Force made its first airdrop of supplies, a total of 27 tons, near several Kurdish refugee camps (Allardice: 1). The primary missions in Northern Iraq consisted of air drop of relief supplies; air cover for security forces; enforcing a no-fly restriction on [all] Iraqi aircraft north of 36 degrees latitude; continuous aerial reconnaissance to include frequent photo reconnaissance; aerial resupply; and troop transport. Most of the air force elements employed in this effort had just returned to their home units from Incirlik, where they had been deployed for the air campaign in northern Iraq that supported DESERT STORM. This experience proved to be the key to immediate operations, as the initial Air Tasking Order, flight routes, and procedures were all derived from the prior operation.[1] The effort quickly became a combined operation, as military forces from the U.S., Britain, France and Turkey set about delivering emergency aid (Bush *j*: 273).

A Change in Plans

Although the air drop program successfully delivered tons of emergency supplies, it quickly became viewed as a "drop-in-the-bucket" in comparison to what was needed. Secretary of State James Baker needed only seven

[1] The author was deployed to the Combined Task Force for PROVIDE COMFORT, where he was Intelligence-Imagery Officer.

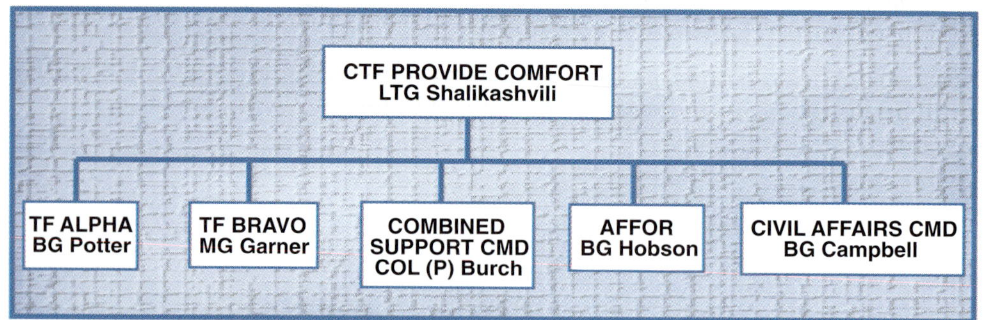

CTF PROVIDE COMFORT. *source: author*

minutes in a Kurdish refugee camp during a 7-9 April 1991 fact-finding visit to Turkey to see that full-scale intervention was necessary (Schorr: 22). Declaring that he had "seen examples of cruelty and human anguish that really do defy description," Baker joined Turkish Foreign Minister Alptemocin in a joint U.S.-Turkish declaration that international support was urgently needed. Baker declared:

> Our relief efforts, including air drops of supplies, have begun, but they alone are not going to be enough. We cannot do this alone. We cannot do this alone with the Turkish Government. Together, we simply cannot cope with this mounting human tragedy (J. Baker: 272).

President Bush immediately directed the U.S. military to expand its mission to sustain the entire refugee population for 30 days and to establish forward ground bases and transit centers for increased efficiency of aid distribution. The most significant change in the original plan, however, came on 16 April, when Bush directed the construction of several resettlement communities in northern Iraq, inside of a security zone, in which refugees and displaced Kurds would be moved, administered, and protected from Iraqi attack by U.S., British, and French ground forces (Bush *j*: 273). The initial plans called for the construction of 12 camps, each with a 20,000-person capacity. But a psychological operation designed to convince many Kurds that it was safe to return to their own homes inside the security zone was successful, and the number of shelters required dropped to only four camps.

As the multinational forces attended to the Kurds' survival needs and prepared to transport them to the security zone resettlement camps in Zakho, it became apparent that the security zone needed to be enlarged to include Al Amadiyah. On 5 May, the security zone was again extended eastward from Al Amadiyah to include the city of Suri. On 11 May, the multinational forces assigned to Joint Task Force Alpha began transporting refugees to Zakho, and on 13 May, the United Nations agreed to accept control and responsibility for the first resettlement camp in Zakho (Author's observations).

As the resettlement operation progressed, it again became apparent that a great number of refugees could be directly resettled in their homes if the security zone were increased to include the provincial capital city of Dohuk, the original home of about 250,000 refugees. On this occasion, the constantly troublesome Iraqi Army refused to withdraw its occupation force, raising the expectation of a major armed conflict between the humanitarian forces and the Iraqi Army. Although the CTF reached an agreement with the Iraqis for the inclusion of Dohuk on 22 May, the coalition forces who entered Dohuk on 25 May were greatly relieved to observe the Iraqi forces withdrawing from their newly prepared fortifications (Author's observations).

On 6 June, the last mountain refugee camp was emptied and the displaced population was successfully transported to the Security Zone. The next day, the CTF transferred all relief operations to the United Nations High Commissioner for Refugees, and on 8 June, the phased redeployment of humanitarian forces began. Operation PROVIDE COMFORT II began on 15 July, as a force of about 5,000 personnel from 6 coalition countries remained at Incirlik Air Base to deter Iraqi aggression against the resettled Kurds. Aerial reconnaissance and armed flights continued over northern Iraq during this phase.

Intelligence Support for Emergency Airdrop Operations

Planning for the humanitarian intervention operation was done entirely "on the fly," as there had been no anticipation that the U.S. would become involved in any relief efforts (Fishel: viii). The main intelligence problem for the initial mission was determining locations, numbers, and conditions of the refugees. Essentially an air mission, the intelligence staff was drawn from the Headquarters U.S. Air Forces Europe Directorate for Intelligence. This intelligence staff deployed from Ramstein Air Base on 6 April with an initial list of refugee camps, provided by British intelligence and U.S. imaging satellites, that guided the U.S. Air Force's first airdrops

(Branch). Satellite and U-2R imagery, both of which were produced in Germany, were provided in hardcopy form to aircrews with appropriate drop zones annotated.

Besides the standard intelligence requirements for an air-drop mission, this operation required intelligence on the culture, customs, politics, lifestyle habits, and history of the Kurds. The condition and needs of the refugees could not be ascertained, however, until U.S. Special Forces personnel entered the camps and provided direct operational intelligence reporting (Branch). This information was not only extremely important for the forces in direct contact with the refugees and the planners who shaped decisions, but also to the psychological operations elements after the mission expanded.

A New Ballgame

On 16 April, President Bush's order to resettle the Kurdish refugees greatly expanded the ground mission and brought a corresponding change in emphasis in intelligence tasking. Already enroute to the NATO base at Incirlik, Turkey, to "sort out the issue with respect to the Army role in the refugee crisis," General Shalikashvili arrived at virtually the same time that President Bush announced that the U.S. with Britain and France would create a security zone in northern Iraq and a multinational military force would protect the refugees and stay until the UN was operational in the area (Fishel: 52). As the new commander of the now-Combined Task Force PROVIDE COMFORT, Shalikashvili directed the establishment of ground bases and the deployment of over 10,000 multinational ground forces into northern Iraq. Although most of the forces that entered Iraq maintained unit and national integrity, the headquarters staffs were fully integrated. Indeed, the chain of command within the intelligence staff was populated with field grade British Army intelligence officers who directly supervised company grade U.S. officers.

Central to the operation were two subordinate forward-deployed task forces, Alpha and Bravo. JTF Alpha had the mission of finding, caring for, and persuading the refugees to come down from the mountains. Located in Silopi, in the Turkish mountains near the Iraqi border, this task force consisted primarily of U.S. Special Forces personnel. JTF Bravo had the mission of establishing and securing temporary camps as close to the major cities that were home to the refugees as possible. Located in the city of Zakho, in northern Iraq, this task force consisted of a wide range of U.S.

and allied military specialists. Rounding out the operational customers of the CTF PROVIDE COMFORT Intelligence Staff, the CTF included an air forces element which included all helicopters, except for Marine aircraft. This element was designated AFFOR and was collocated at Incirlik with the CTF.

An unusual element of the operation was the close working relationship between the military and the civilian aid organizations. Civilian involvement had profound ramifications for intelligence support. Although all of the coalition nations were intelligence-sharing allies, the issue of sharing classified intelligence information was a problem when the personnel from non-governmental agencies increased participation. As civilian participation grew, the use of satellite imagery dwindled drastically. The phrase, "if I can't show it, then I can't use it, so don't send it" became the guideline for intelligence production in support of operational-level requirements. The CTF Intelligence Staff did have, however, full authority to show — but not release — any imagery they felt necessary for mission accomplishment (Branch).

Support to Operating Forces

The initial problem that General Shalikashvili faced was to stop the 1,000-deaths per day casualty rate and stabilize the refugees' situation from one of panic and chaos. The major problems encountered in the mountain camps were:

> polluted water supplies, poor sanitation, diarrhoeal disease, poor rubbish disposal, inadequate tents with large numbers of refugees still living in crowded conditions in animal stables, and the scarcity of drugs and supplies (H. Palmer: 303).

While field-validated operational reports satisfied the requirement for refugee condition and needs assessments, imagery interpreters of satellite and U-2R aerial reconnaissance film ensured that all refugee sites had been located. Signals intelligence played virtually no role in the effort to locate either the Kurds or the Iraqis.

A serious intelligence shortfall initially hindered the ground transportation of supplies and refugees: the shortage of maps. While the air operations could rely on the residual maps from the air campaign at the end of DESERT STORM, there had been no requirement for maps that supported ground movement. As drivers tended to get lost without maps, the CTF Intelligence Staff requested large-scale maps from the Defense Mapping Agency, while the Maps Officer and terrain analysts set about producing limited quantities of maps on a by-request basis. The 497th Reconnaissance Technical Group, through its forward-deployed liaison element, initiated and mass-produced a new and highly popular product: gridded photo-lithographic maps of each city from U-2R imagery.

The security of the Kurds and humanitarian relief workers was probably the highest intelligence priority. This requirement called for the use of dedicated, quick-response, and fast-production tactical reconnaissance. Unfortunately, the tactical photographic processing and interpretation facility that remained at Incirlik Air Base could not be used because there simply was not enough ramp space for reconnaissance planes along with the tremendous number of multinational cargo, fighter, and ground attack planes needed for the operation. Instead, the U.S. Navy provided F-14 Tactical Aerial Reconnaissance Pod System support from a carrier in the eastern Mediterranean Sea.

Finally, the U-2R aerial reconnaissance program supported every aspect of the operation, with the exception of warning intelligence. The sensor system on the U-2R had many advantages over other collection systems: a high-resolution image, broad-area coverage, and releasability to multinational forces. Flown every other day, each mission provided between 8,000 and 10,500 feet of imagery that covered every point of interest in the area of operations.

The time required for flying, processing, and interpreting the film, unfortunately, exceeded the time allowed for tactical warning. Designed as a strategic collection platform, the U-2R program emphasizes broad-area coverage and high resolution over timeliness. Indeed, without a collection system that provides constant surveillance, tactical warning was simply not available to Operation PROVIDE COMFORT. As the most consistent means of intelligence collection under the Intelligence Staff's control, however, the U-2R became the intelligence collection workhorse for Operation PROVIDE COMFORT.

Essentially, the U-2R would fly and image at least eight hours before returning to base; after it recovered, the film was couriered to Ramstein Air Base, Germany, on a dedicated courier aircraft. Upon arrival, personnel from the 497th Reconnaissance Technical Group couriered the film to the production facility at Wiesbaden Air Base, consuming a minimum of another two hours when the autobahns were clear. Once the film reached the photo-processing lab, the processing consumed another eight to nine hours before all of the production film could be delivered to the interpreters at Schierstein Compound. From that point, initial interpretation reports could be transmitted electronically at any time, and select hardcopy images could be produced for special courier, that night, to Incirlik.

In all, electronic reporting normally reached the consumers about 24 hours after the time of imaging. Hardcopy prints, however, were less predictable. Depending on the weather and a consumer's specific request, a hardcopy image taken from a previous mission's film could be produced and arrive at Incirlik within 10 hours, provided the imagery requested could be satisfied with archival imagery, there was no production backlog, and the ground courier could get the material to the special air courier at Ramstein Air Base before its flight time. Otherwise, select imagery that corresponded to the initial readout of the current mission would be received no earlier than 30 hours after the mission flew over the target.

The dedicated air courier from Ramstein Air Base to Incirlik Air Base provided the most timely delivery of imagery and other intelligence materials that was possible. This procedure was established early into the operation and was maintained well after PROVIDE COMFORT II began.

INTELLIGENCE SUPPORT IN CAMBODIA

William E. Whitney
Captain, U.S. Army
August 1995

The UN effort in seeking a resolution to Cambodia's long-standing political conflict represented an unparalleled international diplomatic effort. The UN Transitional Authority in Cambodia (UNTAC) was begun at a time when the UN was mired in the controversy of both the Bosnia and Somalia missions. The mission was unique in its broad mandate, covering a range of operations to alleviate Cambodia's troubles. Massive in size, comprehensive in scope and precise in its mandate, UNTAC set a new standard for peacekeeping operations undertaken by the international community (UN *h*: 3). This paper will examine the history of the Cambodia conflict, the UN's role in it, and each of UNTAC's seven components that required information collection, synthesis of that information, and subsequent integration of that information into UNTAC's mission processes. The information considered here is called "intelligence" anywhere but in the United Nations environment.

HISTORY

Since Cambodia's emergence from French colonialism in the 1950s, the country had suffered not only the effects of the Vietnam War of the 1960s and 1970s, but also the devastating effects of civil conflict and the destructive totalitarian regime of the Khmer Rouge under the leadership of Pol Pot. The Khmer Rouge controlled Cambodia from 1975 to 1979, a period in which approximately 1 million Cambodians perished. Within days of assuming power, the Khmer Rouge evacuated all cities, forcing virtually the entire Cambodian population into the countryside to live and work on a communal basis. Living conditions under the Khmer Rouge were extremely harsh, with collective manual labor for up to 18 hours a day, often with only meager rations of food (Curtis: 2). By 1977, communal cooking and eating were introduced throughout much of the country, and scrounging for food or hoarding was punishable by death.

Vietnamese troops invaded Cambodia in late 1978 to stem repeated and bloody border violations by the forces of Democratic Kampuchea (Khmer Rouge). The Khmer Rouge offered little resistance, and were pushed to the border of Thailand where they were able to regain some of their military strength. The Vietnamese communists installed a new government known as the Phnom Penh regime, under the leadership of Hun Sen, and changed the name of the country to the People's Republic of Kampuchea under the Party of Democratic Kampuchea (PDK) (Heininger: 24).

Wall poster of last victims of the Khmer Rouge at Tuol Sleng prison, Cambodia, 1979. *photo courtesy of NIMA ISLWL, Ground Photo Team*

In 1982, the Khmer Rouge entered into alliance with Cambodia's non-communist resistance forces, establishing the Coalition Government of Democratic Kampuchea (CGDK) under the leadership of Prince Norodom Sihanouk. Prince Sihanouk's political party was known as the United National Front for an Independent, Neutral, Peaceful and Cooperative

Cambodia (FUNCINPEC). The CGDK was a government-in-exile that retained international recognition throughout the 1980s, including membership in the UN (Curtis: 2). This recognition in the UN was seen as an effort to keep the UN seat from falling into Soviet hands via the Vietnamese client regime in Phnom Penh. Furthermore, the CGDK received material support and political backing from the U.S. and the Association for Southeast Asian Nations countries.

The last faction, bringing the total to three, in the struggle against the Phnom Penh regime, was the smaller non-communist party led by former prime minister Son Sann. This party was known as the Khmer People's National Liberation Front (KPNLF) and it formed a loose alliance with Prince Sihanouk to establish the CGDK.

During the 1980s the Cambodian conflict was seen by many as a struggle between China and Vietnam for hegemony over Indochina (Heininger: 10). China backed the Khmer Rouge and Vietnam backed the Phnom Penh regime. The U.S. backed the non-communist resistance forces of Prince Sihanouk and Son Sann, with a determination to oppose Soviet influence in Indochina by stemming Vietnamese aggression. According to reports from a UN fact-finding team sent to Cambodia in 1991, the four factions consisted of more than 200,000 regular soldiers deployed in some 650 locations. Additionally, militias totaling more than 250,000 personnel operated throughout the countryside with over 300,000 weapons of all types and some 80 million rounds of ammunition (UN *h*: 13).

UN INVOLVEMENT

Cambodia was in a state of deep internal conflict and relative isolation from the rest of the world. However, the UN did make attempts to intervene in the Cambodian conflict many years before the Paris Peace Agreements were signed on 23 October 1991. The Security Council first considered the issue in 1979, following Vietnam's December 1978 attack, but lack of unanimity among its five permanent members prevented it from taking any action (UN h: 5).

Waning support from both the USSR and China improved the political climate that paved the way for the UN-brokered peace agreement in Cambodia. China's Deng Xiaoping wanted to clean the slate with Vietnam and remove any lingering animosity from the international community toward China. Specifically, he wanted to rectify the loss of face incurred by his humiliating defeat when China invaded Vietnam early in 1979 to "teach Vietnam a lesson" for its invasion of Cambodia (Heininger: 20). Using the Khmer Rouge as a weapon against Vietnam in Cambodia had not worked, nor was there any prospect for success. China was seeking international acceptance, in the wake of the June 1989 Tiananmen Square massacre, and a settlement in Cambodia could go a long way toward restoring China's image.

In contrast, Vietnamese support for its client regime remained bogged down, largely because Chinese military assistance enabled the Khmer Rouge to keep pressure on the Phnom Penh regime. The Soviet Union's support for Vietnam was predicated on its own competition with China. Support to Vietnam was expensive—both monetarily and politically—and Mikhail Gorbachev's disenchantment with the costs permitted movement toward peace in Cambodia. Gorbachev considered the estimated $3 billion annually to Vietnam as a drain on precious Soviet resources. The battlefield situation in Cambodia was at a stalemate and Vietnam's economy was deteriorating (Heininger: 11).

Finally, in 1989 the path was cleared for a diplomatic settlement in Cambodia. An initiative by the five permanent members of the Security Council led to the brokered Paris Conference on Cambodia, which led to UNTAC's authorization. The negotiations began in July 1989 and culminated with the signing of the Paris Peace Agreement on 23 October 1991, where the four factions agreed to establish the Supreme National Council which would assume the sovereign powers of Cambodia through the transition period. To ensure implementation of the accords, the SNC would delegate "all necessary powers" to the UN for the transitional period, lasting from signing the agreements through the creation of a new government following the elections. The final Paris Agreement consisted of three instruments: the *Agreement on a Comprehensive Political Settlement of the Cambodian Conflict; the Agreement Concerning the Sovereignty, Independence, Territorial Integrity and Inviolability, Neutrality and National Unity of Cambodia; and the Declaration on the Rehabilitation and Reconstruction of Cambodia* (UN *h*: 8-9). On 31 October 1991, in Resolution 718, the Security Council expressed its full support for the Paris Peace Plan, called on all Cambodian factions to comply with the cease-fire, and called on the SNC and all Cambodians to cooperate fully with the UN.

The agreements authorized the Security Council to establish UNTAC. Under the agreements UNTAC's mandate (mission) was to accomplish the following:

> Organize and conduct free and fair elections; coordinate the repatriation of Cambodian refugees and displaced persons; coordinate a major program of economic and financial support for rehabilitation and reconstruction; supervise or control the existing administrative structures in Cambodia; supervise, monitor, and verify the withdrawal of foreign forces, the cease-fire, the cessation of outside military assistance to all Cambodian factions and the demobilization of at least 70 percent of the military forces of each faction; coordinate, with the International Committee of the Red Cross, the release of all prisoners of war and civilian internees; and foster an environment of peace and stability in which all Cambodians could enjoy the rights and freedoms embodied in the Universal Declaration of Human Rights and other relevant international human rights instruments (UN *h*: 9).

The heart of UNTAC's mandate was to take the structure laid out in the Paris Accords and give Cambodia a chance to establish a government that would be strong enough to prevent further civil war. Each mandated task was designed in some way to facilitate that outcome: 1) get the refugees home and reintegrate them into Cambodian society, so their camps would cease to be a staging area for armed insurgents; 2) disarm the factions; 3) keep the troops that were not demobilized in cantonment areas so they could not fight; 4) teach Cambodians not to abuse human rights; 5) develop a civilian police force to help dampen the level of violence; 6) build the structures of a civil society; and 7) get the international community to undertake a massive effort to rebuild Cambodia through economic assistance, liberalization, and investment in an effort to thwart a return to power by the Khmer Rouge.

UNITED NATIONS ADVANCE MISSION IN CAMBODIA (UNAMIC)

Prior to the signing of the Paris Agreements that authorized the creation of UNTAC, several fact-finding missions were sent to Cambodia to survey the situation on the ground and make an assessment of what was needed to facilitate the implementation of an agreement. The UN fact-finding missions were sent to Cambodia, beginning in 1989 and continuing through the summer of 1990, to study the communications and transportation infrastructure, water supply, sanitation, housing, modalities for repatriation and reintegration of refugees and displaced persons, and the country's existing administrative structures (UN *h*: 7).

Following the fact-finding missions and the signing of the Paris Agreements, UNAMIC was established to bridge the gap between the signing of the peace agreement and the time it would take for UNTAC to fully deploy. UNAMIC, authorized by Security Council Resolution 717 (16 October 1991) became operational on 9 November 1991 and consisted of 268 personnel from 23 countries. UNAMIC was organized into a Civil/Military staff, a Military mine awareness unit, and both a logistics and a support unit (Curtis: 7).

The primary goal of UNAMIC was to assist in maintaining the cease-fire, but it was also expected to collect information regarding the number of personnel and equipment in the military elements of the Cambodian factions, to launch a military mine awareness program, and to obtain and provide other information that would help UNTAC (Farris: 42).

Amid an increasing awareness that a mine clearance program was becoming a growing priority, the UN Security Council passed Resolution 728 (8 January 1992), expanding UNAMIC by 1,100 personnel. This increase incorporated a 700-person field engineering battalion that would work with the Office of the United Nations High Commissioner for Refugees (UNHCR) to clear mines from repatriation routes, reception centers, and resettlement areas (UN *h*: 11). Additionally, the mine clearance team would resume its mine clearance training for the Cambodians with hopes they would continue the program once UNTAC departed in late 1993.

UNITED NATIONS TRANSITIONAL AUTHORITY IN CAMBODIA (UNTAC)

On 19 February 1992, the Secretary-General submitted to the Security Council a report detailing the proposed implementation plan for UNTAC. The Security Council endorsed the report, and by its Resolution 745 (28 February 1992) established UNTAC for a period not to exceed 18 months. Upon becoming operational on 15 March 1992, UNTAC absorbed UNAMIC (Curtis: 11).

One of Boutros Boutros-Ghali's first tasks as the new Secretary-General was to name Yasushi Akashi to head UNTAC. Akashi was also named the Secretary-General's special representative for Cambodia. The choice of Akashi to head UNTAC was made in recognition of Japan's growing importance in the region and in the UN. Furthermore, his selection was also a less-than-discreet nudge for Japan to accept world responsibilities commensurate with its economic superpower status (Heininger: 35).

With the selection of Akashi, the international community wished to increase Japan's involvement in UN peacekeeping. Japan's involvement in UNTAC was to go further than it had in the Persian Gulf War, to which it contributed $13 billion but no troops. In its first deployment since World War II, Japan sent eight military observers and a 600-member unit to participate in UNTAC. Although this unit, an engineer battalion, was assigned to rebuild two major highways during a six-month tour and normally remained unarmed, its deployment sparked protests in the Philippines against renewed Japanese militarism. Japan also contributed 75 civilian police to UNTAC (Heininger: 36).

UNTAC Organization

The UNTAC mission was unique and diverse. In the broadest sense the UN mission was to create conditions that would foster the growth of a democratic nation and society in Cambodia. Because peacekeeping in Cambodia represented a new and greatly expanded mission for the UN, UNTAC's organization was also unique (Farris: 42). UNTAC was planned to have nearly 16,000 military, 5,800 international and local civilian staff, 3,600 civil police, and 62,000 Cambodians to help with the elections (Heininger: 41). It was composed of seven distinct operational elements — six civilian components and a military component. Each of these activities required the collection of information and the processing or analysis of that information, before some mission-related action could take place. The contributions of each component toward these activities are discussed below.

Electoral Component

This component was charged with carrying out UNTAC's principal task, holding national elections. The Electoral Component mounted a large-scale education program to inform the general public about the purposes and importance of the election, particularly the integrity of the ballot. Additionally, this necessitated a massive voter registration effort which had to reach into the most remote parts of the country to register the voters, the political parties and candidates, and to actually conduct the election. Eventually, 4.76 million Cambodians were registered, about 96 percent of the eligible population (Farris: 43).

UN Troop Deployments, March 1993.

source: Central Intelligence Agency

The Electoral Law, which established the rules and procedures for the election, was adopted by the SNC on 5 August 1992 and promulgated the following week. The large number of registered voters was, in part, due to the strong desire of the Cambodian people for a chance to express their opinions about the future of Cambodia. However, this also illustrates the diligence put forth by UNTAC to fully understand the situation and develop appropriate procedures for promoting the election process. Since the repatriation effort was not complete, the registration period was extended from its original closing date of 31 December 1992 to 31 January 1993 to allow the registration of the maximum number of voters.

Uncertainty over the PDK's (Khmer Rouge) intentions made it unclear whether voter education, training, and registration would be able to proceed in zones under PDK control. In close cooperation with the UNTAC civilian and military components, UNTAC electoral staff were able to move into some zones where the PDK was operating or present. They experienced high levels of interest on the part of locals and had moderate success in registering some of them as voters. However, UNTAC was denied access to most PDK-controlled areas, which were generally considered to be in Northwest Cambodia and included roughly 5 percent of Cambodia's total population (UN: *h* 29).

Information played a key role in preparing the Cambodians for the elections and informing them about UNTAC, the Paris Agreements, and the public's rights and responsibilities. However, UNTAC was faced with two obstacles. The first was skepticism from the population about UNTAC's intentions toward free and fair elections, resulting from decades of conflict and isolation from the rest of the world. These doubts were further exacerbated by several attempts at misleading propaganda produced by the different factions. The second was the physical obstacle of how to disseminate information to the population. The impact of written materials was lost with low literacy rates throughout the country, and the country's radio and television facilities were old, damaged, and had limited range (Curtis: 4).

UNTAC's solution was to create its own radio station and integrate the different components of UNTAC to mount a massive public education campaign. Radio UNTAC began broadcasting on 9 November 1992, from a transmitter located in Phnom Penh (UN *h*: 30). Its programs focused primarily on the electoral process but also included information about mine awareness and human rights. On 28 January 1993, the SNC decided that the election would take place at fixed polling stations and occur from 23 to 25 May 1993. This followed a campaign period from 7 April through 19 May 1993 (UN *h*: 31).

Human Rights Component

This component was given overall responsibility during the transitional period for fostering an environment in which respect for human rights was to be ensured. Such responsibility included ratification by the SNC of relevant human rights instruments, the development and implementation of a human rights education training program, and the oversight and investigation of complaints about human rights abuses and, where appropriate, taking corrective action (Curtis: 8).

This component had a relatively small staff to conduct educational programs and investigate human rights abuses. Initially, no provisions were made to position human rights officials in the provinces. Even though the staff was beefed up to 33, the unit remained understaffed for the duration of UNTAC's mandate. Additionally, there was an inherent contradiction in mission that separated the Human Rights and Civil Administration Components. For example, there was little communication between the human rights officers and the civil administrators because, as one senior human rights monitor observed, "the civil administrator is trying to work with the existing government while the human rights officer 'tries to tear it down'" (Heininger: 93).

Despite coordination problems within UNTAC, it did make some notable contributions. One was that the four factions signed all the major international human rights instruments. Another was reform in the primitive Cambodian prison system, which subsequently received special attention from the Human Rights Component. UNTAC was able to gain unrestricted access to all prisons throughout Cambodia and found some prisoners had been detained by Phnom Penh authorities for up to 10 years without trial, sometimes for political allegiance rather than criminal activity. By the end of August 1993, the Human Rights Component secured the release of 258 prisoners who had been detained without trial (Heininger: 94). Despite the fact that this component had no enforcement authority, it was aggressive in investigating complaints. From March to December 1992, it investigated 339 cases of human rights abuses, primarily harassment, land disputes and unlawful imprisonment. By November 1992, as fighting increased between the Khmer Rouge and the Phnom Penh regime, the human rights abuses seemed to become more violent, with political overtones. From March to May 1993, the Human Rights Component was able to confirm 200 deaths, 338 injuries and 114 abductions. Through investigation, UNTAC was able to attribute the vast majority of the killings, 131, to the Khmer Rouge and only 15 to the Phnom Penh regime (Heininger: 95).

Red Cross hut along Thai/Cambodia border, 1992. *photo courtesy of NIMA ISLWL, Ground Photo Team*

Civil Administration Component

The functions of this component are a striking departure from previous peacekeeping operations. Civil Administration is one of the fundamental components and one reason why UNTAC was nontraditional. UNTAC, through the Civil Administration Component, insisted on and was granted control over five essential areas of each faction's administrative structures: national defense, foreign affairs, finance, public security, and information. The purpose was to ensure a neutral political environment conducive to free and fair elections by exercising direct supervision or control over the administrative bodies, agencies and offices which could directly influence the outcome of the elections. This was a striking departure from previous peacekeeping operations.

What the UN wanted was to level the playing field prior to the elections. The UN was careful to define UNTAC's mandate in terms of overseeing "existing administrative functions" of all four factions (Heininger: 83). However, it was implied that the administrative agencies of the Phnom Penh regime were the primary target, partly because the Khmer Rouge did not allow the UN into its area and neither non-communist faction had any structures of significance.

This component was also limited in the number of personnel it could field to oversee administrative functions. UNTAC allotted roughly 200 personnel to monitor and control activities in Phnom Penh and the provinces — 95 were allocated to the capital and 123 to the provinces. This minimal presence in the provinces amounted to only five international staff and seven local staff per province (Heininger: 86).

The general strategy of the Civil Administrators was to first evaluate the current administrative mechanisms in place and then to insist on examining the decisions made by the various factions before and after the fact. As the component's staff became more proficient, officials of the Phnom Penh regime resorted to back channels and informal networks for communicating with each other (Heininger: 86). The following example illustrates the tenacity of the Phnom Penh regime and the diligence needed by the Civil Administrators to stay one step ahead of the factions:

> Civil Administration director Gerard Pourcell reported that while civil administrators examined all the instructions and guidance issued by the ministries, often decisions were transmitted informally without UNTAC's knowledge. Sometimes they were deliberately hidden. The Public Security Ministry, over which UNTAC was supposed to have control, transferred a particularly notorious unit, used to harass political opponents, from one ministry to another in order to elude UNTAC. It ended up in the Cultural Ministry, over which UNTAC had no authority (Heininger: 86).

The tools UNTAC had available to control the existing administrative structures included the "codes of conduct and guidelines for management, especially regarding ethical conduct, measures to counter corruption, and measures to ensure non-discrimination" (Heininger: 87). UNTAC also had the right to install its own personnel in the administrative structures and was supposed to have unlimited access to all administrative operations and information. This unlimited access was designed to give UNTAC political leverage—especially over the Phnom Penh regime, though its effectiveness was diminished through actions such as those in the example mentioned.

UNTAC had two additional tools at its disposal to keep the factions in line. It could issue binding directives on an ad hoc basis or it could dismiss or reassign personnel from structures it was monitoring (UNGA A/46/608). However, Yasushi Akashi insisted on cooperation and consensus among the factions, limiting the use of binding directives and rarely reassigning or removing personnel. This was based on an assessment that actions perceived as too harsh, particularly on those members of the regime who were trying to undermine the neutrality of the peace process, could cause the Phnom Penh regime to refuse to cooperate with UNTAC at all (Heininger: 87).

The greatest tool granted the Civil Administrators was the responsibility for investigating complaints about authorities misusing their powers. On 26 June 1992, UNTAC issued a public statement instructing the Cambodian people of their right to complain to the director of UNTAC's Civil Administration office in their province, to UNTAC police at the provincial level, or to UNTAC police or electoral officials at the district level (Heininger: 87). While UNTAC was not able to remedy all complaints, the open-door policy had the unintended benefit of providing an unlimited flow of information about the factions' doings. Additionally, it helped the components work more closely by sharing information and also allowed UNTAC to keep a finger on the pulse of Cambodian activities.

Refugee Repatriation Component

"The task of rebuilding the Cambodian nation will require the harnessing of all its human and natural resources. To this end, the return to the place of their choice of Cambodians from their temporary refuge and elsewhere outside their country of origin will make a major contribution" (UNGA A/46/608). This example is indicative of UNTAC's assessment that successful reintegration of refugees was fundamental to UNTAC's success. UNTAC was to repatriate some 350,000 to 370,000 refugees from the Thai border areas, 170,000 "internal refugees" displaced within Cambodia, and 150,000 demobilized soldiers from the four factions (Heininger: 35). Of these numbers, UNTAC declared that 362,209 refugees were repatriated by the end of UNTAC's mandate. This success can be attributed to several reasons.

The first was the joint participation of the Repatriation Component and the UNHCR in the repatriation process. Since the UNHCR had a long-standing relationship with the Cambodian people, it had a procedural and operational head start over the other UNTAC components in Cambodia. The UNHCR not only had the support of all four factions, it also had a good relationship with both the refugees and the Thai government, which provided refugee camps along the Thai border. Additionally, the UNHCR had a close relationship with the following agencies, that were familiar with Cambodia's refugee problem: the United Nations Development Program, the United Nations Children's Fund, the World Food Program, the World Health Organization, the United Nations Educational, Scientific and Cultural Organization, and the International Labor Organization (UN *h*: 14).

Second, the UNHCR operated with a degree of institutional ambiguity that worked in its favor. UNHCR could legitimately claim independence from UNTAC when it chose to do so (Heininger: 49). This separate status helped the refugee effort to be perceived as more neutral than other UNTAC activities. Although the factions did not cooperate fully in carrying out UNTAC's other tasks, each faction cooperated fully on the return of refugees to Cambodia (Heininger: 39).

Finally, more than half the refugee population registered with the UNHCR to return to the Northwestern provinces of Cambodia—even though most did not originate from that area, the region was littered with mines, and short of agricultural land. The assessment was that refugees desired a place that would allow them to quickly flee across the Thai border if fighting resumed (UN *h*: 19). However, these fears were quickly put to rest since all four factions saw it in their interest to encourage the refugees to return to Cambodia. This was because most refugees were affiliated with a specific faction and thus were seen as a basis of support that could be transferred across the border in preparation for the elections.

Rehabilitation and Reconstruction Component

This component was governed by the Declaration of Reconstruction and Rehabilitation, one of the three main instruments accepted at the Paris Conference on 23 October 1991. The purpose of this component was simply to lay the groundwork for the international community to bring Cambodia out of economic isolation (Heininger: 54). The Declaration determined that international efforts should focus on urgent humanitarian needs (food, housing, and health) and the nation's basic infrastructure needs to include water and power projects, technical work in the field of agriculture, and public administration reform.

The focus of this component was to secure donations from the international community and ensure the activities were carried out following the departure of UNTAC. Donations from the international community totalled more than $880 million which exceeded the Secretary-General's initial request of only $595 million (Heininger: 55-56).

Unlike other components of UNTAC that were designed to carry out mandates, the Rehabilitation Component had no implementation capability. It would only coordinate activities undertaken by NGOs, or existing international and Cambodian institutions (Heininger: 55). The integration of this component into UNTAC is unlike any other peacekeeping activities to date. It was unique to UNTAC's nontraditional functions and indicative of UNTAC's efforts to abide by and implement an existing agreement made by the belligerent parties.

Civil Police Component

The Civil Police Component mandated in the Paris Agreement was modeled on the successful UN operation in Namibia. While the use of civilian police in Namibia broke new ground for UN peacekeeping, in Cambodia, the civilian police were probably the least successful component (Heininger: 79). The Civil Police, numbering 3,600, was the second largest component, but was particularly hampered by seriously undertrained and unqualified staff. Unarmed and without arrest powers, they were nonetheless expected to supervise and control the police of each faction to ensure maintenance of law and order, and the protection of human rights (Farris: 42).

The Civil Police mission devolved into monitoring of the police from the Phnom Penh regime (SOC). This is partly because only the SOC had anything approximating a police force. Initial assessments by UNTAC estimated the SOC police force roughly numbered 47,000 personnel, but they were found to be poorly equipped, had few cars, were largely untrained, and had no standard procedures to follow. The Khmer Rouge police reportedly numbered 9,000 but were indistinguishable from the

Khmer Rouge military forces. The non-Communists had only token forces: 150 FUNCINPEC police under Prince Sihanouk and 400 KPNLF police under Son Sann (UNSec S/23613).

UNTAC civilian police building, Phnom Penh, Cambodia, 1993.

photo courtesy of NIMA ISLWL, Ground Photo Team

In response to the large numbers of unqualified police sent to UNTAC, Boutros Boutros-Ghali issued a memo on 30 November 1992 entitled "Requirements For and Testing of UN Civilian Police Monitors" in an attempt to alleviate the problem (Heininger: 163). The UN had found that a significant number did not possess the minimum requirements for the force: Many spoke neither English nor French (UNTAC's official languages), nor possessed a driver's license, nor had the required six years of police experience, and some had no experience at all (Heininger: 80).

The Civil Police Component eventually was granted arrest powers that brought it very close to crossing the threshold from peacekeeping to peace enforcement. These new arrest powers were deemed necessary following a steep rise in attacks with hand-grenades and automatic weapons against offices of political parties. UNTAC civil police, with the cooperation of the

Military Component, first launched a special operation to curb these attacks by establishing 24-hour protection for 60 political offices considered most at risk. Following the implementation of this protection, no attacks or disruptions occurred, through March 1993, at any political office afforded protection. However, the number of attacks soon began to rise, focused on newly opened political offices in the provinces (UN *h*: 295).

Military Component

The Military Component, led by Australia's Lieutenant General John Sanderson, was the largest of UNTAC's components. It was responsible for the following tasks:

a. Verifying the withdrawal of foreign forces from Cambodia.
b. Supervising the cease-fire and related measures, including disarmament, cantonment and demobilization.
c. Instituting a weapons control program.
d. Assisting in mine-clearing and developing mine awareness.
e. Investigating complaints by factions
f. Providing assistance in the repatriation of Cambodian refugees and internally displaced persons (Farris: 43).

These tasks assigned to the Military Component were considered key not only to ensure a neutral political environment but also to UNTAC's overall success. Without disarmament, confiscation of weapons, and cantonment of the factions' forces, fighting was expected to continue, putting all plans for the country's recovery in danger.

UNTAC operated within the constraints of the consent of the parties, due largely to the efforts of LTG Sanderson and Yasushi Akashi, who resisted the pleas of the three factions who wanted the right to use force against the Khmer Rouge. For example, UNTAC was, as one UN official stated, "diplomatically aggressive, militarily passive" (Heininger: 67). Akashi sought every opportunity to negotiate a solution to UNTAC's impasse with the Khmer Rouge—and was criticized by the factions who wanted to compel the Khmer Rouge to disarm. For instance, Mr. Hun Sen, a Supreme National Council representative, called upon the Secretary-General to invoke Article 29 of the Paris Agreements, and, if necessary, to approve coercive measures to stem widespread violations and intransigence by the Khmer Rouge.

The Military Component was able to collect and use information because of the component's military organization. Not only did the Military Component work closely with and share information with the other components, it possessed a formal military intelligence structure to gather and verify the activities of each faction with regard to the provisions set forth in the Comprehensive Settlement.

The military headquarters was located in Phnom Penh and deployed each of its contingents into sectors throughout the country, corresponding to provincial territories. Each sector would get its share of infantry personnel and military observers, and would be supported with appropriate engineer, aviation, signal, medical and logistical augmentation. Of the nine sectors, seven received one infantry battalion each, and the provinces of Kampong Thom and Kampong Speu each received two battalions (UN *h*: 168).

Within the military headquarters there were two military information cells. One was the Chief of Information, which worked for the Force Chief of Staff, much like a U.S. Army Division Intelligence Office. The other belonged to the Plans Branch, which also worked for the Chief of Staff. Additionally, each contingent had its own military information cell, similar to any found in a traditional peacekeeping operation.

Although intelligence is not mentioned in UNTAC documents, intelligence functions are implied, particularly by the overt activities conducted during the course of the component's attempt to carry out its mandate. The military mandate was premised on the notion that all four factions would willingly participate in the disarmament, demobilization, and cantonment process, and that the Military Component need only verify the factions' adherence to the agreement. For example, each faction, by signing the Comprehensive Settlement, agreed to disclose the following specific information concerning its military forces:

a. Total strength of forces; organization, precise number and location of deployments inside and outside Cambodia.

b. Comprehensive list of arms, ammunition and equipment held by their forces, and their exact locations.

c. Detailed record of minefields and information on booby traps laid by them or other parties.

d. Total strength of police forces and lists of arms, ammunition and equipment (UNGA A/46/608).

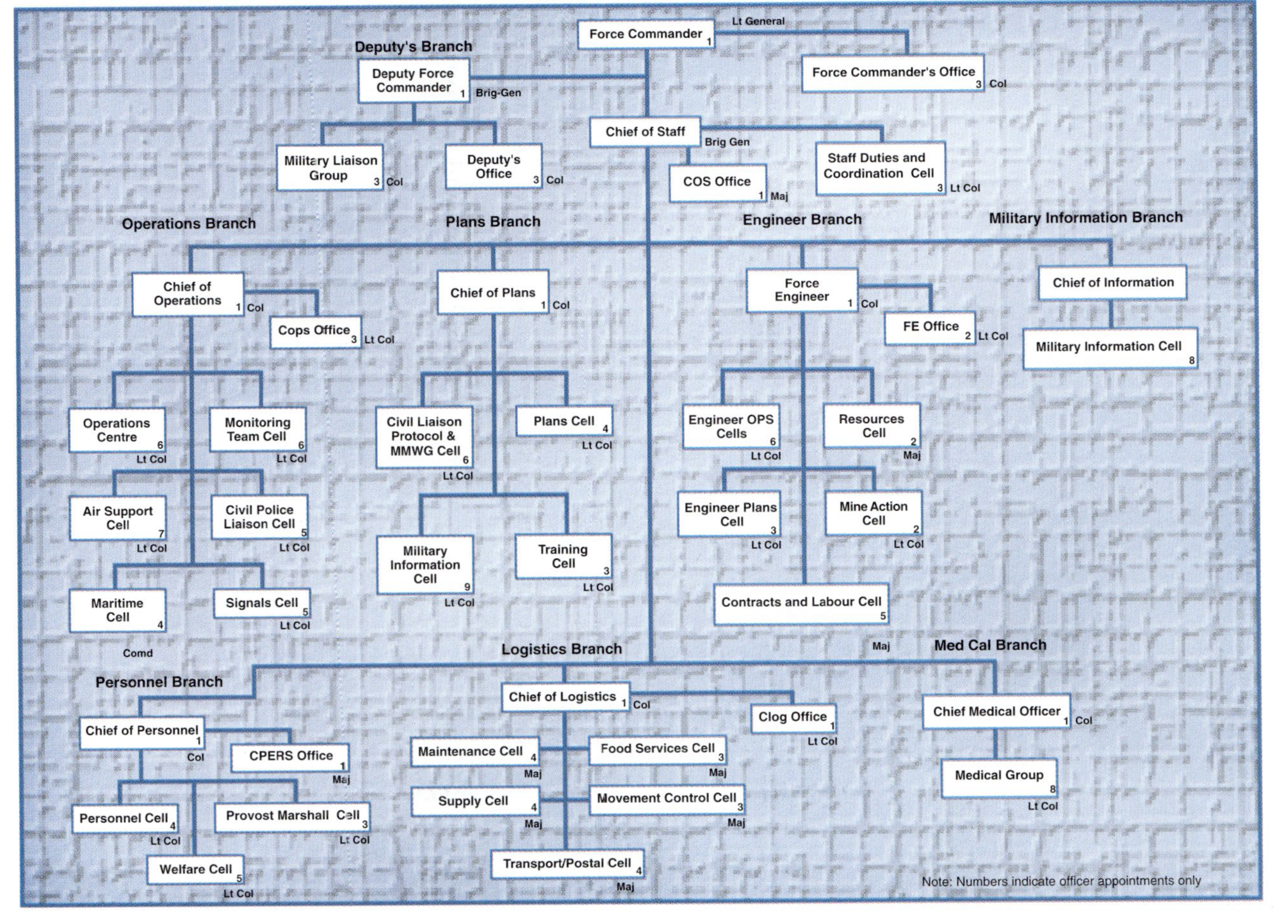

Headquarters UNTAC Military Component.

source: author

120mm projectiles found during mine-clearing operations in Cambodia, 1992. *photo courtesy of NIMA ISLWL, Ground Photo Team*

How could the Military Component monitor and verify compliance with the agreements, especially when the PDK forbade UNTAC from its controlled areas? UNTAC's mandate provided certain measures and specified tasks conducive to collecting and processing raw information that allowed them to verify the accuracy of the information provided by the factions.

To verify the withdrawal of all foreign forces, UNTAC established checkpoints on withdrawal routes, border crossing points and airfields to verify not only the withdrawal, but also that no forces were to return to Cambodia. Twenty-four such ingress/egress points were identified. Seven checkpoints were positioned along the Thai border, nine along the border with Vietnam, two along the border with Laos, one each at the ports of Kompong Som and Phnom Penh, and one each at the airports of Phnom Penh, Battambang, Siem Riep and Stung Treng (UN *h*: 142). Subject to further assessments, additional checkpoints were to be established as necessary. Observers at these checkpoints were also to report, through their contingents to Force Headquarters, any suspected outside military assistance and movements of combatants and arms into Cambodia (UN *h*: 164).

To monitor and verify the cessation of outside military assistance, the naval contingent would patrol the coastal and inland waterways. The Military Component also placed mobile teams at strategic locations within Cambodia to patrol and investigate allegations of arms support to any faction. Additionally, provisions were made in the Comprehensive Settlement with the Governments of Laos, Thailand, and Vietnam to prevent the territories of their respective states from being used to provide any form of military assistance to Cambodian factions. Each of these countries received a liaison officer and a small team to investigate complaints that these countries were allowing assistance from their territories (UN *h*: 143).

Two techniques were used to investigate complaints of suspected non-compliance or violations of any provision set forth in the Comprehensive Settlement. The wording in UNTAC's mandate was carefully orchestrated to allow the Military Component the freedom to investigate complaints in a manner it deemed appropriate. First, any faction making a complaint was to provide personnel to accompany the UNTAC investigators to ensure they were not misled with inaccurate information, including locations of the suspected violation. Second, if the Military Component suspected a violation, they did not have to wait for a complaint. They could simply deploy a verification team to the location, assess the situation, and report their findings through the appropriate channels (UN *h*: 144). Each of these measures resulted in an enormous amount of overt information for UNTAC. It was important that the information be provided, so UNTAC did not rely solely on information provided to them by the different factions that could possibly contain inaccuracies or propaganda.

UNTAC INTELLIGENCE FUNCTIONS

The six civilian UNTAC components had no formal intelligence organization, but were able to receive enormous amounts of information by working closely with the other components and by using the institutional knowledge of those NGOs and international organizations that had been in Cambodia for up to 10 years. Not only did the Military Component's mandate provide a formal intelligence mechanism, but also the enormous size and non-biased activities of this component fostered an environment of popular support for UNTAC among the Cambodian people.

On 29 May 1993, at a meeting of the Supreme National Council, Mr. Yasushi Akashi declared: "In view of the high turnout throughout the country, the absence of violence or disruption during the polling period, the success of the technical conduct of the poll, and the calm and peaceful atmosphere that reigned throughout the polling period, the conduct of the poll has been free and fair" (Heininger: 113). On 16 June 1993, Prince Sihanouk announced the formation of an Interim Joint Administration with Prince Rinarddh and Mr. Hun Sen as Co-Chairman of a Council of Ministers. This council was dissolved on 24 September 1994 at the unveiling of Cambodia's newly promulgated Constitution that established a constitutional monarchy and the Kingdom of Cambodia (UN *h*: 47).

Following the elections and the establishment of an interim government, UNTAC began withdrawing from Cambodia on 2 August 1993. However, violence soon began to increase, and the two Prime Ministers of Cambodia requested a continued UN presence. On 4 November 1993, the Security Council passed Resolution 880 that postponed the withdrawal of the mine clearance team until 30 November, and the elements of the military police and medical unit until 31 December 1993. The Security Council also approved a 20-person Military Liaison Team for a single six-month period that would help the government deal with residual matters pertaining to the Paris Agreements (UN *h*: 335). On 13 May 1994, the Security Council decided not to extend the mandate for the Military Liaison Team. UNTAC no longer existed except for the post-conflict peacebuilding activities that had been coordinated by the Rehabilitation and Reconstruction component.

INTELLIGENCE THEORY AND PRACTICE IN SOMALIA

Robert J. Allen
Lieutenant, U.S. Navy
July 1994

> We have a lot of work to do with the UN, in terms of the UN being able to do a Chapter VII mission in the future and do it more efficiently and better than we did here (Richburg *f*: A18).
>
> UNOSOM II Deputy Commander
> Lieutenant General Thomas Montgomery (USA)

The peace enforcement action in Somalia revealed the challenges of providing intelligence to a UN coalition in a combat situation. Many of the same obstacles to effective intelligence support seen at UN Headquarters in New York were encountered again in the field—with serious consequences. The realities of UN peace enforcement in the field exposed the limits of U.S. capabilities and doctrine for furnishing intelligence to multinational coalitions. In Somalia, the U.S. was able, despite some highly publicized military intelligence and operational failures, to deliver valuable intelligence to UN forces. Most importantly, however, the Somali misadventure demonstrated the danger of a peacekeeping operation becoming a peace enforcement action when political intelligence warnings are not heeded.

EXPANDING MISSIONS

The United Nations Operation in Somalia II (UNOSOM II) represented the third phase of peacekeeping in Somalia. Humanitarian motivations precipitated the initial deployment of UN troops in September 1992. The Security Council authorized the dispatch of 500 lightly armed Pakistani peacekeepers to Mogadishu to secure the city's port and airfield for

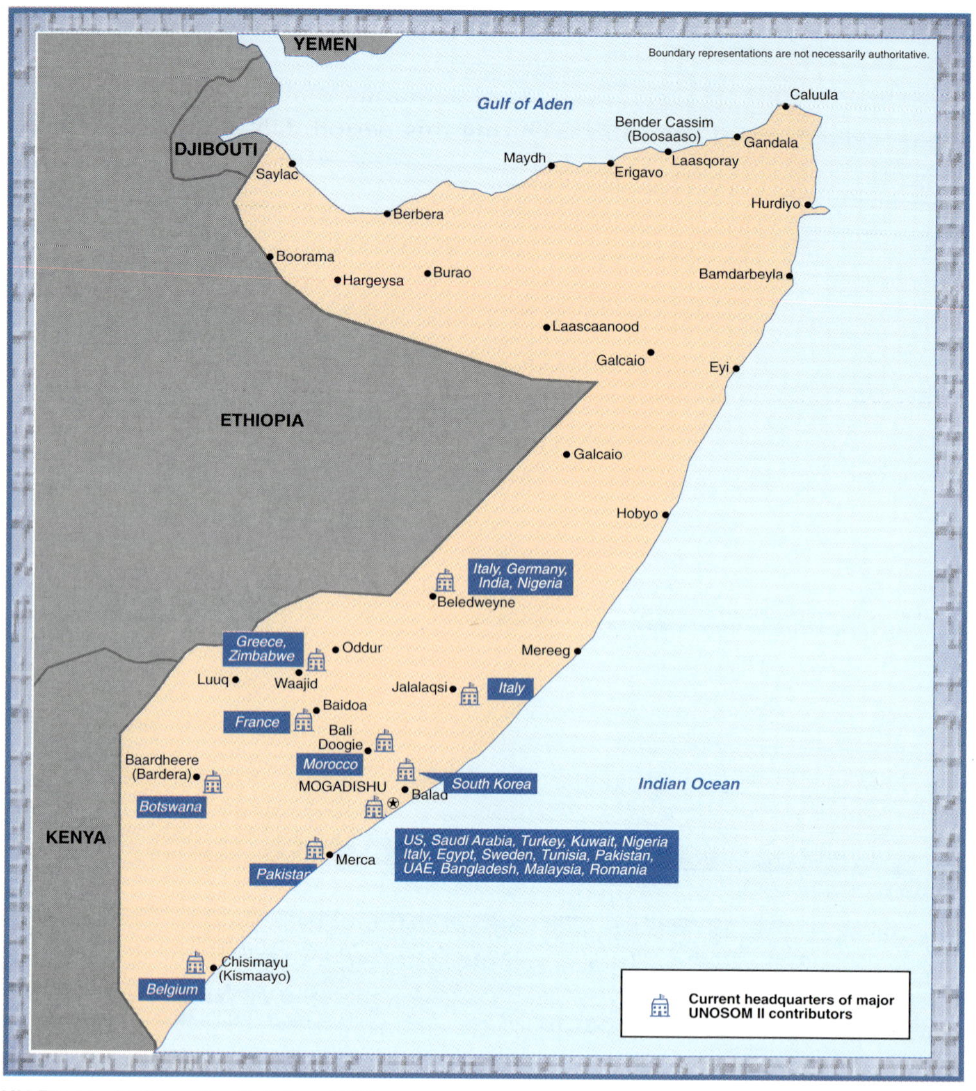

UN Forces in Somalia, October 1993. *source: Central Intelligence Agency*

humanitarian relief shipments. This undertaking was known as the United Nations Operation in Somalia (UNOSOM) (Richburg *b*: A36). The anarchy and lawlessness that exacerbated Somalia's famine prevented the troops from fulfilling their mission and they became virtual prisoners in their compound at Mogadishu International Airport.

A deteriorating security situation and increasing death toll from starvation through October and November 1992 convinced President George

Bush to order a U.S. military operation in Somalia under UN auspices. Operation RESTORE HOPE, a U.S.-led coalition that eventually included 35 countries, provided security for humanitarian relief operations between December 1992 and May 1993. During this period, UN political and military direction of the peace operation was minimal. The Unified Task Force (UNITAF) was firmly under U.S. command. The U.S. military commander, Lieutenant General Robert Johnston (USMC), and chief diplomat, Robert Oakley, met regularly with General Mohamed Farah Aideed, the Somali clan leader who controlled south Mogadishu, the U.S. base of operations (Natsios: 137). They maintained a hands-off policy with the warlord and restricted UNITAF missions to those essential to ensure the flow of humanitarian relief (Richburg *b*: A36). Intelligence operations were directed by the U.S., and necessary information was provided to third countries on a bilateral basis.

Somalis welcoming Admiral Jonathan T. Howe to Kismayo,Somalia, April 1993.

photo courtesy of NIMA ISLWL, Ground Photo Team

UNOSOM II, the UN follow-on to Operation RESTORE HOPE, set a number of precedents. It was the first UN peace operation to receive an explicit Chapter VII mandate (permitting the use of force in accomplishing its mission). It marked the first large-scale participation by U.S. combat troops in a UN peace mission. And it was the first UN peace operation to receive the full benefit of dedicated U.S. intelligence support. The UN Transition Authority in Cambodia (UNTAC) received U.S. intelligence support from May 1992, but did not have a U.S. intelligence center collocated in the country for direct support. The Security Council greatly expanded the missions of peacekeeping forces in Somalia under UNOSOM II, while the number of troops available to perform them was simultaneously being reduced. The mandate authorized under Security Council Resolution 814 included disarming militias, negotiating an agreement on national reconciliation, and organizing the reconstruction of Somalia. It was these intrusions into Somali domestic political affairs that drew UNOSOM II into an unsuccessful urban counterinsurgency campaign between June and October 1993 and severely tested the concept of providing intelligence support to a multinational coalition.

INTELLIGENCE INFRASTRUCTURE

The UN intelligence organization which supported almost 24,000 troops from 32 nations from May 1993 through March 1994 was dominated by the U.S. The key intelligence support elements were the U.S. Central Command (USCENTCOM) Intelligence Support Element (ISE) and the UNOSOM Information Center (UNOSOM IC). The 80-person ISE possessed its own intelligence collection and analysis capabilities to support the 1,200-man U.S. Quick Reaction Force that remained in Somalia after the passing of command to the UN in May 1993. Connectivity through the Joint Deployable Intelligence Support System (JDISS) permitted the ISE to draw upon products of the U.S. Intelligence Community.

Staff support for the UNOSOM IC, like the Department of Peacekeeping Operations Situation Center in New York, was performed by many non-intelligence military personnel. An Italian Lieutenant Colonel served as the Director of the Information Center with a U.S. Army Lieutenant Colonel as his deputy. The U.S. was heavily represented in the 30-man facility, with six to seven seconded U.S. military intelligence professionals (two officers and four to five enlisted service members). An additional three U.S. personnel (two officers and one enlisted member) formed the ISE liaison cell at the UNOSOM IC. U.S., Australian, and New Zealand personnel were considered to constitute the UNOSOM IC's core analytical capability.

Information Sources

U.S. intelligence reports and analysis provided the bulk of the information flow into the UNOSOM IC, mirroring the intelligence sharing relationship at the UN Situation Center in New York. Other national contingents, like the U.S., had their own intelligence assets in Somalia, but did not contribute information to the UNOSOM IC on a regular basis. Belgium, France and Italy had intelligence operations in Somalia, but were reluctant to share information with the UN. The information exchange between the ISE and UNOSOM IC was primarily unidirectional, although the U.S. did receive some useful analytical products back from the UNOSOM IC. The U.S. Intelligence Community at the national level played a minimal role in providing support to the UN. Most intelligence was collected and produced locally.

Dissemination

Information exchange among elements of the intelligence network supporting UNOSOM II was uneven. The JDISS suite purchased by the UN to interface with the ISE and the Department of Peacekeeping Operations' (DPKO) Situation Center in New York failed to live up to its promise as an intelligence exchange tool. The system went off-line in October 1993 and was not communicating effectively with its U.S. counterpart as late as March 1994. Most intelligence materials supplied by the ISE were therefore transferred in a hard-copy format or on computer diskette. The ISE was under no standing orders to route intelligence shared with the UNOSOM IC via the U.S. Communications links back to the U.S. Mission to the UN for transmission to the DPKO Situation Center.

Release Procedures

The decision as to which intelligence was to be shared with the UN in Mogadishu was essentially a "judgment call." Sanitization of materials for release was largely accomplished by fiat — there were no firm guidelines. The elaborate sanitization procedures established in U.S. Intelligence Community concepts of operation were often circumvented because of a perception of shared risk with the UN troops. U.S. personnel were acutely aware, however, that any information released into UN channels was subject to compromise and edited out the more sensitive materials to protect intelligence sources and methods (Sanai).

Security of Information

The UN's lack of any adequate security system fostered concerns over leaks of information in Mogadishu just as it had in New York. In the case of Somalia, it has been charged that the "intelligence network set up for the United Nations and the United States was rife with double agents" (Lorch: A5). Infiltration of UN operations by sympathizers of Somali warlord General Mohamed Farah Aideed was seen as responsible for the compromise of military plans and lost opportunities to capture Aideed and his key lieutenants (Richburg *d*: A1). Security concerns were not limited to Somali citizens employed as contractors by the UN. Certain national contingents were alleged to be particularly unreliable at protecting information (Fineman: A2).

UN Mi-26 at Kismayo Airfield, August 1993. *photo courtesy of NIMA ISLWL, Ground Photo Team*

A former National Security Council official's appraisal of the security problem presented by the U.S. intelligence sharing experience in Somalia was bleak:

> I don't think we are close to working out the operational security aspects when our [U.S.] forces are involved outside the well-honed NATO apparatus . . . Frankly, I think that our security is almost certainly being compromised by the multi-lateral aspect of the operation[.] (Kraemer: A1).

Information Exchange

In the atmosphere of suspicion and recrimination that prevailed in Somalia, international intelligence exchange was severely curtailed and all sensitive information was subject to undue compartmentation. The resulting "breakdown in intelligence between various armies" was blamed by many UN commanders for causing major operational problems (Fineman: A2). In some instances, sensitive documents passed to the UN Information Center were spirited away to the U.S. Intelligence Support Element for protection before the information ever entered suspect UN channels. This perceived need to maintain excessive secrecy for any type of information, including operational, is thought to have contributed to delays surrounding the rescue of U.S. Army Special Forces trapped in Mogadishu during the 3-4 October 1993 firefight (Timms: 1).

Effects of Institutional Inertia

Conduct of intelligence operations by the U.S. and the multinational coalition in Somalia underscored the difficulties inherent in dealing with a UN environment. According to Congressman Jack Reed, a House Permanent Select Committee on Intelligence member who twice visited Somalia during 1993, despite the establishment of the UNOSOM Information Center, UN field operations still reflected a UN culture that "abhors the concept of intelligence" (Sanai). The consequent lack of UN leadership and direction for intelligence operations forced each national contingent to fend for itself without regard for international cooperation. Congressman Reed described the results: "As each subordinate commander scramble[d] to call his home ministry of defense to assemble a picture of the battlefield, coherence and unity of command suffer[ed]." (R. Smith *f*: A19).

U.S. INTELLIGENCE LIMITATIONS

Transfer of command to the UN and a drawdown of U.S. intelligence assets affected overall intelligence capabilities in Somalia, leading to subsequent UN difficulties during the manhunt for Aideed. Senator Dennis DeConcini, chairman of the Senate Select Committee on Intelligence, found the U.S. intelligence operation praiseworthy during a visit in the spring of 1993 — before the withdrawal of most U.S. forces. But a decision to pull out U.S. intelligence personnel along with the combat forces in May 1993 contributed to his later evaluation that the intelligence operation deteriorated following the assumption of UN command (R. Smith *f*: A19).

Technical Assets

Sophisticated U.S. national intelligence collection systems (U-2 reconnaissance aircraft, electronic eavesdropping systems, and spy satellites) proved to be of marginal utility during UNOSOM II's hunt for General Aideed (Sanai). Technical capabilities available to U.S. forces in Somalia (tactical reconnaissance aircraft and various communications intercept systems) fared no better against a low-tech enemy in an urban landscape. Aideed's movements or location produced no discernible visual or electronic signature. He traveled frequently, alone and on foot (Scarborough and Gertz: A1). Antique low-powered walkie-talkies were used for communication. Operating in a crowded low frequency spectrum, they were extremely difficult to detect in an urban environment. The Somalis also used frequency switching and burst transmissions to thwart interception (Sanai). Those communications intercepted revealed few intentions. One Department of Defense official remarked: "You don't pick up any communication by his people talking about what their next move is" (Scarborough and Gertz: A1).

Human Intelligence

Without input from U.S. technical intelligence collection assets, UNOSOM II was heavily reliant upon human intelligence of dubious credibility. Once the UN targeted Aideed, the impartiality of the peacekeepers was lost and they were perceived as another belligerent in Somalia's ancient clan warfare. Clan loyalty prevailed over U.S.-sponsored intelligence collection operations. Suspected informants among Aideed's faction were assassinated and those recruited from rival clans dared not enter south Mogadishu for fear of suffering a similar fate (Richburg *d*: A1; C. Baker: 18). Former National Security Agency Director Lieutenant General William Odom speculated it would take years to penetrate the clans ("Aideed Hunt": A7). Consequently, the CIA was forced to rely upon newly recruited, untested and often unreliable informants (C. Baker: 18). Afraid to operate at night in Mogadishu, they provided little valuable intelligence (Atkinson: A1). Further complicating matters, the UN was fed disinformation by Aideed sympathizers to frustrate efforts to locate him.

UNOSOM II faced a scenario similar to that encountered during the U.S. pursuit of Manuel Noriega. But unlike Panama, there was no significant U.S. human resource intelligence infrastructure in Somalia. Furthermore, the U.S. Special Forces dispatched to Somalia in August 1993 to capture Aideed were completely unfamiliar with the labyrinth presented by Mogadishu. Countries without strong intelligence collection operations were reluctant to share information for security reasons (Sanai).

An entrance of the U.S. Embassy in Mogadishu, Somalia, 1993.

photo courtesy of NIMA ISLWL, Ground Photo Team

Representative Dan Glickman, chairman of the House Permanent Select Committee on Intelligence, criticized the UNOSOM II intelligence operation during September 1993 for insufficient development of a human resources intelligence collection capability (R. Smith *f*: A19). Because of this shortfall, U.S. Army Rangers and Delta Force commandos depended on estimates produced by the UNOSOM IC or on their own visual reconnaissance to locate and track Aideed. Reliance on these intelligence sources resulted in the embarrassing 30 August 1993 raid on the UN Development Program Office and the 14 September 1993 arrest of a key Aideed opponent and UN ally (Atkinson: A1).

Doctrinal Conflicts

The UNOSOM II intelligence performance in Somalia violated six of seven principles promulgated by U.S. intelligence doctrine for multinational operations (U.S. DoD *b*: VIII, 3-5). The principle of *Adjustment [of Intelligence Concepts] to Differences among Nations* was impeded by the general lack of participation by national contingents in the UN intelligence process. *Full Exchange of Intelligence* was prevented by a reluctance to compromise sensitive sources or materials. *Complementary [that is, Coordinated] Intelligence Operations* were not practiced due to the necessity for each contingent to meet its own intelligence needs. *A Multinational Intelligence Center's* efforts to acquire and fuse information were thwarted by a poor information flow. *Unity of Effort Against a Common Threat* was never achieved because of animosities among national contingents. *Determining and Planning Intelligence* requirements, production, and use in advance was made impossible by the rapid turnover of the operation from the U.S. to the UN and the *ad hoc* assembly of its multinational components. It should be clear from UNOSOM II that the principles of U.S. multinational intelligence doctrine are nearly impossible to attain in a UN peace operation.

Italian CH-47C, part of the Somalia peacekeeping forces, 1993.

photo courtesy of NIMA ISLWL, Ground Photo Team

QUALITY OF INTELLIGENCE SUPPORT

Overall, there appears to be little dispute that intelligence the U.S. provided to UN troops in the field was useful (Best: 15). U.S. personnel considered threat warning information as one of the more vital items shared with the UNOSOM IC. The UN generally held U.S.-supplied intelligence in high regard, so much so that Secretary Boutros-Ghali explicitly requested U.S. intelligence support for UNOSOM II (UNSC S/25354: 16). The comments of the Pakistani contingent commander, Brigadier General Ikram ul-Hasan, worried over the prospect of the termination of intelligence support upon ultimate American withdrawal, are reflective of this opinion:

> When you lose the Americans, you lose your force multipliers . . . Most important in combat operations is intelligence input. No intelligence, with no combat helicopters, no force multipliers—how do you fight a guerrilla? You can't (Richburg *c*: A11).

As requested, an intelligence unit was retained in the U.S. Mogadishu liaison office to maintain support to the UN following the withdrawal of U.S. forces in March 1994 (Preston *a*: A14).

Political Intelligence

Difficulties encountered during the execution of military operations, while highlighting military intelligence shortcomings in Somalia, tended to obscure the inability of the U.S. and UN to take into account critical, accurate intelligence on the Somali political situation. Aideed's intentions during the transition period from April to May 1993 were fundamentally misjudged by U.S. and UN policymakers, despite available intelligence reporting indicating the warlord was moving weapons into the capital for an eventual showdown with the UN (Richburg *a*: A1). UN officials were later to admit they "grossly miscalculated the military threat in Somalia" when they assumed command in May 1993 (Richburg *b*: A36).

After the transition from U.S. command of the Somali operation to the UN in May 1993, the Secretary-General's Special Representative, retired Admiral Jonathan Howe, and U.S. envoy Robert Gosende sought to marginalize Aideed in order to fulfill the UN's ambitious goals of national reconstruction. The general and his supporters had made clear their determination to rule Somalia, despite the presence of UNOSOM II, and warned the UN against interference (Quinn-Judge: A12). UN activities such as establishment of a judicial system, a police force, and local government councils and a decision to sponsor a clan conference to replace Aideed threatened to erode the warlord's power base in south Mogadishu.

Policymakers ignored advice and intelligence reports that attempts to isolate Aideed would ultimately backfire and proceeded with plans to inventory heavy weapons as part of the disarmament process (Lippman and Gellman: A1). This action led Aideed to confront the UN in an ambush that killed 24 Pakistani troops in June 1993. The Security Council responded within 24 hours with a resolution calling for the arrest of those responsible, launching the UN into its unsuccessful conflict with Aideed and his militia (Sloyan: C3).

Lessons Learned

It was not the failures of military intelligence or military operations that ultimately doomed UNOSOM II. Political decisions taken in Mogadishu, New York and Washington between March and June 1993 gradually expanded the mandate of a humanitarian peacekeeping operation to a peace enforcement action, despite intelligence warning of the likely consequences. Once the peacekeepers' neutrality was sacrificed — along with their primary source of intelligence, the Somali people — the mission was well down the slippery slope of "mission creep." An artificial coalition of states was then required to conduct an urban counterinsurgency campaign in unfamiliar terrain, while alienated from the local population. UNOSOM II was the ultimate example that intelligence issues in UN peace operations are not just limited to military matters, but involve the political process that could prevent a peacekeeping operation from devolving into a peace enforcement action.

FROM HUMANITARIAN ASSISTANCE TO NATION BUILDING: UN MISSION CHANGE AND ITS IMPACT ON THE INTELLIGENCE PROCESS

Payton A. Flynn
Technical Sergeant, U.S. Air Force
June 1996

The U.S. Intelligence Community had a difficult time in Somalia attempting to collect, process, analyze, and disseminate intelligence between U.S. assets, and especially between coalition forces. The intelligence questions asked, the intelligence collection apparatus deployed and the methods employed to analyze the intentions and capabilities of Somali factions were based on the humanitarian mission of the Unified Task Force (UNITAF). Basically, the U.S. and UN made the wrong assumptions and asked the wrong questions for the follow-on nation-building mission of UNOSOM II, called operation RESTORE HOPE (Hirsch and Oakley: 101-114).[1]

ASKING THE RIGHT QUESTIONS

Intelligence operators and planners in UNOSOM I, UNITAF and UNOSOM II underestimated the Somalis. UNOSOM II assessments noted the Somalis' inability to operate or maintain sophisticated weaponry, a lack of leadership by the clans/militias, the inability of the clans/militias to coordinate operations against UN forces, the lack of command and control to conduct detailed operations, and the UN's advantage over antiquated

[1] Robert B. Oakley, the U.S. Special Envoy to Somalia, and John L. Hirsch served in Somalia during RESTORE HOPE, and their 1995 book reflects their strategic view of the transition from UNITAF to UNOSOM II.

Somali weapon systems. In reality, the Somalis showed considerable capability in all of these areas. The U.S./UN assumed that the majority of factions would not defy any UN forceful action, and concluded that organized resistance against the UN was unlikely.

The U.S./UN failed to identify the intentions of the warlords, especially those of General Aideed. When the mission shifted to disarmament and nation-building, the warlords had the most to lose because their power was based on access to weapons and a threat of violence. The UN's goals for nation-building would decrease the number of weapons available to the Somali warlords and eliminate the threat of violence on the streets of Mogadishu. The mission of the UN was unacceptable to General Aideed, whose goal was to be the leader of Somalia. His personal agenda would be in jeopardy if the UN were able to rebuild Somalia and establish a government chosen by the people. UNOSOM II never anticipated that Aideed would ambush its peacekeepers, and it was not adequately prepared to handle the intelligence or operational aspects of the mission to capture him. An incident in June 1993 illustrates the faulty intelligence estimate process. On 5 June, when Pakistani peacekeepers inspected the Somalia national radio station (controlled by General Aideed) and other Somalia National Alliance weapons storage areas, the results were disastrous. It was an intelligence error to anticipate that General Aideed would allow the UN to search one of his key tactical assets without an organized resistance (Richburg *a*: A1).

INTELLIGENCE TRANSFER

The transfer of intelligence functions between the U.S.-led UNITAF coalition and the UN's UNOSOM II was not properly coordinated. The transition functions were accomplished too quickly. The CENTCOM Intelligence Support Element was not prepared at the start of UNOSOM II to take over the complicated intelligence process and provide timely, accurate and relevant information to decisionmakers. The lack of adequate transition time, coupled with a reduction in personnel, combined to disrupt the intelligence process. The intelligence gap created by the transition left UNOSOM II in the precarious position of continuously "catching up," as most of the time it was reduced to producing only reactive intelligence.

The reduction in personnel from UNITAF to UNOSOM II had a direct impact on intelligence capabilities. The UN was not prepared on 4 May 1993 to take over the operation from UNITAF. Lt Gen Robert Johnston,

USMC, Commander of UNITAF, had drawn down U.S. forces to minimal levels by April 1993. General Colin Powell, then Chairman of the Joint Chiefs of Staff, said in a visit to Mogadishu on 5 April 1993: "We're not in a hurry to get out of here by 1 May, because we don't want to force (Turkish Lt. General) Bir to move too quickly" (Richburg *b*: A36). But facts on the ground dictated otherwise. General Johnston's drawdown forced the UN to take over before it was ready and with reduced troop levels. Coalition forces were reduced from more than 28,000 in January to approximately 16,000 in May, 12,000 less than authorized by the UN Security Council.

In the end, the UN was forced into taking on a mission that it was not prepared to handle. Admiral Howe said: "There was a real issue of are we ready or are we not. I don't think we were properly prepared. We took people out of the city . . . It was a stretching exercise. We were replacing well-equipped, highly trained, well-integrated American forces with splotches of other groups" (Richburg *b*: A36).

The gap created in the intelligence arena due to the decrease in personnel would hamper the intelligence effort from May through October 1993. Senator Dennis DeConcini (D-AZ), Chairman of the Senate Select Committee on Intelligence said: "We had a big contingent, a sizable contingent there, with a good network throughout the country. ...[But we] substantially pulled that down when we pulled out" (R. Smith *f*: A19).

SECURITY AND INTELLIGENCE SHARING

Taking into account the limitations of the UN, the U.S. Intelligence Community security and sanitization procedures for intelligence shared with the UN ended in a security breach. On 27 February 1995, Ambassador Simpson and others from the Somali Liaison Office in Nairobi were exploring the vacated former UNOSOM Force Commander's headquarters and found an unsecured room full of classified U.S. and UN documents and computer disks. Included were large numbers of documents and imagery classified up to U.S. "SECRET/NO FOREIGN DISSEMINATION" and "UN RESTRICTED, LEVEL II," all of which would have been compromised if they had not been discovered ("Documents": 322). Such a compromise could have been extremely damaging in two ways: use of these materials by enemies to identify and settle scores with former U.S./UN Somali intelligence sources and to embarrass the U.S./UN with an onslaught of adverse propaganda.

Security is paramount when sharing intelligence among coalition forces, yet the sharing of intelligence is critical to the success of UN peace operations. In a multilateral environment, security concerns are always present, and downgrading intelligence information to protect sources, without neutralizing the value of the information, is a strenuous task. This problem is compounded when coalition partners have their own agendas and may not trust each other.

POLITICAL CONTEXT

Great political sensitivity is required to deal with individuals and organizations during UN peace operations, especially where a legitimate government does not exist. On 7 and 8 December 1992, the President's Special Envoy for Somalia, Robert B. Oakley, met separately in Mogadishu with the two most powerful Somali faction leaders, Mohammed Farah Aideed and Ali Mahdi, to enlist their cooperation in assuring the arrival of U.S. forces (UNITAF) would go without incident. During the meeting, the U.S. indicated that it would not tolerate violence from faction leaders similar to that imposed upon the 500 Pakistani troops a few months earlier (Oakley: 46). But, more importantly, the meeting sent a message to the other clans/militia, clan elders, civilian leaders, and the rest of the population in Somalia, that Aideed and Mahdi were considered the most powerful men in the war-torn country. As a result, the U.S. had legitimized the leading warlords in Somalia and planted the seeds for future confrontations when the UN would attempt to rehabilitate the country.

UNITAF accommodated the Somali warlords by allowing them to store weapons and ammunition in warehouses outside of Mogadishu as long as the material was not used against the peacekeeping force or against those who were delivering relief supplies. The UNITAF strategy used a hands-off approach with the Somali warlords, to eliminate any hostilities with them, especially General Aideed. Because of this approach, UNITAF, when necessary, negotiated with the Somali warlords. The Americans attempted to appease the warlords, and failed to take advantage of the influence of clan elders and women.

General Aideed became UNOSOM II's worst enemy as it attempted to plan and execute its objectives. He never intended to cooperate with the UN's efforts to disarm the warring factions and establish a new government unless he controlled it. UN civilian officials took initiatives such as installing a new judicial system and local government councils without consulting Aideed. General Aideed launched propaganda attacks against the UN, accusing the organization of attempting to colonialize Somalia ("Somalia: Warlord": 48).

UNOSOM II's objectives seemed clear at the beginning of the mission. But UNITAF was not able to develop sufficient situational awareness to allow UNISOM II to proceed confidently (Allard: 74-76). The lead intelligence element of UNITAF had only seven weeks of training (only three in-theater), only five human intelligence collectors and no significant signals intelligence assets. The intelligence requirements were not sufficiently detailed to address intentions and capabilities, amount of weapons and ammunition, troop strength, organizational structure, command and control, or order of battle on the various Somali factions. The lead intelligence element had the added responsibility of disseminating intelligence to the United Nations and coalition partners under demanding security restrictions. In sum, the intelligence apparatus suffered from major handicaps.[2]

---

2 Editor's note: This excerpt from Payton A. Flynn's thesis is a brief summary of his findings. Information for his thesis was gathered from a variety of DIA, CIA and Pentagon intelligence analysts. The author also benefited from the personal experiences of his thesis chair, John A. Wahlquist, Col, USAF, who was Military Advisor to the U.S. Special Envoy to Somalia in support of operations RESTORE HOPE and CONTINUE HOPE in 1993 and 1994.

Chapter 4
REGIONAL PERSPECTIVES

It is tempting to view the enhanced role of the United Nations in the post-Cold War world solely from an American perspective. In fact, many countries consider the commitment of forces to the UN an essential and non-controversial component of their foreign policies. At the same time, some countries have for 50 years refused to participate. Both ends of the spectrum are illustrated by Sub-Saharan Africa and Japan. For Africans the difficulties of UN nation-building in Somalia hardly came as a surprise. The Congo crisis in the 1960s shaped the African perception of the dangers of UN and great-power intervention in civil war, but they still contributed as part of their role in African regional affairs and on the broader stage of world politics. Japan, on the other hand, used the no-war clause in their post-war constitution to avoid any hint of a return to a power projection capability. Now, attempting to put both World War II and the Cold War behind them, the Japanese see the Security Council and the UN collective security system as a means to attain their proper status in the world community. Involvement in UN peace operations is the first tentative step.

Captain John W. Loffert Jr. takes a broad historical view of Sub-Saharan participation in UN peacekeeping. He evaluates the performance of African military contingents and specific African commanders of peacekeeping operations. He addresses the domestic political and economic motives of the African countries and examines how UN peacekeeping relates to international politics in the region, including the move to obtain influence in the UN Secretariat. Finally, he assesses the capability and prospects for Sub-Saharan contributions to UN peacekeeping in the future.

Second Lieutenant Fae M. Crissman reviews the Japanese quest for a permanent seat on the UN Security Council, an attempt to obtain political status in world politics commensurate with their economic power. Internationalist

Japanese see a seat on the Security Council as a way to put World War II and dependence on the U.S. Security Treaty behind them and assume great-power status. Lieutenant Crissman notes that several obstacles remain in Japan's path: a reluctance of the Japanese public to support the use of force for UN collective security, UN procedural hurdles, and complex group dynamics in the General Assembly.

Second Lieutenant Steven E. Maceda looks at the peacekeeping mission of Japan's Self-Defense Forces. Created to provide rear-area security for Americans fighting the Korean War, the constitutional validity of the Japanese military has been challenged from the start. The Soviet threat was its primary justification. With the end of the Cold War, its *raison d'etre* collapsed. The government's first attempts to contribute Self-Defense Forces to UN peacekeeping met with a political firestorm from the left. Over time, with careful selection of low-risk missions, the Self-Defense Forces have built political support for service outside Japan in a UN context.

SUB-SAHARAN AFRICAN ENGAGEMENT IN UNITED NATIONS PEACEKEEPING

John Wesley Loffert Jr.
Captain, U.S. Army
July 1994

LEVEL OF PARTICIPATION

The end of the Cold War has decreased superpower confrontation and allowed the UN to expand its role in the international environment. M. A. Vogt, a peacekeeping scholar, describes the results of declining superpower authority: "The thawing of superpower relations has created disruptions in

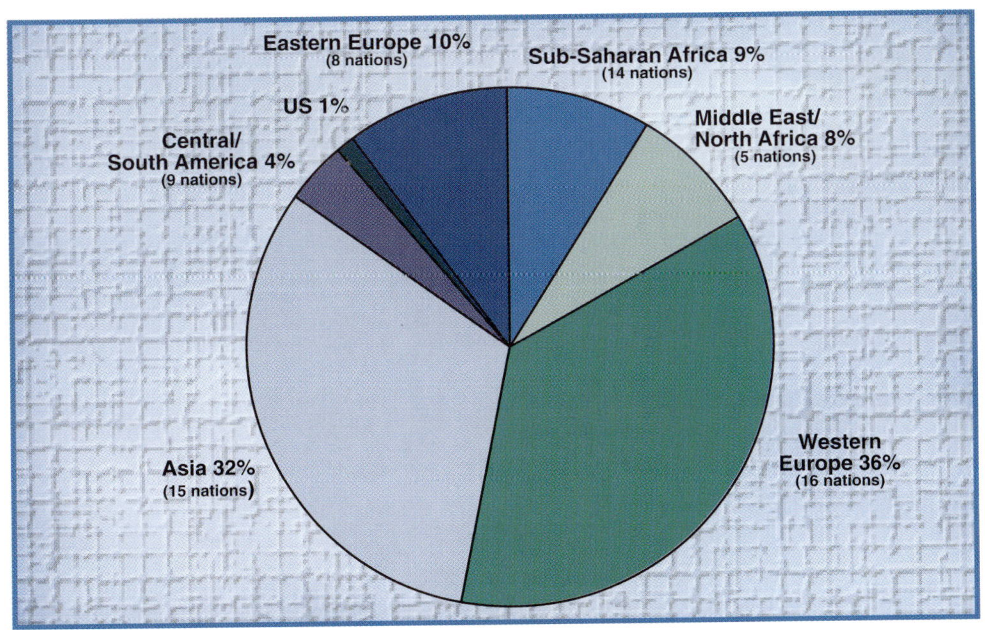

Regional Contributions of UN Peacekeeping Personnel, 1994. *source: author*

the social and political order in many regions of the world and [these] disruptions have led to a higher incidence of armed conflict" (Vogt: 150). The world is increasingly turning to UN peacekeeping operations to stabilize the growing number of civil conflicts and the humanitarian disasters which result. In order to do this, the scope and role of UN peacekeeping has expanded. In the beginning of 1992 there were 11,500 UN peacekeepers deployed worldwide. As of May 1994 there were 70,442 (Hall: 22). To finance this larger peacekeeping force, the peacekeeping budget has nearly doubled to $3.6 billion (Brooks: A1). The countries of Sub-Saharan Africa have been extremely active within this world of UN peacekeeping.

Fifteen countries of Sub-Saharan Africa have participated in nine past UN peacekeeping missions. Fourteen Sub-Saharan African countries are, or have been involved in, nine of the 18 current UN peacekeeping missions. Sub-Saharan African countries provide over 9 percent of all current UN peacekeeping forces (CIA *b*; UN *f*; UN *c*).

BENEFITS OF UN PEACEKEEPING

UN peacekeeping benefits the countries of Sub-Saharan Africa in many ways. Participation in UN peacekeeping increases Sub-Saharan African influence in the UN and opens up numerous UN peacekeeping command positions. UN peacekeeping helps establish a country as a leader in the international community and benefits bilateral relations. Domestically, UN peacekeeping strengthens the government and increases the preparedness of the armed forces.

The extensive Sub-Saharan African involvement in UN peacekeeping has increased Sub-Saharan African influence within the UN. The effect this can have on the nature of UN operations is significant. The current Secretary-General is Kofi Annan, a Ghanaian. His previous position was Under-Secretary-General for Peacekeeping. Annan's position ensures the UN places emphasis on African problems.

Secretary-General Perez de Cuellar also had an African on his staff. Major General Timothy Dibuama from Ghana was the Secretary-General's military advisor in 1978, and facilitated the acceptance and deployment of the Ghanaian contingent to UNIFIL. Active participation in UN peacekeeping, whether with observers or military contingents, enables a country to access key administrative and staff posts within the Secretariat.

Political map of Africa.

source: Central Intelligence Agency

Active participation in UN peacekeeping has also enabled individuals from Sub-Saharan Africa to obtain command positions. The following UN operations were commanded by Sub-Saharan African military officers: ONUC—Lieutenant General Kebbede Guebre (Ethiopia—Apr 62-Jul 63) and Major General Aguiyi Ironsi (Nigeria-Jan 64-Jun 64); UNIFIL—Major General Emmanuel A. Erskine (Ghana—May 78-Feb 81); UNAVEM II—Major General Christ Abutu Garuba (Nigeria); UNIKOM—Major General Timothy Dibuama (Ghana); and UNOMIL—Major General Daniel Opande (Kenya). In addition, several deputy commander positions have been assigned to Sub-Saharan African commanders. The list includes: ONUC—Brigadier General

Iyassu Mengesha (Ethiopia); UNTAG—Brigadier General Daniel Opande (Kenya), Southern Knin Sector; UNPROFOR—Brigadier General J. K. Arap Robs (Kenya); UNOSOM—Major General Mike Nambuya (Zimbabwe); and UNAMIR—Brigadier General Henri Anyidoho (Ghana).

Norwegian People's Aid instructors and students examine human skull in de-mining school, Mozambique, 1993.

photo courtesy of NIMA ISLWL, Ground Photo Team

Expanded international involvement, such as UN peacekeeping, means that a particular country is seen as a leader. This is evident for Ghana, Nigeria, and Kenya, which are all active participants in UN peacekeeping. One of Ghana's and Nigeria's goals in providing military contingents to ONUC in 1960 was to advance their leadership positions in Africa. Ghanaian President Kwame Nkrumah planned to unite Ghana and the Congo by setting up the framework for a unified African state. Congolese Prime Minister Lumumba's death in 1960 shattered this dream, but Nkrumah continued to assert his influence in the UN mission in an effort to foster Ghanaian goals in Africa. The Congo crisis provided Nigeria with the opportunity to give itself a leading role in Africa while drawing some attention away from Nkrumah. The Nigerian military used the deployment to show off the Army as a "symbol of sovereignty" (LeFever and Joshua: 291). Since that time, Nigeria has been actively involved in African policy. With Nigeria as chair, the Organization of African Unity attempted to mediate the crisis in Somalia and readily took up the leadership of the Economic Community of West African States Cease-Fire Monitoring Group (ECOMOG)'s force in Liberia. Kenya assumed a leading role in Africa during its participation in the Namibian UN peacekeeping force, and it was the only Sub-Saharan country to provide a military contingent to UNTAG. After UNTAG, Kenyans stayed in Namibia to help the new government train its military and police forces.

UN peacekeeping benefits a country's bilateral relations as well. The Botswanan Defense Force's deployment to Somalia has greatly increased the Botswanan government's prestige and fostered an improved relationship with

Country	Combat Troops	Observers	Civil Police	Total
Botswana	1180	22	15	1217
Cape Verde		18		18
Congo		27		27
Ghana	1113	54	6	1173
Guinea		1		1
Guinea-Bissau		59	55	114
Kenya	933	83	48	1064
Malawi		5		5
Mali		10	5	15
Nigeria	745	34	45	824
Senegal		44		44
Togo		14	15	29
Zambia	820	8		828
Zimbabwe	1095	25	7	1127
Total	**5886**	**404**	**196**	**6486**
UN Total	**66579**	**2357**	**1506**	**70442**

Sub-Saharan Country Participation in UN Peacekeeping Operations, 1994. *source: author*

the U.S. When Major General John F. Stewart, Deputy Chief of Staff for Intelligence, U.S. Army Europe, visited Botswana in May 1993, he praised the Botswana Defense Force's performance in Somalia and lauded the cooperation and similar goals of Botswana and the U.S. in Africa (Stewart).

The domestic benefits from UN peacekeeping occur on many levels. At the national level, UN peacekeeping strengthens the political leadership by increasing their international prestige, and by funneling the monetary benefits to the local populace. For the military, UN peacekeeping provides training, supplements pay, and facilitates the acquisition of new equipment.

The monetary benefits of UN peacekeeping, funnelled through the soldiers' pay, impacts directly on the home front. UN contingents are monetarily reimbursed by direct UN payments to the contributing government. The government in turn pays its soldiers in accordance with its own policy. For Ghana, this serves two functions. First, the monetary influx into the government is seen as "an important contribution to the people by their armed forces, who have often been regarded as a drain on national resources" (Erskine: 152). While Western countries do not make any profit from UN peacekeeping, developing countries, such as Ghana, gain tremendously. The second benefit involves the enthusiasm and support UN peacekeeping instills in the armed forces. UN peacekeeping improves the standard of living for the Ghanaian soldiers. They are able to buy freezers, coolers, stereo systems, televisions, and household items unavailable on the meager soldier's pay received in Ghana. This increase in the soldier's standard of living is channeled to their families back home. In essence, UN peacekeeping has "enhanced the troops' professional expertise and their standard of living—both are important. Perhaps most important of all, it has reduced the risks to Ghana's political stability" (Erskine: 161).

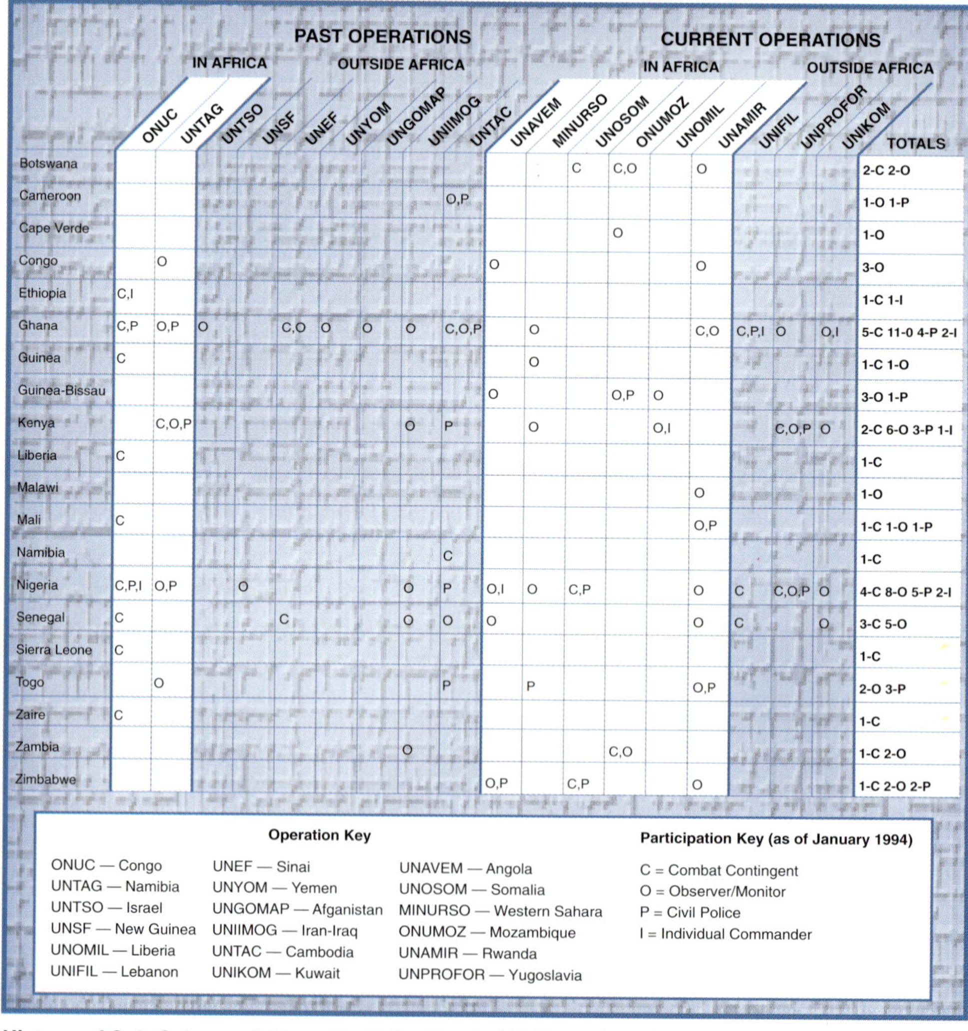

	PAST OPERATIONS									CURRENT OPERATIONS									
	IN AFRICA		OUTSIDE AFRICA							IN AFRICA						OUTSIDE AFRICA			
	ONUC	UNTAG	UNTSO	UNSF	UNEF	UNYOM	UNGOMAP	UNIIMOG	UNTAC	UNAVEM	MINURSO	UNOSOM	ONUMOZ	UNOMIL	UNAMIR	UNIFIL	UNPROFOR	UNIKOM	TOTALS
Botswana												C	C,O		O				2-C 2-O
Cameroon									O,P										1-O 1-P
Cape Verde													O						1-O
Congo		O								O					O				3-O
Ethiopia	C,I																		1-C 1-I
Ghana	C,P	O,P	O		C,O	O	O	O	C,O,P		O				C,O	C,P,I	O	O,I	5-C 11-0 4-P 2-I
Guinea	C										O								1-C 1-O
Guinea-Bissau										O			O,P	O					3-O 1-P
Kenya		C,O,P						O	P		O			O,I			C,O,P	O	2-C 6-O 3-P 1-I
Liberia	C																		1-C
Malawi															O				1-O
Mali	C														O,P				1-C 1-O 1-P
Namibia									C										1-C
Nigeria	C,P,I	O,P		O				O	P	O,I	O	C,P			O	C	C,O,P	O	4-C 8-O 5-P 2-I
Senegal	C				C			O	O	O					O	C		O	3-C 5-O
Sierra Leone	C																		1-C
Togo		O							P		P				O,P				2-O 3-P
Zaire	C																		1-C
Zambia								O					C,O						1-C 2-O
Zimbabwe										O,P		C,P			O				1-C 2-O 2-P

Operation Key

ONUC — Congo
UNTAG — Namibia
UNTSO — Israel
UNSF — New Guinea
UNOMIL — Liberia
UNIFIL — Lebanon
UNEF — Sinai
UNYOM — Yemen
UNGOMAP — Afganistan
UNIIMOG — Iran-Iraq
UNTAC — Cambodia
UNIKOM — Kuwait
UNAVEM — Angola
UNOSOM — Somalia
MINURSO — Western Sahara
ONUMOZ — Mozambique
UNAMIR — Rwanda
UNPROFOR — Yugoslavia

Participation Key (as of January 1994)

C = Combat Contingent
O = Observer/Monitor
P = Civil Police
I = Individual Commander

History of Sub-Saharan African Participation in UN Peacekeeping. *source: author*

In 1991, based on human rights violations, the U.S. and 11 other donor countries suspended all new aid commitments to the Kenyan government. It was within this environment that Kenya began its preparations to send a military contingent to Croatia. The UNPROFOR mission was a perfect opportunity to alleviate the international pressure on the government and supplement the military wages of the soldier. It was hoped that the UN peacekeeping mission would have an advantageous effect on Kenya's external, as well as internal, problems.

Zambia's desire to participate in UN peacekeeping is motivated by the UN money that will be obtained for its military. The Zambian military has suffered budget reductions. Much of the Zambian equipment is outdated Soviet weaponry. A troubled economy and lack of foreign support has meant that much of this equipment is unserviceable. When Zambia was accepted for the UN mission to Mozambique the government had to buy new uniforms for its soldiers to improve the force's appearance. The financial state of the Zambian army is detrimental to morale, and the government is seeking ways to keep the soldiers content and employed. The importance of the UN monetary influx into the Zambian force was highlighted by Defense Minister Benjamin Muila's speech to departing troops on 27 April 1993. He announced that the Zambian military would receive $3 million for its participation in ONUMOZ and that this would significantly increase the standards and capabilities of the army (Reuters *c*).

RESULTS OF OPERATIONAL DEPLOYMENTS

Sub-Saharan African militaries involved in UN peacekeeping operations have performed well under fire, are extremely proficient in civil-military relations, deploy capable forces, and provide specialized equipment perfectly suited for UN peacekeeping.

The Sub-Saharan African contingents have proven themselves when under fire in UN peacekeeping operations from ONUC to UNAMIR. The Nigerians conducted several large-scale joint military operations in the Congo, most notably Operation FRIENDSHIP and the rescue of missionaries in Kasai. In Operation FRIENDSHIP the Nigerians commanded a joint Malaysian-Nigerian force that cleared the remaining mercenaries out of Katanga. In Kasai, the Nigerians launched numerous air assault operations to penetrate into rebel territory and rescue captive missionaries (Ohaegbulam: 116).

The Kenyans in UNPROFOR were one of the few UN forces that did not withdraw in the face of the Croatian offensive in 1993. The Kenyans withstood Croatian artillery and returned fire in an effort to prevent the capture of the Peruca dam in UN-controlled territory. Although they eventually withdrew, their action earned them the respect of both sides ("Croatian Forces").

On 25 February 1993, in support of U.S. Marines, the Nigerians quickly returned fire against Somali militia attempting to block a key intersection in Mogadishu. As the operation progressed, the Nigerians worked closely with U.S. forces to cordon off the area and defuse the situation. This action established the Nigerians as a force to be reckoned with (CJTF Somalia).

The Ghanaians proved their mettle in Rwanda. While other UN forces withdrew in the wake of renewed civil war, the Ghanaians left a battalion in Kigali to maintain a UN presence at the airport. The Ghanaians served as the UN rear guard in Rwanda in the hope that UN forces would be able to reenter the country ("Fighting").

Close cooperation between the military contingent and the local populace is often lacking in a UN operation. Sub-Saharan African detachments excel in civil military operations. One of the first examples of this was Nigeria's successful operation UNION in the Congo in 1960. Establishing a local rapport with the Congolese populace in the turbulent Kasai province, the Nigerian 3rd Brigade was able to provide a secure environment for UN relief agencies (Lefever and Joshua: 359).

In Somalia the Botswana Defense Force coordinated with Non-Governmental Organizations (NGOs) and other UN civil activities. A special Botswanan liaison officer was widely respected for his accessibility and responsiveness to the local NGOs. Through this effort the contingent has been able to establish a successful farming program in Baardheere in cooperation with the World Food Program (CJTF Somalia).

Twelve years of combat in Mozambique gave the Zimbabwean contingent in Somalia valuable experience in the importance of civil affairs operations. The Zimbabwean contingent in Afgooye developed a strong rapport with the Somalis, and the Zimbabwean 12-day police training program is enabling the local populace to regain control of their region (USLO Mogadishu).

	Army	Navy	Air Force	Tanks	Recon/APC	Helicopters	Transport Aircraft
Botswana	6,000		100		10-Shorland, 12-V150, 30-BTR60	2-AS350L	2-Defender, 2-CN235, 2-Skyvan
Cameroon	6,600	1,200	300		8-Ferret, 49-V150, 5-VBLM11	3-Bell206, 3-SE3130, 4-SA319, 4-SA342L	3-C130, 1-DHC4, 4-DHC5D, 2-PA23
Cape Verde	1,100		100		10-BRDM2		
Congo	10,000	300	500	25-T64, 15-TYPE59, 10-TYPE62 3-PT76	25-BRDM1/2, 30-BTR50, 30-BTR60, 20-BTR152	2-SA316, 2-SA318, 1-SA365	5-AN24, 1-AN26
Ethiopia	100,000			350-T54, T62	200-BRDM, BMP, BTR60/152	18-M124, 25-MI8, 2-MI4, 1-UH1, 1-IAR330	6-AN12, 2-DH6
	Figures for Ethiopia are approx due to Independence of Eritrea and split in Armed Forces						
Ghana	5,000	850	1,000		3-SALADIN, 3-EE9, 50 MOWAG PIRANHA	2-M12, 4-SA319	3-F27, 6-Skyvan, 1-C212
Guinea	8,500	400	800	30-T34, 8-T54, 20-PT76	25-BRDM1/2, 2-AML90, 16-BTR40, 10-BTR50, 8-BTR60, 6-BTR152	1-IAR330, 4-MI4, 1-SA316, 1-SA330, 1-SA342	2-AN12, 4-AN14
Guinea Bissau	6,800	300	100	10-T34, 20-PT76	20-TYPE56, 35-BTR40/60/152	1-SA318, 2-SA319	
Kenya	20,500	1,400	2,500	80-Vickers MK3	30-AML90, 38-AML60, 12-Ferret, 8-Shorland, 52-UR416, 52-UR416, 10-PanhardM3	9-IAR330, 4-SA330, 1-SA342, 34-Hughes 500	7-DHC5D, 7-DO28D, 1PA32, 3-DHC8, 5-DHC4, 15-DHC2
Liberia	Military occupied with a Civil War — current data unavailable						
Malawi	10,000	200	200		20-FOX, 10-Ferret, 13-ELAND	4-AS350, 3-SA319, 3-SA330, 1-SA365 2-CH47	4-DO228
Mali	6,900	50	400	21-T34, 19-TYPE62	20-BRDM2, 30-BTR40, 10-BTR60, 10-BTR152	2-MI4, 1-MI8	2-AN2, 2-AN24, 2-AN26
Namibia	8,000				Various BRDM2, Casspir, Wolf, BTR152		
Nigeria	62,000	7,300	9,500	157-T55, 97-Vickers MK3	10-SARACEN, 70-MOWAG, 55-FOX, 100-SCORPION, 60-AML90 75-EE9, 20-SALADIN,	10-AS330, 4-AS332, 2-SA330, 7-CH47 300-4K7FA, 120-AML60 22-BO105	5-C130, 3-H30, 5-G222, 18-DO128, 18-DO280
Senegal	8,500	700	500		10-M8, 4-M20, 30-AML60, 27-AML90, 16-Panhard M3, 12-M3	2-SA318, 2-SA330, 1-SA341	6-F27, 2-MHI521
Sierra Leone	6,000	150			10-MOWAG, 4-SARACEN		
South Africa	47,000	4,500	10,000	250-Oilpant	1,600-ELAND60/90, 100-Roolkat 76, 160-Mamba 1,500-Buffel/Casspir, 1,500-Ratel 20/60/90	63-SA316/319, 63-SA330	7-C130, 19-C47
Togo	4,800	200	250	2-T54	9-SCORPION, 6-M8, 3-M20, 3-AML60, 7-AML90 36-EE9, 2-UBLM11, 4-M3, 30-UR416	1-AS332, 2-SA315, 1 SA319, 1-SA330	2-DHC5, 1-DO27
Zaire	25,000	1,300	1,800	20-TYPE59 40-TYPE62	30-AML60, 30-AML90, 12-M113, 12-YW531, 60-M3	1-AS332, 4-SA319, 4-SA330	8-C47, 5-C130, 3-DHC
Zambia	20,000		1,600	10-T55, 20-TYPE59, 30-PT76	88-DRDM1/2, 13-BTR60	4-AB205, 12-MI8	4-AN26, 4-C47, 2-DC6B, 3-DHC4, 4-DHC5D
Zimbabwe	47,000		1,200	40-T55, 30-TYPE59, 10-TYPE69	34-ELAND, 90-EE9, 95-AML60/90, 8-YW531 40-UR416, 75-CROCODILE/ BUFFALO/HIPPO/HYENA/ LEOPARD	10-AB205, 10-AB412	6-BN2, 11-C212, 10-C47

Sub-Saharan African Military Equipment Suitable for UN Peacekeeping. *source: author*

The frequency with which Ghanaian soldiers are deployed in support of UN operations, such as UNEF II, UNIFIL, UNTAC, and UNAMIR, means that almost every soldier in the Ghanaian military is experienced in UN operations. This experienced manpower pool ensures that any Ghanaian contingent will have many UN veterans capable of functioning in the ambiguous world of UN peacekeeping.

Sub-Saharan Africans bring specially designed personnel carriers on UN deployment. Ironically, these vehicles were developed by South Africa due to the arms embargo placed on the minority government. Now the vehicles, developed to support apartheid, are being used by black African countries in UN peacekeeping worldwide. They are hardened against mines, and their high profile makes them ideal for crowd control and surveillance. Namibia, South Africa, and Zimbabwe all have these vehicles readily available. These vehicles, used in UNTAC and UNOSOM, provide a perfect vehicle for future UN peacekeeping operations ("Troops").

Zimbabwean armored personnel carrier, Somalia, 1993. *photo courtesy of NIMA ISLWL, Ground Photo Team*

One significant issue for Sub-Saharan African peacekeepers is the political agenda of the contributing government and the potential loss of the key element of impartiality. This occurred in the Congo in 1960 when the Ghanaian government expressed its support for Lumumba. Although the

Ghanaian contingent was able to balance this conflict of interest and function effectively under UN control, the effects of political meddling by the Ghanaian government turned the Congolese government and much of the populace against the Ghanaian soldiers (Baynham: 5). The Kenyan government's support of the Southwest Africa People's Organization during UN Transition Assistance Group (UNTAG) operations, while endearing the Kenyan soldiers to the Namibian people, identified them as a potential enemy to the occupying South African Forces. There were several instances where South African Forces fired on Kenyan peacekeepers (U.S. Office Windhoek). The Nigerian soldiers in Somalia became suspect among the local Somalis due to Nigeria's political ties with ex-Somali President Siad Barre. Based on this political relationship, the Nigerian contingent in Somalia was the target of hostile action on several occasions ("Army Moves").

Truck with mud for camouflage, Rwanda, 1994. *photo courtesy of NIMA ISLWL, Ground Photo Team*

Unfortunately, despite the best intentions of the military, domestic problems greatly influence the military's performance in a UN operation. The Nigerians suffered from this problem in Croatia. Faced with growing domestic animosity toward the Nigerian military government and waning public support over policy in Liberia, the Nigerian soldiers in UNPROFOR found themselves distracted from their mission. They were finally brought home to witness a failed democratic election that was followed by sanctions levied on the government by the U.S. and the UK. Faced with growing internal discontent, Nigeria finds that UN peacekeeping provides a convenient source of employment for the military. This is important because the military does not support the result of the failed electoral process in Nigeria. In a state with a long history of military rule and coups, it is in the best interest of the current government to keep the military employed outside the country ("Kenyan").

During a coup in Ghana, the Ghanaian military did not want to bring home its UNEF II force as the UN mission ended. Instead, the Ghanaian commander, General Erskine, lobbied to have the force moved to Lebanon as part of UNIFIL. Keeping the military occupied is seen as a crucial step in protecting the stability of the Ghanaian government. This use of the military takes its toll. Currently the army has almost half its strength deployed outside the country in UN peacekeeping operations. The Ghanaian army is short on logistics and equipment, and the outflow of personnel in the military is exceeding recruitment ("Briefing").

Another shortcoming in Sub-Saharan African military participation in UN peacekeeping involves both the lack of strategic lift assets and logistical support. This has led to the untimely arrival of a contingent or the inability to sustain itself without outside assistance. In an attempt to solve the organic strategic lift problem, some Sub-Saharan African countries have used their domestic airlines to support the mission of a military contingent in a UN peacekeeping operation. This has been most notable in the Ghanaian government's use of Ghana Airways to transport troops to UNEF II, UNIFIL, and UNTAC. Zimbabwe has also used its domestic airlines to fly in logistical support to Nairobi, Kenya for their contingent in Somalia. However, the use of domestic airlines has significant logistical limitations. Much of the military equipment cannot accompany the troops and the contingent cannot deploy into unsecured airfields. For this reason, the Ghanaian contingent in UNTAC was one of the last to arrive and did so without the required logistical support. In the case of Zimbabwe, the supplies flown into Nairobi could not reach the contingent in Somalia because the military lacked the lift to move it and the civilian airline could not fly into Mogadishu (U.S. Mission to the UN *c*).

Nigeria took almost two and a half months to deploy its contingent to Somalia even with U.S. airlift support. The reason for the delay was that it took the Nigerians that long to assemble a suitably equipped force, not the inability of the U.S. to rapidly supply transport aircraft. One of the problems in the Nigerian military is its lack of standardized equipment. Nigeria has military equipment from over 22 different countries. The bulk comes from Austria, Brazil, France, Germany, the U.S., UK, and the former Soviet Union. Much of the equipment is obsolete and nonfunctional. The troubled Nigerian economy has encouraged corrupt officials to procure weaponry not based on the needs of the military, but for kickbacks and commissions ("Middle East"). For this reason the Nigerian military needed more time to assemble a force, complete with operable vehicles, for the Somali mission (USDAO Lagos).

Even if the difficulties of strategic lift are overcome with outside assistance, contingents often face severe logistical shortages on the ground. The Zambian force in Mozambique arrived without any transport and began to patrol its 300-square-mile sector on foot. Only later was it supplied with trucks from the UN. Other Sub-Saharan African countries, such as Botswana, Ghana, and Zimbabwe have had to make substantial equipment requests to the UN before deploying on a UN mission. Most recently, Ghana has produced an extensive list of required assets it needs to help bail out the UN in Rwanda (U.S. Mission to the UN *b*).

AIDS is a problem in Africa. There is growing concern in Croatia over the deaths of one Nigerian and two Kenyans from AIDs. It is uncertain how many other soldiers are HIV- positive. In general, African countries do not test for HIV, and the UN has been lax in its requirements to test contingents before their deployment. Reliable statistics are unavailable, but it is believed that a large percentage of the military in African countries are infected with AIDS. Many countries are unwilling to accept contingents from highly infected areas, and without proper testing many African countries may be limited to peacekeeping duties inside the continent of Africa.

Racism has also affected African military participation in Lebanon and Croatia. There are indications that the black battalions in UNIFIL were widely resented. It has been asserted that "within the Arab world there exists a profound and institutional racism toward black people" (Heiberg: 26). This was brought to the attention of the Ghanaian government early on in the UNIFIL deployment when a Ghanaian woman working in Lebanon was killed with little reaction from the Lebanese government. The Ghanaian administration saw this as a "generally alarming trend confirming . . . abusive treatment being meted out to black Africans abroad, notably in Lebanon and West Germany" ("Inquiry"). The Nigerians faced the same sort of slander in Croatia from the Croatians. This racism does not necessarily overshadow an entire UN operation, but it is an important criterion to consider when deploying black African forces outside of Africa.

Sub-Saharan African contingents have not been prepared for deployments into colder environments. This was evident in Lebanon with the Ghanaians, and in Croatia with the Kenyans and Nigerians. Each contingent overcame the difficulties, but the initial shock of the colder climate reduced their initial effectiveness in the UN operation ("Kenyan": 6).

One of the biggest shortcomings involving Sub-Saharan African military participation in UN peacekeeping, and directly related to their logistical problems, is money. The poor economies of many Sub-Saharan African countries mean they cannot fulfill their peacekeeping pledges without outside help from the UN or its member states. Zimbabwean relations with the UN have become strained due to this factor. Zimbabwe has felt the financial burden of trying to conduct a UN peacekeeping operation in Somalia without timely reimbursement from UN funds. Zimbabwe's weak economy cannot stand the strain. The Zimbabwean government has told the UN that money will now have to be paid before Zimbabwe participates in any future UN operation ("Minister Criticizes"). Zimbabwe carried out this threat when it refused to send troops to Liberia as part of a UN peace mission, and Zimbabwe also turned down a UN request for an additional 1,000 Zimbabwean troops for UNOSOM when the U.S. withdrew ("Minister: UN Offer").

PROSPECTS FOR FUTURE DEPLOYMENTS

The countries of Sub-Saharan Africa have forces and equipment readily available and suitable for most UN peacekeeping operations. In addition, the centralized nature of many Sub-Saharan governments means that the process of putting a peacekeeping force together and obtaining a decision to commit it to a UN peacekeeping operation is greatly expedited, assuming the UN can provide financial support.

Of the 20 countries of Sub-Saharan Africa that have participated in UN peacekeeping, all are currently capable of providing a battalion-size contingent, with the exception of Liberia. In addition, several countries can provide brigade-size or multiple battalion-size contingents. Many of these countries also have logistical assets to support a battalion-size contingent. However, these assets are generally left at home during a deployment and the UN is expected to pick up the cost, and to supply the necessary logistical support. Limited logistical resources require that the assets be used for forces remaining at home.

The militaries of Sub-Saharan Africa offer a viable and readily available source of peacekeeping forces provided certain resources are available: money, strategic lift, and logistical support. With these resources available, Sub-Saharan African military contingents are highly effec-

	UN Experience	1 LT BN	1 LT BDE	CSSS	Willingness to Participate in Future UN Operations
Botswana	C, O	Y	N	Y	Y — Limited due to small size of Army
Cameroon	O, P	Y	N	Y	Y — Unequipped BN offered and rejected by UNTAC
Cape Verde	O	N	N	N	Y — Observers
Congo	O	Y	N	Y	Y — 300 troops promised for UNAMIR
Ethiopia	C, I	Y	Y	Y	Y — BN promised for UNAMIR
Ghana	C, O, P, I	Y	N	Y	Y — 800 man BN recommitted for UNAMIR
Guinea	C, O	Y	N	Y	Y — BN serving in Liberia with ECOMOG
Guinea-Bissau	O, P	Y	N	Y	Y — BN serving in Liberia with ECOMOG, 200 troops promised for UNAMIR
Kenya	C, O, P, I	Y	Y	Y	Y — May limit its involvement only to African operations
Liberia	C	N	N	N	N — Undergoing a Civil War
Malawi	O	Y	N	Y	Y — Observers
Mali	C, O, P	Y	N	N	Y — 20 military observers in Russia
Namibia	C	Y	N	N	Y — Mine-hardened vehicles of critical value to UN
Nigeria	C, O, P, I	Y	Y	Y	Y — Undergoing internal turmoil over failed elections
Senegal	C, O	Y	N	Y	Y — 300 troops promised to support French efforts in Rwanda
Sierra Leone	C	Y	N	Y	Y — Has promised observers to UNOMIG
South Africa		Y	Y	Y	Y — New government still has not established policy
Togo	O, P	Y	N	Y	Y — Observers
Zaire	C	Y	Y	Y	Y — Unlikely due to internal instability
Zambia	C, O	Y	N	Y	Y — Impoverished military
Zimbabwe	C, O, P	Y	Y	Y	Y — Money up front before committing future combat contingents

1 LT BN = Ability to deploy one battalion on a UN mission
1 LT BDE = Ability to deploy one brigade on a UN mission
CSSS = Military has capability to support a battalion sized contingent with logistical assets

Y = Yes
N = No

C = Combat Contingent
O = Observer/Monitor
P = Civil Police
I = Individual Commander

Sub-Saharan African Military Prospects for Future UN Peacekeeping. *source: author*

tive. They serve best in the austere African environment. They excel in civil affairs operations. They do well in the limited combat operations sometimes experienced in peacekeeping.

Because of the lack of wealth in Sub-Saharan African countries, it is essential that the UN provide adequate funding for the force prior to its deployment. This ensures that the unit takes up its peacekeeping duties fully outfitted. If not, soldiers will often deploy without essential individual equipment. The next challenge is to get the force to the desired location in a timely manner and with its equipment. The lack of strategic-lift assets in Sub-Saharan African militaries means that this support will have to be provided by the UN or a reliable donor country like the U.S. Sub-Saharan African countries have been successful in deploying their troops aboard domestic airlines, but this means that the equipment cannot accompany them. If African domestic airlines are used, the troops on arrival will not be prepared to conduct operations. External strategic lift is still needed to move their equipment. The only alternative is to have the equipment already in theater for their use upon arrival. Sub-Saharan African forces lack the logistical sustainability to conduct long-term operations. This support must be provided by third-country UN logistical units. To ensure success, the logistical mechanisms must be in place before the Sub-Saharan African force arrives.

JAPAN'S ASPIRATION FOR INTERNATIONAL POLITICAL STATUS: A BID FOR A PERMANENT UN SECURITY COUNCIL SEAT

Fae Marie Crissman
Second Lieutenant, U.S. Air Force
August 1995

> Japan is prepared, with the endorsement of many countries, to discharge its responsibilities as a permanent member of the Security Council.
>
> Japanese Foreign Minister Yohei Kono

As a major economic power and the second largest financial contributor to the United Nations, Japan desires a commensurate political role (Woodall: 30). Japan wants a permanent seat on the UN Security Council as the symbol of its new status. Although there had been much talk, Japan's campaign was not formal. On 27 September 1994, Japanese Foreign Minister Yohei Kono formally announced Japan's desire for a permanent seat on the United Nations Security Council in the UN General Assembly (UNGA A/48/PV.7).

The question of equitable representation and expansion of the Security Council appeared on the agenda of the UN General Assembly from 1979 until 1990 without being debated (UN *n*: 211). The increasingly active role of the Security Council in the post-Cold War world has made the item more prominent. In 1991, Japan joined a joint commission with India to expand the Security Council. Together with other aspirants to the Council such as Nigeria and Brazil, they helped bring the issue of reform to the top of the UN agenda. On 11 December 1992 the General Assembly requested the Secretary-General to invite member states to submit written comments on a possible review of Security Council membership (UNGA Res 47/62). Eighty states responded. There was widespread agreement that the composition of the Security Council should be expanded, including the number of permanent seats.

THE CASE FOR A JAPANESE SEAT

Since World War II, Japan has not been proactive in international political affairs, but in the new international environment is prepared for greater involvement in the UN, including a UN permanent seat. Japan justifies its place on the Council on the basis of UN reform to enhance the UN's legitimacy in light of new realities. Japan asserts:

1. The emergence of new global powers, which prompts consideration of a limited increase in the number of permanent seats in addition to the current permanent members;
2. The drastic expansion of the UN membership, which requires consideration of an appropriate increase in the number of non-permanent seats to improve the representativeness of the Security Council; and
3. The imbalance that has emerged in the geographical representation within the council, which suggests that we should redress the overall distribution of seats (UNGA A/49/PV.30: 15).

Enhanced legitimacy of the Security Council will be achieved only if the Council improves its effectiveness by inviting the major powers of the current world order to participate in decisions. Just as the absence of the U.S. contributed to the failure of the League of Nations, Japan feels it is time to reassess the realities in 1995 (Ito).

Permanent membership is a symbol of political power. Permanent members have direct influence on the selection of the Secretary-General, control several important posts in the UN Secretariat, enjoy membership in most key committees and prevent Security Council decisions adverse to their interests with the veto (Ueki: 365). Security Council sessions are often closed, and non-members of the debate get only second-hand information. Permanent membership in the Security Council tremendously increases a state's bargaining power in multilateral institutions in general (Pickert: 91).

Although Japan is a major financial contributor, it must run for a non-renewable non-permanent seat without any guarantee of success. Japan feels there should be "no taxation without representation" (Ueki: 365). Currently, Japan finds out about decisions after the fact and is asked to pay without prior consultation. The best way of obtaining information firsthand is by having a permanent seat on the Council. Further, as a major financial contributor to peacekeeping operations, Japan wants its views taken into consideration before decisions are made to assess the anticipated cost of a peacekeeping operation. It is necessary for Japan to help determine whether to send peacekeeping missions, including their deployment length, size and composition. Providing money without representation is not considered effective. Although Japan's contribution to the UN budget is growing, Japan is not able to take part in key UN decisionmaking (UNGA A/C.5/49/L.30: 3).

Japan's absence from the decisionmaking process makes it difficult for the government to build a basis of support from the Japanese people. This complicates the Ministry of Foreign Affairs' efforts to get support from the Ministry of Finance in bureaucratic politics. The UN needs money from Japan, but the government and people are reluctant to provide funds if Japan has not participated in the decisionmaking process. Japan feels that the bid for a permanent seat is not only in Japan's interest, but necessary for the UN as a practical means of building the base of support to justify to the people payments to the UN (Yokota).

POLITICAL COMMITMENT

Although the Ministry of Foreign Affairs and internationalist Japanese leaders want Security Council membership, there is a lack of clear consensus in the bureaucracy, the Diet and among Japanese people. The recent debate in the Diet on the peacekeeping law, the reluctance of the political leadership to use the Self-Defense Forces (SDF) abroad, and the lack of enthusiasm of Japanese to serve as international civil servants reflect an ambivalence toward the UN. Nonetheless, the Diet passed the *Law Concerning Cooperation for UN Peacekeeping Operations (PKO) & Other Operations* in June 1992 (Cho: 2). The PKO Law authorizes a deployment of up to 2,000 persons, including SDF troops, civilian police, and election observers in two broad categories of UN operations:

(1) potentially dangerous United Nations peacekeeping operations (Shinn: 1-3);

(2) supposedly less risky international humanitarian relief operations and logistical support (Yanai: 45-46).

The law was scheduled for parliamentary review in August 1995. The fragile coalition government deferred consideration, avoiding contentious debate on sensitive issues prior to general elections. Government officials say "it is better to wait till the right moment comes for a full revision of the law" (Hayashi and Hidaka: 16).

Beyond Peacekeeping to Collective Security

Member states are not legally obligated to provide forces, but the power structure of the UN as reflected in the responsibilities of the Security Council encourages it. Collective security functions of the Security Council have prompted considerable debate as to whether Japan should seek permanent membership. Yasuhiro Ueki points out:

> A serious question for Japan is whether Japan can be an effective permanent member of the Council without the capability to enforce actions in the event of an aggression. The main function of the Security Council is to maintain international peace and security. Its duties may entail forcible actions, as is outlined in Chapter 7 of the UN Charter. At present, Japan is not willing to use force except for the defense of Japan. Even the new peacekeeping legislation is not adequate to answer the question since it specifically prohibits the military personnel to use force or threaten use of force in carrying out their duties. The new legislation allows use of small firearms only in self-defense (Ueki: 366).

The internationalists in the Diet and elsewhere in the government argue that the Japanese Constitution allows enforcement of Security Council decisions. In August 1992, a majority-sponsored Diet research committee asserted that participation in a regular UN force is different from the threat or use of force renounced in Article 9 and hence it does not contravene the Constitution. The committee was established to study the future of Japanese foreign policy, and was headed by Ichiro Ozawa, Secretary-General of the Liberal Democratic Party (LDP). The committee comprised elite Diet members interested in defense issues (Pickert: 51-52). Not surprisingly, their report met sharp criticism, with several members complaining it provided a constitutional revision by interpretation (Cho: 10).

UNTAC Military Hospital, Cambodia, 1993. *photo courtesy of NIMA ISLWL, Ground Photo Team*

Professor Yokota of Tokyo University argues that if Japan wishes to be viewed as a respected international player, it must avoid hiding behind the constitution. No one can pretend that Japan does not have military capability to offer the UN (Yokota). Japanese use of force abroad is not a constitutional question, but a political question. If Japan is to continue advocating a non-military role in the UN, it will have to legitimize that course and demonstrate how it is in the world's interest as well as Japan's rather than simply explain how the country is constrained by constitutional limits and other special circumstances. However generous Japan might be, other countries will inevitably distrust Japan if it has no intention of getting in harm's way (Schwartz: 26).

Manpower then becomes a fundamental issue. Although the Self-Defense Forces (SDF), previously ignored by the public, has raised its credibility lately, it does not have full trust of the public because of Japan's military past. Shinnichi Yoshida advocates a separate force for peace enforcement operations, a sort of Japanese special forces. However, there has been little public support for this notion, and most from the SDF are against it (Yoshida).

Non-Military Contributions

Sending soldiers is not the only way to cooperate with the UN. Japan's non-military contributions also offer a measure of political commitment. Involvement in humanitarian activities is a crucial aspect of non-military contributions. Dr. Edward Lincoln argues that if Japan really wants to contribute, then the government should get its citizens into the front lines of humanitarian work. He cites examples such as giving medical care and food to Kurds in Iraq or ministering to the victims of Mount Pinatubo in the Philippines as ways Japan can demonstrate its commitment to the UN's goals (Lincoln *a*: 259).

The appointment of Sadako Ogata to be UN High Commissioner for Refugees is a practical step toward a more positive image. She has provided an important positive role model of an involved person dealing with difficult world issues with which Japanese have been relatively uninvolved in the past. Yasushi Akashi has held very high visibility positions as head of the successful UN mission in Cambodia, but has been severely criticized as head of UNPROFOR in the former Yugoslavia.

UN site at Sisophon, Cambodia, 1992. *photo courtesy of NIMA ISLWL, Ground Photo Team*

Yet Japan's tentative commitment to the UN is reflected through a lack of personnel presence in the UN Secretariat. All multilateral organizations have at least informal geographical quotas which determine how many nationals they will accept from a country, but in 1994 Japan was listed as one of 25 underrepresented Member States in the UN Secretariat, filling only 91 of its 223 slots (UNGA A/49/527: 34). The extremely low level of personnel involvement in the UN leaves the impression that commitment to the goals and work of these organizations is superficial.

According to Mr. Naoki Ito of the Ministry of Foreign Affairs, international civil service is not considered prestigious for Japanese school graduates. Since the salary is low, working for the UN is secondary to government positions or private industry. He further argues that if Japan becomes a permanent member, the Japanese government will increase its interest in the UN. Accordingly, graduates may decide to pursue international organization careers (Ito).

Domestic Environment

Although polls indicate public support for the UN, there has been no significant Japanese domestic debate regarding the issue of a permanent seat. The Foreign Ministry is actively working to shift public opinion and is conducting polls to measure public attitudes ("*Yomiuri Shimbun*": 2-2). The results reflect gradual movement toward greater support for a permanent seat. In January 1994, 53 percent of those who gave valid responses to the survey favored the bid, while in October 1994, following Foreign Minister Kono's speech to the UN, those favoring Japan's campaign increased to 56 percent. However, those opposing Japan's bid also increased from 14.8 percent to 18 percent. Of the 18 percent opposed to a permanent seat in October, 31 percent felt permanent membership would oblige Japan to take part in military activities. However, those who opposed any form of Japanese participation in peacekeeping operations were drastically down from 38.8 percent in January to 8.6 percent in October ("UNSC Seat": 16). These results show a gradual shift toward favorable attitudes to the UN, however, there is still a growing negative opinion on peacekeeping operations. The lack of consensus in the Japanese public leads to caution in Japanese politics. Most politicians agree that Japan should have the permanent seat, but do not agree on what level of contributions to the UN Japan should provide to obtain it (Yoshida). The Liberal Democratic Party (LDP) has doubts about the cost of global responsibility. The Socialists are leery of the use of force under any circumstances.

The use of Self-Defense Forces for UN operations is often a source of friction between the ministries. The Ministry of Foreign Affairs advocates peacekeeping involvement, since it would lead to elevation of Japan's international standing. The Ministry of Finance emphasizes the domestic economy, and fears increased demands for Japanese contributions to the UN budget. This conflict was revealed in preparations for Prime Minister

Hosokawa's speech to the UN General Assembly in 1993. He planned to voice Japan's desire to become a permanent member, but the final speech only referred to "a reformed United Nations" (UNGA A/48/PV.4).

UNTAC civil aviation headquarters, Phnom Penh, Cambodia, 1992.

photo courtesy of NIMA ISLWL, Ground Photo Team

There was a similar confrontation in 1995. The Prime Minister planned to voice his support for Japan's bid for a permanent seat on the UN Security Council to the national Diet on 20 January. However, Finance Minister Takemura demanded the sentence supporting the bid for a permanent seat be removed from the speech. Takemura felt that Japan needed to support UN reform, and through that process build support for permanent membership in the Security Council. Kono, the Minister of Foreign Affairs, wanted to seek permanent membership directly, while at the same time supporting UN reform. In the end, Prime Minister Murayama's speech omitted mention of permanent membership in favor of reiterating Japan's commitment to UN reform, while Kono's speech retained a statement that Japan sought a permanent seat on the Security Council, as well as pledging Japanese support for Security Council reform ("Murayama": 11).

The competing interests among the ministries have root in party politics. The current government is an uneasy coalition between the LDP conservatives, headed by Foreign Minister Kono; the socialists, represented by Prime Minister Murayama; and the Sakigake, led by Finance Minister Takemura. The dynamics of this leadership "pit[s] traditional enemies against each other as the heads of competing bureaucracies, causing clashes and power struggles among ministries" (Pickert: 58).

REVISION OF THE UN CHARTER

Japan may wish to be added as a permanent member but any change in the membership of the United Nations Security Council requires an amendment of the UN Charter. In considering the amendment of the Charter, both the explicit requirements in the Charter and the procedural obstacles which are not a matter of treaty language must be considered. The original Charter, signed in 1945, provided for five permanent members, the U.S., the Soviet Union, the UK, France and China, and six non-permanent members elected by two-thirds of the General Assembly for two-year terms, and not eligible for immediate re-election (Simma: 395). Decolonization in the 1950's brought a great increase in UN membership, resulting in amendment of the Charter in 1965 to increase the number of non-permanent members from 6 to 10, and producing the current 15-member Security Council. A review of the 1965 amendment process provides the best indication of the procedural obstacles which Japan will face in an attempt to obtain a permanent seat on the Security Council.

The first proposal to increase the size of the Council was formally introduced by a group of Latin American states at the 1956 session of the General Assembly. The proposal did not pass the General Assembly until 1963 (Goodrich: 195). The ratification process took two more years and the amendment came into force on 1 September 1965.

The UN Charter specifies the amendment procedure. According to Article 108:

> Amendments to the present Charter shall come into force for all Members of the United Nations when they have been adopted by a vote of two-thirds of the members of the General Assembly and ratified in accordance with their respective constitutional processes by two-thirds of the Members of the United Nations, including all the permanent members of the Security Council.

Thus, amendments develop in two phases. The first phase consists of the adoption of a decision on an amendment by the General Assembly or by a review conference. This decision does not formally amend the Charter. The second phase consists of the ratification of the proposal for an amendment by a sufficient number of member states including the permanent members of the Security Council. There is no time limit set for this process. Only when the amendment is ratified by the members is it legally binding.

Although Charter amendments are binding on all member states, they only depend on a qualified majority. The amendment decision requires a two-thirds vote based on the total number of members of the General Assembly. An amendment must be ratified by two-thirds of the member states, including all permanent members of the Security Council. Single ratifications have no legal effects in and of themselves. If a charter amendment fails to obtain the required number of ratifications, those actually made become obsolete. If it succeeds, however, it is again not the single ratification but the composite act of the Organization under Article 108 that creates legal obligations for the ratifying states. That is why ratifications after the fulfillment of the numerical requirement are legally unnecessary, though they may be important for domestic politics. Since amendments can be blocked by the failure to ratify by a single permanent member, this amounts to the right of veto on behalf of the legislatures of the permanent members. When adopting an amendment, the General Assembly may request prompt ratification and also set a time limit. These provisions are not binding, so that belated ratifications are valid and the amendment process remains open for an indefinite period of time.

Charter amendments, upon entering into force, become binding for all member states, no matter what their position on the amendment in the General Assembly or whether they ratified the amendment. The alternative is withdrawing from the UN altogether. The time at which a Charter amendment comes into force coincides with the deposit of the last necessary instrument of ratification with the Secretary-General. The Charter does not specifically require the permanent members to vote in favor of the amendment in the General Assembly, but each permanent member must ratify it through its constitutional process (Simma: 1070).

JAPAN'S STRATEGY

The Foreign Ministry plan to obtain a permanent seat includes both international and domestic efforts. Aggressive multilateral diplomacy, coordinated with the world's largest foreign aid program, supports the campaign in the international arena. On the domestic front, the Foreign Ministry has gone directly to the public, out-maneuvering other bureaucracies (Yoshida). Because of this, there is a hesitancy on the part of the political leaders to speak out on the issue, which adversely affects Japan's strategy for the seat on an international level. The silence leaves the impression of a lack of domestic political support.

Japan got an important boost for its bid when the U.S. expressed support (P. Lewis *d:* A5). Many Japanese expected the U.S. to win the seat for them. The Clinton Administration's aggressive support brought a backlash from the U.S. Senate based on Japan's unwillingness to deploy forces in support of UN enforcement activities, so the overt diplomatic support has been downplayed for fear of offending the new Republican majority in Congress.

Foreign aid is a very large part of Japan's strategy. Japan is the world's number one aid donor, but Japanese foreign aid is distributed to subsidize specific sectors of the Japanese economy (Orr: 146). The Foreign Ministry wants to give foreign aid to UN members in exchange for support (Yoshida). Thus the shift of aid to the UN campaign antagonizes other ministries which want to support their domestic constituencies.

Emphasis on Japan's quest for Security Council status has caused the Foreign Ministry to downplay another key foreign policy objective. Recognition as a full-fledged member is a major goal for Japan. In this regard, deletion of the enemy states clauses of the UN Charter has been a longstanding objective of the Japanese government (Arts 53 and 107). These clauses allow members to take action against "any state which during the Second World War has been an enemy of any signatory to the present Charter" without the authorization of the Security Council. Even though these articles are considered "dead," they still leave open legal argument for military action against Japan without UN authorization and represent an embarrassing reminder of Japan's past.

These articles may be used by Russia to justify occupation of the Northern Islands as a result of the Second World War. The former Soviet Union was reported to have referred to these articles in bilateral negotiations in 1989 to justify the Soviet position. Japan feels it is a second-class citizen in the eyes of the UN Charter (Ueki: 366). By shifting attention to the permanent seat, the Japanese Foreign Ministry may have traded away deletion of the enemy states clause, a realistic step with visible results, for the much more risky and elusive goal of a permanent seat.

UN MEMBER POSITIONS ON SECURITY COUNCIL EXPANSION

Since the 1963 increase of Security Council membership, the question of equitable representation has been avoided for fear of opening a "Pandora's box." The box is open. In response to the 1992 resolution, the overwhelming majority of Member States submitting responses have called for enlargement of the Council. The majority called for a Security Council between 20 and 25 with some proposals as high as 30. Many issues regarding expansion surfaced, including increasing permanent membership, review of veto power, increasing non-permanent membership, addition of a new category of semi-permanent members and deletion of the enemy states clauses. Each of these issues affects Japan's bid, since, as Malaysia's response stated, "any reform which merely facilitates enlargement, specifically through the increase of permanent membership by one or two or even three seats, to the exclusion of other equally important issues is certainly not acceptable" (UNGA A/49/PV.29: 10). In a veiled reference to Germany and Japan, Mexico commented: "reform cannot be confined to satisfying the aspirations of the new economic powers. That would mean failing the international community" (UNGA A/49/PV.29: 2). The issues which will be discussed below are summarized in the accompanying tables showing Member States' positions. The information was taken from speeches to the General Assembly and from written responses to the General Assembly Resolution regarding the "question of Equitable Representation on and Increase in the Membership of the Security Council." Other tables summarize UN Member positions according to press sources from outside Japan, and separately, according to positions reported by the Japanese press.

Each issue raised by UN members may have both positive and negative aspects for Japan. For example, the support for adding permanent members helps Japan's bid, but since there are several countries vying for permanent membership, Japan must compete for the new seats as well as face the argument from the present permanent members that the Council will become too large to function effectively.

Increase in Permanent Membership

Of the key issues concerning an increase in the permanent membership, perhaps the most difficult is whether the new permanent member should have the veto power. Many members call for the abolition or limitation of the veto. Malaysia urged that the negative votes of two permanent members be required for a veto rather than just one. Mexico referred to the veto as an "undemocratic institution" (UNGA A/48/264: 57). Pakistan said the veto was "contrary to the aim of democratizing the United Nations" (A/48/264: 75). Ukraine contended that the General Assembly ought to have the right to override the Council if action was blocked by one veto (A/48/264/Add.3: 8). Fiji said the right of veto should be limited to Chapter VII actions (A/48/264: 38). Guatemala said the veto was "in direct opposition to the sovereign equality of states" and should be revised or eliminated (A/48/264: 38). Ghana too said the veto was "irrelevant, outdated and probably undemocratic" and should be limited to Chapter VII (A/48/264/Add.3: 6). New Zealand argued against the veto and continues to do so today (A/48/264: 68). Yet Japan feels that it deserves to have the same status as the current permanent members.

There is also the question of the qualification for a new permanent member. The majority feel that a country's "contribution to maintenance of international peace and security" should be assessed. However, there is considerable debate as to what exactly these contributions should entail. Political and financial contributions are enough for some, but a sizable number of members feel "a readiness to commit substantial forces to peacekeeping and peace enforcement" is prerequisite to becoming a permanent member (A/48/264: 69). Clearly Japan will have trouble obtaining support if it continues to fall back on its constitution and extends the "freeze" on peace enforcement operations. Belize, India, Indonesia and Nigeria are among the countries to state "the population criterion is of great importance" (A/48/264: 72).

Many members have pointed to the imbalance on the Security Council between developed and developing countries. Developing countries, 133 members, comprise 72 percent of UN membership and feel they have their right to "their democratic share" (UNGA A/49/PV.31: 6; A/49/527: 72). Vietnam shared this concern that "attention be given to the concerns of the developing countries, which make up more than three quarters of total UN membership" (UNGA A/48/PV.62: 2). Any amendment that includes Japanese representation must accommodate the developing countries' desire for representation.

Non-Permanent Membership

Changes have also been proposed to the nature of the non-permanent membership. Several states, including Argentina, Australia, Canada, Ecuador, France, Ghana, Netherlands, New Zealand, Norway, Slovenia and the U.S., have proposed amending the Charter to allow immediate re-election of non-permanent members. This would allow more frequent representation on the Council for a much broader spectrum of members and therefore will have support in the General Assembly. Italy has proposed a third category of membership on the Security Council. Semi-permanent seats without veto would rotate between two countries in a region. The proposal was for five permanent seats; ten semi-permanent seats that would rotate among twenty members in groups of two; and the remaining ten non-permanent seats (UNGA A/48/264: 51-52). This plan appeals to the small states, which account for 125 members of the General Assembly. It would allow the smaller states to take advantage of non-permanent representation because the major states would be represented by the semi-permanent membership. An increase in non-permanent membership or addition of semi-permanent seats will not satisfy Japan, since it wants international recognition on the same level as the permanent members.

VOTE OF THE GENERAL ASSEMBLY

The issue of Security Council expansion will be debated on a theoretical level in the General Assembly, but an amendment resolution comes down to the affirmative votes of two-thirds of the total UN membership. Many members have tossed their names into the hat for permanent membership. Announced and potential candidates include: Germany, India, Brazil, Mexico, Indonesia, Nigeria, Algeria, Ukraine, Jordan and Egypt. The size of this list in itself complicates Japan's bid, but each of these members has a significant political power base in the regional and special interest groups in the General Assembly.

UN MEMBER OFFICIAL STATEMENTS ON SECURITY COUNCIL MEMBERSHIP FOR JAPAN

	Express support for Security Council expansion with conditions	Support increase of permanent members with conditions	with veto	without veto	contribute to maintenance of international peace and security	Assess political contributions	Larger financial burden	Provide forces	At least 2 vetoes to block resolutions	Population	Equitable balance between developed and developing	Proportional by region	Limited enlargement	Support increase of non-permanent seats	Support addition of non-permanent seats	Support review of veto power	Own representation	Permanent	Non-permanent	Efficiency caveat	Explicit support for Japan as permanent member	Support for Japan as permanent member with conditions	Express no clear position	Remove enemy states clause	Amend Charter to allow non-permanent successive terms
Algeria					a		a				a d	b c		a d	a	c d			e						
Antigua, Barbuda			c d									a	a		a										
Argentina												c		a c d											d
Australia		***		a c d					d				a c d		d						d	****		a d	a d
Austria						a c d	a c d	a d			c		a c d	d	d	c d									
Bahamas							a									a							a		
Bahrain												c													
Bangladesh					d							d				c d									
Belarus					d		d					d		d											
Belgium		*			c	a c	a	a				a d		a c d											
Belize					c		a d		c d	a d			a c d	a c d	a d	c d									
Brazil		a			b d						a d	a d		a b d									c		
Bulgaria					d								d	d					* *		d				
Cambodia																							* **		
Canada					a d								a d	a d	a d								c		a
Chile				a c d	a								a c	a c	a c d	a c d			d		c			a	
China											c d	c	c							ac			d		
Colombia				a	a						a c			a d		a c d									
Costa Rica											a			a		a								a	
Croatia					a				d		d		a d	a d		d					d				
Cuba					a						d	d		a d		a b d									
Cyprus												d													
Denmark					a	a	a	a			a				a										
Ecuador											d	a				a d				a	d				a
Egypt*					a			a			a	a b d	d	a	a c	d									
Fiji				a	a		a	a												a					
Finland						a c	c	a c				c	a c			a				a					
France											d		d							a	d		c		d
Gabon		a***												a											
Germany			d		d							d *		d				a b c d							
Ghana												a d	d	a		d					a				d
Greece				a																					
Guatemala														a		a * *									
Guyana											d				d										
Honduras***			a		d								a d		a d		a d								
Iceland****				a									a d	d											
India			a d		b d	a	a d	a c d		a c d	d	c		a c d											
Indonesia			a*****	a		a	a c	a c		a	b c			c		a c d									
Iran											d	d				c d									
Ireland		a									a	a	a							a			c d		
Italy							b			b				b c	a d			a *							
Jamaica					c							c		c	c										
Japan	c				b d	a	a							a b d				d							
Jordan		a									a		a							a					
Kazakhstan										a			a	a	a					a					

a = Response to General Assembly Resolution
b = Statement to 47th General Assembly
c = Statement to 48th General Assembly
d = Statement to 49th General Assembly

e = Africa
f = North Africa Group
g = Arab

* = Response to General Assembly Resolution was as Chairman of Group of Member States of the Caribbean Community
** = Call for Africa: 1 permanent and 6 non-permanent; Asia: 2 permanent and 3 non-permanent; Eastern Europe: 1 permanent and 2 non-permanent; Latin America and Caribbean: 1 permanent and 3 non-permanent; West and Other: 3 permanent and 3 non-permanent.
*** = Call for 3 additional permanent members for Africa and Asia; 1 permanent for West and Other; 1 permanent for Latin American and Caribbean.
**** = Japanese seat does not preclude additional Asia representation.

UN MEMBER OFFICIAL STATEMENTS ON SECURITY COUNCIL MEMBERSHIP FOR JAPAN (Continued)

	Express support for Security Council expansion with conditions	Support increase of permanent members with conditions	with veto	without veto	contribute to maintenance of international peace and security	Assess political contributions	Larger financial burden	Provide forces	At least 2 vetoes to block resolutions	Population	Equitable balance between developed and developing	Proportional by region	Limited enlargement	Support increase of non-permanent seats	Support addition of non-permanent seats	Support review of veto power	Own representation	Permanent	Non-permanent	Efficiency caveat	Explicit support for Japan as permanent member	Support for Japan as permanent member with conditions	Express no clear position	Remove enemy states clause	Amend Charter to allow non-permanent successive terms
Kenya		**										d		d		d									
Lao People's Dem. Rep.							c						c		c							c			
Libyan Arab Jamahirija													c		a d		a b c d								
Liechtenstein														a											
Luxembourg																					a				
Madagascar																a									
Malaysia														a b d	a	a b c d									
Maldives					c							c		c		c									
Malta													d										c		
Mauritania	a											d													
Mauritius				a									a												
Mexico					a							b		a d	d	a b d									
Monaco														a	a										
Mongolia				a d					a		a d	d	a d	a d		a d					d				
Nepal											d	d	a										c		
Netherlands					d	a c	a	a				c			a b	b					a d			a c	a d
New Zealand					a c	a		a	a c				a d	a c	a c d	c	a d								a d
Nigeria			d		a d		a	a		a d		a b c d		a c d				e							
North Korea											c d	a c d		c d											
Norway													a							a					a
Pakistan	a											b		d		a							c		
Panama												a *				c									
Papua New Guinea		c															c								
Paraguay												a				a									
Peru						a	a							a											
Philippines											d	a c d	a	d	d	a c									
Poland						a	a					a	a							a c				a	
Portugal				a	c									a c											
Qatar														a	a *										
Romania														a							a c			a	
Russian Federation													d	d							a c				
Samoa				a		a			a				a	a											
San Marino															d										
Singapore			a		d		a c	a c	a															a	
Slovenia				c			c					c	c	c										c	c
South Korea					a	a									a		a								
Spain				a	a	a					a		d	a	a c										
Sri Lanka					d							c d	c d	d		c									
Sudan												f				a									
Suriname		a										a		a											
Sweden						a	a	a				a		a						a					
Syrian Arab Republic												d	d			c	c							a	
Thailand					c									c	c										
Tunisia					c						d	d		c d				e							
Turkey													a	a	a c d										

a = Response to General Assembly Resolution
b = Statement to 47th General Assembly
c = Statement to 48th General Assembly
d = Statement to 49th General Assembly

e = Africa
f = North Africa Group
g = Arab

* = Response to General Assembly Resolution was as Chairman of Group of Member States of the Caribbean Community
** = Call for Africa: 1 permanent and 6 non-permanent; Asia: 2 permanent and 3 non-permanent; Eastern Europe: 1 permanent and 2 non-permanent; Latin America and Caribbean: 1 permanent and 3 non-permanent; West and Other: 3 permanent and 3 non-permanent.
*** = Call for 3 additional permanent members for Africa and Asia; 1 permanent for West and Other; 1 permanent for Latin American and Caribbean.
**** = Japanese seat does not preclude additional Asia representation.

UN MEMBER OFFICIAL STATEMENTS ON SECURITY COUNCIL MEMBERSHIP FOR JAPAN (Continued)

	Express support for Security Council expansion with conditions	Support increase of permanent members with conditions	with veto	without veto	contribute to maintenance of international peace and security	Assess political contributions	Larger financial burden	Provide forces	At least 2 vetoes to block resolutions	Population	Equitable balance between developed and developing	Proportional by region	Limited enlargement	Support increase of non-permanent seats	Support addition of non-permanent seats	Support review of veto power	Own representation	Permanent	Non-permanent	Efficiency caveat	Explicit support for Japan as permanent member	Support for Japan as permanent member with conditions	Express no clear position	Remove enemy states clause	Amend Charter to allow non-permanent successive terms
U.A.E.													c					g							
United Kingdom														d							a	d		c	
Ukraine					c								d	c d	a c d	a c									
United Rep. of Tanzania				a									a c		a		a c		e	e					
United States														a c d	d							a d			d
Uruguay							a	a																	
Venezuela		d**												d	a c	a c d									
Vietnam											a c	a													
Yemen												a		a		a									
Yugoslavia												a				a									
Zambia	***				c																				
Zimbabwe			d									b		b d		b d									

a = Response to General Assembly Resolution
b = Statement to 47th General Assembly
c = Statement to 48th General Assembly
d = Statement to 49th General Assembly

e = Africa
f = North Africa Group
g = Arab

* = Response to General Assembly Resolution was as Chairman of Group of Member States of the Caribbean Community
** = Call for Africa: 1 permanent and 6 non-permanent; Asia: 2 permanent and 3 non-permanent; Eastern Europe: 1 permanent and 2 non-permanent; Latin America and Caribbean: 1 permanent and 3 non-permanent; West and Other: 3 permanent and 3 non-permanent.
*** = Call for 3 additional permanent members for Africa and Asia; 1 permanent for West and Other; 1 permanent for Latin American and Caribbean.
**** = Japanese seat does not preclude additional Asia representation.

Source: Compiled by author from multiple sources.

No Statement Available From:

Afghanistan
Albania
Andorra
Angola
Armenia
Azerbaijan
Barbados
Benin
Bhutan
Bolivia
Bosnia & Herzegovina
Botswana
Brunei
Burkina Faso
Burundi
Cameroon
Cape Verde
Central African Republic
Chad
Comoros
Congo
Cote d'Ivoire
Czech Republic
Djibouti
Dominica
Dominican Republic
El Salvador
Equatorial Guinea
Eritrea
Estonia
Ethiopia
Gambia
Georgia
Grenada
Guinea
Guinea-Bissau
Haiti
Hungary
Iraq
Israel
Kuwait
Kyrgystan
Latvia
Lebanon
Lesotho
Liberia
Lithuania
Malawi
Mali
Marshall Islands
Micronesia (Fed. States)
Moldova
Morocco
Mozambique
Myanmar
Namibia
Nicaragua
Niger
Oman
Rwanda
Saint Kitts Nevis
Saint Lucia
Saint Vincent & Grenadines
Sao Tome & Principe
Saudi Arabia
Senegal
Seychelles
Sierra Leone
Slovakia
Solomon Islands
Somalia
South Africa
Swaziland
Former Yugoslav Rep of Macedonia
Togo
Trinidad & Tobago
Turkmenistan
Uganda
Uzbekistan
Vanuatu
Zaire

The Non-Aligned Movement

The Non-Aligned Movement (NAM), 111 countries with 12 observers, comprises a significant majority (66 percent) of UN membership. India, a member of the NAM, led the movement to bring Security Council reform to the agenda of the General Assembly. Accordingly, members of the NAM have a high stake in reform and have "expressed their concern that non-aligned countries were extremely under-represented in the Council and underlined that the proposed enlargement should, therefore, be comprehensive in nature so as to enhance the credibility of the Council and to reflect the universal character of the world body" (UNGA A/49/PV.29: 14). The NAM has stressed that "any predetermined selection excluding the non-aligned and other developing countries would be unacceptable to the Movement" (UNGA A/49/PV.29: 14). India and Indonesia each pose a problem for Japan, since they each want permanent membership and are part of both the NAM and Asian Group. Since 123 votes are needed to pass an amendment resolution, the NAM may block any package which does not accommodate the NAM.

Africa

The end of colonization brought a sharp increase in UN membership with 53 African Member States. Despite this sizable percentage of UN membership, Africa does not have permanent representation. Africa is campaigning for permanent representation and does not endorse the introduction of any new categories of membership. It recognizes and advocates "the continuance of the present arrangement of permanent and non-permanent membership only . . . All permanent members should enjoy the same status and privileges and assume the responsibilities incumbent on membership" (UNGA A/49/PV.31: 19). Africa would not accept the second-class status of a permanent seat without veto. The African Group has enough countries to block an amendment resolution. Japan has increased trade and aid to key African countries.

Latin America

Like Africa, Latin America also comprises a significant portion, 33 members, of the UN without permanent representation. Brazil has also expressed its desire to hold a permanent seat. In addition, Brazil has stated that the "appropriate proportionality between the size of the Council and that of the entire membership of the organization" requires "adequate participation of both industrialized and developing countries in a future expansion of permanent members" (UNGA A/49/PV.29: 23). Any expansion which does not take developing countries into consideration will not be acceptable to many member states, including some of the permanent members.

Asia

As far as the Asian Group (26 percent of UN membership) is concerned, history dies hard. Many Asian countries have been reported in the Japanese press to support Japan's bid, but few have actually endorsed Japan in General Assembly speeches. The Japanese bid may be exploited for domestic political purposes in China and Korea. The fear of Japanese militarism was revived when Japan passed its PKO Law. A Chinese spokesperson said that the PKO Law "runs counter to the spirit of the Japanese Constitution" (Pickert: 79). The Prime Minister of Singapore, Lee Kwan Yew, said in a press conference that allowing the Japanese to participate in military operations was like giving chocolate liqueur to an alcoholic. Offering the most resistance to a militarily active Japan, the North Korean Central News Agency announced that the PKO Law "reflects Japan's wild ambitions to become a military power" (Pickert: 79).

Eastern Europe

The end of the Cold War and breakup of the Soviet Union have caused the Eastern European States, 20 members, to be a group not to be forgotten. The Ukraine is an unofficial candidate for a permanent seat by identifying the need for representation of countries with over 50 million people. Additionally, countries from Eastern Europe stipulate that any enlargement must take into account the interests of all regional groups (UNGA A/49/PV.31: 7).

Efficiency Caveat

Any expansion of the Security Council must accommodate regional representation. Many countries point to the lack of permanent representation for Africa and Latin America, despite their sizable percentages of UN membership. However, there are also a significant number that feel any expansion should be limited, so as not to affect the Council's efficiency. This "efficiency caveat" was used by many of the permanent members in their written submission. Russia maintained that the UN "cannot afford a potentially paralyzing major overhaul of machinery that not only is not broken but is actually functioning smoothly" (UNGA A/48/PV.64: 7). In the General Assembly the abundance of issues and interests means Security Council expansion will become additive politics. Each group will demand support for its interests in return for support for other groups. Japan and Germany with the NAM and each of the regional groups have enough influence to gain inclusion of their seat in the proposed amendment. When all the groups have satisfied each other, the amendment will certainly fail the test of efficiency.

RATIFICATION

An amendment to the Charter does not come into effect until the ratification phase is complete. Two-thirds of the UN membership, including the five permanent members, must ratify the amendment through their constitutional processes. Thus the legislatures of the permanent members have an effective veto over Council expansion.

China

In June 1994, President Jiang Zemin said that despite several changes in Japan's political scene, the cooperation between China and Japan is progressing ("Jiang Zemin"). However, China has not yet clarified its stance on the issue of a Japanese permanent seat. China was a victim of Japan's aggression and expansion before and during World War II. "Whether or not Japan earnestly recognizes its aggression against China during World War II will influence whether or not Japan can become a permanent member of the UN Security Council" ("Jiang Rejects"). The official view of the Chinese government is that the question of reforming the Council is complicated and requires sufficient broad-based exchanges of views among UN members before Japan's permanent council membership can be considered ("Spokesman"). Further, China states that

> in any expansion of the Council, the principle of equitable geographical distribution should be observed and full consideration should be given to the aspirations and interests of the developing countries, which account for the majority of the United Nations membership . . . Practices which might lead to the creation of any new imbalances should be avoided (UNGA A/49/PV.31).

	Angola	Brazil	China	DPRK	France	India	Indonesia	Italy	Libya	Malaysia
1. Oppose increase in permanent members								X		
2. Oppose Japan as permanent member				X						
3. Oppose Japan as permanent member with veto										
4. Support Japan as permanent member	X				X					
5. Support Japan as permanent member w/conditions		X					X			X *
6. Support semi-permanent seats								X		
7. Desire own permanent seat		X				X	X			
8. Express no clear position			X						X	

* In context of total UN restructuring and Japanese participation in military activity

	Netherlands	Nicaragua	Russia	South Africa	South Korea	United Kingdom	Ukraine	United States	Vietnam
1. Oppose increase in permanent members									
2. Oppose Japan as permanent member									
3. Oppose Japan as permanent member with veto					X				X
4. Support Japan as permanent member	X	X					X	X	
5. Support Japan as permanent member w/conditions									
6. Support semi-permanent seats	X								
7. Desire own permanent seat									
8. Express no clear position			X	X		X			

Non-Japanese Press-Reported UN Member Positions. *source: author*

In other words, there is an East Asian seat on the Security Council and China is sitting in it.

The issue of Council reform may be used by China as a way to avoid giving Japan a seat. Additionally, China feels that the wealth of a country should not be the sole condition taken into consideration, and that the principle of fair regional distribution, and the principle of unanimity in consultation should be fully honored in approaching this issue. China reserves the right to make a formal decision regarding changes to the Council until other nations' positions have been surveyed. China hints at support for expansion by giving all members a veto. China may favor a unanimity rule. Thus China, by supporting only fundamental reform and membership for a broad spectrum of Non-Aligned Movement members, supports only reforms which would be unacceptable to the other four permanent members. It is unlikely China will support Japan.

France

When the issue of Council reform was first placed on the agenda, France took a very conservative position. In a response to the resolution on Security Council expansion, France argued that "the Council's effectiveness" is "bound up with the fact that it has a limited number of members, which permits it to achieve compromise and reach decisions reflecting as often as not a consensus agreement within the United Nations as a whole" (UNGA A/48/264: 41). However, France seemed to become more flexible in 1994 when it endorsed Germany and Japan as permanent members "with all the prerogatives and obligations of the present permanent members" (UNGA A/49/PV.30: 17). However, France, like China, has concerns about representation for developing countries and is particularly supportive of its former colonies in Francophile Africa: "An increase in the representation of the more advanced countries must not create an imbalance that operates to the detriment of the developing world. This means that if Japan and Germany were to join the Security Council as permanent members, a seat should be given to the developing countries to preserve a desirable balance" (UNGA A/49/PV.30: 17). France endorses a Security Council membership of 20 and immediate re-election of non-permanent members.

Russia

Like China, Russia has not stated a clear position concerning Japan's bid. Russia reiterated the permanent members' catch phrase that "the most important condition for any steps that might be taken must be the strengthening of the Security Council's newly acquired energy and operational effectiveness" (UNGA A/48/264: 82). Indeed, Russia has advocated a limited expansion of up to 20 seats while maintaining the status of the present permanent members (UNGA A/49/PV.31: 10). Russia has taken the position that when expanding the UN Security Council "the principles on which this should be done ought to be determined first, and only then should specific candidates be discussed" ("Panov Views").

Although Japanese press reports Moscow's support for Japan's campaign to become a permanent member, this has not been confirmed by Russia's official statements ("Official"). Although Russia says it does not link this issue to the signing of a peace treaty with Japan, the two issues may, in fact, be very closely related ("Panov: Moscow"). Russia's vote may be very expensive.

	Angola	Argentina	Australia	Bangladesh	Bolivia	Brazil	Caribbean Countries	Chile	China	Costa Rica
1. Express support for Japan as permanent member		X	X	X	X		X	X		X
2. Support Japan as permanent member w/condition	X*					X**				
3. Support Japan as semi-permanent member										
4. Express no clear position									X	

* Support Japan in conjunction with bids of developing countries
** Desire support for own permanent seat

	Croatia	Ecuador	European Union	Fiji	Finland	France	Great Britain	Hungary	Indonesia	Ireland
1. Express support for Japan as permanent member	X	X	X	X	X	X	X	X	X	X
2. Support Japan as permanent member w/condition										
3. Support Japan as semi-permanent member										
4. Express no clear position										

	Italy	Laos	Macedonia	Malaysia	Mongolia	Nepal	New Zealand	Pakistan	Paraguay
1. Express support for Japan as permanent member		X	X	X	X			X	X
2. Support Japan as permanent member w/condition							X*		
3. Support Japan as semi-permanent member	X								
4. Express no clear position						X			

* Without veto

	Philippines	Russia	Singapore	South Korea	Sri Lanka	Thailand	Turkey	Uganda	Ukraine	United States
1. Express support for Japan as permanent member	X	X			X	X	X	X	X	X
2. Support Japan as permanent member w/condition										
3. Support Japan as semi-permanent member										
4. Express no clear position			X	X						

Japanese Press-Reported UN Member Positions. *source: author*

United Kingdom

The UK's initial reaction to expansion was similar to that of France and Russia. While welcoming debate, the UK cautioned against "precipitate action" that "might diminish the Council's effectiveness" and emphasized the need for "a Council which remains able to respond rapidly and effectively" (UNGA A/48/264: 90-91). Like France, the UK relaxed its view, stating "if consensus can be reached certain countries, by virtue of their global interests and their contribution to international security and to United Nations operations, should be invited to accept the responsibilities of permanent membership. In that context, we would support the permanent membership of Japan and Germany" (UNGA A/49/PV.31: 4).

United States

In its written response to the General Assembly resolution, the U.S. asserted the status of the five current permanent members "should remain unaltered" and yet supported permanent membership for Japan and Germany. The U.S. was prepared to consider a modest number of additional seats (UNGA A/48/264: 91-92). In 1994, the U.S. explicitly endorsed permanent membership for Japan and Germany and an increase of 3 non-permanent seats for a total membership of 20, allowing immediate re-election of non-permanent members (UNGA A/49/PV.29: 23-24).

Ratification takes place in the legislative branch. In July 1994, the U.S. Senate attached an amendment to the Foreign Operations Appropriations FY 1995 Bill, asking that "Japan take whatever steps are necessary to enable it to fully engage in any form of UN peacekeeping or peacemaking operation" and "the U.S. should actively support Japan's efforts to gain permanent membership only after Japan takes such steps" (H.R. 4426). Although Japan feels the use of force abroad is a different issue than permanent membership on the Security Council, this clearly is not the feeling in the U.S. Congress. Even though Japan feels the Congressional language is not binding, one of the requirements for amendment to the Charter is ratification by each of the permanent members in their constitutional processes, that is, the U.S. Senate. In general, Japanese trade policies are not well-regarded, especially in the U.S., but it is difficult to tell if this will become an obstacle in the campaign for a permanent seat (Lincoln *b*). The current trade tensions could cause the economic relationship between the U.S. and Japan to boil over into the security arena.

In summary, diplomats from France, the UK and the U.S. have given qualified endorsement of Japan's membership; however, there may be significant opposition within the U.S. Congress and other legislatures. Russia's dispute over the Northern territories may prevent ratification. The people of the UK and France still remember World War II well, and there is a long-standing animosity between China and Japan. Accordingly, an amendment may be blocked from coming into effect if the legislature of any permanent member does not ratify. The ratification phase could take many years and the legislature of a permanent member could simply do nothing, thereby blocking it without directly opposing it.

JAPAN'S PROSPECTS

This issue is an issue which has the conclusion at the beginning.

Shinnichi Yoshida, Deputy Editor, *Asahi Shimbun*

The Search for a Suitable Package

Japan's success is dependent upon a multitude of variables. The necessary first step is the political process in the UN. Many proposals have been put forth by member states. There are several possible outcomes for this issue in the UN:

1. No amendment of the Charter;
2. Amendment with a new category of seats;
3. Amendment increasing non-permanent members;
4. Amendment including additional permanent seats with veto; and
5. Amendment for fundamental reform of the Council.

Non-amendment reform requires the least amount of change and is the most likely to occur. Each of the following options requires more complex amendments to the Charter and is progressively less likely to occur. The final option, fundamental reform, is the least likely because it requires such radical change.

No Amendment: Most Likely

Due to the enormity of the task of reforming the Security Council, one possible outcome is much debate without change. There are so many issues, it will be difficult to obtain a consensus. However, reform is possible without requiring an amendment. One example is Professor Louis Sohn's proposal of "dual seating." Two non-permanent seats would be given to Africa, Asia, Central and South America and the Caribbean, Eastern Europe and Central Asia, and Western Europe and the remaining states. One of these seats would be given "semi-permanent" status and would rotate every two years. The alternate semi-permanent member would be able to participate in the discussion without vote in the period the other semi-permanent member held the seat (Hoffmann: 49).

This proposal requires no amendment to the Charter and merely amends the procedures of the Council. It gives the larger states in each region more recognition, but reduces the smaller states' chances of being elected to the Council. It is criticized as being unfair to the South, since it gives greater weight to European countries like Poland, Italy and Ukraine than might otherwise be the case. It also ignores the problem of the permanent seat distribution (Hoffmann: 50). Although it has disadvantages, some change in Council procedure is likely since it does not involve the complex process of amending the Charter.

Amendment with a New Category of Seats: Possible

There have been many proposals for variations of the current structure of Security Council membership. Australia proposes allowing successive terms for non-permanent members and the creation of eight quasi-permanent seats, allocated among regional groups, together with 10 rotating non-permanent seats which would account for a total membership of 23. In addition to keeping the number of permanent members at five, Italy proposes increasing the number of non-permanent members from 10 to 20. The 10 new seats would be allotted, in turn, to a group of 20 or eventually 30 Member States. This guarantees the continuous presence in the Council of current permanent members and at the same time allows a more frequent presence for 20 to 30 mid-size to large-size countries. The plan also provides more access for the smaller states to the 10 non-permanent seats (UNGA A/49/PV.29: 8-9).

The differentiation in permanent status will be a major factor in the rejection of Italy's proposal. Australia's model gives consideration to maintaining an appropriate balance between permanent to quasi-permanent or non-permanent members and allows rotation of membership of large and small countries (UNGA A/49/PV.31: 12). This proposal is more realistic, but the "second-class" status will not be acceptable for African and Latin American countries who want the same status enjoyed by the current permanent members.

Australia alternatively proposes the creation of five new permanent seats without veto, allocated with three new permanent members coming from Africa and Asia, one from the Group of Western European and Other States, and one from Latin America and the Caribbean. Yozo Yokota, Professor of Law at Tokyo University, says a compromise, even though not satisfying all needs, may be a starting point. The current permanent members would retain their veto status. An intermediate category would be introduced allowing five permanent seats without veto or seats that would be elected for a longer term of five years with the possibility of re-election. The non-permanent seats would be increased by 5 to allow better regional representation for a total Council size of 25 (Yokota). Although this proposal is not the perfect solution, this plan includes the greatest amount of compromise for everyone involved. A package such as the one suggested by Yozo Yokota may have a chance, since it accommodates the regional groups. Even though Japan may not be as happy with this scenario, it will give Japan the permanent status it wants. It also protects the veto power of the current permanent members.

Amendment Increasing Non-permanent Members: Unlikely

Another option is expansion similar to what took place in 1965. The current permanent members would keep their status, and the number of non-permanent seats would be increased to allow more equitable representation. Although this option appeals to the current permanent members, this scenario is unlikely, since it does not satisfy any of the major regional powers. Africa and Latin America will settle for no less than permanent seats in any reform.

Expansion with Additional Permanent Seats with Veto: Unlikely

The U.S. endorses an increase of two permanent seats for Japan and Germany with veto. Furthermore, the U.S. supports 3 non-permanent seats for a total Council membership of 20. The U.S. proposal of adding Japan and Germany alone as permanent members will not be acceptable to countries in Africa or Latin America, since they will still have no permanent representation. Additionally, the U.S. proposal still does not answer the question of involving developing countries in the decisionmaking process.

Fundamental Reform: Least Likely

One academic proposal is a weighted system of voting for the election of all Security Council members. Another fundamental reform proposes the creation of quasi-permanent seats with 10-year renewable terms using UN financial contributions and regional population ranking for selection (Hoffmann: 51-63). Although these proposals provide rational ways for the election of members of the Security Council, they are probably too big a leap from the present system. The renewable-term system allows for future economic and population changes, so that the Charter does not have to be amended every time the international atmosphere shifts. Although this proposal is certainly credible, it is also asking the permanent members to relinquish their power if they cease to satisfy the criteria, which is asking the impossible.

There is no quick-fix answer that will satisfy the desires of the entire General Assembly. The package should increase non-permanent seats for regional representation. The number of permanent seats needs to be kept to a minimum to keep the Security Council effective. Although the permanent members agree to a very limited increase, they will not go along with some of the proposals due to the dilution of their power. On the other hand, the developing countries will not be content with a limited increase by giving Japan and Germany permanent seats. Because of this quandary, it is unlikely that a compromise package will be reached soon.

JAPAN'S DIPLOMATIC AND POLITICAL TASK

Japan's Assets

Japan has many things to offer the UN. It is an economic power to be reckoned with and has the largest foreign aid program. Additionally, Japan is the second-largest financial contributor to the UN budget and has many ways of furthering UN goals. A highly professional diplomatic corps with world-wide representation for Japan also supports large permanent missions at the UN. Japan has extensive trade relationships with private contacts in most countries. Finally, Japan has been carefully building up political capital in the UN.

Japan's Liabilities

The Prime Minister and Cabinet must be enthusiastic campaigners to win support from the public and from UN members. They are riding the fence on this issue. There is a need for a domestic political consensus. The public is actually ambivalent. The working level in the Foreign Ministry is engaged in the campaigning, but this will not be effective without the support and lobbying efforts of the top-level officials. Additionally, Japan lacks an extensive personnel presence in the UN Secretariat to lobby. Although personnel involvement ultimately depends on the willingness of Japanese citizens to work in these organizations, the Japanese government can do a great deal to encourage such participation. Japan thinks it is making its intentions clear with statements in the General Assembly, but the government is often pro forma in presenting its bid.

Japan's primary reason for obtaining a permanent seat is to demonstrate its role as an international political player. Japan's view that participation in Chapter VII enforcement action using the Self-Defense Forces is unconstitutional has its roots in deep-seated domestic political struggles. Although Japan has many non-military options to offer the UN, it will not be viewed the same as human contribution to military operations by UN members.

Japan does not really have a long-term strategy to obtain the permanent seat. By going for the long shot of permanent representation on the Council as its first move, Japan is overlooking a gradual step-by-step process by increasing personnel presence in the UN Secretariat and deleting the enemy states clause. Shinnichi Yoshida suggests that Japan should be focusing on the deletion of the enemy states clause. As Yoshida points out, "a hunter chasing two rabbits won't catch either one" (Yoshida).

PROMISES, PROMISES AND THE BOTTOM LINE

Security Council reform is unlikely to occur in this century or the beginning of the next. There is no consensus on the composition of a reformed Council. Japan has chosen a very difficult goal to achieve. Japanese proposals are transparently self-servicing and conflict with reform which might achieve consensus in the General Assembly. Japan advocates a Security Council membership in the low 20s as the optimal size. Japan also endorses Germany as a permanent member. It is open to other permanent members from developing countries if they have the global reach and the ability to discharge the responsibility. "As a matter of principle, the Japanese government feels there shouldn't be two categories of permanent membership," so Japan wants veto power (Ito). The exclusive club Japan wants to enter will have no members.

The highly-caveated endorsements of the permanent members are vague. The present permanent members are not happy with a large increase, because then it would be much more difficult to obtain the majority it takes to pass a resolution. They agree to a size of 20-23, not more. They set conditions for reform. The permanent members are likely to encourage clients and allies in the General Assembly to push contradictory proposals for reform which reduce the chances for consensus packages. If permanent members are added to the Security Council, it is in the best interests of the current permanent members not to create a new category of permanent membership.

Many members who aspire to permanent membership have expressed support for Japan with strings attached. If Japan agrees to support these countries' bids, the package deal would create Pandora's box, exceeding the limits of members for the efficiency test set by the permanent members.

For most UN members, explicit endorsement for Japan as a permanent member costs nothing. In some cases, "we support Japan's bid" may mean that a country understands or empathizes with Japan's position. Although the member understands why Japan would want a permanent seat, that country may not necessarily endorse Japan at the expense of another preferable solution. In this light, it is understandable there is a significant difference in the number of countries supporting Japan as reported by the press and those in speeches to the General Assembly. Willingness to consider "reform" may just be a cover. By proposing "reforms" which are unacceptable to important constituencies in the UN, a country may say it supports Japan's campaign while knowing most certainly it will not have to vote on the issue. In the end, the members know they will only have the choice of voting in favor of a consensus reform proposal which may or may not accommodate Japan's aspiration.

Japan's constitution is not really an issue in the General Assembly. The members will vote on a consensus proposal, not the specific case of Japan. Japan has enough multilateral support to have its membership included in a package deal. However, the constitution may be an issue in the ratification of the permanent members in their legislatures. The issue is highly political, especially in the U.S., China and Russia.

Instead of embarking on an isolated permanent seat for Japan, it would have been in Japan's best strategic interests to support Council reform in general. A well-thought-out plan for reform, which takes into consideration the views of the developing countries, African and Latin America groups, and preserves the veto prerogatives of the current permanent members, has the best prospects for success. After a suitable package is agreed upon, then Japan would be able to push for a consensus proposal, rather than solicit support for itself. This process would produce a much larger Council than the current permanent members may tolerate. This massive Security Council will lead to inefficiency, and it will be unacceptable to the permanent members. They may then refuse to ratify. Only the political pressure of virtually the entire UN membership might cause them to concede. The 1963 amendment was, in the end, ratified.

IMPLICATIONS

There are two outcomes for Japan's quest for permanent membership on the UN Security Council: success, meaning permanent representation but not necessarily the veto, and failure. A seat on the Council would grant the international status Japan desires and access to the UN decisionmaking process in the collective security functions of the organization. With a veto, Japan would have the discretion to prevent UN action adverse to its interests and considerable leverage in the process of formulating Security Council decisions. Without the veto, Japan would play an enhanced role in multilateral dynamics of the Security Council, but would have to rely on the diplomacy of coalition and consensus-building to achieve its objectives. Japan would be required to move between the military and economic great powers and the regional leaders of the underdeveloped world to maximize its ability to support its policy objectives.

Permanent membership on the Council would also bring an expectation of greater international responsibility. The passive foreign policy of the past will have to be abandoned for a more decisive approach. Japan will be forced to vote on sensitive issues, whereas in the past ambiguous statements have allowed them to avoid taking sides. Japan will be expected to assume a greater political, economic and even military role. Since Japan will have been elected to the Council on the basis of its economic power, the bill will come due in even greater contributions to international organizations.

On the other hand, the most likely outcome is no consensus amendment, no vote on the issue in the General Assembly, and no seat for Japan. Rejection of the Foreign Ministry's argument in both the domestic and international arenas will produce a backlash. The status-conscious Japanese public and bureaucratic elite are likely to use Japan's failure to withdraw their current tentative support for a more active foreign policy in exchange for a more passive approach. As the second-largest contributor to the UN, Japan's failure will erode the domestic political base for increased funding for the UN.

Japanese success or failure adversely affects U.S. interests. If the General Assembly votes in favor of an amendment giving Japan a seat, the U.S. Government will be in an awkward position. The U.S. Senate has already put Japan on notice that it will not approve a Security Council seat unless Japan modifies its position on deployment of troops in support of UN enforcement action. The potentially acrimonious debate in both the U.S. Congress and the Japanese Diet would be detrimental to the U.S.-Japanese relationship.

If Japan obtains a permanent seat, it will almost certainly be part of a package deal which greatly expands the Council. This will make the task of U.S. multilateral diplomacy much more complex. An expanded Council will make it significantly more difficult to obtain the majority needed to pass Security Council resolutions, and the resolutions which are passed are likely to be watered-down to accommodate the interests of more members. Obtaining Japan's vote for U.S. initiatives may require extra pressure, straining Japanese relations.

On a bilateral level, the U.S. has little to lose if Japan fails to gain a seat. The U.S.-Japan Security Treaty and the broader alliance are strong, and Japan's disappointment will have only temporary and marginal effects. However, in the past few years, Japan has provided significant financial support to the UN and international organizations, taking up the slack as U.S. contributions decline. The expected reduction in Japanese support to international organizations as a result of Japanese rejection will reduce the UN's ability to carry out many of the humanitarian and developmental objectives the U.S. supports.

THE PEACEKEEPING MISSION OF JAPAN'S SELF-DEFENSE FORCES

Steven E. Maceda
Second Lieutenant, U.S. Air Force
August 1996

JAPANESE PEACEKEEPING

Japan has created the second-most powerful economy in the world from the ashes of its World War II defeat. Along the way, it established a small but effective military to counter the threat of Soviet invasion. The Japan Self-Defense Forces (SDF) lost this Cold War focus in the early 1990s and experienced a downturn in popularity. Diminished public support resulted in lower quality recruits and a corresponding drop in morale. The SDF and its parent organization, the Japan Defense Agency, had long been second-class citizens in the Japanese government. The removal of the SDF's *raison d'etre* caught the SDF in a vicious cycle of apathy and neglect. Recently, though, Japan's international aspirations have given the SDF a new mission: peacekeeping. Although controversial, peacekeeping is now an appropriate and beneficial mission for the SDF.

The United Nations (UN) has become a shaping force in the so-called new world order, and peacekeeping operations (PKO) are an important tool in the UN's international security kit. Japan has adopted an increasing PKO role since the 1991 Persian Gulf War, reversing the SDF's downward spiral. Public support has rebounded, and SDF is now even more proficient than it was during the Cold War. This rebirth has had its price, however. Domestic political concerns over the legality of Japanese participation in PKO, an underdeveloped command and control structure, resource limitations, and debate within the SDF have limited the extent of Japanese involvement in UN operations. Although barriers to an expanded PKO arrangement still exist inside and outside the military, it is in the SDF's interest that Japan aggressively pursue additional PKO responsibilities.

YESTERDAY'S POLITICS

Following World War II, Japan focused its national energy on economic and commercial growth while keeping itself out of international security affairs. American military strength sheltered Japan from outside aggression. This "neo-mercantilist, neo-isolationist, low profile, low risk strategy" came to be known as the Yoshida Doctrine, after former Prime Minister Shigeru Yoshida (Yasutomo: 323). Without distractions, Japan became the economic power the world knows today.

Japan satisfied its security needs with the U.S.-Japan Security Treaty, signed in 1952 and revised in 1960. This treaty continues to be the backbone of Japan's national security policy. The treaty guarantees American aid should a foreign power attack Japan. Japan needs to commit its own military force only if American bases in Japan fall under direct attack. In addition to the promise of U.S. conventional military force, Japan also nestled snugly under America's nuclear umbrella. The security granted by America led some to argue against the need for the SDF, if not its legality: What purpose did the tiny SDF serve if the U.S. would defend Japan?

Japan's insular view of the world also grew from the belief that regional and global international organizations make effective security instruments. Japan has long allied itself with the UN, proclaiming a UN-centric foreign policy in 1957 (Ueki: 348). Although Japan continued to rely on the U.S. for its security needs, Japan felt that the UN was the proper forum for its diplomatic activity. Japan wanted to maintain friendly relationships across the world to further its own commercial interests. As Japan's economic power grew, so did its interests on the international stage and its responsibilities to the world community. International consideration of Japan's desire for a permanent seat on the UN Security Council (UNSC) reflects its growing role in world events.

In 1992, Prime Minister Kiichi Miyazawa specifically stated Japan's intention of gaining permanent UNSC membership (Inoguchi *a*: 336). Ryutaro Hashimoto, who replaced Socialist Tomiichi Murayama as prime minister in January 1996, also believes that the UN structure needs updating. In his inaugural address, he spoke of gaining a permanent UNSC seat "on the basis of reforms achieved in the United Nations"—reforms guided by Japan's "crucial role" (Hashimoto: 23). To accomplish its goal, Japan is portraying itself as a leader in international affairs and as a nation capable of carrying out the duties of a great power. Only of late, however, with the institutionalization of PKO, has Japan taken its first small step toward fulfilling its responsibility.

Japan began to address the PKO issue in the wake of the 1991 Persian Gulf War. Its failure to provide troops to the international coalition arrayed against Iraq earned it criticism from many nations, including the United States. The 100-member medical team promised by Japan never fully arrived, with only 17 people mustering for duty (Blaker: 22). Although Japan did send a minesweeping contingent to the Gulf, this flotilla did not deploy until after the cessation of hostilities. Rather than send armed forces to the desert, Japan opted to shoulder a large portion of the warfighting bill, contributing some $13 billion to the UN coalition (Ministry of Foreign Affairs of Japan: Sec. 1/2). It soon found, however, that financial contributions to the "new world order" were not enough, especially considering Japan's reliance on Persian Gulf oil. Former Liberal Democratic Party (LDP) General Secretary and reform leader Ichiro Ozawa addressed this in *Blueprint for a New Japan*, arguing that both monetary and personnel contributions toward international peace and stability are in Japan's best interest (Ozawa: 94).

Political ambiguity left the Japanese government's hands tied in 1991. Lacking established procedures for aiding UN missions, the risk-averse bureaucracy reacted with characteristic hesitation (Blaker: 1-42). Japan's leaders, like America's, must consider public opinion when deciding their country's official response to any crisis. Just as U.S. politicians strive to gain public support for a decision to send troops to a hostile region, Japanese leaders must be cognizant of public opinion. Japan also faces the much more fundamental issue of the very legality of participation in an international military effort.

TODAY'S CONTROVERSY

Article 9 of Japan's constitution is at the core of Japan's domestic PKO debate. This section of the Constitution renounces war and the use of force to settle international disputes. It may also be interpreted as forbidding the very existence of the SDF. In this context, Japan's reluctance to send troops to PKO is understandable. However, the radical shifts in international power structure since the end of the Cold War necessitate change if Japan is to continue as one of the world's most powerful countries.

The legal basis of continuing SDF participation in PKO and the problems inherent in today's world raise the issue of constitutional reform. Although Article 9 is not the only area of the Constitution discussed for possible amendment, it is the most contentious (*Japan Echo*). The idea of reform of some kind is becoming acceptable in Japan, as witnessed by the acknowledgment that the Constitution is not a perfect document and is subject to revision as situations change ("Yomiuri": 24). A poll by Japan's leading newspaper, *Yomiuri Shimbun*, showed that support for revision rose from 23 percent in 1986 to 50 percent in 1993. Those opposed to Constitutional amendment fell from 57 percent to 33 percent over the same period (*Japan Echo:* 6).

Ken Moroi outlines three prevailing schools of thought relating to the future security of Japan. The first calls for Japan to act autonomously with regard to its defense. The second wants a strengthened and updated Japan-U.S. alliance. The third is for a UN-centered strategy. Regardless of which path Japan chooses, Moroi feels that Article 9 must be addressed directly. Either it should be amended, or it should receive a new official interpretation. The status quo is simply too inefficient. For pragmatic reasons, he thinks that Japan should use the reinterpretation method. The amendment procedure required by the Constitution is too time-consuming. The world community, and the Japanese people, would like to see the issue resolved soon, but the government itself is holding up the process. Reinterpretation would take less time than an amendment and still address the problem created by the Constitution's ambiguous language. However, the nature of the controversial issue keeps the politicians from acting (Moroi: 15).

Such bureaucratic inertia caused Ichiro Ozawa, one-time Secretary General of the LDP, to press for reform within his party, and later to form his own group, the New Frontier Party. Ozawa wrote in *Blueprint for a New Japan* that the Constitution needed amendment. He wants to add a third paragraph to Article 9, explicitly stating that the renunciation of war and the prohibition on war potential does not ban participation in international operations such as PKO (Ozawa: 110).

THE CONSTITUTION AND THE MILITARY: CREATING THE SELF-DEFENSE FORCES

> Aspiring sincerely to an international peace based on justice and order, the Japanese people forever renounce war as a sovereign right of the nation and the threat or use of force as means of settling international disputes.
>
> In order to accomplish the aim of the preceding paragraph, land, sea, and air forces, as well as other war potential, will never be maintained. The right of belligerency of the state will not be recognized.
>
> Article 9, Japanese Constitution

Japan must fight, or at least address, its own Constitution when attempting to send SDF personnel outside the country. Article 9, above, seemingly prohibits the existence of the SDF. The law remains open to interpretation, however, with strict constitutionalist opponents interpreting the document in the most idealistic sense, and arguing against the SDF and its mission since their inception in 1954. Proponents of the SDF argue that Japan, as a sovereign nation, maintains the right of self-defense, and therefore can possess armaments limited to the minimum necessary for such operations, including PKO. Left-of-center parties raised constitutionality questions about the small minesweeping contingent sent after the Gulf War. Such political haranguing has surrounded the article for decades.

Recipe for Ambiguity: Writing Article 9

Even under the pacifist Constitution, Japan has had a military force since 1950, when it was known as the National Police Reserve. Today, without formal amendment to the law, the SDF is among the most modern armed forces in the world. The post-World War II Constitution, especially Article 9, now shows signs of old age. Constitutional re-evaluation is necessary if Japan truly wants to assume the responsibilities of a great power, especially as UN-sponsored PKO become more important.

James Auer describes the writing of Japan's Constitution in his 1993 article "Article Nine: Renunciation of War." Following World War II, the Supreme Commander for the Allied Powers, General Douglas MacArthur, had his staff prepare a draft constitution for Japan. MacArthur originally intended Japan to have no military capability —even for self-defense. The staff guidance he presented for the first draft of the Constitution said, in part, "Japan renounces [war] as an instrumentality for settling its disputes and even for preserving its own security" (Auer: 71).

MacArthur's staff amended this draft and presented the Japanese government a revised version, similar to the present Article 9. This left some room in the wording of the document for interpretation. The ambiguity increased as the Constitution faced review in Japan's House of Representatives. An amendment committee, chaired by Hitoshi Ashida, examined the Constitution. The committee suggested that the phrase "aspiring sincerely to an international peace based on justice and order" be added to the start of the first paragraph, and that "in order to accomplish the aim of the preceding paragraph" begin the second section. Ashida explained that these changes made the Constitution more emphatic by explicitly stating Japan's sincerity. The final version of the Constitution went into effect on 3 May 1947 (Auer: 73).

Ashida later stated that the amendments made by his commission had the express purpose of allowing Japan to organize a military for self-defense. MacArthur wrote in his memoirs that he had always intended Japan to have self-defense capability (Auer: 72). Regardless of their original intentions, both soon saw Japan develop a military capability.

What Changed: The Birth of the SDF

Following passage of the Constitution, Japan's government interpreted it to mean that Japan reserved the right of self-defense but that the maintenance of armed forces was illegal. Cold War realities and pressure from MacArthur soon forced Tokyo to rethink its position. In 1950, Japan organized a National Police Reserve (NPR) under the direction of MacArthur. The U.S. wanted Japan to provide a measure of rear area security for U.S. bases, and the Korean War's proximity to Japan necessitated some means to defend the country and to "supplement regional, national and municipal police forces: (Wada: 118). This organization drew officers and men from the old Japanese Army. The staffer in charge of NPR organization, Colonel Frank Kowalski, said that the sole purpose of the NPR was to pave the way for an overhauled Japanese army. Prime Minister Shigeru Yoshida, famous for the "Yoshida Doctrine" of placing economic growth as the first national priority, said that such development required Constitutional reform (Auer: 75).

The National Police Reserve evolved into the National Safety Forces (NSF) in 1952, with the addition of a maritime component and strengthening of the land forces. The NSF had its genesis in the peace treaty between the U.S. and Japan, signed in 1952. This treaty presupposed that Japan would begin to take some responsibility for its own defense (Wada: 123). As a transition organization, the NSF underwent another change in 1954, when Japan passed the Self-Defense Forces Law, and the National Safety Forces became the SDF.

The SDF gradually improved its capabilities under four successive defense plans between 1954 and 1976, and by that time comprised 180,000 soldiers, 770 aircraft, and a fleet totaling 214,000 tons (Wada: 118). Tokyo justified the continuing military expenditure by separating unconstitutional "war potential" from acceptable "self-defense potential." The official government interpretation of the Constitution expanded, from the immediate post-war's complete renunciation of any military capability, to the right to acquire power commensurate with the "minimum needed for self defense" (Yoshihiko: 21).

The SDF now has the second largest defense budget in the world, although it remains near one percent of Gross Domestic Product ("The Compass": 9). Japan has more military personnel than the U.S. in the Western Pacific (Auer: 83). Recent passage of the *Law Concerning Cooperation for United Nations Peacekeeping Operations and Other Operations* (the PKO law) enabled Japanese troops to deploy overseas and participate in UN operations. The seemingly inexorable march toward a modern military faced considerable opposition at home, however, both in the judiciary and the Diet, and the issue remains politically sensitive today.

How It Changed: Court Battles

This expansion of power was not effortless. Japanese courts heard four major cases between 1959 and 1977 that pushed the issue of SDF Constitutionality to the front page. Although these cases threatened to upset the basis for the SDF's existence, the Supreme Court in each case avoided the question while maintaining the status quo. In the 1976 issue of *Law in Japan,* Hideo Wada recounts the early struggle for SDF existence.

The Sunakawa Case

Wada begins by describing the Sunakawa decision. In the 1950s, Japanese activists began protesting the construction of U.S. military bases on Japanese soil. One group interfered with activity at the Tachikawa U.S. air base outside the city of Sunakawa, near Tokyo. At their trial, the defendants claimed that the U.S. military was constitutionally prohibited from being in Japan. The trial court's decision had four parts. First, and most basic, it said that although Article 9 does not prohibit self-defense, it does deny Japan's ability to produce war potential for this purpose. Second, the court held that Article 9's enactment was based on the decision of the government to seek security under the UN, and that any Japanese security measures must be undertaken by a UN agent. Third, because the U.S. troops in Japan are under American command, Japan, as a result of U.S. actions, may find itself part of a war it did not want to fight. Finally, the trial court ruled that the government's consent in allowing U.S. forces to be stationed in Japan violated the war potential clause of Article 9 (Wada: 121).

Wada goes on to say that Japan's Supreme Court overturned this decision. It decided that although war potential is forbidden under the Constitution, the right of self-defense allows Japan to "take such measures necessary for self-defense in order to maintain its peace and security and preserve its existence." The court felt that Japan could not rely on the UN for defense purposes. This reason validated the Japan-U.S. security arrangement and meant that foreign troops stationed on Japanese soil do not constitute war potential. The Supreme Court, however, avoided the issue of SDF and military constitutionality by ruling that since the SDF law was passed according to constitutional procedure, and the SDF had already come into being, the question was not subject to judicial review (Wada: 122).

The Eniwa Case

In 1967, a case involving two brothers who cut firing range telephone wires came to trial. The defendants were charged with damaging articles used in connection with military defense. Although the court ruled that the phone lines did not represent military equipment, and thereby avoided a ruling on SDF constitutionality, the prosecution's arguments outlined the government's position on this issue.

Wada describes this stance, saying the prosecution contended that self-defense was a basic right of the state, and, as such, the military capability to exercise this right is a necessary condition of sovereignty. Limits on the size of the SDF are a function of the spirit and intent of the Constitution, and the government had responsibility not to overstep these boundaries. Since the SDF law provided only for defensive armaments to be used in self-defense, it clearly fell within the realm of constitutionality. The prosecution restated the Sunakawa idea of constitutionality based on mere existence of the SDF (Wada: 124-125). Although the SDF remained justified as a *fait accompli*, it met a head-on challenge in 1973.

The Naganuma Case

Under the 1967-71 buildup plan, the SDF built a Nike air-defense missile site on Hokkaido. A suit against the government followed since the site was on a forest preserve. Auer succinctly describes the facts surrounding the case. Illegal construction of a military base damaged the environment, the plaintiffs contended, and the government would stand trial. In 1973, the local district court declared the SDF to be unconstitutional. The court agreed that Japan did maintain the right to self-defense, but that self-defense did not presuppose military capability. The court felt that diplomacy, police action, and various nonmilitary activities provided sufficient self-defense (Auer: 80). The court debunked the government's position of constitutionality based on SDF existence by saying "each country in the modern world maintains troops and military force as necessary for its defense, and under the position of the government, we are led to the rather odd conclusion that none of these countries possesses war potential" (Wada: 126).

On appeal, the Sapporo High Court reversed this decision, stating that the plaintiff had "lost interest of the suit," as the government had rectified the damage done to the forest preserve. The High Court said that the Constitution prohibited aggressive laws, but that since the SDF law was not in and of itself aggressive in tone, the court could not answer the constitutionality question. In 1982, the case reached Japan's Supreme Court, which affirmed the decision of the High Court while dodging the Article 9 controversy (Auer: 81).

The Hyakuri Base Case

The last significant Cold War case involving the SDF and the Constitution is described by Auer. As SDF expansion continued through the 1970s, the government began to purchase land for new bases. One farmer sold his plot not to the government, but to a private individual opposed to the military buildup. After the buyer did not pay, the farmer joined forces with the government, and sued to get his land back. The defendant claimed that the government's case was invalid because SDF unconstitutionality prohibited construction of the base. In 1977, the Mito District Court ruled that self-defense was constitutional, that the SDF did not violate Article 9, and that the question of SDF existence should be left to the political apparatus, not to the courts (Auer: 81). The Hyakuri Base matter never appeared before Japan's Supreme Court.

The End of the Cold War

Japan's highest court never directly addressed the issue of SDF constitutionality. Although the initial Naganuma ruling attempted to do so, the highest courts consistently avoided a definitive ruling. Cold War politics forced much of this situation on Japan. The threat of Soviet aggression overshadowed internal problems, and Japan's relationship with the U.S. guaranteed that the SDF would remain a modern military machine.

Though Japan's courts avoided answering the question of Article 9 during the Cold War, the court system now confronts the issue almost daily. Recent bilateral discussions with the U.S. regarding regional contingency operations and the expansion of the PKO mission guarantee another Article 9 controversy. However, Japan is unlikely to make fundamental changes to its constitution, and will rely instead on further reinterpretation of Article 9, according to the political climate of the time (Takai *b*).

Left-wing opposition groups traditionally choose the strict interpretation of Article 9, which denies the SDF's constitutionality. This argument rings hollow because the SDF's court battles and its long history have gained it a niche, albeit a tiny one, in Japan. The Social Democratic Party (SDP) recently dropped this objection, to become a part of a coalition government. Understanding that they will not abolish the SDF, the SDP and other left-wing groups have other, more compelling arguments (Yamaguchi: 163).

Some of this reasoning is outlined in *Japan Echo's* 1993 essay on Constitutional revision. The SDF was chartered to provide only the minimum needed for self-defense, and its use of force has traditionally been limited to only what is necessary to protect Japan from direct attack. Active participation in UN operations entails the possibility of using force—peace-enforcement operations being the best example. In these instances, Japan itself is not under direct attack, and therefore the SDF is not justified in using its military strength (*Japan Echo*: 6).

The Constitution prohibits Japan from using force against other nations. Since PKO and other UN operations require sending troops to foreign shores, Japan would be using force against belligerent parties. This also goes beyond the bounds of the "minimum necessary for self-defense." When SDF personnel deploy, they are breaking the law merely by leaving Japan. However, left-wingers concede that the Constitution does not explicitly prohibit PKO.

Proponents of Japanese PKO involvement argue that peacekeeping is consistent with Article 9. They do not ignore charges that the SDF is inherently unconstitutional, but the power of Japan's bureaucracy effectively insulates most claims of this nature. America's position in favor of the SDF also deflects criticism within the government. Susumu Takai, an expert on PKO and professor at the National Institute for Defense Studies in Tokyo, doubts that the government will act quickly to defuse the Article 9 controversy. The current government does not want to reopen this politically sensitive issue, and will not do so until a crisis forces its hand (Takai *b*).

The government feels that Japan's participation in PKO is justifiable under the Constitution. Ozawa, in his book, outlines his idealistic view of peacekeeping, which is shared to some degree by the current government. Since Japan is built on trade and commerce, international stability is critical to the country's survival. Fighting disrupts business, and therefore negatively affects Japan's security. Using the SDF for PKO constitutes a use on behalf of Japan's defense (Ozawa: 94). Although this argument stretches the facts somewhat, it is not the best argument the government has to offer.

Ozawa goes on to say that although Article 9 does prohibit Japan from using force against other nations, PKO do not represent a Japanese use of force, per se. When Japan participates in a PKO, it is doing so under UN auspices as a member of an international coalition (Ozawa: 107). Japan legally agreed in principle to these operations in 1956, when it became a member of the United Nations (Ogata *a*: 30). The Diet approved signing the UN Charter, binding Japan to the ideals of the international community.

PKO are not unilateral strikes against other nations. Military operations taken in accordance with Chapter VII of the UN Charter, such as Operation DESERT STORM and the current NATO mission in the Balkans, are not acts of aggression by one state against another. Ozawa therefore feels that PKO do not violate the Constitution's prohibition against the use of force. Rather, Japan is acting as an active, responsible member of the community of nations, as represented by the UN (Ozawa: 110). This is a shift from the relatively passive foreign policy Japan followed during the Cold War. Japan's new-found assertiveness required a vehicle for participation.

THE PKO LAW

Although still faced with a constitutional quandary in the early 1990s, Tokyo needed to take action on PKO to show its resolve to the international community. Political leaders found a way to allow the SDF to join UN forces overseas by passing a special law in 1992 that permits the military to operate overseas provided that the operation in question meets certain criteria. Japan passed the *Law Concerning Cooperation for United Nations Peacekeeping Operations and Other Operations* in June 1992. It went into effect in August of the same year. This law sets forth the preconditions necessary for deployment of the SDF overseas (Takai *a*: 110).

Passing the Law

The law is a compromise between the positions of the LDP and Socialist parties, and, as such, all parties find it lacking in some regard. The Socialists think the law goes too far in allowing SDF involvement, and the most extreme left-wingers still consider the entire law unconstitutional. The LDP feels the law is too restrictive in its application. Some extreme right-wing groups oppose the law on the grounds that Japan loses sovereignty through participation in UN operations (Yanai: 33-75). The law, originally scheduled for review in late 1995, remained too politically sensitive for the bureaucracy to deal with directly. No side felt it could put together a solid enough coalition to guarantee passage of a revised law. As a result, the law was not reviewed as originally scheduled. Today, the law remains in legislative limbo.

The Five Principles

Currently, SDF participation is tightly bound by the PKO law's five conditions describing permissible operations. Only after these criteria are met may the SDF be deployed to a UN operation. Although they are not perfect, Japan continues to use them as its basis for policy. Revision of the principles is an important part of the current review. These five conditions are:

(1) There must be agreement on a cease-fire among the parties to a conflict;
(2) The parties to the conflict, including the territorial state(s), shall have given their consent to the deployment of peacekeeping forces and to Japan's participation in the force;
(3) The peacekeeping forces shall maintain strict impartiality, not favoring any party in the conflict;
(4) Should any of the above requirements cease to be satisfied, the government of Japan may withdraw its contingent; and
(5) The use of weapons shall be limited to the minimum necessary to protect the lives of Japanese military personnel (Takai *a*: 110).

The first condition precludes Japanese involvement in any "peace" operation other than peacekeeping. For instance, peace-making and peace-enforcement missions are excluded because the involved UN force is inserted into a hostile environment to actively restrain fighting parties. This prevented Japan from becoming a player in the United Nations Protection Force in Bosnia, and keeps Japan out of ongoing operations such as the United Nations Force in Cyprus. Socialist objections to the unconstitutional use of force placed this clause in the bill. The LDP considers the clause excessively restrictive and would like to expand the range of Japanese PKO activities.

Requiring the consent of all parties involved alleviates the concern that SDF personnel will engage in the use of force against another country, since all have agreed to the SDF's presence in the particular mission. If everyone concerned agrees that Japan's participation is justified, then the risk of conflict decreases. This condition also arises from Japan's need not to be perceived as an aggressive state, especially in Asia. The memory of the Second World War and occupation lingers on in the region, and manifests itself politically on occasion. For instance, Japan lost the 1978 election for an Asian nonpermanent UN Security Council seat to Bangladesh

(Ueki: 365). More recently, Japan has been involved in a territorial dispute with Korea over tiny islands in the Sea of Japan. However, the country is slowly recovering from its warlike reputation. In September 1992, Japan sent a 600-strong engineer battalion to the United Nations Transitional Authority in Cambodia (UNTAC). Although reaction from Southeast Asian countries was favorable, China and Korea still harbor doubts about Japanese intentions (Yanai: 65). Even today, the SDF cannot operate east of Bangladesh without arousing at least some suspicion (Inoguchi *b*).

The intent of the impartiality clause is to keep the SDF out of combat by maintaining its neutrality. It also attempts to give Japan the "moral high ground" through the implication that Japan is an objective observer. This is an important step in projecting an image of forthrightness to the other countries, especially in Asia. This principle also denies Japan's ability to participate in missions, such as peace-enforcement, where SDF troops may be forced to take sides in a conflict.

The fourth condition means that Japan can unilaterally withdraw the SDF from PKO if the mission evolves into peace-enforcement. This is a concession to domestic politics: The Japanese people do not want blood spilled overseas. Here, Japan is acting similarly to the U.S. Press coverage and casualties combine to degrade popular support for the government very quickly, as the U.S. learned in Somalia. Some fear that this clause weakens Japan's will and encourages violent action against deployed SDF personnel.

The "minimum necessary for self-defense" argument comes out again in the last principle. Fearing that SDF units would be drawn into firefights, Japanese leaders placed responsibility for the decision to use force in the hands of the individual SDF member, rather than with the unit commander. Although designed to prevent armed confrontations between SDF personnel and other parties, the restrictions placed on SDF leaders led to problems in command and control, discussed in more detail below (Takai *b*).

PEACEKEEPING OPERATIONS

Japan applied the PKO law almost immediately. The first test of the law came when Japan sent troops to the United Nations Transitional Authority in Cambodia (UNTAC) in late 1992. In addition to the Cambodia operation, Japan has dispatched SDF contingents to PKO in Mozambique and the Golan Heights, and also to the International Cooperation for Rwandan

Refugees mission based in Zaire. The Japanese have taken care to learn from each operation and apply the lessons to their current activities. All of these missions have been conducted under the terms of the PKO law.

Cambodia

The UN established UNTAC in February 1992 to aid Cambodia's transition from civil war to elected government. Over 20,000 UN peacekeepers from 42 countries participated in the operation. UNTAC's mandate included the following missions: supervision and monitoring of cease-fire and demilitarization operations; verification of the withdrawal of foreign armies; supervision of the Cambodian administrative organizations; assistance in land mine removal; repatriation of refugees; reconstruction of infrastructure; and preparation and management for general elections. Japan sent military observers, election monitors, civilian police, and an SDF engineer unit to Cambodia under the PKO law. Japan participated in UNTAC from September 1992 to September 1993 (Ministry of Foreign Affairs of Japan: Sec 2/8).

UNTAC headquarters, Phnom Penh, Cambodia, 1992. *photo courtesy of NIMA ISLWL, Ground Photo Team*

The military contingent numbered 608 people. A 600-man engineer battalion served a six month tour, after which a similar unit replaced it. Likewise, the eight SDF officers sent as military observers rotated out of country after six months. When added to the 75-member police force and 41 election monitors, 1,332 Japanese deployed to Cambodia. Though no SDF members became involved in hostilities, one civilian police officer was killed in action and four were wounded on 4 May 1993 (Yanai: 62).

The PKO law immediately ran into problems because it did not contain authorization for the SDF to have officers assigned to the UNTAC staff. This hindered support from UNTAC and led to problems with intelligence and liaison between the SDF engineer battalion and UNTAC headquarters. Andrew Kim describes one of the major difficulties this presented to the SDF engineers. Although the SDF had planned for deployment to the river country of eastern Cambodia, inadequate coordination with UNTAC staff resulted in the battalion's dispatch to Cambodia's mountainous southern region. The unit initially did not have the equipment needed for this terrain. On an *ad hoc* basis, the SDF engineers began to receive shipments of supplies appropriate to the hills (A. Kim: 28). Japan learned from this mistake, and took steps in subsequent operations to improve coordination.

The 600-member SDF battalion was to repair Cambodian equipment and facilities. This mission expanded as UNTAC activities increased. The SDF became responsible for the provisioning of UNTAC polling station officers and staff. While most of the newly assigned tasks fell within the purview of the PKO law, others had not been explicitly mentioned in the legislation. The cabinet applied a clause allowing it to approve additional tasks, and the engineers continued to operate (Yanai: 68).

Japan regarded its UNTAC experience as positive, and felt growing confidence in its ability to operate overseas. The country received praise from UN Secretary General Boutros-Ghali for its efforts, and public support for further SDF deployments increased (Ministry of Foreign Affairs of Japan: Sec 2/10).

Mozambique

Following a 14-year civil war, factions in Mozambique signed a cease-fire agreement in October 1992. In December of that year, the UN created ONUMOZ—United Nations Operation in Mozambique—to monitor the cease fire and observe elections. A small SDF contingent deployed with ONUMOZ from May 1993 until the operation's conclusion in January 1995 (Ministry of Foreign Affairs of Japan).

Applying a lesson from UNTAC, the SDF sent five SDF officers to ONUMOZ headquarters to act as planners for the overall transportation mission in Mozambique. This facilitated the operation of Japan's 48-member movement control company. The company was responsible for "technical matters on transport" including resource allocation and customs assistance (Ministry of Foreign Affairs of Japan: Sec 2/9). The liaison officers remained in Mozambique for one-year tours, while the other SDF personnel rotated out after six months. The length of ONUMOZ required two liaison changes and three larger moves, meaning that a total of 154 SDF members deployed to Mozambique (Yanai: 63). ONUMOZ included a total of 3,941 troops, plus 204 military observers and 918 civilian police, so the Japanese contingent represented only a small percentage of UN personnel (UN 1). However, ONUMOZ demonstrated Japan's increasingly assertive PKO role.

Rwanda and Zaire

The PKO law also allows for participation in other UN activities, such as the International Cooperation for Rwandan Refugees conducted by the UN High Commissioner for Refugees (UNHCR). The Japanese government sent an investigative team to the Rwanda-Zaire-Tanzania region at the request of High Commissioner Sadako Ogata. On 12 August 1994, Japan announced that its team recommended an SDF deployment ("SDF Support": 5). The government acceded to the UNHCR request, and on 1 September 1994, then-Prime Minister Murayama ordered the SDF to begin preparations for humanitarian operations in Zaire ("SDF Ordered": 3). The relative speed of Murayama's decision caught the SDF unprepared for the mission, and resulted in inadequate planning and preparation (Takai *b*). Final approval for the mission came on 13 September 1994, as up to 470 SDF personnel were authorized to participate ("Government": 7).

Japan sent 283 Ground Self Defense Force (GSDF) members to Goma, Zaire, near the Rwandan border, to build sanitation and medical facilities. An air component including 118 Air Self-Defense Force (ASDF) personnel went to Nairobi, Kenya, to provide a supply ferry service to the GSDF in Zaire. Coordination with the overall UNHCR mission came from 22 liaison officers. Again, the inclusion of dedicated liaison personnel marked a determination to avoid the mistakes of UNTAC. This humanitarian assistance mission remained in the field from September 1994 until December 1994 (Ministry of Foreign Affairs of Japan).

Egyptian-made grenades, Rwanda, 1991. *photo courtesy of NIMA ISLWL, Ground Photo Team*

A potential for serious political fallout also existed in Zaire. Since the UN Security Council did not pass a resolution approving the mission, the SDF technically was not part of a UN operation. The SDF deployment to Africa was a unilateral Japanese effort. However, the Japanese press and public did not focus on the issue, apparently viewing UNHCR's call for help as a UN stamp of approval (Takai *b*). Fortunately for the government, no serious incident occurred, saving Japan from embarrassment.

The Golan Heights

UNDOF, the United Nations Disengagement Observer Force, was born on 31 May 1974 to oversee the separation of Israeli and Syrian forces. UNDOF has been in place for more than 20 years, with its mandate extended every six months by the UN Security Council. Until Security Council resolution 338(1973), which calls for a just and durable settlement in the Middle East, is implemented, UNDOF will remain in the region (UN *k*).

The Japanese government began to study possible UNDOF participation in November 1994 ("Survey Team": 10). The socialist government of Tomiichi Murayama, which entered office in June 1994, did not want to participate because of the possibility that an SDF contingent in the Middle East might have to use force. The UN subsequently dropped its request that Japan assist a Canadian logistics battalion already on station in the Golan ("UN Not to Seek":5-6). Despite this setback, Japan's government continued its study.

Almost a year after the initial inquiries, on 25 August 1995, Japan decided that it could legally send SDF personnel to the Middle East, under certain conditions. Although the political situation was shifting toward the right, Murayama and his Social Democratic Party (SDP) managed to extract some concessions from its coalition partners. The SDF would not transport weapons or ammunition, could not remain in the Golan for more than two years, and would not become involved in activities directly related to combat ("Coalition": 3). The SDP felt that any SDF deployment without these conditions would violate the PKO law ("Cabinet Approves": 4).

The possibility that the SDF might need to use force continued to concern the SDP. In October 1995, the SDF explained that Japanese weapons in the Golan would face strict controls. The Japanese government would need to authorize the use of force on a case-by-case basis, even in emergencies ("SDF Official": 16). The SDP and its conservative LDP coalition partner continued to bicker over the role of weapons in PKO. When LDP leader Ryutaro Hashimoto took over the premiership in January 1996, Defense Agency Director-General Hideo Usui suggested that the arms-use rules would be reviewed before the deployment ("Japan: Usui": 16).

The SDF began to deploy to the Golan on 31 January 1996, sending a 14-man advance team to conduct liaison with the Canadian battalion being relieved. Additionally, two civilian officers went to UNDOF headquarters, once more reflecting the lesson of UNTAC. The advance team was part of a 43-member transportation company that will rotate out after 6 months ("Japan: Peacekeepers": 21). A 60-member ASDF team will fly C-130 aircraft to the Golan twice a year to deliver supplies (Ono). The Canadians officially turned over their transportation duties on 12 February 1996 ("Japan: Peacekeepers": 21). Although the Murayama government had decided that the SDF would not remain in the Golan for more than two years, there is now talk about lengthening the mission and possibly undertaking additional logistics duties (Ono).

CONSTRAINTS

The scheduled review period for the PKO law passed with no legislative activity, and the law remains in effect. The deployment of the UNDOF contingent is a *de facto* affirmation of the law's validity. The law was also specifically referenced in the April 1996 Acquisition and Cross-Servicing

Agreement (ACSA) between the U.S. and Japan, further reinforcing the law's legitimacy. ACSA will allow Japan to participate in a wider range of activities and on a larger scale.

In each of the SDF deployments, the primary focus has been on transportation and infrastructure support. This is a Japanese strength, and a logical reason for Japanese PKO participation. As world-wide PKO become more important and Japan becomes more involved in UN operations, it may find itself in a situation with insufficient domestic logistics support. This would exacerbate the already high tension in the government and public concerning the constitutional issues involved in Japanese PKO.

To date, Japanese PKO have been very small operations because of political and resource limitations. The resources available to the SDF prohibit the mounting of a large-scale operation of any kind, while political restraints hamper the ability of the SDF to function effectively under some circumstances. The SDF also has command and control problems. The coordination and jointness espoused by the U.S. military has not yet become part of SDF culture. Despite these problems, the SDF has seen an upswing in morale and in the quality of troops since expanding its PKO role.

Japan has a shortage of lift assets for deploying its troops abroad. As desirable as lift might be for PKO, appropriations are constrained by the constitution. However, Japan will acquire a 9,000-ton landing ship in Fiscal Year 1997. This is significant because the ship has been upgraded from 2,000 tons in initial planning to four and one-half times its original design size. The larger ship will allow SDF peacekeepers to transport their equipment to the field more efficiently, and thus enable more effective operations. The ships used to transport the engineer battalion to Cambodia were too small for the mission. According to Lieutenant Colonel Hiroshi Hayashi, UNTAC veteran and SDF spokesman during that operation, the new ship will be a great improvement for the SDF (Hayashi).

Japan also lacks long-range airlifters and air refuelers. The C-130 aircraft used to support the operation in Goma, Zaire, had to stop several times for fuel while en route from Japan. Japan did not have adequate intelligence and weather information on the intermediate stops, taxing the ASDF's capability to operate. Acquisition of new U.S. planes such as the

C-17 would certainly increase the SDF's deployment ability, but such assets can be perceived as having a war-making potential, and political sensitivity virtually prohibits Japanese procurement.

To make up for this deficiency, Japan has in the past asked the U.S. to provide additional lift capacity for PKO, but the U.S. has never agreed to these requests. In the case of Zaire, for instance, the U.S. was not able to spare C-5 airlifters to transport GSDF troops to Goma. The Japanese government leased Russian Aeroflot planes instead (Inoguchi *b*). These aircraft, flown by civilians, ferried the GSDF troops to Africa. The Acquisition and Cross-Servicing Agreement is a formal attempt to rectify Japan's lift shortages while avoiding political controversy over acquiring war potential.

THE ACQUISITION AND CROSS-SERVICING AGREEMENT (ACSA)

As President Clinton prepared for his summit visit to Japan in April 1996, American and Japanese diplomats in Tokyo concluded an arrangement designed to allow SDF and the U.S. military to exchange logistic supplies and services during training exercises and peacekeeping operations. This is not a new step for the SDF and American forces, who have provided each other logistic support on an *ad hoc* basis for years. ACSA, signed on 16 April 1996, is the codification of a long-standing relationship. America has similar understandings with over 20 countries and international organizations.

Although not a treaty subject to ratification by the U.S. Senate, it is a binding executive agreement. This makes it more concrete than other defense accords, such as the Five Power Defense Agreements between the UK, Australia, New Zealand, Singapore and Malaysia. ACSA begins by describing its purpose. The agreement promotes "close cooperation" and enables the Treaty of Mutual Cooperation and Security to function more effectively. Peacekeeping operations (PKO) and humanitarian assistance missions are explicitly mentioned in the preamble, establishing these as a feature in ACSA application ("Agreement Between the Government").

The relative importance of PKO under ACSA is a matter of some contention. Professor Takashi Inoguchi, Senior Vice-Rector at the United Nations University in Tokyo, points out that PKO is merely a sidelight of ACSA, not the agreement's main focus (Inoguchi *b*). Professor Fumiaki Nishiwaki of Japan's National Defense Academy echoed this view, adding that some people in the government were surprised to find PKO mentioned in ACSA (Nishiwaki). Tetsuya Shimauchi, a Senior Research Fellow at the Institute for International Policy Studies, says that ACSA is difficult to apply for PKO outside the area immediately around Japan. Although ACSA does not explicitly forbid its use away from Japan, the government of Japan would take a "long time" to decide if ACSA could be used in this type of situation (Shimauchi; Suzuki).

Article I of the agreement points out the larger framework within which ACSA operates. Again, PKO and humanitarian missions are referenced, and bilateral exercises and training are added as another element of ACSA. The UN Charter is specified as the overarching guide for ACSA application. Significantly, Article II, paragraph 3 states that whenever Japan provides logistic support to U.S. units engaged in UN peacekeeping missions, Japan's PKO law will govern the procedure. The specificity of this clause contrasts with the intentionally vague wording used elsewhere. This suggests a sensitivity on the part of both governments to the ongoing political issue of PKO in Japan. The mention of the PKO law also validates the law's continued applicability, even though its review is not yet complete.

Articles II and III go straight to the heart of the agreement and establish the categories of logistic support, supplies, and services that are covered under the agreement. Although ACSA mentions 15 categories covering a wide spectrum of military support, paragraph 3 of Article 11 specifically states that ACSA does not include ammunition. In the spirit of its pacifist Constitution, Japan banned arms exports to avoid the risk of escalating international conflict. The exclusion of ammunition from ACSA was necessary to ensure that the accord does not challenge Japanese law. However, the Japanese left still criticizes ACSA for allowing the transfer of spare parts for weapons.

ACSA commits neither party to action by stating, "when either party requests the other party to provide logistic support . . . the other party, within its competence, may provide the logistic support, supplies and services requested" (Art II, para 1). This means that neither side incurs any obligation should a situation arise where it is not politically expedient to trade supplies. Contingencies such as an outbreak of hostilities on the

Korean peninsula do not appear to be covered under the present interpretation of ACSA. Secretary of Defense William Perry stressed this point at the joint news conference following the ACSA signing ("Japan: Joint": 5). He wanted the Japanese people to feel that Japan was not committed to the supply of U.S. troops in a potential Korean War. However, there is discussion about the breadth of ACSA's mandate, and some still harbor the belief that ACSA marks another step in the breakdown of Japan's Constitution. The Ministry of Foreign Affairs maintains that ACSA is not the proper framework for logistic support during contingency operations.

ACSA, under Article VI, also prohibits either party from transferring supplies and other support to any third party. This prevents ACSA from being used as a tool for illicit sales. Only the written consent of the providing party can negate this provision. Article VI makes the hypothetical movement of supplies from Japan to South Korea extremely unlikely. Yet some members of the Japanese left still fear the possibility of third-party transfers.

The day before the signing, Chief Cabinet Secretary Seiroku Kajiyama discussed these two points as they relate to Tokyo's ban on arms exports. Kajiyama said that limiting support to only U.S. forces which act in concert with the UN Charter, "firmly upholds" the principle of avoiding international conflict ("Japan: Chief": 16-17). The supporting procedural agreement attached to ACSA articulates the understanding that all transfers will be made consistent with the laws of both nations.

ACSA dictates only that any supplies, services, or other support be repaid in kind to the providing party. Monetary reimbursement is an alternative, but this is not the preferred method. This seems to be an attempt to keep ACSA transactions from becoming points of contention in trade discussions. For instance, Article IV makes clear that neither party may levy excise duties on support provided under the agreement. The procedural agreement, signed at the same time as the larger ACSA, lays out the methods for making payment and determining the cost of services and supplies.

ACSA was designed as a long-range accord. The initial term is 10 years, after which it is automatically extended for additional 10-year periods. The longevity written into the agreement is potentially very important, especially when applied to PKO. The long duration of ongoing peacekeeping operations, coupled with increased participation by both parties, raises the likelihood of ACSA-governed logistic support being applied to a single operation for an extended period.

Party Politics and Governmental Opinions

At the April 1996 summit, the U.S. and Japan agreed to review the security situation in Northeast Asia. Planning for contingencies in the region is a central part of the updated U.S.-Japan security arrangement. As examples of emergencies, Prime Minister Ryutaro Hashimoto used massive refugee flows, refugee rescue operations, and operations requiring use of non-Japanese airports ("Japan: Government": 11-12). The question of cooperation comes with any discussion of dealing with these contingencies. Since no legislation fully defines "emergency," there are still some questions about ACSA's application in such a situation.

Some within the government would like to use ACSA as a framework for logistic support to contingency operations. On 25 April 1996, three days after Hashimoto's statement, Defense Agency Vice Minister Naoaki Murata said that joint training may take place during an emergency ("Japan: DA Vice Minister": 6). This changes the previous government position, reported on 10 April 1996 that joint exercises "normally do not happen during an emergency" ("Japan: Main Points": 10). Murata's statement opens the door toward using ACSA in a Korean or Taiwan Straits scenario via the joint training clause. He said that until an emergency is encountered, the application of ACSA to that situation cannot be determined. Murata qualified his remark by saying that the SDF cannot conduct exercises with the U.S. if the operation would violate Japan's ban on the use of collective self-defense ("Japan: DA Vice Minister": 6). The following day, Defense Agency Director-General Usui told the press at a news conference that "Japan-U.S. joint training will not be held as normal during emergencies" ("Japan: Defense": 6). Usui's damage-control-style statement was published in the 26 April 1996 evening edition of *Nihon Keizai Shimbun,* which had carried Murata's statement in its morning edition.

Japan's largest political parties, the LDP and its reluctant coalition partner, the SDP, have different views on ACSA's application. Both parties agree that ACSA is valid during peacetime joint training and PKO. Both also agree that ACSA forbids the shipment of weapons and ammunition to American forces. LDP Secretary General Yoshinori Ono said that the transfer of arms would "without a doubt, infringe on the Constitution of Japan," but he felt that Japan could act to provide logistics support and medical care if U.S. forces operating out of Japan came under fire ("Japan: LDP Official": 11). Reiterating this view, LDP Policy Research Committee Chairman Taku Yamasaki said that some situations, such as the recent Taiwan Straits tension, fall between emergencies and peacetime operations. Yamasaki felt that the government should decide if logistic support could be granted to Japan-based U.S. forces operating in such situations ("Japan: Article": 8). This would demonstrate the validity of the U.S.-Japan security arrangement and deny, in Ono's words, "the situation of Japan having to build up and possess its own defense capabilities" ("Japan: LDP Official": 11).

The SDP has opposed ACSA from its inception, but has been on the defensive in Japan's recent political struggles over security policy. Ono's SDP counterpart, Kenji Taguchi, urged further discussions not only on logistic support, but also on Japan's military role in both PKO and the U.S.-Japan security pact. Taguchi said that ACSA should not be applied to unilateral U.S. actions, such as aircraft carrier demonstrations off the North Korean coast. The SDP believes that this would constitute an illegal act of collective self-defense ("Japan: SDP Official": 11). The SDP's stalling tactic is designed to prevent the government of Japan from moving before the SDP thinks it is prepared.

Media Response

Predictably, the Japanese press gave a mixed reaction to ACSA. The left-leaning *Okinawa Times* unsurprisingly expressed skepticism about ACSA and the updated security arrangements. An editorial expressed concern that the entire issue of collective self-defense and Japanese participation in military operations would come up again ("Japan: Okinawa": 11). In this respect, they are no doubt correct. The issue is unlikely to be resolved until a crisis demands action on the part of the Japanese government.

Japan's largest papers were split on ACSA. *Asahi Shimbun* and *Mainichi Shimbun* both declared their doubts about increasing Japanese military activism. *Mainichi Shimbun* commented that the U.S. may ask Japan to "shoulder new, extra security responsibility" ("Japanese Media"). If LDP policymakers such as Yamasaki have their way, *Mainichi*'s fear will materialize, as Yamasaki favors expanding the Japan-U.S. security treaty to include not just northeast Asia and the Philippines, but the whole of the Asia-Pacific region as well ("Japan: LDP Proposes": 9).

Yomiuri Shimbun and the business-oriented *Nihon Keizai Shimbun* both favored the conservative position. *Yomiuri* went so far as to criticize ACSA for placing unnecessary limits on Japanese participation in East Asian security affairs. *Yomiuri's* editors recognize the constitutional difficulties involved, but would like the government to rethink the traditional self-imposed restraints on military operations ("Japanese Media").

Ramifications

Observers acknowledge Japan's value as a U.S. springboard into Asia, and ACSA permits a wider range of U.S. operations from Japan, although it does not cover every contingency (Suzuki). It may also facilitate a decrease in U.S. force structure, as some logistic support units may no longer be needed if Japan provides equivalent services. A greater reliance on Japanese parts and services will consequently increase the risk of at least indirect Japanese involvement in what would otherwise be an American unilateral action. However, the resurgence of UN and multilateral activities reduces the possibility of purely unilateral activities.

The PKO mission that Japan is now embracing can greatly benefit from the application of ACSA. The agreement will allow the SDF to utilize American sea and airlift capability for larger scale deployments. The current Japanese contingent in the Golan Heights numbers only the 43-man transportation company, plus the C-130 detachment. The use of more and heavier non-Japanese lift assets will allow Japan to participate in a wider range of PKO activity, while still maintaining its status as a non-power-projection nation.

The geopolitical ramifications of the expanded U.S.-Japan security relationship encompass the security situation in East Asia, and also the global UN forum. ACSA is a small step toward this larger relationship, and appears to be a fairly straightforward document. Article 9 of Japan's Constitution was also straightforward when it was written, but its apparent prohibitions have gradually eroded. In the same way, the U.S.-Japan relationship will only grow closer under ACSA, and logistics sharing will increase.

IMPLICATIONS FOR THE FUTURE

Peacekeeping operations are useful to the Self-Defense Forces, reassuring the public that their SDF is a useful tool, and can be used effectively to promote peace throughout the world. This in turn increases the SDF's popularity and helps to justify its budget, currently hovering near 1 percent of GDP ("The Compass": 9). The positive benefits of undertaking PKO are essential if the SDF is to remain a robust force.

Improving the Self-Defense Forces

The SDF wants approximately 10 percent of its soldiers, sailors, and airmen, about 24,000 people, to experience PKO (Takai *b*). This figure is an ideal that will not be reached at the current level of deployment. Although 1,200 SDF members spent time in the Cambodia operation, only 45 are deployed to the Golan Heights. In an effort to broaden exposure, four Air Force and four Navy personnel deployed as part of the predominantly Ground Self-Defense Force (GSDF) transportation company in the Golan (Ono). If the ongoing SDF and PKO law reviews do not allow larger-scale participation in a broader range of PKO, SDF training will suffer.

Command and Control

Since UNTAC, Japan has consistently deployed advance teams and liaison officers to the UN headquarters in the field. This has been a successful tactic in avoiding the complications faced by the UNTAC engineers. Some command and control problems still exist within the SDF, however.

The SDF executes PKO from the service level. Although a Joint Staff Office (JSO) exists, it does not have a command function outside of joint or combined operations. Since Japanese PKO to date have been single-service operations, the J-3 (operations) component of the JSO has taken on an oversight and monitoring function. In this role, J-3 reports back to the services with feedback, but the services are not bound to accept it. The Japanese setup in many ways mirrors the pre-Goldwater-Nichols-Act U.S. military establishment.

The government is also reconsidering the missions of the SDF and JSO. A favorable review would give the SDF greater latitude in its overseas operations, and allow the purchase of more lift assets. The JSO hopes this review will prompt more coordination among the services and facilitate more efficient operations. Interoperability is becoming a buzzword in SDF circles, and is gaining importance rapidly with the signing of ACSA. The JSO is pushing this, and PKO will be enhanced as a result.

Both the SDF and PKO laws are also under review. Under the current system, PKO unit commanders are hamstrung by their lack of authority to command their troops in hostile situations. The decision to use force against an aggressive party lies in the hands of the individual soldier, not with the commander. This may put whole units at risk should a dangerous condition present itself. If this issue is resolved, and commanders are able to direct their units under fire, then Japan could contribute cease-fire zone monitors to PKO. The current law prohibits this because the potential for using force is considered too high. With revision, cease-fire monitoring operations would meet the five conditions of the PKO law, and SDF troops would have legal authority to participate. However, as the SDF saw in Zaire, tense situations can arise even in humanitarian relief operations. Giving commanders more control would increase unit safety and allow more SDF activity in PKO.

The SDF had inadequate intelligence support, especially during their humanitarian aid mission to Zaire. In the words of Professor Susumu Takai of the National Institute for Defense Studies, "Zaire was a lucky operation" and quite dangerous (Takai *b*). This assignment came up quickly, and did not allow the SDF adequate lead time to prepare. Prime Minister Tomiichi Murayama responded to UNHCR commissioner Sadako Ogata's request for help by ordering the SDF deployment. The GSDF had insufficient information on the local area, resulting in Japanese troops being placed in hostile situations. Fortunately, no SDF troops were involved in violent incidents. There is a need for enhanced education and training prior to deployment. The amount of PKO training the military receives has decreased over time. The Institute for International Policy Studies' Shimauchi, a GSDF officer, said that no formal PKO training takes place within the military, although the GSDF does provide some education to its troops. Some mid-level officers have trained with foreign officers at the UN's Scandinavian PKO facility, but this experience is not widespread. According to Shimauchi, day-to-day job training is adequate for most PKO missions, with only two weeks of specialized training immediately before deployment. This may be sufficient for the logistic and engineering missions that the SDF has so far undertaken, but if expanded participation is to become a reality, the SDF must provide additional training on PKO and UN operations.

Reports of plans for constructing a joint training facility in Malaysia, with the cooperation of the Association of Southeast Asian Nations, have surfaced recently in the Japanese press. If this idea comes to fruition, it would increase defense transparency in the region and promote understanding between Japan and its uneasy Asian neighbors, easing Japan's transition to broader PKO involvement.

Attitudes Within the Military

Prolonged deployments seriously impact family life. This factor has understandably made PKO activities more popular with younger, single personnel than with their married counterparts. Since only volunteers man Japanese PKO missions, the deeply imbedded Japanese reluctance to break the family unit apart, even temporarily, keeps some of the best people away from overseas operations.

Not all SDF officers have accepted the idea that Japan should send peacekeepers overseas. The basic mission of the SDF, and the founding principle for its establishment, is to protect the Japanese home islands from invasion. Cooperation with the U.S. and prevention of regional conflicts are controversial missions, and peacekeeping had never been an SDF concern until the Cold War ended. Some feel that PKO distracts the SDF from their primary mission. This is similar to the opposition heard within the U.S. military that the job of the military is to fight and win wars, not to keep peace in Bosnia or any other place. Within the SDF, this philosophy is more prevalent among the senior ranks, although some younger officers share the view. However, the consensus is that peacekeeping operations are a "good bumper sticker" for the SDF, and that UN operations have helped the quality of the SDF's public relations and its recruiting ability.

Following the Cold War and the collapse of the Soviet threat, the SDF suffered a marked downturn in the quality of its new recruits. Young Japanese did not see the rationale for the existence of the SDF, and fewer and fewer joined the military. The Cambodia operation helped to show off the military's capabilities, showcased the SDF's contribution, and justified the SDF in the eyes of many young people. The quality of both new enlisted personnel and officers rose as a direct result of the PKO experience.

PKO activities have given the SDF the opportunity to undertake a mission beyond preparation for an invasion that is unlikely to occur. No longer is the mission "train, train, train" to repel the Soviet masses. This change appeals especially to the younger generation of SDF personnel, as it breaks the monotony of the normal routine. Some are enthusiastic because they see PKO as a good opportunity to travel abroad.

POLITICS

Article 9 of Japan's Constitution remains a stumbling block for Japanese PKO participation. The current debate is over the "right of collective self-defense," and whether PKO constitute the exercise of this right. Today's interpretation of the Constitution is that while Japan, as a sovereign nation, does have the right to collective self-defense, the Constitution legally bars Japan from exercising it. In effect, Japan has waived the right. Although the best long-term solution would be a revision of the Constitution, the practice of gradual reinterpretation is likely to continue (Inoguchi *b*). Each individual PKO requires that this question be addressed.

The government is not in a position to make fundamental changes. The three-party coalition now in power makes it difficult to pass any legislation that significantly conflicts with any one party's ideology. The SDP will not allow the SDF to grow in perceived power, at least in the near future. If the LDP or the opposition New Frontier Party gained a solid majority, the SDF would find itself with friends in high places. However, the SDP then would have nothing to lose by being steadfast in its opposition. This, warns Hideo Suzuki of the Ministry of Foreign Affairs, could upset the consensus-based Japanese political system, hampering efforts to build up the SDF or revise the Constitution.

Japanese public opinion, like its American counterpart, is notoriously fickle. This prevents Japan from greatly expanding its PKO participation. The Japanese electorate is generally content with the SDF's current level of activity. The mood allows expanded participation, but only on a slowly increasing basis. This incremental change is consistent with the government's gradual reinterpretations of the Constitution. Although it is not hostile toward the SDF, Japanese public opinion prevents the SDF from making great strides in PKO, especially as more and larger operations increase the level of danger involved.

The issue of casualties is a frightening prospect for the SDF. In previous operations, Japan has not suffered any military casualties. Some think that had the policemen killed and wounded in Cambodia been SDF troops, public outcry against the SDF could have risen to a fever pitch. Lieutenant Colonel Hayashi expressed the military's reservations about taking casualties because the effect of SDF deaths on public opinion is unknown. The SDF fears a public backlash against overseas deployment would offset all the positive strides made by the SDF in recent years. The PKO law's fourth condition, which allows Japan to withdraw from UN operations unilaterally, would come into play following any hostile activity. The SDF does not want to be caught in an impossible situation between domestic politics and a deadly operation.

Issues that do not have a direct impact on events in Japan do not interest the Japanese public. The potential controversy surrounding Bosnian PKO participation muted any discussion of the subject. Such an operation promised no tangible benefit for Japan, while the mere act of studying military participation in a European issue was anathema to most Japanese politicians. However, Japan is warming to the prospect of maintaining peace far from its shores. Japan relies on the Middle East's oil, and has come to be more interested in preserving peace in the region. Israel in particular has aggressively pursued Japanese investment and economic participation. The deployment of SDF peacekeepers to the Golan Heights is a sign of Japanese commitment to stability in the region, and will enhance Japan-Israel relations. If Japan's presence there continues beyond the original two-year term and expands to include greater duties, Japan's influence in the region will increase.

LOOKING AHEAD

According to Professor Inoguchi, Japan's continued participation in PKO will take place in remote locations, including additional deployments to Africa and potentially South Asia. This is because such operations are less likely to arouse controversy. Small, isolated operations west of Bangladesh are not haunted by the specter of World War II, and therefore are more acceptable both in Japan and to Japan's neighbors.

Some work is being done to further U.S.-Japan combined PKO. Although the U.S. offered to work with the SDF on this topic years ago, only recently has the SDF undertaken a study. An operation using U.S.

combat troops and Japanese engineers and logistics would be "natural," according to the Institute for International Policy Studies' Shimauchi. However, care must be taken to ensure that Japan and the U.S. do not appear too powerful, especially in the eyes of East Asian countries.

The military threat to Japan has all but disappeared, and increasingly close ties to the U.S. military provide a hedge against a resurgent danger. The post-Cold War world structure is fundamentally different than its bipolar antecedent. Guaranteeing peace and security in a new era requires that powerful nations, including Japan, engage in constructive measures to limit war and solve international disputes.

The SDF should be Japan's primary instrument for accomplishing this task, rather than "checkbook" diplomacy. Since the 1992 deployment to Cambodia, the SDF has seen its popularity and morale rebound from a post-Cold War low. The SDF, always a capable fighting force, never before had the opportunity to display its competence. PKO give Japan the chance to get a return on 50 years of defense spending. To maximize results, Japan needs to allow the SDF the latitude to conduct operations across the full spectrum of PKO. The SDF law, the PKO law, and the Constitution all are due for revision, or at least reinterpretation. Closer ties wrought by the April 1996 Japan-U.S. summit can also enhance Japanese PKO efforts. As the SDF becomes a more effective peacekeeping force, the Japanese public will be more accepting of Japan's limited military role in the world. In the consensus-based Japanese society, a broad base of popular support is essential for continuing success. PKO is a way for Japan to participate in the "new world order," and to develop a new mission for the SDF. Article 9 declares that Japan "aspires sincerely to an international peace based on justice and order." Peacekeeping gives Japan the perfect opportunity to live up to the ideals of its Constitution. The mission can only help the SDF to improve its own readiness and public image. With the Soviet nemesis gone, the SDF should concentrate its efforts on expanding participation in peacekeeping operations.

Chapter 5

NONPROLIFERATION

The UN Security Council resolutions authorizing the multilateral coalition to expel Iraq from Kuwait were followed by UN action establishing the most comprehensive multilateral apparatus to enforce the peace since the occupation of Japan and Germany. Iraq was required to reveal and destroy all of its weapons of mass destruction, and the UN was empowered to monitor Iraqi compliance using an intrusive inspection regime. The role of intelligence in this process was crucial. Working from intelligence tips, the UN soon discovered a massive clandestine nuclear weapons program in violation of the Nonproliferation Treaty and undetected by the International Atomic Energy Agency. A fundamental reform of the IAEA safeguards system followed, establishing new procedures for the use of intelligence in international organizations.

Captain Hudgins traces the history of the IAEA and its role in nuclear nonproliferation. She outlines the legal structure and the inspection process to monitor peaceful use of nuclear energy and to prevent diversion to nuclear weapons. The disclosure of the Iraqi weapons program called into question the whole nonproliferation regime. The IAEA responded with a new set of procedures for safeguards and a willingness to insist on unannounced inspections of undisclosed facilities. Captain Hudgins shows the key role that intelligence played in the political process required to discover the Iraq nuclear program, and the evolution of procedures for the integration of intelligence input into safeguards inspections.

The first test of the new IAEA inspection regime came in North Korea. Master Sergeant Campbell reviews the history of North Korea's nuclear program and relationship with the IAEA. As part of diplomatic efforts to ease tension, on 10 April 1992 North Korea signed a safeguards agreement that included the intrusive inspection provisions implemented in the wake of the Gulf War. Based on the results of inspections and intelligence reporting, the IAEA became suspicious and insisted on spot-inspections of sites which might have evidence of North Korean violations of the Nonproliferation Treaty. North Korea refused and the issue was brought to the UN Security Council, prompting a crisis that ended with the visit to Pyongyang by Former President Jimmy Carter and an agreement by the North to freeze its nuclear program. Sergeant Campbell shows the role of intelligence in the inspection process and the public diplomacy leading to the framework agreement, measures that have settled the crisis at least for the moment.

Overt intelligence sharing is a new way of doing business for the IAEA. Captain Hudgins considers the implications of the new arrangement for U.S. policy, for the U.S. Intelligence Community, and for the IAEA. Sergeant Campbell considers the role of intelligence in public diplomacy, and Theodore Wolff concludes that there is a new counterproliferation mindset in the U.S. Intelligence Community that sees U.S. national interests served by cooperation between the Community and the IAEA.

INTELLIGENCE AND THE INTERNATIONAL ATOMIC ENERGY AGENCY

Audrey D. Hudgins
Captain, U.S. Army
September 1992

OVERVIEW

The collapse of the Soviet Union and the revelations of Iraq's extensive nuclear weapons program have far-reaching implications for the issue of nuclear weapons proliferation. During the Cold War, parity was the governing philosophy of the two great nuclear powers, the United States and the USSR. Deterrence, fostered by nuclear parity, provided an unusually stable global environment. This nuclear duality regulated the regional ambitions of technology-dependent countries, thus ensuring continued global stability. Further, both great powers generally supported the tenets of nuclear nonproliferation and related treaties, thereby controlling the spread of nuclear weapons and related technology. The collapse of the Soviet Union created a thoroughly multipolar world in strategic terms; the concept of deterrence effectively vanished.

Revelations of the Iraqi nuclear weapons development program also contributed to the global nuclear imbalance. The mere existence of that country's nuclear program removed any confidence the world had in the nuclear nonproliferation regime, which consists of three major elements: the International Atomic Energy Agency (IAEA), the Nuclear Nonproliferation Treaty (NPT), and a wide-ranging group of export controls.[1] Iraq proved that despite the existence of the NPT and the concerted efforts of the IAEA and multilateral export control groups, nuclear proliferation remains a serious global problem.

The Director of Central Intelligence, Robert Gates, has emphasized the need to unveil the Intelligence Community and expand its role (U.S. Cong, Senate *f*: 15). The experience with Iraq's nuclear program was a successful test of this new role. The time may have come to consider the adoption of a more flexible intelligence disclosure policy, in recognition of the growing importance of nuclear nonproliferation. Assistance to the IAEA in its verification of the NPT may be the most appropriate mechanism. By setting the example, the U.S. can persuade other countries to invoke a similar strategy. The release of information from the U.S. Intelligence Community to the IAEA is both necessary and feasible in the effort to ensure the successful application of the NPT.

International cooperation in the post-Cold War era is now possible as countries multilaterally pursue common interests. Iraq is a case in point; its naked aggression against Kuwait provided the world the opportunity to come together to halt its threshold nuclear weapons development program. Enhanced cooperation on a number of fronts strengthens the case for U.S. release of intelligence products to the International Atomic Energy Agency. The *Open Skies Treaty, Chemical Weapons Convention, Vienna Document 1992,* and the *Treaty on Conventional Armed Forces In Europe* (commonly referred to as the *CFE Treaty*) all serve as useful paradigms for enhanced international cooperation. Each uses intelligence and information sharing as a tool for transparency. Intelligence release and disclosure has a rich history as well. The U.S. used intelligence as a policy tool during the Cuban Missile Crisis and in anticipation of military action in Grenada. More recently, the Intelligence Community has begun releasing intelligence products to the United Nations in support of peacekeeping operations in Cambodia.

U.S. INTERESTS IN NONPROLIFERATION

The Bush administration maintains that nuclear nonproliferation is a high priority U.S. interest: "The proliferation of advanced weapons poses

---

[1] Export controls, which are beyond the scope of this thesis, are an important part of the nonproliferation regime. These voluntary guidelines, followed by most nuclear suppliers, consist of the NPT Suppliers Controls/Zangger Trigger List, created in 1974, and the London Nuclear Suppliers Guidelines, enacted in 1978. The Coordinating Committee on Multilateral Export Controls (COCOM) covers a broad range of exports, but has a substantial nuclear subset.

an ominous challenge to global peace and stability" (U.S. President *c*: 16). The collapse of the Soviet Union rapidly brought about a new world order, as President Bush has stated; however, the consequences are less than agreeable to the United States:

> [T]he arms race in weapons of mass destruction now going on in the third world is unbridled by any of the instruments the U.S. and U.S.S.R. developed over the years to control a potential crisis. There is no arms control between India and Pakistan and . . . no hotline between Baghdad and Jerusalem (Kitfield: 34).

Regional and Global Stability

The U.S. has an interest in maintaining regional and global stability. In this era of multipolarity and coalition-building, a regional conflict could quite easily escalate. Beyond formidable conventional threats and inherent animosities in every region of the world, the presence of nuclear weapons provides a more urgent dimension to an already troubled international environment. A regional nuclear conflict in the Middle East poses no direct threat to the continental United States, but the global dependence on oil implies that any conflict could have devastating geo-economic effects. If Iraq, for example, had been successful in its nuclear attempts, the strategic balance in the Middle East would have become precarious at best, and deadly at worst.

Nuclear weapons play an important role in many other regions of the world as well. North Korea's nuclear intentions might have been designed to counter U.S. nuclear weapons based in South Korea, or the potential Japanese or Taiwanese threat to the East. In our own hemisphere, Brazil and Argentina until recently pursued a nuclear weapons capability. Nuclear terrorism also poses a grave threat to U.S. interests. As nuclear weapons technology proliferates, terrorist organizations could find a new method for achieving their aims. The strategic interests of the U.S. will continue to be threatened by any hostile entity that possesses nuclear weapons.

The United States can play an active role in containing nuclear proliferation. But the U.S. has experienced difficulty in enforcing its stringent export controls because foreign firms are not subject to U.S. regulations. Stronger international controls would remove the U.S. from this delicate

OLD COLD WARRIORS NEVER DIE
. . . THEY BECOME UN ASSETS

UN Security Council briefing by Ambassador Stevenson, 25 November 1962

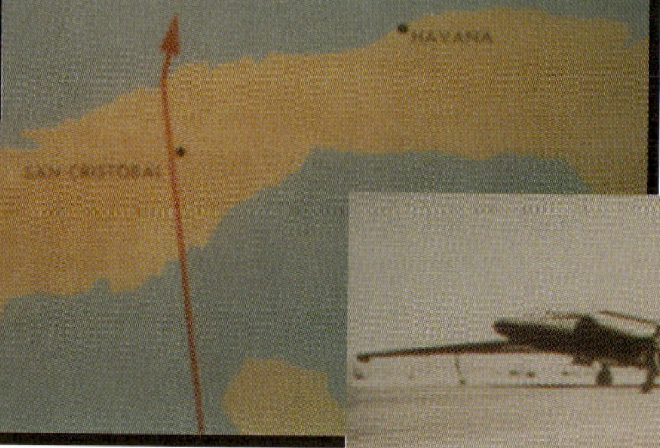

U-2 flight path over Cuba, 1962

U-2 in support of UN Special Commission, under UN Security Council Resolution 687, 1991.

photos used with permission

position with respect to American industry and improve efforts to curb the proliferation of key nuclear technologies.

Nuclear Preeminence

Paramount to U.S. national security interests is maintenance of global nuclear preeminence. A challenge to that preeminence by a renegade, nuclear-capable country may have the effect of reducing U.S. international stature. The U.S. has entered an era of unprecedented cooperation with its former chief adversary and must exploit the situation before a hostile nuclear country upsets regional nuclear balances. Successes in this arena may result in an even stronger and more stable global environment than before the collapse of the Soviet Union.

Nuclear Predictability

Prior to the collapse of the Soviet Union, superpower nuclear relations were analogous to an unending chess game. Each superpower could predict, with reasonable accuracy, its opponent's next move; diplomatic negotiations regarding arms control and disarmament had reached a stable pinnacle. The beauty of this geopolitical situation was that each player was aware of the rules of the game. The new world order has altered the strategic balance; predicting an opponent's capabilities, intentions, and policies has become more difficult. Limiting proliferation will make this problem easier to contend with.

The Brain Drain

The international community could be threatened by the emigration of Soviet nuclear experts. Western proposals for economic assistance to the former Soviet Union could reduce the risk of emigration or circuitous transfer of technology by these individuals. Former Secretary of State James Baker and former German Foreign Minister Hans-Dietrich Genscher advanced proposals designed to halt this brain drain. An international research institute will employ scientists of the Former Soviet Union (FSU) and hopefully limit the spread of nuclear technology ("Genscher": 14-15). China, however, has recently hired a number of weapons specialists from the FSU (Denny: 2). A continued brain drain can only further destabilize the nuclear balance.

Competing Interests

Nonproliferation has been in the U.S. national interest since the development of the atomic bomb. It competes with a host of other national priorities, at times taking a back seat to a more pressing agenda. The Soviet invasion of Afghanistan provides an excellent example. President Carter had chosen in February of 1979 to discontinue aid to Pakistan based on U.S. Intelligence Community concern over Pakistan's nuclear intentions. In December of that same year, the Soviet invasion of Afghanistan boldly challenged the U.S. containment policy and threatened U.S. oil interests in the Persian Gulf, two important national priorities. Because of its geostrategic importance as a refuge for Afghan rebels, the U.S. resumed aid to Pakistan.

More than a decade later, as Soviet influence waned and their withdrawal had begun, aid was again discontinued because President Bush could not certify Pakistan's peaceful nuclear intentions. Nonproliferation had again leaped to the forefront of the American political agenda. During this interval, however, Pakistan was able to gain all equipment and material required for a nuclear weapons program, and the country now possesses the capability to assemble a nuclear device (R. Smith *e*: A18).

Competing priorities within U.S. national interests are not at question here. The Soviet invasion of Afghanistan was a serious threat to the U.S. national interests; America's handling of this situation would impact heavily on its credibility in the international community. What is at question is the use of information held by the U.S. Intelligence Community and its communication of that information to policymakers and international organizations.

The U.S. media were adept at publishing reports on the arrest of Pakistani nationals and individuals, acting on behalf of Pakistan, attempting to illegally export nuclear material for the clandestine weapons program (Hedrick Smith: 38). Allegedly, the U.S. Intelligence Community knew a great deal more about the complexity and extent of Pakistan's, as well as other developing countries', clandestine nuclear programs. Unfortunately, this information was not communicated to individuals and organizations empowered to take action. In the case of Pakistan, U.S. aid and assistance to Pakistan and the Afghan rebels did not permit the U.S. to take action in the nonproliferation arena. However, had this information been communicated to the IAEA, that program may have been slowed or halted.

A HISTORY OF INTERNATIONAL NONPROLIFERATION EFFORTS

The term proliferation has been used frequently in recent years to denote a new intelligence and national security area of interest, although it is not a new concept. Perhaps the earliest impetus for historic weapons proliferation was the invention of gunpowder. Proliferation in the last two centuries has led to the introduction of the rifle to the far reaches of North America, for example, with a devastating effect on native Americans. Further proliferation of firepower in warfare between the first and second world wars radically transformed the nature of war itself.

U.S. development of the atomic bomb during World War II initiated a bilateral arms race that was to spiral upward for the next 40 years. The USSR's desire to achieve nuclear parity with the U.S. was essential to combat "imperialism" and to ensure the USSR's place as a world power. Alarmed by their increasing vulnerability, other countries have since pursued nuclear weapons development programs, some with modest success. Although today nuclear weapons states number only a third of that predicted in the 1960s (Kitfield: 42), international efforts to control nuclear proliferation have not been entirely adequate and are even more important in today's destabilizing global environment.

The International Atomic Energy Agency

International concern regarding nuclear weapons proliferation developed quickly after World War II. The U.S. knew that its monopoly in the nuclear arena would be short-lived and thus suggested the implementation of international safeguards governing the development and use of nuclear technology. In 1945, the U.S., UK, and Canada proposed the creation of a United Nations Atomic Energy Commission (UNAEC) charged with "eliminating the use of atomic energy for destructive purposes" (U.S. ACDA *a*: 89). With little debate, this proposal was adopted by the UN General Assembly on 24 January 1946. Later that year the U.S. introduced the Baruch Plan to the UNAEC. The plan called for the placement of nuclear resources under international control; however, the proposal met with strong Soviet opposition. UNAEC negotiations came to an impasse due to the dichotomy of views on implementation of the Baruch Plan. Thus, in 1948, both the Baruch Plan and the UNAEC were dissolved.

The U.S. then modified its strategy by promoting the peaceful uses of nuclear energy through the "Atoms for Peace" program. President Eisenhower introduced the program to the UN General Assembly in 1953 as a means of shifting interest away from the military applications of nuclear energy (Hiester: 403). The proposal, idealistic in word and spirit, essentially stated that the U.S. agreed to share nuclear technology with any country that would use it peacefully. Previous efforts to control nuclear technology had met with strong resistance from the Soviet Union, primarily because its nuclear weapons development program was dependent on technological information gained from the West. By 1949, Soviet possession of the bomb prompted them to join in the implementation of a nuclear nonproliferation agenda.

Through "Atoms for Peace," efforts to focus international attention on nuclear proliferation issues succeeded, with the creation of the IAEA under the auspices of the United Nations. At the UN international conference assembled in September 1956 to finalize the Statute of the IAEA, much of the controversy centered around the nature and application of safeguards. Many countries perceived a threat to their national sovereignty. Others expressed the concern that the proposed agency would interfere with the economic development of UN member states (Scheinman: 72). In the end, the conference approved the statute.

Treaty on the Non-Proliferation of Nuclear Weapons

The "Atoms for Peace" program was extremely successful in promoting the peaceful use of atomic energy; however, it became clear that many countries sought to utilize "peaceful" nuclear technology as the first step in the development of nuclear weapons. By the mid 1960s the spread of "peaceful" nuclear technology had increased the risk of nuclear war. By 1964 the nuclear powers were five in number: the U.S. (1945), the Soviet Union (1949), the United Kingdom (1952), France (1960), and China (1964). At the time, the international community envisioned great potential for nuclear power. It was estimated that nearly 300 nuclear power plants would be in operation by 1985, prompting concern over the diversion of plutonium (U.S. ACDA *a*: 89). With the rapid spread of nuclear technology and the motivation of many countries to become nuclear-capable, the diversion of plutonium from peaceful use became an increasing possibility. A new fear spread throughout the international community, the fear that dozens of nuclear weapons states would lower the threshold for conflict, and that regional animosities and disputes could escalate into the nuclear realm.

This concern was reflected in the 1964 U.S. proposal to the Eighteen-Nation Disarmament Committee. The proposal called for the nondissemination and nonacquisition of nuclear weapons by nuclear and non-nuclear states, respectively, as well as the implementation of safeguards on the international transfer of peaceful nuclear materials. After three years of debate with the Soviet Union and other members, a coordinated draft treaty was submitted to the Committee. On 12 June 1968, the Treaty on the Non-Proliferation of Nuclear Weapons was approved by the United Nations General Assembly.

The treaty seeks to prevent the spread of nuclear weapons through the pledges of signatory countries and the application of the IAEA program of on-site inspections, audits, and inventory controls, collectively referred to as safeguards. Non-nuclear weapons states pledge to remain as such, and agree to allow inspection of their nuclear facilities in exchange for access to nuclear technology. Nuclear weapons states agree not to assist non-nuclear weapons states in the acquisition of nuclear weapons and pledge to continue their efforts to end the arms race. Currently 146 countries are signatories to the treaty, including all permanent members of the United Nations Security Council. Several countries of nuclear proliferation concern have not acceded to the NPT (Israel, India, Pakistan, Algeria, Argentina, and Brazil); however, in recent months these countries have indicated that this decision is under reconsideration.

In accordance with Article VIII of the NPT, review conferences are held every five years to validate the continued significance of the treaty. The first conference, held in Geneva in May 1975, resulted in a strong consensus for continuation of the treaty. Since that time, three conferences have been held, each provoking more intense debate over the effectiveness of the treaty. The fourth NPT review conference was held from 20 August to 15 September 1990 in Geneva. Key suppliers of nuclear materials, notably Germany and Japan, agreed to make such supplies conditional on all nuclear materials and plants in the recipient state being subject to international safeguards, and constructive proposals were recommended to improve the inspection capacity of the IAEA.

The fifth conference, scheduled for 1995, will likely see a continuation of this trend as revelations of the extent and complexity of Iraq's nuclear weapons program, as well as the possible existence of other clandestine programs worldwide, raise the specter of international concern over nuclear proliferation. The NPT has had limited success in preventing the spread of nuclear weapons material and technology; however, in the absence of the regime, the number of nuclear and near-nuclear weapons states would have grown much more rapidly. With the recent accession of China and France to the NPT, there is hope that the spirit and intent of the treaty can be revitalized. With all five permanent members of the United Nations Security Council signatories to the treaty, universal enforcement might be more likely.

THE EVOLVING ROLE OF THE IAEA

The IAEA's mission is to promote the growth and development of peaceful atomic energy and to administer safeguards to prevent the diversion of nuclear materials to weapons programs. With over 116 members, the Agency monitors over 900 nuclear facilities in more than 50 countries (IAEA, IAEA Bulletin: 69). This responsibility is taken very seriously by the agency, as verification of a country's peaceful nuclear intentions provides confidence and promotes international stability.

Safeguards Before Iraq

Complementing its role as the purveyor of peaceful nuclear technology, the IAEA became the verification mechanism for ensuring that no diversion of nuclear material from peaceful use occurred. The United States, a major participant in the design of the original statute, along with many other countries, pushed diligently for a regime that would be strict, but not infringe on a country's sovereignty. When the IAEA was created, the focus was on the former axis powers of World War II, specifically Germany and Japan. The central concern was to ensure these powers did not obtain this frightening new technology. Thus, the IAEA was charged with a watchdog function over large nuclear fuel cycles. As time went by, and with the inclusion of the NPT mission in its charter, the IAEA became the accountant for nuclear fuel cycles throughout the world. This is no small task, and the IAEA set about creating a material and statistical accountancy system that would detect the slightest diversion of fissile material.

This important mission is carried out through a complex system of safeguards, detailed in INFCIRC 66[2], the agency's safeguards document for non-NPT member states, and in INFCIRC 153, which outlines safeguards procedures for NPT signatories. In accordance with Article III.A.5 of the IAEA Statute, safeguards are applied when the agency provides technical assistance, the signatories to a bilateral or multilateral agreement request it, or a country volunteers (Scheinman: 125). Before the NPT, INFCIRC 66 safeguards agreements were the standard, usually the result of a bilateral or multilateral agreement, but in all cases requiring the transferred nuclear material to be placed under safeguards. With the advent of the NPT, signatory countries were legally bound to accept IAEA safeguards under INFCIRC 153. INFCIRC 153 is more comprehensive, requiring NPT member countries to declare and open for inspection all peaceful nuclear facilities on their territories.

Safeguards under both types of agreement are not unilaterally imposed by the IAEA, but are subject to the conclusion of a safeguards agreement between the agency and a member state. Thus, from their inception, safeguards are accepted voluntarily. The obligation to place its nuclear program under safeguards has been accepted by the member state. Both the NPT and IAEA safeguards are treaties, relying on the integrity of the signatories to perpetuate the validity of the regime.

The agency safeguards system applies to all nuclear facilities listed on the "declared facilities list," which is part of the safeguards agreement reached between the agency and each member country. The agreement applies a myriad of safeguards verification techniques to ensure that no diversion of fissile material from peaceful use occurs. This verification system includes the review of nuclear facility design information, the installation of containment and surveillance equipment, nuclear material accountability, physical inventory verification, and issuance of the annual

[2] INFCIRC stands for "Information Circular," a term used to denote official IAEA documents. The final version of INFCIRC 66 came into force in 1968; INFCIRC 153, in 1970.

Safeguards Implementation Report and Safeguards Technical Report, which describe the results of safeguards activities over the previous year. The Statute allows for access anytime, anywhere, but this authority is limited in the safeguards agreement by "facility attachment," a term in the safeguards agreement which attaches inspection access to facilities containing safeguarded nuclear materials or equipment. In the event that the safeguards information is inadequate, or questions arise as to the adequacy of the declarations, the IAEA has the right to question the target country for further clarification, within the provisions of the safeguards agreement. Despite limits on its authority, the IAEA must be able to carry out its safeguards responsibilities at all times. Failure to do so would require action by the IAEA Board of Governors to settle a dispute.

A Changing Safeguards Approach

Over time, it became apparent that proliferation risks did not lie with those industrialized countries, namely Germany and Japan, for which the IAEA Statute and safeguards agreements were originally intended. Germany's alliance with the North Atlantic Treaty Organization, its economic integration within the European Community, and Japan's security treaty with the United States and its relationships with other countries along the Pacific Rim, contributed to the assurance that these countries would maintain a peaceful nuclear role. The real risks lay with a few countries that choose to advance their own interests over the interests of their neighbors. As a result, a considerable number of other countries may also choose action at the nuclear level in self-defense, because they feel that their sovereignty, security and safety are threatened by the actions of the recalcitrant proliferates.

The IAEA Board of Governors recognized these realities. INFCIRC 66 was modified to make its coverage of safeguarded material more effective. Following the approval of INFCIRC 153, the IAEA Director General established the Standing Advisory Group on Safeguards Implementation which serves as a think tank on the agency's safeguards approach. As an international organization under United Nations auspices, however, the IAEA is the servant of its member states. Past attempts to improve the scope and effectiveness of safeguards in many cases have met with both political and diplomatic opposition.

Undeclared Facilities and Intelligence

The safeguards system eventually agreed upon was fundamentally different in character from earlier, more stringent proposals advanced by the United Nations Atomic Energy Commission (UNAEC). This early view called for safeguards to prevent the diversion of nuclear material, clandestine operation, and the seizure of material or facilities. Political realities and sovereignty issues contributed to a more limited safeguards approach.

Although addressed in the UNAEC report, the issue of clandestine nuclear operations was not discussed in the early years of the IAEA. The potential existence of undeclared facilities was simply not relevant in comparison to the larger discussion of the form international safeguards should take. Further, in a 1964 revision of INFCIRC 26, the predecessor to INFCIRC 66, the right of "pursuit" was added. "Pursuit" refers to the mandatory attachment of safeguards to "successively produced generations of nuclear material" (Scheinman: 128). Thus, the understanding was that the agreed-upon system of safeguards would adequately control the proliferation of nuclear material.

Despite ratification of the Nuclear Nonproliferation Treaty in 1970, international concern over proliferation grew, a by-product of the expanding nuclear energy industry. During negotiations of INFCIRC 153 in that same year, the detection of undeclared facilities was first addressed. The United States proposed that the IAEA be granted the ability to search for undeclared facilities on the basis of information obtained from any source (U.S. ACDA *b*: 4-99). Intelligence, it was understood, would be provided to the Agency to act as a trigger in the safeguards process. The reasons for the limited use of intelligence are as diverse as they are intriguing. First, by and large, safeguards were perceived to be functioning effectively. The complex system of safeguards had revealed few diversions of nuclear material, and in those instances of diversion, the Agency was able to resolve further questions through other means (Jennekens *b*: 14). Second, the IAEA was hesitant to accept intelligence information for fear that developing countries might incorrectly perceive the U.S.-IAEA relationship. Third, on the basis of intelligence information obtained on countries of proliferation concern, the U.S. was accustomed to issuing demarches to target countries or their allies as a means of curtailing proliferation (Spector and Smith: 177). Finally, the U.S. Intelligence Community did not support the release of intelligence because the information was considered too sensitive.

SUMMARY

Since the development of the atomic bomb, the global community has been confronted with the problem of proliferation. Early efforts at international control, through the United Nations Atomic Energy Commission and the Baruch Plan, met with no success. Through the "Atoms for Peace" proposal, the IAEA emerged as the compromise institution, charged with promoting the growth and development of peaceful atomic energy and preventing the diversion of nuclear material from peaceful use. A legal commitment to nonproliferation embodied itself in the Nuclear Nonproliferation Treaty of 1968. Over time, the Agency's safeguards system, originally designed to monitor the World War II axis powers and formally instituted in INFCIRC 66 and 153, evolved in an attempt to meet the challenges of a changing world.

U.S. interests have also evolved to reflect a changing global security environment. Containing nuclear proliferation is vital to global stability. The disclosure of Iraq's extensive and complex nuclear weapons development program has again thrust nonproliferation to the forefront of the American national security agenda.

U.S. INTELLIGENCE, IRAQ, AND NONPROLIFERATION

Audrey D. Hudgins
Captain, U.S. Army
September 1992

THE IRAQ EXPERIENCE

The disclosure of Iraq's nuclear weapons development program eroded international confidence in the nuclear nonproliferation regime. The three important pillars of the regime, it was found, required strengthening. Export control groups reacted quickly to close gaps exploited by Iraq. In April 1992, 27 countries following the Nuclear Suppliers Guidelines, and known as the London Club, agreed to stricter regulations governing the export of sensitive dual-use items. Further, the group decided on a common policy dictating the application of IAEA safeguards on significant exports to non-nuclear weapons states. Altering the Nuclear Nonproliferation Treaty of 1968 (NPT), however, would open a pandora's box; the result might be a weaker, less effective international agreement. Perhaps most importantly, the third pillar of the regime, the International Atomic Energy Agency (IAEA), emerged from the Iraqi experience with a mandate to strengthen its approach to safeguards (Blix *a*: 2).

The experience in monitoring Iraq's nuclear program has been a watershed development. The U.S. Intelligence Community has focused new attention on the IAEA since Iraq's invasion of Kuwait. The Community had suspected the existence of the Iraqi nuclear weapons program for some time, and Director of Central Intelligence Robert Gates has acknowledged that the U.S. Intelligence Community warned policymakers of Iraq's nuclear weapons program (U.S. Cong *f*: 14). The IAEA had similar doubts as to the veracity of Iraq's peaceful nuclear intentions, but the IAEA had not concluded that a violation of the NPT had occurred.

Geography of Iraq's nuclear weapons program. *source: author, modified from IAEA Bulletin, 1992*

The public perception was that the agency's safeguards system should have detected this frightening example of proliferation. However, Iraq's clandestine development of nuclear weapons occurred independently of its safeguarded nuclear program. No diversion of safeguarded nuclear material was detected by the IAEA because none had occurred. Iraq used an intricate web of clandestine supplier networks to obtain the necessary components for its nuclear weapons program. The effort that went into the program was significant and expensive, exploiting technologies long abandoned by the United States because of their cost and inefficiency (Timmerman; Zifferero).

The provision of intelligence by the United States and other countries to the United Nations Special Commission (UNSCOM) and the IAEA has assisted in the intense effort to uncover the extent of Iraq's nuclear weapons program. The Iraqi episode proved that intelligence acts as a force multiplier (Thorne: 20).

INTELLIGENCE IN IRAQ

U.S. nonproliferation policy became more definitive following the Indian nuclear test in 1974. In Congress, the Symington (1976) and Glenn (1977) Amendments to the Foreign Assistance Act of 1961 tied U.S. economic and military assistance to nuclear proliferation concerns, and the Nuclear Nonproliferation Act of 1978 framed U.S. nonproliferation policy (Scheinman: 183-187). Despite these efforts, in the view of some in the IAEA, proliferation was not "discovered" by the U.S. Intelligence Community until the Gulf War. In fact, the Inter-agency Nonproliferation Center, the responsible Intelligence Community element charged with all-source intelligence collection and analysis on proliferation issues, was not established until mandated by Congress in the FY 1991 Intelligence Authorization Bill (U.S. Cong *f*).

The Intelligence Community's hesitation in providing information to the IAEA was overcome by U.S. involvement in the Gulf War. Policymakers provided the impetus needed to formalize intelligence release and disclosure policy in this area. Following the Iraqi invasion, the Intelligence Community quickly made up for lost time. Intelligence release with regard to Iraq began in late 1990; however, the release was limited to the IAEA Special Action Team. A more formalized intelligence relationship with the IAEA began in the Spring of 1991, following approval of United Nations Resolution 687, mandating disposal of Iraq's weapons of mass destruction by the IAEA and UNSCOM. Intelligence continues to play a central role in the Iraq inspections.

Indications of the extent and complexity of the Iraq nuclear weapons program came following release of the "human shields," citizens from the U.S. and other countries used by the Iraqis to deter attacks on key industrial facilities. Spectrographic analysis of the clothes worn by the hostages at Tuwaitha indicated that Iraq might be pursuing electromagnetic isotope separation, a method for producing enriched uranium. This information caused policymakers and the Intelligence Community to approach the situation more seriously, perhaps contributing to the relaxation of traditional intelligence release and disclosure standards (Zorpette: 24; Albright and Hibbs: 15).

The flow of U.S. intelligence information began with the release of Iraqi defector information. Several key defectors provided information that led to the discovery of the electromagnetic isotope separation program and the capture of sensitive Iraqi documents that revealed the extent of their nuclear weapons program. Intelligence was employed in the first case by confirming the existence of calutrons in a timely fashion, the information was passed to the inspection team, enabling them to conduct a no-notice inspection and gain control of the material (Hedges and Cary: 36).

In the second instance, defector information pointed to a robust cache of documents. Iraqi attempts to maintain control of the documents resulted in the famous "parking lot standoff" during inspection no. 6. In the press, this event seemed to mark a turning point in the post-Gulf War battle with Iraq and signaled a redemption of sorts for the IAEA. Intelligence was the reason the team was there in the first place, an important point, but even more significant is the information revealed from the translation of the documents. The translation provided the first solid evidence of Iraq's intention to develop a nuclear weapon, an intention that previously had only been a suspicion (Zorpette: 63; Hedges and Cary: 41; Kay).

These selected examples demonstrate the impact that the provision of intelligence information can have on the compliance and verification process. Without intelligence, inspection teams would have been reduced to blindly roaming the country in search of indications of the Iraqi nuclear program, an undertaking that would have been as senseless as it would have been unproductive. Intelligence, as is now appreciated, provides the "teeth" needed in the successful implementation of international safeguards.

IRAQ: PROBLEMS AND DIFFICULTIES

The IAEA has a requirement for intelligence; as the agency experience in the Iraqi inspections has proved, intelligence was instrumental in uncovering the extent of the nuclear program there. Despite the benefits derived from the use of intelligence information, there were several associated problems and difficulties.

Erroneous Intelligence

The craft of intelligence is not always peering into a "crystal ball," as depicted by some romantics. In fact, during the IAEA inspections in Iraq, the employment of intelligence information was useless in some instances. Information supplied to UNSCOM indicated the possible presence of a heavy water production facility in Northern Iraq. Inspection of the site revealed nothing. On another occasion, intelligence information led the inspection team to a sewer system. In a third example, the IAEA Special Action Team was provided imagery intelligence by a member country indicating the possible existence of an unknown nuclear facility. Questioning of Iraqi officials and inspection of the site revealed a prison. In this case, the imagery analyst perhaps logically reached the conclusion that a nuclear facility existed based on the signature. Many nuclear facilities are heavily guarded and protected. These examples show that intelligence is not an exact science and must be employed carefully (IAEA, IAEA Bulletin: 13).

Countermeasures

The only nuclear site initially declared by the Iraqis was the Al Tuwaitha nuclear center. The second inspection revealed an electromagnetic isotope separation (EMIS) program at Tarmiya industrial center, a site the Iraqis had claimed to be a transformer manufacturing plant. Later inspections revealed that the Iraqis had taken steps to camouflage the facility's true nature. Iraqi officials later revealed that a facility at Ash Sharkat, declared as a non-nuclear plastic coating plant, was intended as a replica of the Tarmiya facility.

Iraq attempted to avert discovery of the true extent of the EMIS program by burying, excavating, and moving EMIS components among several locations on a routine basis. The continual harassment of these Iraqi convoys based on intelligence information overwhelmed Iraqi officials. The Iraqis did not predict this scenario, nor did they appreciate the inspection team's intelligence capability. Over time, however, the inspection methodology became clear and the Iraqis developed countermeasures. As a result, some sources of information became less useful with each inspection.

Measurement and Signature Intelligence

Except for its use in the initial identification of the electromagnetic isotope separation program, Measurement and Signature Intelligence has been contradictory almost to the point of being unusable. Particle samples obtained in Iraq were split among several member countries and the IAEA laboratory at Seibersdorf, Austria for analysis. Each sample analysis revealed different information because the laboratories had varying degrees of detection capability. Additionally, the lengthy analysis timeline allowed the Iraqis to clean up sampling locations, thus preventing inspection teams from obtaining a genuine resample when contradictory analyses were determined to be inconclusive (Donohue and Zeisler: 25).

Communications Security

Communications security (COMSEC) in a hostile environment is necessary to protect information. To Iraq, information on the content and location of planned inspections was of great interest in its effort to thwart the activity. Unfortunately, this information was easily obtained for two reasons.

First, the hotels in which inspectors were lodged were subjected to electronic surveillance. Team member inexperience in the practice of sound COMSEC resulted in several leaks of sensitive information. Further, those team leaders with security experience conducted briefings to enhance awareness of the threat; but in the absence of such experience, no briefing was given.

Underground Cavity Detection

The capability to detect underground cavities has been in existence since the Vietnam conflict, when it was employed to detect tunnels built by the Viet Cong. Since that time detection capability has increased tremendously. In Iraq, several sources indicated the existence of underground facilities, particularly at Tuwaitha. Despite repeated requests, inspection teams were not granted access to this useful equipment from the U.S. inventory, whether it was new or old. Confirming or denying the existence of underground facilities through use of this equipment would greatly enhance confidence in the ability of the inspection teams to fully implement UN Security Council Resolution 687.

THE AFTERMATH

The deterrent value of classical safeguards is significant. A state pursuing clandestine development of nuclear weapons cannot be completely assured that the IAEA will not detect its program. Thus, many countries have not pursued this treacherous path. Unfortunately, as Iraq has proved, a state that chooses to violate its international commitments can do so. Just as an intelligence specialist can remove classified documents from a secure area, a signatory to the Nuclear Nonproliferation Treaty (NPT) can pursue the clandestine development of nuclear weapons, thus thwarting the NPT regime. Iraq's program was stopped before it reached fruition; thus, the experience has become a multifaceted learning point. The IAEA translated its experience in Iraq into positive action in two areas: the Agency's safeguards approach and its use of information.

The Safeguards Approach

The term "misperception" adequately characterizes the global community's understanding of IAEA safeguards. In fact, many view the modern-day safeguards as having the same scope and complexity of early safeguards approaches under the Baruch Plan and the United Nations Atomic Energy Commission Report. The reality is that sovereign countries would not allow such intrusive inspection procedures for fear of compromising their national security interests. The IAEA is the servant of its member states; thus, the issue of sovereignty will forever impact on attempts to strengthen safeguards. In the past, political and diplomatic intransigence on the issue of intrusive safeguards has slowed efforts at reform.

The safeguards system that evolved over time placed great faith in the declarations of member states. This faith was a by-product of the NPT, the treaty that requires the declaration of all nuclear activity. Thus the assumption, however inappropriate in light of recent events, was that member states had declared all nuclear activities. All inspections were carried out in declared facilities on the basis of declared inventories. IAEA inspections were announced in advance and followed a regular schedule in each member country. This safeguards approach revealed no inconsistencies and, in practice, questions were rarely asked.

The mandate for the IAEA-conducted inspections in Iraq was unique; the UN Resolution dictating the disposal of Iraq's weapons of mass destruction allowed a highly intrusive inspection regime. But this mandate will not apply to future IAEA endeavors without a positive shift in public expectations, and thus political action, on the issue of safeguards effectiveness. Disclosure of Iraq's subversion of the nuclear nonproliferation regime unified IAEA member states. If, in the past, political and diplomatic inertia prevented aggressive changes in the Agency's safeguards approach, Iraq's actions have provided new impetus in this arena. Statements strongly supporting nonproliferation efforts have come from NATO, the United Nations Security Council, and Presidents Bush and Yeltsin during their recent summit.

Since the Iraq experience, the Agency has learned the potential benefits of a more aggressive attitude and has acted to apply these lessons. In December 1991, the IAEA Board of Governors deferred action on China's proposed sale of a small nuclear research reactor to Syria while approving a request for a similar transfer from China to Ghana. The move is an attempt to persuade Damascus, a signatory to the NPT, to conclude a safeguards agreement with the IAEA (Wise *b*: 10).

Military compound in Shi'ite southern Iraq, 1991. *photo used with permission*

The IAEA's new aggressive attitude can also be seen in its implementation of the principle of randomization. The IAEA is now considering utilization of short-notice, random inspections as a way to provide an added degree of reliability. Also concerned about the future application of safeguards, the Fourth NPT Review Conference, held in 1990, addressed the need for the IAEA to activate dormant provisions in INFCIRC 153 (Fischer: 33). For example, special inspections have never been conducted by the IAEA but are authorized under Paragraph 73 in the event routine inspections reveal inadequate information.

The IAEA has three tasks: to confirm that nuclear material has not been diverted from peaceful use, to detect its diversion, and to deter its diversion. The safeguards system must be able to stand alone, supported in part by intelligence information. The efforts outlined above, as well as other methods of intensifying the effectiveness of safeguards currently under consideration by the Board of Governors, will allow this to occur. In the long term, international concern and political action will craft a more intrusive safeguards system for a more secure and confident nonproliferation future.

The Role of Information

Information is important in the conduct of the IAEA's mission. The IAEA has available two types of information: in-house information and outside sources. In-house information consists of safeguards confidential information, the reports and related information arising from agency inspections; reports from scientific and technical cooperation visits; and limited nuclear-related export information. Outside sources of information include press reports, scientific and technical journals, government publications and unilateral reporting on nuclear-related exports, proceedings of symposia and conferences, and intelligence information. Information other than safeguards confidential information is referred to as "non-safeguards information." This includes intelligence information. Before Iraq, the IAEA made only a minimal attempt to consolidate this information and analyze it in a systematic manner. The product of studied analysis, it is now realized, can assist in drawing conclusions as to the nuclear intentions of its member states and might have led the IAEA to question Iraq directly on the scope of its nuclear activities.

The Director-General's call for information from any source at the February 1992 Board of Governors meeting demonstrates that the IAEA's operating environment is now marked by an enhanced awareness of the role information can play. The necessity of accepting information from any source was also addressed personally by the Director-General in correspondence to each of the foreign ministers of the nuclear weapons states. Information is power; it gives the agency the ability to conduct its mission more effectively.

In-house and Open Source Information. The IAEA Division for Safeguards Information Treatment is now responsible for analyzing in-house and other sources of information and presenting its conclusions to the Director-General. The Division is also reviewing its organic databases and those available outside the organization to determine what mix is needed to create greater information awareness. Outside sources include the Uranium Institute, the Nuclear Assurance Corporation, the Monterey Institute of International Studies, and the Stockholm International Peace Research Institute (IAEA, IAEA Bulletin: 8). On this basis, the IAEA will be able to conduct a reasoned analysis of member states' declarations and address any inconsistencies before the safeguards agreement is concluded. For those countries that currently have a safeguards agreement, it has been suggested that an annual review occur to ensure a country's continued peaceful nuclear intentions.

Export Information. The Zangger Group and London Club are the primary organizations responsible for the control of nuclear exports. The guidelines are voluntary, but member countries have reported such transfers to these organizations. These records, analyzed by their member governments, provide useful indicators pointing to the existence of clandestine nuclear programs. In the past, this information was rarely provided to the IAEA in a systematic and comprehensive fashion, for fear of compromise. During the Iraq inspections, however, export information was essential in uncovering the depth of the clandestine nuclear program.

A nuclear-related export control list can be likened to an indicator list; the items it contains are essentially a cookbook for a nuclear capability. This is why the great majority of information is not in the public domain. However, with the broad scientific and technical knowledge base in the IAEA, this information can be applied to a study of member states' nuclear intentions. Information that an NPT member state has imported heavy water, for example, may indicate to the IAEA the presence of an unsafeguarded nuclear facility. Of course, not all transfers occur under the export control regime, as Iraq's supplier network proved, but the information would likely reveal inconsistencies.

In April 1990, representatives of the suppliers groups met with senior IAEA officials to suggest improvements in the IAEA capability to analyze this information. Since 1983, these same states have continued to insist on zero real growth in the IAEA budget. The IAEA officials responded by stating that the information would be gladly accepted, but that the provision of raw data would not serve the interests of either party. In this way, the suppliers groups maintain the sensitivity of the details, and the IAEA benefits from this important information. In a related vein, the U.S.-based Monterey Institute has provided the IAEA a proliferation forecasting capability, utilizing a vast computerized database of international nuclear-related commerce ("Nuclear Mercenary").

Since the Iraq experience, the Board of Governors has continued to debate the issue of member-country reporting of nuclear-related exports and imports to the IAEA. There is a consensus that this information is a useful tool in ensuring the effectiveness of safeguards. The Board is considering proposals for the expansion of current nuclear material reporting requirements, and the inclusion in regular reporting channels of activity related to certain non-nuclear material and equipment. This proposal further seeks to verify that exported and imported material and equipment are not diverted from their intended location and use (Jennekens *a*). Whatever the final decision on the form export control information will take, it will certainly benefit the IAEA in its search for undeclared activities.

Intelligence Information. Although the effort by the IAEA in Iraq was the result of a special UN Security Council mandate, in principle, intelligence information can legally and usefully be applied to future Agency endeavors. The IAEA was not empowered with an independent means of verifying a country's peaceful nuclear intentions; thus, it must make use of information provided by member states. The agency has learned a great deal about the use of intelligence information; what remains to be seen is how the IAEA will incorporate intelligence into its routine operations as the IAEA strives to ensure the continued relevancy and effectiveness of safeguards.

The IAEA is beginning to formulate the method in which intelligence will be institutionalized. To its credit, the agency is approaching this task in a comprehensive, well-reasoned manner in an attempt to maintain the confidence of those countries choosing to provide intelligence. However, the IAEA is somewhat inexperienced in the use of intelligence, by U.S. standards. The handling of intelligence by many U.S. government agencies is a routine matter. In contrast, the IAEA rarely dealt with intelligence before the inspections in Iraq. Procedures for successfully employing intelligence are now a critical issue: Should the IAEA use desk officers, secure areas, special access badges? These are questions agency officials now need to address on a day-to-day basis. The IAEA has also contacted several countries for assistance in this task.

Despite this seeming inexperience, the IAEA has a great deal of experience handling sensitive information, experience that can be usefully applied to intelligence information. Safeguards Confidential Information is restricted in its distribution to the member state to which the information applies, to Safeguards Department personnel, and to the Director-General. It consists of information obtained in the implementation of safeguards agreements, which in many instances is commercially sensitive, proprietary information.

From the agency perspective, intelligence complements rather than replaces in-house information. The mix of intelligence and other information may be likened to a pyramid. The base is 95% of the pyramid, consisting of source material derived from safeguards confidential information, open source and technical journals, and other information. The tip is 5% of the pyramid, and represents information derived from intelligence sources. Intelligence can act as a confirmation of information the Agency already has, or as a starting point in a thorough analysis of in-house information.

The experience in Iraq proved that the IAEA is capable of handling intelligence information. As a result, the U.S. Intelligence Community and the IAEA have extended this cooperation to other regions of the world, namely North Korea and Iran. The usefulness of intelligence can be seen in the IAEA's handling of North Korea. Hans Blix, IAEA Director General, travelled to Pyongyang to make final arrangements for the IAEA's first inspection, required under the provisions of the safeguards agreement. At that time, the IAEA apparently utilized information provided by the U.S. Intelligence Community to challenge the veracity of North Korea's nuclear declaration (Sanger: A7). During a recent IAEA mission in Iran, Iranian officials asked the Agency to identify locations they wished to visit. On the basis of intelligence and other information from member states, IAEA officials picked a number of sites, all of which were visited (Wise *a*: A29). Future negotiations with other countries might also be aided by the international use of intelligence.

The number of clandestine programs that exist throughout the world remains to be seen, but it has become clear that neither the IAEA nor the U.S. Intelligence Community can accomplish in isolation the objectives called for by their common interests. The IAEA verification regime is best supported by the employment of foreign intelligence information, as the Iraq experience has proved.

U.S. INTELLIGENCE AND THE NORTH KOREAN "NUCLEAR CRISIS"

William E. Campbell
Senior Master Sergeant, U.S. Air Force
August 1996

Inspections without intelligence input are unguided searches with little chance of detecting well-conceived violations.

David Kay

NORTH KOREA

North Korea joined the IAEA in September 1974 and signed the NPT in 1985, but failed to negotiate a new full scope safeguards agreement with the IAEA within the prescribed 18-month period.[1] Although delays were not entirely North Korea's fault—the IAEA initially forwarded the wrong paperwork—many believed that Pyongyang was postponing signing the agreement in an effort to develop nuclear weapons. North Korea delayed signing the safeguards agreement, citing three preconditions: the withdrawal of U.S. nuclear weapons from South Korea; termination of annual U.S.-Republic of Korea (ROK) joint military exercises, known as Team Spirit, which the North claims are rehearsals for nuclear war; and finally, the right to withdraw from the safeguards accord any time Pyongyang felt threatened by the hostile actions of nuclear states. The IAEA considered these stipulations unsatisfactory because the actions of third parties had no bearing on the bilateral agreement between the IAEA and North Korea (Mack: 87).

---

1 North Korea concluded an older INFCIRC 66 Rev. 2 agreement with the IAEA in 1977, placing a Soviet-supplied research reactor along with its related nuclear materials under IAEA safeguards ("Agreement Between the IAEA and DPRK").

U.S. intelligence satellites first identified North Korea's indigenously produced nuclear reactor at its Yongbyon nuclear complex, 60 miles north of Pyongyang, during 1984-5, while the reactor was still under construction. The U.S. quietly urged the Soviet Union, which trained North Korea's initial cadre of nuclear technicians and scientists and supplied it with its first nuclear research reactor, to respond to this North Korean development (Song: 478). Equally concerned about the spread of nuclear weapons, the Soviet Union pressured North Korea to join the NPT in December 1985. In return for signing the Treaty, North Korea received long-term economic cooperation and continued nuclear-related technical assistance from the Kremlin, including a pledge of additional Soviet reactors for electrical power generation (Bermudez: 595).

Intelligence Enters the Public Domain

In early 1989, the U.S. shifted its diplomatic efforts to the public domain. Although North Korea had signed the NPT in 1985, it still had not concluded a full scope safeguards agreement with the IAEA. Information derived from U.S. intelligence concerning the continued construction at the Yongbyon complex was leaked to the South Korean press, the *Washington Post,* and the *New York Times,* among others, in 1989, increasing international concerns over North Korea's nuclear ambitions.

Jane's Defense Weekly featured a story about the Yongbyon complex in September 1989. In the article, the author cited U.S. intelligence sources who estimated North Korea could produce a "nuclear device (an experimental, non-deliverable nuclear system) within five years and a deliverable nuclear bomb shortly thereafter" (Bermudez: 597). The article, based in part on leaked intelligence derived from U.S. military satellite photographs, indicated that the indigenously-built reactor at Yongbyon was a 30-Megawatt reactor constructed from declassified blue prints of the 60-Megawatt Calder Hall reactor first built in the United Kingdom in 1956. In addition to the reactor first detected by U.S. intelligence during the mid 1980s, U.S. satellites in 1989 also revealed "four to five additional facilities under construction in the Yongbyon area" (Bermudez: 597). One site was identified as a test site for nuclear detonations and another as a nuclear reprocessing facility. It was later reported that U.S. and ROK intelligence detected approximately 70 small-scale explosions at the test site between the mid 1980s and 1991 (Hibbs *a*: 5). Intelligence sources believed the site was used to test various high-explosive triggering devices, a necessary step in nuclear weapons development. North Korea apparently stopped testing at this site or shifted to underground tests once they were informed that the U.S. was aware of their activities (Hibbs *e*: 17).

In February 1990, Japanese press released the first photograph of the construction of North Korea's nuclear site near Yongbyon. According to the *Daily Yomiuri* article, Tokai University scientists displayed a photograph of the Yongbyon complex taken from the French SPOT commercial satellite ("First Picture"). The unclassified imagery confirmed the existence of the nuclear reprocessing center under construction at the complex and provided the first hard evidence available in the public domain of North Korea's nuclear ambitions.

By U.S. estimates, the reprocessing facility, later identified by North Korean officials as a "Radiochemical Laboratory," was designed to extract plutonium from spent nuclear fuel for weapons production. It is the largest facility of its kind outside of the United States. In addition, U.S. intelligence sources, the following April, confirmed that North Korea had been operating an unsafeguarded 30-Megawatt, graphite-moderated reactor at Yongbyon since shortly after signing the NPT in 1985 (Hibbs and Usui: 8). This reactor was believed capable of producing enough plutonium for one nuclear bomb a year. An older Soviet-supplied research reactor, also located at Yongbyon, had been in operation since the late 1960s. This modified 2-Megawatt thermal reactor, along with a 0.1-Megawatt critical assembly, has been under IAEA safeguards since 1977 (Monsourov: 26). Both facilities were already subject to IAEA safeguards provided under the older INFCIRC 66-type agreement.

The Post-Gulf War Era

North Korea's nuclear program received little attention until the issue resurfaced after the Gulf War. The failure of U.S. intelligence to detect Iraq's clandestine nuclear program, North Korea's development of a long-range ballistic missiles, and Pyongyang's failure to conclude a new full scope safeguards agreement raised concerns in the international community over North Korea's nuclear intentions. Despite repeated efforts by the IAEA to conclude an agreement, North Korea was still holding to its preconditions for signing the safeguards accord. In February, South Korea officially asked the IAEA to impose sanctions against North Korea should it fail to sign a safeguards agreement by June 1991.

U.S. diplomatic efforts were renewed, in early 1991, to bring North Korea into compliance with the NPT. Partly aimed at appeasing the North Koreans and also the result of the post-Cold War military drawdown, President George Bush announced in September 1991 that the U.S. would withdraw all tactical nuclear weapons from foreign soil. This announcement was offset later in November when the U.S. announced it would postpone planned troop reductions for Korea, a signal of U.S. resolve. In December, ROK President Roh Tae Woo declared that South Korean soil was free of nuclear weapons.

The situation improved significantly following the ROK President's announcement. Although the agreement was never fully implemented, North and South Korea initialed, on New Year's Eve 1991, the Joint Declaration for a Non-Nuclear Korean Peninsula. This agreement banned all aspects of nuclear weapons production, possession, or deployment on the Korean peninsula and provided for bilateral inspections of all nuclear-related facilities. Early the next month, the ROK announced the suspension of joint Team Spirit exercises. Following the announcement, North Korea signed a full scope safeguards agreement, often referred to as INFCIRC 403, without preconditions. In the meantime, CIA Director Robert Gates, in his testimony before the House Foreign Affairs Committee, claimed that North Korea was a few months to two years from producing a nuclear bomb, further raising suspicions about North Korea's nuclear program (Fessler: 480).

After several delays, the safeguards accord was ratified by the North Korean legislature and entered into force on 10 April 1992. Early the following month, North Korea submitted an initial report, pursuant to the safeguards agreement, declaring its nuclear facilities and materials to the IAEA (UNSC S/25556: 4). In addition to declaring gram quantities of plutonium, the report listed seven facilities the DPRK claimed constituted the full disclosure of its nuclear program (MacLachlan: 13).

IAEA Inspections Begin

IAEA Director-General Blix conducted an unprecedented visit of North Korea's nuclear facilities during 11-16 May 1992. The purpose of the trip, although not officially an inspection, was to familiarize the IAEA with North Korea's nuclear program. The Director-General met with senior DPRK officials, held discussions with nuclear experts, and toured several of North Korea's nuclear-related facilities. He and his staff visited facilities at the Yongbyon complex, including among others, the unsafeguarded 5-Megawatt experimental reactor in operation since 1986, a 50-Megawatt reactor under construction, and the partially operational fuel reprocessing facility North Korean officials referred to as the Radiochemical Laboratory. In addition, the IAEA team visited a 200-Megawatt reactor under construction near Teachon, uranium ore processing plants in Pakchon and Pyongsan, the Institute of Atomic Energy, and the nuclear research center at Kim Il-Sung University. During the visit, IAEA officials became the first "outsiders" to be granted access to North Korea's indigenous nuclear program that, like most aspects of North Korean society, is based on a policy of self-reliance (Blix *a*).

Between May 1992 and November 1993, IAEA inspectors conducted six *ad hoc* inspections of North Korea's declared nuclear facilities to determine the correctness and completeness of the information provided to the IAEA. Tasks undertaken during these inspections, among other duties, included taking material samples at the radiochemical laboratory that the DPRK had identified as a spent fuel reprocessing facility in its initial report. Analysis of the material samples taken would determine the extent of North Korea's reprocessing activities at the laboratory. North Korea previously stated that the Radiochemical Laboratory had been used only once to reprocess spent fuel. According to Mr. Blix, North Korean officials admitted to reprocessing a "tiny amount" of plutonium at this facility from the DPRK's 5-Megawatt experimental reactor. The reprocessing coincided with the removal of a few damaged fuel rods from the reactor's core during late 1989 and early 1990 (UNSC A/25556: 4). Experts in the U.S. believed this plutonium was recovered, instead, from the Soviet-supplied reactor during the 1970s (Hibbs *f*: 15) Despite having initially denied the allegation, North Korean officials later admitted, in early 1993, to reprocessing a small quantity of plutonium from the reactor in 1975 (Hibbs *c*: 8).

During the first inspection in May, IAEA inspectors were granted access to all areas that they had requested, including the Radiochemical Laboratory. IAEA inspectors, however, became increasingly suspicious of North Korea's nuclear ambitions during subsequent inspections. Test results of the material samples suggested that North Korea had extracted more weapons grade plutonium than admitted. There were inconsistencies between the DPRK's Initial Report and the test results from the samples taken at the laboratory and from the declared plutonium (UNSC S/25556: 5). While the DPRK claimed only one reprocessing campaign, analysis of the samples indicated that North Korea had extracted plutonium on four occasions. The IAEA believed that North Korea had reprocessed spent fuel at the Laboratory, once each year between 1989 and early 1992 (R. Smith *d*: A1).

The IAEA made extensive efforts to resolve the discrepancies during the inspections that followed. According to the Blix report:

> [T]he Agency undertook additional sampling activities, requested access to operating records of the relevant facilities, solicited clarifications from the DPRK authorities and requested that Agency officials be permitted to visit two sites located in the Nyongbyon Nuclear Research Centre that the Agency had reason to believe were related to nuclear waste (UNSC S/25556: 5).

IAEA inspectors requested and received access to the two suspect waste sites during the 3rd inspection in September. Inspectors determined that the first site was not nuclear related. They were granted access to the above-ground level of the second facility, however, U.S. intelligence later provided to the IAEA (R. Smith *d*: A1) data indicating that the building had a second level below-ground (UNSC S/25556: 5).

During high-level talks in Vienna, in December, the IAEA expressed its concerns over the inconsistencies that had emerged during previous inspections. The agency requested to revisit the second facility to determine the use of the lower level of the building and to take samples. In an IAEA cable sent to the DPRK in late December, Director General Blix indicated that a second site in the complex may also require IAEA inspection (UNSC S/25556: 5). The DPRK responded that these sites were military related and non-nuclear and therefore, not subject to IAEA safeguards (UNSC S/25556: 5).

During meetings held in late January 1993, North Korea continued its assertion that the sites were military and had no connection to its nuclear program and also added another reason for refusing access to these facilities. Referring to U.S. intelligence, the North Koreans objected to the inspections because the IAEA was requesting access to these facilities based on third-party information (UNSC S/25556: 6).

North Korea Challenges Special Inspections

The crisis escalated in early 1993. The DPRK continued its refusal to grant access to the two sites during the IAEA's sixth inspection visit, in January. Senior leaders from both sides again met in Vienna, in February, but failed to reach a settlement of the issue. As a result, Director General Blix brought the matter to the attention of the IAEA Board of Governors (UNSC S/25556: 6).

Fearing a repeat of its experiences with Iraq, the IAEA requested "special inspections" of the two sites suspected to hold the key to North Korea's nuclear past (UNSC S/25556: 6). The IAEA's reputation was at stake, as was possibly the non-proliferation regime itself. The agency's status as the world's nuclear watchdog was already tarnished by its inability to uncover Iraq's nuclear program, secretly carried out by Baghdad despite annual IAEA inspections. This was only the third time in the IAEA's 30-year history that such a request had been made and the first time the agency had requested UN backing. Although not specifically termed as special inspections, the agency had "requested and received access to undeclared sites in Iran and South Africa" (Woolsey: 38). During the latter, IAEA officials conducted a short-notice visit to a non-declared site in South Africa in 1993 that U.S. intelligence suspected was nuclear related (Hibbs *b*: 18). In effect, North Korea's refusal was a direct challenge to the IAEA's efforts to strengthen its safeguards regime.

During the February Board of Governors meeting, U.S. intelligence supplied the IAEA with an unprecedented array of U.S. satellite photographs that were displayed as evidence of North Korea's failure to fulfill its obligations under the NPT. In addition, Director General Blix produced test results from previous inspections that showed that kilogram quantities of plutonium were missing from North Korea's inventory (UNSC S/25556: 6). This evidence drew an immediate response from the IAEA. At the conclusion of the 4-day closed session, the Board adopted a resolution calling upon the DPRK to "urgently" extend its full cooperation to the IAEA by positively responding to the agency's request for access to the additional information and to the alleged waste sites (UNSC S/25556: 52).

Again North Korea refused. On 10 March, the Minister for Atomic Energy of the DPRK, Choi Hak Gun, issued the government's official response. The Minister stated that the DPRK could not consider the IAEA's request for special inspections because the resumption of Team Spirit exercises in South Korea had forced his country into a "state of semi-war" (UNSC S/25556: 56). Two days later, North Korea announced its intentions to withdraw from the NPT — the first member state to officially announce its withdraw from the Treaty since it entered into force in 1970 (UNSC S/25405: annex). The withdrawal would be effective at the end of the 90-day notification period provided in the Treaty. In addition to the "unjust" resolution which the DPRK claimed was based on fabricated intelligence information, North Korea cited the resumption of Team Spirit joint military exercises and the continued presence of U.S. nuclear weapons in South Korea as the basis for its withdrawal from the Treaty (UNSC S/25407: annex).

North Korea claimed its decision to withdraw from the NPT was within its rights under the Treaty. Article X.1 of the NPT provides that any member state can withdraw from the Treaty provided there are "extraordinary events," in relation to the Treaty, that "have jeopardized the supreme interests of its country." North Korea claimed that the U.S. was threatening it with nuclear weapons. The official statement renouncing the Treaty stated that Pyongyang's decision to withdraw would "remain unchanged until the United States stops its nuclear threats against the DPRK and the IAEA secretariat returns to its principle of independence and impartiality" (UNSC S/25407). The IAEA's position, on the other hand, was that the Safeguards Agreement remained in force as long as the DPRK was a party to the NPT (UNSC S/25556: 6). Pursuant to Article 26 of the agreement signed by North Korea, the DPRK would remain a party to the NPT during the 90-day notification period. Therefore, North Korea's nuclear facilities remained subject to IAEA safeguards.

The international community took seriously North Korea's decision to withdraw from the NPT. If North Korea developed nuclear weapons, the U.S. feared it would touch off a regional nuclear arms race.

The urgency expressed in the U.S., however, was not echoed by many elsewhere. Many Asian diplomats, for example, blamed the U.S. for escalating the nuclear crisis. Diplomatic officials from Japan, China, and Russia criticized the U.S. decision to hold Team Spirit exercises and its efforts to push IAEA special inspections, claiming these actions were underlying reasons for North Korea's announcement to withdraw from the NPT (Hibbs *h*: 1).

On 18 March, the IAEA's Board of Governors, meeting in special session, adopted a second resolution on the North Korean issue (UNSC S/25445: 3). In the resolution, the Board expressed its concerns over the DPRK's announcement to withdraw from the NPT and confirmed that the DPRK's safeguards accord with the IAEA remained in force. Additionally, the Board requested that the Director-General take all necessary steps to resolve the issue and report back to the Board on 31 March.

The Board of Governors met again in special session in late March to discuss the implementation of safeguards in North Korea. The Director-General concluded that North Korea was in non-compliance with Articles 3, 71, 73 and 77 of its safeguards agreement. The Board adopted another resolution, on 1 April, declaring that North Korea was "in non-compliance with its obligations under its Safeguards Agreement with the Agency." The IAEA also stated its intention to report the matter, as required by Article XII.C of the IAEA Statute, to the full membership of the IAEA, and to the UN Security Council and the General Assembly (UNSC S/25556: 14-15).

Following intensive debate and negotiations among members of the Security Council, the Council's President issued a statement, on 8 April, expressing concern over the situation and the refusal of North Korea to open its nuclear facilities to IAEA inspections (UNSC S/25556). The members of the Council, in the presidential statement, also reaffirmed the importance of the NPT and encouraged the IAEA to continue its deliberations with the DPRK to resolve the situation satisfactorily. Still, North Korea refused to cooperate with the IAEA. On 22 April, Russia increased the pressure when Moscow notified the DPRK that it had terminated bilateral nuclear cooperation as a result of the DPRK's announcement to withdrawal from the NPT.

The following week, North Korea denounced the IAEA resolution and called for bilateral talks with the United States, which Pyongyang claimed was the only way to resolve the impasse (Shigemura: A28). North Korea also spelled out its conditions for remaining in the NPT. The demands were: (1) the cancellation of future Team Spirit exercises; (2) inspections of both ROK and U.S. military installations in South Korea; (3) a U.S. pledge that it would not use nuclear weapons against North Korea; (4) the U.S. must abandon its nuclear umbrella over South Korea; and, (5) the U.S. must respect North Korea's socialist system. Many in the U.S. believed that the changing nature of North Korean demands was a pretext for stalling international inspections. Despite the rhetoric, during mid-May, North Korea allowed IAEA inspectors to conduct maintenance checks of monitoring devices and to replace film in surveillance cameras at the declared facilities in the Yongbyon complex.

On 11 May, the UN Security Council passed Resolution 825 without dissension (China and Pakistan abstained), a resolution expressing its "grave concern" and calling upon the DPRK to reconsider its withdrawal from the NPT and "to reaffirm its commitment to the Treaty." Continuing, the Council further requested that the DPRK honor its obligations under the Treaty and called upon other nations to persuade North Korea to find a solution.

U.S.-DPRK Talks Begin

The first in a series of bilateral talks were held in New York from 2 to 11 June. Following the first round of negotiations, the U.S. and North Korea issued a joint statement outlining the principles agreed upon by the two sides. The agreed principles included assurances to refrain from the threat and use of force, to support "peace and security in a nuclear-free Korean Peninsula" that included the "impartial" application of safeguards, "respect for each other's sovereignty," "noninterference in each other's internal affairs," and mutual "support for the peaceful reunification of Korea." More important, North Korea announced it unilaterally decided to suspend, at least temporarily, its withdrawal from the NPT ("U.S.-North Korea": 32).

A second round of high-level talks between the U.S. and the DPRK were held in Geneva during early July. The two sides released a joint statement at the conclusion of negotiations, outlining Pyongyang's agreement to exchange its graphite-moderated reactors for light water reactors that are less suitable for plutonium production. The U.S. agreed, in return, to support and assist the DPRK in this initiative. In addition, the North announced its willingness to pursue consultations with the IAEA concerning inspections and with South Korea on the implementation of the joint declaration ("U.S.-North Korea": 32).

In the meantime, the IAEA continued to press North Korea to comply with its obligations under the NPT. The DPRK again allowed IAEA inspectors to maintain surveillance equipment at the two Yongbyon facilities, in August. IAEA and DPRK officials meeting in Pyongyang in early September failed, however, to make any progress in their negotiations. North Korea, in fact, refused to discuss IAEA suggestions for overcoming the hurdles to resuming full-scope safeguards inspections. The DPRK held to its position that, under the "current circumstances," it was enough that North Korea allow IAEA inspectors to perform routine maintenance of the monitoring equipment.

At the opening session of the Board of Governors meeting, on 21 September, Director General Blix reported on the IAEA's lack of progress on the North Korean nuclear issue. He also informed the Board that the IAEA had requested routine and *ad hoc* inspections to begin in late September and, as of the meeting, North Korea had not responded. At the conclusion of the meeting, the Board adopted a resolution placing the North Korean issue on the agenda of the IAEA's General Conference scheduled for the following week (IAEA Doc 291). North Korea argued that the resolution violated its sovereignty. Claiming it had made every effort to resolve the issue, Pyongyang attempted to transfer blame for the standoff to the U.S. for plotting to undermine its socialist regime and to the IAEA for continually demanding special inspections and for using third-party intelligence.

International support was building behind the IAEA. On 1 October, the IAEA General Conference adopted a resolution expressing "grave concern" over North Korea's failure to discharge its safeguards obligations and urging the DPRK to "cooperate immediately" with the IAEA to implement the safeguards agreement (IAEA Doc 1250). The resolution, however, failed to refer the issue to the UN Security Council. Seventy-two states voted in favor of the resolution, 2 voted against and 11 abstained. North Korea and Libya voted against the resolution, while China led the list of countries that abstained. North Korea expressed regret over the passing of the resolution and reiterated the DPRK's position that the resolution violated its sovereignty.

During October and November, the situation became more urgent because negotiations between the DPRK and the IAEA had broken off. Negotiations with the U.S. had tapered off and were limited to working-level discussions. Time was also running out for the safeguards monitoring equipment in North Korea's declared facilities, which would soon require servicing. As a result, the IAEA submitted a report to the UN General Assembly outlining North Korea's continued non-compliance with its safeguards obligations. Director-General Blix also reported to the UN General Assembly that inspectors would no longer be able to verify the safeguards unless they were granted immediate access to the facilities (UNGA Res A/48/14). The General Assembly passed a resolution expressing "grave concern" over the situation and urged North Korea to "immediately cooperate" with IAEA inspectors (UNGA Res A/48/14). North Korea was the only member to vote against the resolution.

Just prior to the General Assembly meeting, the DPRK informed the IAEA that it was ready to accept limited inspections of its declared facilities for the purpose of maintaining safeguards equipment (Blix *b*). The North claimed that checking the seals and maintenance of equipment was sufficient for the IAEA to insure the continuity of safeguards. The IAEA declined the offer on the basis that all inspections, routine and *ad hoc*, were long overdue. North Korea had not allowed routine inspections of its facilities since February. Speaking before the IAEA Board of Governors in early December, Dr. Blix concluded that the safeguards system in place at North Korea's declared facilities could no longer provide adequate assurances that these facilities were being used for peaceful purposes (IAEA Doc 1253). North Korea and the IAEA resumed working-level discussions in December; however, little progress was made.

The U.S. increased the stakes in January 1994 when it announced plans to deploy advanced weapons and a national intelligence support team to South Korea. The Clinton Administration was becoming increasingly concerned that North Korea was close to developing a bomb. These fears were fueled, in part, by a revised intelligence estimate released earlier in December that stated North Korea had extracted enough plutonium for two bombs in 1989 (Hibbs *g*: 9). Moreover, the Intelligence Community believed that the DPRK had separated 8.5 to 12 kilograms of plutonium as opposed to the 80 grams claimed by North Korea (Hibbs *e*: 17). North Korea abruptly agreed to IAEA inspections of the seven declared nuclear facilities the following month (IAEA Doc 1255). The two undeclared waste sites, however, remained off limits to IAEA inspectors (UNSC S/1994/254: 5).

IAEA Inspections Resume

During mid-March 1994, IAEA inspectors conducted the first inspection of North Korean nuclear facilities in over a year. During the visit, however, North Korean officials prevented inspectors from conducting key checks at one facility and from taking samples from two key cells in the Radiochemical Laboratory (UNSC S/1994/322: 5). These tests were necessary to determine North Korea's reprocessing activities since the last IAEA inspection. In addition, inspectors found that some seals on monitoring devices had been broken. Pyongyang's failure to cooperate with inspectors prompted the IAEA Board of Governors, on 21 March, to find North Korea in "further non-compliance" with INFCIRC 403 and to refer the matter to the UN Security Council and the General Assembly (UNSC S/1994/322: 3).

Later that afternoon, the UN Security Council began intense deliberations on a response to the IAEA resolution. The result was short of U.S. expectations. The Council's President issued a statement calling upon the DPRK "to allow the IAEA inspectors to complete the inspections activities" (UNSC S/PRST/1994/13). The statement represented a compromise between the U.S., which wanted a resolution condemning North Korea's actions, and China, which believed the measure was too strong. Shortly thereafter, the U.S. announced the resumption of plans for Team Spirit '94, which was canceled earlier in March as a reward for North Korea allowing inspections. Clinton Administration officials also announced they would formulate plans to pursue international economic sanctions against North Korea (Fulghum: 22).

North Korea Discharges Fuel Without IAEA Supervision

The crisis deepened in mid-May when the DPRK announced that it had begun discharging the 8,000 spent fuel rods from its 5-Megawatt reactor at Yongbyon without close IAEA supervision. North Korea refused to allow the IAEA to observe the core discharge based on its "unique status" under the NPT. The IAEA considered this a violation of the safeguards accord, since removal of the rods, without safeguards measures, would destroy evidence of North Korea's past refueling activities. (IAEA Doc 1269).

Prior to the announcement, U.S. intelligence and the IAEA estimated that, based on Pyongyang's outdated refueling equipment, it would require 90 days to remove the entire core of spent fuel rods. Instead, two weeks after refueling got underway, IAEA inspectors at the Yongbyon complex reported that half of the core had been discharged. North Korea was using indigenous refueling equipment previously unknown to the IAEA or U.S. intelligence (Hibbs *d*: 1). U.S. officials had assumed that, based on the intelligence estimates, they would have more than a month to negotiate an agreement with the DPRK to allow IAEA inspectors to tag the discharged fuel rods. The rapid refueling of the reactor meant that North Korea would likely complete the process before a settlement could be reached. Unless IAEA inspectors were allowed to map the irradiated fuel rods as they were removed, the IAEA would no longer be able to verify DPRK claims that the rods removed from the reactor's core were the original ones loaded in 1986. U.S. intelligence believed that North Korea had discharged and refueled the reactor during a 100-day outage in 1989 (Hibbs and Hart: 5).

Despite the lack of progress in this area, IAEA inspectors were permitted to complete some verification activities at the Radiochemical Laboratory during mid-May. The safeguards measures included performing gamma mapping (Hibbs *d*: 1) and taking smear samples from the plutonium glovebox area that was off-limits to IAEA inspectors during the previous inspection. Additionally, inspectors were allowed to service the surveillance cameras and replace seals at the laboratory (UNSC S/1994/601: 2).

IAEA and DPRK officials met again in Pyongyang, in late May, to find a solution to the reprocessing dilemma, but again no agreement was reached. The lack of progress prompted the UN Security Council to issue yet another presidential statement on the North Korean situation on 30 May. The President, on behalf of the Council's members, expressed "grave concern" over the discharge activities at North Korea's 5-Megawatt reactor and "strongly urged" the DPRK to proceed with refueling only in the manner prescribed by the IAEA. If North Korea followed IAEA guidelines, it would preserve the rods, allowing for fuel measurements at a later date (UNSC S/PRST/1994/28).

In June, the IAEA's Board of Governors officially condemned North Korea's actions. The Board adopted another resolution that "deplored" the DPRK's failure to comply with previous resolutions on the matter (IAEA Doc 1273). As a result, the Board suspended non-medical support to North Korea. Three days later and in response to the resolution, the DPRK announced its immediate withdrawal from the IAEA. North Korea justified its decision based on the "unjust" Board of Governors resolution, which the DPRK claimed imposed "sanctions" that threatened the sovereignty of their country ("Minister of Foreign Affairs of the DPRK"). The U.S. also announced plans to pursue international sanctions against North Korea in the UN, although China continued to oppose the measure strongly.

Former President Jimmy Carter visited Pyongyang on a mission to defuse the crisis. Following the Carter visit, President Clinton announced that North Korea agreed to freeze its nuclear program and to resume diplomatic talks (Clinton *e*). U.S.-DPRK talks resumed in July, but were interrupted by the death of North Korea's only leader, Kim Il Sung. Talks resumed again in August. The IAEA General Conference once again adopted a resolution, in September, expressing its "grave concern" and "urging" the DPRK to "cooperate immediately" with the agency (IAEA Doc 1286). The U.S. and the DPRK finally reached an accord on the disposition of North Korea's nuclear program in October.

The agreement obligates North Korea to freeze its nuclear program under IAEA supervision and eventually dismantle its graphite-moderated reactors. In exchange, North Korea will receive two light water reactors by a target date of 2003, at which time North Korea must allow *ad hoc* and routine inspections of its nuclear facilities. The U.S., in the meantime, will facilitate the annual delivery of 500,000 tons of heavy oil to fuel North Korea's energy needs. In addition, the U.S. and the DPRK agreed to open liaison offices in each other's capitals as an initial step toward full diplomatic relations. Both sides also agreed to move toward full normalization of economic relations by reducing barriers to trade and investment.

While the framework requires North Korea to remain a party to the NPT, it provides an interim period of about 9 years in which IAEA routine and *ad hoc* inspections are prohibited. North Korea is not obligated to provide a full accounting of its nuclear activities until that time.

CONCLUSION

THE FUTURE OF INTELLIGENCE SHARING WITH THE INTERNATIONAL ATOMIC ENERGY AGENCY

Audrey D. Hudgins
Captain U.S. Army
September 1992

Nuclear proliferation has been a concern since the world entered the nuclear age. Early international efforts to operate and control nuclear fuel cycles, envisaged in the Baruch Plan, met with failure. In the years following, the use of atomic energy became a national rather than international endeavor. To aid the spread of peaceful nuclear technology and to prevent its diversion to military use, in 1957 the International Atomic Energy Agency (IAEA) was created. Some characteristics of this international inspectorate were appropriate only to the time in which it originated. Former World War II enemies of the Allied victors were the targets of the safeguards regime. Following ratification of the Nuclear Nonproliferation Treaty (NPT) of 1968, the IAEA safeguarded nuclear cycles the world over.

By design, the agency's mission was strictly one of inspection and verification through safeguards agreements. The detection of clandestine nuclear activities was a mission of the major powers. Disclosure of the extent and complexity of Iraq's nuclear weapons program eroded the level of confidence that the international community had in the nuclear inspection and regulatory abilities of the IAEA.

But Iraq was a failure of far greater proportions. Although the IAEA might be faulted for its lack of aggressiveness in inspection techniques, safeguards are simply one component of a comprehensive nuclear nonproliferation regime. Iraq violated all relevant aspects of this regime. Through its accession to the NPT, Iraq pledged not to acquire nuclear weapons. Iraq subverted the export control regime by clandestinely obtaining nuclear equipment and material. Finally, Iraq violated its safeguards agreement with the IAEA. The Iraqi nuclear weapons program showed that a signatory to the NPT could evade the IAEA, the U.S. Intelligence Community, and all other international scrutiny. As a result of this experience, all of these parties now realize the importance of global cooperation in the fight against nuclear proliferation.

Time has been the ultimate arbiter for international cooperation. Old enemies of World War II are now friends and allies. The Berlin Wall has fallen, and the two Germanies are now one. The collapse of the Soviet Union and the end of the Cold War have formed a new global environment. Bilateral arms control and disarmament treaties have evolved into multilateral confidence and security building measures. The United Nations has finally emerged as an effective promoter of international peace and security.

The IAEA, an organization under the auspices of the United Nations, has reaped the benefits of enhanced cooperation. In 1991, the U.S. Intelligence Community, the IAEA, and the United Nations Special Commission on Iraq (UNSCOM) joined forces to rid Iraq of its weapons of mass destruction. Despite its failure in some areas, intelligence has been the key to success. The U.S. Intelligence Community must now further define its role in a new international security environment. In order to ensure its continued effectiveness, the Intelligence Community must protect its sources and methods. But the Intelligence Community serves the policymaker, who, in turn, serves the national interest. The U.S. National Security Strategy defines nuclear proliferation as one of those interests. In order for U.S. and global concern over proliferation to be addressed, countries must choose to give the IAEA the tools it needs to do its job. Intelligence is one of these tools.

The Problem of National Interest

Nuclear proliferation presents a great threat to U.S. national security. Regional arms races can be destabilizing, potentially causing major shifts in the strategic power balance. Gaps in the export control regime and the threat of Soviet nuclear scientist emigration only accelerate this dangerous nuclear timeline.

The United States, and its intelligence community, must display vigilance and resolve. Unfortunately, nuclear proliferation cannot compete successfully with other national priorities, as demonstrated in the case of Pakistan in the 1980s. The U.S. must carefully weigh a myriad of factors when making short- and long-term policy decisions. The U.S. inability to certify Pakistan's peaceful nuclear intentions and Pakistani ties to the Iraq problem indicate that nuclear proliferation is a continuing policy concern.

The Problems of the IAEA

Conflicting national interests have plagued states throughout history. The IAEA, representing over 116 countries, has had its share of conflicting "international interests."

Safeguards Effectiveness. Safeguards effectiveness has been debated at the IAEA since its creation. Concerns over sovereignty and divergent views on the role of safeguards have contributed to diplomatic and political stalemate. The Iraq issue focused new attention on this issue. For example, the IAEA followed a routine, predictable inspection schedule. States pursuing clandestine development of a nuclear weapons program could clean up their operation prior to inspection and thus give the appearance of compliance with applicable safeguards. Iraq is a recent, yet classic example of this evasive strategy.

Never before had a country been caught violating its safeguards agreement with the IAEA. The Board of Governors came to the realization that IAEA safeguards are only as good as their implementation. This convergence of opinion has resulted in positive changes in the inspection process to ensure stricter compliance. The IAEA Board has implemented a short-notice, random inspection methodology and will soon adopt safeguards measures designed to detect clandestine activity.

Export Controls. Export control groups, and their member states, have expressed a traditional reluctance to provide export information to the IAEA because of its proprietary, commercially sensitive nature. During the inspections in Iraq, however, this information was essential in uncovering the depth of the clandestine nuclear program. The IAEA's handling of export information was very successful.

Iraq showed that many gaps exist in the field of export controls. The export control groups, one of the three pillars of the nuclear nonproliferation regime, have taken steps to enhance the comprehensiveness of export control guidelines. The inspections in Iraq also proved that greater cooperation between these groups and the IAEA produces a synergistic effect, making the regime as a whole stronger. A greater understanding and appreciation has developed between the two groups that will likely continue into the future.

A Lack of Aggressiveness. Historic evolution has framed the agency's safeguards approach. Until very recently, an aggressive application of safeguards was deemed discriminatory and prejudicial to a member's sovereign interests. The absence of assertiveness perhaps allowed Iraq to proceed unencumbered with its weapons development program. The Agency has since realized the benefit of a more aggressive attitude. Recently, IAEA inspectors have requested access to a number of suspected Iranian and North Korean nuclear facilities not declared by those states in their safeguards agreements. This trend will likely continue as the IAEA strives to deter proliferation.

Counterintelligence Problem. The IAEA is responsible for safeguarding the peaceful use of the atom, but is also the international purveyor of nuclear technology. With 85 percent of inspection personnel from non-nuclear weapons states, the IAEA must balance its approach. A lack of balance might actually make the IAEA a proliferant, as was the case with the director of the Iraqi national safeguards program. Nonetheless, this example has raised the IAEA's awareness of the dangerous potential of proliferation.

The IAEA and Nuclear Proliferation

The IAEA is a unique organization. Its role as the purveyor of peaceful nuclear energy gives the agency a full understanding of global nuclear activity and allows unparalleled insight into the prospects for illegal nuclear activity. Its staff of scientists and technicians are able to evaluate information available through the open press, scientific and technical journals, and a number of in-house and other information sources to enhance this understanding. Finally, through its safeguards system, the IAEA has the authority to question a target country or perform inspections to determine the purpose of suspected nuclear activity. No other organization, national or international, has the authority or the ability to perform all these tasks.

The IAEA safeguards system has three components:

1) deter the diversion of nuclear material to non-peaceful use,
2) detect the diversion of nuclear material to non-peaceful use, and
3) confirm by inspection that nuclear material is not diverted from peaceful use.

The last two components are adequately addressed through the current safeguards approach. The first component has two implied tasks, the detection and deterrence of clandestine nuclear facilities, which have received new attention since Iraq's clandestine nuclear weapons program was revealed. It is now understood that the current safeguards system does not adequately address the issue of deterrence.

Deterrence is the key to a successful nuclear nonproliferation regime. Many factors enable deterrence to be effective. First, and perhaps foremost, is the ability of intelligence to detect clandestine nuclear activity. Countries cannot be fully confident that such activity will go undetected. Second, the political and economic impact of illegal proliferation can be a significant deterrent. When international concern is raised, political isolation and economic sanctions might persuade a proliferant to cease nuclear activity. Finally, the destabilizing effects of regional nuclear proliferation are a viable deterrent. Conventional military and nuclear arms races flourish at the cost of economic progress, a price many states cannot afford.

The IAEA's central role in the nuclear nonproliferation regime has continued despite the missteps in handling the problem of Iraq. In order to ensure an effective regime, the IAEA must be empowered with the ability to deter illicit activity. The use of intelligence by the IAEA will provide this deterrent capability.

The Future of Intelligence and the IAEA

The IAEA safeguards system is simply not designed to detect diversions such as Iraq's, and the IAEA is not in a position to develop an organic intelligence collection capability. The agency does not possess the resources for such a venture, and the great majority of member states would not support its creation. Moreover, member countries already have unilateral capabilities in place. The IAEA must therefore rely on the member states to provide intelligence information. The experience in Iraq has proved that intelligence is a useful and necessary complement to a successful IAEA safeguards regime.

The IAEA is charged with the verification of safeguards on declared nuclear facilities. The safeguards program, much like the NPT, relies on the integrity of the signatories. A country's clandestine nuclear weapons development program is designed to subvert this pledge. Foreign intelligence information is the means to ensure that states are fulfilling the letter and spirit of the regime. Those that sign the treaty have pledged they will not develop nuclear weapons. Intelligence can be used simply to verify this pledge. Further, most countries motivated to possess a nuclear weapons capability are willing to do whatever is necessary to achieve that goal. The use of intelligence by the IAEA is a means of ensuring that the agency is doing whatever is necessary to achieve its goal of halting the spread of weapons of mass destruction.

Just as revelations of the Iraqi program alerted the IAEA to its own inadequacies, it also provides a warning to potential proliferants. The next offender may be harder to expose. This argues for more sharing of intelligence in the future. It can be hoped that the U.S. Intelligence Community's relationship with the IAEA, born of necessity and sustained by success, can continue well into the future. The cost is only as much as the U.S. chooses to bear, and the benefits are many.

U.S. INTELLIGENCE AND NUCLEAR DIPLOMACY

William E. Campbell
Senior Master Sergeant, U.S. Air Force
August 1996

A principle function of intelligence is to support policymakers in achieving national security objectives. This was clearly demonstrated during the North Korean nuclear crisis. U.S. objectives vis-a-vis North Korea were focused and clearly defined throughout the Bush and Clinton Administrations, although the two administrations adopted slightly different strategies to achieve these goals. In June 1992, in a joint statement with Russian President Boris Yeltsin, President George Bush applauded North and South Korea's efforts in concluding the Joint Denuclearization Declaration as a positive step toward strengthening the nuclear non-proliferation regime and adding to the peace and security in Northeast Asia ("Joint Statement": 18). President Clinton reiterated these goals, in July 1993, when he outlined his priorities for security in the Asian Pacific region. Speaking before the ROK National Assembly, President Clinton renewed U.S. commitments to the security of the South Korea and to the goals of a nuclear-free Korea and a strong international non-proliferation regime (Clinton *f*).

Measured against these objectives, the contributions of U.S. intelligence to U.S. strategy during the North Korean "nuclear crisis" were extremely important. Information supplied by U.S. intelligence served as the impetus for the actions taken by both the U.S. and the IAEA to persuade North Korea to freeze its nuclear program and eventually allow international inspections. Moreover, in describing the intelligence needs of the policymaker, Director of Central Intelligence (DCI) R. James Woolsey, in a statement before the Senate Governmental Affairs Committee in 1993, said:

> Too often the value of intelligence is measured by how it adds to our knowledge of a particular subject. But knowledge alone is no longer sufficient. Policymakers need more than facts, they need information that they can use — actionable intelligence (Woolsey: 38).

Indeed, U.S. intelligence provided the "actionable" intelligence necessary to first pressure North Korea to join the NPT in 1985 and to conclude a safeguards agreement in 1992. It provided the evidence that prompted the IAEA to demand special inspections in 1993, and to generate the international support needed to finally pressure the DPRK to freeze its nuclear program in 1994.

John Macartney, author of the widely disseminated *Intelligence: A Consumer's Guide,* also considers the use of intelligence information to be a tool of both foreign policy and diplomacy (Macartney: 472). In the realm of foreign policy, the U.S. supplied the IAEA with an unprecedented array of intelligence information necessary for the IAEA to undertake its mission in North Korea. The U.S. possesses the world's most costly intelligence apparatus, with highly sophisticated technical collection capabilities ranked second to none. As a foreign policy tool, sharing intelligence with the IAEA is a valuable means of ensuring the successful implementation of U.S. policy and serves as evidence of U.S. commitment to stemming the spread of weapons of mass destruction.

Intelligence, again according to Macartney, becomes a diplomatic tool when it is used publicly (Macartney: 472). While intelligence may not necessarily be a diplomatic tool, it certainly supports this instrument of national power. A popular example he cites was the effective use of U-2 imagery during UN Ambassador Adlai Stevenson's televised speech before the UN Security Council during the 1962 Cuban missile crisis. Since that time, this practice has become commonplace. As a more recent example, during a UN Security Council meeting in 1995, UN Ambassador Madeleine K. Albright displayed U-2 photographs that depicted mass graves in eastern Bosnia — evidence of Serbian crimes against humanity (Cassata *a*: 2665).

The U.S. used intelligence to effectively support public diplomacy throughout the North Korean nuclear crisis. A notable example was the display of U.S. satellite photographs during the February 1993 IAEA

Board of Governors meeting in Vienna. U.S.-supplied imagery provided compelling evidence of North Korea's nuclear ambitions and showed that Pyongyang was attempting to hide alleged nuclear waste sites from IAEA inspectors. The incriminating photographs, combined with the results of earlier IAEA inspections, provided the IAEA with concrete evidence of North Korea's failure to disclose the full extent of its nuclear program. This information also served as the basis for the Board of Governors resolution that called for special inspections of the suspect sites. This was the first step in the diplomatic process to bring North Korea into compliance with international norms.

While the display constitutes the most significant and undoubtedly the most dramatic presentation of U.S. intelligence during the crisis, it amounts to a relatively small portion of the intelligence made available to the public since 1989. U.S. officials from the Intelligence Community and other government agencies made public statements, briefed the media, and testified before open Congressional committees concerning North Korea's nuclear program. Given the uncharacteristically wide dissemination of intelligence information and the frequency of these "leaks," it is reasonable to conclude that many were condoned by officials, if not authorized, as part of a larger effort to draw attention to the issue and to substantiate U.S. initiatives in this area.

Prior to 1989, efforts to pressure North Korea to accept international safeguards where undertaken in diplomatic channels. This practice is often referred to as quiet diplomacy. Evidence of North Korea's covert nuclear activities, supplied by U.S. intelligence, provided the catalyst for these actions. U.S. diplomatic efforts achieved positive results in 1985, when the Soviet Union persuaded the DPRK to accede to the NPT. This approach was effective, at that time, because the Soviet Union still exercised some influence over North Korea. Quiet diplomacy, however, failed to persuade North Korea to conclude a full-scope safeguards agreement with the IAEA. By the late 1980s, as the Soviet Union neared collapse, Soviet aid and subsequently its leverage over the DPRK had all but disappeared. Consequently, a shift in strategy was warranted.

In addition, several other trends favor the release of intelligence information to the public. First, it reflects the greater public awareness of the activities of the U.S. government and the Intelligence Community. An element of this openness policy includes, among other things, expanded relations between the Intelligence Community and the media. In 1993, for instance, CIA personnel gave over 250 briefings to the press on a variety of subjects, including North Korea's nuclear weapons program (Gries: 366). Second was the need to build an international consensus against North Korea's continued disregard for the NPT. The U.S. realized it would require near-unanimous global support to pressure the DPRK first to conclude a safeguards accord and to open its facilities to international inspection, and later to freeze its nuclear program and remain in the Treaty. The media proved to be valuable for this purpose.

The third reason was political. Information was leaked by Republicans on Capitol Hill and the White House to support opposing positions over the Clinton Administration's handling of the North Korean issue (Fallows: 45). Finally, information was used, in part, to build public support at home — a lesson learned from the Vietnam era. Informing the public of the threat presented by North Korea's continued non-compliance and outlining U.S. policy options were designed to build domestic support for further U.S. actions. Additionally, while the information was undoubtedly intended to build U.S. resolve, it was also focused on the socialist regime in Pyongyang. Although clearly stating U.S. policy vis-a-vis North Korea did not lay the foundation for the use of force, it signaled to the DPRK that the U.S. had not ruled out the military option.

Whether used as a tool of policy or public diplomacy, U.S. intelligence supplied information that was actionable for both the U.S. and the IAEA. Knowledge backed by persuasive evidence that North Korea was pursuing a clandestine nuclear weapons program gave decisionmakers the impetus to respond.

No Intelligence Community Consensus

While U.S. intelligence provided valuable insight into North Korea's nuclear ambitions and served as the catalyst for most diplomatic actions toward the DPRK, the information was, as Andrew Mack described it, "circumstantial, fragmentary, contested, and often contradictory" (Mack: 87). As a result, the Intelligence Community was split (and remains so today) over the extent of North Korea's nuclear weapons program. The fact that North Korea was pursuing a bomb was uncontested among U.S. intelligence agencies. This had been the Community consensus since early 1991 (Hibbs *g*: 9). Rather, the Intelligence Community was divided over how close the DPRK was to building one. Department of Defense and CIA analysts assessed that North Korea was much closer to developing a bomb than analysts from the Departments of State and Energy believed (Mack: 89).

Although circumstantial, there was evidence to support claims that North Korea was pursuing a bomb. This contention was based on North Korea's advanced industrial capabilities, its technical know-how, evidence of high-explosive testing during the late 1980s, its pursuit of dual-use equipment used in the manufacture of or as components in nuclear weapons, and the development of an extensive plutonium production capability (Hibbs *g*: 9). Critics of the Department of Defense/CIA position, particularly at the Department of State, cautioned that there was little direct evidence to support this position.

This dissension was evident in both the open and classified domains. Public statements by senior administration officials between 1992 and 1994 reflected the different views of the intelligence agencies. In February 1992, Robert M. Gates, DCI during the Bush Administration, stated that "North Korea could build a nuclear weapon within a few months to a couple of years" (Fessler: 480). James Woolsey, who replaced Mr. Gates as DCI, took a more moderate position. During Senate testimony in February 1993, he stated, "[There] is a real possibility that North Korea has already manufactured enough fissile material for at least one nuclear weapon" (Woolsey: 34). His assessment followed the Community-wide consensus at the time: that North Korea had reprocessed between 8.5 and 12 kilograms of plutonium, enough for one to two bombs (Hibbs and Hart: 5). However, during this speech, he did not speculate on the DPRK's ability to produce a nuclear weapon using the fissile fuel. Secretary of Defense William Perry further confused the issue in May 1994 when, during a speech to the Asia Society, he quoted DCI Woolsey as "estimat[ing] that the plutonium from the last unloading already may have been used to build at least one nuclear device" (Perry: 27). While the difference between the two statements is subtle, the implications are striking. The latter statement suggested North Korea may have completed nuclear bomb development. It is possible that the Secretary of Defense was referring to a different statement by DCI Woolsey, although it is more likely that his statement reflected the Department of Defense position on North Korea's weapons program.

Criticisms of Information Sharing

Despite Intelligence Community successes in the area of non-proliferation, critics of information sharing often cite two valid concerns that warrant discussion. The first is the protection of sources and methods of U.S. intelligence when shared with the UN. The U.S. routinely briefed IAEA officials on developments in North Korea throughout the crisis. While these briefings were most often limited to senior IAEA personnel and briefing materials were seldom left behind, these officials do not have security clearances and many are non-U.S. citizens. Much of the information, however, must be given wider dissemination if it is to be useful. Since it is a safe assumption that there are members of foreign intelligence organizations on the IAEA staff, the possibility of compromising sources and methods increases once the information is disseminated.

The use of intelligence as a tool of public diplomacy also raises concerns about compromising sources and methods. Again the intelligence supplied to the February 1993 Board of Governors meeting serves as an excellent example. The U.S. supplied intelligence (primarily satellite imagery) for the Board meeting as evidence of North Korea's nuclear activities. Although this meeting was closed to the IAEA's general membership, several representatives of the 35-member board are from countries whose interests run contrary to those of the United States. Understandably, the Intelligence Community was reluctant to release the information for this reason. According to a *Washington Post* article at the time, CIA analysts tried on several occasions to prevent the State Department from releasing the photographs to the Board. But their protests were overruled first by DCI Robert M. Gates during the Bush Administration and later by the Clinton White House (R. Smith *d*: A1). Despite the risks of compromising sources and methods, senior officials held firmly to the position that the evidence was necessary if the IAEA was to do its job.

The second concern is the security afforded to information once it is released to the UN. The UN has only limited safeguards in place for protecting information provided by member states (Commission: 129). In March 1995, Republicans on Capitol Hill requested that President Clinton suspend intelligence sharing for UN peacekeeping operations due to a security violation discovered while UN forces were withdrawing from Somalia. U.S. forces, earlier in March, had discovered volumes of classified materials supplied by the U.S. in an unguarded UN office (Cassata *b*:

826). David Kay, a former IAEA inspector, credits this "UN fiasco," along with the lack of secure areas and cleared personnel, with the U.S.'s growing reluctance to share intelligence with the IAEA (Kay 1996).

While solutions to these concerns are not readily obvious and are outside the scope of this paper, these issues are valid. Yet, the need to share intelligence remains. The Commission on the Roles and Capabilities of the U.S. Intelligence Community best summarized the issue in its final report, in which it stated:

> [T]here are a range of activities undertaken by multinational bodies — from peacekeeping operations to enforcing internationally imposed sanctions to dealing with humanitarian crises — which either involve U.S. military or civilian personnel directly, or where the United States has a strong interest in seeing the activity succeed. To the extent that the United States has information important to the success of these activities, it is in the interest of the U.S. to find a way to share it (Commission: 129).

Certainly, the quest for weapons of mass destruction poses a serious threat to U.S. interests worldwide. As the remaining superpower with global commitments, it is a vested interest of U.S. to prevent the spread of these weapons and to preserve the international nuclear non-proliferation regime.

Foreign intelligence sharing is not a new concept. In fact, the U.S. has been sharing information derived from intelligence with its close allies since World War II. Established procedures have long existed for exchanging classified information between friendly governments and within multinational defense organizations, such as the North Atlantic Treaty Organization, or NATO (Macartney: 472). In the post-Cold War era, the window of information sharing has opened wider to include international bodies such as the UN and the IAEA.

Without question, the need to share intelligence with UN or UN-affiliated organizations will continue as these organizations increase their role in world politics. The U.S. is dedicated to supporting the efforts of the UN as it takes a more active role in world affairs. The role of U.S. intelligence in supporting these endeavors is well demonstrated. In 1993, then-DCI Woolsey proclaimed the commitment of the U.S. to supplying the information required by the UN to complete its mandate (Woolsey: 38). A major step toward improving this support, in the area of non-proliferation, was the creation of the DCI's Nonproliferation Center. This interagency organization serves as a focal point for coordination and dissemination of intelligence regarding the proliferation threat.

Despite its limitations, U.S. intelligence contributed to the successful implementation of U.S. policy with regard to North Korea. It functioned as a tool of both foreign policy and public diplomacy, providing policymakers with the "actionable" information necessary to freeze North Korea's nuclear program, at least for now. For the IAEA, intelligence support has become an indispensable part of its improved safeguards regime. Its performance, however, shows that greater emphasis should be placed on human source collection to provide insight into the capabilities and intentions of potential proliferators. Technical collection, as demonstrated by the North Korean example, can not always satisfy this requirement.

FROM IRAQ TO NORTH KOREA: THE ROLE OF THE COUNTERPROLIFERATION MINDSET

Theodore William Wolff, Jr.
Defense Intelligence Agency
August 1996

The United States Government is committed to halting the proliferation of nuclear weapons. Therefore it is important for government officials to understand the intelligence methodologies employed by the Intelligence Community (IC) for this counterproliferation goal. In their 1991 effort against post-Gulf War Iraq, the IC, working in conjunction with the International Atomic Energy Agency (IAEA), developed a whole new approach to nuclear counterproliferation. The new approach grew out of the failure of both the IC and IAEA to detect the scope of Iraq's nuclear program.

The IC's and IAEA's new approach successfully overcame Iraqi concealment efforts, and when these two organizations applied their new methodology against North Korea, they achieved similar success in overcoming deception. Without the methodological changes instituted by the IC and IAEA for dealing with Iraq, their future successes against North Korea would have been severely limited.

IMPLICATIONS FOR THE FUTURE

Just as the lessons learned from Iraq influenced North Korea analysis, the methodologies employed against North Korea have utility in other counterproliferation problems. While there are many nuclear proliferation challenges in the world today, the threat posed by Iran is especially relevant to this discussion. Like Iraq and North Korea, Iran has signed the NPT treaty and is under IAEA safeguards. Experience with Iraq and North

Korea showed the IAEA and United States that signing the NPT did not guarantee compliance.

The IAEA has not found any NPT violations or breeches of nuclear safeguards in Iran (Foreign Policy Association: 21). The U.S. is nonetheless suspicious of Iran's nuclear intentions. The U.S. cites Iran's effort to obtain heavy water research reactors, uranium enrichment technology, and spent fuel reprocessing as evidence that the Islamic regime is bent on acquiring nuclear weapons technology (U.S. DoD OSD *b*: 14). In the future, Iran will expand its array of operational nuclear reactors with assistance from Russia, France, and China (Gerardi and Aharinejad: 208-210). Once these projects are complete, Iran will possess a nuclear infrastructure capable of producing weapons grade fissile material, the key hurdle on any pathway to the bomb (Gerardi and Aharinejad: 212).

When the new array of Iranian nuclear facilities becomes operational, it will pose a strong proliferation threat. The best method for the international community to counter Iran's program is the application of the same mindset developed on Iraq and used for North Korea. While Iran and the U.S. may never engage in a comprehensive bilateral denuclearizing accord, the intelligence methodologies are relevant and directly applicable. The IAEA should aggressively apply its new procedures to Iran. The U.S. should support the IAEA Iranian inspections with information on any suspected proliferation activity. The IAEA and U.S. Intelligence Community should apply the same probing skepticism against Iran that was shown Iraq and North Korea. The driving synergism of the counterproliferation mindset can help assure future Iranian compliance with NPT.

The intelligence and inspection methodologies developed for Iraq and North Korea nuclear analysis also have broader applications in the fields of chemical and biological weapons control. While the NPT treaty is verified via the IAEA, treaties limiting chemical and biological weapons are also evolving on-site inspection regimes. Each regime will require the same kind of intelligence support given the IAEA. The Chemical Weapons Convention and the Biological Weapons Convention treaties seek to ban chemical and biological weapons. The Chemical Weapons Convention provides for a highly intrusive inspection regime of on-site inspections, and the U.S. is currently negotiating to establish a Biological Weapons Convention on-site protocol.

The analytical demands of chemical/biological weapons detection increases the need for a shared counterproliferation mindset between any international chemical/biological on-site inspection agency and the U.S. Intelligence Community. The dual-use nature of the industrial infrastructure required for producing these weapons makes IC-international organization cooperation essential, perhaps more so than with nuclear activity:

> [E]xternal visual signatures, such as those that might be observed through overhead photography, can provide clues of CW (chemical weapons) production activities but are rarely conclusive and must be supplemented with evidence from onsite inspections (U.S. Cong *c*: 15).

When the demand for verification of the Chemical and Biological treaties increases, the U.S. Intelligence Community and on-site inspection regimes can build upon the precedent of cooperation established by Iraq and North Korea analysis. The precedent of international organizations pursuing these goals is not new: UNSCOM had a broad mandate under UN Security Council Resolution 687 for removing from Iraq all weapons of mass destruction including nuclear, biological, and chemical assets. In the future, we are likely to witness an increased demand for the unique capabilities of the counterproliferation mindset.

Chapter 6

UN ROLE IN RESOLVING THE KOREAN CONFLICT

The North Korean People's Army's attack across the 38th parallel on 25 June 1950 was the first serious challenge to the UN system of collective security, and the Cold War will not really end until the Korean Peninsula is reunified. The United Nations has formally been involved in attempts to resolve the Korean problem since 1947 and is actively engaged today. At the Demilitarized Zone, U.S. troops flying the UN flag are as close to war as any on the planet, and yet the UN is also behind the lines on the other side of the DMZ actively promoting the economic development of North Korea. A key intelligence question is: What are the prospects for a peaceful resolution of the Korean conflict? In a UN context, the follow-up questions are: What are the prospects for a UN role in a negotiated settlement? and, How could it be accomplished?

UN Secretary-General Boutros-Ghali's *Agenda for Peace* called for a comprehensive and preemptive approach to peacemaking. He advocates UN involvement in solving the underlying problems which lead to conflict in the first place, using the UN as a mechanism to bring the parties into a process to resolve the conflict. In *An Agenda for Development*, he proposes economic cooperation and development as a means to build common interest and understanding as the basis for peace.

Since the end of the Cold War the UN has been involved in comprehensive peacemaking in Mozambique, Cambodia and El Salvador, providing a mechanism to end decades of civil war fueled by superpower confrontation. Captain Hoyle analyzes these three cases as possible models for a UN role in Korea. She reviews UN involvement in Korea since 1947 and analyzes the stated positions of North and South Korea toward peaceful reunification. She then provides an assessment of the suitability of the UN's approach to the Korean problem, pointing to some areas where the parties' positions are close to agreement and others which may require third-party intervention.

The hardest part seems to be getting dialogue started. Master Sergeant Curran sees the incentive of economic gain from the multilateral development of the Tumen River area as a possible catalyst. He outlines the plans of the UN Development Program for a free trade area as a way to open at least a small crack in the door to North Korea through international trade, shipping and manufacturing. Although only a small step, the UN project is one of the few areas where North and South Korea are actively cooperating.

PROSPECTS FOR UNITED NATIONS PARTICIPATION IN KOREAN REUNIFICATION

Jennifer Morsch Hoyle
Captain, U.S. Army
August 1996

THE UNITED NATIONS IN KOREA

The United Nations has played a significant role in the problem of the unification and independence of Korea since September 1947 and maintains a presence on the Korean peninsula today. The UN has provided guiding principles for reunification, has mobilized forces to halt aggression, and has established commissions to assist North and South Korea in their search for common ground. The continued stalemate and division of the peninsula is a relic of the Cold War, the end of which has brought renewed hope of a reunified Korea.

This paper will address the prospects for the UN's participation in assisting North and South Korea to reunify, based on the changing role of the UN and its recent peace operations in Cambodia, El Salvador, and Mozambique. The UN's experience and lessons learned from its past involvement in Korea and in recent transitional regimes may provide the necessary assistance in facilitating a well-planned framework set of procedures to reunite the governments, factions, militaries and peoples of the divided nation.

Since September 1947, the United Nations has played a significant role in the "problem of the independence of Korea" (Bailey: 2) and maintained a presence on the Korean peninsula in one form or another. The various UN commissions on Korea, the Military Armistice Commission, and the Unified Command all reflect international interest in the peaceful reunification of Korea. Korean attempts of the early 1990s to solve the problem between themselves were followed by stalemate in the last few years. A look at what divides North from South and the role the UN has played in that division provides a valuable perspective for future attempts to bring unity and peace to the peninsula.

20TH CENTURY HISTORY OF KOREA'S DIVISION

For 13 centuries, Korea spent its political and social history as a unified nation under the Shilla Kingdom. During the early 20th century, Korea lost its autonomy as the Japanese formally annexed it in 1910 after their successes in the Sino-Japanese War of 1895 and the Russo-Japanese War of 1904-1905. In 1945, during the Yalta and Potsdam conferences and after Japan's surrender in World War II, world leaders from the U.S., Great Britain, and the Soviet Union agreed to divide the Korean peninsula. Their intent was not only to disarm the Japanese military forces, placing the Soviet Union in the north and the U.S. in the south, but to find a way to reunify the peninsula. In 1950, North Korea attempted to reunify the nation by force, attacking the South in a conflict that ended with an armistice in 1953. Since then, Korea has remained a nation divided along the 38th parallel, seeking to mend its physical and ideological rifts, borne of years of armed stand-off and deep-seated distrust (Korean Overseas Information Service *a*: 308).

Japanese Colonial Rule

International involvement in Korea followed a long history of foreign occupation of the peninsula. Japan fought its war with China on Korean soil in 1894-95, on the peninsula that had acted as a cultural bridge between the two nations for centuries. The Japanese remained in Korea after asserting strong influence over the peninsula, making it a Japanese protectorate after the Russo-Japanese war of 1904-1905. Japan annexed Korea in 1910 and maintained violent and ruthless rule until World War II. During the Cairo Conference of 1943, Britain's Winston Churchill, American Franklin Delano Roosevelt, and China's Chiang Kai-shek determined the need for a free and independent Korea, due primarily to the peninsula's suffering under Japanese colonial rule, but also to its strategic significance. The Korean peninsula offered the U.S. and Britain access to the Asian continent, while it could serve China as a buffer from future Japanese aggression, protecting the mainland nations (Fairbank, Reischauer and Craig: 912-913).

Temporary Solution

In 1945, during the Yalta and Potsdam conferences and after the Japanese had been pushed out of the peninsula, the Soviet Union and the U.S. agreed to temporarily divide the Korean peninsula at the 38th parallel. The intent was to provide a Soviet haven in the north and to maintain an American stronghold in the south. "A line or zone had to be found that was far enough north not to jeopardize the future role of the United States, but also far enough south so that the Russian Army could not have already crossed it" (Fehrenbach: 19). Although the Soviet Union agreed to a temporary demarcation line, the allied powers failed to agree on the issue of Korea's future.

During the December 1945 Council of Foreign Ministers meeting in Moscow, the ministers agreed to set up a provisional democratic government in Korea to assist the country in rehabilitation and recuperation after suffering 40 years of Japanese occupation. The Joint U.S.-USSR Commission was formed to consult with the Korean democratic parties and social organizations to work out a trusteeship system consisting of the four great powers: Britain, China, the United States, and the Soviet Union. The members of this commission, however, disagreed on the definition of "democratic parties and social organizations" (Bailey: 1). The Soviets refused to consult with any Korean who had criticized the Moscow agreement on trusteeship, a rather large group of potential (and U.S.-supported) Korean leaders. The joint commission met again in 1946, but agreement continued to elude the group, leading to posturing for separate elections in the North and South.

The United States insisted on national unification through the process of free elections. This proposal directly opposed the underlying Soviet plan to retain the 38th parallel (Weathersby: 6) in order to maintain the balance of power on the peninsula and to control North Korea. For the Soviets, North Korea offered more than strategic significance. Korea offered a great source of economic resources such as monazite, a black, sandy, radioactive material used in the production of atomic bombs (Weathersby: 21). The Soviet nuclear program was in the process of developing a weapon expected to alter the balance of power in years to come.

At its 1947 meeting, the joint commission remained deadlocked on the election issue. The Soviets accused the U.S. of purposely involving majority parties and groups that opposed the Soviet plan for trusteeship, which included fostering "close and friendly" relations with Korea (C. Park: 72). At this impasse, the U.S. threatened to refer the entire matter to the UN General Assembly. This initial involvement of an organ of the UN began the contentious relationship between the UN and the Korean peninsula that still exists today.

EVENTS LEADING TO THE KOREAN WAR

Author at Panmunjom, Korea. North Korean observer in background. *photo used with permission*

Disagreements between the U.S. and Soviet Union on ways to reestablish a unified government in Korea led to Korea's role as a pawn in the stand-off that became the Cold War and eventually manifested itself in the armed struggle that became the Korean War.

Initially the economy in the North prospered, in great part due to Soviet assistance. After 40 years of Japanese occupation, South Korea was left in political chaos, without any modern political tradition to direct the country's governmental, economic, or social efforts, and the South suffered rapid decline. In addition, the Soviet halt of commercial travel between the north and south further aggravated the state of the South Korean economy. The Korean People's Party established itself in a South Korea wrought with political tensions and a confused American occupation force headed by Lieutenant General John R. Hodge. Due to this growing conflict, the Truman administration selected a popular figure from the Korean rebellion against the Japanese, Syngman Rhee, to govern South Korea. Truman believed Rhee was the only political figure powerful enough to adequately respond to U.S. interests in the region (Hoyt: 16).

While the South attempted to establish some stability, North Korea continued to blossom under Soviet tutelage. Kim Sung-chu, a Korean who fled his occupied homeland to join the Chinese Communist Army in 1937, returned as a Soviet Army captain to assist the Korean Volunteer Army in establishing a united and independent Korea. The Soviet plan was to establish a North Korea government that would follow Soviet policy. Kim Sung-chu changed his name to Kim Il-sung, his *nom de guerre*, and was groomed for the responsibility of taking charge of the state (Hoyt: 278). The Soviets actively assisted North Korea in establishing a viable fighting force and armed it with technologically advanced weapons. By the end of 1948, Soviet aid had successfully conferred the upper hand on the peninsula to North Korea in terms of military strength and equipment, political control, and economic power. The Soviet Union withdrew its forces, leaving behind a group of military advisers to provide continual guidance and supervision (Weathersby: 22).

In response to a U.S. initiative, the United Nations General Assembly proposed free elections throughout Korea (UNGA Res 112(II)). North Korea did not comply, since the Soviets had successfully established a *de facto* government and they were not inclined to sacrifice their interests in exchange for a political infrastructure sympathetic to those of the U.S. The South moved ahead as proposed by the United Nations and elected Dr. Syngman Rhee, recognized by the U.S. as the elected leader of the entire Korean peninsula. This international slight to Kim Il-Sung would fester until June 1950.

General Assembly Formula for Korea's Reunification

The General Assembly, in its 14 November 1947 Resolution, proposed key elements to achieve the reunification of Korea, establishing the framework for elections. It recognized the rightful claims to independence of the people of Korea and acknowledged that freedom and independence could only be fairly and correctly resolved with the participation of the representatives of the Korean people. The General Assembly outlined the modalities for achieving an independent Korea through observed elections to choose the aforementioned representatives, enabling them to constitute a National Assembly and establish a national government. It further recommended that the government institute its own national security force and dissolve all military formations not involved with national defense, take over the functions of government from the military commands and civilian authorities of North and South Korea, and arrange for the complete withdrawal of occupying forces from Korea as early as possible.

The UN General Assembly established the UN Temporary Commission on Korea to facilitate and expedite its programs for Korea to achieve national independence and the withdrawal of occupation forces. The UN encouraged its member states to assist the UN commission in fulfilling its responsibilities in any way possible. However, the commission failed to achieve the participation of representatives from the north and south. The commission's efforts to re-establish the national independence of Korea stalled, opening the door for unilateral action by the north.

American policy also gave the appearance of confusion. Secretary of State Dean Acheson disagreed with President Truman that Korea was even within America's sphere of influence, a view he publicized in what is referred to as "Truman's invitation to North Korea." In a speech to the National Press Club in early 1950, Secretary Acheson declared that "Korea was not inside the zone of primary American national security concerns . . . [and that], if . . . attacked, Korea would be allowed to fall" (Hoyt: 18). This statement built North Korea's confidence and significantly tipped the scales in favor of war in 1950.

Korean War

On 25 June 1950, at 0400 hours, the North Korean People's Army swept across the 38th parallel, taking South Korea and the international community by surprise. North Korea's attack was an attempt to reunite the peninsula by force and, while it failed to accomplish that goal, it placed the "problem of Korea" on the agenda of the international community for the rest of the century (Y-H. Park: 62).

Responding to reports of the invasion, President Harry S. Truman requested an emergency meeting of the UN Security Council (UNSC) and authorized the dispatch of U.S. ground and naval forces, augmented by Britain and Australia, to provide immediate support to South Korea (Hoyt: 29). The UN subsequently asked the U.S. to take charge of a unified command comprising military forces provided by members of the UN and to conduct operations against North Korean forces under the UN flag.

The war lasted until 1953, when an armistice agreement went into effect. North Korea failed to achieve its objective of unifying the peninsula under its control, leaving a permanent division that remains today, as a remnant of Cold-War politics (Y-H. Park: 62). The deep-seated distrust and suspicion between the North and South is borne of the power struggle epitomized by the Korean War. North Korea's surprise attack on its neighbor to the south, and the destruction which ensued, caused a rift so deep that it is only now beginning to heal. Korea's recovery process is due in large part to the international attention and assistance it has received and the desire of the Korean people to unify their country.

Overview of the UN's Role

The UN's initial involvement in "the problem of Korea" was at the initiative of the U.S., when it referred the election issue to the General Assembly in 1947. The U.S. attempt to unify Korea under American influence through democratic elections met with disdain from the Soviet members of the Joint U.S.-USSR Commission, resulting in an unresolved impasse that required UN mediation. The Soviets and the Americans took sides in the struggle for power on the Korean peninsula. The U.S. supported and provided for UN-sanctioned elections in the south to ensure the establishment of a democratic government. The Soviets installed a communist regime under Kim Il-sung in the north, and Korea became the centerpiece of the ideological struggle between East and West.

The absence of the Soviet Union from its place at the Security Council, in protest over refusal to admit communist China, allowed the UNSC to play a significant role in the international response to North Korea's attack against the Republic of Korea. The UNSC authorized the use of force by the U.S. and its allies. In its infancy, the UN was motivated to take action in Korea in order to erase the past mistakes of the League of Nations, which failed to take action in Manchuria in 1932 (Fairbank, Reischauer and Craig: 708).

When the USSR returned to the UNSC to take the Presidency of the Security Council, a rotating responsibility, further action by the Security Council on Korea was prevented by the Soviet veto. The U.S. sponsored the Uniting for Peace Resolution (UNGA Res 377A(V)) allowing the General Assembly to act in the stead of the UNSC when the use of the veto blocked action by the Security Council. This enabled the U.S. to cancel the effects of a Soviet veto with the collaboration of its major allies and small states that resented the veto power of the five permanent members. The Uniting for Peace Resolution also enabled the U.S. to mobilize effective international pressure in the General Assembly when the Soviet veto in the Security Council had prevented action. Thus, the United States was able to claim UN authorization for its actions in Korea. The struggle between the Chinese- and Soviet-backed North Koreans and the U.S.- and West-supported South Koreans played out in the public forum of the UN Headquarters in New York and on the battlefields of the Korean peninsula (Claude: 150).

UNITED NATIONS PRESENCE IN KOREA

The UN's attempts to solve the "problem of the independence of Korea" have been exercised by a series of subsidiary organs established by the UN Security Council and the General Assembly, including the United Nations Temporary Commission on Korea, the UN Commission on Korea, the Unified Command, the UN Commission for the Unification and Rehabilitation of Korea, and the Military Armistice Commission, which carried the United Nations through the initiation of hostilities against North Korea and the stalemate for the past 40 years. The UN authority vested in each of these organizational groups has changed over the years, as South Korea has become more independent and as the prospects for unification have entered and exited the realm of reality.

United Nations Temporary Commission on Korea

In response to the U.S. referral of the Korean election issue, the General Assembly appointed the UN Temporary Commission on Korea (UNTCOK) (UNGA Res 112(II)). Its mission was to consult with representatives of the Korean people throughout the peninsula in fulfilling the Assembly's recommendations to hold elections for a national assembly before 31 March 1948, and to arrange for the withdrawal of all armed forces from Korea as proposed by the Soviets in 1947. In the interest of equitable geographical distribution, UNTCOK consisted of representatives from Australia, Canada, China, El Salvador, France, India, the Philippines, Syria, and the Ukrainian Soviet Socialist Republic. The temporary commission was authorized to consult with the Interim Committee, which had been created to investigate matters that occurred between the annual fall sessions of the General Assembly.

The UNTCOK was plagued with problems. Infighting and accusations abounded between the American political adviser and what he believed to be a British clique led by Australia and Canada. He also questioned the loyalty and commitment of the representatives to their assigned mission, believing they were more interested in "home life, luxurious living, bright lights, new scenes, and varied entertainment . . . placing their national interests above . . . the welfare of . . . the Korean people" (Bailey: 3).

Despite its internal problems, UNTCOK was able to conduct liaison and consult with American leaders in South Korea on election and withdrawal issues. The Soviet commander in North Korea, however, would not even accept receipt of correspondence from UNTCOK's chairman, making access to the north for election purposes impossible. Since the General Assembly was not in session, UNTCOK sought advice from the UN Interim Committee. The result was a green light for UNTCOK to hold elections in accessible parts of Korea, that is, South Korea. The decision to hold elections only in the south sparked protest even from several pro-American political leaders considered to be likely presidential candidates. The popular Kim Koo, chairman of the Korean Independence Party, and Dr. Kim Kiu-sic, chairman of the South Korean legislative assembly and previously backed by the U.S., participated in a conference sponsored by Pyongyang that condemned unilateral elections in South Korea, faulted the U.S. for delaying the unification process, and demanded the withdrawal of occupation forces.

Despite North Korea's disapproval, elections were held in South Korea on 10 May 1948. UNTCOK coordinated with the National Elections Committee, observed voter registration, oversaw the voting process, and declared the election "a valid expression of the free will of the electorate" (Bailey: 5) and Dr. Syngman Rhee became the first President of South Korea. Since the election had been supervised and monitored by an agent of the UN in accordance with UN resolutions, President Rhee claimed authority over the entire Korean peninsula. On 15 August 1948, the U.S. military government formally terminated operations and began to withdraw its troops, leaving behind a Korean Military Advisory Group of approximately 500 personnel (Ridgway: 15).

In its last report to the General Assembly, UNTCOK declared that South Korea had achieved a lawful government via valid elections and the Government of the Republic of Korea (ROK) was firmly in control. The commission also recommended the establishment of a permanent commission on Korea to "facilitate the removal of barriers caused by the division of Korea and to bring about the unification of Korea" (UNGA Res 195(III)). The General Assembly approved UNTCOK's report in its 1948 session, and the United Nations Commission on Korea superseded UNTCOK in December 1948.

United Nations Commission on Korea

The United Nations Commission on Korea (UNCOK) consisted of the same members as the UNTCOK, except for Canada and the Ukrainian SSR, who had not felt entirely comfortable with UNTCOK's activities and were dropped from membership. Its goal was to serve as a stabilizing influence on the Korean peninsula, deterring North Korean aggression through its presence. The commission renewed efforts to gain access to the north, but to no avail. By 28 July 1949, UNCOK had observed and verified the withdrawal of U.S. forces, but could not provide similar confirmation to the General Assembly of the withdrawal of Soviet troops from North Korea. In the South, UNCOK's operations were severely limited, with the Rhee government citing security and safety reasons. More likely, they were imposed to "intimidate Korean dissidents" (Bailey: 7), although President Rhee maintained that was not the case.

UNCOK reported to the General Assembly that the situation in Korea was rapidly declining, based on internal opposition to the new South Korean government and the increase in border skirmishes (UNGA A/936: 34), but the Assembly merely took note of the report and extended the Commission (UN *o*: 291). In October 1949, however, the General Assembly did expand the UNCOK's mandate to include observing and reporting on "any developments which might lead to or otherwise involve military conflict in Korea" (UNGA Res 294(IV)). Indications of North Korea's plans to unify the peninsula by force were reported to UNCOK by ROK officers who knew of the North Korean buildup along the border (UNGA A/936: 33). When UN officials questioned the U.S. military assistance group commander about the reports, they were assured that the activities were routine (Hoyt: 15).

The North Korean attack on 25 June 1950 came as a surprise, not only to those in the Republic of Korea, but to the UN as well. While UNCOK tried to verify the gravity of the situation, the North Korean People's Army pushed southward toward Seoul. Reports reached the Far Eastern Air Force Headquarters in Japan four hours after commencement of the attack. In the U.S., members of the media picked up the story and "informed" the State Department through their anxious inquiries (Fehrenbach: 19). At the same time, North Korea sent a communique to the UN claiming that it was acting in self-defense against a South Korean attack, an assertion that did little to impress the Security Council. North Korea's allegation did cause the UN

Secretary-General to request a report from UNCOK before making a decision. However, UNCOK reported that, indeed, North Korea had launched the attack and that the situation "may endanger the maintenance of international peace and security," (UNSC S/1496: 2), but did not clearly characterize the event. The Security Council felt it had insufficient information to decide whether the attack constituted a breach of peace and an act of aggression, because UNCOK did not assert that the action was a definitive danger to international peace and security. As a result, the UNSC's resolution referenced "a breach of the peace" and called for a cease-fire and the withdrawal of North Korean forces (Bailey: 13). Meanwhile, President Truman dispatched both U.S. air and sea forces in support of the South Korean troops. UNCOK sent four cablegrams to update the UNSC and suggested mediation to preclude further deterioration of the military situation (UNSC S/1496; S/1507). The Secretary-General attempted to solicit military assistance from members of the UN, but with little success. China, the USSR, North Korea, and other Communist nations responded with a letter disagreeing with the Security Council's decisions on Korea, since two of the five permanent members had not concurred. The USSR was boycotting Security Council meetings in protest over China's absence, and the People's Republic of China was absent because its seat was occupied by Chiang Kai-shek's Nationalists (Kang: 10).

The Unified Command

At the 7 July meeting, the Security Council adopted the Anglo-French proposal which solved the problem of the failure of individual member states to provide military assistance to the Republic of Korea. It authorized the establishment of "a unified command under the United States," authorized the use of the UN flag, and invited the contribution of forces from the UN member states. The unified command eventually consisted of 16 nations providing combat units, including the U.S., Australia, Britain, France, Greece, the Netherlands, the Philippines, Thailand, Turkey, Belgium, Luxembourg, Canada, Colombia, Ethiopia, New Zealand, and South Africa; Denmark, India, Italy, Norway, and Sweden provided medical units (UNSC S/1588: 1).

The UN gave the Unified Command, also called the United Nations Command (UNC), the authority to repel the North Korean attack, to restore international peace and security to the peninsula, and to provide command

and control of all UNC forces. It also requested that the U.S. provide the Security Council with reports on the course of action taken under the command (UNSC S/1588): 1).

North Korea initially enjoyed success in its surprise attack, taking control of Seoul, South Korea's capital, within 72 hours. UN forces were pushed to the southern tip of South Korea at Pusan, but rallied with the successful amphibious landing at Inchon. Under General Douglas MacArthur, UN forces pushed the Korean People's Army northward past the 38th parallel to the Yalu River. China responded to the threat to its border with Korea by augmenting North Korea's forces, and the struggle between the Chinese-backed North and the UN-supported South ensued, ending in stalemate.

Armistice negotiations took over 2 years and were conducted as hostilities continued. The Unified Command's negotiating team consisted of U.S. and ROK representatives sitting across from representatives of North Korea and the People's Republic of China. Negotiations were plagued by adjournments, arguments, and disruption, preventing any progress toward a cease-fire (Bailey: 74). On 27 July 1953, the Commander in Chief of the UN Command, the Supreme Commander of the Korean People's Army, and the Commander of the Chinese People's Volunteers finally signed the armistice agreement, which established the Military Demarcation Line (MDL) and created a 4-kilometer buffer zone known as the Demilitarized Zone (DMZ). With the cease-fire in 1953, the UNC's focus switched to preventing a return to hostilities and maintaining the institutional mechanisms created to supervise the implementation of the armistice agreement (UN Command: 5).

For the past 43 years, the UNC has had the mission of implementing and maintaining the Armistice Agreement, keeping watch over the situation in Korea. The UNC has "defended the ROK and executed crisis management . . . and war deterrence missions . . . in accordance with the Armistice" (S. Lee). The UNC also staffs the Military Armistice Commission, which investigates armistice violations and reports annually, and as needed, to the UNSC.

Today, the UNC continues its "role of deterring war and maintaining security of the Korean peninsula" (S. Lee) while it attempts to implement the Armistice Agreement. The breakdown of relations between the north and south makes it difficult for the UNC to communicate with the North Korean People's Army, though it continues attempts to re-establish military-to-military communications (UN Command: 9,14). It maintains around-the-clock presence in Panmunjom to answer any calls from the north. The UNC monitors activity along the DMZ through special investigative teams and continues to report to the UNSC annually, and the commander provides periodic testimony before the U.S. Congress.

The Armistice Agreement, while still in effect, has lost much of its relevance over the years due to non-compliance and changing regional and peninsular conditions. The current situation dictates a move toward a comprehensive peace settlement between North and South Korea and reunification.

The UN Commission for the Unification and Rehabilitation of Korea

With the institution of a unified command, UNCOK became obsolete. A new commission was formed to continue work on Korean unification issues and to assist the unified command in handling relief and support operations. On 7 October 1950, the United Nations General Assembly established the UN Commission for the Unification and Rehabilitation of Korea (UNCURK) (UNGA Res 376(V)).

Initially, UNCURK consisted of seven nations: Australia, Chile, the Netherlands, Pakistan, the Philippines, Thailand, and Turkey. Chile and Pakistan eventually withdrew in 1970 and 1972, respectively. In addition to taking over UNCOK's missions, UNCURK turned its attention to the war in Korea. The Unified Command, under General Douglas MacArthur, had been established in July 1950 and had entered into war with North Korea. UNCURK assisted the Unified Command with civilian population relief and support operations. During its tenure, UNCURK was never able to achieve Korea's unification, though Canada suggested that it be "reorganized in a way acceptable to both South and North Korean governments" (C. Park: 158). With its unification mission unfulfilled, and with no further need for relief operations, UNCURK was disbanded in November 1973 (UNGA A/9027: 24).

The Military Armistice Commission

On 27 July 1953, representatives of North Korea, China, and the UN Command signed the Armistice Agreement. Twelve hours after the

Author in Korea. *photo used with permission*

signing, the cease-fire went into effect. The following day, the Military Armistice Commission (MAC) held its first meeting. Established by the Armistice Agreement, the MAC is not a UN organ but a vehicle by which the UNC maintains military-to-military connection with North Korea. The MAC consisted of ten senior officers: five appointed by the Commander in Chief, UN Command, and five appointed by the Supreme Commander of the Korean People's Army and the Commander of the Chinese People's Volunteers. Their specific duty was to "supervise the implementation of [the] Armistice Agreement and to settle through negotiation any violations" (Wellens: 230) of it, acting as intermediaries in transmitting communications between the commanders of the opposing sides. They were also responsible for marking the Military Demarcation Line (MDL) which served, and still exists, as the dividing line between north and south. The two sides were directed to withdraw at least two kilometers from the MDL, forming a 4-kilometer Demilitarized Zone (DMZ), to minimize the likelihood of incidents between the opposing forces and prevent the occurrence of further aggression. The MAC ensures the DMZ is sustained as a buffer zone, and is responsible for prescribing the number of civil police required to do so, as well as specifying the weapons the police are authorized to carry. The MAC maintains sole authority for granting permission for crossings of the DMZ. When unauthorized crossings occur, the MAC reports the violations or its corrective action to the commanders of both sides. The MAC can also dispatch Joint Observer Teams to investigate reported violations in the DMZ. The MAC usually meets five times a year in a formal setting at the Joint Security Area located within the DMZ at Panmunjom, Korea. Rather than negotiating on violations of the Armistice Agreement, however, the representatives end up making or denying allegations of violations (Bailey: 201), which allows little progress toward open dialogue, much less unification. Of the commissions described, only the MAC still exists. It is a first-step measure in building trust through negotiations between the north and south, a trust that is required for any successful headway in the quest for unification (Clough: 32).

UN involvement in Korea began with a proposed general framework for achieving independence and reunification. Today the Unified Command is poised to prevent North Korean aggression, and the MAC provides opportunities for dialogue. The stalemate in Korea has been reflected in the United Nations, as East and West have faced off against each other. Now that East-West cooperation has begun, North and South Korea also need to free themselves of the chains of the Cold War. An agreement to cooperate with each other, as well as Russia, the U.S., China, and the rest of the world will enable Korea to develop as a nation. The international interest in and encouragement for a unified Korea implies an expanded UN role in the current post-Cold War era.

UN PEACEKEEPING OPERATIONS IN TRANSITIONAL REGIMES

The end of the Cold War brought an increased demand for UN peacekeeping and enforcement missions to deal with the rise in global instability and widespread violence manifested most often in local and regional conflicts. A comparison of the number of peacekeeping operations (PKOs) reveals that during the Cold War, between 1948 and 1987, the UN installed 13 PKOs; after the Cold War, in one-tenth that time (1988-1992), the UN established 10 PKOs (Liu: 38).

Why did the end of the Cold War cause the floodwaters of local conflict to overflow the dam? During the Cold War, the world lived under a "bipolar stalemate, imposed by mutual fear of nuclear war, establish[ing] a dangerous but rather stable deterrent to conflagrations of global magnitude" (Hoopes: 1). The bipolar powers had also suppressed local conflicts within their spheres of interest or taken sides in civil wars which were allowed to fester. It is not that these local conflicts did not exist, but that the end of the Cold War "simply removed the lid from many cauldrons of ethnic, religious, and territorial animosity" (Hoopes: 1).

With the end of the Cold War, the character of relations between the superpowers changed from competition to cooperation. The permanent members of the UNSC are shouldering increased responsibility within the UN and contributing forces for peacekeeping missions with more authority and a greater capability to enforce decisive measures. The Gulf War is a prime example of the success of the increased power of the Security Council. The UN effectively authorized a collective security force and conducted enforcement measures, involving 38 nations, against Iraq for its invasion of Kuwait (Liu: 38). After defeating Saddam Hussein, the Security Council has maintained the pressure on Iraq to destroy its capability to use weapons of mass destruction and to protect the Kurd and Shi'ite minorities.

THE CHANGING DEFINITIONS OF PEACE OPERATIONS

The increased demand for UN intervention has led to an expansion of the definition of UN peace operations. The UN had used PKOs to contain and control armed conflicts between two governments and their armies, and UN peacekeepers were basically lightly armed cease-fire monitors. In the post-Cold War era, the UN became involved in conflicts including not only legitimate governments, but factions, liberation movements, and other armed elements engaged in internal conflict. The increased number of players, coupled with their inability or unwillingness to cooperate with the UN, causes significant problems and makes PKOs much more complex.

UN Secretary-General Boutros-Ghali introduced the most recent additions to the concept of UN peace operations in his *An Agenda for Peace* (UN *b*). He includes the UN in activities that apply directly to the intrastate conflict of the post-Cold War era. UN efforts to provide peace and security span the spectrum from pacific non-use of force measures to those achieved by military might (Duke: 386). Peacemaking and peacekeeping are closely interrelated—peacekeeping promotes peacemaking by creating on-the-ground conditions (Thakur and Thayer: 255) conducive to negotiations, while peacemaking provides hope for a peaceful resolution, motivating the parties to cooperate with a peacekeeping force. Peacemaking operations also aim to provide a peace "which will survive the withdrawal of the peacekeepers" (Thakur and Thayer: 240), further inducing a move toward cooperation with the UN. The concept of peace-building involves rebuilding a nation's institutions and infrastructure to create conditions conducive to peace, a goal similar to that of peacekeeping. Protective engagement utilizes military forces and resources to provide safe havens or a secure environment to facilitate humanitarian operations, one way to provide hope for people in a desperate situation. Peace-enforcing makes use of military force to create cessation of hostilities or stop aggression, actions that necessarily preface peacekeeping and peacemaking operations.

COMPREHENSIVE PEACE SETTLEMENTS

One type of UN peace operation has involved overseeing the implementation of comprehensive peace accords in an effort to end civil war among political factions within a country that had been divided along Cold War ideological lines (Ratner: 14). The United Nations Transitional Authority in Cambodia (UNTAC), the United Nations Observer Mission in El Salvador (ONUSAL), and the United Nations Operation in Mozambique (ONUMOZ) each constitute UN involvement in a transitional regime as part of a comprehensive peace settlement to a civil war.

Each of these transitional challenges closely resembles the current stalemate in Korea as North and South seek a solution to unification. The incentive for North Korea to accept similar assistance from the international community comes from degraded economic and social conditions.

The common framework of procedures used by the UN for nation-states experiencing transition from civil war is applicable to Korean unification. The shared, and often competing, components of UN transitional regimes address the numerous political and social conditions of the nation-states. They include various aspects of power-sharing, constitution development and reform, human rights, elections, military forces, civil administration, civil police, repatriation, and rehabilitation. The UN experience in Cambodia, El Salvador, and Mozambique offers mechanisms that may be of use in resolving the problem of Korean reunification.

Cambodia

Cambodia was the product of the great-power compromise at the Geneva Conference of 1954. The French withdrew from Indochina, leaving an armistice between the pro-French governments in Cambodia and South Vietnam and various anti-French communist resistance movements. In Cambodia, Prince Norodom Sihanouk was installed as the head of state of the royalist government of Cambodia while the Khmer Rouge, supported by the Soviets and the Communist Chinese, were left in control of the northwest corner of the country. Prince Sihanouk was deposed by an American-backed general, Lon Nol. He was eventually overthrown by the Khmer Rouge, who tried to create a Maoist peasant utopia by eliminating all Western influence. The resulting purge killed up to four million Cambodians, almost one-half of the population. In the late 1970s, the Vietnamese invaded, forcing the Khmer Rouge back to their bases in the northwest of the country (UN *h*: 6).

The UN considered the Cambodian issue in 1979, as control of the country kept changing hands, but no action was taken. The battle for control of the country was waged between the Government of Phnom Penh, installed by the Vietnamese, and coalition forces which included the destructive regime of the Khmer Rouge. In 1982, three groups which opposed the Vietnamese-backed Government, the Khmer People's National Liberation Front (KPNLF), the Party of Democratic Kampuchea (PDK or Khmer Rouge), and the United National Front for an Independent, Neutral, Peaceful and Cooperative Cambodia (FUNCINPEC), formed the coalition party of the National Government of Cambodia and occupied a seat in the UN until the Paris Agreements (UN *h*: 5).

Due to the continuing conflict and its heavy toll on the Cambodian people, the coalition leader and the Government's Prime Minister held their first meeting in December 1987. This initial contact paved the way for face-to-face talks between the four parties in July 1988 and the subsequent Paris Conference from 30 July-30 August 1989. In Paris, the four parties, with the help of the five permanent members of the UN Security Council and the Secretary-General, developed a broad strategy for peace, though they failed to reach a comprehensive settlement.

As a result of the first steps toward peace, the five permanent members of the Security Council met and achieved a settlement framework which they announced in August 1990. The four Cambodian factions accepted the framework, which established a primary role for the UN in "supervising and controlling the activities of Cambodia's existing administrative structures" (UN *h*: 8) and forming a Supreme National Council (SNC) to oversee and protect the sovereignty of the country. All that remained was to negotiate the framework into a peace agreement, which the five permanent members, the Co-Chairmen of the Paris Conference (France and Indonesia), and the Secretary-General achieved by 26 November 1990. The Council concurred and the first ceasefire in 12 years went into effect in Cambodia.

In anticipation of success in the peace negotiations, the President of the Supreme National Council requested the UN to send observers to Cambodia as an act of good faith toward the promise of peace and to monitor the fragile cease-fire. The Security Council established the UN Advance Mission in Cambodia (UNAMIC) on 16 October 1991 (UN *h*: 119). UNAMIC deployed after the signing of the Paris Agreements, assisting in the maintenance of the cease-fire and providing liaison with the SNC for the deployment of the UN Transitional Authority in Cambodia (UNTAC). UNAMIC also conducted mine-awareness training for civilians, a mission that was expanded to include training Cambodians in mine-clearing operations and repairing roads and bridges.

UNTAC was the comprehensive transitional regime provided for in the Peace Plan Agreements. It absorbed the missions of UNAMIC when it arrived in Cambodia. The seven primary components of UNTAC's mission were human rights, elections, military, civil administration, police, repatriation, and rehabilitation.

In the area of human rights, UNTAC's mission was to foster an environment ensuring basic human rights, based on internationally accepted human rights instruments. Its mandate was to conduct education and general oversight of the human condition of the Cambodian people. Part of UNTAC's oversight responsibility included investigating rights abuses, which decreased over time.

The electoral role of UNTAC was quite extensive, ensuring free and fair general elections and providing an election law and a code of conduct. Its implied duties included conducting civic education on the importance of elections and the integrity of the ballot, training for electoral staff, registration of voters and political parties, and polling. The parties agreed that once a constituent assembly was elected, they would draft a new constitution to govern the "new" nation-state.

Perhaps the most challenging duty of UNTAC was to assist all parties in reaching agreement on military issues. While security and stability were necessary first steps toward achieving confidence-building, UNTAC met with resistance in its attempt to disarm and demobilize the forces of the four factions. The Khmer Rouge refused to cooperate with the peace plan or the UN, obstructing UNTAC's ability to investigate non-compliance with the military provisions of the Agreements, and prevented successful demobilization. Where possible, UNTAC verified withdrawal of forces and supervised the cease-fire, weapons control, and mine-clearing operations.

A key concern of the parties was the maintenance of an impartial civil administration. The UNTAC supervised and controlled agencies dealing with foreign affairs, national defense, finance, and public security, to prevent the Cambodian faction from using the government. UNTAC's Information and Education Division provided public information concerning the Paris Agreements, UN peace-keeping, and the public's rights and responsibilities. Cambodia's police forces operated under UNTAC supervision during the transition. The UNTAC police component provided one policeman for every 3000 Cambodians (UN *h*: 14) to ensure the maintenance of law and order.

In conjunction with the United Nations High Commissioner for Refugees, UNTAC participated in repatriation efforts to ensure refugees and displaced persons were able to return to Cambodia and live in safety, security, and dignity. In a three-stage operation, UNTAC supervised the transportation of 360,000 refugees to final destinations in Cambodia. Part of UNTAC's rehabilitation responsibilities included providing humanitarian and resettlement needs such as food, security, health, housing, and education to the refugees. The limited land available delayed repatriation efforts, but UNTAC was able to settle most of the refugees or pay compensation. To continue its rehabilitation mission, UNTAC supervised the restoration, maintenance, and support of Cambodia's basic infrastructure, rebuilding or improving its utilities, major roadways, railways, ports, airports, telecommunications, and banks.

Although occasional attacks by Khmer Rouge forces in the northwest provinces continue even today, UNTAC left "encouraging legacies" (UN *h*: 55) for Cambodia's government and people: introduction to the democratic process and a chance to find a political rather than military solution to Cambodia's problems.

El Salvador

El Salvador's decade-long civil conflict was a product of long-standing social and economic inequities, exacerbated by years of repressive armed force and domination by public security bodies (UN *i*: 6). The UN became involved when the General Assembly urged the Government of El Salvador to halt its human rights abuses (UN *i*: 67). In early 1981, full-scale civil war broke out between the Government of El Salvador and a coalition of resistance groups, the *Frente Farabundo Marti para la Liberacion Nacional* (The Farabundo Marti Front for National Liberation, or FMLN). For more than a decade, the armed struggle consumed El Salvador, until both parties wearied of the fighting and its severe impact on the population. Realizing that no military solution was in sight and support from the superpowers was waning in light of the unfounded cooperation between the U.S. and USSR, the Government and the FMLN turned to the UN. Negotiations began with talks between the UN Secretary-General, the Secretary-General of the Organization of the American States, and the five Central American countries of Costa Rica, El Salvador, Guatemala, Honduras, and Nicaragua. The result was the *Procedure for the Establishment of a Firm and Lasting Peace in Central America* (UN *i*: 9), signed in August 1987 and known as the "Guatemala Procedure" or *"Esquipulas II,"* which established the UN Observer Group in Central America (ONUCA) to implement future peace agreements. On 15 September 1989, the Government of El Salvador and the FMLN agreed to begin formal dialogue to end their conflict. However, they were unable to agree on several major issues, and negotiations broke down. In December 1989, the Government and the FMLN requested Secretary-General assistance to commence an uninterrupted negotiating effort to settle the conflict and eliminate its root causes (UN *i*: 105).

The UN's success in assisting the Government of El Salvador and the FMLN in reaching agreements paved the way for the creation of the UN Observer Mission in El Salvador (ONUSAL). The Security Council, at the request of the Parties, established ONUSAL "to monitor all agreements concluded between the two parties . . . [and to] verify the compliance by the parties with the Agreement on Human Rights." Both the Government and the FMLN agreed to constitutional reforms in the judicial system and human rights, the electoral system, and the armed forces, dealing with each issue separately. Human rights concerns were written directly into the Constitution to ensure complete attention and in support of the creation of the "National Council for the Defence of Human Rights." The mission to monitor and provide "extensive, systematic human rights oversight" belonged to ONUSAL, and the "Commission on the Truth" was formed, composed of three UN Secretary-General appointees to investigate "serious acts of violence." In the interest of electoral reform, the Agreements called for the establishment of a Supreme Electoral Tribunal to replace the existing Central Board of Elections, giving the Tribunal the highest administrative authority and jurisdiction with respect to electoral matters. The Government of El Salvador also requested that ONUSAL verify and observe the elections (UN *i*: 288).

The initial mission of ONUSAL with respect to military issues was to observe and verify all aspects of the cease-fire and to achieve a separation of forces. This had to be accomplished to allow ONUSAL the flexibility to demobilize the FMLN ex-combatants and conduct a widespread turn-in of weapons. ONUSAL was able to reduce the size of the armed forces, retain quality soldiers, and redefine the military mission to focus on defending El Salvador's sovereignty and territorial integrity.

A primary concern of ONUSAL in civil administration and rehabilitation areas was the issue of land ownership. The UN Secretary-General proposed that the Government provide a guarantee preventing landholders from being evicted from their holdings and establishing a ceiling on the number of beneficiaries of land transfers. To meet rehabilitation requirements, ONUSAL made use of land holdings exceeding the constitutional limit to meet the needs of those without land. The status quo was honored in landholding situations in designated conflict zones until suitable arrangements could be made. Both ONUSAL and the UN Secretary-General served as mediators, and ONUSAL maintained public security with the help of the Auxiliary Transitory Police. In order to monitor the maintenance of public order, ONUSAL used its Police Division while the newly organized National Civil Police was trained and commissioned into service (UN *i*: 20-25).

Mozambique

Mozambique experienced 16 years of civil war until the Government of Mozambique and its guerrilla opposition, the *Resistencia Nacional Mocambicana* (National Mozambican Resistance, or RENAMO), came to the negotiating table to discuss the peace process for the good of the country, resulting in the *General Peace Agreement for Mozambique*. The conflict had destabilized the government and drained its resources, while both sides were unsuccessful in achieving a military victory (UN *j*: 14).

The face-off between the Marxist-Leninist party government and its opposition, strengthened by external support from the neighboring countries of Southern Rhodesia and South Africa, brought about a deepening humanitarian crisis which was exacerbated by periodic severe droughts. By 1987, the civil war had devastated the economy, forcing the government to rely on foreign assistance and abandon its Marxist-Leninist philosophy in the interest of economic reform. The government's economic and political reforms helped lead the way to the possibility of negotiations with the armed opposition group. Both sides felt the devastating effects of the civil war and the drought, and at last realized that they had reached a military impasse and, therefore, sought a peace agreement.

Negotiations began in 1988 in Rome. With the help of intermediaries from the Catholic Church, the negotiations entered the final stages in 1992, as the UN's role as an "impartial guarantor" of the peace process emerged. The Government and RENAMO agreed that they needed impartial management of the peace process, and thus requested international assistance from the UN and the Organization of African Unity. At the request of the parties, the UN established the UN Operation in Mozambique (ONUMOZ) to verify and monitor the peace agreement signed by the Government and RENAMO. The UN had already been involved in Mozambique, providing international humanitarian support in 1983-84 and appointing the UN Special Coordinator for Emergency Relief Operations in 1987 to integrate the "objectives of the emergency programme with those for economic rehabilitation and development" (UN *j*: 131). ONUMOZ further expanded the UN role in Mozambique, not only to serve as an impartial monitor, but as an honest broker in helping to reduce the level of distrust between the parties.

In their agreement, the Government and RENAMO identified a number of issues particular to the transition regime that called for UN assistance. The human rights concerns had been addressed by the UN previously, but ONUMOZ was charged with coordinating, monitoring, and assisting humanitarian relief operations to continue building a climate of trust and cooperation between all parties. In addition, ONUMOZ undertook the reconstruction of hospitals, schools, and other social facilities, as well as establishing a "reintegration programme" for demobilized soldiers (UN *j*: 154).

In preparation for its role in the elections, ONUMOZ deployed an Electoral Division consisting of 148 electoral officers and 1200 international observers. Its mission was to participate in and conduct an electoral education campaign on the role of opposition parties and to provide resources to enable new groups to organize for the election. During the campaign, ONUMOZ monitored the electoral process, provided oversight, strengthened the organizational capability of parties contesting the election, and provided any required technical assistance.

The ultimate goal of ONUMOZ's work with the armed forces was to achieve demobilization of the opposition forces and to integrate them into society in the interest of peace-building. Upon arrival, ONUMOZ monitored and verified the cease-fire, with an eye to achieving a separation of forces and the complete withdrawal of foreign forces. Part of the demobilization process was the collection, storage, and destruction of weapons, as well as monitoring and verifying the disbanding of private and irregular armed groups. ONUMOZ also authorized special security arrangements for vital infrastructure, such as roads, hospitals, and schools, to provide a sense of continuity and safety. The UN established a trust fund to transform RENAMO from a guerrilla force to a political party, thus giving the opposition group a peaceful means of voicing its views on state matters.

The issue of a UN role in monitoring the civilian police was not initially addressed in the Agreement, though the UN Secretary-General, in his report on ONUMOZ (UNSC S/24642: 1-5) suggested that it would be useful as a confidence-building measure and to assist in the security of the electoral process. The Parties took his suggestion and, as a result, the UN sent 128 police officers to monitor civil liberties and provide technical advice to Mozambique's National Police Affairs Commission.

With the extensive assistance of the UN High Commissioner on Refugees, ONUMOZ successfully achieved its goal in the area of repatriation through the resettlement of over four million people, of which one million were refugees. They returned home to resume farming and other economic activities (UN *j*: 5).

COMPARISON OF UN ROLES

The United Nations has had varying roles in peace operations throughout its history — these studies are only a sample. As global situations change, so does the degree of participation of the UN in peace operations that support affected nation-states. In Cambodia, the UN played a critical role in launching the peace process by offering possible solutions to the inability or unwillingness of the four factions to reach agreement on a peace settlement. The framework achieved by the five permanent members of the UNSC, and accepted by the four Cambodian factions, set the stage for negotiations which translated the settlement framework into a peace agreement. In El Salvador, the UN was brought in by invitation once the parties had decided to give peace a chance. Though no less important, the UN role in El Salvador was one of mediation and establishing standard operating procedures for the conduct of negotiations. The UN was an active participant in the process, providing international verification prior to the ceasefire to build confidence, but its overall function was to serve as a facilitator to the parties in their quest for peace.

Mozambique required only limited participation of the UN in helping it to implement its peace plan. The Government and its guerrilla opposition achieved successful negotiations with the help of the Catholic Church and the international community, requiring specific UN assistance only as they neared the final stages. The UN served in more of an overseer role to verify and occasionally supervise the progress of the peace plan.

Key elements of transitional regimes include the issue of power-sharing as parties face the problems of cross-recognition and acceptance. The development or revision of a constitution documents decisions on power-sharing, as well as providing protection of basic human rights and freedoms. Measures that translate the promises of guaranteed human rights into action play a large part in transitional regimes, as civil wars are often characterized by grave human rights abuses. Elections epitomize the success of transitional regimes in achieving a free and fair system, allowing the people to choose their political leaders. It is likely the most important of the components. Failure to enable the people to voice their political views through free elections denies the new government a legitimate base. Agreement on issues of military force, civil administration, and police creates a sense of national security for the parties to a transitional regime. Years of civil war or armistice make the parties to a peace agreement insecure and skeptical. Addressing these issues up front provides the parties a documented, and often UN-enforced, peace process. Repatriation and rehabilitation are confidence-building measures. Transitional regimes that emerge from civil wars or temporary peace arrangements can regain the trust of the citizens through reuniting families and rebuilding their lives.

This broad framework identifies issues of concern for nation-states divided by civil war, and experiencing transition toward a comprehensive peace plan. The situation on the Korean peninsula is ripe for such a transition as reunification gains attention and the need for a comprehensive peace agreement rises. Using the components of transitional regimes in this framework may be useful in analyzing the positions of North and South Korea on the issue of reunification.

KOREAN REUNIFICATION PROPOSALS

Over the years, North and South Korea have each offered solutions to the problem of reunification. The late Kim Il-sung, former leader of North Korea, first advanced the idea of establishing a confederal system as an interim step toward reunification in August 1960. During his 1980 speech to the Sixth Congress of the Workers' Party, Kim Il-sung put forth a comprehensive policy for reunification, producing a method of establishing a Democratic Confederal Republic of Koryo (ancient name for Korea) with concrete principles and complicated prerequisites (National Unification Board (NUB) *a*: 101). South Korea made its first overture toward North Korea in President Park Chung Hee's August 15 Declaration in 1970, where he broke from the former policy of avoiding contact with communists and suggested measures to gradually remove numerous barriers between the two sides (Korean Overseas Information Service *a*: 311). Since then, both North and South Korea have proffered various suggested solutions in the interest of reunification.

Of global concern is the hate and mistrust that exists between the leaders and kindred people of each state, preventing them from achieving compromise on the path toward unification. An exploration of the points of contention between the two states' proposals reveals areas of potential compromise which might be achieved with outside assistance.

SOUTH vs. NORTH

The current unification policies of South and North Korea have evolved over the years and as global events have unfolded. South Korea has embraced western democracy, which has colored its unification policy, tempered its attitude toward the North, and enhanced its international standing. In spite of decreasing support from its once-staunch allies, Russia and China, North Korea has maintained the isolationist policy established by the late Kim Il-sung and continued by his son and designated heir, Kim Jong-Il. The policies differ primarily in philosophy and process, as reflected in the names of each country's blueprint for unification. The South calls its proposal the "Korean National Community Unification Formula" (NUB *a*: 116), indicating a gradual process of adding various factors to achieve unification. The North refers to its policy as the "Formula for Creating a Democratic Confederation of Koryo" (NUB *a*: 102), foretelling an immediate change in the political and governmental structure of each country. South Korea's reunification philosophy is based on the values of freedom and liberal democracy, with the intent of building a single Korean national community. It is governed by a set of principles agreed to by both states in the 4 July 1972 South-North Communique (Seong: 77), including independence, peaceful unification, and a democracy conducive to grand national unity (NUB *b*: 14)

North Korea's philosophy is governed by *Chuche*, its ideology of self-reliance introduced by Kim Il-Sung. It fuels the mission of the North Korean Workers' Party to increase the leadership role of the working class and fights to unite all forces "behind the banner of the worker-peasant alliance" (Oh: 27). The premise of *Chuche*, a Marxist-Leninist theory, is to encourage North Koreans to survive and prosper within the limitations of available resources and national capabilities. The overriding goal of this isolationist policy is to expel "American imperialist forces from South Korea and [frustrate] the return of Japanese militarism to the Korean peninsula" (Oh: 27).

South and North Korea approach the process of unification from opposite ends of the spectrum. The South proposes a gradual, three-phased approach, the end result being a unified Korea with one system and one government. The North promotes immediate unification of the peninsula under a confederation of two states, each with its own system and government.

South Korea's Unification Policy

The three phases of South Korea's unification policy are described as Reconciliation and Cooperation, Formation of a Korean Commonwealth, and a Unified Single Nation State (Korean Overseas Information Service *b*: 2). The first phase, Reconciliation and Cooperation, is an effort to replace the distrust and lingering hostility from the past with confidence-building measures. It includes mutual recognition of each other's systems, energized exchanges and cooperation, and resolution of humanitarian issues such as reuniting dispersed families.

The second phase, Formation of a Korean Commonwealth, promotes peaceful coexistence and co-prosperity, encouraging the North and South to join together in a single socio-economic community. It facilitates a special intra-national relationship between the two (as opposed to the existing state-to-state relationship) and establishes a joint council of presidents and council of ministers to ease political integration while parliamentary delegates representing both sides develop a unified constitution.

Phase three, Development of a Unified Single Nation State, encompasses full integration of the North and South as they form a joint legislature and united government under democratic procedures in accordance with a unified constitution.

North Korea's Unification Policy

North Korea's suggested confederation system is the cornerstone of its unification policy. The concept of a confederation has been elaborated in a series of proposals over the years. In October 1980, Kim Il Sung outlined North Korea's unification policy at the Party Central Committee in the form of "Prerequisites" and "Principles" (Kim Il Sung: 57-58). The prerequisites were designed to ensure compliance prior to any unification plan, including the replacement of the "incumbent Seoul regime . . . in favor of a . . . people's democratic regime" (NUB *a*: 109). The prerequisites contradict both the espoused principles for the formation and operation of a confederal government, as well as Kim Il Sung's 1993 "Ten-Point Programme" (UNSC S/25577: 2-4).

The mandatory prerequisites to a confederation system include:

a. Liquidating the South's military fascist rule and achieving its democratization, replacing the present regime with one that is acceptable to the North.

b. Repealing the South's Anti-Communist and National Security Laws and abolishing its "tyrannical offices," possibly nullifying the existing U.S.-ROK Mutual Defense Treaty.

c. The mutual legalization of all political parties and social organizations, including the Communist Party, and guaranteeing the freedom for those parties to conduct political activities.

d. Achieving dialogue and forming a peace agreement between North Korea and the U.S. thereby effectively eliminating the role of South Korea and accomplishing U.S. withdrawal of troops from the South.

e. Ending U.S. interference in Korea's internal affairs (NUB *a*: 103-109).

Components	South Korea	North Korea	Potential for Compromise
Power Sharing		◆ (yellow)	● (yellow)
Political Parties		◆ (orange)	
Constitution			
Development	■	▲	● (yellow)
Human Rights	■	◆ (blue)	● (green)
Elections	■		● (yellow)
Organize			
Conduct	■		● (brown)
Military	■	◆ (blue)	● (green)
Civil Administration	■	◆ (orange)	● (yellow)
Foreign Affairs	■	◆ (yellow)	● (yellow)
National Defense	■	◆ (yellow)	● (yellow)
Peace Zone	■		● (yellow)
Police			
Repatriation	■		● (yellow)
Rehabilitation			● (yellow)

● (green) = Agreement; no outside mediation required
● (yellow) = Compromise likely between parties; may require mediation
● (brown) = Policies diametrically opposed; will likely require mediation
■ = Addressed in South Korean unification policy
▲ = Alluded to in North Korea's principles
◆ (orange) = Addressed in North Korea's prerequisites
◆ (yellow) = Addressed in North Korea's principles
◆ (blue) = Addressed in North Korea's ten-point programme

Unification Policies.

source: author

The key role of the prerequisites is to set the stage for the confederal government, in essence forming a government in the South that is conducive to the aims of the North. This idea contradicts those set forth in the principles that are meant to guide the formation and operation of the confederal government. In its Principles, the North advocates a unification process similar to that suggested by the South. However, it is widely believed that North Korea's emphasis on Principles instead of Prerequisites is a propaganda technique and may in fact be intentional to prevent the unification under any system other than a confederal one (NUB *a*: 109).

North Korea's Principles include:

a. Both sides of Korea unify the fatherland on principles of independence, peaceful unification, and great national unity, while retaining their ideologies and systems.
b. North and South form a unified national government, recognizing and tolerating their existing ideologies and systems and maintaining their regional autonomy.
c. North and South form a Supreme National Confederal Assembly under which they create a confederal government office to guide the regional governments of each side.
d. Call the confederal state the "Democratic Confederal Republic of Koryo" in honor of the previous unified condition of the peninsula and reflecting the common political ideal of democracy (Seong: 77).

The North proposed the *Ten-Point Programme of Great Unity* (UNSC S/25577: 1-4) in 1993. It is the most definitive and positive overture toward unification, since it can be implemented in the presence or absence of a confederal system (NUB *a*: 107). North Korea will not, however, implement any portion of its program until a confederal system is established, which implies the "democratization" or cessation of the existing South Korean government and refers back to the true emphasis placed on the mandatory Prerequisites.

The *Ten-Point Programme of Great Unity* consists of:

1. A unified state, independent, peaceful and neutral, which should be founded through the unity of the north and south and should represent all parties.
2. Basing unity on patriotism and the spirit of national independence.
3. Achieving unity on the principles of promoting coexistence, coprosperity, and common interests, making reunification the top priority.

4. Achieving unity through ceasing all political disputes between fellow countrymen.
5. Elimination of the state of military confrontation between the North and the South, and organization of allied national forces.
6. Ensuring freedom of debate on and activity for reunification and allowing political freedom of choice.
7. Protecting the material and spiritual wealth of individuals and organizations, encouraging exchange and cooperation in the areas of science, culture and education, and the promotion of the uniform development of science-technology, national culture, and national education.
8. Achieving trust and understanding through the free and guaranteed use of transportation and communications throughout the country.
9. Strengthening the solidarity between people of the north, the south, and overseas through organizations and political parties.
10. Rewarding those who contribute to the cause of national reunification and ensuring "those who turned their back on the nation . . . be treated leniently" (UNSC S/25577: 4).

SUMMARY OF KEY DIFFERENCES

The differences between the two reunification policies can be generally expressed in two categories: those areas that may be solved through bilateral compromise and those which probably will be resolved only with outside assistance.

A study of common components of UN transitional regimes reveals similar issues that apply to the sensitive nature of Korean reunification. Not only are these key issues the same problems that may require the aid of a third party; they also present opportunities for the states to reach compromise. The essential components of UN transitional regimes include the issues of political power sharing, constitution development, human rights, elections, military forces, civil administration, police force, repatriation, and rehabilitation. The unification policies of the North and South address several of these components.

Issues specific to the question of Korean reunification that are especially sensitive and may require assistance from a third party or organization include the deep-rooted differences in philosophy (democratic values and freedom vs. *Chuche*), the process or formula for achieving a unified Korea (a single nation-state with one system and one government vs. a confederation of two states each with its own system and government), and the method of founding a Unified Korea (democratic general elections in both the South and North vs. negotiations at a conference of delegates from political and civic groups).

Although North Korea's *Chuche* ideology continues today, its isolationist policy has brought the economic and social condition of the country to its knees. Even North Korea's acceptance of rice from Japan contradicts the ideology upon which its entire society is based, and serves as a sign to the possible loosening of the tight reins of self-reliance.

The proposal of an interim arrangement en route to a single nation-state is key to the second phase of the South's gradual approach. The purpose of the Korean commonwealth is to institutionalize peace through re-establishment of "a sense of national community" (Korean Overseas Information Service *a*: 321). The concept is for several joint organizations to determine and discuss alternative ways of integrating the two states. Economic concerns may prevent North Korea's plans for immediate formation of a confederal state and encourage some type of interim arrangement that could be facilitated by an agreed-upon third party. The question of elections by the people or by a panel of delegates can be solved through the appointment of an election committee, comprising representatives from both states and supervised by an approved international organization, meeting the stated requirements of the North and South.

Numerous issues in the quest for unification are potential opportunities for compromise between the North and South. The questions of equal power sharing and political organization can be solved with the South continuing to embrace liberal democratic ideals, to include free speech, in an effort to offer confidence-building measures to North Korea and enabling the Communist Party to exist as a political entity.

Although the South vocally supports a joint effort in developing a unified constitution, the North implies a similar intent and purpose in its *Ten-Point Programme*. The North alludes to jointly-developed guidance to support and protect national rights and interests. Both the North and South indicate a desire to ease military tensions on the peninsula, the South, through the establishment of a Peace Zone, and the North, through the elimination of military confrontation.

In the area of civil administration, both the North and South agree that a joint organization should be formed. The South proposes the formation of joint councils of presidents and ministers, while the North advocates forming a joint supreme national confederal assembly. It is conceivable that a unified Korea may want to initially handle joint foreign affairs and national defense with the assistance of an international agency. The South directly addresses the issue of repatriation in its Reconciliation and Cooperation phase through its milestone of reuniting dispersed families. The North's policies of guaranteeing free use of transportation and communications, promoting stability in people's lives, and elevating the well-being of all people are positive moves in the direction of making repatriation a primary goal.

UNITED NATIONS PARTICIPATION IN KOREA'S REUNIFICATION

Korea's long-standing face-off since the Korean War has made it an international and regional concern. Though not actively engaged in a civil war, North and South Korea continue to confront each other across the Demilitarized Zone (DMZ), keeping tensions high on the peninsula. In 1947 the General Assembly identified key elements to the process of reunifying the Korean peninsula. It recognized freedom, independence, and fair representation as principles that drive reunification and manifest themselves in the conduct of free and fair elections and the establishment of a self-sufficient government, to include a national security force and the withdrawal of occupying forces (UNGA A/C.1/218/Rev 1: 1-2). Since the end of the Cold War, the UN has had renewed opportunities to fulfill its Charter to maintain international peace and security, governed by the principles of freedom, independence, and fair representation, in its various missions and operations throughout the world. Perhaps the time is right for the UN to play a role in the reunification of Korea, similar to the roles it has played in UN transitional regimes, and complete the task begun in 1947.

SIMILARITIES BETWEEN TRANSITIONAL REGIMES AND KOREA

The end of the Cold War has affected North Korea considerably, taking away its primary supporter and leaving it in social, if not political, disarray. Like Cambodia, El Salvador, and Mozambique, Korea has lost its link to superpower confrontation. North Korea has made overtures toward unification since the end of the Cold War, recognizing its isolationist policy of the past no longer has reliable Russian support. Neither China nor the United States is interested in expending precious economic resources to maintain a posture of military confrontation.

Components	Cambodia	El Salvador	Mozambique	Korea
Power Sharing	●	❍	●	●
Political Party	●	●	●	●
Constitution	●	●	❍	●
Human Rights	●	●	●	●
Educate/Investigation	●	❍	❍	❍
Oversight	●	●	●	❍
Elections	●	●	●	●
Organize	●	●	❍	❍
Conduct/Fairness	●	❍	❍	●
Observe	●	●	●	❍
Register Voters	●	●	❍	❍
Monitor Compliance	●	●	●	❍
Educate Voters	●	❍	●	❍
Military	●	●	●	❍
Maintain Cease-fire	●	❍	●	●
Mine-Awareness/Clearing	●	❍	●	❍
Supervise	●	❍	❍	❍
Verify Withdrawal	●	❍	●	❍
Regroup/Demobilize	●	❍	●	❍
Purify	❍	●	❍	❍
Training Awareness	●	❍	❍	❍
Civil Admin	●	●	❍	❍
Good Offices/Liaison	●	❍	❍	❍
Foreign Affairs	●	❍	❍	●
National Defense	●	❍	❍	●
Finance/Information	●	❍	❍	❍
Public Security	●	❍	●	❍
Land Issues	●	●	❍	●
Police	●	●	●	❍
Supervise	●	❍	●	❍
Replace	❍	●	❍	❍
Repatriation	●	❍	●	●
Rehabilitation	●	●	●	●

● = Component present ❍ = Component lacking

Transitional Regimes.

source: author

As in Cambodia, El Salvador, and Mozambique, full military victory has not been achieved in Korea. There appears to be no military solution to the problem of unifying the Korean peninsula. Recent overtures, in the way of reunification proposals, imply North and South Koreans are seriously considering a political solution. In the reunification proposals of North and South Korea, the potential for compromise and international assistance exists. Although not assured, the examples of Cambodia, El Salvador, and Mozambique may provide possible options to Korea's challenges.

The issue of power-sharing is a point on which the North and South could reach a compromise, particularly in light of El Salvador's success in achieving political legitimacy of the FMLN and Mozambique's success in transforming an armed opposition group, the National Mozambican Resistance, into a political party. These achievements were due in great part to the work of ONUSAL and ONUMOZ, respectively, and indicate a potential for UN assistance if North and South cannot reach a compromise between themselves.

In their individual proposals, North and South Korea indicate a potential for the development of a unified constitution. The South addresses the issue directly, while the North alludes to some type of governing document in its Principles. Both Cambodia and El Salvador formed joint bodies to create or reform their constitutions, with the advice of UNTAC and ONUSAL, respectively.

The issue of elections is a point of contention between North and South Korea which requires further negotiation and may call for impartial, outside assistance. The South supports the ideal of elections, while the North doesn't address it at all. While all three transitional regimes held free and fair elections with the help of the UN, they accomplished this only after reaching a peace agreement.

The North and South both address the issue of the military in their proposals but disagree on the mode of unifying the force. Although El Salvador and Mozambique were successful in this endeavor, in Cambodia the Khmer Rouge maintains a military force although its activities are limited to a relatively small sector of the country. To reach agreement on this subject, North and South Korea will likely require assistance from an outside party.

Repatriation is specifically addressed by South Korea's proposal for reunification and is similar to the agreements in El Salvador and Cambodia. Honoring land ownership and providing humanitarian and resettlement aid will apply to the many families that live separated by the DMZ. The UN was deeply involved in land and humanitarian issues with the UNHCR, and such a role seems relevant to the situation in North and South Korea.

Though not every component of the referenced transitional regimes and Korea's reunification proposals are identical, they are similar in intent and provide valuable lessons learned. The study of UN involvement in transitional regimes provides an initial blueprint for the potential participation of the UN in the reunification of Korea.

The involvement of the UN in Korea has always reflected the attention of the superpowers. The superpowers have been able to protect their client states by virtue of their status on the UN Security Council. As Russia grows more comfortable with its Security Council cooperation with the United States, and China continues to grow as an economic and military power, the potential for these permanent members of the Security Council to have a significant role in Korea's reunification rises. Support of UN participation in the reunification of Korea would provide Russia and China a face-saving gesture to compensate for the global isolation suffered at the outset of the Korean War. The United States maintains its direct role in Korea by supporting the UN Command with a commander, staff, and significant troop presence. It is likely that American allies, such as Western Europe, Japan, and other Asian countries will view the UN role in Korea's reunification as opportunities to invest in Korea economically and politically, and in the interest of international peace and security.

THE UN AND KOREA — FUTURE PARTNERS?

It is apparent that the possibility exists for North and South Korea to rely on shared common bonds to make unification a realistic goal. Though the states approach the issue of unification from different perspectives, many elements of their proposals are similar. The opportunities for compromise are not only pathways toward successful unification, but may heal the wounds that have festered since the Korean War. The UN's success since the end of the Cold War in providing the mechanisms for UN transitional regimes may encourage an invitation to the international organization, which would allow North and South Korea to participate in the transition process.

Permanent membership in the Security Council gives the United States, Russia, and China a mechanism to protect their interests in the Korean peninsula while providing leverage in the North and South Korean governments to press for compromise and guarantee the enforcement of a comprehensive peace agreement. The large UN peacekeeping force that would be required, and the economic assistance that would be necessary, would engage Japan, other Asian countries, and Western Europe in the process. In the end, despite years of protestations to the contrary, North and South Korea may turn to the United Nations for assistance in achieving peaceful reunification.

NORTH KOREA'S PARTICIPATION IN THE TUMEN RIVER ECONOMIC DEVELOPMENT AREA: CATALYST FOR PEACE?

Bradley J. Curran
Master Sergeant, U.S. Marine Corps
August 1996

The United Nations Development Program (UNDP) is sponsoring a regional program of cooperative economic development with China, North Korea, South Korea, Mongolia and Russia called the Tumen River Area Development Program (TRADP). The vision is to transform the Tumen River basin into an international shipping, trading, and manufacturing center.

Korea's Tumen River basin has been of economic and strategic interest to China, Russia, and Japan for hundreds of years. In the 1930s, the Japanese had ambitious plans to develop the area, but they were not implemented. The TRADP can trace its origins to 1979, when the UNDP established an office in Pyongyang to help North Korea improve its international trade efforts. North Korea gradually began to increase participation in UN-sponsored economic programs.

In July 1990, a UNDP-sponsored Northeast Asia academic and business conference, attended by representatives of the U.S., Japan, China, the Soviet Union, Mongolia, South Korea and North Korea, stated that the Tumen River is the key to the economic development of the region and there was "great potential for economic cooperation" (UNDP *c*). The UNDP endorsed a 20-year plan to develop the Tumen River area. Then the UNDP, China, Mongolia, Russia, South Korea, and North Korea, with observers from Japan, the World Bank, and the Asian Development Bank, met in Pyongyang in 1991 and formed the first intergovernmental organization in Northeast Asia for economic and trade cooperation. Funding was provided by the UNDP, the United Nations Conference on Trade and Development, Canada, Finland and South Korea. The project was named the Tumen River Economic Development Area (TREDA) and efforts to attract foreign investors began in earnest (Carter: 11).

North Korea's contribution to the TREDA is access to the ice-free ports of Najin-Sonbong at the mouth of the Tumen River on the Sea of Japan. North Korea has devoted scarce resources to develop a Free Economic and Trade Zone (FETZ) at Najin-Sonbong. This FETZ development is assisted by the UNDP and coordinated with the other TREDA nations as part of a 20-year, three-phase plan.

Why would the communist North Koreans, with a history of isolation and hostile intentions to outsiders, be interested in cooperation with the United Nations and capitalist countries for economic development?

NORTH KOREA'S INTENTIONS

North Korea has been politically controlled by the Korean Workers Party led by Kim Il Sung, and now by his son, Kim Chong Il, since liberation from Japan in 1945. The cornerstone of the Kims' power has been the *Chuche* policy of self reliance. To justify their harsh suppression of any dissent, the Kims have fostered hatred of their rivals in South Korea and their supporters in the UN, the U.S., and Japan.

With the collapse of the Soviet Union and free market reforms in China, North Korea has lost her political allies and barter-based trade arrangements, and has been increasingly forced to deal with the realities of the international marketplace. North Korean leaders have two main goals in establishing their free trade zone: first, to gain hard currencies to buy food, fuel, and consumer goods, and then to learn market economic mechanisms and international trade.

Need for Food

In a recent North Korean videotape, Kim Chong Il stated "I feel we need to expand to the western world to feed the people" ("Kim Chong Il": 37). Hunger and discontent are widespread in North Korea. The leaders must address food, heating oil, and consumer goods shortages to remain in

Tumen River Area Development Program (TRADP): Regional Perspective.

source: Central Intelligence Agency

power. North Korea must gain the level of foreign trade needed to meet the basic food, shelter, and heating needs of its isolated people.

Despite lip service to their *Chuche* philosophy of self-reliance, North Korea has accepted shipments of South Korean and U.S. rice. So far they have received only a small part of the 70,000 tons needed to overcome an "increasingly desperate" situation largely provoked by widespread flooding that destroyed a significant portion of the 1995 harvest (R. Smith *b*: A1). Some in South Korea say that the North is exaggerating the damage done to crops by last summers floods and that food aid will only increase the Army's stocks, but meanwhile there are unprecedented flows of hungry refugees into China.

International Trade and Market Reforms

North Korea is also using the TREDA as a vehicle to earn cash and learn international trade. Deputy Director-General for the Bureau for Cooperation with International Organizations, Choi In Yon, said that

> Sonbong is very important to the development of Northeast Asia and can become an important gateway to Europe. It is time not for confrontation but rather understanding. DPRK's traditional trading relationships are changing. There has been much internal discussion on the issue since 1988. The DPRK's centrally planned economic system will not change (UNDP *e*: 4).

Many analysts say that North Korea's tentative new openness is driven purely by economic necessity and is limited to damage control. There are compelling reasons to think that its ideas for economic reform are more permanent. North Korea's self-imposed isolationism has left it vulnerable, and it has set in motion changes in international economic policy. The government will channel all foreign investment through a single DPRK governmental agency and restrict it to a free trade zone (Zumwalt: B4). China and Vietnam took similar early steps as they made economic reforms without political reform (Shirk). Kim Il Sung signalled these changes in his economic philosophy in 1991, when he announced a policy of encouraging foreign investment within North Korea (Zumwalt: B4). Kim seemed to follow the Chinese in this regard. One of Deng Xiaoping's goals in China in the late 1970s was to acquire foreign technologies, and he began to establish "windows" with foreign partners in coastal cities (Gurtov: 218, 222). North Korean propaganda began to acknowledge the need for increased trade with capitalist countries and began to state that this was not necessarily a contradiction of *Chuche* policy. This was justified by saying that trade would first benefit ethnic Koreans outside of North Korea ("Equality": 22).

Transportation Infrastructure in the Tumen River Development Program area.

source: Central Intelligence Agency

By establishing this free trade zone, North Korea hopes to learn international trade techniques while keeping its population relatively free of contamination by foreign influences. North Korean reforms are what Chinese Foreign Minister Huang Hua called a socialist market economy for modernization (Huang Hua: 179). Like Lenin, who used the New Economic Policy to save the Soviet Union from total economic collapse, Kim Chong Il has been offering incentives for foreign trade and investment. Before a meeting of 20 economists from Japan and other countries, he stated, "we would like to learn what we can from capitalist society as much as possible," but went on to say that "everything is finally decided by myself" (Croddy: 272).

Chuche is being allowed to include high technology trade even with the hated Japanese and Americans (Pak: 6). North Korea would like Japan to lift its ban on the export of high-tech and other advanced expertise to North Korea, remove discriminatory export insurance and tariffs, exchange trade offices, and provide know-how on the exploration of seabed oil deposits ("N. K. Asks": 1).

The North Koreans admit privately that they are still learning from the PRC's experience (Garrett and Glaser: 541). The Chinese have always explained to visiting North Korean economic managers that the PRC's economic opening has had pluses and minuses — a point underscored by Tiananmen. Deng Xiaoping once acknowledged the inevitability of a little cultural pollution by saying that "if you open the door, some flies will come in" ("Making": 38). Perhaps some of North Korea's practical leaders see international joint ventures as a way to introduce market mechanisms through the back door. This practical flexibility in economic matters towards capitalist countries, especially in trade, technology transfer, and foreign investment is continuing (Kim Hakjoon: 88). The Tumen River Economic Development Area (TREDA) and the Najin-Sonbong free trade zone give North Korea a degree of control over its economic future. By participating, they can effect gradual economic changes needed for economic growth while maintaining political power based on Chinese and Vietnamese models.

Compared to the development efforts of other Asian countries, the TREDA effort thus far may look unimpressive. The ambitious foreign investment goals and the participation of North Korea are looked at with skepticism. Marcus Noland of the Institute for International Economics in Washington reflects the majority view in the United States concerning North Korea's Najin-Sonbong free trade zone: "[T]here has been almost no investment . . . there is absolutely no infrastructure there. None. There's just a big muddy field" (Quoted in K. Sullivan: A21). Chong-Sik Lee of the University of Pennsylvania says that "implementation of the plan will require an investment of at least $4 billion and North Korea has yet to attract major foreign investors" (Lee *a*: 11).

The purpose of this paper is to look at the facts of the UN's TREDA plan and North Korea's participation so that we can draw implications for Northeast Asia and the United States.

THE TUMEN RIVER PROJECT

TREDA's origins can be traced back to 1979, when the UNDP and the UN Industrial Development Organization (UNIDO) began to assist North Korea and other nations of Northeast Asia to increase international trade. From 1990 to the present, the UNDP and the five nations involved have held a series of meetings and formed intergovernmental organizations to coordinate goals to take advantage of the Tumen River basin's abundant natural resources and excellent location for transit trade. When the UNDP was invited to establish an office in Pyongyang in 1979, the international community began to expand international trade beyond the traditional North Korean barter system with communist China and the Soviet Union. As North Korea's primary international partners have adopted market reforms, North Korea has increased participation with the UNDP, and the result is the current TREDA plan to cooperatively develop the Tumen River basin economy.

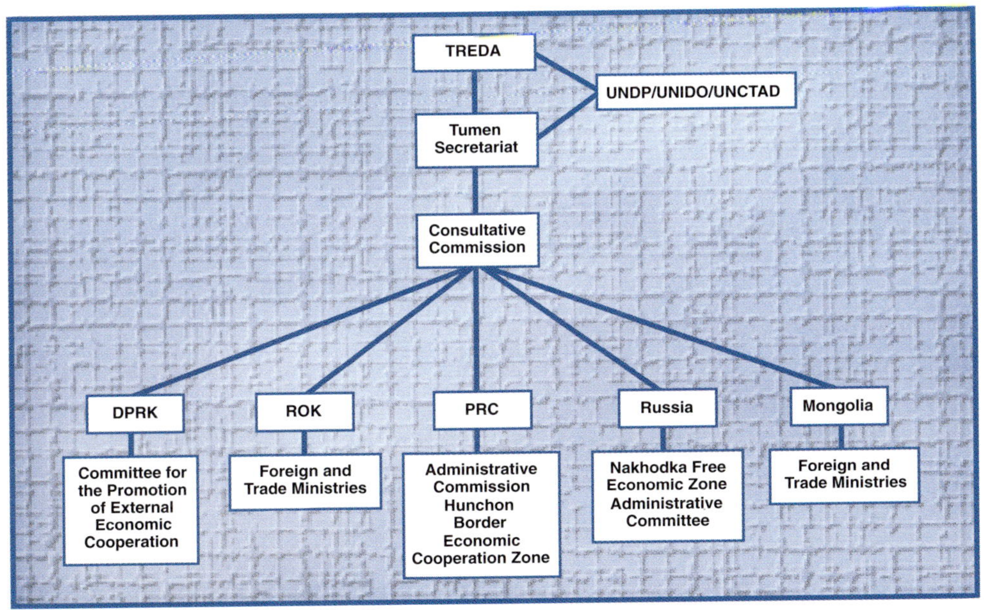

TREDA Organization. *source: UNDP C*

Vision

The goal is to transform the Tumen River basin into an international shipping, trading, and manufacturing center. The strategy adopted by the Tumen Secretariat is to build TREDA as the base for developing the economy of the broader Northeast Asia hinterland (UNDP *a*).

Foreign capital, technology, and marketing expertise is now required. Investment brochures advertise that the Tumen River region of Northeast Asia has a powerful set of comparative advantages over Hong Kong, Singapore, South Korea, Japan, India, Malaysia, Thailand and the southern coast of China:

- Access to Japanese, South Korean, and Chinese markets
- Abundant natural resources
- Excellent agricultural export base
- Low-cost manufacturing base
- Very low-priced and well-located land
- Low-cost power
- Inexpensive human resources
- Export processing zones with major tax incentives
- Excellent location for transit trade (UNIDO: 1).

Location is an important incentive for TREDA investors. By sea, the markets of Eastern Russia, Japan, South Korea and the U.S. are more cheaply accessible than from Southeast Asia. By rail, there is access to Russian, Chinese, European and, in the future, Mid-Eastern and Indian markets. Rail is cheaper and quicker than ships. Niigata to Hamburg by ship is a journey of 21,300 km and 40 days. By rail it is only 10,000 Km and 10 days, at half the price (UNIDO: 5).

A significant part of TREDA's long-term strategy is to entice container shipping companies to use Najin as a hub between Europe and Japan. Containers would be shipped to Najin from Niigata and then by rail through the DPRK and China, linking up with the Trans-Siberian railway. The new container facilities at Najin are set to alter the whole economics of doing business in Yanbian and northeast China. North Korea's ice-free ports make it easy to export bulk commodities from landlocked northeast China, Mongolia, and Siberia. Costs of labor, land, transport, raw materials, utilities, and taxes are a fraction of those in Japan, South Korea, and Taiwan. Duty-free export processing zones with skilled labor are one-third the price levels of China's southern coastal areas, though a bit more than Malaysia, Indonesia, and India. There is a small but well-trained core of technically skilled workers available throughout the region (UNDP *c*: preface).

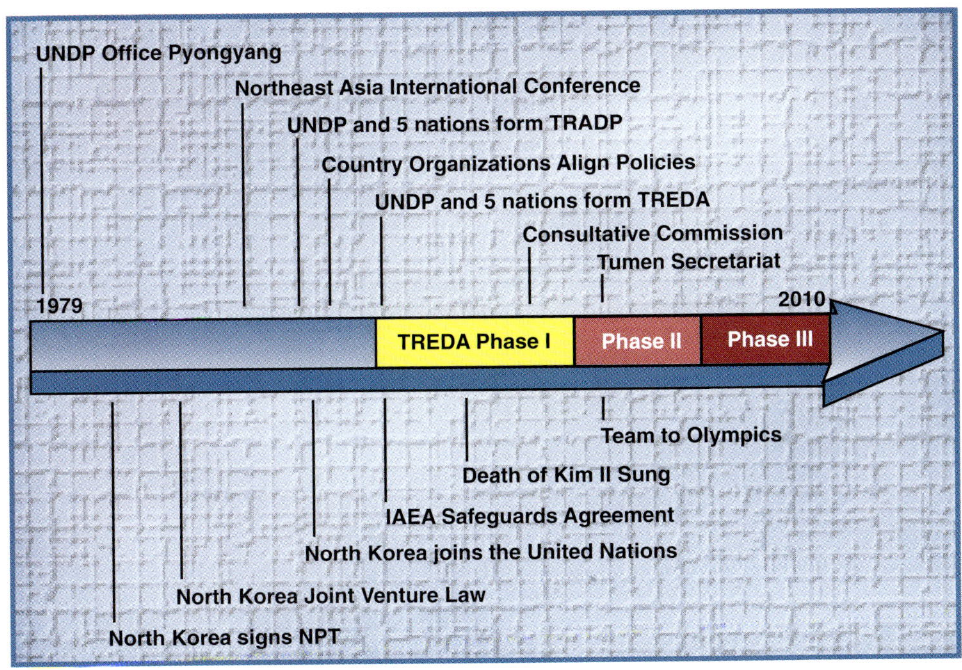

TREDA Plan phases. *source: UNDP C*

Development Strategy

TREDA's cooperative strategy has four steps: 1) create an "enabling" environment, 2) improve available services, 3) expand trade, and 4) attract investment and new technology to improve market access (UNDP *c*: 18).

To accomplish this, TREDA has developed a three-phase, 20-year plan calling for "enabling environment" and coordination preparations to be completed by 1995, infrastructure and service improvements to be completed by 2000, and complete development and activation for international trade and investment to be accomplished by 2010.

Each TREDA country is individually and cooperatively executing this 3-phase plan, with UNDP coordination, to take advantage of their human, land, water, forestry, mineral and tourism resources. Service sectors of transportation, power, telecommunications, water, tourism, and business will be developed simultaneously with light and heavy industry to attract foreign investment. These resources, services, and industries are being developed under UNDP coordination to ensure that there is no adverse impact on the environment and that the plan is executed using sound economic analysis using real world market prices (UNDP *c*: A2)

NATIONAL INTERESTS

Each of the five countries participating in TREDA has economic and political interests in the project. In addition, countries and private corporations in Asia, Europe, and North America hope to gain long-term profit and influence in Northeast Asia.

North Korea

Within the framework of the TREDA, the North Koreans are participating by developing a Free Economic and Trade Zone (FETZ) in the Najin-Sonbong area and declaring Chongjin a free port. Najin and Sonbong are ports on the Sea of Japan (East Sea to Koreans) and the Tumen River estuary.

North Korea has drawn up a coordinated three-phase, 20-year plan for participation in the TREDA that dovetails the overall TREDA plan. The main objective of the first phase (1993-95) is to improve Najin-Sonbong as an international cargo transit point by rebuilding and upgrading the existing infrastructure of railways, roads, and ports. The desire to simultaneously create a favorable investment climate is proceeding, though with difficulty.

The goal is to turn Najin into a container-exclusive port in the future. The North Koreans hope it will become the largest port in continental Northeast Asia, with a 70-million-ton freight capacity annually (DPRK). The port is the heart of the Najin-Sonbong Free Economic and Trade Zone. It is located 93 kilometers by road from Hunchon in China, and will be the major outlet for exports by container from Yanbian Province, China. North Korea is betting on growing dependence by China and Japan on Najin-Sonbong as a transshipment point .

South Korea

South Korean President Kim Young Sam is determined to persuade Pyongyang to resume peace talks by offering the carrot of economic cooperation. Many South Korean businessmen take that as a green light to set up business with the North (Shim *a*: 63). South Korea must provide the lion's share of money and technical expertise to bring North Korea into a modern economic system. Foreigners will naturally follow their lead or invest in North Korea through South Korean companies, the same way they invest in China via Hong Kong companies.

The South Korean government is concerned that the North Korean economy might collapse, prompting a desperate North Korean attack against South Korea. South Korea closely watched German reunification and concluded that a gradual merging, eased by increasing North-South trade and investment, is most desirable (Shim *b*: 15). Since 1988, businesses in the South have been allowed limited trade with the North, but the amounts are still small compared to investments in the PRC and Vietnam. South Korea is divided into two camps: embargo and encircle the North, or trade with them to gain access and influence. Many South Korean conglomerates have shown interest in investing and operating in North Korea's FETZ, but government security issues have taken precedence. The strategy of South Korean industrial groups Daewoo and Lucky-Goldstar is to transfer garment and footwear factories to the North, for production and export to the South. Samsung Electronics wants to produce televisions and to invest in railroads and roads linking Chongjin with China through the Najin-Sonbong FETZ. SangYong wants to invest in the building blocks of infrastructure: cement, oil, and construction (Shim *a*: 63).

The industrialists' enthusiasm for trade with the North is gradually penetrating the South's foreign ministry bureaucracy. The ministry of trade, industry, and energy has suggested it is time to break the link between economic cooperation and the nuclear issue. Still, North Korea's long-term desire is economic investment by Japan and the West to give it more independence from the South ("South Korea": 163).

China

China is the short-term key to the success of the project. No other country has greater influence in North Korea, and Chinese government officials have been pushing North Korea to adopt their development model (Garrett and Glaser: 541). Chinese cooperation with the ethnic Koreans inside their borders is a key. Already a steady stream of refugees is crossing the border illegally, looking for food. In the event of economic collapse, China will have to deal with the refugees from North Korea if the government implodes or starts a war with the South (Glain and Cho: A6).

China regards the ethnic Korean province bordering North Korea as a potential breakaway province. China recognizes the possibly that South Korea, with its authoritarian democracy, may eventually rule the entire peninsula and is reluctant to provide excessive support to the North, which could drive the South toward friendlier relations with Japan and Russia. China wants a stable border with its traditional "little brother" and access to the Sea of Japan, while lessening Japanese influence in Northeast Asia. They have a stake in making sure that North Korea's economic and security promises are kept ("South Korea": 163). Chinese foreign ministry officials have said that, "We want to encourage North Korea to move forward toward a market economy. Those countries that live on aid cannot develop" (Garrett and Glaser: 541).

Russia

Russia is also encouraging North Korea to liberalize, fearing collapse and instability in Northeast Asia. A war on the Korean peninsula or a hostile nuclear-armed North Korea may mean Japanese rearmament and continued tension over Russian-occupied islands claimed by Japan. Russian participation in the TREDA has been extensive despite concern that Nakhodka and Vladivostok traffic may diminish while the Chinese and North Koreans benefit. They want to ensure that the free trade zone border areas are not reconfigured to their disadvantage ("Russian": 4). Russia is also said to have cut freight train service to North Korea for lack of payment of bills, complicating export of timber through North Korea until or unless a foreign investor steps in (Kristof: A1).

Mongolia

Mongolia is counting on the development within the TREDA area to have a positive impact on its economy. Improved transportation and investment mean easier access to Mongolia's vast natural resources by foreign investors and increased consumer goods trade for their people (UNDP *c*: 2).

Asia and Europe

Japan has had a long and profitable interest in the Tumen River area. Japanese economic ambitions in Northeast Asia are basically the same today as they were in 1905. Japan covets the rich natural resources of Manchuria and North Korea, especially coal and timber. Japan would like to build a rail link from the Tumen River area leading all the way to markets and other sources of raw material in eastern and western Europe. Korean and Manchurian coal mean less dependence on Arab oil, and rail links also provide an alternative to shipping oil via the Hormuz and Malaccan Straits. A stable and economically open North Korea, or perhaps a unified Korea in the future, will restore the ancient trade conduit between Japan and China. Japanese companies would like to make more use of North Korea's cheap and educated work force and would like to see a Trans-Asian natural gas pipeline from Siberia to South Korea, with a branch line to Japan.

Japan does not discourage the pro-Pyongyang ethnic Koreans living in Japan from sending large amounts of cash or investing in North Korea. In 1994 a joint Russian-Japanese project to build a $5 million bulk fertilizer facility to export Russian bulk chemical fertilizer to Japan was approved ("TRADP": 5). Japan does not want a quick reunification of Korea through explosion or implosion. A gradual reunification, where they can continue to invest in the North to gain influence, is in their interests ("South Korea": 163). Though suspicions of Japan run deep throughout Asia, Pyongyang is courting $458 million in Japanese investments in Najin-Sonbong ("Let's Make": 7).

Among the nations of East Asia, there is little distinction between corporate and national interests. Large multinational companies are routinely used to help reach foreign policy goals. Fear that the world might divide into regional trading blocks is driving the interests of Asian and European investors. Members of the Association of South East Asian Nations are exploring new areas for trade in the Pacific. Members of the European Union see the possibility of a Western Hemisphere trading block and do not want to be left out of an Asian trading block dominated by China and Japan.

TREDA hopes to attract mining and ore processing companies to develop the extensive mineral resources of the participating countries, especially those of Mongolia. A high priority of the TREDA nations is to have an assessment of the economic potential of these mineral resources done as soon as possible. Increased exploration will help develop the region by requiring infrastructure development, export earnings, and raw materials for industrial development.

The Najin-Sonbong Free Trade Zone is a center for wood processing, importing timber from Russia under Korean labor contracts. Foreign partners with marketing skills and advanced technology would make a massive and profitable difference (UNIDO: 7). Investors in the timber industry do have some negative points to consider. During the Japanese occupation of Korea, many Koreans went to work in the forests of Manchuria and Sakhalin and were treated as virtual slaves. Even today, North Korean timber workers in Russia are often sent as political prisoners. Even volunteers are subject to harsh conditions and "reeducation" upon their return to North Korea ("ROK: DPRK": 67).

United States

Strategically thinking U.S. businessmen and diplomats see short- and long-term benefits from supporting the TREDA, and North Korea's FETZ in particular. Participation will provide access and influence in North Korean business, diplomatic, and military circles, which will open the way for investment in North Korea. In the long term, U.S. investment contributes to lessening military tension and ensures that the U.S. has an economic and security role to play in Northeast Asia after Korean unification. Investment in TREDA will also encourage close economic cooperation between China and Japan, which will lessen the likelihood of an arms race between these two dominant East Asian powers.

U.S. sanctions against doing business with North Korea have been partially lifted. U.S. law permits American companies to engage in telecommunications and banking as long as the transactions do not originate or end in America. Limited exporting and importing of selected materials such as magnesium are permitted. United States magnesium and telephone companies have profited in North Korea's part of TREDA ("North Korea Plans": A11). Though the State Department does not encourage it, as there is no diplomatic presence as yet, Americans are free to travel to North Korea, and there is no longer a limit on how much they can spend ("Going There": A8).

The Nuclear Non-proliferation Treaty compliance negotiations sent fuel oil for electric generation to the Najin-Sonbong FETZ, and plans to jointly search for the remains of missing-in-action servicemen in North Korea has improved relations (Shorrock: 1A). Plans for an exchange of official liaison offices in Pyongyang and Washington are being negotiated. The Clinton administration's national security policy of "enlargement and engagement" is a good vehicle to begin a policy of assisting TREDA and North Korean economic development.

GEOGRAPHY

Northeast Asia's Tumen River forms the boundary of the Peoples Republic of China (PRC) (Manchuria), the Democratic Peoples Republic of Korea (DPRK) (North Korea), and Russia (Primorsky Territory). The Tumen originates on Mt. Changpu, (Mt. Paektu in Korean), and flows southeast to the Sea of Japan (the East Sea to Koreans). The Tumen River is frozen from December to March of each year and sometimes floods during the rainy season of July and August.

Russia and China are on the northern and the DPRK is on the southern bank. This area of the Tumen River, joining the frontiers of the PRC, Russia, and the DPRK, is centrally located in Northeast Asia. On the continent, the Tumen River basin backs the great resource-rich hinterland stretching from Northeast China to Mongolia and Siberia (UNDP *b*: 18). The sea does not freeze in the winter due to warm currents. There are about 855,000 ethnic Koreans in the Yanbian semi-autonomous province of China which borders North Korea. There are about 10,000 ethnic Koreans in Posyet, Russia, on the North Korean border.

HISTORY

The Japanese began the modern development of the Tumen River basin. After defeating the Russians in 1905, they eventually dominated most of Northeast Asia, annexed Korea, set up a puppet state in Manchuria, and controlled parts of the Soviet Far East such as Sakhalin Island. The Japanese Army and industrialists made detailed strategic plans for the development of Korea and Manchuria. Though they oppressed the Korean people, the Japanese built ports, roads, railroads, power plants, and modern schools in the area. The Japanese concentrated on control and expansion of the railroads, and on the coal and iron industries. The Japanese effectively used their military and industrial technology to advantage to colonize a land where natural resources were abundant, labor was cheap, and the native political regimes were weak and divided (Lee *b*: 11-15).

Additional development plans for the Tumen River basin were not implemented because Japan was defeated in World War II. The Soviet Union hoped to integrate aspects of the communist Chinese and North

Korean economies with its own, but nationalism and ideological schisms intervened, and there was little additional development of the area. In spite of the fact that the nations of Northeast Asia had rich natural resources and centrally planned economies based on communist ideology, political tension resulted in an inward orientation for trade and development. During this period trade was mostly based on barter arrangements.

UNDP INITIATIVE

In 1979, the United Nations Development Program (UNDP) established an office in Pyongyang, Democratic Peoples Republic of Korea (DPRK), and began to develop contacts to support North Korea's development and investment potential. North Korean leader Kim Il Sung acknowledged that his *Chuche* policy of maintaining national integrity and self sufficiency could be enhanced by international trade and commerce. To assist the DPRK in improving its international trade environment, dominated by Cold War security concerns, the UNDP committed $58 million between 1979 and 1996 to economic modernization projects (UNDP *f*: 1).

The United Nations system, primarily UNIDO operating under the auspices of the UNDP, began conducting the initial coordination and research throughout Northeast Asia that eventually resulted in the formation of the UNDP Tumen River Area Development Program (TRADP) and the Tumen Secretariat. The first step was for the UNDP, assisted by the United Nations Industrial Development Organization (UNIDO) and the United Nations Conference on Trade And Development (UNCTAD), to help North Korea write a joint venture law that passed in 1986, enabling them to expand their trade contacts (UNDP *f*: 14). In July of 1990, an international conference on the economic development in the region of Northeast Asia was held in Changchun, China, sponsored jointly by the East-West Center of the United States, the Asian Pacific Society of China, and the UNDP. There were over sixty participants from the Peoples Republic of China, the DPRK, the Republic of Korea, the Mongolian Peoples Republic, the Soviet Union, Japan and the United States.

Originally, the Conference planned to discuss economic development of the region in general but instead focused its attention on the development of the Tumen River as the key to international cooperation in Northeast Asia. Scholars of Northeast Asian Studies call the Tumen River basin the "Golden Triangle" of the region because of the strategic importance for economic development and great potential for international economic cooperation (UNDP *b*: 18).

The economic miracle of the South Koreans, the PRC's success with limited market reforms and Free Trade Zones in the 1980s, the collapse of the Soviet economy and government in 1991, and the failing economies in Mongolia and North Korea led the governments in the area to consider additional economic options. After discussions in Bangkok and New York between UNDP resident representatives and government counterparts, the UNDP Northeast Asia Sub-Regional Program for Technical Cooperation sponsored a meeting in July 1991 at Ulaanbaatar, Mongolia, to consider the following: expansion of temperate zone food crops, sub-regional air pollution and energy usage, new and renewable sources of energy, and promotion of trade and investment, especially in the Tumen River Area. The participants decided that the Tumen River basin's location has enormous potential for regional and international land, sea and air routes matching Russian, Chinese, and DPRK natural resources and labor with ROK and Japanese capital, technology, and management expertise (UNDP *b*: 18).

A UNDP reconnaissance mission travelled to North Korea in August and September 1991 and recommended development of the Tumen River area as a center for global trade to and from Northeast Asia including a land bridge to Central Asia and Europe. The mission recommended a coordinated 20-year plan and a UNDP regional commission to secure the confidence of the international investment community to finance about $30 billion for long-term development of facilities and to eliminate destructive competition (UNDP *e*: 5-1). At the request of the five Tumen River area countries, a meeting was held in Pyongyang, North Korea, in October of 1991, which inaugurated the Tumen River Area Development Program (TRADP) and established the Program Management Committee, the first inter-governmental organization in Northeast Asia committed to economic and technical cooperation (UNDP *c*: preface).

The principal sponsor of TRADP was the UNDP, which coordinated with UNIDO to carry out investment promotion programs. Other funding was provided by the Canadian International Development Agency, Finland, and the Republic of Korea (UNDP *c*: preface). The UNDP's role was and is to facilitate closer economic integration and mutual cooperation between the five participating countries: North Korea, Mongolia, PRC, ROK, and Russia. Each country is responsible for its own cooperative and consultative efforts. The TRADP has been supported by the International Trade Center and received observers from Finland, Canada, Japan, the World Bank, and the Asian Development Bank (UNDP *a*: 1). The 1992 Program Agreement signed by all five countries includes provisions to cooperate in the TREDA, abide by international law, and work to ensure TREDA is attractive for international investment, trade, and business. The TREDA area defined in the agreements is:

> the terrain located within the conceptual boundary lines from Chongjin in the DPRK, through Yanji in the PRC, to Nakhodka in the Russian Federation. TREDA specifically incorporates Najin-Sonbong Free Economic and Trade Zone in the DPRK, the Yanbian Korean Autonomous Prefecture in the PRC, which includes the Special Economic Zones of Yanji and Hunchon, and Vladivostok and the Free Economic Zone of Nakhodka, including Vostochny, and Primorsky Krai towns and ports south of those cities, in the Russian Federation ("Agreements on the Establishment").

The current population of the TREDA area provides a market of about 3.5 million, with 2.1 million in the Yanbian Prefecture of China, 1.2 million in the southern part of the Primorsky Krai of Russia, 137,000 in eastern Mongolia, and 140,000 in the northern part of the North Hamgyong Province of North Korea. There are 35 million potential consumers living within 500 km of Hunchon, China, the center of the fastest growing area of the Tumen River basin (UNDP *c*: 3).

The UNDP has outlined the TRADP development plans in a series of "Collected Papers." These are a series of nine reports written by Canadian and Australian consultants, detailing the strategy to attract foreign investment, and coordinate infrastructure and resource development (UNDP *d*). These working documents are based on input and amendments from the TREDA participant government representatives, and provide detailed recommendations for infrastructure development, trade and industry investment areas, environmental protection, tourism statistics, and telecommunications services. The reports are published separately to facilitate distribution to individuals or groups with special interests.

On 6 December 1995, in New York, representatives from each of the five TRADP countries signed agreements to cooperate and coordinate on environmentally sound development, and to establish an intergovernmental consultative commission and a coordination committee. These organizations are now responsible for the program, with continuing UNDP assistance. The consultative commission agreement is particularly interesting. Although still technically at war, both North and South Korea signed it. The agreement apparently gives the UN and interested non-government organizations unprecedented access to North Korean economic plans and statistics ("Agreements on the Establishment").

To create an enabling environment, governments in the region have made official commitments to institutions such as TREDA, have begun the formal process to align trade policies to World Trade Organization rules, and are working on standardizing regulations for transportation, licensing, and pollution to help create a business climate that enables private and public investors to develop industry, businesses and trade.

The TREDA governments' commitment to international institutions such as the World Bank, the International Monetary Fund (IMF), and Asian Development Bank (ADB) is intended to build investor confidence. However, with respect to North Korea no significant progress has been made. For now, international investors can only look to the willingness of these governments to spend their own scarce resources on the project and to their active participation in joint ventures and adoption of laws and regulations based on the early Chinese free trade zones (Tejno).

When the five participant nations of TREDA met in Ulaanbaatar in 1991 to discuss economic cooperation and development, there were no procedures or venues available to start the process of opening up trade. The UNDP and UNIDO, because of their previous economic development and aid work in each country, were selected by the governments as facilitators to assist and encourage on-going development (UNDP *c*: 13).

IMPLICATIONS

The good chance that over the next 15 years TREDA will be successful, has far-reaching economic and political implications for North Korea, the other TREDA nations, Japan, and the United States.

North Korea's economy may be able to stabilize and gradually improve by attracting foreign investment and through participation in the global economy. North Korea can earn the foreign exchange necessary to avoid starvation and enable the Communist Party to maintain control. The success of Najin-Sonbong can lead the North Koreans to expand or establish additional FETZ's in other parts of the country. The North Korean experience may be similar to that of the Chinese and Vietnamese governments as Communist Party elite gain wealth and independent ideas from foreigners.

Accepting capitalistic practices raises questions in North Korea about the *raison d'etre* of the communist political system. The Korean Workers Party's job is to protect the workers from exploitation by the "imperialists" and their "running dogs" (Lee *a*: 15). These concerns must of necessity be downplayed, as they were in China and Vietnam, when the immediate need to feed the people takes precedence. The official propaganda reflects plenty of room for maneuver for the North Koreans to save face by claiming they are self-reliantly caring for all Koreans.

A gradual reunification process could continue as the economic cooperation between North and South Korea increases, lessening the impact of the political differences. On the other hand, Chinese communists have felt no need to yield political power despite their adoption of capitalistic cooperation with Hong Kong and Taiwan. North Korea could remain a separate political entity for a very long time and maintain close economic relationships to South Korea, the other TREDA nations, Japan, and the United States that will reduce the possibility of war.

TREDA does not have to succeed to the optimistic levels envisioned by the UN and the TREDA participants to have a positive impact. The TREDA participants and Japan will gain comparative advantages over other developing areas if they cooperate to maximize the resources of each TREDA country. Utilizing Najin-Sonbong as a transportation hub is the major contribution to simplifying the logistics of trade between the countries of Northeast Asia.

The implications for a successful TREDA and North Korean FETZ for the United States can be good both economically and politically. As TREDA becomes a hub of trade in Northeast Asia, American corporations will have easier and cheaper access to the area. Economic cooperation among the TREDA countries and Japan will lessen the possibility of conflict. If the United States does not support TREDA's efforts, a reduced economic and security role in Northeast Asia will result.

CONCLUSION

North Korea's participation in the TREDA is a watershed change in economic policy, not a short-term defense measure due to shortages of food and fuel. Its goals of obtaining sufficient food and fuel and learning the lessons of controlled market economics will be reached with or without U.S. assistance. In North Korea, security policy and foreign trade policy are interlinked. In North Korean's eyes, the country has made security changes and concessions to the international community in order to revive its economy. North Korea has also made significant economic and policy changes and shifted its propaganda line. Kim Chong Il must now deal with his own hard-liners, who complain about appeasing enemies and lost sovereignty because of compliance with the Nuclear Nonproliferation Treaty, UN Food Aid, and TREDA cooperation with the UN and South Korea.

The North Korean military is spearheading the reforms, based on Chinese, Vietnamese and Laotian models, to help them maintain political control while meeting economic needs (Zumwalt: B4). This may lead to additional FETZs being established and the eventual spread of market reforms beyond the barracks and the FETZ to the rest of the economy as benefits become more visible. Selected communications, computer, and chemical technologies will be imported, allowing North Korean military modernization on the pattern of Deng Xiaoping's "four modernizations." Profit will trickle down to the party and population. Improved living standards for all will protect Kim Chong Il and be impossible to retreat from, thus institutionalizing limited capitalism.

The North Korean leaders face a dilemma. Whether they succeed or fail at keeping the loyalty of the army and attracting foreign investment, they will eventually lose their absolute control over the people. To succeed economically, there must be increased access to information. If they do not allow access to information, their economy cannot grow. If they allow the freedoms necessary for a healthy economy, their people will not trust them any longer. The North Korean regime loses control either if they succeed too well in their TREDA cooperation or because they do not cooperate with TREDA enough.

The TREDA market is potentially as large as the European Union. TREDA and North Korea's FETZ may succeed with or without U.S.

participation. By supporting TREDA and North Korea's participation, U.S. foreign policy goals can be met. The Clinton administration's national security policy of "engagement and enlargement," the nuclear nonproliferation agreement negotiations, the proposal for "four-way talks" between North and South Korea, China and the United States (R. Smith *a*: A25), the agreement on a U.S./DPRK joint search for servicemen missing in action, and the proposal to end sanctions against North Korea in exchange for a halt to Pyongyang's sales of ballistic missiles are starting points for continued negotiations with the North Koreans (Gertz *c*: A20). Allowing U.S. business to gradually increase participation in North Korea's Najin-Sonbong FETZ would give the United States some access and influence in North Korea.

A foundation for greater U.S. influence in Northeast Asia, based on mutual economic and political interests, could be established if eventual Korean reunification lessens our military role. Encouraging the North Korean FETZ may have the additional benefit of weaning the North Koreans from dependence on weapons sales to gain hard currency. The North Koreans may also find that the political costs of maintaining a nuclear power program are prohibitive if they can meet their energy and security needs through trade.

Chapter 7
CONGRESSIONAL OVERSIGHT

The lack of a domestic consensus on U.S. participation in world government is nothing new. In negotiating the Treaty of Versailles, President Wilson was unable to build the domestic political consensus necessary to obtain ratification. A joke that circulated in Geneva went that the two great American inventions during World War I were the League of Nations and the cocktail, and that the U.S. Congress proceeded to outlaw both. The balance of powers in the U.S. Constitution means there is inherent tension between the executive and legislative branches whenever the issue of allocation of decisionmaking power arises. It mattered little that the shift to an emphasis on multilateral diplomacy came gradually in the Reagan and Bush Administrations, as the U.S. moved toward cooperation with the Russians in the UN. The Clinton Administration faced the traditional balance of powers debate as it contributed to the UN's enhanced role in peacekeeping and peacemaking. Placing U.S. soldiers under UN operational command and sharing intelligence with the UN were the key issues in this round of the ongoing debate.

William O'Hara traces the evolution of President Clinton's Presidential Decision Directive-25 (PDD-25) on reforming multilateral peace operations. He sets the context with a review of constitutional provisions on the conduct of foreign affairs and the controversy concerning joining the League of Nations and the UN. The War Powers act is analyzed because UN peace operations may place U.S. troops in a combat situation. For example, a domestic political crisis erupted as U.S. Rangers under UN command were killed in the streets of Mogadishu. While the Congress has given explicit approval and tacit consent to various U.S. deployments in UN peace operations, there is a lack of consensus in Congress on a general policy and any Administration would have a very thin base of domestic political support for putting Americans at risk in UN operations.

Joseph Hays focuses on one key provision of PDD-25 that authorized enhanced information support to the UN. Although the idea was first proposed by President Bush in the UN General Assembly, there was resistance even then in Congress and the U.S. Intelligence Community. Many in Congress felt that intelligence sharing with the UN, a multilateral institution, risked exposing sources and methods. As part of the debate on the balance of powers, the issue of intelligence sharing became an election-year political football when sensitive U.S. documents were found abandoned by the UN unit as it evacuated its headquarters in Somalia. After a highly partisan debate, no action was taken. It appears that the Congress sees some positives in intelligence sharing with the UN if it is handled in a professional manner. As with the issue of U.S. troops under UN command, the base of support for the policy is thin.

PDD-25: A CASE STUDY OF LEGISLATIVE AND EXECUTIVE BRANCH CONFLICT

William D. O'Hara III
U.S. Air Force Air Intelligence Agency
August 1995

THE MAKINGS OF AN EXECUTIVE — LEGISLATIVE BRANCH CONFLICT

The development of President Clinton's Presidential Decision Directive-25 (PDD-25) on reforming multilateral peace operations serves as a case study of the conflict between the executive and legislative branches over the use of U.S. forces in the new world order.[1] The roots of this conflict date back to the Constitution and the history of U.S. participation in international organizations. Using the evolution of PDD-25 as its focus, this paper examines this debate and its implications for the future.

The current UN definition of peacemaking is "action to bring hostile parties to agreement, essentially through such peaceful means as those foreseen in Chapter VI of the Charter of the United Nations" (UNSC S/24111, para 20). Peacekeeping is defined as "the deployment of a United Nations presence in the field, hitherto with the consent of all the parties concerned, normally involving United Nations military and/or police personnel and frequently civilians as well. Peacekeeping is a technique that expands the possibilities for both the prevention of conflict and the making of peace" (UNSC Doc S/24111, para 20). PDD-25 does not differentiate between

1 Presidential Decision Directive 25, Clinton Administration's Policy on Reforming Multilateral Peace Operations, 3 May 1994. (Hereinafter PDD-25) The directive is classified. The reference is to the unclassified version available in International Legal Materials published by the American Society of International Law, usually cited as 33 I.L.M. 70 (1994).

peacekeeping and peacemaking. It uses the term "peace operations" to describe the entire spectrum of activities, from traditional peacekeeping to peace enforcement, in which the UN may authorize the use of force (PDD 25: 1).

The use of U.S. troops in UN operations is a very sensitive topic. The argument centers on this question: Why should young Americans die for issues that are not vital to the nation's survival? If the issue were critical, the U.S. would act unilaterally. This debate makes it extremely hard to build a domestic political consensus for participation in UN operations.

The UN is also in the unenviable position of receiving the world's most intractable problems. When issues are so difficult that they cannot be solved bilaterally or regionally, the last hope is to turn to the UN. This then creates a gap between expectations and the UN's ability to solve the problem.

This paper begins with a historical review which centers on the Constitution, the War Powers Resolution, the UN Charter, and the UN Participation Act. The first two deal with the separation of powers among the branches of government and the war powers granted to the executive and the legislature. The debate centers on the power to declare and conduct wars. These "war powers" are granted by the Constitution to both the President and Congress. Article 1, section 8, of the Constitution gives Congress the ability to declare war, while Article 2, section 1, gives the President, as Commander in Chief, the ultimate power to conduct war. Controversy between the executive and legislative branches has focused on the extent to which the President, as commander, can commit U.S. forces abroad in the absence of a congressional declaration of war. In addition to the powers laid out in the Constitution, Congress also passed, over President Nixon's veto, the War Powers Resolution. Although dismissed by successive presidents as unconstitutional and regarded by many in Congress as unworkable, the War Powers Resolution is the law of the land and calls for congressional authorization of troop deployments of over 60 days to potentially hostile areas.

The UN Charter and UN Participation Act, both ratified by Congress in 1945, set forth procedures for the involvement of U.S. troops in UN military operations. However, the Cold War effectively blunted these initiatives. There were two notable exceptions: The Korean conflict and the Gulf War showed how the laws and procedures were both used and ignored.

The paper next examines presidential actions regarding U.S. participation in UN military operations. The end of the Cold War brought new optimism that the UN could take a more active role in peacekeeping and peacemaking. Presidents of both parties believed the UN should do more to solve the world's conflicts and that the United States should actively support the UN in doing so. President Bush called for member states to have military units, trained for peacekeeping duties, available to the UN on short notice. President Clinton came into office with an even more aggressive agenda for U.S. participation in UN operations.

Within months of assuming power, President Clinton directed the National Security Council to formulate a more active policy on U.S. support to UN peacekeeping operations. A draft policy statement supported the rapid expansion of UN peace enforcement operations around the world and accepted the idea of UN command over U.S. troops. The resultant congressional uproar over this draft and the public outcry over the killing of 18 U.S. soldiers in Somalia caused the administration to scale back its proposed policy. When finally signed on 3 May 1994, Presidential Decision Directive 25 was called the "first comprehensive U.S. policy on multilateral peace operations suited to the post-Cold-War era" (Reuters *d*). Its concepts have been incorporated into such key documents as the National Security Strategy, the National Military Stratcgy, and Defense Planning Guidance.

The administration did not initially consult Congress when developing PDD-25. After a draft of the policy was leaked to the press, there was an immediate congressional backlash. This caused revisions to the original directive. Simultaneously, the legislative branch became wary of the UN and the possible erosion of its war powers. In addition to developing a new peacekeeping policy, the executive branch was also committing troops to UN operations. Congressional response to these actions has generally fallen into one of three categories: first is agreement, as in resolutions affirming President Bush's deployment of troops to Somalia; the second category is the "sense of Congress," which expressed negative attitudes toward possible U.S. troop involvement in UN operations in Haiti or Bosnia, but were not binding; the third, and most drastic, is to cut off funds for further U.S. military operations.

These conflicts between the executive and legislative branches have become even more highly charged due to the change of leadership in the

Congress. The switch from a Democratic to Republican majority in both the House and Senate has increased Congress' hostility toward the UN and U.S. participation in UN military operations. Proposed legislation working its way through the Congress would prohibit placing U.S. troops under a foreign UN commander, and cut the level of U.S. financial support for UN peacekeeping operations. Even if not enacted, these bills show a Congress increasingly skeptical of the UN.

The outcome of this debate has been a shifting of power from the executive branch to the legislative branch. This will impact on the way the United States conducts foreign relations and is perceived by other nations of the world.

UN PEACEKEEPING IN A CONSTITUTIONAL CONTEXT

To appreciate how the development and implementation of PDD-25 fits into the executive and legislative conflicts over the use of U.S. troops, one must first understand the documents and legislation which provide the backdrop for the current environment. These are the United States Constitution, the UN Charter, the UN Participation Act, and the War Powers Resolution.

U.S. Constitution

The founding fathers wanted to establish a system of checks and balances to ensure no one branch of government became dominant. This was especially true regarding the raising, maintaining, and control of the armed forces. The Constitution divides these responsibilities between the President and the Congress. It gives Congress the power to "declare War . . . raise and support Armies . . . provide and maintain a Navy . . . make Rules for the Government and regulation of the land and naval Forces . . . provide for calling forth the Militia to execute the Laws of the Union, suppress Insurrections and repel Invasions . . . and to make all Laws" (Art I, Sec 8) necessary to carry out these actions.

However, the Constitution also states "The President shall be Commander in Chief of the Army and Navy of the United States, and of the Militia of the several States, when called into the actual Service of the United States" (Art II, Sec 2). This language has at times put the President and Congress at loggerheads with respect to sending troops into combat. Congress has only declared war five times,[2] but presidents have committed U.S. troops to combat situations more than 200 times without a formal declaration (Glennon: 89). Congress attempted to clarify this gray area between declaring war and waging war when it enacted the War Powers Resolution.

UN Charter

The end of the Cold War effectively ended the need for unilateral deployments of U.S. troops to fight the communist threat. However, it also brought with it the hope that the United Nations could do more to solve the world's conflicts. This in turn has led to executive vs. legislative conflicts over the use of U.S. troops in UN operations.

Instead of fighting the communist evil empire, U.S. forces under the auspices of the UN have fought warlords in Somalia and installed a president in Haiti. These operations have led to the same war powers debate between the executive and legislative branches. The debate still centers on a President sending U.S. forces into hostile situations without formal congressional approval.

To understand how this situation developed, it is necessary to review the congressional debate concerning ratification of the Covenant of the League of Nations. A key issue in the 1920 debate over the Covenant centered on Article 10. Some thought this clause would bind the U.S. into a war against the nation's will. Article 10 provided:

> The Members of the League undertake to respect and preserve as against external aggression the territorial integrity and existing political independence of all Members of the League. In case of any such aggression or in case of any threat or danger of such aggression the Council shall advise upon the means by which this obligation shall be fulfilled.

Members of Congress, led by Senator Henry Cabot Lodge, opposed the Covenant, fearing that a vote in the League would require the U.S. to enter into a conflict. President Wilson argued that a unanimous vote in the League would be required to invoke Article 10. Furthermore, the U.S. representative to the League of Nations would not vote on such a resolution

---

2 The War of 1812, the Mexican War, the Spanish-American War, and both World Wars.

without instructions from Washington. However, such a vote would be an executive prerogative and therefore this assurance failed to persuade the Congress. The United States never joined the League of Nations.

The framers of the UN Charter at the San Francisco Conference in 1945 avoided any language which could be perceived as an automatic requirement to use force. Article 43 of the Charter provides that all members undertake to make available to the Security Council, in accordance with a special agreement, armed forces and assistance for the purpose of maintaining internal peace and security. These agreements "shall be subject to ratification by the signatory states in accordance with their respective constitutional processes" (Art 43). Therefore, the UN Charter is constructed so that Article 42, the only provision authorizing the use of force, is immediately followed by the provision for raising of an armed force which specifically acknowledges each country's constitutional process in the creation of such an armed force (Art 43).

However, the Security Council has never made an Article 43 agreement with any member state. In 1946, the Security Council directed the Military Staff Committee to draw up recommendations on basic principles which would govern Article 43 agreements. On 30 April 1947, the committee submitted its report. It contained 25 articles on which the permanent members of the Security Council had reached agreement and 16 articles on which they had not. The areas where no agreement could be reached included a timetable for withdrawing UN forces after use, the location of troops when not used by the UN, whether or not assistance and facilities included the provision of bases, and how specific the initial agreement should be about the nature of contributions. Intransigence on the part of the Soviet Union effectively killed the idea of consummating any Article 43 agreements. The Security Council dropped the idea of such agreements, and the Military Staff Committee became a moribund institution (Boulden).

United Nations Participation Act

The legislation which implemented the UN Charter for the United States was the United Nations Participation Act (Pub. L. 79-264). Enacted in 1945, this legislation specified the procedures by which the U.S. was to carry out its obligations under the Charter. It authorized the President to negotiate agreements with the Security Council to provide U.S. military forces on call to the Security Council for actions under Article 43 of the

UN Charter (Pub. L. 79-264, sec 6). The Act states that these agreements are subject to approval of the Congress by Act or joint resolution. However, once an Article 43 agreement has been made, further congressional authorization is not necessary before committing the troops to a UN operation.

Congress believed the UN needed a rapid response capability to be a creditable deterrent in preventing or containing breaches of the peace. They did not, however, wish to abdicate their war powers role. It was envisioned that these agreements would be for a small number of troops which could serve in a police action, but not large enough to participate in a war (Stromseth: 615-618).

In 1949 the Act was amended to allow the President to detail U.S. forces to the UN, but only in certain capacities (Pub. L. 81-341). The amended Act states that the President may assign up to 1,000 U.S. troops to the UN to serve in noncombat positions such as observers and guards (Pub. L. 81-341, sec. 7). These troops can support UN operations for the settlement of disputes; however, they can not be involved in any enforcement actions

War Powers Resolution

In response to the Vietnam conflict and to assert its control over the war-making process, on 7 November 1973 Congress passed the War Powers Resolution over President Nixon's veto (Pub. L. 93-148). It states that the President may send troops into hostilities, or imminent hostilities, only when Congress has declared war, given specific authorization, or in the event of attack upon the U.S. or its forces. The President must consult Congress beforehand or report to Congress within 48 hours of his decision. This notification starts a 60-day timetable after which the troops must be withdrawn or Congress must either provide authorization for the troops or extend the 60-day limit.

Presidents of both parties have acted in ways which effectively nullify the resolution. In situations all over the world, presidents from Ford to Clinton have finessed the War Powers Resolution. When notifying Congress of the use of troops, they have used the terms "consistent with" or "taking note of" rather than "in compliance with" the resolution (Ford). This has been to avoid language which could have been understood to accept the constitutionality of the resolution (Eastland: 23). Even members of Congress recognize the resolution's shortcomings. Referring to the resolution's 60-day timetable for withdrawing troops from hostile action, Senator Sam Nunn said, "It's never going to work. It's never worked in the past; it's never going to work. That automatic trigger makes any president reluctant to acknowledge that hostilities are imminent" (Doherty *c*: 323).

The nebulous nature of the resolution can be seen in the decisions, or more precisely the non-decisions, handed down by the judicial branch in cases dealing with war powers, such as Lowry v. Reagan (676 F. Supp. 333 (D.D.C.) 1987). The President was challenged by some members of Congress in response to the reflagging of Kuwaiti tankers in 1987. A federal district court dismissed the case, stating that a decision by the judicial branch would have risked the problem of numerous positions taken by various branches of government (Glennon: 93). Likewise, on three other occasions during the Reagan administration (El Salvador, Nicaragua, and Grenada) when members of Congress filed suit to have military actions ruled unconstitutional and illegal, the federal courts said Congress itself must challenge the President directly, not use the courts to do so (Biskupic: 36)

Enforcement under Chapter VII

Both the Korean and Persian Gulf conflicts provide important examples of U.S. military action performed under the auspices or with the approval of the UN. Korea was the first major military emergency of the Cold War. As such, both President Truman and Congress felt strong, decisive measures had to be taken against communist aggression and to uphold the fledgling UN.

At the outset of the invasion of South Korea by North Korea, the Security Council, on 25 June 1950, declared that there was a breach of the peace. The Council called for hostilities to cease and for the North Korean troops to withdraw. Two days later it adopted a second resolution which *recommended* "that the Members of the United Nations furnish such assistance to the Republic of Korea as may be necessary to repel the armed attack and to restore international peace and security in the area" (UNSC Res 83, 1950). Without citing Chapter VII explicitly, these resolutions were adopted using the language of Chapter VII, Article 39, of the UN Charter. This article permits the Security Council to determine the existence of any threat to the peace, breach of the peace, or act of aggression. It allows the

Council to make recommendations or decide what measures should be taken to maintain or restore the peace.

Truman had already ordered U.S. air and sea forces to support South Korea on 26 June (Fisher: 33). However, he used the UN Security Council resolutions as justification for the action. Truman stated:

> The Security Council called upon all members of the United Nations to render every assistance to the United Nations in the execution of this resolution. In these circumstances I have ordered United States air and sea forces to give the [South] Korean Government troops cover and support. (Truman: 492).

Because of the emergency situation, neither the UN nor Congress objected. Although Truman met with congressional leaders on June 27 and informed them of what was happening, he never asked for their authorization. Congress played no role in this action. The only immediate response it took was to extend the draft. In fact, Senate Majority Leader Scott Lucas advised Truman not to seek a congressional resolution supporting his deployment of troops to Korea. Lucas thought if the President were to go to Congress it might have sounded as if he were asking for a declaration of war (Stromseth: 632). President Truman presented a message to a joint session of Congress on 19 July, but never asked for legislative action.

There was very little objection in Congress to Truman's actions. Most members articulated support for this decision, believing Korea was to be a police action rather than a war. That Congress agreed with the President's actions, recognized it was an emergency situation, and sought to stand firm with the President as U.S. troops were sent into battle, all help explain why they took no actions.

A more recent example of U.S. troops participating in a UN-authorized military action is the Gulf War. Unlike the Korean conflict, Congress exercised, at least nominally, some of its war powers. Shortly after the 2 August 1990 Iraqi invasion of Kuwait, the Security Council passed resolutions condemning the attack, demanded withdrawal of Iraqi forces from Kuwait, and imposed economic sanctions on Iraq (UNSC Res 661, 662, 1990). President Bush, on 8 August, announced he was initiating Operation DESERT SHIELD. U.S. troops were sent to Saudi Arabia and the Persian Gulf to stop any further advance of Iraqi troops. The following day, the President reported this deployment to Congress, "consistent with" the War

Powers Resolution, and stated that he did not believe hostilities were imminent (Bush *a*; CR 1 Oct 90, H8441; 2 Oct 90, S14333). Both houses of Congress passed resolutions which commended President Bush's leadership and supported the "defensive" deployment of troops to the Gulf region, but did not authorize the President to start a war.

Like President Truman during the Korean conflict, President Bush used the UN to justify, or at least rationalize, the troop deployment. He declared:

> The United Nations has provided enormous leadership to the whole world community in pursuing this objective and voting the sanctions necessary to carrying it out. And let's be clear, as the deployment of the force of the many nations shows and as the votes in the United Nations show, this is not a matter between Iraq and the United States of America. It is between Iraq and the entire world community (Bush *h*: 1281)

Congress was careful during the period before the Gulf War not to legislate away its war powers. Yet neither did it aggressively pursue them. The attitude of Congress was to support the initial deployment of troops, yet be clear about the bounds of its support. Senator Daniel Patrick Moynihan stated, "The resolution does not give the President a blank check" (CR 28 Sep 90, S14190). Congress was wary of the President taking the resolution and using it as an authorization to go to war.

On 8 November 1990, President Bush announced that he was sending an additional 150,000 troops to the Gulf to provide an offensive capability (Bush *i*). Again he used the UN to justify the action. In a speech from the White House, he said:

> We are not alone in these goals and objectives. The United Nations, invigorated with a new sense of purpose, is in full agreement . . . Yesterday's UN Security Council resolution [authorizing the use of force] was historic. Once again, the Security Council has enhanced the legitimate peacekeeping functions of the United Nations (Bush *g*: 1948).

This raised congressional concerns over the possible usurpation of its war powers. Many leading Democrats, including Senate Majority Leader George Mitchell and Senator Sam Nunn, warned the President not to start an offensive without congressional authorization (Wiesskopf: A1). However, they did not urge that the Congress be called back from recess.

Others members, however, sought to stop any presidential action through the intervention of the judicial branch. On 20 November, 56 members of Congress filed a lawsuit to restrain the President from commencing hostilities without prior congressional consent. As if resigned to the fact that the War Powers Resolution was unworkable, the suit never raised it as an issue (Dellums v. Bush, 1752 F. Supp. 1141 (D.D.C. 1990)). Before the case was decided, the Security Council passed Resolution 678 on 29 November. It authorized the use of "all necessary means" to drive Iraq from Kuwait after 15 January 1991. On 13 December, the court ruled that the case was not ready for decision because only a small minority of the Congress was seeking redress. This followed the historical precedent of the court not wishing to become involved in matters of war powers. The fact that only a handful of congressmen participated in this action further shows Congressional reluctance to exercise its war powers to the fullest. However, it did not totally abdicate them either.

It was the increasing congressional concern over the use of force in the Gulf that finally persuaded President Bush, on 8 January 1991, to request from the House and Senate a resolution supporting the use of all necessary means to implement Security Council Resolution 678 (Stromseth: 648). After intense debate, on 12 January, Congress passed Joint Resolution 77, which authorized the President to use force in accordance with Security Council Resolution 678 after notifying the Speaker of the House and President Pro Tempore of the Senate that all other means had failed (HJ Res. 77, CR 12 Jan 91). President Bush, at his signing of the joint resolution, reiterated his belief that this did not constitute a change in the executive branch's view of its authority to use the Armed Forces or the constitutionality of the War Powers Resolution (Stromseth: 654-655).

Although Congress did not fully exercise its war powers, neither was it derelict in its duties. Congress could have defined the Gulf War as a police action, as it did during the Korean crisis, and left all action to the President. Congress, however, insisted that its authorization was needed before any offensive actions could be taken. This foreshadowed Congress' future increased involvement in the debate over U.S. troops in UN operations.

THE EVOLUTION OF U.S. PEACEKEEPING SINCE 1992

> The need for enhanced peacekeeping capabilities has never been greater....as much as the United Nations has done, it can do much more (Bush c: 1697).

These words, spoken by President George Bush in a September 1992 address to the United Nations General Assembly, heralded the beginning of increased U.S. emphasis on UN peacekeeping. The end of the Cold War, marked by the disintegration of the Soviet Union, optimized the use of the UN to carry out peacekeeping operations. No longer was the Security Council hobbled by superpower conflicts. As envisioned by President Bush and others, the "New World Order" would allow the UN to take a more active role in peacekeeping operations. The drafting and implementation by the Clinton administration of Presidential Decision Directive 25, reforming multilateral peace operations, constituted the first major policy review of U.S. participation in UN operations since the end of the Cold War.

From President Bush's deployment of troops to Somalia in December 1992 to the July 1995 fall of so-called "safe areas" in Bosnia, the UN has had numerous fiascoes. In Somalia, U.S. troops became entangled in the UN's "nation building" effort and that country's clan infighting. After 18 Army soldiers were killed in a 3 October 1993 battle with followers of a Somali warlord, domestic support for U.S. participation in the UN operation evaporated. In Haiti, the military rulers continually disregarded the UN and its efforts to install the democratically elected President. On 11 October 1993, armed Haitians prevented civil engineers on the USS *Harlan County* from coming ashore to aid in UN-sponsored reconstruction projects. In the 1994 civil war in Rwanda, squabbling among UN Security Council members delayed both peacekeeping and humanitarian missions from rapidly relieving the misery. This delay resulted in millions of refugees. And in the former Yugoslavia, the UN Protection Force was unable to ensure its own safety, let alone that of the civilians caught in the crossfire of that civil war.

During this same time, Congressional attitude toward the UN has gone from support to distrust and contempt. Initially, Congress supported the humanitarian effort in Somalia, but when the mission changed to nation building and American troops were being killed, support vanished. Congress was also annoyed at being left out of the Clinton administration's development of its new peacekeeping policy. Finally, the November 1994 election which brought the Republicans to power in Congress further fueled the lawmakers' concerns regarding the administration's UN position. Several bills have been introduced to reduce U.S. contributions to the UN, forbid UN command over U.S. troops, and unilaterally lift U.S. support of the UN arms embargo on Bosnia.

President Bush

President Bush welcomed UN Secretary-General Boutros-Ghali's 1992 proposal to strengthen the United Nations (Boutros-Ghali *b*). The President made five proposals for member states to consider:

- Designate specially trained units for peacekeeping.
- Develop the UN's planning, crisis management, and intelligence capabilities.
- Institute multinational training.
- Ensure adequate and equitable financing.
- Designate stockpiles for humanitarian emergencies (Bush *c*: 1698-1699).

President Bush also directed the Secretary of Defense to place a new emphasis on peacekeeping and pledged to work with the UN to best employ airlift, logistics, communications and intelligence capabilities to support peacekeeping operations.

President Clinton

As a candidate for President, Governor Clinton spoke of his desire for a standing UN deployment force. In an April 1992 speech, he called for the creation of an international army whose troops would be ready to fight for peace. This army, as envisioned by Clinton, would be "standing at the borders of countries threatened by aggression, preventing mass violence against civilian populations, providing humanitarian relief and combating terrorism" (Clinton *c*).

In one of his first foreign policy initiatives, President Clinton instructed the National Security Council, in February 1993, to formulate a more active policy on peacekeeping. An inter-agency group headed by Deputy National Security Advisor Samuel R. Berger was formed, and the administration began conducting an intensive inter-agency review of the U.S. role in peacekeeping (Sciolino *b*: A8). By 18 June 1993, senior officials at State, Defense, and the Joint Chiefs of Staff had reached general agreement on what was then called Presidential Review Directive 13 (PRD-13) (Smith and Preston *a*: A1).

The draft PRD proposed major shifts in U.S. policy for contributions to UN operations. It would allow U.S. forces to plan, train for and participate in UN peacekeeping activities when justified by U.S. interests, not just when the U.S. could make a unique contribution. Traditionally, the U.S. contributed only a unique capability, such as an engineering unit, which no other country could provide. The U.S. did not, however, contribute infantry units, since other countries had this capability. Under the new draft rules, the U.S. could contribute infantry units. The draft also indicated the U.S. would be more inclined to allow UN command of U.S. troops. This draft was to codify the administration's policy, which Ambassador Albright called "assertive multilateralism" (M. Albright *a*: 464).

According to press reports, the final draft of PRD-13 was approved, on schedule, in a 14 July interagency meeting of senior officials headed by Samuel Berger (Gellman *b*: A1). The President was expected to sign the policy by August. However, the draft was leaked to the Washington Post in early August.

This version of PRD-13 reflected fundamental shifts in U.S. policy toward the UN. It:

- Supported the "rapid expansion" of UN peace enforcement operations.
- Formalized the President's acceptance of UN command over U.S. troops.
- Rejected the Secretary General's call for a standing UN rapid deployment force.
- Listed a set of capabilities to be contributed on a case-by-case basis.
- Endorsed 100 new staff members for the peacekeeping office at UN headquarters.
- Proposed Germany and Japan pay for these improvements (Gellman *b*: A1).

The administration felt these policy changes were very sensitive. The draft PRD was classified. The press, however, using leaked material and quoting anonymous sources, presented an accurate picture of how the policy was developing.

A State Department official familiar with PRD-13 said it went beyond the Bush administration's acceptance of a multilateral approach to regional conflicts and reflected the Clinton administration's belief that military responsibilities must be shared in the post-Cold-War world. This official also said, "The difference with this administration is that it envisions the United States, in principle, taking part in any peacekeeping operation in any capacity" (Holmes: A1).

The first clear application of the draft policy occurred during the week of August 11, when Ambassador Albright wrote the Secretary General asking for a cost estimate of a proposed peacekeeping operation in the former Soviet republic of Georgia. She also asked for the project length, basis of the cost, precise responsibilities of the peacekeepers, and what would determine when they had fulfilled these responsibilities (Holmes: A1).

Senator John McCain visiting members of the Implementation Force in Bosnia-Herzegovina, 1996.

photo used with permission

As PRD-13 was being leaked to the press, the first sounds of concern emanated from Capitol Hill. Many members of Congress were reported to be furious that PRD-13 had been developed without consulting them (Rubin: A23). The press reported that this congressional backlash caused two redrafts of PRD-13 even before cabinet-level administration officials were getting their first look at the document in September (Gellman *a*: A1). The main changes concerned committing U.S. troops to UN operations. Successive drafts moved away from routinely committing U.S. forces to UN control.

The information leaked also concerned the UN Secretary General and other UN member states. Changes had to be made to accommodate them. In the August draft, U.S. commanders were not to obey orders which were "...illegal under U.S. or international law, or are militarily imprudent or unsound." The Secretary General said that if other nations were also to follow such rules, it would destroy a coherent UN command. The draft deleted the reference to "imprudent or unsound." If a U.S. commander received illegal orders, or orders which were outside the UN mandate, the new policy directed him to appeal up the UN chain of command and then to his U.S. commanders (Gellman a: A1).

Secretary of State Warren Christopher was still bothered by the imprecise language used in PRD-13. Press reports indicated a meeting was held at the White House at his request on 17 September 1993. Chaired by National Security Advisor Anthony Lake, the meeting was called to set specific criteria for U.S. involvement in various types of UN operations. The outline hammered out at the meeting required justifying the operation in terms of United States national interests, and limited situations in which American troops would serve under UN command (Sciolino b: A8). The U.S. would cede control only if it was a small mission with a remote likelihood of casualties. It also laid out a set of criteria for involvement in UN operations which included: the degree of national interest, cost, a guaranteed exit strategy, and the likelihood that the action would produce lasting benefits (Robbins: 24). An unnamed senior administration official said, "it was not enough to say that the United States might be involved in future United Nations operations. We have to define what type of operation, and whether it would be something the United States has an interest in, or will only succeed if the United States leads" (Sciolino *b*: A8).

The National Security Council also redrafted another section of PRD-13 to assuage State and Defense officials regarding their authority and financial responsibilities over peacekeeping operations. The compromise gave the State Department responsibility to control and pay for peacekeeping operations performed under Chapter VI of the UN Charter, while the Department of Defense would run peace-enforcement operations under Chapter VII, which authorized the use of force.

On 23 September 1993, Madeleine Albright, in a speech at the National War College, gave a glimpse of the modified PRD-13. She said it was necessary to consider a set of factors in deciding on U.S. involvement in UN operations. These factors could be addressed by questions:

- Is there a real threat to international peace and security?
- Does the proposed peacekeeping mission have clear objectives, and can its scope be clearly defined?
- Is a cease-fire in place, and have the conflicting parties agreed to a UN presence?
- Are thc financial and human resources available to accomplish the mission?
- Can an end point to UN participation be identified? (M. Albright *d*).

President Clinton's address to the UN General Assembly on 27 September 1993 further reflects a shift from "assertive multilateralism" to a cautious approach when dealing with the UN. He stated, "The United Nations simply cannot become engaged in every one of the world's conflicts. If the American people are to say yes to UN peacekeeping, the United Nations must know when to say no" (Clinton *b*: 651).

As the executive branch backed away from its previous views of the UN, support in Congress for peacekeeping operations evaporated due to the 3 October 1993 Somalia debacle in which 18 U.S. Army Rangers were killed. Sensing this mood in Congress, Secretary of Defense Les Aspin, on 26 October, urged National Security Advisor Anthony Lake to revise PRD-13 yet again. Secretary Aspin wanted senior policymakers to "go back to the drawing board with it, [and] send it to the deputies' committee" for redrafting by lesser officials (Williams and Devroy: A6).

The *Washington Post* reported that the administration was trying to develop two sets of criteria to determine the level of U.S. involvement in UN operations. The first set would determine when the U.S. could support a UN peacekeeping operation politically and financially. The second would establish criteria for involvement of U.S. troops in UN operations. In testimony before the Senate Foreign Relations Committee, UN Ambassador Madeleine Albright said "as a practical matter . . . when large-scale or high-risk operations are contemplated and American involvement is necessary, we will be unlikely to accept UN leadership" (Williams and Devroy: A6). She went on to say that use of U.S. combat troops would be infrequent. The most likely support would consist of logistics, intelligence, public affairs, and communications.

On 16 November, the House Government Operations Subcommittee on Legislation and National Security had scheduled the Secretary of State, Secretary of Defense, and U.S. Ambassador to the UN to appear for a hearing on the U.S. role in UN peacekeeping operations. At the last minute, the White House announced that ongoing discussions on peacekeeping policy would prevent those people from attending the hearing (Morrison: 2859). At this point PRD-13 went underground. Between November 1993 and January 1994 press reporting on PRD-13 ceased. It was not until early February 1994 that PRD-13 again was in the news. A government official said the final draft had been approved by outgoing Secretary of Defense Aspin, the Secretary of State, and the national security advisor (Hitchens: 4). Anthony Lake, in an article for the *New York Times,* wrote that the administration had completed a policy review of peacekeeping (Lake: D17).

The new policy contained four main elements: 1) a list of questions to ask before U.S. troops are committed to an operation: What is the threat to the U.S. national interest? Is there a clearly defined mission? A distinct end point? How much will it cost? Are the resources available? What is the likelihood of success?; 2) reduce the U.S. share of paying for peace operations from 30 percent to 25 percent; 3) bring modern management and financial accountability to the UN; 4) a new division of responsibility for peace operations between the State and Defense departments.

The *Washington Post* again reported that the President would soon sign the PRD. It said the PRD would set high thresholds for the use of U.S. troops in UN operations, especially if combat was likely. The larger the operation and the more likely there would be fighting, the less likely U.S. troops would be under the operational command of non-U.S. commanders. The report also noted that the PRD would change the long-standing

U.S. policy of taking part in UN operations only when American capabilities are "unique," to taking part when their skills are especially needed or their presence would attract other participants. Although this relaxed the old policy, it was not as forthcoming as the one previously considered by the administration. Language was removed which had said U.S. forces could engage in peacekeeping operations on a case-by-case basis. It added lists of conditions, including the need for a prior domestic consensus. With respect to the issue of command, this version stated that the U.S. chain of command remains intact, even if Americans are under the operational control of a foreign commander. The *Post* also noted that aides from the Defense and State Department had begun briefing congressional staffs on the new directive and top officials would soon visit key lawmakers (Williams: A24).

The President was expected to sign the directive in a matter of weeks. But again PRD 13 disappeared for another two months. Finally, on 3 May 1994, President Clinton signed the PRD, renamed Presidential Decision Directive 25 (PDD-25). In a press conference to announce its release, Anthony Lake, the National Security Advisor, called PDD-25 the "first comprehensive U.S. policy on multilateral peace operations suited to the post-Cold-War era" (Reuters *d*). He stated that the outcome of the PRD process was that properly conceived and well-executed peacekeeping can be a very important and useful tool of American foreign policy. He acknowledged the contributions by members of Congress which had been incorporated into the final policy. According to Ambassador Albright, the new policy was "not designed to expand UN peacekeeping, but rather to help fix it, to make multilateral peace operations more selective and more effective" (Sciolino *a*: A1). The goal of the policy, she said, was "to ensure that we refrain from asking the UN to undertake missions it is not equipped to do and to help the UN to succeed in missions we would like it to do" (Sciolino *a*: A1).

PDD-25, in its final form, addresses six major issues: first, it ensures the U.S. supports the right operations; second it reduces U.S. costs for peacekeeping operations; third, it clearly defines the policy regarding the command and control of U.S. forces in UN operations; fourth, it reforms and improves the UN's capability to manage peacekeeping operations; fifth, it improves the way the U.S. government manages and funds peacekeeping operations; and sixth, it enhances the cooperation between the Congress and the executive branch on peace operations. These issues are described in more detail below.

- **Ensuring the U.S. supports the right operations:** PDD-25 lays out strict questions to ask about a UN operation, depending on the level of U.S. support. These three support levels are: 1) voting for peace operations in which no U.S. troops will be involved; 2) sending U.S. personnel to participate in an operation; and 3) significant U.S. participation in operations which are likely to involve combat. Some of the questions to be asked include: Does the participation advance U.S. interests, and have both the unique and general risks to American personnel been weighed and considered acceptable? Is U.S. participation necessary for the operation's success? And does a determination exist to commit sufficient forces to achieve clearly defined objectives?

- **Reducing U.S. costs:** The policy states that the administration is committed to reducing the U.S. share of peacekeeping operations down to 25 percent, from 31.7 percent, by 1 January 1996. The administration will also inform the UN of Congress's likely refusal to fund U.S. peacekeeping assessments at a rate higher than 25 percent after Fiscal Year 1995.

- **Defining the policy regarding the command and control of U.S. forces:** PDD-25 emphasizes that the President will never relinquish command of U.S. forces. However, as Commander-in-Chief, the President has the authority to place U.S. forces under the "operational control" of a foreign commander, when doing so serves American security interests. The greater the U.S. participation, the less likely the U.S. will agree to have a non-U.S. UN commander exercise overall operational control.

- **Improving the UN's management:** The policy recommends 11 steps to strengthen UN management of peace operations and directs U.S. support for strengthening the UN's planning, logistics, information, and command and control capabilities. Some of the recommendations include the reorganization of the UN's Department of Peacekeeping Operations to include separate divisions for plans, information and research, operations, and logistics. It also suggests the UN should establish a trained civilian reserve corps, a modest airlift capability, and a rapidly deployable headquarters team, all of which would eliminate delays once a mission has been authorized.

- **Improve U.S. government funding:** Responsibility for management and funding of peacekeeping operations will be divided between the Department of Defense and Department of State. Sanctioned UN operations that involve U.S. combat troops, and operations where combat is likely, whether U.S. forces are involved or not, will be managed by the Defense Department. The State Department will retain lead management and funding responsibility for traditional peacekeeping operations that do not involve U.S. combat units.

- **Enhance cooperation of Congress, the executive, and the American public:** The proposals for attaining this goal include informing Congress of votes in the UNSC on new or expanded peace operations and to supporting legislation along the lines of that introduced by Senators Mitchell, Nunn, Byrd, and Warner to amend the War Powers Resolution. This legislation would introduce a consultative mechanism and eliminate the Resolution's 60-day withdrawal provisions.

From "Assertive Multilateralism" to "Just Say No"

The development of President Clinton's policy on U.S. support to UN peacekeeping operations can be traced through newspaper headlines from August 1993 to May of 1994:

"Wider UN Police Role Supported"	5 August 1993
"U.S. Narrows Terms for its Peacekeepers"	23 September 1993
"U.S. Would Keep Control of Its Forces in UN Operations"	17 February 1994
"New U.S. Peacekeeping Policy De-emphasizes Role of the UN"	6 May 1994

It is interesting to note how the Clinton administration refined its views regarding five key issues concerning UN peacekeeping from candidate Clinton's speeches, through PRD-13, to PDD-25.

Evolution of President Clinton's View of the UN

Issues	Candidate Clinton	PRD-13	PDD-25
Increased UN peacekeeping	+	+	—
UN Rapid Deployment Force	+	—	—
UN control of U.S. Forces	+	+	—
Reducing UN costs	+	+	+
Increasing UN peacekeeping staff and capabilities	0	+	+

+ favorable view;
— negative view;
0 no stated view

source: author.

Although the 1992 presidential election focused on domestic issues, candidate Clinton gave two major speeches on foreign policy. In both he spoke of the UN and his vision of its role in the world. In his speech to the Los Angeles World Affairs Council on 13 August 1992, Clinton declared, "the world of multilateral action holds promise as never before" (Clinton *d*). This message was echoed by Madeleine Albright at her confirmation hearing when she said, "with the end of the Cold War, the United Nations is poised to play a central and positive role for peace" (Albright *b*).

Candidate Clinton also called for a rapid deployment force under the control of the UN. In his speech delivered to the Foreign Policy Association in New York on 1 April 1992, he envisioned "a small force that could be called up from units of national armed forces and earmarked and trained in advance," showing a willingness to put U.S. troops under UN control (Clinton *c*). Candidate Clinton also said he would seek to reduce the U.S.'s financial share of peacekeeping operations and ask other countries to shoulder more of the fiscal burden.

The main difference between candidate Clinton's UN proposals and PRD-13 was the abandonment of the idea of a UN rapid deployment force and, instead, settlement for a list of capabilities the U.S. might contribute on a case-by-case basis. The proposed directive also called for new staff members and increased capabilities for the UN's peacekeeping headquarters. The similarities between the Review Directive and candidate Clinton's position included supporting the rapid expansion of UN peace enforcement operations, routinely placing U.S. forces under UN control, and reducing U.S. payments for peacekeeping operations.

The administration's policy on reforming multilateral peace operations in PDD-25 was very different from both candidate Clinton's views and the earlier version of PRD-13. His policy statement shifted from enthusiasm for the UN, to caution, and finally to skepticism. Instead of a rapid expansion of UN peacekeeping operations, President Clinton declared, "if the American people are to say yes to UN peacekeeping, the United Nations must know when to say no" (Clinton b: 651). Instead of routine UN control of U.S. troops, PDD-25 states, "on a case by case basis, the President will consider placing appropriate U.S. forces under the operational control of a competent UN commander" The only consistent theme throughout the evolution of this policy was the desire to reduce the U.S.'s financial share of UN peacekeeping operations and ask other nations to pick up more of the collective burden.

CONGRESSIONAL RESPONSE

PDD-25 was not developed in a vacuum. Although initially drafted without congressional input, once the draft policy was leaked, the congressional response and the ensuing interaction with the executive branch led to significant changes. Congress also reacted to U.S. participation in the UN operations in Somalia, Haiti, and Bosnia.

Congress has several means at its disposal to rein in the power of the President. The most drastic is to use the "power of the purse" to cut off funding for a specific program and forbid any other funds from supporting it. This in effect kills the program. Congress can also require certain actions to take place before any money is spent. Congress can require reports or other documentation to be produced and submitted to them before the money is available for use. Congress also can express itself through a "sense of the Congress" clause placed in legislation. This method clearly lets the executive branch know Congressional thoughts on an issue. Although these clauses do not carry the weight of law, the President will know to expect a fight if he acts contrary to their stated opinion.

Somalia

In response to the August 1992 images of suffering in Somalia, the Senate, in the middle of the presidential campaign, urged President Bush to seek UN action and "work with the United Nations Security Council to deploy [a sufficient number of] security guards with or without the consent of the Somalia faction" (CR 3 Aug 1992: S11227) to protect food shipments to Somalia.

As the situation in Somalia continued to deteriorate, President Bush, on 4 December 1992, announced that U.S. troops would be sent to Somalia (Bush *b*). He also met with Speaker of the House Thomas Foley and other top lawmakers, who subsequently declared their support for the operation. Foley said, "the President has acted wisely, and in a circumstance where he had very little choice without grave humanitarian consequences" (Towell *b*: 3759). When asked about the War Powers Resolution, which requires the President to seek congressional approval whenever troops are sent into hostilities or where imminent hostilities are expected, Foley said, "the statement is that there is no imminent likelihood of hostilities." Foley added, "we will be monitoring the situation closely. If hearings are indicated, they'll be held. But there is strong bipartisan support among the leadership for the action the President is taking" (Davis: 3760).

This lack of assertive action by Congress set the tone for the early stages of the Somalia mission. Except for a few dissenting voices, Congress took no action until disaster struck the UN mission.

Somalia was one of the first significant foreign policy issues for the newly elected President Clinton and Congress. The Senate, on 4 February 1993, two months after the initial deployment of troops, retroactively approved the operation. The resolution authorized the use of force in support of the UN-sponsored operation to establish a "secure environment" to deliver supplies to Somalia. It sidestepped the War Powers Resolution by describing the deployment as "consistent with" the law's terms (CR 4 Feb 1996: S1363). The measure set no deadline for withdrawing U.S. troops but urged the new Clinton administration to consult with the UN Secretary-General on organizing the UN force that would replace U.S. troops. The Senate's goal was to permit U.S. soldiers to withdraw at the earliest possible date. The resolution was sponsored by a bipartisan group which included Senate Majority Leader George Mitchell, Minority Leader Bob

Dole, chairman of the Senate Foreign Relations Committee Claiborne Pell, and ranking member Jesse Helms.

However, there were concerns in the Senate that Congress was avoiding its constitutional responsibilities. On 25 March, Senators Sam Nunn and Carl Levin urged the President to seek congressional authorization for continued deployment of U.S. troops to Somalia. Senator Nunn said, "it's extremely important that the President consult with and seek support of Congress "before the changeover to a UN-led operation ("Senators": 772). He contended that U.S. participation in this new force would set a precedent for future multilateral peacemaking and humanitarian missions. Senator Levin echoed Nunn's call but argued that Clinton should seek congressional authorization regardless of whether U.S. troops would be placed under non-U.S. command. Both senators faulted Congress for taking no formal responsibility for U.S. participation in Somalia. No action was taken in response to these calls.

On 1 May 1993, a 28,000-strong UN peacekeeping force took over responsibility from the U.S. for securing the flow of relief supplies and pacifying the country. Of the 5,000 U.S. troops left, 3,000 were logistics troops and 2,000 were part of a rapid deployment force (Crigler: 66).

The House did not act on Somalia until 25 May 1993, when it passed its Somalia resolution (CR 25 May 1993: H2763-2765). Like the Senate version passed in February, it authorized U.S. forces in Somalia, explicitly citing the War Powers Resolution, and retroactively authorized the U.S.-led deployment that began in December 1992. The House version differed from the Senate's in that it placed a one-year deadline and explicitly authorized the participation of U.S. personnel in the UN-led force. In debating the inclusion of the reference to the War Powers Resolution, Representative Harry A. Johnston said, "My gosh, if we ever want this establishment, the U.S. Congress, to be relevant to the situation, then we [must] acknowledge the War Powers Act is the law of the land" (Bowens *b*: 1373).

The elapse of three months between the Senate and House passage of this resolution reflected the low level of congressional interest. In addition, after the House approved its resolution, the Senate had the option of accepting the House version of the legislation, or requesting a conference to resolve the differences in the two resolutions. However, no action was ever taken and the resolutions never became law.

Soon the political and security situations in Somalia began to deteriorate. In response to ambushes on UN forces, President Clinton deployed aircraft to support U.S.-led strikes in Somalia. These were followed by a full-blown multinational ground assault on 17 June 1993 ("U.S. Bolsters": 1498). As the situation in Somalia began to heat up, Congress became aware of PRD-13, and the draft directive was leaked to the press. Members were upset that they had not been consulted. Senator Robert Byrd echoed this sentiment when he wrote:

> The plan [PRD-13] would allow American soldiers to serve under foreign commanders on a regular basis. Before adopting any directive embracing their policy, the administration should allow Congress to debate it thoroughly. If the plan is carried out, we would face more than the dubious prospect of sending U.S. troops into battle under foreign command. We might also become militarily involved in operations that the American people don't properly understand or support (Byrd: A23).

He viewed PRD-13 as a way for the President to order U.S. troops to serve in UN combat operations without congressional approval.

The failure to consult on PRD-13, and the deteriorating situation in Somalia, prompted Congress to assert its oversight responsibility. On 9 September, using the 1994 National Defense Authorization Bill as a vehicle for debate, the Senate passed a non-binding "Sense of Congress" resolution stating that "Congress believes the President should by 15 November 1993 seek and receive congressional authorization in order for the deployment of U.S. forces to Somalia to continue" (CR 9 Sep 1993: S1298). This resolution marked the first time the Senate had addressed the deployment since the UN assumed control of the operation. Byrd, who forced the Senate debate, said "the United Nations' mandate to disarm the warlords and rebuild a civil society in Somalia, approved by the UN Security Council, was never addressed, never debated or never approved by this body" (E. Palmer: 2399). Senator Byrd expressed concern that the President was using UN Security Council resolutions as justification for taking actions which the Congress would not authorize. Echoing Senator Byrd's remarks, Representative Benjamin Gilman said, "While we weren't looking, the United Nations and the administration changed the mission. It was shifted from feeding hungry people to nation-building" (Doherty *b*: 2655). The House passed an identical resolution on September 28 (HR 2401, CR

28 Sep 1993: H7106). This shift in the mission, with no attempt by the administration to garner congressional or public support, eroded the President's political base in Congress.

On 3 October 1993, 18 U.S. troops were killed and 80 wounded during a raid on a suspected warlord's headquarters. Public and congressional support for continued deployment evaporated. In an attempt to avoid direct congressional action, sponsored by Senator Byrd, which would have immediately pulled troops out of Somalia, President Clinton promised that "all American troops will be out of Somalia no later than 31 March 1994, except for a few hundred support personnel in non-combat roles" (Clinton *g*). To ensure this would happen, the Senate relied on its most effective weapon to check the executive branch from further actions. It used its "power of the purse" to bring the situation in Somalia to an end. After much debate, the Senate endorsed the President's proposal for a 31 March pullout, but cut off funds for the operation after that date (Pub. L. 103-139, sec 8141). This was a significant constitutional assertion of authority by the Congress. It marked the first time since the Vietnam conflict that either house of Congress had voted to use the power of the purse to terminate funding for an overseas military mission (Towell *a*: 2898).

Although the death of the American soldiers was the catalyst for this action, it also coincided with increasing congressional concerns over U.S. participation in UN operations. Senator Byrd, a staunch defender of Congressional war-making authority, said, "we put an end to this business of the appearance of the UN leading us around by the nose, and we put Congress in the front seat and on the front row as it should be under the Constitution" (Doherty *a*: 2824).

The congressional actions on Somalia established a pattern for future executive and legislative interaction over U.S. participation in UN operations. The initial goal, when President Bush deployed troops, was to feed the people of Somalia. Congress and the public were behind this action. However, after President Clinton was elected, the UN passed resolutions, backed by the administration, which changed the mission to rebuilding the country. This fit in with the administration's declared policy of "assertive multilateralism," and the spirit of the initial drafts of PRD-13. There was little debate on this change in mission, and even less attempt by the administration to build congressional or public support. When the situation in Somalia worsened, the administration's political base evaporated. Congress asserted its role as a check against an over-stepping executive. Using its power of the purse, it reined in the President's policy, which had negligible support outside of the administration.

Haiti

As a result of the Somalia experience, the Congress was much more sensitive to the actions of the President and the UN Security Council regarding Haiti. In September 1991, the Haitian military overthrew that country's democratically elected President, Jean-Bertrand Aristide. In response, the UN imposed an oil and arms embargo. This prompted the military leaders to sign a UN-brokered accord to step down and restore the elected government by 30 October 1993. However, the Haitian military leadership did not comply with the agreement (Towell *a*: 2898).

On 11 October 1993, armed Haitians prevented U.S. and Canadian engineers aboard the USS *Harlan County* from coming ashore to aid in rebuilding projects that were part of a UN-brokered agreement. Tensions further increased when Haiti's military rulers defied the UN agreement to permit the return of deposed President Aristide. President Clinton responded by dispatching Navy ships to enforce the UN embargo on oil and arms. Leaders of the Congressional Black Caucus, who were strong supporters of the drive to restore Aristide, urged President Clinton to take forceful action to resolve the problem. However, most of the rest of the Congress could not see what U.S. interests would be served. Senator Phil Gramm stated, "I don't understand why the President seems determined to use American military power in regions where it is not clearly applicable" (Bowens *a*: 2825).

To show its concern regarding actions toward Haiti, on 21 October 1993 the Senate passed a resolution to express the sense of the Senate that all U.S. military operations in Haiti should be authorized by Congress unless the deployment is vital to the country's national interests or to protect U.S. citizens (CR 21 Oct 1993: S14072). Congress also used the 1994 Defense Appropriations Act to express its position on Haiti. It inserted a "Sense of Congress" clause to set limitations and conditions for expending funds for U.S. military operations in Haiti. Funds could only be obligated or expended for military operations in Haiti if authorized by Congress, needed to protect U.S. citizens, vital to the national security interests of the United States, or if the President sent a written report to Congress justifying and explaining the action. This report was to answer a set of questions: 1) Is the deployment of U.S. troops justified by national security interests? 2) Are the mission and objectives most appropriate for the military? 3) Are the forces deployed necessary and sufficient to accomplish the objectives? 4) Are there clear objectives established? 5) Has an exit strategy has been identified? 6) Have the financial costs have been estimated? (Pub. L. 103-139, sec 8147). These are the same questions that Ambassador Albright stated had already been incorporated into the draft presidential directive on peacekeeping to determine whether a UN operation should receive U.S. support (Albright *d*). Requiring the administration to provide answers to these questions to Congress was thereby implying that the administration was not following its own policy in regard to Haiti.

By 1994, Congress had become concerned that the President might unilaterally undertake an invasion of Haiti to install Aristide. Congress made its opinion clear when, on 29 June 1994, it passed a "Sense of Congress" resolution repeating the provisions laid out in the 1994 Appropriations Act (CR 29 June 1994: S7932-S7937).

Congressional ire was raised even further when the administration went to the UN and got the Security Council to approve a resolution calling for the use of all necessary means to restore exiled President Jean-Bertrand Aristide to power (UNSC Res 940, 1994). As in Somalia, there was little popular support for using force to install Aristide and the President went to the UN seeking just such authorization. The Senate responded by voting 100-0 in favor of an amendment stating that the UN Resolution does not constitute authorization for the deployment of U.S. armed forces to Haiti under the Constitution or War Powers Resolution (CR 3 Aug 1994: S10415-S10433).

As the situation in Haiti seemed headed toward an invasion, President Clinton dispatched a high-level delegation to Haiti to persuade its military leaders to step down. The delegation of former President Jimmy Carter, retired General Colin Powell, and Senator Sam Nunn reached an agreement with the military rulers of Haiti in which they agreed to step down and accept the deployment of U.S. troops. On 19 September 1994, U.S. troops deployed to Haiti. Both the House and Senate passed non-binding resolutions commending the President and the special delegation to Haiti, supporting the U.S. forces in Haiti, and calling for a withdrawal of U.S. troops as soon as possible (H Cong Res 290, CR 19 Sep 1993: H9208-H9221 and S Res 259, CR 21 Sep 1994: S13048-S13081). Yet this did not imply a real basis of support. On 6 October, the Senate and House passed another pair of non-binding resolutions chiding the President for not seeking or welcoming congressional approval before the deployment of troops. They supported a prompt and orderly withdrawal of U.S. forces from Haiti as soon as possible and called for a series of detailed reports on the cost, scope, and projected timetable of the operation. The resolutions did not constrain the mission or limit its duration; however, neither did they authorize the operation.

Bosnia

In addition to Somalia and Haiti, the situation in Bosnia also eroded congressional and public support for UN peacekeeping operations. Since its 1992 inception, the UN Protection Force (UNPROFOR) has been severely criticized. Sent to the former Yugoslavia to safeguard humanitarian relief efforts, UNPROFOR has been largely impotent. Because it did not have the firepower or mandate to resolve the civil war, UNPROFOR relied on the good graces of the warring factions to provide humanitarian assistance. Although the U.S. did not have combat forces in Bosnia, it provided combat aircraft through NATO. President Clinton also pledged up to 25,000 troops as part of a 50,000-troop NATO deployment to enforce any agreed-upon settlement (Lowenthal). However, Congress, using the 1994 Defense

UNPROFOR personnel on patrol in Bihac, Bosnia. Serb soldier in background, Muslim child in foreground, 1994.

photo used with permission

Appropriations Act as a vehicle, reminded the President that he should consult with Congress if any U.S. action were to be taken in Bosnia. The Act stated, "it is the sense of Congress that none of the funds made available by the Act should be available for the purposes of deploying United States Armed Forces to participate in the implementation of a peace settlement in Bosnia-Herzegovina, unless previously authorized by the Congress" (Pub. L. 103-139, Sec 8146).

Sarajevo Soccer field, 1995. *photo used with permission*

The Appropriations Act also stated the sense of Congress that none of the funds appropriated should be obligated for costs incurred by the military serving in any operations under Chapter VI or VII of the UN Charter or Security Council Resolution unless the President consults with the bipartisan leadership of Congress (Pub. L. 103-139, sec 8153). It included a "Sense of Congress" provision which stated that the President should consult Congress before placing troops under a foreign command (other than NATO and other treaty alliances). Additionally, the Act stated the President should submit a report within 48 hours of placing troops under foreign command which outlines the mission, objectives, U.S. interest, command and control arrangements, estimated cost, and anticipated duration of the operation (Pub. L. 103-139, sec. 9002). Although not binding, this clearly laid down a marker of congressional expectations for the President, if he were to place troops under foreign command.

The 1995 Defense Appropriation and Authorization Acts restated the same language but added guidance for lifting the arms embargo on the government of Bosnia and Herzegovina. It stated that the President, or his representative, should introduce a UN Security Council resolution to terminate the arms embargo if the Bosnian Serbs do not accept an international peace proposal (Pub. L. 103-337, sec 1404). This however, was not mandatory and no actions were undertaken. In July 1995, both houses of Congress voted overwhelmingly to require the President to unilaterally lift the Bosnian arms embargo. President Clinton vetoed the legislation, but an override vote is expected when Congress returns from its summer recess (Cooper and Devroy: A1).

PDD-25

What transpired in Somalia, Haiti, and Bosnia served to weaken the political support in Congress for UN and multilateral actions. Therefore, in March 1994, administration officials attempted to rebuild support for its UN policy by briefing PRD-13 to key members of Congress. Some were bothered by the fact that the UN Secretary-General had been briefed back in August 1993, a full year before the administration had come to Congress (Gellman *a*: A1). In response to these briefings, a group of 12 Republican senators (among them Dole, Stevens, McConnell, Nickels, Lugar, Warner, Helms, and Thurman) weighed in with their inputs to the draft PRD in a 24 March letter to the National Security Advisor (CR 23 Jan 1994: S7550-S7552). To accommodate the Senators and try to gain congressional support, the administration accepted many of the recommendations. The proposed policy was changed to state that American national interests are the foremost criteria for all decisions to support UN operations. Additionally, it would apply the criteria laid out in the directive to evaluate ongoing peace operations when they come up for regular renewal, and added specific recognition of the unique risks to American military and civilians. The administration did not agree with all the Senators' proposals. The policy as signed did not include the recommendation to rein in the power of the Secretary General or change the section of PRD-13 on U.S. funding of UN operations.

On 3 May 1994, President Clinton signed the directive on UN peace operations. This brought to a close over a year of debate, re-drafting, and inter-branch fighting over the development of U.S. policy on supporting UN operations. What emerged was a much watered-down version of the initial draft policy. Once signed, Draft PRD-13 became PDD-25.

The New Congress

UN issues played a part in the November 1994 congressional elections. The House Republicans included proposals regarding the UN as part of their "Contract with America." They promised that if they became the majority in the House they would introduce a bill within the first 100 days to limit U.S. participation in UN operations. In the elections, the Republicans swept to power in both the House and the Senate. This new Congress felt it was elected with a mandate for change. One area for this change was U.S. support for UN peace operations. Congress' reasons for this attitude were four-fold. 1) they did not believe in the administration's policy of "assertive multilateralism," 2) Congress felt that the administration's real feelings on supporting the UN, evidenced by the initial drafts of PRD-13, were out of the mainstream, 3) the President had circumvented Congress on Haiti and Somalia by going to the UN Security Council for resolutions the Congress would have never approved, 4) these resolutions were then used by the administration as justification for its actions.

The new Congress felt that it needed to enact legislation to assert its oversight concerning U.S. military involvement in UN peace operations. The two "hot button" issues both the Senate and House wished to address were foreign command over American troops and reducing U.S. monetary support to UN peace operations. Congress has, in turn, put new legislation on the agenda which, if enacted, will have a monumental impact on the way the legislative and executive branches address the issue of U.S. military participation in UN peacekeeping operations.

On 4 January 1995, Senate Majority Leader Robert Dole introduced a bill to clarify the war powers of Congress and the President in the post-Cold War period. Called the Peace Powers Act of 1995 (S5, CR 4 Jan 1995: S101-S103), it would fundamentally change the way the President and Congress interact regarding the deployment of U.S. troops. The bill was originally introduced in the previous Congress as the Peace Powers Act of 1994 (S 1803, CR 24 Oct 1994: S2143), but the bill went nowhere. With

Republicans in the majority, Dole believed the bill had a good chance to be enacted into law. The new legislation provided for repealing the War Powers Resolution, including the provision that troops must be withdrawn from overseas action within 60 days unless Congress approves the mission. The measure prohibited the President from placing U.S. troops under a foreign commander of a UN operation unless he determined it is in the interest of national security or if authorized by Congress. Additionally, the bill provided for reduction of the U.S. payment to the UN by the amount spent by the Defense Department in support of peacekeeping activities.

Legislation with similar restrictions on U.S. participation in UN action was introduced in the House on 4 January 1995 as the National Security Revitalization Act; it contains many of the same ideas (HR 7, CR 4 Jan 1995: H123). Its two key UN-related provisions on command of U.S. troops and payments to the UN mirror the Senate version. Both the House National Security and International Relations Committees approved the National Security Revitalization Act, with the UN measures intact, on 31 January. It was passed by the full House on 16 February 1995 (CR 16 Feb 1995: H1890).

Intelligence sharing with the UN has also become an issue of concern in the new Congress. PDD-25 notes that the U.S. will "share information, as appropriate," taking into account established procedures. However, due to allegations of leaks by the UN during the Somalia mission and the discovery of a box of classified information left behind after the UN pullout from Somalia, some members of Congress want to limit intelligence sharing with the UN. Both the House and Senate have proposed legislation which seeks to limit presidential discretion to share intelligence as provided for in PDD-25. The House version, contained in the National Security Revitalization Act, directs the President to develop guidelines for the transfer of intelligence to the UN. In the Senate, however, Senator Olympia Snowe has introduced a much more restrictive bill which would prohibit the U.S. from passing "intelligence information involving sensitive sources and methods" to the UN (S. 420, 15 Feb 1995).

In the time between the initial deployment of troops to Somalia in 1992 and the summer of 1995, Congress has taken a wide spectrum of actions in its conflicts with the executive branch over U.S. support to UN peace operations. It has used congressional resolutions to applaud presidential actions, as in the initial Somalia deployment, and to chide the President for not seeking or welcoming congressional approval before the deployment of troops to Haiti. Congress has used the authorization and appropriations bills to express the sense of Congress regarding Haiti and Bosnia. It has also used these bills to request reports from the President if he were to take certain actions. The new Congress, seated in January 1995, has introduced legislation which would put limits on how American troops and funding are used to support UN peace operations. Congress also used its most potent weapon, its power of the purse, to cut off funding to the Somalia operation to ensure the withdrawal of American troops.

RESULTS AND IMPLICATIONS

The result of the development and implementation of the Clinton administration's policy toward U.S. participation in UN peace operations has been a shift of power. In both foreign affairs and war powers there has been a shift from the President to Congress. There has also been a clear erosion of the U.S. commitment to the UN. These shifts in turn point toward certain possible implications for the future.

Results

The past few years have witnessed a shift in the balance of certain powers from the executive to the legislative branch. This trend is evident in Congress' attempt to exert control over foreign policy, specifically regarding U.S. support to UN peace operations. During the Cold War, Congress tended to defer to the President's foreign policy decisions. Most issues were seen as good vs. evil, U.S. vs. USSR, or democracy vs. communism. The fall of the Soviet Union and the Berlin Wall changed this situation. With the country's very survival no longer at stake, Congress has taken a more active role in trying to shape foreign policy. In fact, Congress holds a "virtual veto" over support to new UN peace operations. In mid-June 1995, congressional leaders told President Clinton that they would support the establishment of such a force for Bosnia, but were not willing to pay for it. President Clinton had to promise the European allies that he would "do my dead-level best to argue the case in Congress" that the U.S. should help pay for the operation (Devroy: A12). The U.S. delegation to the UN was compelled to oppose the initial draft UN resolution creating the rapid reaction force. Not until the resolution was rewritten, dropping all references to how the force would be funded, was it adopted by the UN Security Council. In another sign of growing Congressional influence over foreign affairs, both houses of Congress passed legislation which would require the President to lift the Bosnian arms embargo. In spite of presidential lobbying, the bills passed overwhelmingly in both Houses (Cooper and Devroy: A1).

Although not as dramatic, there has also been a gradual erosion of the war powers of the executive branch. In 1993, Congress, for the first time in 20 years, used its "power of the purse" to cut off funds for an overseas military mission, effectively killing U.S. participation in the UN peacekeeping effort in Somalia. Additionally, the House's National Security Revitalization Act and the Senate's Peace Powers Act of 1995, if passed into law, would prohibit the President from placing U.S. troops under a foreign UN commander unless the President declares the UN deployment vital to U.S. national security interests. These examples show an increasingly assertive Congress using its constitutional power to restrain the war powers of the President. These actions however, have not constrained the President from exercising his power as Commander in Chief. The most recent example has been President Clinton's deployment of troops to Haiti without first receiving congressional approval.

Implications

The assertion and then retraction of the Clinton administration's policy of "assertive multilateralism" will have long-term effects on the conduct of U.S. foreign policy. The President has lost some of his prerogative for unilateral action, and Congress has gained influence in the conduct of foreign affairs. As may be seen in the debate over funding the Bosnia rapid reaction force, the executive branch is no longer the sole spokesperson for U.S. foreign policy. Foreign leaders now visit the Senate Majority Leader and the Speaker of the House (Devroy and Swardson: A29). If this trend continues, there is a danger that allies may not trust the U.S. President's word, and enemies may disregard the threat of any U.S. retribution.

U.S. influence in the UN will surely decline. Proposals in Congress to reduce U.S. payments to the UN, put restrictions on UN command of U.S. troops, and to limit intelligence sharing, all show a Congress increasingly skeptical of the UN. This attitude of mistrust makes it all the more likely that Congress will try to reduce the current level of support. Additionally, it is probable that Congress will try to impose firm limitations on any future U.S. military participation in UN operations.

These actions may hamper the ability of the President to use the UN as an instrument for peacekeeping and peacemaking. If U.S. support for the UN declines, so will its ability to influence the UN in support of U.S. foreign policy objectives. President Bush used the UN masterfully to get the international community behind the effort to expel Iraq from Kuwait. President Clinton also used the UN Security Council to get a resolution allowing the use of force to install President Aristide in Haiti. As Congress reduces funding for the UN, the President may find it more difficult to gather support for resolutions and other UN actions beneficial to U.S. foreign policy.

The final implication is the possible reduction of U.S. leadership, not only in the UN, but also in the world. As has been demonstrated in Bosnia, if the U.S. does not take a leadership role across the whole spectrum of support to UN operations, such as placing troops on the ground, its influence on the other participants, allies and enemies alike, is greatly reduced. Some countries may view the lack of support for the UN as a sign of isolationism. If countries believe the U.S. is withdrawing somewhat from the international stage, other nations will fill the perceived vacuum and the U.S. could lose some of its leadership in the world.

OVERSIGHT OF U.S. INTELLIGENCE SUPPORT TO UN PEACEKEEPING OPERATIONS

Joseph G. Hays III
U.S. Department of State
August 1996

INTRODUCTION

Conflicts between the Congress and the executive branch on foreign policy issues have their basis in the U.S. Constitution. The separation of powers, established by the Constitution, makes the President Commander in Chief and gives him the authority to speak for the nation on foreign policy issues, while giving to the Congress the power to fund U.S. Government programs, regulate trade, confirm ambassadorial nominees, approve treaties, and declare war.

This division of foreign policy responsibility results in a tug-of-war between the Congress and the executive over foreign policy issues. The over-arching Soviet strategic threat faced by the U.S. following the Second World War tended to lessen this conflict. While there were certainly foreign policy confrontations between the Congress and the executive during the Cold War, most notably as a result of the war in Vietnam, the perceived threat of global Communism and the very real threat of nuclear annihilation tended to create a bipartisan consensus on a general foreign policy framework, obscuring the constitutionally inherent friction between the Congress and the executive on foreign policy issues. The shared perception of the Congress, the executive, and the public that there was indeed an over-arching threat to U.S. security, enhanced the power of the executive relative to the Congress, reduced friction between the Congress and the executive, and muted partisan foreign policy debate.

The end of the Cold War eliminated not only this perception of a strategic threat to the U.S., but also made much of the existing foreign policy framework irrelevant, and eliminated the impetus for a consensus on foreign policy issues between the Congress and the executive as well as between the two major political parties. The result has been a reappearance of the historic conflict between the executive and the Congress over foreign policy issues. The lack of an over-arching threat to national security has resulted in a Congress more willing to challenge the executive on foreign policy issues, and an increase in the partisan nature of the foreign policy debate.

However, this congressional assertiveness is uneven and inconsistent, with the Congress apparently willing to defer to the executive on issues which have traditional Cold War overtones and clear strategic national interests, such as relations with Russia and the newly independent states of the former Soviet Union, while asserting itself on other issues such as U.S. involvement in Somalia and support for UN peacekeeping operations, where U.S. interests seem less clear.

Peacekeeping has in fact become the single most contentious foreign policy issue between the Congress and the executive. It is not only the prime example of the resurgence of conflict over foreign policy between the Congress and the executive, but also an example of the partisanship that now increasingly characterizes congressional debate on foreign policy issues (Rosner: 66).

Two bills to restrict intelligence sharing with the UN, the *International Peacekeeping Policy Act of 1993* and a provision contained in the *Peace Powers Act of 1994,* were introduced following the deaths of 18 U.S. Army Rangers in Mogadishu, Somalia, in October 1993. While neither bill moved beyond the committee stage, they nevertheless represent the beginnings of congressional assertiveness on the issue of intelligence sharing with the UN, and an indication of increasing partisan alignment on the whole issue of U.S. involvement with the UN. Following the 1994 congressional elections, the new Republican majority in the Congress introduced two bills to restrict the ability of the executive to share intelligence with the UN: a provision contained in the *Contract With America* and the *International Peacekeeping Policy Act of 1995.*

A CHRONOLOGY OF EVENTS AND LEGISLATION AFFECTING INTELLIGENCE SHARING WITH THE UN

Sep 92:	UN Secretary General proposes a significant expansion of UN peace operations in his Agenda for Peace.
Nov 92:	President Bush begins intelligence sharing with the UN in support of peace operations with National Security Decision Directive 74.
Mid 93:	President Clinton seeks to expand U.S. participation in UN peace operations with Presidential Review Directive 13. PRD-13 encounters opposition in Congress and the executive branch and is withdrawn.
Oct 93:	18 U.S. Rangers killed in Mogadishu, Somalia.
Nov 93:	International Peacekeeping Policy Act of 1993: Single issue bill to restrict intelligence sharing.
Jan 94:	Peace Powers Act of 1994: Contains a provision to restrict intelligence sharing.
May 94:	President Clinton approves Presidential Decision Directive 25, a revision of PRD-13. PDD-25 significantly expands U.S. intelligence support to the UN.
Nov 94:	Republicans assume control of Congress.
Jan 95:	*Contract With America*: Contains a provision to restrict intelligence sharing.
Feb 95:	Peacekeeping Policy Act of 1995: A single issue bill to restrict intelligence sharing.
Feb 95:	UN mishandling of U.S.-supplied intelligence occurs in Mogadishu, Somalia.
May 95:	A Bill to Restrict Intelligence Sharing With the UN: Single issue bill to restrict intelligence sharing.
Jun 95:	Foreign Relations Revitalization Act of 1995: Contains a provision to restrict intelligence sharing.
Dec 95:	Senate-House Conference on the Foreign Relations Revitalization Act of 1995 contains additional restrictions on intelligence sharing.
Apr 96:	President vetoes the Foreign Relations Revitalization Act of 1995.
May 96:	Intelligence Authorization Act for Fiscal Year 1997: Contains provision restricting intelligence sharing.

The pivotal event for congressional opposition to intelligence sharing with the UN was the mishandling by the UN in Somalia of U.S.-provided intelligence. In late February 1995, U.S. personnel discovered several cartons of U.S. intelligence documents and photographs that had been abandoned by the UN at the UN compound in Mogadishu. Following an investigation by both the UN and the U.S., it became apparent that UN control of U.S.-provided intelligence was less than adequate, and the potential for compromise of U.S. intelligence sources and methods was high. This mishandling of U.S.-provided intelligence not only resulted in an increase in the number of Republican-sponsored bills to restrict intelligence sharing with the UN, but also changed the nature of this legislation, from stand-alone bills to amendments to major legislation such as the *Foreign Relations Authorization Act* and the *Intelligence Authorization Act.*

The issue has become such a focal point for congressional-administration friction on foreign policy, and is so bound up in partisan politics, that there is virtually no chance of a congressional-administration compromise on the issue similar to that reached during the debate on the *Contract With America.*

In the near term, the administration will likely succeed in expanding intelligence sharing, as the proposed legislation presently has little chance of success. The issue has generated virtually no public interest, and the threat of a Presidential veto therefore remains effective. Single issue bills usually have a small constituency and therefore a slim chance of passage if there is significant opposition. As for major legislative initiatives containing restrictive intelligence sharing provisions, Congress is reluctant to delay important legislation by risking a presidential veto over such an obscure issue.

However, the Congress will likely be ultimately successful in passing legislation to restrict intelligence sharing with the UN. The Congress has asserted itself on the issue and expressed concerns over administration policies, while the administration has failed to build a consensus for its policies either with the Congress or the public. This places the administration in a precarious position when any future mishandling of U.S. intelligence occurs. The next episode will undoubtedly be more serious than the February 1995 Somalia incident, where the material was discovered by U.S. personnel. The next incident is likely to generate a bipartisan Congressional and public reaction that may very well lead to the passage of restrictive legislation.

EXECUTIVE BRANCH INITIATIVES TO EXPAND INTELLIGENCE SHARING WITH THE UN

As a result of the East-West conflict during the Cold War, the UN, instead of becoming the primary forum for international dispute resolution as envisioned by the framers of the UN Charter, was instead relegated to a rather narrowly defined and limited role by power politics practiced by the U.S. and USSR. As a result, those situations in which UN forces were deployed in a peacekeeping role were few, and the limited functions of UN peacekeepers came to be well defined.

With the exceptions of Korea and the Congo, these traditional UN peacekeeping operations utilized forces designed to serve as an impartial buffer force between parties to a conflict, with their main function being to observe and report on cease-fire violations. As these UN forces were deployed with the consent of all parties to the conflict, and only after the cessation of hostilities and the imposition of a cease-fire, there was little expectation that they would engage in sustained combat. Consequently, traditional UN peacekeeping forces were generally infantry units, relatively low-cost, small, lightly armed, and easily supported. Since the possibilities of significant combat were remote, the combat effectiveness of these UN forces and the capabilities and competence of the UN Headquarters organization which supported the forces were rarely factors in the success of traditional UN peacekeeping operations (Ruggie: 6).

In the late 1980s, there was a dramatic expansion of UN peace operations, as well as a change in the character of these operations. From the establishment of the UN until 1988, there were 13 UN peace operations, the vast majority of which were of the traditional peacekeeping type, with small, lightly armed UN forces operating with the consent of the parties to the conflict, introduced only after the cessation of hostilities (Roberts: 95). From May 1988 to October 1993, however, 20 additional UN peace operations were undertaken, and many of these peace operations involved the UN in duties unrelated to traditional peacekeeping. Now, the UN found itself not only monitoring and even running elections in El Salvador, Namibia, Mozambique and Cambodia, but also engaged in peace enforcement operations in the former Yugoslavia and Somalia. These peace enforcement operations were significantly different from earlier, traditional UN peacekeeping operations. UN forces found themselves operating in areas where hostilities were still ongoing, where their presence had not been requested by all or even some of the parties to the conflict, and where they faced the possibility of becoming engaged in major sustained combat with one or more opposing forces. As a result, UN forces engaged in peace enforcement operations came to resemble large, heavily armed conventional military forces with all the personnel, equipment, supply, communications, and intelligence support such a force requires (Roberts: 99).

The main reasons for the expanded number of peace operations were the ability of the UN Security Council to reach an agreement to act during crises; the loss of the restraining influence of the superpowers on their clients; the dissolution of the Soviet Union; and a series of UN-brokered peace agreements in Angola, Iran-Iraq, and Central America which required peacekeeping forces to monitor cease-fire agreements (Roberts: 99). By the time of the Iraqi invasion of Kuwait in the summer of 1990, many observers believed that the UN might finally be able to become the forum of choice for conflict resolution. The remarkable coalition formed under UN auspices, which liberated Kuwait in 1991, did much to reinforce this view.

Against this background, UN Secretary-General Boutros-Ghali issued his *Agenda for Peace* in June 1992, which called for a vastly expanded UN role in peace operations. He recommended that:

- The Security Council assume more peacekeeping burdens rather than authorizing member nations to take action on its behalf.
- Agreements be made, as provided for in Article 43 of the UN Charter, for member states to make military forces, facilities and assistance available to the UN.
- The Security Council guarantee the permanent availability of such peacekeeping forces.
- Peace enforcement forces be on call and more heavily armed than peacekeeping units, that they be made up of volunteers and be extensively trained within their national commands.
- Peacekeeping and peace enforcement forces be placed under the command of the Secretary General.

The Bush Administration

While the Bush administration did not fully endorse all the recommendations of the *Agenda for Peace,* there was a general belief among administration officials that, with the end of the Cold War and an increase in the number of international conflicts, the Security Council could and should now play a more central role in international efforts to resolve these conflicts. President Bush, in a speech to the UN General Assembly on 21 September 1992, recommended that the Security Council consider the recommendations contained in the *Agenda for Peace,* and indicated that the U.S. would:

- Support UN efforts to strengthen the ability of the UN to prevent, contain and resolve conflict.
- Train its forces for the full range of peacekeeping and humanitarian relief operations, which would be coordinated with the UN.
- Inform the UN of the availability of its unique military resources and capabilities and work with the UN to employ U.S. airlift, logistics, communications and intelligence capabilities to support peacekeeping operations (Bush *c*: 1698-1699).

In the area of intelligence support to UN peace operations, this speech represented a major policy shift. Now the U.S. was offering to provide U.S. intelligence to support UN peace operations.

This policy shift, in which the U.S. pledged to utilize U.S. intelligence capabilities to support UN peace operations, was a recognition that UN peace enforcement operations, when compared with traditional peacekeeping operations, would require vastly improved intelligence support if they were to be successful. Such peace enforcement operations would require strategic military and political intelligence for pre-deployment planning; operational intelligence support to deployed UN forces regarding the disposition, capabilities, and intentions of potentially hostile forces; and tactical intelligence to support UN forces that might find themselves engaged in sustained combat. None of these intelligence requirements had been perceived as being necessary to support traditional UN peacekeeping operations, and the UN on its own was unable to provide its forces with such intelligence support (Hugh Smith: 175-176).

President Clinton's Assertive Multilateralism

The Clinton administration initially sought to significantly expand U.S. participation in UN peace operations as part of its pursuit of "assertive multilateralism" (Berdal *a*: 32), the idea that the U.S. should work through international organizations to achieve its foreign policy goals (Bolton). The administration's first attempt to draft a policy to support this expanded U.S. participation was *Presidential Review Directive 13* (PRD-13), the draft of which was circulated for interagency review in mid-summer 1993 (Berdal *a*: 30).

The deaths of 18 U.S. Rangers in Mogadishu, Somalia, on 13 October 1993, forced a major reassessment of the directive and marked the end of any further administration public support for the idea of "assertive multilateralism" (Albright a: 464; c: 51). It was not until May 1994 that the directive, now renamed *Presidential Decision Directive 25, U.S. Policy on Reforming Multilateral Peace Operations,* was formally approved. The deaths in Somalia increased congressional opposition to U.S. involvement in UN peace operations and served as the triggering event for the first congressional legislation to restrict the ability of the President to share intelligence with the UN (Bolton).

The directive, as issued in 1994, contained specific guidelines for U.S. support of and participation in UN peace operations, command and control of U.S. forces participating in UN operations, proposals to reduce the costs of UN peace operations, and proposals to improve UN management of such operations. While PDD-25 contained significant limitations on the participation of U.S. forces in UN peace operations, compared to earlier drafts of the directive, the directive in fact expanded the policy of providing U.S. intelligence support to UN peace operations that had been initiated under the Bush administration. According to PDD-25, the U.S. would share intelligence with the UN to support peace operations as appropriate, while ensuring full protection of sources and methods. PDD-25, while backing away from participation of U.S. combat forces in UN peace operations, recognized that many of these operations were nevertheless in the interests of the U.S., and sought to utilize support to the UN by the U.S. Intelligence Community to help ensure the success of these operations.

The Process of Providing Intelligence Support to the UN

The procedures for providing intelligence support to UN peace operations, which were developed by the Clinton administration, are known as the Concepts of Operations or the CONOP process. This process is highly restrictive, providing only specific types of intelligence to the UN, through narrowly defined channels, and only in support of specific peace operations. The administration has long chafed under the restrictions imposed by the CONOP process, and administration officials have made clear a desire to significantly expand intelligence sharing with the UN well beyond the current process (Gaffney *b*: A12).

Currently, to receive U.S. intelligence to support a peace operation, the UN must formally request such intelligence support via the U.S. Mission to the UN, which in turn transmits the request to the Department of State where it is reviewed by the Bureau of Intelligence and Research (INR). If INR determines that the request is consistent with U.S. foreign policy objectives and interests, the request is forwarded to the Special Assistant to the Director of Central Intelligence for Foreign Intelligence Relationships (Gati c). This CIA office then drafts a narrowly defined CONOP, outlining the types of intelligence to be provided, the organizations tasked to provide the intelligence support, and the mechanisms by which this support will be provided. The draft CONOP is then circulated among the various agencies and departments involved for coordination (Gati *c*).

Through the CONOP process, the DCI has designated the Defense Intelligence Agency (DIA) as the Executive Agent for U.S. Intelligence Community support to most UN peace operations. Since the institution of the CONOP process, the U.S. Intelligence Community has provided support to the following UN peace operations:

- **UNTAC, UN Transitional Authority in Cambodia:** In effect 1992-1994. A variety of all-source information was provided through the Australian Force Commander.
- **UNOSOM, UN Operation in Somalia:** In effect 1993-1995. A variety of all-source intelligence was provided to UN Headquarters in New York City and to deployed UN forces through USCENTCOM.
- **UNPROFOR, UN Protection Force, Yugoslavia:** Approved August 1993.Information provided included reconnaissance aircraft photo mosaics, artillery order of battle, threat information, maps, charts and daily intelligence summaries.
- **UNAMIR, UN Assistance Mission in Rwanda:** Approved June 1994. Information provided included reconnaissance aircraft photo mosaics and refugee migration data.
- **UNAVEM III, UN Angola Verification Mission:** Approved September1995. Information provided included briefings and intelligence summaries.
- **UNMIH, UN Mission in Haiti:** Approved July 1994. Information provided included pre-deployment intelligence on airfields, ports, force protection, daily intelligence summaries and tactical imagery.
- **UNHCR Burundi:** Approved September 1995. Information provided included imagery-derived information on refugee situation (U.S. DoD *i*).

In addition to these mission specific CONOPS, there are two additional CONOPS for intelligence support to UN peace operations. The first is a medical intelligence CONOP, in effect since 1994, which provides the UN with unclassified medical data on epidemic health threats, regional health warnings, medical facilities and environmental threats. DIA serves as the executive agent for this CONOP, with information provided by the Armed Forces Medical Intelligence Center. The second non-mission-associated CONOP, in effect since September 1995, provides immediate warning of any information which indicates a direct threat against UN personnel anywhere in the world. In this case, any watch center within the U.S. Intelligence Community is authorized to pass the threat information directly to the UN element at risk.

DIA support to UN peace operations is three-tiered. Joint Chiefs of Staff Directorate of Intelligence (J-2) representatives are assigned to both the U.S. Mission to the UN and to the UN Situation Center at UN Headquarters. These individuals monitor the transfer of intelligence to the UN, provide feedback from the UN concerning the intelligence provided by the U.S., and assist the UN in drafting requests for intelligence (U.S. DoD *j*).

The UN Support Desk at the National Military Joint Intelligence Center serves as the clearing house for virtually all intelligence support to UN peace operations. Sanitized intelligence is provided to the UN Support Desk by the Defense Intelligence Agency, Central Intelligence Agency and National Security Agency, as specified in each individual CONOP, for forwarding to the U.S. Mission to the UN. The mission then serves as the final reviewing authority before intelligence is passed to the UN. Finally, J-2 provides sanitized intelligence to Unified Commands which have ongoing UN operations within their areas of responsibility, for transmission directly to U.S. elements which may be deployed with UN forces. In addition, Commanders in Chief of the Unified Commands are given authority to provide sanitized tactical intelligence acquired by their own theater assets to UN forces.

Intelligence reports on significant military and political developments make up the bulk of the materials provided to the UN, although a substantial quantity of imagery, primarily tactical and U-2 reconnaissance aircraft photo mosaics, have also been provided.

Beyond the Current Process

The executive branch wants to be more forthcoming and would like to increase intelligence sharing with the UN beyond that currently provided for through the CONOP mechanism. In congressional testimony in May 1995, the Assistant Secretary of State for Intelligence and Research, Toby Gati, stated that the U.S. should share intelligence with the UN even when it was not in the interest of the U.S. to do so. Her rationale was that through routine sharing of intelligence with the UN, the U.S. could ensure that the UN would be more inclined to use U.S.-provided intelligence when it was in the interest of the U.S. for the UN to do so (Gaffney *b*: A12).

The administration's use of expanded sharing of U.S. intelligence as a means to influence the UN on a variety of issues is clearly hampered by the restrictive nature of the current process, which provides for intelligence sharing with the UN in only narrowly defined cases.

While the current administration would like to significantly expand intelligence sharing with the UN, the issue has become such a point of friction between the executive and the Congress, and is so tied up in an increasingly partisan foreign policy debate, that it is not politically feasible to expand intelligence sharing with the UN through a presidential directive, especially in an election year.

As a consequence, the Administration has decided instead to attempt to expand intelligence sharing with the UN beyond the current process by revising bureaucratic directives and procedures of the intelligence agencies, achieving a *de facto* policy shift while avoiding a formal articulation of a change in policy. A Director of Central Intelligence (DCI) Directive, issued by DCI John Deutch, contains a number of provisions which lay the procedural foundation for a significant increase in the sharing of intelligence with the UN and is the first step in this policy shift (CIA *a*).

The Director of Central Intelligence Directive

Director of Central Intelligence Directive 1/7-1, *Security Controls on the Dissemination of Intelligence Information,* which became effective on 15 June 1996, revises policies, controls and procedures for the dissemination and use of intelligence information and related materials. The basic policy of DCI Deutch, which underlies the directive, is his desire "that intelligence be written for the consumer, allowing for the widest dissemination of timely, tailored intelligence possible" (CIA a, App C). Consumers are identified as U.S. policymakers and warfighters and others such as the UN and international organizations. The directive states that the goal of this policy is to "produce intelligence at the collateral, uncaveated level to the greatest extent possible, thus allowing dissemination to all U.S. 'need-to-know consumers' and for release in gisted form to all appropriate foreign governments." The directive makes clear that it is the policy of the DCI that intelligence products be produced so they may be released to foreign governments and the UN, either by removing references to sources and methods from the body of the product and including such information in removable annexes, or by producing a "tear line" version of the product which does not contain references to sources and methods and which can then be shared with foreign governments and international organizations.

The criteria for sharing U.S. intelligence with foreign governments or with the UN are listed by the directive as follows:

- Such sharing of intelligence promotes the interests of the U.S.
- Does not pose unreasonable risk to U.S. foreign policy or national defense.
- Is limited to a specific purpose and is normally of limited duration.

In the directive, DCI Deutch states that classifiers of intelligence information shall take a:

> risk management approach when preparing information for dissemination. In the interest of the widest possible dissemination of information to policy makers, warfighters and other consumers, classifiers shall carefully consider whether there is a need to mark material with any dissemination control marking and to use control markings only in the limited instances authorized by this directive.

The directive, by abolishing some dissemination controls and severely restricting the ability of originators to utilize the remaining dissemination controls, ensures that the vast majority of U.S. intelligence produced in the future will be eligible for dissemination to the UN. The policy guidance contained in the directive is that the U.S. Intelligence Community "needs an updated intelligence product line that is releasable from the inception — a flow of reporting based on all available sources that is written from the outset to be given broad U.S. dissemination and appropriate foreign release." This anticipates that not only will the majority of U.S. intelligence produced in the future be eligible for release to the UN, but that it will be produced from the outset with the intention that it be released.

This initiative by the administration, to expand intelligence sharing with the UN through changes in bureaucratic and administrative procedures, avoids the congressional and public scrutiny that the drafting of a formal policy change would certainly generate.

CONGRESSIONAL RESPONSES

Beginning in the fall of 1993, eight bills have been introduced in the Congress to restrict the ability of the President to share intelligence with the UN. The evolution in the character of these bills, from single issue bills to provisions included in major legislation, as well as the increasingly restrictive nature of the legislation, reflects the post-Cold War lack of consensus on U.S. foreign policy objectives, the reemergence of congressional foreign policy assertiveness and friction with the executive, and the increasingly partisan nature of the debate on foreign policy issues, especially apparent in an election year.

Although there was considerable congressional interest in the issue of intelligence support to UN peace operations, particularly during the debate over Presidential Decision Directive 25, the actual introduction of legislation to restrict the ability of the executive to share intelligence with the UN did not begin until the fall of 1993, and has been defined by three events:

- The deaths of 18 U.S. Rangers in Somalia in October 1993.
- The congressional elections in the fall of 1994.
- The mishandling by the UN of U.S.-provided intelligence in Somalia in February 1995.

Each of these events led to congressionally-sponsored legislation to restrict intelligence sharing with the UN, and influenced the character of the legislation as well as the response of the executive branch to the proposed legislation.

The public perception of the failure of UN peace operations in Somalia and Bosnia, the increasing number, violent nature and financial cost of these peace enforcement operations, coupled with the view of many members of the Congress that the administration had been unable to convincingly articulate what U.S. national security interests were served by U.S. participation in many such operations, led to increasing congressional assertiveness on the issue of U.S. intelligence support to UN peace operations.

As each of the three events noted above unfolded, the congressional response was an increase in the number of legislative initiatives to restrict the ability of the executive to share intelligence with the UN, as well as a change in the nature of legislation — from single issue bills to amendments to major legislation — intended to restrict the ability of the President to share intelligence with the UN.

LEGISLATIVE INITIATIVES TO RESTRICT INTELLIGENCE SHARING WITH THE UN

Bill Number	Date Introduced	Type of Bill	Legislative Disposition
October 1993: U.S. Rangers Killed in Somalia			
H.R. 3503	11/10/93	Non Appropriations	Failed to move out of committee.
H.R. 3744	01/24/94	Non Appropriations	Failed to move out of committee.
November 1994: Republicans Gain Control of Congres			
H.R. 7	01/04/95	Non Appropriations	Passed by House only.
S. 420	02/15/95	Non Appropriations	Failed to move out of committee.
February 1995: Mishandling of U.S. Intelligence In Somalia			
S. 858	05/25/95	Non Appropriations	Failed to move out of committee.
S. 908	06/09/95	Appropriations	Amended by Helms/Kerry. Senate passed House version.
H.R. 1561	05/03/95	Appropriations	Passed by the Congress; vetoed by the President.
H.R. 3259	04/17/96	Appropriations	Amended by Combest; Amendment to Brownback Amendment

Legislative Initiatives Following the Deaths of Rangers in Mogadishu in October 1993

On 3 October 1993, 18 U.S. rangers were killed and 78 wounded during an assault on the headquarters of Somali warlord Mohammed Farah Aidid in Mogadishu. While U.S. personnel killed during the assault had been under U.S., not UN, command and supported by U.S., not UN, intelligence, there was nevertheless a suspicion in the Congress that UN security lapses had contributed to U.S. fatalities. It was no surprise then that following the losses in Mogadishu, several bills were introduced in the Congress to restrict the ability of the executive branch to share intelligence with the UN in support of peace operations.

The first of these bills was the *International Peacekeeping Policy Act of 1993, H.R. 3503,* a single-issue bill introduced on 10 November 1993 by Representative Olympia Snowe, (R-ME). Representative Snowe's bill would have prevented the expenditure of funds appropriated to the Department of State international peacekeeping account, or the expenditure of any funds appropriated to the Department of State under any law, to pay for assessed or voluntary contributions to United Nations peacekeeping, unless the President certified to the Congress that the peacekeeping operation met a number of foreign policy guidelines. One of the guidelines specified in the bill was that no U.S. intelligence information involving sensitive sources and methods of intelligence gathering would be provided to the UN to support the operation. The bill was referred to the Committee on Foreign Affairs, and no additional action was taken.

The second bill introduced following the losses in Somalia was known as the *Peace Powers Act of 1994, H.R. 3744.* Introduced on 26 January 1994 by Representative Henry J. Hyde, (R-IL), the bill dealt with a number of issues related to U.S. participation in UN peace operations, and contained one section which specifically addressed U.S. intelligence support to UN peace operations. The provisions of this section of the act would have required the President to enter into a written agreement with the UN Secretary-General before any U.S. intelligence information could be provided to the UN. Such a written agreement was to specify:

- The types of intelligence to be provided to the UN.
- The circumstances under which intelligence may be provided to the UN.
- The procedures governing who at the UN would have access to U.S.-provided intelligence.
- The procedures to be followed by the UN to protect the information from disclosure not authorized by the agreement.

Under the provisions of this bill, the President could delegate specified authorities and assign the duties of the President to the Secretary of Defense or the DCI.

Upon its introduction, Representative Hyde's bill was referred to the House Committee on Foreign Affairs, the House Armed Services Committee, and the House Permanent Select Committee on Intelligence (HPSCI), but no additional action was taken.

Although the sponsors recognized that there was little possibility that this legislation restricting the ability of the executive to share intelligence with the UN would progress beyond the committee stage, introduction of the bills nevertheless served as an indication of increasing congressional concern with the issue, and both bills contained language that would reappear in subsequent legislation. Executive branch reaction to the legislation was virtually non-existent. With a Democratic majority in both houses of the Congress, there was virtually no chance that either bill would become law, and the administration apparently saw no need to react to either bill.

Legislative Initiatives Following the 1994 Congressional Elections

In the new Congress following the 1994 congressional elections, two pieces of legislation were introduced to restrict the ability of the executive to share intelligence with the UN: the *Contract with America, H.R. 7,* and the *International Peacekeeping Policy Act of 1995, S. 420.* Increasing congressional assertiveness on the issue was driven not only by the new Republican majority in the Congress, but by the perceived failure of UN peacekeeping operations in Somalia, the apparent failure of the UN to stem the conflict in the former Yugoslavia, congressional misgivings over the deployment of U.S. forces to Haiti in the Fall of 1994, and significant increases in the costs of UN peace operations. UN failures on the ground, coupled with doubts in the Congress over whether U.S. national interests were really at stake in such operations, drove congressional assertiveness on the larger issue of UN peacekeeping operations and on the associated issue of U.S. intelligence support to these operations. Peacekeeping and U.S. involvement with the UN had now become the primary focus of foreign policy conflict between the Congress and the executive.

Contract With America

Introduced on 4 January 1995, the *Contract With America, H.R. 7,* was a sweeping series of legislative initiatives addressing a number of widely varied Republican campaign promises. One section of the contract specifically addressed intelligence sharing with the UN and contained language which would have severely limited U.S. intelligence sharing with the UN to support peace operations (H.R. 7, sec 512). This portion of the *Contract With America* drew heavily on the language of Representative Hyde's *Peace Powers Act of 1995,* and was the first attempt by the Republicans to pursue the issue since achieving a majority in the Congress. As such, it was the first legislative initiative on the issue to generate significant opposition from the executive branch. The larger issue of U.S. involvement in UN peace operations had by now become a partisan issue, and the more narrow issue of U.S. intelligence support to the UN was rapidly becoming so as well. The increasingly partisan debate, coupled with subsequent events in Somalia, would make the hearings on the *Contract With America* the last time the administration would seek to make its case before the Congress for continued U.S. intelligence support to UN peace operations and the last time the administration and the Congress would reach a compromise on the issue.

The congressional and public furor that ensued after the deaths of 18 U.S. Rangers in Somalia in October 1993, had quickly convinced the administration that commitment of U.S. combat forces to UN peace operations would be significantly more difficult in the future. However, in the administration's view, there were continuing areas of instability throughout the world which affected U.S. interests, and UN peace operations remained the best tool to deal with such crises. Limited in its ability to ensure the success of such operations by committing U.S. combat forces, the administration had turned to intelligence sharing with the UN as an alternative means of attempting to ensure that these UN peace operations would be successful.

By the time the *Contract With America* was introduced in the House of Representatives, the U.S. was supplying the UN with increasing quantities of various types of intelligence to support UN peace operations. Indeed, Representative C.W. Bill Young (R-FL) stated during the 19 January 1995 Congressional hearings on the *Contract With America* that, as of January

1995, the Defense Intelligence Agency alone had provided more than 9,000 pieces of secret intelligence to the UN (Gertz *a*: A8).

As originally drafted, the portion of the *Contract With America* that addressed U.S. intelligence support to UN peace operations contained the following provisions:

- The U.S. could provide intelligence to the UN, but only in accordance with a written agreement between the President and the UN Secretary General.
- This agreement was to specify:
  - The types of intelligence to be provided to the UN.
  - The circumstances under which this intelligence was to be provided.
  - The procedures to be followed by the UN to limit access and to protect the information against unauthorized disclosure.
- The agreement was to become effective only if the President transmitted it to the Senate and House Intelligence and Foreign Affairs Committees.

As expected, the administration opposed these provisions and, during hearings held by the House Permanent Select Committee on Intelligence on 19 January 1995, Assistant Secretary of State for Intelligence and Research, Toby Gati, and others presented the administration's opposition to these restrictions on intelligence sharing with the UN. Assistant Secretary Gati testified in open as well as closed session, while the remaining witnesses testified in closed session.

Committee chairman Larry Combest (R-TX), opened the hearing by noting the changing nature of UN peace operations, the marked increase in the number of such operations in recent years, and the call by some for the more efficient use of intelligence to better protect UN peacekeepers (Combest).

The ranking minority member, Norm Dicks (D-WA), articulated the administration view that there was presently in place an effective system for sharing intelligence with the UN, and that provisions in the *Contract With America* would remove the element of flexibility which then existed and would not improve current procedures or promote the security interests of the United States. He continued that the current method of providing intelligence to the UN had as its fundamental principle the protection of sources and methods, and that he was unaware of any concerns within the Intelligence Community that the current system did not work well. He stated that the proposed legislation would be unconstitutional, as it would intrude into the constitutional duties of the President. Representative Dicks concluded by stating that he opposed the legislation but was willing to work with Chairman Combest to resolve any legitimate concerns surrounding the provision of U.S. intelligence to the UN (Dicks *a*).

U.S. personnel in street scene in Somalia, 1993. *photo used with permission*

During her testimony, Assistant Secretary Gati stated the administration's position that the legislation would be counterproductive and unconstitutional, and would, "undermine the constructive steps we have taken to improve the efficiency and effectiveness of UN missions through the modest use of our intelligence assets." According to Gati, the sharing of intelligence with the UN had been a success story that would be wiped away by provisions in the *Contract With America* (Gati *a*).

Gati continued that the proposed legislation would impose unconstitutional restrictions on Presidential action, as it would prevent the President from sharing intelligence with the UN except pursuant to a written agreement between the U.S. and UN. According to Gati, the provisions of this written agreement, as specified by the legislation, would unconstitutionally limit the President's disclosure of information during the course of diplomatic communications. Gati stated that under the Constitution the President is the voice of the U.S. in the field of international relations, and he must therefore be able to decide what information he may use or reveal in diplomatic exchanges. More specifically, when the information concerns national security, the President has the constitutional responsibility to determine what he will say or not say in diplomatic communications, and the proposed legislation would conflict with that responsibility.

Gati added that U.S. intelligence sharing was in support of Presidential Decision Directive 25, which called for timely intelligence support for UN peace operations, and that the process was implemented in strict accordance with guidance issued by the Director of Central Intelligence, which gave clear priority to protecting intelligence sources and methods.

She made the point that U.S. intelligence sharing with the UN was not a "blank check" arrangement, but that intelligence was shared with the UN only to support specific operations and only after a determination had been made by the Department of State that support of the operation was consistent with U.S. foreign policy objectives.

Gati also assured the committee that sharing of intelligence with the UN had not compromised U.S. intelligence sources and methods and that U.S. national security had not been compromised by the current arrangements. She continued that, while there had been compromises of U.S.-provided intelligence by the UN, none were considered major, none had resulted in harm to Americans, and action had been taken to prevent further disclosures. During her unclassified testimony before the committee, she did not provide further details of these compromises.

In the closed session which followed her public testimony, press reports indicate that Gati detailed current U.S. procedures for sharing intelligence with the UN, outlined UN peace operations that have received U.S. intelligence support, and provided details of UN compromises of U.S. provided intelligence (Gertz *a*: A8).

Although Ambassador Montgomery, the CIA witness during the hearings, testified in closed session, the CIA's position was reflected in a

19 January 1995 letter to committee chairman Combest, from Admiral William Studeman, Acting Director of the CIA. According to Admiral Studeman, provisions in the *Contract With America* would make it extremely difficult if not impossible to provide meaningful intelligence support to the UN and would undermine the constructive and innovative steps the CIA had taken in recent years to improve the timeliness and value of intelligence support to the UN and its related activities (Studeman).

Following this testimony, committee members on both sides of the aisle became generally convinced that the current arrangements for sharing intelligence with the UN were adequate, and that if there had been some compromises of U.S.-provided intelligence in the past, these had been relatively minor and isolated and had not endangered U.S. intelligence sources and methods. Thus, by the time the full committee mark-up of the intelligence sharing provisions of the *Contract With America* was held on 27 January 1995, there seemed to be general agreement among committee members that the legislation as originally drafted would make the current U.S. intelligence sharing arrangements with the UN unworkable, and that the section should be revised.

Chairman Combest and ranking minority member Dicks reached a compromise on the issue and presented a proposed amendment during the full committee markup on 27 January 1995. Chairman Combest, in opening remarks, stated that testimony during the previous week had provided the committee a better understanding of what intelligence sharing with the UN involved (Combest). He continued that the general conclusion among committee members was that intelligence sharing with the UN should continue, that most members of the committee were satisfied that guidelines and procedures had been established to control the sharing of intelligence with the United Nations, and that U.S. intelligence sources and methods were being protected. He stated that testimony during the previous week's hearing had made it clear that the result of the proposed legislation would be to bring intelligence sharing with the UN to a halt, primarily because it was highly unlikely that the U.S. would be able to negotiate a formal written agreement with the UN. For this reason, the committee recommended that the requirement for a formal written agreement be deleted from the legislation. However, the committee still recognized that there were legitimate concerns dealing with protection of U.S. sources and methods and, for this reason, the proposed amendment adopted by the committee would require that before U.S. intelligence is provided to the UN, the President must ensure that the Director of Central Intelligence, in consultation with the Secretaries of State and Defense, had established guidelines governing the provision of intelligence to the UN that protected U.S. sources and methods. According to chairman Combest, in an effort to improve the committee's oversight of intelligence sharing with the UN, the committee had added a reporting requirement to the proposed amendment that would require the administration to inform the appropriate committees in both the House and Senate on a semi-annual basis of the types of intelligence provided to the UN and the purposes for which it was provided. In addition, the amendment would require the President, within 15 days of the event, to report to the two intelligence committees any UN compromise of U.S.-provided intelligence.

In his opening remarks at the hearings on 27 January ranking minority member Dicks stated that the bipartisan amendment which he and chairman Combest were proposing would delete the requirement that a formal agreement between the President and the UN Secretary General be drafted before U.S. intelligence could be shared with the UN. He continued that it was his judgment that the legislation, as originally worded, would unconstitutionally intrude on the President's authority to conduct foreign relations and would severely restrict the President's flexibility to provide intelligence to the UN to respond to unforeseen situations. He stated that the amendment which he and chairman Combest were offering would provide for the sharing of U.S. intelligence with the UN on a case-by-case basis, while ensuring the protection of sources and methods. Representative Dicks stated that the proposed amendment would in no way change the current process by which intelligence was provided to the UN, which he and chairman Combest felt was currently operating in the interests of the U.S. (Dicks *b*). The amendment was adopted by the full committee.

There was, however, a lingering doubt among many Republicans concerning the incident, and a feeling that they could not simply drop the provisions of the *Contract With America* which had sought to restrict intelligence sharing with the UN. For his part, Speaker Gingrich apparently wanted to proceed with the legislation as originally drafted. There were Republicans who felt that a "Sense of the Congress" amendment should be attached to the compromise language to address Republican concerns.

Drafts of two amendments were circulated. These amendments declared:

(A) It is the sense of the Congress that:

(1) The Director of Central Intelligence pursuant to his authorities under section 103 (c) of the National Security Act of 1947, 50 U.S.C. S403-3 (c) (6) has taken adequate steps to protect intelligence sources and methods when the U.S. provided intelligence to the United Nations.

(2) The Director would ensure that the Permanent Select Committee on Intelligence of the House of Representatives and the Select Committee on Intelligence of the Senate are kept informed about intelligence assistance provided by the U.S. to the United Nations.

(B) It is the sense of the Congress that:

(1) The U.S. should provide intelligence support to the United Nations only when it is in the United States' interest to do so, and only if such support does not compromise intelligence sources and methods; and

(2) That the President should periodically, as appropriate, notify the type of intelligence support that has been provided to the United Nations, and the circumstances under which such support was provided, to the Committee on International Relations and the Permanent Select Committee on Intelligence of the House of Representatives and to the Committee on Foreign Relations and the Select Committee on Intelligence of the Senate.

While they reflected Republican unease with the compromise on the issue, ultimately, neither of the proposed "Sense of the Congress" amendments were adopted.

The amendment to the intelligence sharing provisions of the *Contract With America,* brokered by the HPSCI and the administration, was also adopted by the House International Relations Committee (HIRC) during a three-day markup session, with the committee voting out the bill on 31 January. Unlike the Intelligence Committee deliberations, the International Relations Committee markup was characterized by sharp political differences over the bill, with very little evidence of the traditional bipartisanship which had normally prevailed within the committee.

The House adopted the *Contract With America*, including the amended provisions on intelligence sharing on 16 February 1995.

International Peacekeeping Policy Act of 1995

On 15 February 1995, Senator Olympia Snowe (R-ME) introduced the *International Peacekeeping Policy Act of 1995, S. 420,* which proposed restrictions on the funds available to the State Department for peacekeeping operations and prohibited the sharing of sensitive intelligence information with the UN. This bill contained language identical to that contained in Senator Snowe's earlier bill, the *International Peacekeeping Policy Act of 1993, H.R. 3503,* which she had introduced while serving as a Representative in November 1993. If passed by the Senate, Snowe's bill would have required reconciliation with the weaker legislation passed by the House in the amended version of the *Contract With America* (Cassata *b*: 826).

Senator Snowe's bill was referred to the Committee on Foreign Relations; however, as was the case with her previous bill introduced in the House, it failed to move beyond committee. The administration, confident that it had reached a compromise with Congress during hearings on the *Contract With America,* did not see the necessity to react to this bill.

The debate over the intelligence sharing provisions of the *Contract With America* was the end of bipartisan consensus on the issue of intelligence support to UN peace operations. The subsequent discovery of U.S.-supplied intelligence found abandoned in Somalia, which occurred only two weeks after the passage of the *Contract With America* by the House, convinced those Republicans who had been swayed by administration arguments in support of intelligence sharing with the UN that they had been misled by administration witnesses (Spence). The mishandling of U.S. intelligence in Somalia ended the brief congressional-administration compromise on the issue, and was the last time the administration would really seek to make a case for intelligence sharing before the Congress. Subsequent administration reaction to legislation restricting the ability of the President to share intelligence with the UN would consist only of veto threats.

The Incident in Mogadishu

The mishandling of U.S. intelligence by the UN in Somalia in February 1995 became the pivotal issue in the debate between Congress and the executive branch over intelligence sharing with the UN in support of peace operations. It solidified the partisan divisions on the issue, led to the introduction of a wave of additional legislation aimed at severely restricting the ability of the executive branch to share intelligence with the UN, and changed the nature of congressional legislative initiatives from single issue bills with little chance of passage, to amendments attached to significant legislation such as the authorization bills for the State Department and Intelligence Community. The incident so soured relations between the Congress and the executive on the issue that there was little administration reaction to the flurry of legislation driven by the incident, other than the threat of vetoes.

In February 1995, as the UN mission in Somalia, UNOSOM II, prepared to evacuate under the protective cover of the U.S. Coalition Task Force UNITED SHIELD, Ambassador Daniel Simpson and other U.S. personnel were staying in the offices of the Deputy UN Forces Commander on the UNOSOM II compound in Mogadishu, Somalia. On the evening of 27 February, Ambassador Simpson, the State Department Regional Security Officer for Mogadishu, John Tolly, and U.S. military personnel discovered a large quantity of U.S. classified material in unlocked UNOSOM II intelligence offices adjacent to the Deputy UN Force Commander's office. At the time of the discovery, UNOSOM II personnel had abandoned the offices in preparation for CTF assumption of control of the UNOSOM II compound on February 28 (U.S. DoD *p*).

Among the items left behind were U.S.-supplied intelligence documents which had been sanitized and provided to the UN at the UN RESTRICTED level; daily intelligence reports on the political situation in Somalia; tactical U.S. intelligence reports marked SECRET NOFORN, indicating that they were not releasable to UN personnel; and U.S.-produced tactical imagery of Mogadishu, with various targets labeled. There were also 54 computer diskettes containing interviews with and names of Somali informants. U.S. personnel destroyed all of the material except for a 100-document sampling and the computer diskettes. Eight U.S. classified documents not marked for release to the UN were found in the sampling.

This incident occurred only five weeks following the House Permanent Select Committee on Intelligence hearings on the *Contract With America,* where administration witnesses had assured committee members that the procedures for sharing U.S. intelligence with the UN were sound and designed to prevent the compromise of U.S. intelligence sources and methods. It was this testimony by administration officials that had convinced committee members to vote for compromise language which significantly relaxed provisions in the *Contract With America* restricting the ability of the President to share intelligence with the UN, a position which was also adopted by the House International Relations Committee and was ultimately contained in the final version of the legislation passed by the House only two weeks before the discovery in Somalia.

As might be expected, the incident produced a swift reaction from members of the Congress, who felt they had been out-maneuvered by an administration whose officials had been less than forthcoming concerning intelligence sharing arrangements with the UN during their recent Congressional testimony. In a statement to the press on 24 March 1995, the Chairman of the House National Security Committee, Representative Floyd Spence, (R-SC), stated:

> We received lots of assurances that this wasn't a problem and the administration strongly opposed a House Republican proposal that a formal intelligence sharing arrangement be put in place. The administration's assurances ring hollow now. The administration should stop the flow of intelligence materials to the UN, conduct a full scale investigation and develop an effective policy to ensure that U.S. classified materials are not carelessly disclosed around the world (Spence).

The fallout from the incident was the introduction of additional legislation to restrict U.S. intelligence sharing with the UN; a shift in the nature of this legislation, from single-issue bills to amendments to major legislation; and an increase in the politicization of the issue. As this incident would prove so crucial to congressional interest in the issue, the incident itself, as well as the views of various officials involved in the investigation deserve closer examination.

On 3 March 1993, the Chairman of the Joint Chiefs tasked the U.S. Commander In Chief, U.S. Central Command, the unified commander responsible for operations in Somalia, to investigate the possible compromise of U.S. classified material that had been provided to UNOSOM II and discovered by Ambassador Simpson and his party. The investigation was initiated on 8 March 1995 and completed on 29 March 1995 (Shalikashvili).

On 13 March, in a letter to Ambassador Madeleine Albright, the U.S. Permanent Representative to the UN, Senator Snowe stated her deep concern over press reports in the 12 March *Washington Post* regarding the possible misuse of U.S. classified information by the UN in Somalia, and requested a personal meeting with Ambassador Albright to discuss the issue. In addition, she stated that such security failures were one reason that she had introduced legislation in the last Congress that would have permitted the payment of U.S. contributions only for UN peacekeeping operations where the President has certified that the United States would not be providing sensitive intelligence information to the UN, (the *International Peacekeeping Policy Act of 1993,* introduced by Representative Snowe in November 1993). She continued that in her new position as Chairman of the Foreign Relations Subcommittee on International Operations, which had jurisdiction over the United Nations and international peacekeeping activities, she had reintroduced this legislation as the *International Peacekeeping Policy Act of 1995* (Snowe).

The letter continued that the mishandling of U.S. intelligence by the UN in Somalia was contrary to specific assurances that the administration had given to members of the Congress. She stated that she hoped Ambassador Albright was prepared to explain the nature of these assurances and whether the administration had ended the dangerous practice of routinely providing sensitive intelligence information to a UN peacekeeping bureaucracy that was institutionally incapable of reliably protecting such information.

On 16 March 1995, a letter drafted by Representative Floyd Spence (R-SC), Chairman of the House National Security Committee, and signed by the Republican leadership of both houses, was sent to President Clinton (U.S. Congress *a*). The letter expressed strong concern over the discovery of the U.S. intelligence material in Mogadishu, and indicated that the potential for the compromise of intelligence sources and methods was significant. The letter continued that given the gravity of the situation, the drafters were concerned that the selection of the U.S. Central Command Inspector General, as the sole U.S. investigative authority, inappropriately narrowed the scope and reach of the ongoing review. They requested that the Inspectors General of the Department of Defense, Department of State and Central Intelligence Agency be tasked to undertake concurrent investigative reviews of the incident to ensure the broadest possible focus on all aspects of how this material came to be in the possession of the UN and the circumstances under which UN personnel had abandoned the material.

On patrol in Somalia, 1993.

photo used with permission

The letter requested the immediate suspension of intelligence sharing arrangements with the UN for the purpose of supporting peacekeeping operations, unless the provision of such intelligence was necessary to protect the life or safety of deployed forces. It requested that this suspension remain in effect until the completion of the investigation into the Somalia incident and a subsequent thorough review and modification of procedures was conducted.

The letter continued that while the drafters recognized that the U.S. had a continuing national interest in being able to share, on a case-by-case basis, intelligence information with the UN, it should be clear that the regular provision of sensitive U.S. intelligence information required a reciprocal commitment from the UN to protect any such information from disclosure or compromise, as well as an assessment of the ability of the UN to uphold such a commitment.

In a response dated 6 April 1996, and addressed to Senator Dole, President Clinton indicated that the Department of Defense had begun a thorough investigation not only of the Somalia incident but also of other intelligence sharing arrangements with the UN. He continued that pending the results of these reviews, he had directed that only intelligence information necessary to protect the safety and operational security of UN forces be provided (Clinton *a*).

President Bush visiting U.S. soldiers in Somalia, December 1992. *photo used with permission*

On 22 March, the ranking Democrat on the Senate Select Committee on Intelligence (SSCI), Senator Bob Kerrey (D-NE), disputed a charge made by Senator Snowe that in addition to the Somalia incident, there had been three other compromises of U.S.-provided intelligence by the UN since February 1993. Kerrey said that the incident in Somalia was a case of U.S. forces leaving classified information behind, not bungling by the UN. When asked to elaborate on the charges of UN compromises of U.S. provided intelligence, Senator Snowe stated that she could not provide any additional details due to the classified nature of the information, but stated that she had received the information from persons in a position to know.

A Department of Defense press release dated 18 April 1995 summarized the results of the U.S. Central Command investigation into the Somalia incident. According to the release, the investigation included a thorough review of approximately 100 U.S. and UN classified documents, including two examples of tactical imagery and 54 computer disks. The operational environment in Somalia necessitated the on-site destruction of the remaining documents prior to the successful evacuation of the remaining UNOSOM II forces.

The investigation concluded that:

- From all available evidence, U.S. national security was not compromised, nor were U.S. forces or U.S. intelligence sources or methods put in jeopardy.
- Of all the documents reviewed, only one contained sensitive material which should not have been passed to UNOSOM II at the time, but no harm was caused to intelligence sources or methods because of this error.
- Seven other documents were appropriate for release to UNOSOM II, but U.S. personnel had failed to remove classification markings and relabel the documents UN RESTRICTED before release to UNOSOM II.
- U.S. procedures for intelligence sharing were sound, and except as noted, were followed by U.S. personnel.
- The information security practices followed by UNOSOM II forces prior to their evacuation were not in consonance with U.S. or UN policy and standards (U.S. DoD *p*).

On 6 April 1995, the Chairman of the Joint Chiefs of Staff, General Shalikashvili, USA, forwarded to Secretary of Defense William Perry the U.S. Central Command report of investigation. In his review of the investigation, the Chairman concluded that to prevent further problems, the U.S. must ensure that sound information security practices and procedures were developed and enforced and that when providing appropriately sanitized information to UN forces, the U.S. must be satisfied that the deployed UN contingent is organized to properly receive, handle, and dispose of the material in a safe and timely manner (Shalikashvili). General Shalikashvili indicated that he concurred with the conclusions of the report, which called into question UNOSOM II's information security practices and substantiated the conclusion that UN security management and execution in this case were unsatisfactory. He noted that, in his opinion, the problem in Somalia resulted from poor execution by both U.S. and UN personnel and not from inadequate policy or written guidance.

Most significantly, the Chairman strongly endorsed the U.S. policy of providing the UN with selected U.S. intelligence, because it could be crucial to the success of UN operations. He concluded by making a number of recommendations to improve UN handling of U.S.-provided intelligence.

On 17 April 1995, Deputy Secretary of Defense John Deutch transmitted the U.S. Central Command report to the various congressional committees concerned. In the cover letter which accompanied the report, he stated that it remained in the interest of the U.S. to make certain that UN operations, with or without the participation of U.S. forces, are effective, not least because they can act as force multipliers for the U.S. Making properly sanitized intelligence information available to selected UN operations was an important factor in assuring the success of such operations. He noted that the Congress had made clear its concern that this intelligence-sharing relationship with the UN must work properly, and that the Defense Department understands and fully shares these concerns. He indicated that the Department of Defense, in conjunction with the Department of State and other agencies, would consult closely with the congressional committees concerned as various recommendations and initiatives that resulted from the Somalia investigation were initiated (Deutch).

On 18 April 1995, Ambassador Inderfurth and a Joint Chiefs of Staff representative briefed UN peacekeeping officials on the U.S. investigation findings and recommendations. At this meeting, the U.S. offered assistance to the UN in strengthening its information security program (Batten).

On 25 April 1995, a U.S. delegation met with UN peacekeeping officials to discuss specific assistance the U.S. was willing to provide and delivered a letter outlining this U.S. assistance, which included:

- Assistance in developing standard information security procedures for receiving, handling, storing and destroying sensitive information.
- Assistance in developing standard operating procedures tailored to particular contingencies and locations.
- Training for UN personnel at the Department of Defense Security Institute in Richmond, VA (Batten).

On 11 May 1995, the UN presented an Aide-Memoire to the U.S. which documented the results of the UN investigation into the Somalia incident and at the same time accepted the offer of U.S. training assistance. The

Aide-Memoire began with the assertion that the documents discovered by Ambassador Simpson and other U.S. personnel on the evening of 27 February 1995 had in fact been purposely left in the unlocked UN intelligence office by the UNOSOM II officer in charge of the documents so that U.S. CTF personnel would have access to the documents and could take any that they wished. The UN asserted that it had intended to ship any documents not taken by CTF personnel to Nairobi on the morning of 28 February. UN investigators interviewed the CTF officers involved, who asserted that while they had indeed been offered the documents, they had informed UNOSOM II personnel more than a week before that they had no need for the documents. Further questioning of the UNOSOM officers involved indicated that they apparently still believed that CTF personnel desired the documents and, when they discovered the documents missing on the morning of 28 February, they had assumed that CTF personnel had removed all the documents (UN *a*).

The Aide-Memoire continued that when Ambassador Simpson and an aide, accompanied by a security officer, came upon the documents, the Ambassador improperly concluded that this was the result of UNOSOM II's negligence. Instead of consulting with other CTF officers or his UNOSOM II hosts, in keeping with the CTF's close working relations with UNOSOM II, Ambassador Simpson decided to treat this incident as a compromise of sensitive U.S. intelligence documents and report it to Washington without even mentioning the incident to the UN Special Representative or the UN Force Commander.

The UN report continued that, despite these facts, there were undoubtedly inadequate UNOSOM II arrangements relating to the security of the documents. The door to the UNOSOM II intelligence office was unlocked; there was no listing of material to be turned over to the CTF, destroyed, or evacuated to Nairobi; and while UNOSOM II's procedures regarding security were generally sound, they may not have been specific enough in dealing with procedures to be followed during an evacuation. The Aide-Memoire concluded that while more detailed security instructions for the field mission should have been prepared, in the UN's view, Ambassador Simpson's actions were highly inappropriate. He was a guest of UNOSOM II at the time he came across these documents and consequently should have brought the matter to the attention of senior UNOSOM II personnel before reporting the incident to Washington. The Aide-Memoire added that

Ambassador Simpson's actions were even more unfortunate in light of the fact that the U.S. investigation itself had concluded that there had been no compromise of highly classified information and that there had also been security lapses in U.S. procedures in the transfer of information to UNOSOM II.

Despite the general acceptance among U.S. officials that this particular incident in Somalia did not compromise U.S. intelligence sources and methods, it was by no means the first compromise of U.S. intelligence by the UN during the Somalia operation. According to U.S. officials, the UN in Somalia had repeatedly failed to adequately safeguard classified information provided by the U.S. "There were earlier incidents in which information was passed to one (Somali) faction or another" said a senior U.S. official (Smith and Preston *b*: A1).

Surprisingly, there were no congressional hearings on the Somalia incident, although administration officials met with a number of members to brief them on the incident and on subsequent administration initiatives with the UN to improve UN information security procedures.

Congressional Reaction to the Mishandling of Intelligence

As might be expected, the mishandling of U.S. intelligence by the UN in Somalia generated a flurry of congressional legislative initiatives to restrict intelligence sharing with the UN. While some of these initiatives were similar to the single-issue bills introduced previously, and failed to move out of committee, most were provisions of major legislation, a significant change which reflected the increasing assertiveness of the Congress on this issue.

Introduced 25 May 1995, by Senator Snowe, *A Bill to Restrict Intelligence Sharing With the UN, S. 858,* was a single-issue measure which sought to impose even more severe restrictions on the administrations's ability to share intelligence with the UN than had been contained either in the *Contract With America* or in her previous bill, the *International Peacekeeping Policy Act of 1995*. This latest bill sought to force the administration to declare to the Congress that the provision of U.S. intelligence to the UN was in the vital national interest of the U.S.

Senator Snowe's bill would have prohibited the sharing of U.S. intelligence information with the UN or any organization affiliated with the UN unless the President certified to the appropriate committees of the Congress that the Director of Central Intelligence, in consultation with the Secretaries of Defense and State, had established the following requirements which had been formally agreed to and implemented by the UN for protecting U.S. intelligence sources and methods:

- The adoption by the UN of formal security violation and background clearance procedures.
- The agreement by the UN to protect U.S.-provided intelligence in a manner certified by the Director of Central Intelligence to be comparable to U.S. standards.
- Agreement by the UN to notify the U.S. of any unauthorized disclosure of U.S.-provided information
- Agreement by the UN to allow U.S. law enforcement personnel to participate in the investigations of such unauthorized disclosures.
- Prohibitions on access to U.S.-provided information by nationals of countries not otherwise eligible for receipt of such information.
- Prohibitions on access to U.S.-provided intelligence information by the governments of any country designated by the Secretary of State as a state supporter of terrorism.
- Prohibitions on access to U.S.-provided intelligence by governments not eligible for direct provision of such information by the U.S. through existing bilateral agreements.
- Other measures designed to protect U.S. provided intelligence information from unauthorized disclosure that were in accordance with provisions of the National Security Act of 1947 (S. 858 Placed in the Senate).

Many of the requirements called for in Senator Snowe's bill were clearly impractical, such as the adoption by the UN of background clearance procedures and the participation by U.S. law enforcement personnel in UN investigations of compromises of U.S.-supplied intelligence. In addition, the bill would have effectively prevented the administration from sharing U.S. intelligence information with any member of the UN that was not already eligible to receive such information through bilateral agreements with the U.S., thereby bringing to a halt virtually all intelligence sharing with the UN.

The bill, however, contained a further provision which stated that all these restrictions could be waived if the President provided written certification to the appropriate committees of the Congress that it was in the vital national security interest of the U.S. to share intelligence with the UN and that all possible measures had been taken to protect the information. Such certification would, however, have to be made for each instance intelligence was provided to the UN or for each document provided.

Like the compromise version of the *Contract With America,* Senator Snowe's bill contained a reporting provision which would have required that the President report quarterly to the Foreign Affairs and Intelligence Committees of the House and Senate on the types and quantities of intelligence provided to the UN and the purposes for which it was provided. Even more restrictive, and unlike any legislation on the issue previously introduced, Senator Snowe's bill would have prohibited the President from delegating or assigning the duties of the President contained in the bill. Although this bill was referred to the Senate Foreign Relations Committee on the day it was introduced, there was no additional congressional action.

Introduced by Senator Helms (R-NC) on 9 June 1995, the *Foreign Relations Revitalization Act of 1995, S. 908,* was the authorization bill for the Department of State for fiscal years 1996-1999. The major thrust of Senator Helms' bill was an attempt to force the consolidation of U.S. Foreign Affairs Agencies, abolishing the Agency for International Development, the U.S. Information Agency and the Arms Control and Disarmament Agency. However, one section of the bill dealt exclusively with U.S. intelligence sharing with the UN. As the result of an amendment offered by Senator Snowe, who also served on the Senate Foreign Relations Committee, this section incorporated wording identical to that contained in her *Bill to Restrict Intelligence Sharing With the UN,* which she had introduced several weeks earlier (Gaffney *a*: A20).

On 14 December 1995, the Senate passed an amendment to Senator Helms' bill which had been agreed to by Chairman Helms and Senator John Kerry (D-MA) (Helms-Kerry Amendment No. 3100 to S. 908). The amendment incorporated language contained in both the compromise version of the *Contract With America* and Senator Snowe's *Bill to Restrict Intelligence Sharing With the UN.* It stripped from the bill the list of specific restrictions on intelligence that had been incorporated from Senator Snowe's bill, and instead substituted language similar to that contained in the compromise version of the *Contract With America* passed by the House in February 1995.

The Helms-Kerry amendment prohibited the sharing of U.S. intelligence with the UN unless the President certified to the appropriate committees of the Congress that the Director of Central Intelligence, in consultation with the Secretaries of State and Defense, had established procedures and had worked with the UN to ensure the implementation of procedures for protecting U.S. intelligence sources and methods from unauthorized disclosure. The requirement to work with the UN to ensure implementation of the procedures was new and had not been contained in either the *Contract With America* or Senator Snowe's bill.

Drawing from language contained in Senator Snowe's bill, the amendment provided that the above requirements could be waived by the President upon written certification to the appropriate committees of the Congress that providing such information to the UN was in the national security interest of the U.S. The requirement from Senator Snowe's bill that such national security interests be deemed vital, was deleted from the amendment. The amendment also deleted the requirements, contained in Senator Snowe's bill, that the President certify that all possible measures to protect U.S. intelligence provided to the UN had been taken, and that the President make such certifications to appropriate congressional committees for each instance such information was provided or for each document provided to the UN.

The amendment retained a reporting requirement, as had been the case in both the *Contract With America* and Senator Snowe's bill, but adopted the semi-annual reporting requirement contained in the *Contract With America* instead of Senator Snowe's more restrictive quarterly reporting requirement. The Helms-Kerry Amendment also included the requirement to report the types and volume and the purposes for which U.S. intelligence was provided to the UN, a more restrictive requirement which had been included in Senator Snowe's bill, instead of the provision in the *Contract With America,* which had not required reporting of the volume of intelligence provided to the UN.

On 14 December 1995 the Senate passed the companion House measure, the *American Overseas Interests Act of 1995, H.R. 1561,* in lieu of the Senate Version of the Helms bill. No further action was taken on the Helms bill.

The *American Overseas Interests Act of 1995, H.R. 1561,* was introduced in the House on 3 May 1995 by Representative Gilman, (R-NY). In its original form, it contained no language dealing with intelligence sharing with the UN. On 14 June 1995, it was received in the Senate and on 14 December 1995, the Senate amended it by incorporating into it all the provisions of Senator Helms' *Foreign Relations Revitalization Act of 1995* and passing the resulting measure. The bill, now retitled the *Foreign Relations Revitalization Act of 1995,* contained the provisions of the Helms bill, as amended by the Helms-Kerry compromise, restricting intelligence sharing with the UN.

Since the Senate version of the bill was now substantially different from the version of the *American Overseas Interests Act of 1995* passed earlier by the House, the Senate called for a conference and appointed conferees. The bill was reported out of conference on 7 March 1995. The resulting conference report revised language in the version previously passed by the Senate. The section of the conference report dealing with intelligence sharing with the UN contained the following provisions:

- Required that procedures be established and implemented at the UN to prevent release of U.S.-supplied intelligence to foreign nationals not otherwise eligible to receive such information.
- Required that these provisions be at least as stringent as those maintained by nations with which the U.S. regularly shares similar types of intelligence.
- These requirements could be waived if the President certified to Congress that providing such information to the UN was in the U.S. national security interest.
- Provided that such a wavier must be executed by the President for each instance such information was provided to the UN or for each document provided.
- Required quarterly reports to Congress on the type, volume, and purposes of intelligence shared with the UN.
- Required a reporting annex containing a counterintelligence and security assessment of all risks, including an evaluation of any potential adverse impact on national collection systems, of providing intelligence to the UN, together with information on how such risks have been addressed (H.R. 1528).

The conference report drew on language contained in both the original unamended portion of the *Foreign Relations Revitalization Act,* which in turn had been taken from Senator Snowe's bill, and on language contained in the final Senate version of the *Foreign Relations Revitalization Act,* which had been amended by the Helms-Kerry amendment. The requirement that U.S. interests be deemed vital national security interests, which had been included in Senator Snowe's bill, was not included in the conference report. However, the waiver provision in the conference report did require that a waiver be made by the President for each instance such information was provided to the UN or for each document provided, as had been required in the earlier, more restrictive bills. The reporting requirement adopted by the conference report, which called for quarterly reports from the President to various Congressional Committees on the type, volume, and purposes of intelligence provided to the UN, was drawn from the two earlier, more restrictive bills rather than from the Helms-Kerry compromise amendment, which had contained a semi-annual reporting requirement. The requirement for an annex containing a counterintelligence and security assessment of the risks involved in providing intelligence to the UN was a new requirement.

On 12 March the House agreed to the conference report, and the report was subsequently agreed to by the Senate on 28 March. On 5 April, the bill was presented to the President, who vetoed the measure. The House failed to override the President's veto by a vote of 234-188.

The *Intelligence Authorization Act for Fiscal Year 1997, H.R. 3259,* was introduced in the House on 17 April 1996. On 22 May, Representative Sam Brownback (R-KS) introduced an amendment to the bill which would have restricted intelligence sharing with the United Nations. Representative Brownback's proposed amendment was identical to language contained in the final version of the *Foreign Relations Revitalization Act* that had been vetoed by President Clinton (H.R. 3259 Introduced).

The proposed amendment generated considerable debate on the House floor and was opposed by Representative Norm Dicks, (D-WA). Representative Dicks, in opposing the proposed amendment, stated that it would place:

> new unworkable restrictions on the U.S. sharing information with the UN — even when it is in the national interest to do so. It would make it extremely difficult to provide intelligence support to these UN activities which are supportive of U.S. foreign policy goals.

> The administration is opposed to the Brownback amendment. This amendment is identical to language contained in the conference report on the *American Overseas Interests Act,* which was vetoed by the President. As the President noted in his veto message, this amendment would unconstitutionally infringe on the President's power to conduct diplomatic relations and limit presidential control over the use of state secrets (H.R. 3259 Introduced).

Representative Dicks continued that the waiver process outlined in the amendment was too cumbersome to be practical, and that the amendment, like original versions of both the *Foreign Relations Revitalization Act* and the *Contract With America,* did not allow the President to delegate any provisions of the amendment. He concluded by stating that while he did not believe legislation to restrict the ability of the President to share intelligence with the UN was necessary, provisions regarding intelligence sharing with the UN contained in the Helms-Kerry amendment were certainly preferable to the amendment proposed by Representative Brownback.

Representative Combest (R-TX) spoke next, noting that while he agreed with the intent of Representative Brownback, he was concerned that the proposed amendment could prevent the timely sharing of intelligence with UN commands where U.S. troops were assigned and might, therefore, endanger American lives. He then proposed an amendment to the Brownback amendment. His proposal, identical to the Helms-Kerry amendment, passed on a voice vote and was incorporated into the bill. The bill passed the House on 22 May 1996 and was placed on the Senate calendar on 23 May 1996. As of August 1996, there had been no Senate action on the House bill (H.R. 3259 Introduced).

As the executive branch has continued to move forward with initiatives to expand intelligence sharing with the UN in support of peace operations, the Congress has become increasingly assertive on the issue, as evidenced by the evolution of congressionally sponsored legislation to restrict the ability of the executive to share intelligence with the UN from single-issue bills with little chance of passage, to provisions now included in major legislation.

Executive reaction to such Congressional legislative initiatives moved from simply ignoring such initiatives to active opposition and presidential vetoes. Following the intelligence breach in Somalia, the issue has become so politicized that it is now impossible to achieve any bipartisan consensus for the administration's position. The administration has abandoned any attempt to articulate its position and simply uses the veto to protect intelligence sharing with the UN.

THE CONGRESSIONAL — EXECUTIVE STALEMATE AND IMPLICATIONS FOR THE FUTURE

The constitutional tension between the Congress and the executive over foreign policy has become reinvigorated following the end of the Cold War. The re-emergence of this friction has in large measure been driven by the disappearance of the strategic threat posed by the Soviet Union. Congress has generally been willing to defer to the President on foreign policy issues which involve a strategic threat to the U.S. During the Cold War a wide range of foreign policy issues were affected by the strategic threat from the Soviet Union. This enhanced the power of the executive relative to the Congress and tended to mute partisan debate over foreign policy issues.

For its part, the administration is frustrated with the constraints imposed on intelligence sharing by the current narrowly defined and restrictive concept of operations process. The administration would like to significantly expand intelligence sharing with the UN, not only to help ensure the success of peace operations, but as a means to influence the UN on a variety of issues. There is a recognition within the administration, however, that relations with the Congress on the issue have deteriorated to the point that a formal declaration of such a policy shift is impossible.

The problem for the Congress is that as a political issue, intelligence sharing with the UN is minor, obscure and generates little public interest. Therefore, despite congressional attempts to insert restrictive language into major legislation, the President's threats of veto remain effective, for the Congress does not want to be seen delaying important legislation for what is viewed by the public as a minor issue. However, the resulting congressional and public furor over any future compromise of intelligence in a UN setting could make even the administration's veto threats ineffective in stopping future legislation to restrict intelligence sharing with the UN.

Chapter 8

FUTURE ISSUES

The prospects for the UN in the maintenance of international peace and security, and the potential role for intelligence in support of that objective, depend on the nature of the UN as an international organization of nation states. The tension between the quest for collective security and the interests of states remains. The end of the global confrontation between the U.S. and the USSR facilitated UN decisionmaking and made action possible but did not greatly alter the configuration of physical or political power in international relations. The future of peace operations and the role of intelligence in a UN context have changed significantly, but the conflict between national interest and multilateral process continues.

Major Crone analyzes the UN Charter as a basis for the expanded use of force in UN peace operations. He sees a post-Cold War change in the UN's responsibility to maintain international peace and security, and in any sovereign state's capability and right to use force. Analyzing Boutros-Ghali's definitions of peacekeeping in terms of the UN Charter, Crone finds support for these concepts. The end of superpower paralysis has allowed the UN to assert authority to intervene for humanitarian purposes. However, the Charter also recognizes the state's right to self-defense and prohibits the UN from intervening in domestic affairs. Post-Cold War euphoria prompted UN activism, but results have been mixed. When the UN has used force in the context of civil wars, the power of nationalism has prevailed.

Margaret Mitchell employed a case studies approach to the problem of using UN peacekeepers for humanitarian intervention, looking at UNPROFOR in the Former Yugoslavia, UNOSOM in Somalia, and UNAMIR in Rwanda. Impartiality is necessary for peacekeeping but cannot be maintained when the peacekeepers use force. Neutrality is the first casualty in a humanitarian intervention, and the UN becomes part of the problem. She concludes that humanitarian crises which require use of an external military force are man-made and cannot be solved by providing humanitarian aid.

Intelligence in a UN context contains inherent opportunities and risks. Lieutenant Commander Quigley shows how intelligence assets may be applied to enforcement of international environmental law. The intelligence tool can become a deterrent on behalf of an international legal regime, but at some cost: some resources are no longer dedicated to the supporting country's defense. Captain Hudgins looks at the weakness of the IAEA safeguards regime and the counterintelligence risk of relationships between the IAEA and intelligence. Iraq and North Korea were successes, but the next generation of proliferators have been put on notice. Intelligence sharing with the IAEA is useful, necessary, and difficult. It should be a component of the U.S. intelligence role in nonproliferation but should not replace a unilateral capability. Lieutenant Allen cautions that it is unrealistic to expect U.S. intelligence provided to the Security Council or to the UN bureaucracy to outweigh the political pressure to approve UN missions with flawed mandates. Even so, the U.S. and other members of the Security Council should employ their national intelligence agencies to assess the prospects for a proposed UN operation and vote against those with little chance for success.

THE USE OF FORCE UNDER THE EMERGING UN SYSTEM

Gary L. Crone
Major, U.S. Air Force Reserve
September 1995

JUST CAUSE

The Christian approach to war has been guided by the teachings of St. Thomas Aquinas. The cornerstone of his thinking was the idea of "just cause." To conduct a just war, certain conditions must be met:

1. There has to be proper authority (private individuals could not declare war).
2. Just cause must exist.
3. The nation waging the war must have the right intentions to achieve some good and not to be merely fighting out of malice, hatred or revenge.

In *De Jure Belli ac Pace,* Hugo Grotius began to develop a secular doctrine independent of religious beliefs. Grotius developed four principles of warfare:

1. Only lawful authority could undertake war.
2. War could be used to defend persons or property.
3. Preemptive strikes were permissible to thwart anticipated dangers, provided the danger was "immediate and imminent."
4. War was a proper instrument to inflict punishment on a state that caused injury to another state.

Today the emerging international system retains the doctrine of state sovereignty as the centerpiece of international diplomacy. Modern interpretations of the UN Charter are challenging the right of states to exercise the use of force under the doctrine of sovereignty. Just as the international system is evolving, the doctrine of sovereignty is also evolving. The UN

Charter is providing UN member-states with new opportunities to shape the UN's role of enforcing peace and security. The UN is taking advantage of the renewed cooperation in the UN General Assembly and the Security Council to expand its military operations into areas traditionally considered internal disputes. These interventions in the internal affairs of other states are often controversial and costly in money and human casualties. Simultaneously, member-states are evaluating whether their national interests justify the costs of such operations.

UNDERSTANDING THE LEGAL LIMITS OF PEACEKEEPING

The UN has traditionally used force to maintain or restore international peace and security through peacekeeping operations. The term peacekeeping, however, does not appear anywhere in the United Nations Charter. Legal scholars generally accept the position that traditional peacekeeping operations are outgrowths of Chapter VI of the UN Charter. The complexity of modern peacekeeping operations, however, raises new questions regarding state sovereignty. Many missions have involved intervention and use of force without the consent of the disputing parties. Understanding the extent to which UN operations may intervene in internal affairs of state, therefore, first requires a basic understanding of peacekeeping principles.

LEGAL EVOLUTION OF PEACEKEEPING

The Meaning of the Term "Peacekeeping"

The term "peacekeeping" has evolved through diplomatic dialogue in the United Nations. Most writings on United Nations peacekeeping include references to the United Nations Charter as a basis for conducting peacekeeping operations. The origin of the term "peacekeeping" is covered in many Congressional Research Service (CRS) Reports to Congress. Marjorie Ann Browne, a Specialist in International Relations, Foreign Affairs and National Defense Division of the CRS, has written "United Nations Peacekeeping: Historical Overview and Current Issues," which provides the basic background, definitions and general principles of the origins of the term peacekeeping. As Browne points out: "In the absence of a permanent United Nations peace or police force, UN peacekeeping has evolved on an *ad hoc* basis" (3). The United Nations members have agreed to establish peacekeeping operations for a variety of reasons over the course of its history. The operations or missions traditionally took the form of observer missions.

Traditional Principles of Peacekeeping

Peacekeeping missions, by design, recognize the sovereignty of the disputing states. The central concepts of observer missions are contained in *The Blue Helmets, A Review of United Nations Peace-keeping*. The book traces certain principles fundamental to all observer peacekeeping missions. These principles include consent of the host governments, agreement of the Security Council, availability of troops, agreement to a cease-fire by the conflicting parties, unrestricted access, freedom of movement, and a neutral United Nations force (UN *g*). Traditional peacekeeping principles were outgrowths of Cold War politics and an international system that had to operate under a modified sovereign state system, or superpower state system. Under the superpower state system, the inability of the United States and Soviet Union to cooperate in the Security Council prevented the UN from exercising authority over the use of force. With the removal of Cold War politics from the Security Council, the UN Charter is now shaping a new and evolving international system.

PEACEKEEPING TERMINOLOGY

New Terminology Reflects Changes in Old Legal Norms

The emerging international system has created what is often called "second generation" peacekeeping missions. These missions contain new terms and language in an attempt to capture the tenets of an emerging international system. These tenets now include peacekeeping, peacemaking, preventive deployment, and peace-building. This new system is moving toward greater globalism and continues to de-emphasize the sovereignty of the state. Global markets now transcend traditional state borders. Ideals, such as international human rights, also transcend national borders and influence the political debates of the UN over when and how to use force to secure international peace. Many of these ideals loom on the horizon as potential general principles of international law that could bind individual state action.

The idea of peacekeeping evolved during the Cold War, when the ability of the Security Council to use the available tools under the UN Charter was extremely limited. Cold War politics, as a practical matter, left the UN unable to act without the consent of the disputing parties. The veto power under the Security Council rules of procedure generally ensured the UN could not act as a unified body. Since most international conflicts during the Cold War involved bipolar politics, the Security Council rarely acted as a united body.

Modern Meaning of Peacekeeping

UN Secretary-General Boutros-Ghali recently defined the term peacekeeping in *An Agenda for Peace* (UN *b*). Boutros-Ghali says that peacekeeping:

> [i]s the deployment of a United Nations presence in the field, hitherto, with the consent of all the parties concerned, normally involving United Nations military and/or police personnel and frequently civilians as well. Peacekeeping is a technique that expands the possibilities for the prevention of conflict and the making of peace (45).

Under Boutros-Ghali's definition, consent remains the key factor in any peacekeeping operation. Simply put, if you do not have the consent of all disputing parties, and the UN passes a resolution to use force against any of the parties, the operation is not a peacekeeping operation.

The justification for peacekeeping resides under Chapter VI of the Charter. An example of a Chapter VI peacekeeping operation is the United Nations mission in the Western Sahara (MINURSO). In MINURSO, military observers are in place to monitor the cease-fire between Moroccan and POLISARIO forces. Other examples include UNFICYP in Cyprus, and UNTSO and MFO in the Middle East.

Chapter VI (Peacekeeping Operations)

Chapter VI provides an implied basis for peacekeeping operations. Under this Chapter, members to any dispute that "endanger[s] the maintenance of international peace" (Art. 33) must first seek peaceful solutions to their disputes. Chapter VI spells out the options members agreed to follow in resolving disputes. These options serve as the basis for which states have agreed to restrain their sovereign right to use force in the resolution of disputes. The options available to the disputing parties include negotiation, arbitration, judicial settlement, resort to regional agencies or arrangements, or "other peaceful means of their own choice" (Art. 33). The "other peaceful means" has traditionally included requesting the UN to provide peacekeeping forces with the consent of the disputing parties.

If the disputing parties are unable to resolve the dispute through the options available under Chapter VI, they "shall refer it to the Security Council" (Art. 36). Chapter VI also gives the Security Council authority to:

> investigate any dispute or any situation which might lead to international friction or give rise to a dispute, in order to determine whether the continuance of the dispute or situation is likely to endanger the maintenance of international peace and security (Art. 34).

This Article provides the Security Council with the authority to investigate and decide whether a threat to international peace exists. The Article also clearly implies that the Security Council is expected to take action if the disputing parties have failed to resolve their dispute.

Peacemaking

Peacemaking is also defined in Boutros-Ghali's *An Agenda for Peace.* Boutros Ghali says that peacemaking is:

> action to bring hostile parties to agreement, essentially through such peaceful means as those foreseen in Chapter VI of the Charter of the United Nations (UN *b*: 49).

Peacemaking clearly implies the use of diplomatic tools short of the use of force. Traditional peacekeeping operations could also be justified under the catchall phrase "other peaceful means of their choice," since such operations require the consent of all parties. These missions generally are observer or noncombatant operations. As such, peacemaking and peacekeeping are essentially Chapter VI operations. Consequently, there is no meaningful legal difference between peacekeeping operations and peacemaking operations regarding state sovereignty. Both require consent of the states involved.

Preventive deployment

Boutros-Ghali also introduced a variation of the traditional peacekeeping concept with the idea of preventive deployment. This concept expands international jurisdiction to the UN to intervene in the internal affairs of a state before the commencement of hostilities. As such, it reduces the traditional restraints on UN peacekeeping operations under Chapter VI. Boutros-Ghali has provided examples of when such operations would occur:

> [I]n conditions of national crisis there could be preventive deployment at the request of the Government or all parties concerned, or with their consent; in inter-State disputes such deployment could take place when two countries feel that a United Nations presence on both sides of their border can discourage hostilities; furthermore, preventive deployment could take place when a country feels threatened and requests the deployment of an appropriate United Nations presence along its side of the border alone (UN *b*: 49).

Boutros-Ghali considers preventive deployments "of critical importance" in humanitarian operations. Boutros-Ghali also recognizes that preventive deployment must "respect the sovereignty of the State" and occur "with the consent of the affected country and, in principle, on the basis of an appeal by that country." Exercising the expanded international jurisdiction of the UN to take preventive action, therefore, is preconditioned on consent. The need for consent keeps preventive deployment operations clearly in the realm of traditional peacekeeping concepts and Chapter VI of the UN Charter. An example of preventive deployment was the deployment of one thousand troops, military observers, and civilian police to Macedonia in 1993. Consequently, no significant legal difference exists between the authority to conduct preventive deployments and traditional peacekeeping operations.

Peacekeeping, peacemaking, and preventive deployments essentially are all Chapter VI operations.

Peace-building or nation-building

Another idea introduced in *An Agenda for Peace* was post-conflict peace-building. Peace-building expands UN international jurisdiction to periods after the hostilities have ended. Peace-building involves rebuilding institutions and infrastructures of a country after a conflict has ended, to give peace a chance to survive. Peace-building is the flip side of preventive deployment. Under a peace-building idea, Boutros-Ghali envisions the use of military personnel for such activities as demilitarization of a nation or region. Demilitarization, for example, could include the removal of mines from a combatant's territory.

Ambassador Albright, Lieutenant General Rose, Ambassador Redman and General Shalikashvili confer at the 1994 opening of the U.S. Embassy in Sarajevo.

photo used with permission

An example of peace-building or nation-building was the United Nations Transitional Authority in Cambodia (UNTAC). UNTAC placed military and civilian personnel in Cambodia to help the people of Cambodia reestablish a sovereign, independent state. UNTAC helped establish a multiparty transitional government in Cambodia in September 1993. After the transitional government was formed, UNTAC left the country. Peace-building is an extension of peacekeeping. Boutros-Ghali has explained:

> [T]he link becomes evident between peacekeeping and peace-building. Just as demilitarized zones may serve the cause of preventive diplomacy and preventive deployment to avoid conflict peace-building [serves] as a measure for heightening the sense of security and encouraging the parties to turn their energies to the work of peaceful restoration of their societies (UN *b*: 62).

Peace-building, therefore, is a form of peacekeeping distinguished only in terms of when it occurs on the continuum of maintaining and establishing peace under Chapter VI.

Peace-building assumes the cooperation of an existing host nation government that is internationally recognized as legitimate and capable of exercising sovereign jurisdiction in the international system. Since peace-building requires the cooperation of the host nation, the UN's ability to implement peace-building operations is also preconditioned on consent. Since the cooperation of the nation involved is a prerequisite for peace-building operations, peace-building is also essentially a Chapter VI operation for purposes of state sovereignty issues.

The UN has expanded its peacekeeping missions to include peacemaking, preventive deployment, and peace-building. This expansion of UN international jurisdiction into the internal affairs of a state potentially conflicts with the doctrine of nonintervention.

INTERVENTION FOR PEACE

In 1988 a significant event occurred in world politics when the Soviet Union and the United States chose to cooperate more in the United Nations. UN operations involving the use of force increased after 1988 as the Security Council no longer deadlocked over the establishment of United Nations military missions. State leaders and the Secretary-General of the United Nations began expanding their vision of the role that the United Nations would play in suppressing acts of aggression. Since 1988, the UN has created 20 military operations, 13 of which continue today. Many of these missions are intranational in nature, involving intervention in the internal affairs of a sovereign state or failed state. These operations authorize the introduction of forces on the ground to stop ongoing hostilities. As such, they are more likely to place UN forces in open combat than traditional observer missions.

The use of the "peace" language in describing non-traditional peacekeeping missions clouds the legal issues of state sovereignty. These intranational missions are a post-Cold War development, reflecting an evolving international social order. Under the evolving social order, states are more inclined to recognize internal disorder as a threat to international peace. This threat to international peace thus opens the door to UN member-states' requests for the UN to take collective action against the individual state to restore peace.

In this sense, the emerging international system is recognizing that any threat to peace, even intranational disorder, is international in nature. The post-Cold War direction of the UN has seemingly recognized a concept of international peace that transcends state sovereignty rights. This globalization process is serving as a catalyst for the UN to exercise increased jurisdiction over traditionally internal affairs of state.

Discussions abound on the utility of UN involvement in countries where ethnic conflicts thrive, such as in Bosnia, Cambodia, the Western Sahara, and Somalia. For example, the question in Bosnia is whether the United Nations can play a successful role in halting ethnic civil war. The issues are charged with political and moral questions that often color the legal analysis used to justify the operations. The moral question, as in Bosnia, is often whether United Nations intervention is morally justified even if the Charter does not allow intervention.

Others are raising moral issues about the use of United Nations forces in the internal affairs of a state. In a *World Press Review* article dealing with the United Nations intervention in Somalia, the author of "When and How to Send in Troops," argues that the end of the Cold War does not justify interference or neocolonialism in the Third World even if ethnic feuds threaten the very existence of a nation (Sid-Ahmed: 10). He argues the original intent of the United Nations was to control the behavior between states. He believes UN operations were never intended to resolve internal disputes.

In an editorial of the *London Financial Times,* Robert Graham offers an opinion that Article 51 of the United Nations Charter, regarding acts of war, clearly suggests that organized armed attacks against states must occur before nations can intervene in the internal affairs of other nations (C3). He argues, for example, that Bush and Reagan incorrectly applied the United Nations Charter as justification for invading Panama and bombing Libya. Graham's analysis underscores a continuing conflict between state sovereignty rights and the right of intervention. A question, therefore, exists about when and under what conditions the UN Charter permits intervention in internal disputes.

Chapter VII (Enforcement Operations)

Chapter VII of the UN Charter provides the implementing procedures for an enforcement action delegated to member-states, and is the heart of

UN warmaking. The language in the Chapter is interesting from a legal standpoint. On the one hand, the Security Council is required to determine the existence of a threat to international peace and to decide what measures shall be taken to restore international peace and security (Chap. VII, Art. 39). On the other hand, however, the Security Council "may" but is not required to actually do anything to bring an end to the dispute.

Enforcement strategies under the UN Charter fall generally into two categories: military and nonmilitary. Military enforcement strategies are commonly called *peace enforcement.* Peace enforcement is defined in Gareth Evans' *Cooperating for Peace.* He defines peace enforcement as "the threat or use of military force, in pursuit of peaceful objectives, in response to conflicts or other major security crises" (Evans: 12). Evans' definition does not preclude internal conflicts under the "other major security crises" category. Under his definition, the UN could intervene if the UN determined the conflict presented the international community with a "major security crisis."

Identifying Internal Conflict and Civil War

UNIKOM observer in southern Iraq, May 1991. *photo used with permission*

Inherent in the UN Charter, however, are limitations regarding the intervention by the UN as a multilateral body in the internal conflicts of sovereign political entities. Chapter I of the UN Charter, which contains the Purposes and Principles of the UN, specifically states in Article 2 (7) that:

> Nothing contained in the present Charter shall authorize the United Nations to intervene in matters which are essentially within the domestic jurisdiction of any state or shall require the Members to submit such matters to settlement under the present Charter.

The language in Article 2 creates a tension between the traditional international law concept of nonintervention, and enforcement actions authorized under Chapter VII. A question thus arises, under the Charter, about when an enforcement action, whose purpose is the intervention in internal matters of state, is permitted under the Charter and international law.

Unlike peacekeeping operations, enforcement actions, under the present Charter, do not require the consent of the disputing parties. Enforcement actions, therefore, are not subordinate to the domestic jurisdiction of the state granting consent under the doctrine of state sovereignty. As such, enforcement actions, although dubbed "peace" enforcement, are really actions of the UN waging war on or in a state. Enforcement actions are authorized under Chapter VII of the UN Charter. Chapter VII controls the procedures for UN enforcement actions. As such, it provides the legal basis for using force, under the auspices of the UN, to conduct warfighting.

Whether a UN operation is a peacekeeping operation or an enforcement action has real ramifications on the manner and scope in which the UN may intervene in the internal affairs of a state. If the operation is a peacekeeping operation under Chapter VI, the UN must have the consent of the parties and recognize the sovereignty of the state. If the UN is implementing an enforcement action, no such consent is needed. Consent is not needed because the UN Charter already allows the Security Council to usurp the domestic jurisdiction of the state through the provisions of Chapter VII.

Sanctions

Nonmilitary enforcement actions take the form of sanctions. The UN Charter anticipates the Security Council will contemplate using sanctions before any military action. The controlling article is Article 41. It states:

> The Security Council may decide what measures not involving the use of armed force are to be employed to give effect to its decisions, and it may call upon the Members of the United Nations to apply such measures. These may include complete or partial interruption of economic relations and of rail, sea, air, postal, telegraphic, radio, and other means of communication, and the severance of diplomatic relations.

The Charter anticipates the Security Council will consider adopting sanctions before using force to restore peace. The legal implication is that the Security Council should not use force unless sanctions are considered first.

Intervention When Sanctions are Inadequate

Chapter VII also provides actions the security Council may take after considering sanctions, or if sanctions fail. Article 42 of Chapter VII states:

> Should the Security Council consider that measures provided for in Article 41 would be inadequate or have proved to be inadequate, it may take such action by air, sea, or land forces as may be necessary to maintain or restore international peace and security.

Two facts are clear under Article 42. First, the Security Council may act without first using sanctions if the Council determines sanctions "would be inadequate." Secondly, even if sanctions would fail or have failed, the Security Council is not required to take any further action. The Charter language merely says the Council "may" take action. Action is not mandatory.

Sanctions restrict a state's ability to engage in conduct normally reserved to the sovereign government of the state. Evans defines sanctions as:

> measures, not involving the use or threat of military force, designed to compel or bring to an end a course of action by a state or party; they function primarily by denying access to goods, services or other externally provided requirements necessary or important to maintenance of their economic, social or political infrastructure or well-being (Evans: 12).

Examples of UN sanctions were the mandatory UN Security Council arms embargo and General Assembly oil embargo against South Africa. The use of sanctions against South Africa limited that country's ability to interact in the international community. The imposition of these two sanctions clearly restricted South Africa's ability to exercise its sovereign rights as a state. The effects of sanctions were to limit South Africa's ability to function within the international system until South Africa changed its racial policies and reformed its government. Scholars generally agree the UN sanctions played a major role in effecting fundamental political change in South Africa.

Although political and economic sanctions may not involve the use of force, sanctions may indirectly restrain a state's sovereign right to use force. A desired effect of the sanction might be to adversely affect a state's ability to effectively wage war. The sanction provisions under the Charter, therefore, provide the members of the UN with a nonmilitary means to restrain a state's ability and desire to use force.

The Issue of Nonintervention

Although the Charter gives the UN authority to use force, the legal concept of nonintervention recognized under Article 1 of the Charter places a duty on states to refrain from acting. Gordan points out: "Nonintervention is a fundamental principle of international law based upon the sovereignty, equality, and political independence of States. It imposes a duty on States to refrain from intervention in the internal affairs of other States" (519-520). Although literature on nonintervention has traditionally focused on unilateral intervention, the obligation also extends to organizations such as the UN. The difficulty the UN faces when intervening in internal conflicts is that "classical theory of sovereignty permits outside support for an incumbent government against internal political rebellion or succession, but considers similar support for insurgent contingents illegal" (Gordan: 530). The classical approach, therefore, tends to favor the sovereign rights of the incumbent government and does not support internal intervention. Whenever an incumbent government resists UN intervention, the UN must resolve the tensions between the sovereign right of a state under the legal principle of nonintervention and the international jurisdiction of the UN to enforce the purpose of the UN, which is to maintain international peace.

UN Authority to Intervene

The fact that traditional international norms under a state-based system recognize the idea of nonintervention does not mean the doctrine of nonintervention remains static. As Gordan points out, the exact limits and boundaries of nonintervention are "incapable of precise and permanent definition, however, because domestic jurisdiction is determined by the development of international relations, which is dynamic" (Gordan: 530). The "dynamic" nature of international relations, therefore, can cause international legal norms to continue to evolve as political relationships change between states.

In the UN, the former legal counsel to the United Nations, Paul Szasz, has enunciated six factors he believes gives the UN jurisdiction over internal conflicts under the emerging international system. They are:

1. Major acts of internal outrage during the conflict;
2. Disputes of a considerable, sizc, intensity, and length;
3. The likelihood of insurgency, or groups of countries assisting both sides;
4. Actual or potential spill-over across international borders;
5. Classification of the conflict as a colonial conflict; and
6. Some part of the dispute is subject to international agreement (Szasz: 345).

The UN is probably more likely to intervene as the number of Szasz factors present in a crisis also increase. Factors 3-6 clearly have international earmarks. Factors 1-3 fall into the "major" crisis category Gareth Evans enunciated, and the UN could interpret them as international in nature.

INTERVENTION FOR HUMANITARIAN PURPOSES

The UN has traditionally dealt with humanitarian relief problems through its various international commissions and organizations. International relief organizations have existed for decades. Intervention in the internal affairs of a state for humanitarian purposes without the consent of the affected nation, however, is a recent phenomenon at the UN.

Humanitarian intervention, in many ways, is the most difficult form of internal intervention to justify under the existing international legal system. Although humanitarian intervention may be popular for political, moral, or religious reasons, current principles of international law constrain the UN from acting. The use of force is presently based on secular justifications. The UN may, therefore, have a justification to intervene if the ideal, such as humanitarian reasons, is one accepted as a general principle of international law. If the civilized nations recognize specific humanitarian principles, the principles could meet the general principle requirements under Article 38 of the statute of the International Court of Justice.

The UN must also consider whether the intervention is based on a human rights violation. If a legitimate government exists, the UN cannot justify intervention under Chapter VI without the consent of the state in which the humanitarian assistance is needed. If the humanitarian problem does not threaten international peace, the UN could not proceed under Chapter VII. Regional organizations could not act under Chapter VIII unless a basis for intervention existed under the principles recognized in Chapter VI or VII.

LIMITATIONS ON THE GROUNDS FOR HUMANITARIAN INTERVENTION

If the UN can intervene for purely humanitarian reasons in the internal affairs of a state or failed state, the humanitarian right must be one that is either already recognized under the UN or one that is a generally recognized principle of international law that the UN has the authority to enforce. The modern notion of human rights adopted in Boutros-Ghali's *An Agenda for Peace* is the most recent example of an increasing movement among international political scholars. Boutros-Ghali's notion rests on the belief that "all peoples, both collectively and individually, [possess] fundamental human rights that are not subject to the sole jurisdiction of the individual state" (UN *b*: 61). Boutros-Ghali apparently is seeking to expand the basic notions of self-determination and independence to include other human rights akin to an international "Bill of Rights." If the UN accepts Boutros-Ghali's approach, the UN jurisdiction over traditional state sovereignty and human rights would expand. The expansion would broaden UN justifications to intervene in the internal affairs of another state for humanitarian reasons.

Under the present UN Charter, the UN cannot interfere in the purely domestic affairs of a state. Boutros-Ghali's notion of fundamental, international human rights, however, restricts a state's sovereign right to determine what freedoms to grant its citizens. Entrusting the UN to protect fundamental rights would give the UN jurisdiction not only to determine what human rights are international, but also to use force to ensure the international rights are available to all citizens of the world. Under Boutros-Ghali's interpretation of the UN Charter, the UN, acting as a multilateral body, has the legal authority to use force against an individual state to conduct humanitarian operations.

Humanitarian Intervention Doctrine is Evolving

As David Kresock observes:

> [S]tates have asserted the right to intervene in the affairs of another state when attempting to protect [their] nationals within the jurisdiction of a foreign state, to protect the nationals of a third state, or even to protect the nationals of the state against which it directs corrective steps (Kresock: 213).

As Kresock points out, though, the doctrine of humanitarian intervention has not been widely accepted for two reasons: 1) lack of consensus on the definition of humanitarian intervention, and 2) the potential for powerful states to abuse the doctrine.

Despite the apparent widespread acceptance that a state could violate another state's territorial integrity to rescue nationals, the principle that an international body or a state could intervene to end human rights violations does not exist under the traditional sovereign state system. Under the system that is currently evolving, however, the case for humanitarian intervention is gaining support. Scholars today add some perspective to humanitarian intervention by contending that the modern doctrine of sovereignty should give way to the concept of "popular sovereignty." He points out:

> International law is still concerned with the protection of sovereignty, but, in its modern sense, the object of protection is not the power base of the tyrant who rules directly by naked power or through the apparatus of a totalitarian political order, but the continuing capacity of a population freely to express and effect choices about the identities and policies of its governors (Reisman: 872).

This approach represents an important change in philosophy. Although similar to Boutros-Ghali's *An Agenda for Peace,* Reisman's approach completely shifts the focus of sovereignty from the leaders to the people. Under Reisman's definition, humanitarian intervention would not violate state sovereignty because the aid is aimed at the population, not the government.

Language in UN Charter Supports Intervention

Reisman's approach has support in the UN Charter. Under paragraph three of Article 1, the Charter states one of the purposes of the UN is:

> To achieve international co-operation in solving international problems of an economic, social, cultural, or humanitarian character, and in promoting and encouraging respect for human rights and for fundamentals freedoms for all without distinction as to race, sex, language, or religion.

Although the Charter does not list human rights violations as a specific basis for the use of force, the Charter clearly anticipates that the UN, as a multilateral body, could agree on what constituted fundamental freedoms. Once the UN has agreed, as a body, on what constitutes a fundamental human right, that right would become a general principle of international law under the present international legal system.

Since states have ceded the sovereign right to define fundamental rights to the UN, the UN could probably enforce the human rights as an extension of the right to use force to maintain peace and security.

The purposes of Article 1 also lend credence to the argument that humanitarian intervention is justified if it is the only way the UN can achieve cooperation in solving international problems of a "humanitarian character." Humanitarian intervention, under Article I, would serve as the preserver of fundamental human rights and as the preserver of sovereignty itself. Kresock has argued a similar point:

> As with the doctrine of "sovereignty," international law must evolve to view all peoples, both collectively and individually, as possessing fundamental human rights which are not subject to the sole jurisdiction of the individual state (Kresock: 235).

Additionally, nothing in the UN Charter defines human rights as a domestic issue. Under Chapter VII, only matters that are "essentially" domestic are exempt from UN intervention. Since the Charter does not define human rights issues as domestic, the UN arguably has a basis to treat human rights violations as a violation of a generally accepted principle of international law. Since human rights protection is a purpose of the UN, the use of force to maintain human rights as a precondition of peace seems merited under the present Charter.

The scope and authority of the UN to use force, as spelled out in Chapter I, Article 2 of the Charter, also does not prohibit humanitarian intervention. Article 2 states, in pertinent part:

> All Members shall refrain from the threat or use of force against the territorial integrity or political independence of any state, or in other manner inconsistent with the Purposes of the United Nations.

Since advocating fundamental human rights is a stated purpose under the Charter, humanitarian intervention is clearly consistent with the purpose of the UN. What is more important, Article 2 only restricts the use of force by the UN if the force is "against" the territorial integrity or political independence of the state. Since humanitarian intervention is not directed "against" territory, it does not violate Article 2. Also, since the intervention does not attempt to dictate the form of government of the people, humanitarian intervention would not violate the common law doctrine of nonintervention.

Failed States

The recent cases of Somalia and Cambodia show the need for drastic humanitarian intervention to prevent massive loss of life from starvation and sickness in cases where the state as an institution has ceased to exist. Nowhere is the tension greater between the purpose of the UN to foster and protect humanitarian rights and the traditional principles of nonintervention than in cases of "failed states." A failed state no longer has a legitimate government that can exert domestic jurisdiction or its sovereign rights in the international arena. The principle of nonintervention does not apply in a failed state because the doctrine presumes an incumbent government exists and the government can exercise sovereignty rights in the international arena.

The issue of whether a failed state has any legal protection under the doctrine of sovereignty is a recent phenomenon. For the failed state, the UN seems to have apparent authority under the Charter to intervene with an enforcement action if the internal conflict threatens international peace. The apparent authority would derive from the idea that since no government existed to assert sovereignty rights, the UN would not be violating a government's rights by intervening. Also, the action would not be an intervention in the internal affairs of a state since, the "state" as a sovereign institution, no longer existed.

Another issue arises if the internal intervention deprives people living in a state the right to self-determination, freedom, and independence (Perkins: 171). Scholars generally accept the notion that the right to self-determination can exist independent of state sovereignty. If the right exists independently of the state, the right would not disappear with the failing of the state as a sovereign institution. In Somalia, for example, the state ceased to exist as an institution, but the people living in Somalia still retained certain fundamental rights under the international system. These rights included self-determination and independence. Any intervention by the UN that violated the right to self-determination, therefore, would violate international law.

Although self-determination principles limit the form of UN intervention, the UN can probably intervene, provided self-determination rights are protected. UN enforcement operations in failed states seem appropriate and legal, provided the UN ensures that the principles of self-determination, freedom, and independence are protected during any intervention.

Scholars also agree that exercising self-determination-related rights are prerequisites for establishing a legitimate government. A failed state, therefore, cannot emerge as a sovereign state unless the people in the failed state have an opportunity to exercise their right to self-determination. Since self-determination-related rights are prerequisites to the reestablishment of a legitimate sovereign government, the UN probably could not successfully conclude an internal intervention mission unless the UN also set mission objectives that protected and encouraged people in the failed state to successfully exercise their self-determination rights.

Dissenters could argue that any intervention into the state violates the political integrity of the state. This argument might be persuasive in the absence of the UN Charter. Under the Charter, however, states have already ceded domestic jurisdiction to the UN for determining fundamental human rights and procedures to intervene without state consent. Under the Charter humanitarian intervention seems justified, provided the following criteria are met:

1. A fundamental human right is violated;
2. The UN has decided sanctions would be ineffectual or have failed;
3. Force is not directed at changing or altering the territory of the state; and
4. The right to self-determination is protected.

Meeting the above criteria would preserve the fundamental human rights postulated under the Charter. The above criteria are also consistent with the evolving notion of nonintervention and state sovereignty.

PRACTICAL LIMITATIONS

Despite the existence of a legal basis for internal intervention, using the enforcement action provisions of the UN Charter has practical limitations. Recent examples in Cambodia and Somalia display the difficulties of internal intervention.

The Secretary-General established a 20-member military liaison team in Cambodia to report progress on reconstruction in Cambodia after UNTAC left the country. The team reported that internal security had become more precarious since UNTAC left Cambodia, banditry was widespread, and that large influxes of refugees threatened the success of reconstruction ("Cambodia": 38).

Difficulties in Cambodia show that the success of any UN intervention in the internal affairs of a state will ultimately depend upon the state's ability to reconcile the very difficulties that caused the intervention in the first place. Any UN intervention operation presumes the people of the state will eventually assume the sovereign responsibilities of the state institution and cease to be a ward of the UN.

In Somalia, a UN Commission of Inquiry was established in 1993 to report on the United Nations Operation in Somalia (UNOSOM II). The Commission reported on both the humanitarian mission and the political and security situation in Somalia. The findings of the Commission revealed several limitations inherent in any UN intervention in the internal affairs of a state. The findings also reflect the inability of the UN to replace the social institutions of the failed state.

The Commission reported that forced disarmament in Somalia:

> had proved unattainable without exposing military and civilian international staff to hostile attacks resulting in casualties. Therefore, in the present context, forced disarmament of the militia under Chapter VII of the UN Charter should be abandoned ("Somalia: UNOSOM": 23).

The Commission report clearly acknowledged the limitations of trying to conduct operations traditionally left to the sovereign state. The report went on to recommend:

> [T]he UN should refrain from undertaking further peace enforcement actions within the internal conflicts of States and that it should, where necessary, continue peacekeeping operations of the traditional type under its Charter ("Somalia: UNOSOM": 23).

The second recommendation underscored the difficulty inherent in intervening in internal affairs even if the UN had the international jurisdiction to supersede state sovereignty. The basis for the recommendation was the conclusion that "states are not prepared to accept substantial casualties for causes unrelated to their national interests." The "national interest" factor places severe practical limitations on the UN's ability to sponsor internal intervention. In future operations, the question of UN authority to intervene may becomc secondary to the larger practical issue of whether member states feel intervention is necessary for their own national interests.

The current situation in Bosnia-Herzegovina represents the present tension between the need for internal intervention and the will to intervene. Under the Reisman approach and Boutros-Ghali's vision, the UN probably has the authority to intervene in the internal affairs of Bosnia for humanitarian reasons. The documented plight of refugees and "ethnic cleansing" occurring in Bosnia give the UN a basis for intervention. The same internal conflicts are also threats to rcgional peace that would warrant an enforcement action under Chapter VII. The limited and wavering involvement in UN military operations by its member-states reflects, in part, the practical problem of getting states to accept substantial casualties for a cause that is unrelated to their national interests. Without a strong connection between the internal threat and national interests, states will continue to be reluctant to apply the jurisdiction of the UN in support of internal intervention enforcement operations.

CONCLUSION

The international system is operating under a set of international legal principles that have evolved over the past several hundred years. A principle undergoing reevaluation today is the doctrine of sovereignty and its relationship to the use of force. The social interdependence of states continues to drive changes in the doctrine of sovereignty, especially with the end of the Cold War.

With the end of the Cold War, states appear willing to let the UN use the language in the UN Charter to further restrain the sovereign rights of states to use force. Secular principles will continue to drive the legal justifications for using force. The principles which form the emerging international system will include justifications for an expansion of the UN's international jurisdiction into the internal affairs of states to promote peace and for humanitarian purposes.

Although the UN will enjoy expanded jurisdiction under the emerging international system, state nationalism will continue to limit the UN's ability to successfully intervene in the internal affairs of a failed state or for a humanitarian purpose. Nationalism will cause states to consider whether their national interests are at stake before entering into any peacekeeping or enforcement action under the UN Charter. Nationalism will also continue to block attempts to establish a UN standing army. Although a lofty ideal, states are not prepared to completely cede their sovereign right of self-defense to the UN. The UN, as a practical matter, does not possess the institutional ability to replace the state regarding all uses of force. Thus, the doctrine of nonintervention will continue to play a role in the emerging international system. The UN will begin looking to regional organizations to resolve international disputes as a substitute for the UN's inability to effectively intervene in all areas of the globe where threats exist to international peace and security.

Many of these regional organizations, however, are not organized to use force to restore or maintain peace in their regions. States that comprise these regional organizations also retain the same nationalistic policies that prevent the UN from garnering support for peacekeeping or enforcement operations. Limitations in the Charter language will continue to prevent regional organizations from conducting enforcement actions without Security Council approval.

The Security Council will continue to play a pivotal role in any UN peacekeeping or enforcement action. Under the present Charter, the UN is unlikely to restrain a state from using force unless the permanent members of the UN decide that UN action is in their own national interest. The present UN Charter also gives the permanent members of the Security Council the latitude to use force in violation of the UN Charter and purpose, since the UN is unable to effectively enforce sanctions or the use of force without the cooperation of the permanent members of the Security Council.

The UN Secretary-General will continue to explore new avenues for using the language under the UN Charter to restrain the right of a state to use force to resolve disputes. His efforts will continue to underscore the fact that the language in the UN Charter is the centerpiece for the evolving international system and the changing role of the state as a social institution. Nations, for their part, will continue to steer a course which promotes the principles and purposes of the UN Charter. But they will also retain sufficient sovereign rights to ensure they may take military action independent of the UN for self-defense and to maintain their own national security.

HUMANITARIAN INTERVENTION: THE USE OF UN PEACEKEEPERS IN NON-TRADITIONAL ROLES

Margaret T. Mitchell
U.S. Department of State
April 1996

> The logic of peacekeeping flows from political and military premises that are quite distinct from those of enforcement; and the dynamics of the latter are incompatible with the political process that peacekeeping is intended to facilitate.
>
> UN Secretary-General Boutros-Ghali
> January 1995

The role of the United Nations in the post-Cold War environment has changed significantly. UN Secretary-General Boutros-Ghali has advocated a more aggressive security role. This role includes the use of UN peacekeepers in non-traditional situations, such as humanitarian interventions. This study looks at how effective UN peacekeepers are when used as a humanitarian intervention force. For purposes of this paper, humanitarian intervention means interference in the internal affairs of another country, using force or threat of force, for humanitarian goals. It is the argument of this paper that, to be effective, UN peacekeepers cannot operate under traditional peacekeeping guidelines when conducting a humanitarian intervention. Case studies of UN missions in Somalia, Rwanda, and the former Yugoslavia are used to examine the validity of this hypothesis.

Humanitarian intervention is incompatible with traditional peacekeeping. Under traditional peacekeeping guidelines, UN forces are in-country with the consent of the host government, they are neutral and impartial, and they use force only in self-defense. An intervention force, on the other hand, violates all of these guidelines: an intervention requires offensive use of force; host-country permission is not necessarily obtained in advance (often because there are competing authorities, which are part of the problem); and it is impossible to remain neutral when, in order to carry out the UN's mandate, force must be used against one or more of the parties to the conflict.

This study concludes that the way the UN so far has authorized humanitarian interventions is not effective because:

1. It is easy for the UN to lose its neutrality and become part of the problem;
2. Neutrality cannot be maintained if using force, but offensive use of force is necessary, at least initially;
3. By compromising their neutrality, the UN forces can become legitimate targets;
4. The types of humanitarian crises that require military force are man-made and therefore cannot be resolved just with the provision of humanitarian aid.

UN OPERATION IN SOMALIA

Motive

- Heavy loss of human life
- Widespread material damage
- Threat to stability and peace in the region
- Protection for organizations providing humanitarian assistance
- UNSC "deeply disturbed by the magnitude of the human suffering"
- Provision of secure environment for humanitarian relief operations

Mandate

UNOSOM was authorized to assist the Secretary-General in obtaining and maintaining a cease-fire and to provide urgent humanitarian assistance. Six months after UNOSOM's establishment in April 1992, the Secretary-General and Security Council decided more aggressive action was needed and, acting under Chapter VII authority, authorized a U.S.-led coalition (UNITAF) to ensure the delivery of humanitarian assistance. The transfer of authority in May 1993 from UNITAF to UNOSOM II led to a much broader mandate, also under Chapter VII authority. This mandate basically called for the UN forces to try to stop the civil war and also to continue humanitarian relief operations. In February 1994, under UNSC Res 897, the mandate was revised, the main difference being that UN forces would not use coercive measures but would rely on the cooperation of the Somali parties.

UN OPERATION IN SOMALIA (Continued)

Conclusion

Street scene in Somalia, 1993. *photo used with permission*

UNOSOM was an effective humanitarian operation, but it also illustrates why humanitarian interventions are so very different from traditional PKOs. The humanitarian crisis in Somalia was man-made and when the UNITAF forces arrived they upset the political economy of Somalia. This economy was based on control of the food supply. By flooding the market with food, UNITAF depressed prices, and the warlords lost some of their influence. Food had become the warlords' primary weapon; by taking it away, the UN forced them to look for other means to coerce their opponents.

UN peacekeepers did not abide by traditional guidelines, yet UNOSOM was perceived as a peacekeeping failure. The "failure" was not something the U.S. could justifiably blame on the UN because the U.S. wrote the mandate. The failure in Somalia was the U.S. unwillingness to thoroughly support an operation it had created. Even before the loss of American service personnel, it was clear the situation would require a large investment in time, personnel and money. Without the U.S. backing, the UN alone could not rebuild Somalia's civil society or economy.

RWANDA

Motive

- Hutu forces rampage, massacre hundreds of thousands of Tutsis
- Humanitarian crisis of enormous proportions
- Deep concern about systematic and widespread killings
- Security and support needed for humanitarian operations

Mandate

UNAMIR I was initially established at the request of the warring parties to monitor compliance with the Arusha Accords. A secondary part of the mandate was to assist in coordination of humanitarian relief operations. Non-compliance by the parties to the accords led to a delay in the full deployment of UNAMIR. When the April 1994 mass genocide began, UNAMIR was ill-prepared to assist. The French were authorized in June 1994, acting under Chapter VII authority, to conduct a strictly humanitarian operation (Operation Turquoise), protecting refugees and displaced persons and allowing the distribution of humanitarian relief. This two-month operation served as a transitional force until UNAMIR II contingents could be deployed.

Conclusion

The UN deployed to Rwanda in an attempt to help with the provision of humanitarian assistance and the security and protection of refugees, but it was not an operation that combined elements of Chapter VI and VII. Operation Turquoise was authorized under Chapter VII because the French would not conduct the mission otherwise. The UN is currently confronted with a situation that cannot be handled without massive resources, both financial and personnel, and without a great deal of international political will.

UNAMIR I was to be an observer group that would facilitate the implementation of the Arusha Accords. The rapid escalation of violence following the deaths of the presidents of Rwanda and Burundi caught the UN off-guard and quickly overwhelmed the small UN contingent in the country. Operation Turquoise was only able to provide assistance and security for those already in refugee camps.

Use of force in Rwanda was not seriously considered. The Rwandan crisis reflected a lack of will on the part of the UN to use the necessary means required to take control of the situation. Even had the UN decided to use the overwhelming force that would have been necessary to quell the violence, the massacre would have been over long before most troops had arrived. There would have been little left to do beyond protecting the fleeing refugees. Peacekeeping forces in Rwanda could only have operated under Chapter VII guidelines because the only way to stop the crisis would have been with force, had the UN been able to deploy rapidly.

UN PROTECTION FORCE IN THE FORMER YUGOSLAVIA

Motive

- Heavy loss of life, refugees, displaced persons, urgent humanitarian needs
- Deliberate armed attacks by the Bosnian Serbs against civilians
- Widespread rape of women
- Detention camps for civilians reminiscent of Nazi concentration camps.

Mandate

The UN Protection Force (UNPROFOR) was mandated to escort humanitarian convoys, protect designated "safe areas," and monitor compliance with cease-fires and the military flight ban. Regional organizations—particularly the North Atlantic Treaty Organization (NATO)—were authorized under Chapter VII of the UN Charter to use "all necessary means" to support UNPROFOR in performance of its mandate.

Conclusion

The original mandate of UNPROFOR was to create conditions of peace and security required for the negotiation of an overall settlement of the Yugoslav crisis. The mission quickly developed a large humanitarian component to deal with predominantly man-made, often deliberate, crises. UNPROFOR quickly became a hostage to the whims of warring factions. The UNPROFOR operation was the first post-Cold War mission in which the UN tried to conduct a Chapter VI operation using elements of Chapter VII. It became clear very quickly that this would not work.

In an early example of the UN forces' hands being tied, in 1992 a UN convoy carrying a Bosnian government official was stopped by Bosnian Serb soldiers. While checking the UN forces' papers, a Bosnian Serb soldier leaned into the UN vehicle and shot the government official. The UN did nothing because they were not directly attacked; the Bosnian Serbs later said the soldier had been disciplined. When NATO forces conducted bombing runs (until August 1995), the targets were selected so as to make a point with the combatants, but were intended not to antagonize them (for example, hitting an airfield runway but not going after the aircraft). In these and other cases the UN was seeking to preserve its role as a neutral mediator and (unintentionally) allowed the Bosnian Serbs to capitalize on this effort.

The Bosnian Serbs quickly figured out how to get what they wanted from the UN—aid convoys were frequently stopped, delayed, or turned back by the Serbs. When it appeared NATO was serious about conducting air strikes, UN forces were taken hostage and sometimes handcuffed to potential military targets in the area the strikes were to take place.

Implementation Force compound in Bosnia-Herzegovina, 1995. *photo used with permission*

So far the most effective humanitarian interventions have been UN-authorized, but led by Great Powers. Humanitarian interventions are time-consuming and expensive operations, best handled, at least initially, by a force willing to be aggressive and to risk casualties. Once a situation is stabilized, then a UN operation could take over. However, the UN and the international community must realize that neither can respond equally well everywhere, every time.

Examining the topic of humanitarian intervention today is important because technological advancements and global interdependence have made the world a much smaller place and have led to higher visibility of crises. The Intelligence Community should be concerned with this issue because by understanding the problems that peacekeeping forces can encounter when trying to conduct a humanitarian intervention, analysts can provide a more refined assessment to policymakers. Policymakers benefit as well because they can better appreciate what to

Stabilization Force (SFOR) in Bosnia and Herzegovina, March 1997. *source: Central Intelligence Angecy*

ask of the Intelligence Community and how to allocate resources more effectively.

The explosion of ethnic conflicts has led to civil wars and massive refugee flows. Many of the new states created by the downfall of the Eastern Bloc and superpower patronage are calling for UN involvement in conflict mediation, humanitarian assistance, and border disputes. The droughts, famines, and civil wars of Africa, which pre-date the collapse of the Soviet Union, are also putting more demands on the UN. This, at least partially, is because mass media are able to give the world instantaneous pictures and reports of the devastation countries are suffering.

All of these global changes, together with the Secretary-General's more aggressive stance on UN security concerns, have led to a greater willingness on the part of the UN, the Security Council in particular, to become involved at many levels. It has also placed a greater emphasis on humanitarian issues and precipitated increased use of peacekeeping forces, particularly to conduct humanitarian interventions.

> The effectiveness of peacekeeping operations derives from a combination of factors — the physical presence of armed soldiers who will return fire if they are fired upon, the moral authority of the UN, the pressures of world public opinion. These work together to deter the hostile parties from taking rash military action. If UN forces take the initiative in using force against any combatant who might be threatening the peace, they have violated the UN's most basic peacekeeping principle — to intervene only with the consent of the parties. When they shoot, the forces have clearly lost the consent of those at whom they are shooting (UN *d*: 7).

This statement reflects the UN's view of peacekeeping — neutral forces interposed between conflicting parties, with the consent of those parties, to help maintain peace. If the UN takes sides or uses force, it becomes part of the problem at the root of the dispute. Often those disputes lead to the humanitarian crises that have recently overwhelmed the UN.

The need for armed interference implies that consent from authorities within the country is lacking. Lack of consent and use of force lead to the assumption on the part of forces within the country that these outside parties are not neutral, or at least not necessarily supportive of "their" position. Any actions to aid one element are likely to be interpreted as opposition against other elements. An intervention does not mean commitment to full-scale war but, since the intervening forces are frequently going into countries experiencing civil wars, they must be able to conduct appropriate military operations as required by the situation.

Understanding the differences between the two types of missions, humanitarian intervention and peacekeeping, is a step toward establishing a viable method of humanitarian intervention. Based on actions by the Secretary-General and mandates authorized by the Security Council, the UN appears to think that it should be responsible for the conduct of humanitarian interventions.

If humanitarian interventions are to be effective, international contingents cannot abide by traditional peacekeeping guidelines. Chapter VI of the UN Charter was intended for pacific settlement of disputes, and Chapter VII for collective security. Combining the two has proven to be extremely difficult. Secretary-General Boutros-Ghali has said:

> International problems cannot be solved quickly or within a limited time . . . Their resolution requires patient diplomacy and the establishment of a political process that permits, over a period of time, the building of confidence and negotiated solutions to long-standing differences . . . It is necessary to resist the temptation to use military power to speed them up. Peacekeeping and the use of force (other than in self-defense) should be seen as alternative techniques and not as adjacent points on a continuum, permitting easy transition from one to the other (UNGA A/47/277 Supplement: 9).

Several overall conclusions can be drawn. First and foremost, it is easy for the UN to lose its neutrality and become part of the problem. UN forces in Bosnia were eventually seen as part of the problem even though they were there to help provide humanitarian aid, using force if necessary. They rarely used force and were unable to stop or stem the violence causing the crisis. When they tried to use force, they encountered a second problem, namely, neutrality cannot be maintained if using force. By compromising their neutrality, the UN forces became legitimate targets of war. And without a credible threat to conduct offensive operations, international contingents can become hostages to the combatants. Another problem inherent in humanitarian crises of the kind that require military force is the fact that they are man-made. Merely providing humanitarian aid will not resolve the problem. Somalia illustrated the difficulty in providing humanitarian aid but not following through and dealing with the root causes of the crisis.

Finally, the most effective solution so far has been the use of a coalition/multinational force such as UNITAF. This last is probably the most-telling conclusion about the future of humanitarian interventions: the UN is not currently capable of conducting an offensive military operation. Peacekeepers are "a military force that is not in the business of threatening or using weapons except for self-defense" (J. Goldman: 15-16). Once a situation is stabilized by a non-UN coalition force, it could then be turned over to a UN peacekeeping force.

Coalition operations are expensive, and unless the international community is willing to pay, in terms both of money and lives, it must carefully choose when, where, and how to get involved. In the long run, if humanitarian interventions only provide immediate relief to afflicted civilian populations, without leading to a peace agreement, these crises will keep recurring. Nothing is more dangerous to the credibility of the UN than to threaten the use of force and then fail to use it or use it ineffectively (Roper: 12). Further studies might look at the effectiveness of multinational coalition peacekeeping forces. In the Gulf War, the coalition was able to repel Iraqi troops from Kuwait, but how effective would such coalitions be at resolving humanitarian crises and their root causes? Thus far, the operations the UN has conducted have all been mixed UN and coalition operations. Another study might examine the possibility of a UN peacekeeping force conducting a full Chapter VII humanitarian intervention and the effect this could have on the UN's primary diplomatic objectives. Diplomacy is the first and favored role of the UN. The UN was created as a world organization of last resort to avoid war or conflict. How would the UN change if it became an agency able to conduct war as well as stop it? Is this feasible? Or would the nation-state system as we know it have to change in a radical fashion?

DRIFTNET FISHERY ENFORCEMENT: A NEW INTELLIGENCE PROBLEM

William J. Quigley
Lieutenant Commander, U.S. Coast Guard
August 1995

> The more clearly we understand the complex interrelationships between the different parts of our world's environment, the better we can understand the regional and even global effects of local changes to the environment. Increasing competition for the dwindling reserves of uncontaminated air, arable land, fisheries and other food resources, and water, once considered "free" goods, is already a very real risk to regional stability around the world. The range of environmental risks serious enough to jeopardize international stability extends to massive population flight from man-made or natural catastrophes, such as Chernobyl or the East African drought, and to large-scale ecosystem damage caused by industrial pollution, deforestation, loss of biodiversity, ozone depletion, and ultimately climate change. Strategies dealing with environmental issues of this magnitude will require partnerships between governments and non-governmental organizations, cooperation between nations and regions, and a commitment to a strategically focused, long-term policy for emerging environmental risks (U.S. President *a*: 15).
>
> President William Clinton

In *A National Security Strategy of Engagement and Enlargement,* President Clinton concludes that the decisions made today on the environment will affect U.S. national interests in the next 20 to 30 years. One recent portentous decision was the adoption of a worldwide moratorium on exploitation of large-scale high seas pelagic driftnet fisheries. This fishery pollutes the oceans with discarded plastic nets and potentially can devastate the biodiversity of the open ocean.

WHAT ARE DRIFTNETS?

> Gill nets, so called because they are designed to trap fish by their gill plates, are single-panel curtains of nylon twine or more commonly monofilament plastic line, suspended in the water column and either anchored (set) or allowed to float free (drift). Trammel nets are a type of gill net comprising a small-mesh curtain sandwiched between two larger, loosely hung nets. Gill nets can be miles long. The Japanese salmon fishery, comprising 172 catcher boats and four enormous factory ships, uses nine-mile-long, twenty-six-feet deep gill nets. This totals 1,548 miles of drifting monofilament net that is released each night (Heinonen: 62).

Gillnets or driftnets date to Biblical times. They were designed to ensnare and catch fish by their gill plates or opercula. More recently, the Japanese have an extensive history of using driftnets in their high seas salmon fishery since prior to World War II. The Japanese expanded their off-shore salmon driftnetting during the mid-1970s. Also during the late 1970s Japan, the Republic of Korea, and Taiwan commenced using driftnets for squid. During the 1980s and early 1990s, driftnetting expanded in the Pacific Ocean, the eastern Atlantic Ocean, and the Mediterranean Sea, targeting salmon, squid, and albacore tuna (Manville: 205).

During the 1980s, the American public became more concerned with the direct and indirect impacts of these large-scale fisheries. Large-scale driftnets were extremely efficient. The driftnets were called "walls of death" by many environmental groups because of the indiscriminate manner of entangling and catching targeted fish. Besides the targeted species, the driftnets were also effective at capturing non-targeted fish, as well as marine mammals, sea birds, sea turtles, and other living marine resources. "Ghost nets," those lost or discarded at sea, continued to catch an estimated 125,000 marine mammals and 750,000 seabirds per year in the North Pacific alone.

The driftnet threat is two-fold, one from incidental catch, and the second from catch which is entangled but not accounted for by lost or discarded nets. During a limited 1989 open-ocean observers program, National Marine Fisheries Service observers reported that 32 Japanese driftnet vessels caught 3 million targeted squid, 914 dolphin, 141 porpoises, 52 northern fur seals, 539 albatross, 32 puffins, 8,536 shearwaters, 17 petrels, and 22 sea turtles. These numbers reflect only the incidental catch which had died, and do not account for the resources which were released alive but probably injured. Additionally, these numbers do not reflect those animals which were caught in "ghost nets." The National Marine Fisheries Service estimated that vessels lose 0.06 percent of their nets per night. With a reported 40,000 nets in use during the late 1980s, that would equate to approximately 14 miles of driftnets lost each day (Manville: 206).

Driftnets have caused similar concern in the northwest Atlantic Ocean. Hundreds of harbor porpoises are entangled in gillnets each year, posing a threat to the long-term survival of that species of marine mammal. In 1987 the National Marine Fisheries Service and other U.S. and Canadian scientists conducted a harbor porpoise survey and worked on methods to better estimate the size of the harbor porpoise population. During the survey, they concluded that harbor porpoises were attracted to the gillnets as a source of food. Therefore, the elimination or reduction of incidental catch of the harbor porpoises would require seasonally prohibiting many of the area's best fishing ground to gillnets, as the porpoise would likely concentrate there in search of food (Polacheck: 63-70).

Driftnetting, in general, did not become a public concern until as recently as 1990. Environmental groups began to increase public sensitivity to the harmful effects of plastics, including driftnets, on the wildlife and the marine environment. In addition, in 1991 the Pacific Seafood Processor's Association reported that the Japanese intercepted high levels of Pacific northwest salmon on the high seas and were selling them in the Asian market. These developments induced more aggressive measures in the U.S. Congress (Manville: 206).

ENFORCEMENT LEGISLATION

The 46th session of the United Nations General Assembly adopted UN Resolution 46/215 on 12 February 1992. The resolution called for a worldwide moratorium on large-scale pelagic driftnet fishing effective 31 December 1992. The resolution was designed to protect fish, marine mammals, seabirds, and other living marine resources that were taken by the world's driftnet fleets (UNGA Res A/RES/46/215).

Prompted by the U.S.-sponsored UN resolution, the U.S. Congress passed the *High Seas Driftnet Enforcement Act* on 2 November 1992. The act stated that large-scale drift fishing on the high seas was highly destructive to the ocean ecosystem, including anadromous fish and other living marine resources of the United States. The act prohibited large-scale driftnet fishing by U.S. nationals and vessels within the U.S. Exclusive Economic Zone (EEZ), and by U.S. nationals on the high seas. It also denied port privileges and provided for sanctions against countries whose registered vessels conducted large-scale driftnet fishing beyond their own EEZ (Pub. L. 102-582).

The *High Seas Driftnet Enforcement Act* also required that the Secretary of Transportation, the Secretary of Commerce, and the Secretary of Defense enter into an agreement concerning the use of U.S. surveillance capabilities to locate and identify vessels that are in violation of the U.S. law or international agreement. A Memorandum of Understanding (MOU) was signed by these three parties on 11 October 1993. The MOU identified the Office of Naval Intelligence as the action office for the Department of Defense (DoD); the National Marine Fisheries Service (NMFS), Office of Enforcement, as the action office for the Department of Commerce; and the Commandant, U.S. Coast Guard, Office of Law Enforcement and Defense Operations, as the action Office for the Department of Transportation. The DoD agreed to use, on a not-to-interfere basis, all-source intelligence assets to monitor, collect, and report the location and identity of vessels in violation of the U.S. law or international agreements. Not-to-interfere was defined as collecting during the course of normal operations, not a dedicated patrol solely in support of this mission. Additionally, the DoD would sanitize to the lowest possible classification level the information identifying and locating those vessels in violation. Finally, all of the parties agreed to bear costs incurred during the collection and dissemination of the information on vessels in violation of the *High Seas Driftnet Enforcement Act* or other international agreements affecting living marine resources.

More recently, a Chairman, Joint Chiefs of Staff Instruction established DoD responsibilities in the detection and monitoring of high seas driftnet fishing (U.S. DoD CJCS). The Instruction called for the use of maritime monitoring and collection assets to detect, track, and identify vessels in violation of the worldwide driftnet moratorium.

ENFORCEMENT OPTIONS

There are two primary enforcement options available to the U.S. for the UN's Large-Scale Pelagic Driftnet Moratorium. First, the U.S. and the UN can negotiate shiprider agreements with countries involved with the driftnet fisheries. Secondly, and the more likely option, the United States will conduct surveillance of the high seas and report on vessels in violation of the worldwide moratorium.

In the past the U.S. has proposed high seas driftnet fishing vessel visit and verification MOUs. One submitted to the Government of Taiwan by the United States in February 1994 was rejected. It called for officials of one side to visit and verify fishing vessels flying the other side's flag if found using or equipped for the use of large-scale pelagic driftnet equipment. The visiting officials would verify the fishing vessel's flag and registration, and could examine the vessel together with its equipment and other records, including fishing gear, catch, and logs. Any evidence of activities inconsistent with the UN resolution would be forwarded to the other side. The American Institute in Taiwan, acting on behalf of the U.S. government, proposed that the MOU, if signed, remain in effect for 3 years (U.S. Secretary of State *b*). A similar agreement is now in effect with the People's Rcpublic of China (U.S. Secretary of State *a*).

More probably, the U.S. will provide surveillance using all-source intelligence assets to fuse information for the U.S. Department of State, so that it may take diplomatic action. The former Secretary of Defense Les Aspin suggested shifting intelligence assets to this mission:

> The first thing that I think we have to answer in the commission is what is it that the intelligence agencies now — whatever there is — ought to be focused on? The old target of the efforts was the Soviet Union in all of its parts. What is the target now, or targets? What is it that this apparatus is going to organize to do? . . . Open sources are now available on lots of questions that were not available before, and that complicates the question. What is it that clandestine collection brings to the party? What does an intelligence organization bring to the party? Those are the questions that need to be addressed when you get to that third set of targets. It's even more so when you get to the fourth set of targets, which is the new agenda targets — economics, environmental, health care. The

> agency is involved in getting requests to get involved in a lot of issues of that kind, where clearly in those areas the primary source of information would probably be the open source. But still there's the question: Is there an ingredient that can be added by the Intelligence Community? Is there something that they can add to the mix, to that fourth category of targets? (Aspin).

Les Aspin's comments provide some insight into the future missions and orientation of the Intelligence Community. His fourth category of intelligence targets includes both economics and the environment. The Large-Scale High Seas Pelagic Driftnet Moratorium falls under both of these headings. Fisheries is an industry that can affect the economic well-being of a country and, of course, a fishery employing driftnets affects marine life on the high seas and is also a source of plastics pollution.

Some analysts have suggested that the fisheries problem may be best handled as an Indications and Warning problem, given the potential for armed conflicts on the high seas. Although there have been isolated incidents of naval exchanges during fisheries conflicts, fisheries, in general, and the high seas driftnet fishery in particular, are economic and environmental problems only. Fisheries are not likely to be accepted by the Defense Indications and Warning Community as a formal warning problem. Nonetheless, the methodology of scenario and indicator construction for individual driftnet fishery problems, does hold promise for the effective application of intelligence capabilities against the problem of large-scale high seas driftnet moratorium enforcement.

Environmental and economic intelligence requirements will become increasingly important to the U.S. populace and, therefore, to the U.S. Intelligence Community. The Department of Defense already has a legislated requirement to support the high seas driftnet moratorium. The national imagery system should also be used to assist in monitoring the moratorium, as all of the intelligence disciplines should be fused to meet the needs of the consumer.

INTELLIGENCE AND NONPROLIFERATION

Audrey D. Hudgins
Captain, U.S. Army
August 1992

> The very idea of change . . . will dominate international life . . . the unthinkable and the not-even-thought-about will be commonplace. . . we have an opportunity to . . . redefine the very mission of intelligence in the new world which we face (Quoted in Weiser: A14).
>
> DCI Robert Gates

Nuclear proliferation has been a concern since the world entered the nuclear age. Early international efforts to operate and control nuclear fuel cycles, envisaged in the Baruch Plan, met with failure. In the years following, the use of atomic energy became a national rather than international endeavor. To aid the spread of peaceful nuclear technology and to prevent its diversion to military use, in 1957 the International Atomic Energy Agency (IAEA) was created. Some characteristics of this international inspectorate were appropriate only to the time in which it originated. Former World War II enemies of the Allied victors were the targets of the safeguards regime. Following ratification of the Nuclear Nonproliferation Treaty (NPT) of 1968, the IAEA safeguarded nuclear cycles the world over.

By design, the agency's mission was strictly one of inspection and verification, as reflected in the safeguards agreements. The detection of clandestine nuclear activities was a mission of the major powers. Disclosure of the extent and complexity of Iraq's nuclear weapons program eroded the level of confidence that the international community had in the nuclear inspection and regulatory abilities of the IAEA.

But Iraq was a failure of far greater proportions. Although the agency might be faulted for its lack of an aggressive approach to inspections, safeguards are simply one component of a comprehensive nuclear nonproliferation regime. Iraq violated all relevant aspects of this regime. Through its accession to the NPT, Iraq pledged not to acquire nuclear weapons. Iraq subverted the export control regime by clandestinely obtaining nuclear equipment and material. Finally, Iraq violated its safeguards agreement with the IAEA. The Iraqi nuclear weapons program showed that a signatory to the NPT could evade the IAEA, the U.S. Intelligence Community, and all other international scrutiny. As a result of this experience, all of these parties now realize the importance of global cooperation in the fight against nuclear proliferation.

Time has been the ultimate arbiter for international cooperation. Old enemies of World War II are now friends and allies. The Berlin Wall has fallen and the two Germanies are now one. The collapse of the Soviet Union and the end of the Cold War have formed a new global environment. Bilateral arms control and disarmament treaties evolved into multilateral confidence and security building measures. The United Nations has finally emerged as a more effective promoter of international peace and security.

The IAEA, an organization under the auspices of the United Nations, has reaped the benefits of enhanced cooperation. In 1991, the U.S. Intelligence Community, the IAEA, and the United Nations Special Commission on Iraq (UNSCOM) joined forces to rid Iraq of its weapons of mass destruction. Despite its failure in some areas, intelligence has been the key to success. The U.S. Intelligence Community must now further define its role in a new international security environment. In order to ensure its continued effectiveness, the Intelligence Community must protect its sources and methods. But the Intelligence Community serves the policymaker, who in turn serves the national interest. The U.S. National Security Strategy defines nuclear proliferation as one of those interests. In order for U.S. and global concern over proliferation to be addressed, countries must choose to give the IAEA the tools it needs to do its job. Intelligence is one of these tools.

The Problem of National Interest

Nuclear proliferation presents a great threat to U.S. national security. Regional arms races can be destabilizing, potentially causing major shifts in the strategic power balance. Gaps in the export control regime and the threat of Soviet nuclear scientist emigration only accelerate this dangerous nuclear timeline. The United States and its Intelligence Community must display vigilance and resolve. Unfortunately, nuclear proliferation does not compete successfully with other national priorities, as was the case with Pakistan in the 1980s. The U.S. must carefully weigh a myriad of factors when making short- and long-term policy decisions. The U.S. inability to certify Pakistan's peaceful nuclear intentions and its involvement in the Iraq problem indicate that nuclear proliferation is a continuing policy concern.

The Problems of the IAEA

Conflicting national interests have plagued states throughout history. The IAEA, representing over 116 countries, has had its share of conflicting "international interests."

Safeguards Effectiveness. Safeguards effectiveness has been debated at the IAEA since its creation. Concerns over sovereignty and divergent views on the role of safeguards have contributed to diplomatic and political stalemate. The Iraq issue focused new attention on this issue. For example, the IAEA followed a routine, predictable inspection schedule. States pursuing clandestine development of a nuclear weapons program could clean up their operation prior to inspection and thus give the appearance of compliance with applicable safeguards. Iraq is a recent, yet classic example of this evasive strategy.

Never before had a country been found in violation of its safeguards agreement with the IAEA. The Board of Governors came to the realization that IAEA safeguards are only as good as their implementation. This convergence of opinion has resulted in positive changes in the inspection process to ensure stricter compliance. The IAEA Board has implemented a short-notice, random inspection methodology and will soon adopt safeguards measures designed to detect clandestine activity.

Export Controls. Export control groups, and their member states, have expressed a traditional reluctance to provide export information to the IAEA because of its proprietary, commercially sensitive nature. During the inspections in Iraq, however, this information was essential in uncovering the depth of the clandestine nuclear program. The IAEA's handling of export information was very successful.

Iraq showed that many gaps exist in the field of export controls. The export control groups, one of the three pillars of the nuclear nonproliferation regime, have taken steps to enhance the comprehensiveness of export control guidelines. The inspections in Iraq also proved that greater cooperation between these groups and the IAEA produces a synergistic effect, making the regime as a whole stronger. Greater understanding and appreciation have developed between the two groups that will likely continue into the future.

A Lack of Aggressiveness. Historic evolution has framed the Agency's safeguards approach. Until very recently, aggressive application of safeguards was deemed prejudicial to a member state's sovereign interests. The absence of an aggressive approach perhaps allowed Iraq to proceed unencumbered with its weapons development program. The agency has since realized the benefit of a more aggressive attitude. Recently, IAEA inspectors have requested access to a number of suspected Iranian and North Korean nuclear facilities not declared by those countries in their safeguards agreements. This trend will likely continue as the IAEA strives to deter proliferation.

Counterintelligence. The IAEA is responsible for safeguarding the peaceful use of the atom, but is also the international purveyor of nuclear technology. With 85 percent of inspection personnel from non-nuclear weapons states, the IAEA must balance its approach; a lack of balance might actually make the IAEA a proliferant, as was the case with the director of the Iraqi national safeguards program. Nonetheless, this example has raised the IAEA's awareness of the dangerous potential of proliferation.

The IAEA and Nuclear Proliferation

The IAEA is a unique organization. Its role as the purveyor of peaceful nuclear energy gives the agency an understanding of global nuclear activity and allows unparalleled insight into the prospects for illegal nuclear activity. Its staff of scientists and technicians are able to evaluate information available through the open press, scientific and technical journals, and a number of in-house and other information sources to enhance this understanding. Finally, through its safeguards system, the IAEA has the authority to question or perform inspections to determine the purpose of suspected nuclear activity. No other organization, national or international, has the authority or the ability to perform all these tasks.

The IAEA safeguards system has three components: 1) to deter diversion, 2) to detect diversion, and 3) to confirm by inspection that nuclear material is not diverted from peaceful use. The last two components are adequately addressed through the current safeguards approach. The first component has two implied tasks, the detection and deterrence of clandestine nuclear facilities, which have received new attention since Iraq's clandestine nuclear weapons program was revealed. It is now understood that the current safeguards system does not adequately address the issue of deterrence.

Deterrence is the key to a successful nuclear nonproliferation regime. A myriad of factors enable deterrence to be effective. First, and perhaps foremost, is the ability of intelligence to detect clandestine nuclear activity. No country can be fully confident that such activity will go undetected. Second, the political and economic impact of illegal proliferation can be a significant deterrent. When international concern is raised, political isolation and economic sanctions might persuade a proliferant to cease nuclear activity. Finally, the destabilizing effects of regional nuclear proliferation are a viable deterrent. Conventional military and nuclear arms races flourish at the cost of economic progress, a price many states cannot afford.

The IAEA's central role in the nuclear nonproliferation regime has continued relevancy despite missteps in handling the problem of Iraq. In order to ensure an effective regime, the IAEA must be empowered with the ability to deter illicit activity. The use of intelligence by the IAEA will provide this deterrent capability.

The Future of Intelligence and the IAEA

The IAEA safeguards system is simply not designed to detect diversions such as Iraq's and the IAEA is not in a position to develop an organic intelligence collection capability. The agency does not possess the resources for such a venture, and the great majority of member states would not support its creation. Moreover, member states already have a formidable intelligence capability in place. The IAEA must therefore rely on member states to provide intelligence information. The experience in Iraq has proved that intelligence is a useful and necessary complement to a successful IAEA safeguards regime.

The IAEA is charged with the verification of safeguards on declared nuclear facilities. The safeguards program, much like the NPT, relies on the integrity of the signatories. A country's clandestine nuclear weapons development program is designed to subvert this pledge. Foreign intelligence information is the means to ensure that states are fulfilling the letter and spirit of the regime. Those that sign the treaty have pledged they will not develop nuclear weapons. Intelligence can be used simply to verify this pledge. Further, most states motivated to possess a nuclear weapons capability are willing to do whatever is necessary to achieve that goal. The use of intelligence by the IAEA is a means of ensuring that the agency is doing whatever is necessary to achieve its goal of halting the spread of weapons of mass destruction.

Just as revelations of the Iraqi program alerted the IAEA to its own inadequacies, they also provide a warning to potential proliferants. The next offender may be harder to expose. This argues for more sharing of intelligence in the future. It can be hoped that the U.S. Intelligence Community's relationship with the IAEA, born of necessity and sustained by success, can continue well into the future. The cost is only as much as the U.S. chooses to bear, and the benefits are many.

PEACE OPERATIONS

Robert J. Allen
Lieutenant, U.S. Navy
July 1995

It's the Member States Stupid! (Quoted in Preston *b*).

Alvaro de Soto, Executive Assistant to the UN Secretary-General

EXCEEDING THE BOUNDARIES OF PEACEKEEPING

The problems experienced by the U.S. and UN in meeting the world body's intelligence support requirements are symptomatic of the difficulties of executing Secretary Boutros-Ghali's *Agenda for Peace*. Conditions upon which the well-understood and limited concept of UN peacekeeping depended in the past have largely been abandoned by modern multi-dimensional peace missions. An established cease-fire, consent of the parties to the presence of the UN, and the impartiality of the peacekeepers are no longer prerequisites for the deployment of a UN force into a conflict zone. The absence of functioning governments in these *de facto* wars has prompted the UN Security Council to intervene in the internal affairs of many states whose sovereignty was once considered inviolable. As a consequence, the UN finds itself confronting "armed groups outside the control of recognized political authorities" in its attempts to bring peace (P. Lewis *b*: A10).

William J. Durch, a peacekeeping expert at the Henry L. Stimson Center, warns of the dangers of this development:

> UN peacekeeping has succeeded primarily where local peoples and political factions have both needed and supported the UN's presence. Any operation designed to intervene in situations in

> which there is only partial local consent is not peacekeeping, but something else, and it usually runs into a whole string of problems, as the trials of UN forces in Angola, Bosnia, and Western Sahara currently [February 1993] attest. If the UN's member states continue to send the organization's peacekeepers into politically unstable situations, they risk the political and financial collapse of what has been to date one of the international community's most useful tools for containing and seeking to resolve regional conflicts (Durch *c*: 18).

NATIONAL INTEREST VS. PEACE OPERATIONS

In actuality, a Security Council vote to mount a peace operation is not so much an expression by UN member states — especially the Permanent Five (U.S., Russia, PRC, UK, France) on the Security Council — that a conflict involves their vital national interests, but rather an admission that it does not. The *Washington Post's* lament that the new U.S. government guidelines on "Reforming Multilateral Peace Operations" (PDD-25) relegate peace operations to "a sometime tool for third-level American interests, after other interests meant to be served by American's own defense forces and its alliances," ("Peace-Keeping": C6) is an accurate assessment of how most governments have prioritized UN peace operations. More often than not, the Security Council decision to deploy a UN force represents an international lowest common denominator: an agreement to "do something," no matter how ill-conceived.

This frail consensus begins to unravel as peacekeeping becomes peace enforcement. Above all, a UN peace operation represents an artificial coalition that lacks the conjunction of national interests that underlies an alliance. As a consequence, the absence of shared national interests makes the peace operation's command and control fragile and its tolerance for casualties low. The tendency demonstrated in Somalia for national contingent commanders to disobey UN orders and contact their national capitals for instructions underscores this first weakness (Richburg *a*: A1). The assessment by General Maurice Baril (the Secretary-General's Military Advisor) concerning the lesson to be drawn from the Somali peace enforcement experience illustrates the latter point: "[C]ountries won't send their sons and daughters to die unless a vital national interest is at stake. And it's hard to show that humanitarian relief [and any peace operations by extension] is a vital national interest" (Brooks: A1).

U.S. POLICY: BURDEN SHARING ON THE CHEAP?

The U.S. has chosen to provide intelligence support to specific UN peace operations on a case-by-case basis in accordance with U.S. national interests. Presidential Decision Directive 25 predicates any future U.S. support for and participation in UN peace operations upon advancement of U.S. interests. Critics charge that criteria elaborated in this policy are so restrictive "as to scope mission, duration, resources and risk that only the easiest, cheapest, safest peacekeeping operations could likely be approved under them, and many of the current operations could not" ("Peace-Keeping": C6). After the domestic political uproar caused by casualties in Somalia, provision of intelligence support to the UN gives the U.S. one option for participating in future peace operations without undue risk to combat personnel.

Canadian MG Lewis MacKenzie believes that U.S. combat troops should be kept out of UN peace operations. He notes: "You don't get your picture on the cover of *Newsweek* by killing Canadians. You've got to kill Americans." He suggests that, among other forms of support, the U.S. provide satellite imagery to the UN rather than combat forces (Rowley: A3). Indeed, as early as September 1993, with Congressional unease growing over UN operations in Bosnia and Somalia, U.S. Ambassador to the UN Madeleine Albright noted "specialized areas such as logistics, training, intelligence, communications and public affairs" held the greatest promise for future U.S. contributions to peace operations (Goshko: A19).

U.S. CONSTRAINTS

U.S. government policy that has been established for sharing intelligence with the UN is not universally accepted either by the U.S. Congress or the Intelligence Community. Senator Robert Dole has been a particularly vocal critic of the U.S. intelligence relationship with the UN. Concerns over the extent to which UN intelligence capabilities would be expanded under PDD-25 led Senator Dole to introduce legislation in January 1994 to restrict U.S. support for that undertaking. Section 16 of Senate Bill S. 1803 would require a formal agreement between the U.S. and UN to be concluded governing intelligence sharing. As a formal agreement, it would be subject to review by both the Senate Select Committee on Intelligence and House Permanent Select Committee on Intelligence (Best: 12).

Elements of the U.S. Intelligence Community, especially those outside the Department of Defense, remain wary of an intelligence relationship with the UN. The threat to sensitive intelligence sources and methods is the primary concern of the community. Beyond this legitimate and often-stated risk, budgetary considerations in an era of dwindling resources may eventually force the U.S. to limit any expansion of intelligence support to UN peace operations. This will especially be true if supporting the UN competes with higher priority U.S. intelligence interests such as nonproliferation. Richard Best, a national defense analyst with the Congressional Research Service, observes that "[i]n budget planning sessions, it is difficult to defend devoting collection and analytical resources...on targets whose importance at best is problematical (Best: 18).

DEPENDENCE UPON MEMBER STATES: PITFALLS FOR THE UN

The combination of fiscal constraints on the U.S. Intelligence Community and the proclivity of the Security Council to authorize peace operations in regions of marginal interest to the U.S. and the other major powers is bound to present the UN problems in garnering adequate intelligence support from its member states. As William Durch explains:

> Reliance on major powers for data could fail the UN . . . when an issue or a region important to the organization had not routinely received attention from the major powers' intelligence agencies; that is when its priorities failed to mesh with those of its most powerful members (Durch *c*: 8).

The paucity of U.S. human intelligence assets available in Somalia, due to its relatively low priority in American foreign policy, is an example of such a failure caused by UN reliance on a major power. Refusal by the U.S. to sanction UN intervention in Burundi during November 1993, and its initial opposition to deployment of an expanded peace operation in Rwanda in April 1994, should serve as warnings to the UN that it may not always be able to depend on the U.S. for intelligence support if UN activities are not in accord with high-priority U.S. interests, or the clear interests of our friends and allies.

Dependence on the U.S. and other member states for intelligence support could also fail the UN if national interests are perceived to be influenced by an ongoing or proposed peace operation. Nations will be either unwilling to provide sensitive information to a UN intelligence organization that cannot ensure security—as occurs now at the UN Situation Center and occurred in Somalia—or will feed in information with a distinct bias. Those states whose interests are most closely associated with regions of conflict are likely to have the best information, but also the greatest incentive to provide filtered or biased information. While U.S. and UN officials maintain that information from a single nation cannot be relied upon for UN decisionmaking, effective U.S. domination of the system may ultimately place the UN in a dilemma. Moreover, the potential to cause political embarrassment exists when a decision made by the UN is based on a member state's information. For example, target-of-attack intelligence in a peace enforcement environment might form the basis for a UN assault that inadvertently kills civilians.

Information-Flow Disconnects

The U.S. has aided the UN in creating an intelligence structure oriented toward the conduct of military operations. The structure envisions intelligence information collected, analyzed, and produced at higher-level intelligence facilities (the U.S. National Military Joint Intelligence Center in the Pentagon and the UN Situation Center at UN headquarters in New York), and then disseminated down to an operational commander in the field, the UN Force Commander, through both military and diplomatic channels. Simultaneously, relevant tactical information from the UN Force Commander is expected to move upward to decisionmakers in UN headquarters via the Situation Center. The system breaks down because the UN intelligence cycle is dysfunctional and discontinuous at all levels.

Tactically relevant information provided to the Situation Center is extremely limited. The intelligence provided is rarely disseminated down to the field because of inadequate communications capability. Intelligence that is collected in the field by UN peace missions (considered the best information because of its human intelligence content) is not routinely disseminated back to the Situation Center because it is not needed by the Center's customers. Information critical for the protection and operations of UN troops in the field can only be supplied by intelligence resources located in-country, as the situation in Somalia demonstrated. Unfortunately, provision and practice of intelligence support to

UN peace operations challenges U.S. multilateral intelligence doctrine.

The Consumer: The Critical Issue

Discontinuities in information flow within the current UN intelligence support organization point to the underlying issue that remains unresolved: Who is the ultimate consumer of intelligence? A divergence of views exists between the U.S. Department of Defense and the UN Department of Peacekeeping Operations as to where the emphasis of intelligence support should be placed. U.S. intelligence support networks currently in place are oriented toward supporting military operations in the field. UN efforts are focused toward informing policymakers in the UN bureaucracy. U.S. government policy advocates an enhancement of the latter capability. Neither approach, working through the Situation Center, is likely to be successful, given the UN's structure and management of peace activities.

Any tactical information fed into the Situation Center, whether from the U.S., other member states, or the field, is just that — information, and not intelligence. Intelligence influences decisionmakers' choices, but other than seconded military officers in the UN situation center, there are no military decisionmakers within the UN Department of Peacekeeping Operations (DPKO). The DPKO is a staff support organization of the Secretary-General and Security Council. It is concerned with the political, diplomatic, and logistical aspects of peace operations, not the orchestration of military operations. This lack of an effective military command and control capability proved a major UN failing in Somalia. Like the rest of the UN, DPKO decision and policymaking relies upon careful deliberation and consensus building, hardly a process in need of the rapid intelligence exchange capability promoted by the U.S.

The UN vision of intelligence support aiding the organization's policymakers to make better informed choices about peace activities also faces numerous stumbling blocks inherent to the UN environment. Policymaking for the full scope of UN peace activities requires the same consensus building necessary within the DPKO, with the added bureaucratic impediment of coordination of the process across many competitive UN Departments (DPKO, Department of Political Affairs, Department of Humanitarian Affairs). Forecasting of global trends and disputes to provide early warning of crises requires intelligence input and analysis. Member states are reluctant to contribute information into that process out of concern over security and sovereignty. National interests filter the availability and content of information member states are willing to share with the UN. As William Durch asserts:

> [W]here the SG's [Secretary-General's] good offices and UN action might help to head off, later larger troubles, what the UN needs and what it can get from member states may not be a good match (Durch *c*: 8).

Analysis the UN performs on information received from member states or in open sources will be suspected of partiality if input is dependent upon a few states or analysis is perceived to be performed by nationals of a few countries. The negative U.S. reaction to Soviet efforts to dominate the abortive Office of Research and Collection of Information (ORCI) under Secretary Perez de Cuellar is relevant in this regard.

WHAT DIFFERENCE CAN INTELLIGENCE MAKE?

Obstacles encountered in providing effective intelligence support to UN policymakers on peace activities beg the question of whether better intelligence input in the UN context would make a difference in the world body's decisionmaking process. Can intelligence provide the UN the means to "know when to say no" to a peace operation with a limited chance of success, as President Clinton has asked? (Marcus: A1). Would information that helped to accurately discern an operation's scope, duration, and cost in dollars and lives dissuade the UN from embarking on a peace mission? The debates in the Security Council prior to passage of the resolution which expanded the mandate in Somalia from humanitarian assistance to open combat with General Aideed, and later authorized deployment of a peace mission into the carnage of Rwanda, suggest the members of the Council had a full appreciation for the existing conditions, yet authorized these actions nonetheless.

The UN is, above all, a reflection of international politics and the desires of its most powerful members, expressed thorough the Security Council. As former U.S. Assistant Secretary of State Chester Crocker notes:

> It is simply irresponsible (as well as dishonest) for American commentators to blast "the UN" for problems arising from ill-conceived or poorly drawn [peace operation] mandates. We need forcefully to remind ourselves, our media and our public opinion

> that the UN Security Council is a mirror of the action, inactions, fudges and fantasies of its leading members, who can veto anything they do not like (Crocker: C4).

It is unrealistic to expect intelligence information provided to or produced by the UN bureaucracy to overcome the currents of world politics or compensate for fundamentally flawed decisionmaking by a Security Council which dispatches UN troops into a civil war. While U.S. and other nations' intelligence agencies may be able to deliver information of tactical significance to forces in the field, as was seen in Somalia, or supply the DPKO with data to facilitate mission planning, the ultimate success of UN missions depends upon their deployment where conditions for their success exist. Most important among these are consent of the belligerents to the mission and impartiality of the peacekeepers in performance of their mission. Success of peace operations that are mounted in contradiction to recognized conditions for peacekeeping, without effective command and control for military operations, and with inadequate logistics is open to question. It is the responsibility of the U.S. and the other fourteen members of the Security Council — especially the Permanent Five — to employ the available capabilities of their national intelligence agencies to assess the prospects of a proposed UN peace mission and vote against those with little chance to succeed.

REFERENCES CITED

Abizaid, John P., LTC, USA. "Lessons for Peacekeepers." *Military Review* 73, no. 3 (March 1993): 11-19.

Abizaid, John P. and John R. Wood, LTCs, USA. *Peacekeeping Operations: A Trip Report.* March 1993.

"Agreement Between the Government of the United States and the Government of Japan Concerning Reciprocal Provision of Logistic Support, Supplies, and Services Between the Armed Forces of the United States of America and the Self-Defense Forces of Japan." n.p., 1996.

"Agreement Between the International Atomic Energy Agency and the Government of the Democratic People's Republic of Korea for the Application of Safeguards to the Research Reactor Facility (IRT)." *United Nations Treaty Series* 1065, no. 799 (20 July 1977), part 2.

"Agreements on the Establishment of the Tumen River Area Development Coordination Committee by the governments of the DPRK, the PRC and the Russian Federation, signed in New York." n.p., 6 December 1995.

Albright, David and Mark Hibbs. "Iraq's Nuclear Hide-and-Seek." *Bulletin of the Atomic Scientists* 47, no. 7 (September 1991): 14-23.

Albright, Madeleine K. (*a*) "Myths of Peacekeeping." *U.S. Department of State Dispatch* 4, no. 26 (28 June 1993): 464-467.

________. (*b*) "Statement at Confirmation Hearing of U.S. Ambassador to the United Nations." Statement before the Senate Foreign Relations Committee, Washington, DC, 21 January 1993. *U.S. Department of State Dispatch* 4, no. 5 (12 April 1993): 229-231.

________. (*c*) "Testimony Before the Senate Foreign Relations Committee on U.S. Role in UN Peacekeeping, 20 October 1993." *Foreign Policy Bulletin* 4, nos. 4 and 5 (January/April 1994): 50-54.

________. (*d*) "Use of Force in a Post-Cold-War World." Speech at the National War College, 23 September 1993.

Allard, Kenneth. *Somalia Lessons Learned.* Washington, DC: National Defense University Press, 1995.

Allardice, Robert B., MAJ, USAF. "Summary — CTF PROVIDE COMFORT." *Joint Universal Lesson Learned Report* 71024-35616, 10 January 1992.

Army-Air Force Center for Low-Intensity Conflict. *Peacekeeping Tactics, Techniques and Procedures.* Alexandria, VA: Defense Technical Information Service, 1989.

"Army Moves to Prevent Killings in Peacekeeping Operations" (text). *Lagos Radio* (16 September 1993) 0600 GMT AB1609110993. Extracted by FBIS Abidjan. 16 September 1993.

Aspin, Les. Remarks at the American Bar Association Breakfast. Subject: "The Future of the CIA." International Club, Washington, DC, 19 January 1995.

Atkinson, Rick. "The Raid That Went Awry." *Washington Post,* 30 January 1994, A1.

Auer, James E. "Article Nine: Renunciation of War." In *Japanese Constitutional Law.* Eds R. Luney and Takahashi Kazyuki. Tokyo: University of Tokyo, 1993, 69-86.

Ayers, Charles M., LTC, USA. *Peacekeeping Tactics, Techniques and Procedures.* Langley AFB, VA: Army-Air Force Center for Low-Intensity Conflict, April 1989.

Bailey, Sydney D. *The Korea Armistice.* New York: St. Martin's Press, 1992.

Bair, Andrew S. and Edward P. Joseph. "What Happened in Yugoslavia?; Lessons for Future Peace-Keepers." Unpublished conference paper for National Defense University's Topical Symposium on *Military Coalitions and the UN: Implications for the U.S. Military.* Washington, DC, 2-3 November 1993.

Baker, Caleb. "Manhunt for Aideed: Why the Rangers Came Up Empty-Handed." *Armed Forces Journal International* 133, no. 5 (December 1993): 18.

Baker, James. "Iraqi Refugees: The Need for International Assistance." *U.S. Department of State Dispatch 2,* no. 15 (15 April 1991): 271-272.

Bateman, Robert L. LT, USA. "U.S. Battalion Operations in the Multinational Force and Observers." *Infantry* 82, no. 4 (July-August 1992): 7-10.

Batten, Peter. Deputy to the Under Secretary of Defense (Policy), Policy Support/ International Security/National Disclosure Policy Committee. Information Paper: "Possible Compromise of Classified Information by UNOSOM Forces During Operation UNITED SHIELD in Somalia." 16 May 1995.

Baynham, Simon. *The Military and Politics in Nkrumah's Ghana.* Boulder, CO: Westview Press, 1988.

Beigbeder, Yves. *The Role and Status of International Humanitarian Volunteers and Organizations: The Right and Duty to Humanitarian Assistance.* Dordrecht, Netherlands: Martinus Nijhoff Publishers, 1991.

Berdal, Mats R. (*a*) "Fateful Encounter: The United States and UN Peacekeeping. *Survival.* Vol 36 No. 1. Spring 1994. 30-50.

________. (*b*) "Whither UN Peacekeeping?" *Adelphi Paper* 281. London: Institute of Strategic Studies, October 1993.

Bermudez, Joseph S., Jr. "North Korea Set to Join the Nuclear Club?" *Jane's Defense Weekly* 12, no. 12 (23 September 1989): 594-597.

Best, Richard A., Jr. "Peacekeeping: Intelligence Requirements." *CRS Report for Congress* 94-394F. Washington, DC: Congressional Research Service, Library of Congress, 6 May 1994.

Betts, Richard K. *Surprise Attack: Lessons for Defense Planning.* Washington, DC: Brookings Institution, 1982.

Binnendijk, Hans, and Patrick Clawson, eds. *Strategic Assessment 1995: U.S. Security Challenges in Transition.* Washington, DC: Institute for National Strategic Studies, National Defense University, 1995.

Biskupic, Joan. "War Powers: Constitution's Conflicting Clauses Underscored by Iraq Crisis." *Congressional Quarterly* 49, no. 1 (5 January 1991): 33-36.

Blaker, Michael. "Evaluating Japanese Diplomatic Performance." In *Japan's Foreign Policy After the Cold War: Coping with Change.* Ed. Gerald L. Curtis. Armonk, NY: East Gate, 1993, 1-42.

Blix, Hans. (*a*) "IAEA DG Blix May 16 Beijing Press Conference on the North Korean Nuclear Program." American Embassy Beijing message to U.S. Department of State and others. 17 May 1992.

________. (*b*) "Press Conference by Director-General of IAEA." 1 November 1993. URL: gopher://gopher.undp.org/5000.00/briefings/93_11.

"Blood on the Border." *Asiaweek*, 3 November 1995, 35.

Bolton, John R. "Learning the Limits: The Politics and Priorities of the United Nations in the New World Order." Speech at The University of London, 13 February 1995 (Federal Document Clearinghouse Inc., LEXIS/NEXIS, Inc.).

Boulden, Jane. "Background Notes on Article 43." P*roceedings of the Workshop on Military Implications of United Nations Peacekeeping Operations,* 17 November 1992, Vol II, sponsored by the National Defense University, Institute of Strategic Studies.

Boutros-Ghali, Boutros. (*a*) *An Agenda for Peace*, 1995. 2d ed. New York: United Nations, 1995.

________. (*b*) *An Agenda for Peace: Preventive Diplomacy, Peacemaking and Peace-Keeping.* New York: United Nations, 1992.

________. (*c*) *Building Peace and Development 1994, Annual Report on the Work of the Organization.* New York: United Nations, 1994.

Bowens, Gregory J. (*a*) "Haiti: The Next Showdown." *Congressional Quarterly* 51, no. 41 (16 October 1993): 2825.

________. (*b*) "House Backs Measure Allowing U.S. Role in UN Operations." *Congressional Quarterly* 51, no. 22 (29 May 1993): 1373.

Branch, Patrick. CTF PROVIDE COMFORT Intelligence Staff. Interview by author, 8 July 1993.

"Briefing for Visit of USS Whidbey Island." Message from American Embassy Accra to USS Whidbey Island and others, 15 November 1993.

Brooks, Geraldine. "Globocop." *Wall Street Journal*, 28 December 1993, A1, A4.

Browne, Marjorie Ann. (*a*) "United Nations Peacekeeping: Historical Overview and Current Issues." *CRS Report for Congress* 90-96F. Washington, DC: Congressional Research Service, Library of Congress, 31 January 1990.

________. (*b*) "United Nations Peacekeeping Operations, 1988-1993: Background Information." *CRS Report for Congress* 94-193F. Washington, DC: Congressional Research Service, Library of Congress, 28 February 1994.

Budianski, Stephen and others. "Saddam's Revenge." *U.S. News and World Report,* 15 April 1991, 26-31.

Burns, Arthur Lee and Nina Heathcote. *Peace-keeping by U.N. Forces.* Westport, CO: Greenwood Press, 1975.

Bush, George. (*a*) "Address to the Nation Announcing the Deployment of United States Armed Forces to Saudi Arabia." *Weekly Compilation of Presidential Documents* 26, no. 32 (8 August 1990): 1216-1218.

________. (*b*) "Address to the Nation on the Situation in Somalia." *Weekly Compilation of Presidential Documents* 28, no 49 (4 December 1992): 2329-2331.

________. (*c*) "Address to the UN General Assembly in New York City, 21 September 1992." *Weekly Compilation of Presidential Documents* 28, no. 39 (28 September 1992): 1697-1701.

________. (*d*) "Cease-Fire Holds in Persian Gulf; Iraq Commanders Agree to Allied Terms." *Facts on File*, 7 March 1991, 149-150.

________. (*e*) "Question-and-Answer Session with Reporters in Hobe Sound, Florida, 3 April 1991." *Weekly Compilation of Presidential Documents* 27 no. 14 (5 April 1991): 381-384.

________. (*f*) Resolving Global Conflicts and Disarmament: Building Economic Partnerships. *Vital Speeches of the Day* 59, no. 1 (15 October 1992): 2-5.

________. (*g*) "The President's News Conference, 30 November 1990." *Weekly Compilation of Presidential Documents* 26, no 48 (3 December 1990): 1948-1956.

________. (*h*) "The Presidents' News Conference on the Persian Gulf Crisis." *Weekly Compilation of Presidential Documents* 26, no. 34 (22 August 1990): 1281-1287.

________. (*i*) "The President's News Conference on the Persian Gulf Crisis." *Weekly Compilation of Presidential Documents* 26, no 45 (8 November 1990): 1789-1795.

________. (*j*) "U.S. Expands Kurdish Relief Efforts." *U.S. Department of State Dispatch* 2, no 16 (22 April 1991): 273.

Byrd, Robert C. "The Perils of Peacekeeping." *New York Times*, 19 August 1993, A23.

"Cabinet Approves SDF Mission to Golan Heights" (text). Tokyo *Kyodo* (29 August 1995). *FBIS Daily Report—East Asia*, 29 August 1995, 4.

"Cambodia: Task of Nation-Building 'Monumental'." *UN Chronicle* 31, no. 2 (June 1994): 38.

Campbell, Larry, COL, USA. Chief, Department of Defense Peacekeeping Office at the Pentagon. Interview by author, 20 May 1993.

Carter, Holly Ornstein. "A Field of Dreams in Northeast Asia." *Choices, The Human Development Magazine of the UNDP*, October 1995. 11-13.

Cassata, Donna. (*a*) "A Venerable Cold Warrior Finds New Missions." *Congressional Quarterly* 53, no. 34 (2 September 1995): 2665.

________. (*b*) "Can the UN Keep a Secret?" *Congressional Quarterly*. 53, no. 11 (18 March 1995): 826.

Central Intelligence Agency. (a) Director of Central Intelligence Directive 1/7: *Security Controls on the Dissemination of Intelligence Information*. 16 April 1996.

________. (*b*) "Sub-Saharan Africa: Involvement in Peacekeeping." Chart. Washington DC: GPO, September 1993.

"Charter Committee Reports Progress Regarding UN Fact-Finding Process." *UN Chronicle* 27, no. 2 (June 1990): 32-34.

Cho, Sung Yoon. *Japan's International Peace Cooperation Law and the Japanese Constitution*. Monograph. Washington, DC: Law Library of Congress, December 1992.

CJTF Somalia. Message to CINC USCENTCOM and others. Subject: "Press Briefing of 26 February 1993." 26 February 1993.

Claude, Inis L., Jr. *Swords Into Plowshares: The Problems and Progress of International Organization*. 4th ed. New York: McGraw-Hill, 1984.

Clinton, President William J. (*a*) Letter to Senate Majority Leader Robert Dole. Subject: "Response to Congressional Concerns Over U.S. Intelligence Material Found in UNOSOM II Compound, Mogadishu, Somalia." 6 April 1995.

________. (*b*) "Confronting the Challenges of a Broader World." Address to the UN General Assembly. New York, 27 September 1993. *U.S. Department of State Dispatch* 4, no. 39 (27 September 1993): 649-653.

________. (*c*) "Foreign Policy Speech." Presented to the Foreign Policy Association. New York, 1 April 1992. Transcribed by Federal News Service.

________. (*d*) "Foreign Policy Speech." Presented to the Los Angeles World Affairs Council. Los Angeles, 13 August 1992. Transcribed by Federal News Service.

________. (*e*) "President's Press Conference, 16 June 1994." *Foreign Policy Bulletin* 5, no. 1 (July/August 1994): 31-33.

________. (*f*) "President's Remarks to the Korean National Assembly, Seoul, July 10, 1993." *Foreign Policy Bulletin* 4, no. 2 (September/October 1993): 16-19.

________. (*g*) "U.S. Military Involvement in Somalia." Address to the Nation. *U.S. Department of State Dispatch* 4, no. 42 (18 October 1993): 713-714.

Clough, Ralph N. "U.S.-Korean Relations in the Year 2000." In *Korea: The Year 2000*. Vol. 5 of Ethics and Foreign Policy Series. Eds, Han Sung-Joo and Robert J. Myers, Lanham: MD: University Press of America, 1988, 19-35.

"Coalition Endorses Peacekeepers to Golan Heights" (text). Tokyo *Kyodo* (25 August 1995). *FBIS Daily Report—East Asia*, 25 August 1995, 3.

Cohen, Roger. "UN Military Aide Says Plight of Gorazde Is Exaggerated." *New York Times*, 30 April 1994, A3.

"Collection of Laws and Regulations," Pyongyang: The Committee for the Promotion of External Economic Cooperation of the DPR of Korea, 1994.

Combest, Rep. Larry (Texas). "Opening Statement: Full Committee Markup of the National Security Revitalization Act, H.R. 7." House Permanent Select Committee on Intelligence, 27 January 1995. Federal Document Clearing House, LEXIS-NEXIS, Inc., 10 May 1996.

Commission on the Roles and Capabilities of the United States Intelligence Community. *Preparing for the 21st Century: An Appraisal of U.S. Intelligence*. Washington, DC: GPO, 1 March 1996.

Constantine, G. Ted. *Intelligence Support to Humanitarian-Disaster Relief Operations*. Washington, DC: Center for the Study of Intelligence, Central Intelligence Agency, 1995.

Cooper, Kenneth and Ann Devroy. "House Votes to Lift Embargo on Bosnia." *Washington Post*, 2 August 1995, A1.

Covenant of the League of Nations. 2 Bevar 48-58, *1919 Foreign Relations of the United States* (Paris Peace Conference, XIII) 55, 740, 743: Senate document 51, 66th Cong, 1st sess.

Crigler, T. Frank. "The Peace-Enforcement Dilemma." *Joint Force Quarterly* No. 2 (Autumn 1993): 64-70.

"Croatian Forces Seize Maslenica Cove Area" (text). Belgrade *Tanjug* (23 January 1993) 2104 GMT LD2301213693. Translated by FBIS London, 23 January 1993.

Crocker, Chester A. "Peacekeeping We Can Fight For." *Washington Post*, 8 May 1994, C1, 4.

Croddy, Eric. "Chuche, The Political Economy of the DPRK." *Jane's Intelligence Review* 8, no. 6 (June 1996): 271-277.

Curtis, Grant. "Transition to What? Cambodia, UNTAC and the Peace Process," Discussion Paper 48. Geneva, Switzerland: United Nations Research Institute for Social Development, November 1993.

Davis, Phillip A. "Hill Backs Sending Troops." *Congressional Quarterly* 50, no. 48 (5 December 1992): 3760.

Dedring, Juergen. "Early Warning and the United Nations." *Journal of Ethno-Development* 4, no. 1 (July 1994): 98-104.

DeMars, William. "Waiting for Early Warning: Humanitarian Action After the Cold War." *Journal of Refugee Studies* 8, no. 4 (December 1995): 390-410.

Democratic People's Republic of Korea (DPRK). Committee for the Promotion of External Economic Cooperation. *The Golden Triangle*. 1994 (40-minute Video Cassette).

Denny, Sharon. "China Hires Weapons Experts." *Defense News* 7, no. 33 (17-23 August 1992): 2.

Deutch, John. Deputy Secretary of Defense. Letter to Senator Larry Combest, Chairman, House Permanent Select Committee on Intelligence. Subject: "Transmittal of the Report of Investigation from the United States Central Command Concerning the Circumstances Surrounding Classified Information Found at the UNOSOM Compound in Mogadishu on 27 February 1995." 17 April 1995.

Devroy, Ann. "U.S. Stance at UN Dismays Allies: New Force for Bosnia Approved, but No Means of Paying for It." *Washington Post*, 17 June 1995: A12.

Devroy, Ann and Anne Swardson. "G-7 Leaders Urge Bosnian Truce, Recommitment to Peace Process." *Washington Post*, 16 June 1995, A29.

Dicks, Rep. Norm (Washington). (*a*) "Opening Statement: Committee Hearing on Intelligence Support to the United Nations." House Permanent Select Committee on Intelligence, 19 January 1995. Federal Document Clearing House, LEXIS-NEXIS, Inc., 10 May 1996.

________. (*b*) "Opening Statement: Full Committee Markup of the National Security Revitalization Act, H.R. 7." House Permanent Select Committee on Intelligence, 27 January 1995. Federal Document Clearing House, LEXIS-NEXIS, Inc., 10 May 1996.

Di Rita, Lawrence T. "C'mon, Baby — Do the Multilateral." *National Review*, 4 October 1993, 42-44.

Dmitrichev, Timour F. "Conceptual Approaches to Early Warning — Mechanisms and Methods: A View from the United Nations." *International Journal of Refugee Law* 3, no. 2 (1991): 264-271.

"Documents Mishandled in Somalia Exit." *Facts on File* 55, no. 2840 (4 May 1995): 322.

Doherty, Carrol J. (a) "Byrd's Caution: A Vietnam Legacy." *Congressional Quarterly* 51, no 41 (16 October 1993): 2824.

________. (*b*) "Contrary Paths to Peacekeeping Converge in Wake of Violence." *Congressional Quarterly* 51, no. 39 (2 October 1993): 2655-2657.

________. (*c*) "The Reluctant Warriors." *Congressional Quarterly* 51, no. 7 (13 February 1993): 323.

Donohue, D.L. and R. Zeisler, "Behind the Scenes: Scientific Analysis of Samples from Nuclear Inspections in Iraq." *IAEA Bulletin* 34, No. 1 (1992): 25-32

Druke, Luise. *Preventive Action for Refugee Producing Situations*. 2d ed. Frankfurt am Main: Peter Lang, 1993.

Duke, Simon. "The United Nations and Intra-State Conflict." *International Peacekeeping* 1, no. 4 (Winter 1994): 375-393.

Durch, William J. (*a*) "Introduction." In *The Evolution of Peacekeeping: Case Studies and Comparative Analysis*, Ed William J. Durch, 1-14. New York: St. Martin's Press, 1993.

________. (*b*) "Running the Show: Planning and Implementation." In *The Evolution of Peacekeeping: Case Studies and Comparative Analysis*, Ed William J. Durch, 59-75. New York: St. Martin's Press, 1993.

________. (*c*) *The United Nations and Collective Security in the 21st Century*. Carlisle Barracks, PA: U.S. Army War College, February 1993.

Eastland, Terry. "War Powers Resolution Redux." *Wall Street Journal*, 17 November 1993, 23.

Economist Intelligence Unit (EIU). *Ethiopia, Eritrea, Somalia, Djibouti: EIU Country Report*, 1st Quarter, 1993.

Eliasson, Jan. "The Humanitarian Challenges for the UN: Lessons to be Learned from Bosnia and Somalia?" *Brown Journal of World Affairs* 1, no. 2 (Spring 1994): 179-201.

"Equality and Mutual Benefit," *Foreign Trade of the DPRK*, January 1996, 22.

Erskine, Emmanuel A., LTG. *Mission with UNIFIL: An African Soldier's Reflections*. New York: St. Martin's Press, 1989.

Evans, Gareth. *Cooperating for Peace*. St. Leonards, AS: Allen and Unwin Pty Ltd., 1993.

Fairbank, John K., Edwin O Reischauer and Albert M. Craig. *East Asia: Tradition and Transformation*. Rev. ed. Boston: Houghton Mifflin Company, 1989.

Fallows, James. "The Panic Gap: Reactions to North Korea's Bomb." *National Interest* 38 (Winter 1994/1995): 40-45.

Farris, Karl. "UN Peacekeeping in Cambodia: On Balance, A Success." *Parameters* 24, no. 1 (Spring 1994): 38-50.

Fehrenbach, T.R. *This Kind of War: The Classic Korean War History*. Washington: DC: Brassey's, 1994.

Fessler, Pamela. "Gates Tells of Enduring threats to U.S., World Security." *Congressional Quarterly* 50, no. 9 (29 February 1992): 480.

"Fighting Continues in Kigali" (text). Paris *AFP* (20 June 1994) 1202 GMT AB2006125594. Extracted by FBIS Abidjan. 23 June 1994.

Fineman, Mark. "UN Continues to Have Bad Luck in Somalia." *Los Angeles Times*, 31 August 1993, A2.

"First Picture Shows North Korea." *Daily Yomiuri*, 1 February 1990. LEXIS-NEXIS, Inc., 10 May 1996.

Fischer, David. "Consequences of the Iraq Case for Non-Proliferation Policy." in *Nichtverbreitung von Kernwaffen: Neue Probleme und Perspektiven, Arbeitspapiere zur Internationalen Politik* 66. Bonn, GM: Europa Union Verlag, 1991.

Fishel, John T. *Liberation, Occupation and Rescue: War Termination and DESERT STORM*. Carlisle Barracks, PA: U.S. Army War College, 31 August 1992.

Fisher, Louis. "The Korean War: On What Legal Basis Did Truman Act?" *The American Journal of International Law* 89, no. 1 (1995): 21-39.

Fleitz, Frederick H. *Worldwide Peacekeeping Operations 1993.* Washington, DC: Central Intelligence Agency, 1992.

Ford, Gerald. Letter to Hon. James O. Eastland, President Pro Tempore of the Senate, 12 April 1975.

Foreign Policy Association. *Great Decisions.* Ripon, WI: Ripon Community Printers, 1995.

Freeman, Waldo D., MG, USA, CDR Randall J. Hess, USN and LTC Manuel Faria, Portuguese Army. "The Challenges of Combined Operations." *Military Review* 72, no. 11 (November 1992): 3-11.

Friedman, Thomas L. "Clinton, at UN, Lists Stiff Terms for Sending U.S. Force to Bosnia." *New York Times*, 28 September 1993, A1, A16.

Fulghum, David A. "U.S. Pressures North Korea to Shed Nuclear Weapons." *Aviation Week and Space Technology*, 28 March 1994, 22-23.

Gaffney, Frank. (a) "Mending the Sieve of Shared Secrets." *Washington Times.* 26 July 1995, A20.

________. (*b*) "The Deforming of Intelligence." *Washington Times.* 7 May 1996, A12.

Garrett, Banning and Glaser, Bonnie. "Looking Across the Yalu: Chinese Assessments of North Korea." *Asian Survey* Vol 35, no. 6 (June 1995): 528-545.

Gati, Toby. (*a*) "Statement by Assistant Secretary of State Before the House Permanent Select Committee on Intelligence, Hearing on Intelligence Support to the UN." 19 January 1995. Federal Document Clearing House, LEXIS-NEXIS, Inc.

________. (*b*) "Statement by Assistant Secretary of State for Intelligence and Research before the Senate Select Committee on Intelligence. "Worldwide Threats to the United States." 10 January 1995. Federal Document Clearing House, LEXIS-NEXIS, Inc., 10 May 1996.

________. (*c*) Assistant Secretary of State for Intelligence and Research. Letter to Ambassador Hugh Montgomery. Subject: "UN Request for Intelligence on Guatemala and Burundi." 1 February 1996.

Gellman, Barton. (*a*) "U.S. Reconsiders Putting GIs Under UN: Concern over Somalia and Bosnia Prompts Backlash in Congress." *Washington Post*, 22 September 1993, A1.

________. (*b*) "Wider U.N. Police Role Supported: Foreigners Could Lead U.S. Troops." *Washington Post*, 5 August 1993, A1, A22.

"General Boutros on Parade." *Economist*, 31 July 1993, 36.

"Genscher Launches Nonproliferation Initiative" (text). Duesseldorf Handelsblatt (20 January 1992). *FBIS Daily Report — West Europe* 21 January 1992, 14-15.

Gerardi, Greg J. and Maryam Aharinejad. "An Assessment of Iran's Nuclear Facilities." *The Non-Proliferation Review* 2, no. 3 (Spring/Summer 1995): 207-213.

Gertz, Bill. (*a*) "Administration Plays Down Leaks of U.S. Secrets by UN." *Washington Times*. 20 January 1995, A8.

________. (*b*) "New UN Service Cited As A Soviet Propaganda Tool." *Washington Times*, 12 March 1987, 1A.

________. (*c*) "U.S. Will Pull Sanctions if Pyongyang Halts Missile Program," *Washington Times*, 5 June 1996, A20.

Glain, Steve and Nanju Cho. "China Seeks to Halt Flow of North Korean Refugees." *The Wall Street Journal*, 9 February 1996. A6.

Glennon, Michael J. "The Gulf War and the Constitution." *Foreign Affairs* 70, no. 2 (Spring 1991): 84-101.

"Going There-North Korea is Looking to Foreigners." *The Oregonian*, 28 March 1995, A8.

Goldman, Jan. "A Changing World, A Changing UN." *Military Review* 124, no. 9 (September 1994): 12-18.

Goldman, Ralph M. *Is it Time to Revive the Military Staff Committee*? California State University: National Defense University Press, 1990.

Goodrich, Leland M., Edvard Hambro and Anne Patricia Simons. *Charter of the United Nations Commentary and Documents*. New York: Columbia University Press, 1969.

Gordan, Ruth. "United Nations Intervention in Internal Conflicts: Iraq, Somalia and Beyond." *Michigan Journal of International Law* 15, no. 1 (Winter 1994): 519-530.

Gordenker, Leon. "Early Warning of Refugee Incidents." In *Refugees and International Relations*. Eds. Gil Loescher and L. Monahan. New York: Oxford University Press, 1989, 355-371.

Gorman, Robert F. *Historical Dictionary of Refugee and Disaster Relief Organizations*. Metuchen, NJ: Scarecrow Press, Inc., 1994.

Goshko, John M. "U.S. Lists Stiff Conditions for Troop Role in UN Peacekeeping." *Washington Post*, 24 September 1993, A19.

"Government Approves Dispatch of Troops to Rwanda" (text). Tokyo *Kyodo* (13 September 1994) *FBIS Daily Report—East Asia,* 13 September 1994, 7.

Graham, Robert. Editorial. *London Financial Times*, 20 December 1992: C3.

Gries, David D. "Opening Up Secret Intelligence." *Orbis* 37, no. 3 (Summer 1993): 365-372.

Grove, Eric. "UN Armed Forces and the Military Staff Committee: A Look Back." *International Security* vol. 17, no. 4 (Spring 1993): 172-182.

Gurtov, Mel. "Swords into Market Shares: China's Conversion of Military Industry to Civilian Production." *The China Quarterly*, No. 134 (June 1993): 213-241.

Hall, Brian. "Blue Helmets, Empty Guns," *The New York Times Magazine*. 2 January 1994, 20-25, 30, 38, 41, 43.

Hammarskjold, Dag. *United Nations Emergency Force*. Summary study of the experience derived from the establishment of the force. UN Document A/3943, 9 October 1958.

Liddell Hart, B.H. *Strategy*, 2d revised edition. New York: Meridian, 1991.

Hashimoto, Prime Minister Ryutaro. "Japan's Hashimoto Gives Speech to Diet Session" (text). *FBIS Daily Report—East Asia*, 22 January 1996, 19-27.

Hayashi, Hiroshi, LTC. Assistant Professor of Strategy, National Defense Academy, Yokosuka, Japan. Interview by author, 26 June 1996.

Hayashi, Manami and Tetsuo Hidaka. "Political Parties Delay Review of PKO Law" (text). Tokyo *Yomiuri Shimbun* (6 August 1995). *FBIS Daily Report—East Asia*. 10 August 1995, 16-17.

Hayden, Michael V., Brig Gen, USAF. "Warfighters and Intelligence: One Team—One Fight." *Defense intelligence Journal* 4, no. 2 (Fall 1995): 17-30.

Hedges, Stephen J. and Peter Cary. "Saddam's Secret Bomb." *US News and World Report*, 25 November 1991, 34-42.

Heiberg, Marianne. *Observations on UN Peace Keeping in Lebanon*. Oslo: Norsk Utenrikspolitish Institutt, 1984.

Heininger, Janet E. *Peacekeeping in Transition: The United Nations in Cambodia*. New York: The Twentieth Century Fund Press, 1994.

Heinonen, Kurt C. "Gill Nets: O. What a Tangled Web." *Oceans*, 18, no. 6 (November 1985): 62-68.

Hibbs, Mark. (*a*) "Biggest North Korean Reactor Site Not Believed for Weapons Plutonium." *Nucleonics Week* 35, no. 41 (13 October 1994): 5.

________. (*b*) "IAEA Inspected North Korean Sites U.S. Intelligence Now Says Are Key." *Nucleonics Week* 34, no. 5 (4 February 1993): 18.

________. (*c*) "Isotopics Show Three North Korean Reprocessing Campaigns Since 1975." *Nuclear Fuel* 18, no. 5 (1 March 1993): 8.

________. (*d*) "North Korea Has Machines to Refuel Faster Than West's Experts Thought." *Nucleonics Week* 35, no. 22 (2 June 1994): 1.

________. (*e*) "North Korea Needs 6-9 Months to Reprocess Discharged Core." *Nucleonics Week* 35, no. 21 (26 May 1994): 17.

________. (*f*) "North Korea Thought to Have Separated PU in the 1970s with Soviet Help." *Nuclear Fuel* 17, no. 13 (22 June 1992): 15.

________. (*g*) "No U.S. Agency Consensus on DPRK Nuclear Progress." *Nucleonics Week* 35, no. 1 (6 January 1994): 9.

________. (*h*) "U.S. To Blame for Escalating North Korean Crisis, Asians Say." *Nucleonics Week* 43, no. 11 (18 March 1993): 1.

Hibbs, Mark and Kathleen Hart. "IAEA, U.S. Agencies Underestimated North Korea's Refueling Capacity." *Nuclear Fuel* 19, no. 12 (6 June 1994): 5.

Hibbs, Mark and Naoaki Usui. "Soviet Warning to North Korea Viewed As Signal to Tokyo, Seoul." *Nucleonics Week* 32, no. 16 (18 April 1991): 8.

Hiester, D. W. "Nuclear Proliferation: A Cause for Optimism?" In *At Issue: Politics in the World Arena*, ed. Steven Spiegel. New York: St. Martin's Press, 1988.

Hilderbrand, Robert C. *Dumbarton Oaks: The Origins of the United Nations and the Search for Postwar Security*. Chapel Hill, NC: The University of North Carolina Press, 1990.

Hirsch, John L. and Robert B. Oakley. *Somalia and Operation RESTORE HOPE*. Washington, DC: Institute of Peace Press, 1995.

Hitchens, Theresa. "Clinton Redirects Peacekeeping Policy." *Defense News*, 7 February 1994, 4.

Hoffmann, Walter. *United Nations Security Council Reform and Restructuring*. Monograph no. 14. Livingston, NJ: The Center for UN Reform and Education, December 1994.

Holmes, Steven A. "Clinton May Let U.S. Troops Serve Under UN Chiefs." *New York Times*, 18 August 1993, A1.

Hoopes, Townsend. *Whither UN Peacekeeping*? College Park, MD: Center for International and Security Studies at Maryland, 1994.

Horn, Carl von. *Soldiering for Peace*. New York: Van Rees Press, 1966.

Hoyt, Edwin P. *The Pusan Perimeter: Korea 1950*. New York: Military Heritage Press, 1984.

H.R. 4426, amendment 2272. Proposed by Senators Helms and Roth, and passed by voice vote on 14 July 1994. *Congressional Record*, 14 July 1994, S9006ff, S9044f, 1994.

Huang Hua. Former Foreign Minister of China. "The Market Economy in China." *Security Dialogue* 24, no. 2 (June 1993): 175-179.

Hunter, Horace L., COL, Ret., USA. Political-Military Advisor to the Army-Air Force Center for Low Intensity Conflict. Interview by author, 3 June 1993.

"IAEA Director Views Nuclear Policies." Berlin *Die Welt*. AU0208192593. *FBIS Daily Report—Western Europe*, 3 August 1993, 1-4.

Inoguchi, Takashi. (*a*) "Japan's United Nations Peacekeeping and Other Operations." *International Journal* 50, no 2 (Spring 1995): 325-342.

________. (*b*) Senior Vice-Rector, United Nations University, Tokyo, Japan. Interview by author, 18 June 1996.

"Inquiry Ordered into Girl's Death in Lebanon" (text). Accra Domestic (30 May 1987), 2000 GMT AB302129. Extracted by FBIS Abidjan. 30 May 1987.

International Atomic Energy Agency (IAEA). Document 291. "Safeguards Inspection in Democratic People's Republic of Korea to be Included in Agenda of IAEA General Conference." 23 September 1993. URL: gopher://gopher.undp.org/00/uncurr/press_release/iaea.

________. Document 1250. "IAEA General Conference Adopts Resolution on Nuclear Safeguards Implementation in Democratic People's Republic of Korea." 1 October 1993. URL: gopher://gopher.undp.org/00/uncurr/press_release/iaea/93_10.

________. Document 1253. "IAEA Director-General Comments on 'Declared' Nuclear Installations and Material in Democratic People's Republic of Korea." 6 December 1993. URL: gopher://gopher.undp.org/00/press_releases/iaea/93_12.

________. Document 1255. "Agreement Reached on Inspection Activities of Nuclear Facilities in Democratic People's Republic of Korea." 15 February 1994. URL: gopher://gopher.undp.org/00/press_releases/iaea/94_02.

________. Document 1269. "IAEA Proposes Sending A Team to Democratic People's Republic of Korea to Discuss Arrangements on Safeguards Measures." 20 May 1994. URL: gopher://gopher.undp.org/00/press_releases/iaea/.

________. Document 1273. "IAEA Board Finds That Democratic People's Republic of Korea Continues to Widen Its Non-Compliance With Safeguards Agreement." 14 June 1994. URL: gopher://gopher.undp.org/00/press_releases/iaea/94_06.

________. Document 1286. "IAEA General Conference Adopts Resolutions on Safeguards, Radioactive Waste and Technology Transfer." 23 September 1994. URL: gopher://gopher.undp.org/00/press_release/iaea/94_09.

________. *IAEA Bulletin*, Safeguards and Non-Proliferation 34, no. 1 (1992): entire issue.

International Peace Academy (IPA). (*a*) *Peacekeepers Handbook*. New York: International Peace Academy, 1978.

________. (*b*) *Peacekeepers Handbook*. New York: Pergamon Press, 1984.

International Refugee Documentation Network (IRDN). (*a*) *Circular* no. 13, December 1995.

________. (*b*) *Conference on the Future of the International Refugee Documentation Network*, 8-9 May 1992, Crete. Geneva: IRDN, Centre for Documentation on Refugees, Office of the United Nations High Commissioner for Refugees, 1992.

Ito, Naoki. Deputy Director of UN Policy Division, Japanese Ministry of Foreign Affairs, Tokyo. Interview by author, 5 June 1995.

"Japan: Article Discusses Collective Self-Defense Rights" (text). Tokyo *Shimbun* (12 April 1996). *FBIS Daily Report — East Asia,* 19 April 1996, 8.

"Japan: Chief Cabinet Secretary Kajiyama on ACSA Conclusion" (text). WWW, Japanese Ministry of Foreign Affairs (18 April 1996). *FBIS Daily Report — East Asia*, 18 April 1996, 16-17.

"Japan: DA Vice-Minister on ACSA, Emergency in Far East" (text). Tokyo *Nihon Keizai Shimbun* (26 April 1996), morning edition, 2. *FBIS Daily Report — East Asia*, 29 April 1996, 6.

"Japan: Defense Chief Rejects ACSA Application in Emergencies" (text). Tokyo *Nihon Keizai Shimbun* (26 April 1996), evening edition, 2. *FBIS Daily Report-East Asia*, 29 April 1996, 6.

Japan Echo "How To Improve the Constitution: Four Views." 20, no. 2 (Summer 1993), 1-13.

"Japan: Government Starts Emergency Legislation Discussion" (text). Tokyo *Mainichi Shimbun* (23 April 1996), 1. *FBIS Daily Report — East Asia*, 23 April 1996, 11-12.

"Japan: Joint News Conference on ACSA Conclusion Reported" (text). WWW, Japanese Ministry of Foreign Affairs (16 April 1996). *FBIS Daily Report — East Asia*, 16 April 1996, 5.

"Japan: LDP Official Supports Logistics Support to U.S." (text). Tokyo *Asahi Shimbun* (30 March 1996), 7. *FBIS Daily Report—East Asia*, 3 April 1996, 11.

"Japan: LDP Proposes Wider Scope for Security Treaty with U.S." (text). Tokyo *Kyodo* (21 April 1996). *FBIS Daily Report—East Asia*, 22 April 1996, 9.

"Japan: Main Points of ACSA with U.S. Forces Decided" (text). *Nihon Keizai Shimbun* (10 April 1996), morning edition, 2. *FBIS Daily Report—East Asia*, 10 April 1996, 10.

"Japan: Okinawa Paper on Japan-U.S. Summit" (text). *Okinawa Times* 18 April 1996), 5. *FBIS Daily Report—East Asia*, 22 April 1996, 11-12.

"Japan: Peacekeepers Assume Full Duties in Golan Heights" (text). Tokyo *Kyodo* (23 February 1996). *FBIS Daily Report—East Asia*, 26 February 1996, 21.

"Japan: SDP Official Discusses Logistical Support to U.S." (text). Tokyo *Asahi Shimbun* (30 March 1996), 7. *FBIS Daily Report—East Asia*, 3 April 1996, 11-12.

"Japan: Usui Hints at Arms-Use Review for SDF Missions" (text). Tokyo *Kyodo* (26 January 1996). *FBIS Daily Report—East Asia*, 30 January 1996, 16.

"Japanese Media Divided in Reaction to ACSA." FBIS foreign media note, 16 April 1996. Downloaded from FBIS online.

Jennekens, Jon. (*a*) IAEA Deputy Director General for Safeguards. Interview by author, 24 June 1992.

________. (*b*) "IAEA Safeguards — Emerging Issues." Paper presented at the Fourth International Conference on Facility Operations-Safeguards Interface. Albuquerque, New Mexico, 29 September-4 October 1991.

"Jiang Rejects Stopping Nuclear Tests" (text). OW2406121995 Tokyo *Kyodo*. 1148 GMT, 24 June 1995. FBIS Okinawa JA. 24 June 1995.

"Jiang Zemin Interviewed by Japan's NHK" (text). OW1006123794 Beijing *Xinhua* Domestic Service. 1024 GMT, 10 June 1994. FBIS Okinawa, JA. 10 June 1994.

"Joint Statement on Korean Nuclear Nonproliferation, 17 June 1992." *Foreign Policy Bulletin* 3, no. 1 (July/August 1992): 17-18.

Kam, Ephraim. *Surprise Attack: The Victim's Perspective*. Cambridge, MA: Harvard University Press, 1988.

Kane, Hal. *The Hour of Departure: Forces That Create Refugees and Migrants*. Washington, DC: Worldwatch Institute, 1995.

Kang Sung-Hack. "South Korea's Policy Toward the United Nations." In *The United Nations and Keeping Peace in Northeast Asia*. Ed. Sung-Hack Kang. Seoul: The Institute for Peace Studies, 1995, 1-42.

Kaufmann, Johan. *United Nations Decision Making*. Netherlands: Sijthoff and Noordhoff International Publishers, 1980.

Kay, David. Director General, Uranium Institute and former Leader, UN Res 687 (mandating Iraqi disposal of Iraq's weapons of mass destruction) Special Action Team. Interviews by authors, 29 June 1992 and 9 February 1996.

"Kenyan Soldiers and the Cold War in Sarajevo." *Daily Nation*, 15 April 1993, 6.

Kim, Andrew, LTC, USAR. "Japan and Peacekeeping Operations." *Military Review* 74, no. 4 (April 1994): 22-33.

"Kim Chong Il: The North Korean Enigma" *Economist*, 21 October 1995, 37-38.

Kim Hakjoon. "North Korea After Kim Il-Song and the Future of North-South Korean Relations." *Security Dialogue*, Volume 26, No. 1 (March 1995) 73-91.

Kim Il Sung. *Overall Report on Programs Made at Party Central Committee on Worker's Party Congresses*, vol. 3. Seoul, Korea: National Unification Board, 1981.

Kitfield, James. "The Perils of Proliferation," *Government Executive* 22, no. 10, (October 1990), 34-42.

Korean Overseas Information Service. (*a*) *A Handbook of Korea*. 9th ed. Seoul: Korean Overseas Information Service, 1993.

________. *(b) Unification Policy*. Seoul: Korean Overseas Information Service, April 1996.

Kraemer, Sven. Quoted in Rowan Scarborough and Bill Gertz, "Aideed's Simplicity Baffles Rangers." *Washington Times*, 1 September 1993, A1.

Kresock, David M. "'Ethnic Cleansing' in the Balkans: The Legal Foundations of Foreign Intervention." *Cornell International Law Journal* 27 (Winter 1994): 202-239.

Kristof, Nicholas D. "UN Says North Korea Will Face Famine as Early as This Summer." *New York Times*, 14 May 1996, A1.

Lake, Anthony. "The Limits of Peacekeeping." *New York Times*, 6 February 1994, D17.

Lancaster, John and Keith B. Richburg. "UN Rejected Somali Overture: Memo Details Secret Talks." *Washington Post*, 17 October 1993, A1.

Landers, Daniel F. "The Defense Warning System." *Defense Intelligence Journal* 3, no. 1 (Spring 1994): 21-32.

Lee Chong-Sik. (*a*) "Political Economy of North Korea." Joint Military Intelligence College Fourth Annual Workshop on Asian Politics, June 1994.

________. (*b*) *Revolutionary Struggle in Manchuria: Chinese Communism and Soviet Interest 1922-1945*. Los Angeles: U. of California Press, 1983.

Lee Suk Bok, MG, ROK. Deputy Chief of Staff, Combined Forces Command and Senior Member, United Nations Command Military Armistice Commission, Seoul. Interview by author, 14 May 1996.

Lefever, Ernest W. and Wynfred Joshua. *United Nations Peacekeeping in the Congo 1960-1964*, vol 2. Washington, DC: Brookings Institution, 1966.

"Let's Make a Deal." *Asiaweek* (newsmap), 24 May 1996, 7.

Lewis, Paul. (*a*) "Reluctant Warriors: UN Member States Retreat from Peacekeeping Rules." *New York Times*, 12 December 1994, A22.

________. (*b*) "UN Is Developing Control Center to Coordinate Growing Peacekeeping Role." *New York Times*, 28 March 1993, A10.

________. (*c*) "UN's Top Troop Official Sees No Need for War Room" *New York Times International*, 27 December 1992, A12.

________. (*d*) "U.S. Backs Council Seats for Bonn and Tokyo." *New York Times*, 30 January 1993, A5.

Lewis, Robert D., MAJ, USA. *Combined Joint Task Force Provide Comfort: What Are We Trying to Do? What is the Way Ahead?* Newport, RI: Naval War College, 1992.

Lincoln, Edward J. (*a*) *Japan's New Global Role*. Washington, DC: The Brookings Institution, 1993.

________. (*b*) Special Economic Advisor to the Ambassador, U.S. Embassy to Japan, Tokyo. Interview by author, 5 June 1995.

Lippman, Thomas W. and Barton Gellman. "A Humanitarian Gesture Turns Deadly: Distracted Clinton Administration Missed Signs of 'Peacemaking' Gone Sour." *Washington Post*, 10 October 1993, A1.

Liu, F.T. *United Nations Peacekeeping and the Non-Use of Force*. Boulder, CO: Lynne Rienner Publishers, 1992.

Loescher, Gil. (*a*) "The International Refugee Regime: Stretched to the Limit?" *Journal of International Affairs* 47, no. 2 (Winter 1994): 351-377.

________. (*b*) "The United Nations, the UN High Commissioner for Refugees, and the Global Refugee Problem." In *United States Policy and the Future of the United Nations*. Ed. Roger A. Coate, 139-165. New York: The Twentieth Century Fund Press, 1993.

Lorch, Donatella. "Last of the U.S. Troops Leave Somalia." *New York Times*, 28 March 1994, A5.

Lowenthal, Mark M. "Peacekeeping and U.S. Foreign Policy: Implementing PDD-25." *CRS Issue Brief*. Washington, DC: The Library of Congress, 7 December 1994.

Macartney, John. "Intelligence: A Consumer's Guide." *International Journal of Intelligence and CounterIntelligence* 2, no. 4 (Winter 1988): 457-486.

Mack, Andrew. "North Korea and the Bomb." *Foreign Policy* 83 (Summer 1991): 87-104.

MacKenzie, Lewis. *Peacekeeper: The Road to Sarajevo*. Vancouver: Douglas and McIntyre, 1993.

MacKinlay, John. *The Peacekeepers: An Assessment of Peacekeeping Operations at the Arab-Israeli Interface*. London: Routledge, 1989.

MacKinley, John and Jarat Chopra. "Second Generation Multinational Operations," *Washington Quarterly* 15, no. 3 (Summer 1992): 113-131.

MacLachlan, Ann. "North Korea Admits to Producing Small Quantities of Plutonium." *Nuclear Fuel* 17, no. 10 (11 May 1992): 13.

Madding, Gene. Arms Control Intelligence Staff representative on sensor issues to US Mission in Vienna. Interview by author, 23 June 1992.

Mahiga, Augustine. Coordinator, Rwanda-Burundi Special Unit, Office of the United Nations High Commissioner for Refugees. Interview by author, 1 May 1996.

"Making Chaste." *Economist*, 10 February 1996, 38.

Malone, Michael D., CMDR, USN, William H. Miller, CMDR, USN, and Joseph W. Robben, LTC, USMC. *Lebanon: Lessons for Future Use of American Forces in Peacekeeping*. Naval War College Research Report. Newport, RI: Naval War College, 1985.

Manville, Albert M, III. "Aleutian Island Plastics, Pelagic Drift and Trawl Net Problems, and Their Solutions." *Transactions of the Fifth-Sixth (sic) North American Wildlife and Natural Resources Conference*. Washington, DC: Wildlife Management Institute, 1991.

Marcus, Ruth. "Clinton Seeks Limits In Peace-Keeping." *Washington Post*, 28 September 1993, A1.

"Massive Emergencies, Large-Scale Repatriations Confront UNHCR." *UN Chronicle* 32, no. 1 (March 1995): 88.

McCarthy, Mary. "The National Warning System: Striving for an Elusive Goal." *Defense Intelligence Journal* 3, no. 1 (Spring 1994): 5-19.

McDermott, Anthony and Kjell Skjelsbaek. *The Multinational Force in Beirut 1982-1984*. Miami: Florida International University, 1991.

McHugh. Lois. "Refugees in U.S. Foreign Policy." *CRS Report for Congress* 95-23F. Washington, DC: Congressional Research Service, Library of Congress, 7 December 1994.

Mentz, John W. COL (USAF). Deputy Director, Tactical Systems, Directorate for Conventional Arms Control and Compliance, Office of the Secretary of Defense. Interview by author, 23 April 1992.

Michaels, Margeurite. "Blue-Helmet Blues." *Time*, 15 November 1993, 66.

"Middle East and Asia." In *Foreign Military Markets*. Greenwich, CT: Forecast International, Defense Markets Service, 1993.

"Minister Criticizes UN Tactics in Somalia" (text). Johannesburg Channel Africa Radio (11 August 1993), 1100 GMT MB110814493. Extracted by FBIS Mbabane. 11 August 1993.

"Minister: UN Offer Not Enough to Deploy Troops in Liberia" (text). Gaborone Radio (9 February 1994), 1910 GMT MB0902205394. Extracted by FBIS Mbabane. 9 February 1994.

Ministry of Foreign Affairs of Japan. "Building Peace: Japan's Participation in United Nations Peace-Keeping Operations" (July 1994). Downloaded from Ministry of Foreign Affairs home page, http://www.nttls.co.jp/infomofa.

Minister of Foreign Affairs of the DPRK letter to the U.S. Secretary of State, 13 June 1994; in USUN message to the U.S. Department of State. Subject: "Notification of DPRK to Withdrawal from IAEA." 14 June 1994.

Monsourov, Alexandre Y. "The Origins, Evolution and Current Politics of the North Korean Nuclear Program." *Nonproliferation Review* 2, no. 3 (Spring/Summer 1995): 25-38.

Moroi, Ken. "The Case for Reinterpreting Article 9." *Japan Echo* 20, no. 2 (Summer 1993): 15-18.

Morrison, David C. "Wanted: Peacekeeping Policy." *National Journal*, 27 November 1993, 2859.

Mortimer, Edward. "Iraq: The Road Not Taken." *The New York Review of Books*. 16 May 1991, 3-7.

"Murayama, Ministers Deliver Policy Speeches" (text). Tokyo *Kyodo* (20 January 1995). *FBIS Daily Report—East Asia*. 20 January 1995, 3-17.

Murry, Norm, LTC, USAF. USAF Plans, Operations and Issues Office at the Pentagon. Interview by author, 26 May 1993.

Mylroie, Laurie. "How We Helped Saddam Survive." *Commentary* 92, no. 1 (July 1991): 15-18.

National Unification Board. (*a*) *A Comparison of Unification Policies of South and North Korea*. Seoul: n.p., 1990.

________. (*b*) *To Build a National Community through the Korean Commonwealth: A Blueprint for Korean Unification*. Seoul: n.p., 1989.

Natsios, Andrew S. "Food Through Force: Humanitarian Intervention and U.S. Policy." *Washington Quarterly* 17, no. 1 (Winter 1994): 129-144.

Nishiwaki, Fumiaki. Professor, National Defense Academy, Yokosuka, Japan. Interview by author, 26 June 1996.

"N.K. Asks Japan for Aid, Citing Big Change in Economic Policy." *Korea Herald*, 17 May 1996, 1.

"North Korea Plans Exports to U.S., First Since 1950s." *The Wall Street Journal*, 9 June 1995, A11.

"North Korea to Open Its Air Space to Others," *The New York Times*, 3 August 1996, 5.

"'Nuclear Mercenary' Threat Seen in Nuclear-Rich, Cash-Starved Ex-Soviet Republics." *PR Newswire*, 13 March 1992.

Oakley, Robert B. "An Envoy's Perspective." *Joint Force Quarterly* No. 2 (Autumn 1993): 44-55.

"Official Renews Support for Japan's UN Bid" (text). OW2006013795 Tokyo *Kyodo*. 0100 GMT, 20 June 1995. FBIS Okinawa JA. 20 June 1995.

Ogata, Sadako. (*a*) "The Changing Role of Japan in the United Nations." *Journal of International Affairs* 37, no. 1 (Summer 1983): 29-42.

________. (*b*) "The Interface Between Peacekeeping and Humanitarian Action After the Cold War." In *New Dimensions of Peacekeeping*. Ed. Daniel Warner and others, 119-127. Dordrecht, Netherlands: Martinus Nijhoff Publishers, 1995.

________. (*c*) United Nations High Commissioner for Refugees. Interview by author, 3 May 1996.

Oh Il-Hwan. "The Aims and Characteristics of North Korea's United Front Strategy." *Vantage Point* 19, no. 3 (March 1996): 27-36.

Ohaegbulam, Festus Ugboaja. *Nigeria and the UN Mission to the Democratic Republic of the Congo: A Case Study of the Formative Stages of Nigeria's Foreign Policy*. Tampa, FL: University Presses of Florida, 1982.

Ono, Hedeki, CDR, SDF. Command and Coordination Section, J-3, Joint Staff Office, Japan. Interview by author, 19 June 1996.

Orr, Robert M., Jr. *The Emergence of Japan's Foreign Aid Power*. New York: Columbia University Press, 1992.

Owada, Hisashi. Statement by H.E. Mr. Hisashi Owada on the Question of Equitable Representation and Increase in the Membership of the Security Council, Agenda Item 33, UN General Assembly, 49th Session, Plenary Meeting, 13 October 1994.

Ozawa, Ichiro. *Blueprint for a New Japan*. Translation by Louisa Rubinfien. Tokyo: Kodansha International, 1994.

Pacific Armies Management Seminar (PAMS). United Nations Peacekeeping Operations: The Seventeenth PAMS Conference Papers. 21-30 January 1993. New Delhi, India.

Pak Chong Ku, "Exports Processing Center," *The Pyongyang Times,* 21 October 1995, 6.

Palmer, Elizabeth A. "Senate Demands Voice in Policy But Shies From Confrontation." *Congressional Quarterly* 51, no. 36 (11 September 1993): 2399.

Palmer, Helen. "Turkey, Iran, Iraq: Refugee Health Care." *The Lancet*, 3 August 1991, 303-304.

"Panov: Moscow Wants 'New Level' of Russian-Japanese Ties" (text). LD2503151395 Moscow Interfax. 1438 GMT, 25 March 1995. FBIS London UK. 25 March 1995.

"Panov Views Moscow's Stance on Expanding UNSC" (text). LD2809093494 Moscow tar-Tass world Service. 0800 GMT, 28 September 1994. FBIS London UK. 28 September 1994.

Park Chung Hee. *To Build a Nation*. Washington, DC: Acropolis Books Ltd., 1971.

Park, Young-ho. "Issues and Prospects for Cross-Recognition: A Korean Perspective." *The Korean Journal of National Unification* 3 (1994): 49-62.

"Peace-Keeping Guidelines." *Washington Post*, 8 May 1994, C6.

Pelletiere, Stephen C. *Humanitarian Operations and the Middle East: The Hostility Factor.* Carlisle, PA: Strategic Studies Institute, U.S. Army War College, 1993.

Perez de Cuellar, Javier. *UN Yearbook*. Lake Success, NY: Department of Public Information, 1982.

Perkins, John A. "The Right of Counterintervention." *Georgia Journal of International and Comparative Law* 17, no. 2 (Summer 1987): 171-227.

Perry, William. "Korea: Nuclear Nonproliferation in Jeopardy." Secretary of Defense William Perry's Speech to the Asia Society, Washington, May 3, 1994. *Foreign Policy Bulletin* 5, no. 1 (July/August 1994): 27-29.

Pickert, Mary Alice. *Japanese Involvement in Cambodia — Embarking on an Activist Foreign Policy*. BA Thesis. Amherst, MA: Amherst College, 18 April 1995.

Polacheck, Tom. "Harbor Porpoises and the Gillnet Fishery: Incidental Takes Spur Population Studies." *Oceanus* 32, no. 1 (Spring 1989): 63-70.

Pomfret, John. "Two UN Officials Accuse U.S. of Prolonging War in Bosnia." *Washington Post*, 30 April 1994, A18.

Preston, Julia. (*a*) "U.N. Moves Toward New role in Somalia." *Washington Post*, 5 February 1994, A14.

________. (*b*) "Vision of a More Aggressive UN Is Dimming." *Washington Post*, 5 January 1994, A24.

Quinn-Judge, Paul. "From Surgical Strike to Standoff: Creation of a Quagmire." *Boston Globe*, 9 December 1993, A12.

Ramcharan, B.G. *The International Law and Practice of Early-Warning and Preventive Diplomacy: The Emerging Global Watch*. Dordrecht, Netherlands: Martinus Nijhoff Publishers, 1991.

Ratner, Steven R. *The New UN Peacekeeping: Building Peace in Lands of Conflict After the Cold War*. New York: St. Martin's Press, 1995.

Reisman, W. Michael. "Sovereignty and Human Rights in Contemporary International Law." *American Journal of International Law* 84, no. 4 (October 1990): 866-876.

Reuter Library Report. "Somalia Underlines Limits of High-Tech U.S. Spying." 8 October 1993.

Reuters News Service. (*a*) "North Korea Thanks U.S. for Donation of Food." *Washington Times*, 9 February 1995, A15.

________. (*b*) "Senator Objects to UN's Peace Plan for Cambodia." *Los Angeles Times*, 6 May 1991, A11.

________. (*c*) "Zambian Peace Troops Leave for Mozambique." 27 April 1993.

Reuters Transcript Service. (d) "Policy on Multilateral Peacekeeping Operations," 6 May 1994.

Richburg, Keith B. (a) "Aideed Exploited UN's Failure to Prepare." *Washington Post*, 5 December 1993, A1+.

________. (*b*) "In War on Aideed, UN Battled Itself." *Washington Post*, 6 December 1993, A36.

________. (*c*) "Pakistani Says UN Bungled on Aideed." *Washington Post*, 3 November 1993, A11.

________. (*d*) "UN Mission in Somalia Seen Beset by Infiltrators." *Washington Post*, 7 September 1993, A1.

________. (*e*) "UN Report Criticizes Military Tactics of Somali Peacekeepers." *Washington Post*, 5 August 1993, A22.

________. (*f*) "U.S. Completes Pullout from Somalia." *Washington Post*, 26 March 1994, A1, A18.

Ridgway, Matthew B. *The Korean War*. Garden City, NY: Doubleday and Company, 1967.

Rivlin, Benjamin and Leon Gordenker, eds. *The Challenging Role of the UN Secretary-General: Making 'The Most Impossible Job in the World' Possible*. Westport, CT: Praeger Publishers, 1993.

Robbins, Carla Anne. "Clinton Rethinks U.S. Global Peacekeeping Role, Draws New Criteria for Joining U.S.-Led Missions." *Wall Street Journal*, 27 September 1993, A24.

Robbins, Carla Anne and others. "No War, No Peace." *U.S. News and World Report*, 1 April 1991, 18-20.

Roberts, Adam. "The Crisis in Un Peacekeeping." *Survival* 36, no. 3 (Autumn 1994): 93-120.

"ROK: DPRK Heightens Surveillance of Loggers in Siberia" (text). Seoul *Naewoe Tongsin* (7 Mar 96), E1-E3. *FBIS Daily Report—East Asia*, 19 April 1996, 67.

Roper, John and others. *Keeping the Peace in the Post-Cold War Era: Strengthening Multilateral Peacekeeping*. New York: The Trilateral Commission, 1993.

Rosner, Jeremy D. *New Era, New Partnership: Congress, the Executive, and National Security after the Cold War*. Washington, DC: Carnegie Endowment for International Peace, 1995.

Rostow, Eugene V. "Should UN Charter Article 43 Be Raised From the Dead?" *Global Affairs* 8, no. 1 (Winter 1993): 109-124.

Rowley, Storer H. "Canadian Vet of Bosnia Warns U.S.: Keep GIs off UN Front Lines." *Chicago Tribune*, 12 January 1994, A3.

Rubin, Trudy. "It's Too Soon to Put U.S. Troops Under Foreign UN Commanders." *Philadelphia Inquirer*, 20 August 1993, A23.

Ruggie, John G. "The United Nations: Stuck in a Fog Between Peacekeeping and Enforcement." In *Peacekeeping: The Way Ahead*. McNair Paper no. 25, Washington, DC: National Defense University, November 1993.

Ruiz, Hiram A. "Emergencies: International Response to Refugee Flows and Complex Emergencies." *International Journal of Refugee Law* Special Issue (July 1995): 148-163.

"Russian Regional Leaders Fight $25 billion Trade Zone." *American Metal Market* 103, no. 126 (30 June 1995): 4.

Rusu, Sharon. *(a)* "Refugees, Information, and Solutions: The Need for Informed Decision-Making." *Refugee Survey Quarterly* 13, no. 1 (Spring 1994): 4-10.

________. *(b)* "Terms of Reference—COIP." Document, 5 November 1992, obtained by author at the Centre for Documentation and Research, Office of the United Nations High Commissioner for Refugees, Geneva.

Sanai, Ruth. "Why Can't they Find Aidid?" (text). Associated Press Wire Service, 6 October 1993.

Sanger, David E. "North Korea to Drop First Veil from Nuclear Sites." *New York Times*, 4 May 1992, A7.

Saracino, Peter. "Polemics and Prescriptions: Interview with a Peacekeeper General." *International Defense Review* 26, no. 5 (May 1993): 370-371.

Sarkesian, Sam C. "The Demographic Component of Strategy." *Survival* 31, no. 6 (November/December 1989): 549-564.

Sauer, Frank, SGM, USA. Non-Commissioned Officer in Charge, U.S. Department of Defense Peacekeeping Office, Pentagon, Washington, DC, 12 May 1993.

Scarborough, Rowan and Bill Gertz. "Aidid's Simplicity Baffles Rangers." *Washington Times*, 1 September 1993, A1.

Scheinman, Lawrence. *The International Atomic Energy Agency and World Nuclear Order.* Washington, DC: Resources for the Future, 1987.

Schorr, Daniel. "Ten Days That Shook the White House." *Columbia Journalism Review* 30, no. 2 (July/August 1991): 21-22.

Schwartz, Frank J. *Trading Dangers: Japanese Security in the Post-Cold-War World.* New York: Japan Society, 1993.

Sciolino, Elaine. (*a*) "New U.S. Peacekeeping Policy De-emphasizes Role of the UN." *New York Times,* 6 May 1994, A1.

________. (*b*) "U.S. Narrows Terms for Its Peacekeepers." *New York Times*, 23 September 1993, A8.

"SDF Official on Use of Arms in Golan Heights" (text). Tokyo *Kyodo* (5 October 1995). *FBIS Daily Report—East Asia*, 17 October 1995, 16.

"SDF Ordered to Prepare for Rwandan Mission" (text). Tokyo *Kyodo* (1 September 1995). *FBIS Daily Report—East Asia*, 1 September 1994, 3.

"SDF Support for Rwanda Aid Recommended" (text). Tokyo *Kyodo* (12 August 1994). *FBIS Daily Report—East Asia*, 15 August 1994, 5.

Segal, David R., Theodore P. Furukawa and Jerry C. Lindh. "Light Infantry as Peacekeepers in the Sinai." *Armed Forces and Society* 16, no. 3 (Spring 1990): 385-403.

Seong Ho Jhe. "Replacing the Military Armistice Agreement on the Korean Peninsula." In Vol. 19, no. 1 of *Korea and World Affairs*. Seoul: Research Center for Peace and Unification of Korea, 1995, 67-86.

"Senators Seek Action on Somalia Role." *Congressional Quarterly* 51, no. 13 (27 March 1993: 772.

Sewall, John O.B. "Implications for UN Peacekeeping." *Joint Force Quarterly* No. 3 (Winter 1993-1994): 29-33.

Shalikashvili, John M. GEN., USA, Chairman of the Joint Chiefs of Staff, Memorandum for the Secretary of Defense. CM-742-95. Subject: "Transmittal of Report of Investigation: Discovery of Classified Material Left by UNOSOM During Operation United Shield." 5 April 1995.

Shigemura, Tomokazu. "UN Envoy Discloses Conditions for Returning to NPT." Tokyo *Mainishi Shimbun* 21 April 1993. *FBIS Daily Report—East Asia*, 21 April 1993, A28.

Shim Jae Hoon. (*a*) "Bridging the Divide." *Far Eastern Economic Review*, 14 September 1995, 63.

________. (*b*) "The Image Cracks." *Far Eastern Economic Review*, 29 February 1996, 14-15.

Shimauchi, Tetsuya. Senior Research Fellow, Institute for International Policy Studies, Tokyo. Interview by author, 21 June 1996.

Shinn, Rinn-Sup. "Japanese Participation in United Nations Peacekeeping Operations." *CRS Report for Congress* 92-665F. Washington, DC: The Library of Congress, 24 August 1992.

Shirk, Susan L. *How China Opened Its Door: The Political Success of the PRC's Foreign Trade and Investment Reforms*. Washington, DC: The Brookings Institution, 1994.

Shorrock, Jim. "Fuel Shipment to 'Energize' North Korean Trade Zone." *Journal of Commerce and Commercial*, 9 January 1995. 1A.

Shuger, Scott. "What American Hasn't Learned from Its Greatest Peacekeeping Disaster." *Washington Monthly* 21, no. 9 (October 1989): 40-50.

Sid-Ahmed, Muhammed. "When and How to Send in Troops: Somalia and the Sovereignty Issue." *World Press Review*, March 1993, 10.

Siegel, Adam B. *A Chronology of U.S. Marine Corps Humanitarian Assistance and Peace Operations*. Alexandria, VA: Center for Naval Analyses, 1994.

Simma, Bruno. *The Charter of the United Nations: A Commentary*. New York: Oxford University Press, 1994.

Sloyan, Patrick J. "A Look At...The Somalia Endgame: How the Warlord Outwitted Clinton's Spooks." *Washington Post*, 3 April 1994, C3.

Smith, Hedrick. "A Bomb Ticks in Pakistan." *New York Times Magazine*, 6 March 1988, 38.

Smith, Hugh. "Intelligence and UN Peacekeeping." *Survival* 36, no. 3 (Autumn 1994): 174-192.

Smith, R. Jeffrey. (*a*) "4-Party Peace Taks Plan Unclear, N. Korean Says." *Washington Post*, 28 April 1996, A25.

________. (*b*) "Extra U.S. Food Assistance Planned for North Korea." *Washington Post*, 7 June 1996, A1.

________. (*c*) "N. Korea and the Bomb: High-Tech Hide-and-Seek." *Washington Post*, 8 October 1993, A1.

________. (*d*) "N. Korea and the Bomb: High-Tech Hide-and-Seek; U.S. Intelligence Key in Detecting Deception." *Washington Post*, 27 April 1993, A1.

________. (*e*) "Pakistan Official Affirms Capacity for Nuclear Device: Foreign Minister Vows to Contain Technology." *Washington Post*, 7 February 1992, A18.

________. (*f*) "Tracking Aideed Hampered by Intelligence Failures." *Washington Post*, 8 October 1993, A19.

Smith, Jeffrey and Julia Preston. (*a*) "U.S. Plans Wider Role in UN Peacekeeping; Administration Drafting New Criteria." *Washington Post*, 18 June 1993, A1.

________. (*b*)"U.S. Probes Security for Somalia Files; Secret Documents Left Unprotected by UN." *Washington Post*, 12 March 1995, A1.

Snowe, Sen. Olympia J. (Maine). Letter to Ambassador Madeleine Albright, U.S. Permanent Representative to the UN. Subject: "Possible Misuse of U.S. Classified Information Provided to the UN Peacekeeping Operation in Somalia." 13 March 1995.

"Somalia: UNOSOM II Mandate Renewed, Humanitarian Aspect Stressed." UN *Chronicle* 31, no. 3 (September 1994): 21-23.

"Somalia: Warlord at Large." *Economist*, 12 June 1993, 48.

Song Young Sun. "The Korean Nuclear Issue." *Korea and World Affairs* 15, no. 3. (Fall 1991): 471-493.

"South Korea: Trading With the Enemy." *Euromoney*, 30 September 1994, 163.

Spector, Leonard S., and Jacqueline R. Smith. *Nuclear Ambitions: The Spread of Nuclear Weapons 1989-1990*. Boulder, CO: Westview Press, 1990.

Spence, Rep. Floyd (South Carolina). "Press Release: Congressional Leadership to Clinton: Suspend Intelligence Sharing With UN." Press Release: House National Security Committee, 16 March 1995, Federal Document Clearing House, LEXIS-NEXIS, Inc., 10 May 1996.

"Spokesman Comments on Japan's UNSC Membership Bid" (text). OW1509111394, 15 September 1994. FBIS Okinawa. 15 September 1994.

Stewart, John F., Jr., MG, USA. "Major General Stewart's Botswana Visit." Message from American Embassy Gaborone to USCINCEUR and others, 14 May 1993.

Story, Ann E., LTC, USAF. (*a*) Chief, Stability Operations Division at the Army-Air Force Center for Low-Intensity Conflict. Interview by author, 3 June 1993.

________. (*b*) *Peace Support Operations: A Concept Whose Time Has Come*. Langley AFB, VA: Army-Air Force Center for Low-Intensity Conflict, 2 April 1993.

Stromseth, Jane E. "Rethinking War Powers: Congress, the President, and the United Nations." *The Georgetown Law Journal* 81, no. 3 (March 1993): 597-673.

Studeman, William O. ADM, USN. Acting Director of Central Intelligence. Letter to Representative Larry Combest, Chairman of the House Permanent Select Committee on Intelligence. Subject: "Concern Over the Proposed Section 512 of H.R. 7." 19 January 1995.

Sullivan, Gordon R. GEN, USA. "All-Capable Readiness: The United States Army in the Post Cold-War World." *NATO's Sixteen Nations: Defense of the USA* 37, no 6 (Special Issue 1992): 25-33.

Sullivan, Kevin. "N. Korea Touts Free-Trade Area: Stalinist State Invites Capitalists to Remote Northern Region." *Washington Post*, 20 July 1996, A21.

Survey Team to Golan Heights Under Study" (text). Tokyo *Sankei Shimbun* (6 November 1994), morning edition, 1. *FBIS Daily Report—East Asia*, 9 November 1994, 10-11.

Suzuki, Hideo. Assistant Director, Japan-U.S. Security Treaty Division, North American Affairs Bureau, Ministry of Foreign Affairs, Tokyo. Interview by author, 19 June 1996.

Szasz, Paul C. "Role of the United Nations in Internal Conflicts." *Georgia Journal of International and Comparative Law* 13, Supplement (Winter 1983): 345-354.

Takai, Susumu. (*a*) "Japan: A Hesitant but Interested Partner." *International Defense Review: Defense 1995*: 107-112.

________. (*b*) Professor of International Law, National Institute for Defense Studies, Tokyo. Interview by author, 19 June 1996.

Tejno, Soren. Program Manager, East Asian Division, Regional Bureau for Asia and the Pacific, United Nations Development Program. Interviewed by author, 20 March 1996.

Thakur, Ramesh and Carlyle A. Thayer, eds. *A Crisis of Expectations: UN Peacekeeping in the 1990s*. Boulder, CO: Westview Press, 1995.

"The Compass Swings: A Survey of Tomorrow's Japan." *Economist*, 13 July 1996, pullout section.

Thoolen, Hans. "Information Aspects of Humanitarian Early Warning." In *Early Warning and Conflict Resolution*. Eds. Kumar Rupesinghe and Michiko Kuroda, 166-180. New York: St. Martin's Press, 1992.

Thorne, Leslie. "IAEA Nuclear Inspections in Iraq." *IAEA Bulletin* 34, no. 1 (1992): 16-20.

Timmerman, Kenneth R. *The Death Lobby: How the West Armed Iraq*. Boston, MA: Houghton Mifflin, 1991.

Timms, Ed. "U.S. Assesses Lessons Amid Somalia Pullout." *Dallas Morning News*, 22 March 1994, 1.

Towell, Pat. (*a*) "Clinton's Policy Battered, But His Powers Are Intact." *Congressional Quarterly* 51, no. 42 (23 October 1993): 2896-2898.

________. (*b*) "Suffering Spurs Unprecedented Step as UN Approves Deployment." *Congressional Quarterly* 50, no. 48 (5 December 1992): 3759-3763.

"TRADP (Tumen River Area Development Program) Overview of Foreign Investment and Infrastructure," Promotional Literature, 1995, 1-8.

"Troops, Armored Vehicles to Leave for Cambodia 25 May 1994" (text). Johannesburg SAPA (24 May 1994) 2051 GMT MB2505060793. Extracted by FBIS Mbabane. 22 May 1993.

Truman, Harry S. *Public Papers of the President*, 1950: 492.

Ueki, Yasuhiro. "Japan's UN Diplomacy: Sources of Passivism and Activism." In *Japan's Foreign Policy After the Cold War: Coping with Change*. Ed. Gerald L. Curtis, 347-370. New York: East Gate/M.E. Sharpe, 1993.

Underdown, Dr. Michael. Director, Tumen Secretariat. Facsimile to the author. 23 May 1996.

United Nations. (*a*) Aide Memoire: Investigation by the UN Secretariat into allegations made by the Government of the United States that classified information provided by the U.S. military personnel in UNITAF and UNOSOM to UNOSOM II had been seriously compromised. 11 May 1995.

________. (*b*) *An Agenda for Peace* 1995. New York: Department of Public Information, 1995.

________. (*c*) *Blue Helmets: A Review of United Nations Peacekeeping*, 2d revised edition (New York: Department of Public Information, 1990.

________. (*d*) Pamphlet 3PI/905-40005. *United Nations Peacekeeping—The Facts*. New York: Department of Public Information, 1987.

________. (*e*) *Peacekeeping Operations Chart*, 1992. New York: United Nations, 1992.

________. (*f*) *Summary of Contributions to Peace-Keeping Operations by Countries as of 31 May 1994*. New York: UN Department of Public Information, 1994.

________. (*g*) *The Blue Helmets: A Review of United Nations Peace-Keeping*. 2d rev. ed. New York: Department of Public Information, 1990.

________. (*h*) *The United Nations and Cambodia*. Vol 2 of The United Nations Blue Book Series. New York: Department of Public Information, 1995.

________. (*i*) *The United Nations and El Salvador*. Vol 4 of The United Nations Blue Book Series. New York: Department of Public Information, 1995.

________. (*j*) *The United Nations and Mozambique*. Vol 5 of The United Nations Blue Book Series. New York: Department of Public Information, 1995.

________. (*k*) "United Nations Disengagement Observer Force (UNDOF)." Downloaded from UN home page, July 1996.

________. (*l*) "United Nations Operation in Mozambique (UNOMOZ)." Downloaded from UN home page, July 1996.

________. (*m*) *1982 Yearbook of the United Nations*. Lake Success, NY: Department of Public Information, 1983.

________. (*n*) *1993 Yearbook of the United Nations*. New York: Martinus Nijhoff Publishers, 1994.

________. (*o*) *Yearbook of the United Nations, 1948-49*. Washington, DC: UN Information Centre, 1949.

United Nations Command Military Armistice Commission (UNCMAC). "UNCMAC Command Briefing." Briefing text provided to author at UNCMAC Headquarters, Yongsan Barracks, Korea, 13 May 1996.

United Nations Development Program (UNDP). (*a*) *Gateway to Northeast Asia, A New Investment Frontier*. New York: UNDP, n.d., 1-16.

________. (*b*) "Northeast Asia Sub-Regional Program for Technical Cooperation." Consultation With Participant Governments, Ulaanbaatar Regional Bureau, 6-7 July 1991, 18-20.

________. (*c*) Report A. *Northeast Asia's Tumen River Economic Development Area 1994 Collected Papers, A Regional Development Strategy for the Tumen River Area and Northeast Asia*. New York: PDP Australia, n.d.

________. (*d*) Report C. *Northeast Asia's Tumen River Economic Development Area 1994 Collected Papers, Conceptual Infrastructure Master Plan.* New York, Consultant: CPCS Ltd., n.d.

________. (*e*) Tumen River Area Development. *Mission Report, Consultation With Participant Governments.* Pyongyang: n.p., 18 October 1991.

________. (*f*) *UNDP in the DPRK, Investment Opportunities and Sustainable Human Development*. Pyongyang: n.p., October 1995.

United Nations General Assembly (UNGA). A/936. Report of the United Nations Commission on Korea. 28 July 1949.

________. A/9027. Agenda Item 41. 28 November 1973.

________. A/46/608, S/23177. Final act of the Paris conference on Cambodia. 30 October 1991.

________. A/47/277. An agenda for peace — preventive diplomacy, peacemaking and peace-keeping: Report of the Secretary-General pursuant to the statement adopted by the Summit Meeting of the Security Council on 31 January 1992. 17 June 1992.

________. A/47/594. Report of the Secretary-General. Strengthening of the coordination of emergency humanitarian assistance of the United Nations. 30 October 1992.

________. A/48/PV.4. Address by Mr. Morihiro Hosokawa, Prime Minister of Japan. 27 September 1993.

________. A/48/PV.62. Question of equitable representation on and increase in the membership of the Security Council and related matters. 23 November 1993.

________. A/48/PV.64. Question of equitable representation on and increase in the membership of the Security Council and related matters. 24 November 1993.

________. A/48/264 and addenda 1-10. Question of equitable representation on and increase in the membership of the Security Council: replies received from Member States. 20 July 1993.

________. A/48/403. Comprehensive review of the whole question of peace-keeping operations in all their aspects administrative and budgetary aspects of the financing of the United Nations peace-keeping operations. improving the capacity of the United Nations for peace-keeping: report of the Secretary-General. 14 March 1994.

________. A/48[49]/PV.7. Address by Mr. Yohei; Kono, Foreign Minister of Japan. 27 September 1994.

________. A/49/PV.29. Question of equitable representation on and increase in the membership of the Security Council and related matters. 13 October 1994.

________. A/49/PV.30. Question of equitable representation on and increase in the membership of the Security Council and related matters. 13 October 1994.

________. A/49/PV.31. Question of equitable representation on and increase in the membership of the Security Council and related matters. 14 October 1994.

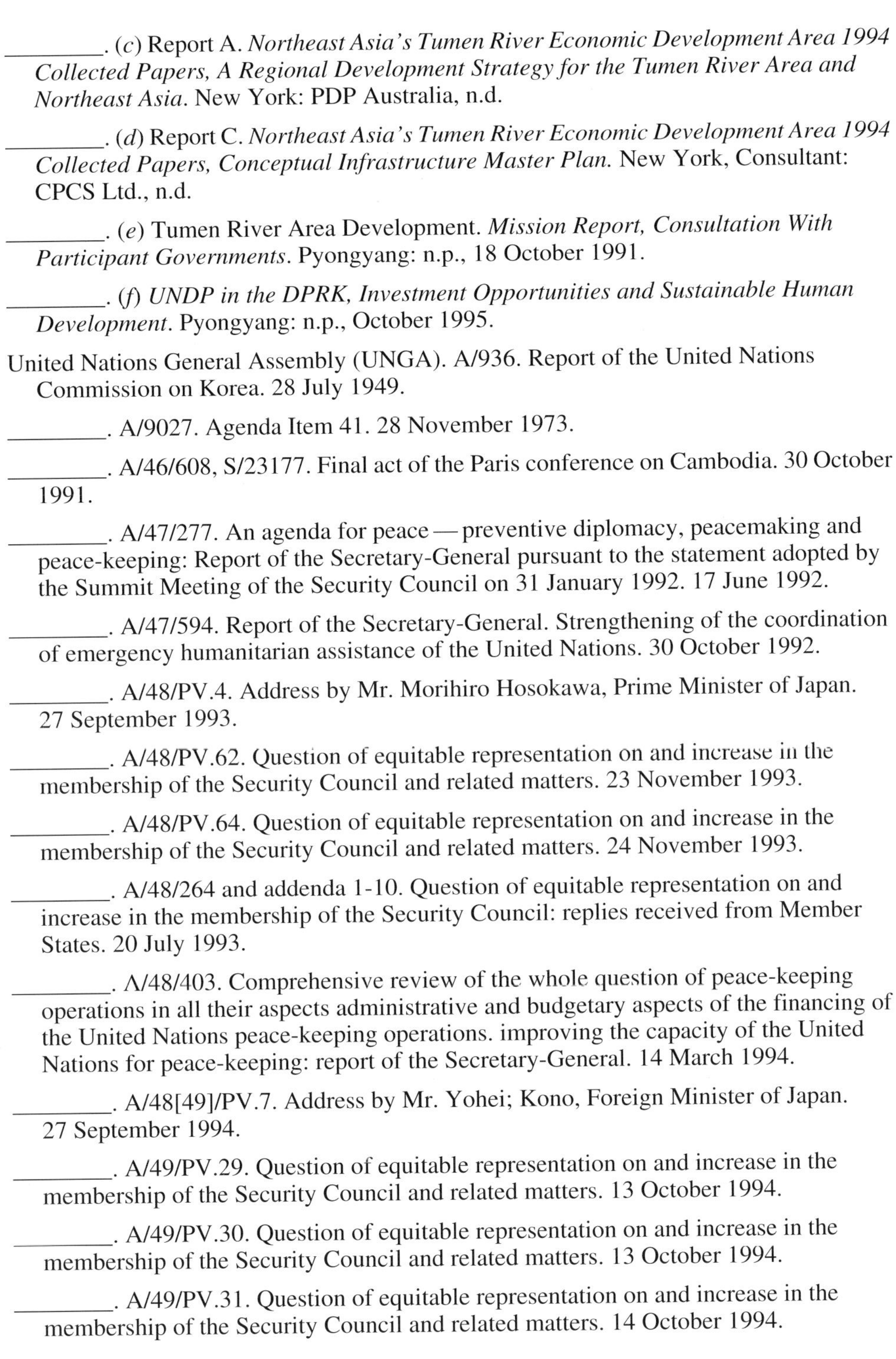

________. A/49/177. Report of the Secretary-General. Strengthening of the coordination of emergency humanitarian assistance of the United Nations. 2 September 1994.

________. A/49/336. Review of the efficiency of the administrative and financial functioning of the United Nations. Restructuring of the United Nations Secretariat: Report of the Secretary-General. 24 August 1994.

________. A/49/527. Human resources management: composition of the Secretariat. 17 October 1994.

________. A/C.1/218/Rev.1. The problem of the independence of Korea. 4 November 1947.

________. A/C.5/49/L.30. Scale of assessments for the apportionment of the expenses of the United Nations. 21 December 1994.

________. Resolution 112 (II). The problem of the independence of Korea. 14 November 1947.

________. Resolution 195 (III). The problem of the independence of Korea. 12 December 1948.

________. Resolution 294 (IV). The problem of the independence of Korea. 21 October 1949.

________. Resolution 376 (V). The problem of the independence of Korea. 7 October 1950.

________. Resolution 377A (V). Uniting for Peace. 3 November 1950.

________. Resolution 428(V). Annex: The Statute of the Office of the United Nations High Commissioner for Refugees. 14 December 1950.

________. A/RES/46/215. Resolution adopted by the General Assembly: large-scale pelagic drift-net fishing and its impact on living marine resources of the world's oceans and seas. 12 February 1992.

________. A/RES/47/62. Question of equitable representation. 11 December 1992.

________. A/RES/48/14. Report on the International Atomic Energy Agency. 1 November 1993.

________. A/RES/48/42. Comprehensive review of the whole question of peace-keeping operations in all their aspects. 10 December 1993.

United Nations High Commissioner for Refugees (UNHCR).(*a*) *A UNHCR Handbook for the Military on Humanitarian Operations*. Geneva: UNHCR, 1995.

________. (*b*) Brochure. *UNHCR by Numbers*, January 1995.

________. (*c*) *Collection of International Instruments Concerning Refugees*. Geneva: UNHCR, 1979.

________. (*d*) Executive Committee of the High Commissioner's Programme. Sub-Committee on Administrative and Financial Matters. Lessons Learned from the Rwanda Emergency, 7 June 1995. EC/1995/SC.2/CRP.21.

________. (*e*) *Handbook for Emergencies — Part I: Field Operations*. Geneva: UNHCR, 1982.

________. (*f*) *Handbook for Emergencies—Part II: Management, Administration and Procedures*. Geneva: UNHCR, 1983.

________. (*g*) "Refugees at a Glance." *Monthly Digest of UNHCR Activities*, February 1996.

________. (*h*) *The State of the World's Refugees: In Search of Solutions*. Oxford: Oxford University Press, 1995.

________. (*i*) Training Module. *Working With the Military*. Geneva: UNHCR, January 1995.

________. (*j*) *UNHCR Manual*. Geneva: UNHCR, 1991.

________. (*k*) *UNHCR Manual*. Geneva: UNHCR, 1993.

________. (*l*) *UNHCR Manual*. Geneva: UNHCR, 1995.

United Nations Industrial Development Organization (UNIDO). *Tumen River Economic Development Area Investment Guide*. United Kingdom: Reynolds Press Printers Ltd., n.d.

"UN Not to Seek SDF Help in Golan Heights" (text). Tokyo *Kyodo* (27 January 1995). *FBIS Daily Report—East Asia*, 27 January 1994, 5-6.

United Nations Secretariat (UNSec). (*a*) Department of Humanitarian Affairs. ST/SGB/Organization. 12 December 1994.

________. (*b*) Department of Humanitarian Affairs. Humanitarian Early Warning System: Progress and Prospects. 1995.

________. (*c*) Department of Political and Security Council Affairs. ST/SGB/Organization. January 1974.

________. (*d*) Information and Research Briefing Handout. 25 April 1995.

________. (*e*) Organizational Manual: Functions and Organizations of the Department of Peace-keeping Operations. ST/SGB/Organization. 22 March 1995.

________. (*f*) Secretary-General's Bulletin: Department of Political and Security Affairs. ST/SGB/Organization. 27 January 1975.

________. (*g*) S/23613, Report of the Secretary-General on Cambodia. 19 February 1992.

________. (*h*) The Office for Research and the Collection of Information. ST/SGB/Organization. 3 October 1988.

United Nations Security Council (UNSC). S/1496. Complaint of aggression upon the Republic of Korea. 25 June 1950.

________. S/1507. Cablegrams from the United Nations Commission on Korea. 7 July 1950.

________. S/1588. Resolution concerning the complaint of aggression upon the Republic of Korea adopted at the 476th Meeting of the Security Council on 7 July 1950.

________. S/24111. An Agenda for Peace, preventive diplomacy and peace-keeping. Report of the Secretary-General pursuant to the statement adopted by the Security Council, 31 January 1992. 17 June 1992.

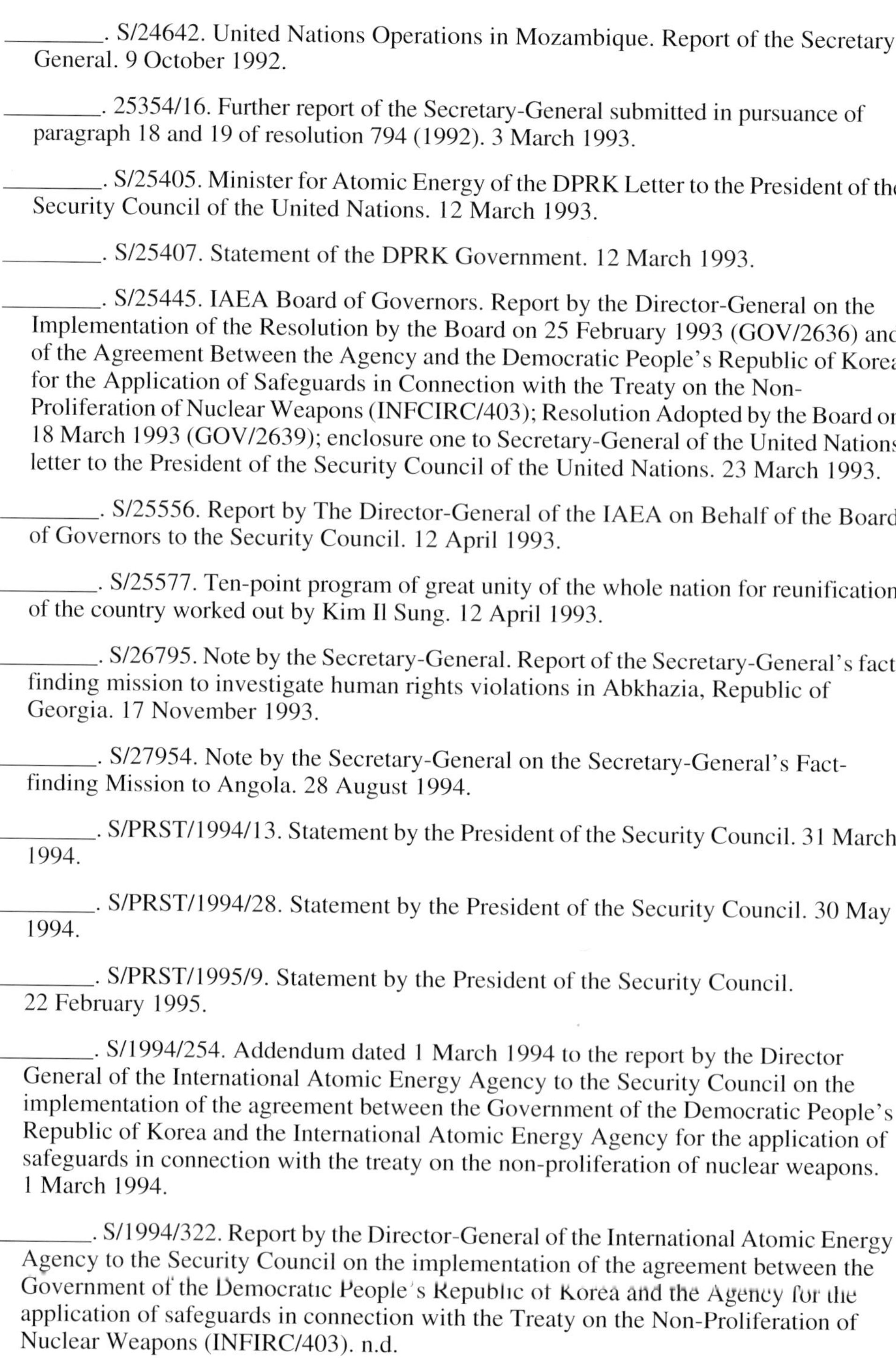

________. S/24642. United Nations Operations in Mozambique. Report of the Secretary-General. 9 October 1992.

________. 25354/16. Further report of the Secretary-General submitted in pursuance of paragraph 18 and 19 of resolution 794 (1992). 3 March 1993.

________. S/25405. Minister for Atomic Energy of the DPRK Letter to the President of the Security Council of the United Nations. 12 March 1993.

________. S/25407. Statement of the DPRK Government. 12 March 1993.

________. S/25445. IAEA Board of Governors. Report by the Director-General on the Implementation of the Resolution by the Board on 25 February 1993 (GOV/2636) and of the Agreement Between the Agency and the Democratic People's Republic of Korea for the Application of Safeguards in Connection with the Treaty on the Non-Proliferation of Nuclear Weapons (INFCIRC/403); Resolution Adopted by the Board on 18 March 1993 (GOV/2639); enclosure one to Secretary-General of the United Nations letter to the President of the Security Council of the United Nations. 23 March 1993.

________. S/25556. Report by The Director-General of the IAEA on Behalf of the Board of Governors to the Security Council. 12 April 1993.

________. S/25577. Ten-point program of great unity of the whole nation for reunification of the country worked out by Kim Il Sung. 12 April 1993.

________. S/26795. Note by the Secretary-General. Report of the Secretary-General's fact-finding mission to investigate human rights violations in Abkhazia, Republic of Georgia. 17 November 1993.

________. S/27954. Note by the Secretary-General on the Secretary-General's Fact-finding Mission to Angola. 28 August 1994.

________. S/PRST/1994/13. Statement by the President of the Security Council. 31 March 1994.

________. S/PRST/1994/28. Statement by the President of the Security Council. 30 May 1994.

________. S/PRST/1995/9. Statement by the President of the Security Council. 22 February 1995.

________. S/1994/254. Addendum dated 1 March 1994 to the report by the Director General of the International Atomic Energy Agency to the Security Council on the implementation of the agreement between the Government of the Democratic People's Republic of Korea and the International Atomic Energy Agency for the application of safeguards in connection with the treaty on the non-proliferation of nuclear weapons. 1 March 1994.

________. S/1994/322. Report by the Director-General of the International Atomic Energy Agency to the Security Council on the implementation of the agreement between the Government of the Democratic People's Republic of Korea and the Agency for the application of safeguards in connection with the Treaty on the Non-Proliferation of Nuclear Weapons (INFIRC/403). n.d.

________. S/1994/601. Director-General of the IAEA letter to the Secretary-General of the United Nations, 19 May 1994; annex to Secretary-General of the United Nations letter to the Security Council of the United Nations. 20 May 1994.

________. S/1995/157. Letter dated 23 February 1995 from the Secretary-General addressed to the President of the Security Council. 24 February 1995.

"UNSC Seat, U.S.-Japan Friction Issues Polled" (text). Tokyo *Kyodo* (8 January 1995). *FBIS Daily Report—East Asia*, 9 January 1995, 16.

United Nations Truce Supervision Organization (UNTSO). *Notes for the Guidance of Military Observers on Appointment*. New York: UN Field Operations Division, 1988.

U.S. Arms Control and Disarmament Agency (ACDA). (*a*) *Arms Control and Disarmament Agreements: Texts and Histories of the Negotiations*. Washington, DC: GPO, 1990.

________. (*b*) *Final Report: Prospects and Directions for Improvements in International Safeguards*, Vol. II (Washington, DC: ACDA, 24 February 1987.

U.S. Army. (a*)* Command and General Staff College. *Techniques and Procedures for Tactical Decisionmaking*. Ft. Leavenworth, KS: USACGSC, 1991.

________. (*c*) Deputy Chief of Staff for Operations and Plans. Political-Military Division. "Peacekeeping Operations Briefing Outline," June 1992.

________. (*d*) Field Manual (FM) 34-1. *Intelligence and Electronic Warfare Operations*. Washington, DC: Department of the Army, July 1987.

________. (*e*) FM 34-3. *Intelligence Analysis*. Washington, DC: Department of the Army, March 1990.

________. (*f*) Intelligence Center and School (USAICS). Student Handout: "Intelligence Requirements, Sources and Agencies in Low Intensity Conflict." Fort Huachuca, AZ: Military Intelligence Officer's Advanced Course, 1992.

________. (*g*) FM 100-20. *Low-Intensity Conflict*. Washington, DC: Department of the Army, July 1986.

________. (*h*) FM 100-20. *Military Operations in a Low-Intensity Conflict*. (FM 100-20/ Air Force Pamphlet 3-20). Washington, DC: Department of the Army, 5 December 1990.

________. (*i*) FM 100-23. *Peace Operations*. Washington, DC: Department of the Army, December 1994.

U.S. Atlantic Command (USACOM). *Tactics, Techniques, and Procedures (TTP) for Migrant Camp Operations*. Norfolk, VA: USACOM, 15 April 1995.

"U.S. Bolsters Forces for Somalia Action." *Congressional Quarterly* 51, no. 24 (12 June 1993): 1498.

U.S. Congress. (*a*) Letter to President Clinton. Subject: "Concern Over the Discovery of an Unsecured Cache of Sensitive U.S. Intelligence Materials by American Forces Covering the Withdrawal of UN Forces From Somalia." 16 March 1996.

________. (*b*) *Creation of the Multinational Force and Observers for the Sinai*, Hearings and Markup before the Committee on Foreign Affairs on HJ resolution 349, 96th Congress, 1st Session, 21, 28 July and 27 October 1981. Washington, DC: U.S. GPO, 1981.

U.S. Congress. (*c*) Office of Technology Assessment. *Technologies Underlying Weapons of Mass Destruction*. Washington, DC: GPO, 1993.

U.S. Congress. Senate. (*d*) Committee on Foreign Relations. *Civil War in Iraq*. 102d Cong, 1st sess, November 1991. Committee Print 102-27.

________. (*e*) Committee on Foreign Relations. *Staff Reform of United Nations Peacekeeping Operations: A Mandate for Change*. 103d Cong, 1st sess. 1993. Staff Print 103-45.

________. (*f*) Committee on Governmental Affairs. *Weapons Proliferation and the New World Order*. Hearings, 102nd Cong., 2nd sess., 15 January 1992.

U.S. Defense Attache Office Lagos. Message to CINC USEUCOM and others. Subject: "Two-Year Training Plan — Federal Republic of Nigeria." 6 January 1993.

U.S. Department of Defense (DoD). Chairman, Joint Chiefs of Staff (CJCS). "Operational Support of High Seas Driftnet Fisheries Enforcement." CJCS Instruction 2410.01, 12 March 1995.

________. (*a*) JCS. Joint Pub 2-0. *Joint Doctrine for Intelligence Support to Operations*. Washington, DC: GPO, 5 May 1995.

________. (*b*) JCS. Joint Pub 2-0. *Joint Doctrine for Intelligence Support to Operations*. Washington, DC: GPO, 12 October 1993.

________. (*c*) JCS. Joint Pub 3-0. *Doctrine for Joint Operations*. Washington, DC: GPO, 1 February 1995.

________. (*d*) JCS. Joint Pub 3-07. *Joint Doctrine for Military Operations Other Than War*. Washington, DC: GPO, 16 June 1995; Final Draft, April 1993.

________. (*e*) JCS. Joint Pub 3-07. *Joint Operations in Low-Intensity Conflict*. Washington, DC: GPO, October 1992.

________. (*f*) JCS. Joint Pub 3-07.3 (Draft). *Joint Tactics, Techniques and Procedures for Peacekeeping Operations*, 1993 and 1992.

________. (*g*) JCS. Joint Pub 3-57. *Doctrine for Joint Civil Affairs*. Washington, DC: GPO, 21 June 1995.

________. (*h*) JCS J2M (Intelligence Directorate, Threat Management Branch). Memorandum. "Briefing at UN DPKO, Regarding Discovery of Classified Material in Somalia." 18 April 1995.

________. (*i*) JCS. J2M. Briefing Package. "U.S. Intelligence Support to the United Nations Peacekeeping/Humanitarian Operations." 1 October 1995.

________. (*j*) JCS J2M UN Support Desk. Information Paper: UN Intelligence Support. National Military Joint Intelligence Center, 9 May 1995.

________. (*k*) JCS J2P (Intelligence Directorate, Policy Branch). Information Paper. "Intelligence Support for United Nations Peacekeeping Operations." 1 December 1993.

________. (*l*) JCS J5. U.S. Delegation to the U.N. Military Staff Committee. Information Paper. "U.S. Representation to the United Nations Military Staff Committee." n.d.

________. (*m*) Joint Warfighting Center. *Joint Task Force Commander's Handbook for Peace Operations*. 28 February 1995.

________. (*n*) *National Military Strategy*. Washington, DC: GPO, 1992.

________. (*o*) *National Military Strategy*. Washington, DC: GPO, 1995.

________. (*p*) *News Release: Results of Investigation into Somalia Classified Documents*. Washington, DC: Office of Assistant Secretary of Defense (Public Affairs). No. 205-95, 18 April 1995.

________. Office of the Secretary of Defense (OSD). (*a*) Message to Secretaries of the Military Departments. Subject: "United Nations Truce Supervision Organization." 20 July 1973.

________. (b) *Proliferation: Threat and Response*. Washington, DC: GPO, 1996.

U.S. European Command (USEUCOM). (*a*) *After-Action Review for Operation SUPPORT HOPE 1994*. Heidelberg, Germany: USEUCOM, 1994.

________. (*b*) *Operation PROVIDE COMFORT After Action Report*. Heidelberg, Germany: USEUCOM, 29 January 1992.

U.S. General Accounting Office (GAO). *UN Peacekeeping: Lessons Learned in Managing Recent Missions*. Washington, DC: GAO, December 1993.

U.S. Liaison Office Mogadishu. Message to U.S. Secretary of State and others. Subject: "Zimbabweans Assist Police in Afgoye AOR." 31 March 1994.

U.S. Marine Corps (USMC). Marine Corps Intelligence Activity (MCIA). *Generic Intelligence Requirements Handbook*. Quantico, VA: MCIA, 1995.

U.S. Mission to the United Nations. (*a*) *Global Humanitarian Emergencies*, 1996. New York: USUN, February 1996.

________. (*b*) Message to the Office of the Secretary of Defense and others. Subject: "UNAMIR Equipment Requirements for the Ghanaian Infantry Battalion." 8 June 1994.

________. (*c*) Message to U.S. Secretary of State. Subject: "Status of UN Airlift Request." 11 May 1992.

"U.S.-North Korea Statement, New York, June 11, 1993." *Foreign Policy Bulletin* 4, no. 1 (July/August 1993): 32.

U.S. Office Windhoek. Message to U.S. Secretary of State and others. Subject: "Kenyan Contingent to Stay After Independence." 10 March 1990.

U.S. President. (*a*) *A National Security Strategy of Engagement and Enlargement*. Washington, DC: The White House, July 1994.

________. (*b*) *A National Security Strategy of Engagement and Enlargement*. Washington, DC: The White House, February 1996.

________. (*c*) *National Security Strategy of the United States*. Washington, DC: The White House, August 1991.

________. (*d*) Presidential Decision Directive 25, "Clinton Administration's Policy on Reforming Multilateral Peace Operations." 3 May 1994.

U.S. Secretary of State. (*a*) Message to American Embassy Beijing. Subject: "1994 U.S. Coast Guard High Seas Driftnet Patrol PRC Shiprider Program." 14 July 1994.

________. (*b*) Message to American Institute in Taiwan. Subject: "Proposed High Seas Driftnet Fishing Visit and Verification MOU." 7 February 1994.

Vogt, Margaret A. "The Problems and Challenges of Peace-Making: From Peace-Keeping to Peace Enforcement," in *The Liberian Crisis and ECOMOG: A Bold Attempt at Regional Peacekeeping*, ed. M.A. Vogt. Lagos, Nigeria: Gabumo Publishers, 1992.

Wada, Hideo. "Decisions Under Article 9 of the Constitution — The Sunakawa, Eniwa, and Naganuma Decisions." *Law in Japan: An Annual* 9, no. 117 (1976): 117-128.

Wallace, Stephen O., LTC, USA. "Joint Task Force Support Hope: The Role of the CMOC in Humanitarian Operations." *Special Warfare* 9, no. 1 (January 1996): 36-41.

Waller, Douglas and others. "The Day We Stopped the War." *Newsweek*, 20 January 1992, 16-25.

Watson, Russell. "A New Victim in Lebanon," *Newsweek*, 29 February 1988, 32-33.

Weathersby, Kathryn. *Soviet Aims in Korea and the Origins of the Korean War, 1945-1950: New Evidence from Russian Archives*. Tallahassee, FL: Florida State University, November 1993.

Weiser, Benjamin. "The Once and Future Spy Mission." *Washington Post*, 2 November 1991, A14.

Wellens, Karel C., ed. R*esolutions and Statements of the United Nations Security Council (1946-1992): A Thematic Guide*. 2d Rev. ed. Dordrecht, NL: Academic Publishers, 1993.

Wiesskopf, Michael. "Democrats Criticize Gulf Policy: Buildup of forces Faulted as Rushing Down Path of War." *Washington Post*, 12 November 1990, A1.

Williams, Daniel. "Clinton Peacekeeping Policy to Set Limits on Use of U.S. Troops." *Washington Post*, 6 February 1994, A24.

Williams, Daniel and Ann Devroy. "U.S. Limits Peacekeeping Role: Administration Delays Policy on Putting GIs Under UN Banner." *Washington Post,* 25 November 1993, A6.

Wilson, James L., BG, USA. Former Commander, Joint Task Force SAFE HAVEN. Interview by author, 3 April 1996.

Wise, Michael. (*a*) "Atomic Team Reports on Iran Probe: No Weapons Research Found by Inspectors." *Washington Post*, 15 February 1992, A29.

________. (*b*) "Nuclear Sale to Syria Blocked." *Independent*, 7 December 1991, 10.

Wood, Chris. "Keeping the Peace," *McClean*'s, 29 August 1988, 14-15.

Woodall, Brian. *Japan's Changing World Role: Emerging Leader or Perpetual Follower?* Policy Forum Series. New York: Japan Society, 1993.

Woolsey, James. "The Proliferation of Weapons of Mass Destruction: CIA Director's Testimony." *Foreign Policy Bulletin*, 3, no. 6 (May/June 1993): 34-38.

Yamaguchi, Jiro. "The Gulf War and the Transformation of Japanese Constitutional Politics." *Journal of Japanese Studies* 18, no. 1 (Winter 1992): 155-172.

Yanai, Shunji. "The Japanese PKO Experience." *The Japanese Annual of International Law* No. 36 (1993): 33-75.

Yasutomo, Dennis T. "The Politicization of Japan's Post-Cold War Multilateral Diplomacy." In *Japan's Foreign Policy After the Cold War: Coping with Change*. Ed. Gerald L. Curtis, 323-346. Armonk, NY: East Gate, 1993.

Yokota, Yozo. Professor of International Law, Tokyo University. Interview by author, 9 June 1995.

Yomiuri Constitution Study Council. "An Initial Proposal on Japan's Constitution." *Japan Echo* 20, no. 2 (Summer 1993): 23-30.

Yomiuri Shimbun News Service. "53% Support Permanent Seat for Japan in UNSC, Says Poll," 5 June 1994, 2-2.

Yoshida, Shinnichi. Deputy Editor, *Asahi Shimbun*, Tokyo. Interview by author, 9 June 1995.

Yoshihiko, Seki. "Concluding the Debate on War—Renouncing Article 9." *Japan Echo* 20, no. 2 (Summer 1993): 19-22.

Zifferero, Maurizio. IAEA Deputy Director General and Leader of UNSC Res 687 (mandating Iraqi disposal of Iraq's weapons of mass destruction) Special Action Team. Interview by author, 25 June 1992.

Zorpette, Glenn. "How Iraq Reverse-Engineered the Bomb." *IEEE Spectrum* 29, no. 4 (April 1992): 20-24, 63-65.

Zumwalt, James. "Perceivable Winds of Change in North Korea?" *Washington Times*, 14 May 1995, B4.

Appendix A
INTELLIGENCE IN A UN CONTEXT: A SELECT BIBLIOGRAPHY

Justin L. Abold
Second Lieutenant, U.S. Air Force
December 1996

Books

Adelman, Howard, Astri Suhrke, and Bruce Jones. *Early Warning and Conflict Management: Genocide in Rwanda*. Fantoft-Bergen, Norway: Michelson Institute, September 1995.

Andrew, C., and J. Noakes, eds. *Intelligence and International Relations 1900-1945*. Exeter Studies in History No. 15. United Kingdom: University of Exeter, 1987.

Bakou, Serge. *UNESCO et subversion*. Paris: Union Nationale Inter-Universitaire Centre D'Etudes Et De Diffusion, 1985.

Behrstock, Julian. *The Eighth Case: Troubled Times at the United Nations*. Lanham, MD: University Press of America, 1987.

Bullock, Harold E. *Peace by Committee: Command and Control Issues in Multinational Peace Enforcement Operations*. Maxwell AFB, AL: Air University School of Advanced Airpower Studies, February 1995.

Centre for International and Strategic Studies. *Multilateral Verification And The Post-Gulf Environment: Learning from the UNSCOM Experience*. Toronto, Canada: York University, 1992.

Copp, DeWitt, and Marshall Peck. *Betrayal at the UN: The Story of Paul Bang-Jensen*. New York: The Devin-Adair Company, 1961.

Druke, Louise. *Preventive Action for Refugee Producing Situations.* 2d ed. Frankfurt am Main: Peter Lang, 1993.

Durch, William J., ed. *The Evolution of UN Peacekeeping.* New York: St. Martin's Press, 1993.

Eriksson, Par, Nils Marius Rekkedal and Wegger Stommen. *Intelligence in Peace Support Operations* (A Joint Report by the Swedish and Norwegian Defense Research Establishments). Stockholm: Defence Research Establishment, 1996.

Gasparini Alves, Pericles. *Evolving Trends in the Dual Use of Satellites.* New York: UN Institute for Disarmament Research, UNIDIR/96/29, 1996.

Gordenker, Leon. "Early Warning of Refugee Incidents." In *Refugees and International Relations*. Eds. G. Loecher and L. Monahan, 355-371. New York: Oxford University Press, 1989.

Greenwood, Ted, Harold Feiveson, and Theodore B. Taylor. *Nuclear Proliferation: Motivations, Capabilities, and Strategies for Control.* New York: McGraw-Hill Book Company, 1977.

Hiester, D. W. "Nuclear Proliferation: A Cause for Optimism?" *In At Issue-Politics in the World Arena,* ed. Steven Spiegel. New York: St. Martin's Press, 1988.

Huss, Pierre J. and George Carpozi Jr. *Red Spies in the U.N.* New York: Coward-McCann, Inc., 1965.

International Peace Academy. *Peacekeeper's Handbook.* New York: Pergamon Press, 1986.

Jasani, Bhupendra, and Troshminomi Sakata, eds. *Satellites for Arms Control and Crisis Monitoring*. Oxford: Oxford University Press, 1987.

Kay, David. "Preventive Approaches: Expectations and Limitations for Inspections." In *Weapons of Mass Destruction: New Perspectives on Counterproliferation*. Eds. Stuart E. Johnson and William H. Lewis, 181-192. Washington, DC: National Defense University Press, 1995.

Lewis, William H., ed. *Military Implications of United Nations Peacekeeping Operations*. Washington, DC: National Defense University, 1993.

Loescher, Gil. *Refugee Movements and International Security.* London: Brassey's, 1992.

Ramcharan, B.G., ed. *International Law and Fact-Finding in the Field of Human Rights*. The Hague, Netherlands: Martinus Nijhoff, 1982.

________. *The International Law and Practice of Early-Warning and Preventive Diplomacy: The Emerging Global Watch*. Dordrecht, Netherlands: Martinus Nijhoff Publishers, 1991.

Rehbein, Robert E., Major, USAF. *Spies in Blue: The Dilemma of American Intelligence Support to United Nations Peacekeeping Operations*. Kingston, Ontario, Canada: Queen's Centre for International Relations, 1995.

Shevchenko, Arkady N. *Breaking With Moscow*. New York: Alfred A. Knopf, 1985.

Shultz, Richard H. and Roy Godson. *The Strategy of Soviet Disinformation*. New York, NY: Berkley Books, 1984.

Smithson, Amy. "Multilateral Aerial Inspections: An Abbreviated History." In *Open Skies, Arms Control, and Cooperative Security*. Eds. Michael Krepon and Amy Smithson, 113-134. New York: St. Martin's Press, 1992.

Soviet Spies in the Shadow of the U.N. Belgium: Ligue De La Liberte, 1969.

Thatcher, Margaret. *The Downing Street Years*. London: Harper Collins, 1993.

Thoolen, Hans. "Information Aspects of Humanitarian Early Warning." In *Early Warning and Conflict Resolution*. Eds. K. Rupesinghe and M. Kuroda, 166-180. New York: St. Martin's Press, 1992.

Tobiassen, Leif Kr. The Reluctant Door: *The Right of Access to the United Nations*. Washington, DC: Public Affairs Press, 1969.

Yardley, Herbert O. *The American Black Chamber*. New York: Ballantine Books, 1981.

Monographs, Journals, and other Scholarly Works

Adam, John A. "Part 2: Working to Halt Proliferation." *IEEE Spectrum* 29, no. 4 (April 1992): 66-71.

Albright, David and Mark Hibbs. "Iraq's Nuclear Hide-and-Seek." *Bulletin of the Atomic Scientists* 47, no. 7 (September 1991): 14-23.

Allen, John R., Lieutenant Colonel, USMC. "Humanity on Humanitarian Operations: How Much Violence is Enough?" *Marine Corps Gazette* 79, no. 2 (February 1995): 14-36.

Andriole, S.J., and R.A. Young. "Towards the development of an integrated crisis warning system." *International Studies Quarterly* 21, no. 15 (March 1977): 107-150.

Australian Safeguards Office. "Iraq and North Korea Implications for Safeguards." Nuclear Issues Briefing Paper 15, March 1995. Downloaded from *America Online*.

Baker, Caleb. "Manhunt for Aideed: Why the Rangers Came Up Empty-Handed." *Armed Forces Journal International* 131, no. 5 (December 1993): 18.

Berdal, Mats R. *Whither UN Peacekeeping?* Adelphi Paper 281. Institute for Strategic Studies. London: Brassey's, October 1993.

________. "Fateful Encounter: The United States and UN Peacekeeping." *Survival* 36, no. 1 (Spring 1994): 30-50.

Bermudez, Joseph S. Jr. "North Korea's Nuclear Infrastructure." *Jane's Intelligence Review 6, no. 2* (February 1994): 74-79.

Beyer, Gregg A. "Human Rights Monitoring and the Failure of Early Warning: A Practitioner's View." *International Journal of Refugee Law* 2, no. 1 (1990): 56-82.

Blix, Hans. "Non-Proliferation and Verification in the 1990s: Securing the Future." *IAEA Bulletin* 34, no. 1 (1992): 2-5.

Boldrick, Michael R. "Three Schools of Thought on Nuclear Proliferation." *Parameters* 25, no. 1 (Spring 1995): 138-144.

Bozeman, Adda B. "Statecraft and Intelligence in the Non-Western World." *Conflict 6*, no. 1 (1985): 1-35.

Brand, David L., Captain, USA, Paul J. Bryson, SGT, USA, and Alfred Lopez Jr., SPC, USA. "Intelligence Support to the Logistician in Somalia." *Military Intelligence* 20, no. 4 (October-December 1994): 5-8.

Brody, Reed. "Early Warning, Early Action." *Refugees* 92 (April 1993): 8-10.

Carter, Dan. "Marine Corps Counterintelligence in Somalia and Beyond." *Defense Intelligence Journal* 4, no. 1 (Spring 1995): 83-89.

Cassata, Donna. "A Venerable Cold Warrior Finds New Missions." *Congressional Quarterly* 53, no. 34 (2 September 1995): 2665.

________. "Can the U.N. Keep a Secret?" *Congressional Quarterly* 53, no. 11 (18 March 1995): 826.

Centre for Refugee Studies, York University. "Towards Practical Early Warning Capabilities Concerning Refugees and Displaced Peoples." *International Journal of Refugee Law* 4, no. 1 (1992): 84-89.

Charny, I. "A genocide early-warning system." Vol. 14 of *The Whole Earth Papers*. New Jersey: Global Education Associates, 1980.

"Charter Committee Reports Progress Regarding UN Fact-Finding Process." *UN Chronicle* 27, no. 2 (June 1990): 32-34.

Chung, Hyun. "North Korea's Nuclear Ambitions and the Current Nuclear Non-Proliferation Regime." *The Korean Journal of International Studies* 25, no. 3 (Autumn 1994): 229-257.

Clarke, Walter and Robert Gosende. "Keeping the Mission focused: The Intelligence Component in Peace Operations." *Defense Intelligence Journal* 5, no. 2 (Fall 1996): 47-69.

Cleary, Michael J., Lieutenant Colonel, USAR. "Civil Affairs Information Collection in Kuwait City." *Special Warfare* 8, no. 2 (April 1995): 11-13.

Cleminson, F. R. "Ongoing Monitoring and Verification: Learning from the IAEA/UNSCOM Experience in Iraq." *Korean Journal of Defense Analysis* 7, no. 1 (Summer 1995): 129-154.

Colby, William. Remarks in "Disarmament — New Realities: Disarmament, Peace-building and Global Security." Panel discussion at a conference held at the United Nations 22-23 April 1993. New York: United Nations, 1993, 254-55.

Connaughton, Richard M. "Command, Control, and Communications." In *Military Implications of United Nations Peacekeeping Operations*. Institute of National Strategic Studies *McNair Paper* 17. Ed. William H. Lewis, 9-23. Washington, DC: National Defense University Press, 1993.

Constantine, G. Ted. *Intelligence Support to Humanitarian-Disaster Relief Operations*. Monograph. Center for the Study of Intelligence. Washington, DC: Central Intelligence Agency, December 1995.

Cooper, Pat. "Peacekeepers in Bosnia to Get Revamped Intelligence Feeds." *Defense News* 11, no. 16 (22-28 April 1996): 36.

Costa, Christopher P., Captain, USA. "Changing Gears: Special Operations Intelligence Support to Operation PROVIDE COMFORT." *Military Intelligence* 18, no. 4 (October-December 1992): 24-28.

Dean, Jonathan. "A Stronger UN Strengthens America." *Bulletin of the Atomic Scientists* 51, no. 2 (March/April 1995): 45-54.

Dedring, Juergen. "Early Warning and the United Nations." *Journal of Ethno-Development* 4, no. 1 (July 1994): 98-104.

Della-Giustina, John. E., Captain, USA. "Intelligence in Peace Operations: The MID in Cuba, 1906-1909." *Military Intelligence* 20, no. 4 (October-December 1994): 18-22.

DeMars, William. "Waiting for Early Warning: Humanitarian Action After the Cold War." *Journal of Refugee Studies* 8, no. 4 (December 1995): 390-410.

Dembinski, Matthias. "North Korea, IAEA Special Inspections, and the Future of the Nonproliferation Regime." *The Nonproliferation Review* 2, no. 2 (Winter 1995): 31-39.

Di Rita, Lawrence T. "C'mon, Baby — Do the Multilateral." *National Review*, 4 October 1993, 42-44.

Dmitrichev, Timour F. "Conceptual Approaches to Early Warning — Mechanisms and Models: A View from the United Nations." *International Journal of Refugee Law* 3, no. 2 (1991): 264-271.

Donath, Jaap. "A European Community Intelligence Organization." *Defense Intelligence Journal* 2, no. 1 (Spring 1993): 15-33.

Donohue, D.L., and R. Zeisler. "Behind the Scenes: Scientific Analysis of Samples from Nuclear Inspections in Iraq." *IAEA Bulletin* 34, no. 1 (1992): 25-32.

Druke, L. "UNHCR and the Need for 'Early Warning.' " *Refugee Abstracts* 8, no. 4 (December 1989).

Eriksson, Par. "Intelligence in Peacekeeping Operations." Paper prepared for ISA Annual Convention, San Diego, 16-20 April 1996. Stockholm: Swedish National Defence Research Establishment, 1996.

Farris, Karl, Colonel, USA. "UN Peacekeeping in Cambodia: On Balance, a Success." *Parameters* 24, no. 1 (Spring 1994): 38-50.

Fischer, David. "Consequences of the Iraq Case for Non-Proliferation Policy." in *Nichtverbreitung von Kernwaffen: Neue Probleme und Perspektiven, Arbeitspapiere zur Internationalen Politik* 66. Bonn, GM: Europa Union Verlag, 1991, 33.

Fischer, Wolfgang, and others. "The Role of Satellites and Remote Data Transmission in a Future Safeguards Regime." In *International Nuclear Safeguards 1994*. Vienna: International Atomic Energy Agency, 1994.

Fishel, John T. *Liberation, Occupation and Rescue: War Termination and DESERT STORM*. Carlisle Barracks, PA: U.S. Army War College, 31 August 1992.

Fisher, Louis. "The Korean War: On What Legal Basis Did Truman Act?" *The American Journal of International Law* 89, no. 1 (1995): 21-39.

Fitz-Simons, Daniel W. *Australian Intelligence Collection in Combined Peacekeeping Operations*. Discussion Paper No. 3. Washington, DC: Joint Military Intelligence College, February 1996.

Flemming, Stephen B. *Organizational and Military Impacts of High-Tech Surveillance and Detection Systems for UN Peacekeeping*. Study. Project Report 535. Ottawa: Operational Research and Analysis Establishment, Department of National Defense, 1992.

Fleitz, Frederick H. *Worldwide Peacekeeping Operations 1993*. Washington, DC: Central Intelligence Agency, 1992.

Fontaine, Marc. "Tactical Military Intelligence, IPB and the UN." *Peacekeeping and International Relations* 24 (1 November 1995): 9.

Gerardi, Greg J. and Maryam Aharinejad. "An Assessment of Iran's Nuclear Facilities." *The Non-Proliferation Review* 2, no. 3 (Spring/Summer 1995): 207-213.

Gold, Philip, Major, USMC. "Civil Affairs for the Eighties." *Marine Corps Gazette* 66, no. 10 (October 1982): 58-63.

Goldman, Alan R. "The Threat Environment in Peace-Related Operations." *Military Intelligence Professional Bulletin PB34-96-2* 22, no. 2 (April-June 1996): 35-39.

Gordenker, L. "Early-Warning of Disastrous Population Movement." *International Migration Review* 20 (1986): 170-189.

________. "Early-Warning of Refugee Incidents: Potentials and Obstacles." Paper presented to the Refugee Studies Programme Seminar, Queen Elizabeth House, Oxford, 26 November 1986.

Graham, James. "Intelligence and Peacekeeping: Definitions and Limitations." *Peacekeeping and International Relations* 24 (1 November 1995): 3.

Gries, David. D. "Opening Up Secret Intelligence." *Orbis* 37, no. 3 (Summer 1993): 365-372.

Hayden, Michael V., Brigadier General, USAF. "Warfighters and Intelligence: One Team — One Fight." *Defense Intelligence Journal* 4, no. 2 (Fall 1995): 17-30.

"High Tech Commo, Sensors Bolster U.S., Allies Peacekeeping in Bosnia." *National Defense* 80, no. 516 (March 1996): 18-19.

Hooper, Richard. "Strengthening IAEA Safeguards in an Era of Nuclear Cooperation." *Arms Control Today 25*, no. 9 (November 1995): 14-18.

"IRENE — International Refugee Electronic Network." *International Journal of Refugee Law* 3, no. 2 (1991): 330-331.

Jasani, Bhupendra. "The Value of Civilian Satellite Imagery." *Jane's Intelligence Review* 5, no. 5 (May 1993): 235-239.

Jennekens, Jon. "IAEA Safeguards — Emerging Issues." Paper presented at the Fourth International Conference on Facility Operations-Safeguards Interface. Albuquerque, New Mexico, 29 September-4 October 1991.

Jonah, J.O.C. "Monitoring of Factors Related to Possible Refugee Outflows and Comparable Emergencies." Address to the United Nations Commission on Human Rights. February 1989.

________. "ORCI: The UN Secretary-General's New Arm of Analytical Information and Early-warning." Paper prepared for the International Seminar on the Reduction of the Risk of War. Warsaw, 24-25 April 1989.

Jones, Garrett. *Intelligence Support to United Nations Activities*. Student Paper. AD-A263-869. Carlisle Barracks, PA: U.S. Army War College, 25 April 1993.

Jones, Peter. "Peacekeeping and Aerial Surveillance." 3 parts. *Peacekeeping & International Relations* 22 (March-April 1993): 3-4; 22 (September-October 1993): 3-5; 23 (July-August 1994): 5-7.

Jongman, A.J. "Contemporary Conflicts." PIOOM 7, no. 1 (Winter 1995): 14-23.

Jurado, Sonia R., and Paul F. Diehl. "UN Peacekeeping and Arms Control Verification." *Contemporary Security Policy* 15, no. 1 (April 1994): 38-54.

Kanninen, T. "Frameworks for Monitoring Emergent or Ongoing Conflicts: Possibility and Feasibility of an Internationally Standardized Framework." Paper presented to International Studies Association Convention. London, 28 March — 1 April 1989.

Kay, David. *Denial and Deception: Iraq and Beyond.* Monograph. Intelligence Studies Section, Working Group on Intelligence Reform. Washington, DC.

________. "Iraq and the IAEA." Lecture presented to the Potomac Chapter of the National Military Intelligence Association. Washington, DC, 21 March 1996.

Kellar, Charles S., Major, USA. *Organizing Anarchy: Planning for Refugee Support Operations.* Monograph. School of Advanced Military Studies. Fort Leavenworth, KS: U.S. Army Command and General Staff College, 1995.

Kerley, E.L. "The Powers of Investigation of the United Nations Security Council." *American Journal of International Law* 55 (1961): 892-918.

Killinger, Mark H. "Improving Safeguards Through Enhanced Information Analysis." *The Nonproliferation Review* 3, no. 1 (Fall 1995): 43-48.

Kirschten, Dick. "Mission Impossible." *The National Journal* 325, no. 44 (30 October 1993): 2576.

Krepon, Michael and Jeffrey P. Tracey. "'Open Skies' and UN Peacekeeping." *Survival* 32, no. 3 (May/June 1990): 251-263.

Krepon, Michael, and others. *Commercial Observation Satellites and International Security.* New York: St. Martins Press, 1990.

"Lawmakers Fear UN Cannot be Trusted With US Intelligence." *Tactical Technology* 5, no. 12 (14 June 1995). Accessed on LEXIS-NEXIS, 10 May 1996.

Leach, Raymond J., Major, USMC. "'Information' Support to U.N. Forces." *Marine Corps Gazette* 78, no. 9 (September 1994): 49-50.

Leurdijk, D.A. "Fact-Finding: The Revitalization of a Dutch Initiative in the UN." *Bulletin of Peace Proposals* 21, no. 1 (1990): 59-69.

Levin, Mark. "Loose Lips." *National Review*, 11 March 1996, 50-51.

Lewis, William, and John O.B. Sewell. "United Nations Peacekeeping: Ends Versus Means." *Joint Forces Quarterly* 1 (Summer 1993): 48-57.

Loescher, Gil. *Peacekeeping: The Way Ahead?* McNair Paper 25. Washington, DC: Institute for Strategic Studies, National Defense University, November 1993.

Macartney, John. "Intelligence: A Consumer's Guide." *International Journal of Intelligence and Counterintelligence* 2, no. 4 (Winter 1988): 457-486.

Mansourov, Alexandre Y. "The Origins, Evolution, and Current Politics of the North Korean Nuclear Program." *The Nonproliferation Review* 2, no. 3 (Spring-Summer 1995): 25-38.

McCorkle, C.M. "Foodgrain disposals as early warning famine signals: a case from Burkina Faso." *Disasters* 11, no. 4 (1987): 273-281.

McPherson, Denver E., Major, USA. "Intelligence and the Peacekeeper in Haiti." *Military Intelligence Professional Bulletin PB34-96-2* 22, no. 2 (April-June 1996): 43-47.

Newhouse, Peter. "Global Warning." *Refugees* 90 (July 1992): 14-15.

Oseth, John M., Lieutenant Colonel, USA. "Intelligence and Low-Intensity Conflict." *Naval War College Review* 37, no. 6 (November-December 1984): 19-36.

Rababy, David A., Captain, USMC. "Intelligence Support During a Humanitarian Mission." *Marine Corps Gazette* 79, no. 2 (February 1995): 40.

Ramcharan, B.G. "Principles for the Conduct of Early-Warning at the United Nations." Summary of Proceedings of Conference at Ralph Bunche Institute. New York University, 1989.

________. "Early-Warning at the United Nations. A First Experiment." *International Journal of Refugee Law* 1, no. 3 (1989): 379-386.

________. "Humanitarian Good Offices in International Law." In *The Good Offices of the United Nations Secretary-General in the Field of Human Rights*. The Hague: Martinus Nijhoff, 1989.

Refugee Policy Group. *Early-Warning: An Analysis of Approaches to Improving the International Response System to Refugee Crisis*. Washington, DC: May 1983.

Renninger, J. "Early Warning. What Role for the United Nations?" Paper presented to UNITAR/USSR Association for the United Nations Roundtable on the "Future Role of the United Nations in an Interdependent World." Moscow, 5-9 September 1988.

Roos, John G. "The Perils of Peacekeeping: Tallying the Costs in Blood, Coin, and Readiness." *Armed Forces Journal International* 132, no. 5(December 1993): 13-18.

Rupesinghe, K. "Notes toward a research programme: ethnic violence, human rights, and early warnings." *UNESCO Yearbook on Peace and Conflict Studies* (1989): 191-233.

________. "The Quest for a Disaster Early-Warning System." *Bulletin of Peace Proposals* 18 (1987): 217-227.

Rusu, Sharon. "Refugees, Information, and Solutions: The Need for Informed Decision-Making." *Refugee Survey Quarterly* 13, no. 1 (Spring 1994): 4-10.

________. "The Role of the Collector in early Warning." *International Journal of Refugee Law*, Special Issue (September 1990): 65-70.

Saracino, Peter. "Polemics and Prescriptions." *International Defense Review* 26, no. 5 (May 1993): 370-371.

Scheinman, Lawrence. "Lessons From Post-War Iraq for the International Full-Scope Safeguards Regime." *Arms Control Today* 23, no. 3 (April 1993): 3-15.

Schlesinger, Stephen. "Cryptanalysis for Peacetime: Codebreaking and the Birth and Structure of the United Nations." *Cryptologia* 19, no. 3 (July 1995): 217-235.

Schmeidel, Susanne. *From Root Cause Assessment to Preventive Diplomacy: Possibilities and Limitations of the Early Warning of Forced Migration*. Ph.D. Dissertation. Columbus, OH: Ohio State University, 1995.

Schmid, A. J. "Five Styles of Conflict and Two Crises Thresholds." *PIOOM* 7, no. 1 (Winter 1995): 4-7.

Shelton, David L., Major, USMC. "Intelligence Lessons Known and Revealed During Operation RESTORE HOPE Somalia." *Marine Corps Gazette* 79, no. 2 (February 1995): 37-42.

Shoham, J. "Does nutritional surveillance have a role to play in early warning of food crisis and in the management of relief operations?" *Disasters* 11, no. 4 (1987): 282-285.

Shulsky, Abram N., and Gary J. Schmitt. "The Future of Intelligence." *National Interest* 38 (Winter 1994/1995): 63-73.

Smith, Hugh. "Intelligence and UN Peacekeeping." *Survival* 36, no. 3 (Autumn 1994): 174-192.

Smithson, Amy. "Open Skies Ready for Takeoff." *Bulletin of the Atomic Scientists* 48, no. 1 (January/February 1992): 17-19.

Snider, L. Britt. *Intelligence and Law Enforcement*. Monograph. Intelligence Studies Section, Working Group on Intelligence Reform. Washington, DC.

Snyder, Lynda and David P. Warshaw. "Force Protection: Integrating Civil Affairs and Intelligence." *Military Intelligence* 21 (1 October 1995): 26.

Sutterlin, J.S. "The Objectives, Requirements and Structure of a War Risk Reduction Centre Within the United Nations." Paper presented to Conference on the Establishment of Multilateral War Risk Reduction Centres. Warsaw, 24-25 April 1989.

Thornberry, Cedric. "Civil Affairs in the Development of UN Peacekeeping." *International Peacekeeping* 1, no. 4 (Winter 1994): 471-484.

Trevan, Timothy T. Remarks in *Disarmament—New Realities: Disarmament, Peace-building and Global Security : Panel Discussion at a Conference Held at the United Nations*, 20-23 April 1993. New York: United Nations, 1993, 262.

United States Institute of Peace. "The North Korean Nuclear Challenge: The Post-Kim Il Sung Phase Begins." Special Report. Washington, DC. Downloaded from *America Online*, 21 December 1995.

Van der Denner, J.M.G. "On Peace." PIOOM 7, no. 1 (Winter 1995): 39-41.

Vick, James A., Captain, USA. "Intelligence Support to Operation 'GIT'MO.' " *Military Intelligence* 19, no. 2 (April-June 1993): 6-9, 50.

Wallace, Stephen O., Lieutenant Colonel, USA. "Joint Task Force Support Hope: The Role of the CMOC in Humanitarian Operations." *Special Warfare* 9, no. 1 (January 1996): 36-41.

Wenger, William V., Lieutenant Colonel, USAR, and Fredric W. Young, First Lieutenant, USAR. "The Los Angeles Riots and Tactical Intelligence." *Military Intelligence* 18, no. 4 (October-December 1992): 30-34.

Wilson, Thomas R. "Joint Intelligence and Uphold Democracy." *Joint Force Quarterly* 7 (Spring 1995): 54-59.

Woods, William A., First Lieutenant, USAR. "Operation GUANTANAMO: Civil Affairs in Action." *Special Warfare* 6, no. 4 (October 1993): 39-41.

Woolsey, James. "The Proliferation of Weapons of Mass Destruction, CIA Director's Testimony." *Foreign Policy Bulletin*, 3, no. 6 (May/June 1993): 34-38.

Zorpette, Glenn. "Part 1: How Iraq Reverse-Engineered the Bomb." *IEEE Spectrum* 29, no. 4 (April 1992): 20-24+.

Zumach, Andreas. "US Intelligence Knew Serbs Were Planning an Assault on Srebrenica." *Newsletter on International Security Information Policy*, no. 47 (16 October 1995): 1.

U.S. Government Publications

Albright, Madeleine K. "Advancing American Interests Through the United Nations." *U.S. Department of State Dispatch* 6, no. 8 (20 February 1995): 125-130.

Batten, Peter. Deputy to the Under Secretary of Defense (Policy), Policy Support/International Security/National Disclosure Policy Committee. "Possible Compromise of US Classified Information by UNOSOM Forces During Operation UNITED SHIELD in Somalia." Information Paper. 16 May 1995.

Best, Richard A. Jr. "Intelligence Technology in the Post-Cold War Era: The Role of Unmanned Aerial Vehicles." *CRS Report for Congress*, 93-686F. Washington, DC: Congressional Research Service, Library of Congress, 26 July 1993.

________. "Peacekeeping: Intelligence Requirements." *CRS Report for Congress*, 94-394F. Washington, DC: Congressional Research Service, Library of Congress, 6 May 1994.

Bolton, John R. "Statement Before the House Appropriations Committee, Commerce, Justice, State and Judiciary Subcommittee." 25 January 1995. Federal Document Clearing House, Accessed on LEXIS-NEXIS, Inc. 10 May 1996.

Bush, George. "Address to the UN General Assembly in New York City, 21 September 1992." *Weekly Compilation of Presidential Documents* 28, no. 39 (28 September 1992): 1697-1701.

Center for Advancement of Language Learning. *Refugee/Migrant Support Operations Training Support Package, S2/Intelligence*. Fort Leavenworth, KS: U.S. Army Combined Arms Center, n.d.

Central Intelligence Agency. *Director of Central Intelligence Directive 1/7: Security Controls on the Dissemination of Intelligence Information.* 16 April 1996.

Central Intelligence Agency, Directorate of Intelligence. *World Wide Humanitarian Aid: An Overview of the Relief System.* RTT 94-100009. February 1994.

Clinton, President William, J., Letter to Senate Majority Leader Robert Dole. Subject: "Response to Congressional Concerns Over U.S. Intelligence Material Found in UNOSOM II Compound, Mogadishu, Somalia." 6 April 1995.

Combest, Rep. Larry (Texas). "Opening Statement: Committee Hearing on Intelligence Support to the United Nations." House Permanent Select Committee on Intelligence, 19 January 1995.

________. "Opening Statement: Full Committee Markup of the National Security Revitalization Act, H.R. 7." House Permanent Select Committee on Intelligence, 27 January 1995.

________. Letter to Admiral William O. Studeman, USN, Acting Director of Central Intelligence. Subject: "Invitation to Appear at Hearings of the House Permanent Select Committee on Intelligence on 19 January 1995." 10 January 1995.

Commission on the Roles and Capabilities of the United States Intelligence Community. *Preparing for the 21st Century: An Appraisal of U.S. Intelligence.* Washington, DC: GPO, 1 March 1996.

Daschle, Sen. Tom (South Dakota). *Press Release: Conference Report on H.R. 1561.* 14 March 1996.

Deutch, John. Deputy Secretary of Defense. Letter to Representative Larry Combest, Chairman, House Permanent Select Committee on Intelligence. Subject: "Transmittal of the Report of Investigation from the United States Central Command Concerning the Circumstances Surrounding Classified Information Found at the UNOSOM Compound in Mogadishu on 27 February 1995." 17 April 1995.

Dicks, Rep. Norm (Washington). "Opening Statement: Committee Hearing on Intelligence Support to the United Nations." House Permanent Select Committee on Intelligence, 19 January 1995.

________. "Opening Statement: Full Committee Markup of the National Security Revitalization Act, H.R. 7." House Permanent Select Committee on Intelligence, 27 January 1995.

Dole, Sen. Robert (Kansas). "Statement Before the Senate Committee on Foreign Relations." 21 March 1995.

"Focus on the United Nations: UN Peacekeeping Operations." *U.S. Department of State Dispatch* 6, no. 18 (1 May 1995): 377-379.

Gati, Tobi T. Assistant Secretary of State for Intelligence and Research. Letter to Ambassador Hugh Montgomery. Subject: "UN Request for US Intelligence on Guatemala and Burundi." 1 February 1996.

________. "Statement by Assistant Secretary of State for Intelligence and Research before the House Permanent Select Committee on Intelligence Hearing on Intelligence Support to the UN." 19 January 1995.

________. "Statement by Assistant Secretary of State for Intelligence and Research before the Senate Select Committee on Intelligence: Worldwide Threats to the United States." 10 January 1995.

INR Press Guidance. *Intelligence Sharing With the UN. U.S. Department of State*, Bureau of Intelligence and Research. 1 November 1995.

Shalikashvili, John M., General, USA, Chairman of the Joint Chiefs of Staff. Memorandum for the Secretary of Defense. CM-742-95. Subject: "Transmittal of Report of Investigation — Discovery of Classified Material Left by UNOSOM During Operation UNITED SHIELD." 5 April 1995.

Snowe, Sen. Olympia J. (Maine). Letter to Ambassador Madeleine Albright, U.S. Permanent Representative to the UN. Subject: "Possible Misuse of U.S. Classified Information Provided to the UN Peacekeeping Operation in Somalia." 13 March 1995.

Spence, Rep. Floyd, (South Carolina). "Press Release: Congressional Leadership to Clinton: Suspend Intelligence Sharing With UN." House National Security Committee, 16 March 1995.

Studeman, William O., Admiral, USN. Acting Director of Central Intelligence. Letter to Rep. Larry Combest, Chairman of the House Permanent Select Committee on Intelligence. Subject: "Concern over the Proposed Section 512 of H. Rept. 7." 19 January 1995.

Talbott, Strobe. "The Case for the United States in the United Nations." *U.S. Department of State Dispatch* 6, no. 37 (11 September 1995): 681-682.

U.S. Arms Control and Disarmament Agency (ACDA). "Prospects and Directions for Improvements in International Safeguards." *Final Report.* Vol. II, 24 February 1987.

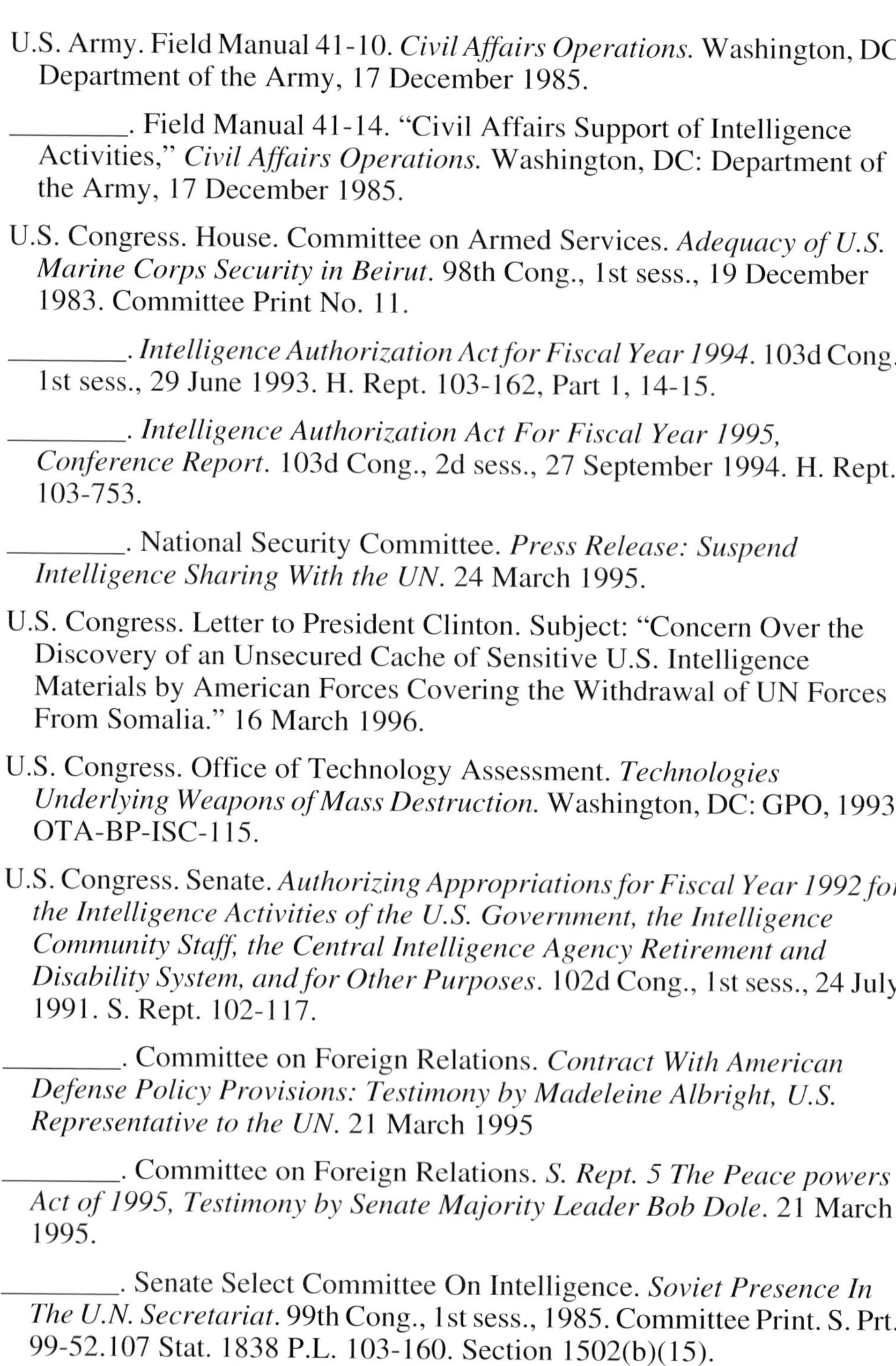

U.S. Army. Field Manual 41-10. *Civil Affairs Operations.* Washington, DC: Department of the Army, 17 December 1985.

________. Field Manual 41-14. "Civil Affairs Support of Intelligence Activities," *Civil Affairs Operations.* Washington, DC: Department of the Army, 17 December 1985.

U.S. Congress. House. Committee on Armed Services. *Adequacy of U.S. Marine Corps Security in Beirut.* 98th Cong., 1st sess., 19 December 1983. Committee Print No. 11.

________. *Intelligence Authorization Act for Fiscal Year 1994.* 103d Cong., 1st sess., 29 June 1993. H. Rept. 103-162, Part 1, 14-15.

________. *Intelligence Authorization Act For Fiscal Year 1995, Conference Report.* 103d Cong., 2d sess., 27 September 1994. H. Rept. 103-753.

________. National Security Committee. *Press Release: Suspend Intelligence Sharing With the UN.* 24 March 1995.

U.S. Congress. Letter to President Clinton. Subject: "Concern Over the Discovery of an Unsecured Cache of Sensitive U.S. Intelligence Materials by American Forces Covering the Withdrawal of UN Forces From Somalia." 16 March 1996.

U.S. Congress. Office of Technology Assessment. *Technologies Underlying Weapons of Mass Destruction.* Washington, DC: GPO, 1993. OTA-BP-ISC-115.

U.S. Congress. Senate. *Authorizing Appropriations for Fiscal Year 1992 for the Intelligence Activities of the U.S. Government, the Intelligence Community Staff, the Central Intelligence Agency Retirement and Disability System, and for Other Purposes.* 102d Cong., 1st sess., 24 July 1991. S. Rept. 102-117.

________. Committee on Foreign Relations. *Contract With American Defense Policy Provisions: Testimony by Madeleine Albright, U.S. Representative to the UN.* 21 March 1995

________. Committee on Foreign Relations. *S. Rept. 5 The Peace powers Act of 1995, Testimony by Senate Majority Leader Bob Dole.* 21 March 1995.

________. Senate Select Committee On Intelligence. *Soviet Presence In The U.N. Secretariat.* 99th Cong., 1st sess., 1985. Committee Print. S. Prt. 99-52.107 Stat. 1838 P.L. 103-160. Section 1502(b)(15).

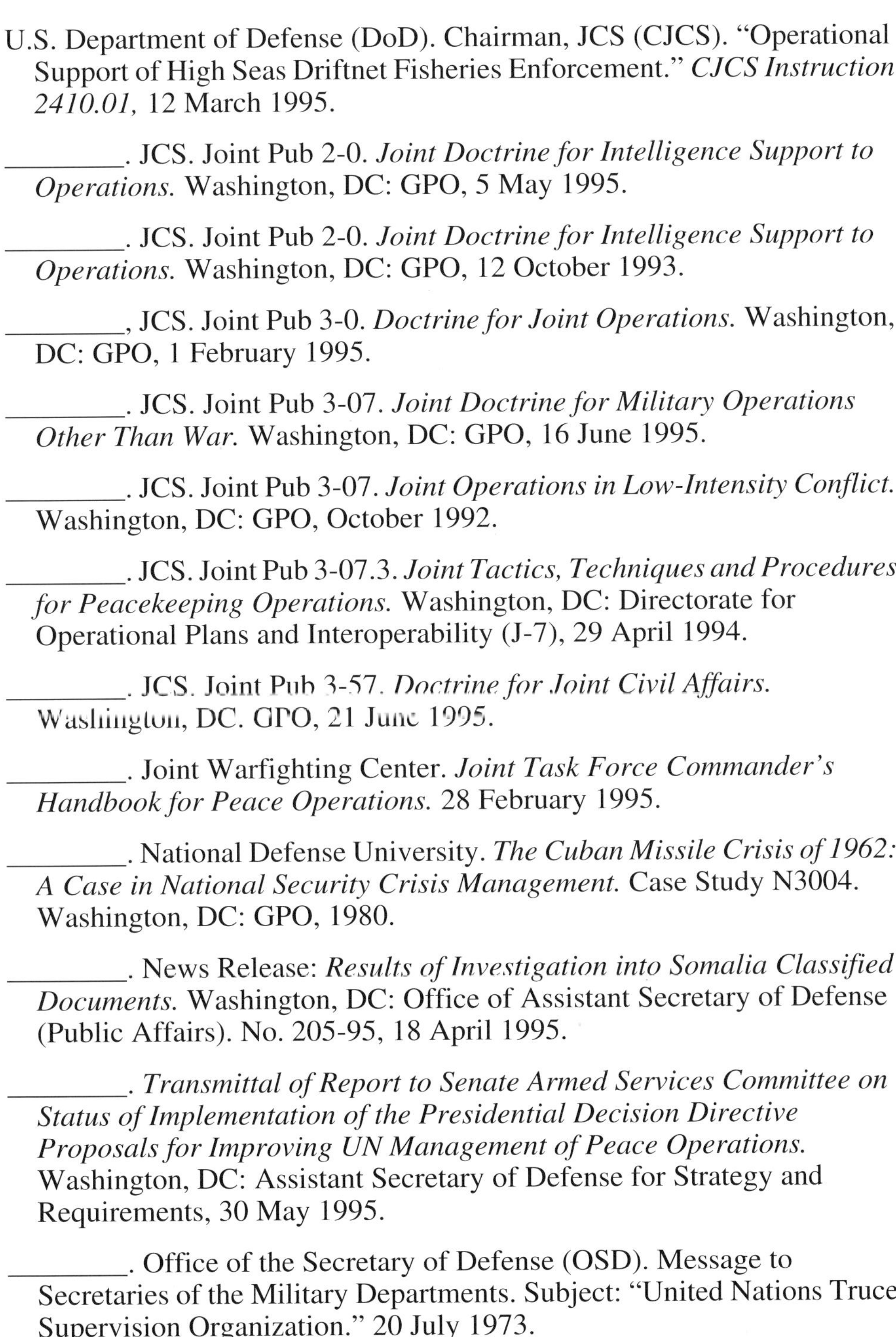

U.S. Department of Defense (DoD). Chairman, JCS (CJCS). "Operational Support of High Seas Driftnet Fisheries Enforcement." *CJCS Instruction 2410.01,* 12 March 1995.

________. JCS. Joint Pub 2-0. *Joint Doctrine for Intelligence Support to Operations.* Washington, DC: GPO, 5 May 1995.

________. JCS. Joint Pub 2-0. *Joint Doctrine for Intelligence Support to Operations.* Washington, DC: GPO, 12 October 1993.

________, JCS. Joint Pub 3-0. *Doctrine for Joint Operations.* Washington, DC: GPO, 1 February 1995.

________. JCS. Joint Pub 3-07. *Joint Doctrine for Military Operations Other Than War.* Washington, DC: GPO, 16 June 1995.

________. JCS. Joint Pub 3-07. *Joint Operations in Low-Intensity Conflict.* Washington, DC: GPO, October 1992.

________. JCS. Joint Pub 3-07.3. *Joint Tactics, Techniques and Procedures for Peacekeeping Operations.* Washington, DC: Directorate for Operational Plans and Interoperability (J-7), 29 April 1994.

________. JCS. Joint Pub 3-57. *Doctrine for Joint Civil Affairs.* Washington, DC: GPO, 21 June 1995.

________. Joint Warfighting Center. *Joint Task Force Commander's Handbook for Peace Operations.* 28 February 1995.

________. National Defense University. *The Cuban Missile Crisis of 1962: A Case in National Security Crisis Management.* Case Study N3004. Washington, DC: GPO, 1980.

________. News Release: *Results of Investigation into Somalia Classified Documents.* Washington, DC: Office of Assistant Secretary of Defense (Public Affairs). No. 205-95, 18 April 1995.

________. *Transmittal of Report to Senate Armed Services Committee on Status of Implementation of the Presidential Decision Directive Proposals for Improving UN Management of Peace Operations.* Washington, DC: Assistant Secretary of Defense for Strategy and Requirements, 30 May 1995.

________. Office of the Secretary of Defense (OSD). Message to Secretaries of the Military Departments. Subject: "United Nations Truce Supervision Organization." 20 July 1973.

U.S. General Accounting Office. *UN Peacekeeping: Lessons Learned in Managing Recent Missions,* Report GAO/NSIAD.94.9. Washington, DC: December 1993.

U.S. Marine Corps (USMC). Marine Corps Intelligence Activity (MCIA). *Generic Intelligence Requirements Handbook.* Quantico, VA: MCIA, 1995.

U.S. Mission to the United Nations. *Global Humanitarian Emergencies,* 1996. New York: U.S. Mission to the United Nations, February 1996.

U.S. President. *Presidential Decision Directive 25,* "Clinton Administration's Policy on Reforming Multilateral Peace Operations." 3 May 1994.

Whitehead, John C. Chairman, United Nations Association of the United States. Letter to Rep. Benjamin Gilman, Chairman House International Relations Committee. Subject: "Concern Over Provision of the National Security Revitalization Act That Would Limit U.S. Support for UN Peacekeeping." 25 January 1995.

UN Documentation

Commonwealth of Independent States: Council of Heads of State Decisions on Settlement of Conflicts, Peacekeeping Forces and Military Training. UN Doc A/51/62, S/1996/74, 31 January 1996. 35 I.L.M. 783 (1996).

International Atomic Energy Agency. "Agreement Reached on Inspection Activities of Nuclear Facilities in Democratic People's Republic of Korea." IAEA/1255, 15 February 1994.

________. "IAEA Board Finds That Democratic People's Republic of Korea to Widen Its Non-Compliance with Safeguards Agreement." IAEA/1273, 14 June 1994.

________. "IAEA Director-General Comments on 'Declared' Nuclear Installations and Material in Democratic People's Republic of Korea." IAEA/1253, 6 December 1994.

________. "IAEA General Conference Adopts Resolution on Nuclear Safeguards Implementation in Democratic People's Republic of Korea." IAEA/1250, 1 October 1993.

________. "IAEA General Conference Adopts Resolutions on Safeguards, Radioactive Waste and Technology Transfer." IAEA/1286, 23 September 1994.

________. "IAEA Proposes Sending Team to Democratic People's Republic of Korea to Discuss Arrangements on Safeguards Measures." IAEA/1269, 20 May 1994.

________. "IAEA Resolutions Seek to Strengthen Nuclear Safeguards, Prevent Illicit Trafficking, Promote Technical Cooperation." IAEA/1299, 25 September 1995.

________. "Safeguards Inspection in Democratic People's Republic of Korea to be Included in Agenda of IAEA General Conference." IAEA/291, 23 September 1993.

International Refugee Documentation Network (IRDN). *Conference on the Future of the International Refugee Documentation Network*, 8-9 May 1992, Crete. Geneva: IRDN, Centre for Documentation on Refugees, Office of the United Nations High Commissioner for Refugees, 1992.

Joint Inspection Unit. *The Coordination of Activities Related to Early-Warning of Possible Refugee Flows*. JIU/REP/90/2.

Permanent Representative of the DPRK to the United Nations. Letter to the President of the Security Council of the United Nations. Official Record. A/25405. 12 March 1993. *United Nations Documents and Publications Comprehensive Collection*. Microfiche edition, 1996.

United Nations. Aide Memorie: Investigation by the UN Secretariat Into Allegations Made By the Government of the United States That Classified Information Provided by the US Military Personnel in INTAF and UNOSOM to UNOSOM II Had Been Seriously Compromised. 11 May 1995.

United Nations. General Assembly. A/41/324. International Co-operation to Avert New Flows of Refugees—Note by the Secretary-General. New York, 13 May 1986.

________. A/47/277. Report of the Secretary General. *An Agenda For Peace*. 17 June 1992.

________. A/47/594. Report of the Secretary-General. Strengthening of the Coordination of Emergency Humanitarian Assistance of the United Nations. 30 October 1992.

________. A/48/1. Report of the Secretary General on the Work of the Organization. 10 September 1993.

________. A/49/177. Report of the Secretary-General. Strengthening of the Coordination of Emergency Humanitarian Assistance of the United Nations. 21 June 1994.

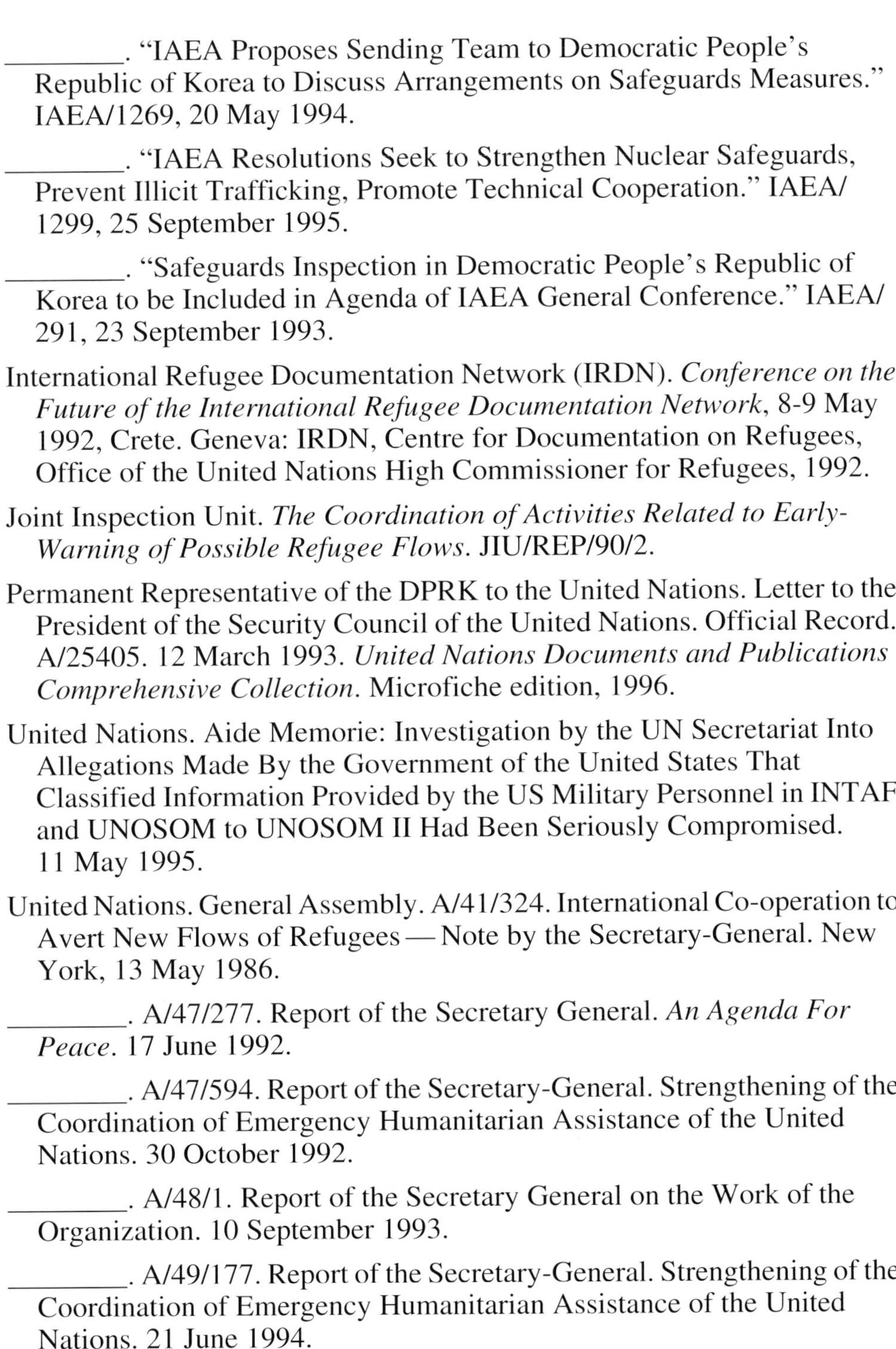

________. A/50/60. Report of the Secretary General. *Supplement To An Agenda For Peace*. 3 January 1995.

United Nations High Commissioner for Refugees (UNHCR). "Information Requests." Geneva: UNHCR, CDR, 1993-1994.

United Nations Secretariat (UNSec). Department of Humanitarian Affairs. Humanitarian Early Warning System: Progress and Prospects, 1995.

________. The Office for Research and the Collection of Information. ST/SGB/Organization. 3 October 1988.

________. The Office for Research and the Collection of Information. Secretary-General's Bulletin. 1 March 1987. ST/SGB/225.

United Nations Truce Supervision Organization (UNTSO). *Notes for the Guidance of Military Observers on Appointment.* New York: UN Field Operations Division, 1988.

General Press Articles

Batten, Effie. "Marines Blame Drone Crashes on Equipment." *European Stars & Stripes,* 18 July 1996, 1.

Barkho, Leon. "U.N. Team Enters Building in Baghdad." *Washington Post*, 10 March 1996, A21.

Beelman, Maud S. "From Croatian Isle, U.S. Team Mounts Secret Surveillance of Bosnia." *Washington Times*, 5 February 1995, A1.

Bennet, James. "On Eve of African Relief Talks, Aid Donors Argue Over Numbers." *New York Times,* 22 November 1996, 1.

Block, Robert. "UN Left 8,000 to Die in Bosnia." *The Independent* (United Kingdom), 30 October 1995, 1.

Caires, Greg. "Army KIOWA Warriors Provide Intel, Security in Bosnia, Troops Say," *Defense Daily,* 6 November 1996, 212.

Capaccio, Tony. "Paper Describes Islamic Militants Threat In Bosnia." *Defense Week*, 4 December 1995, 1.

Carollo, Russell. "In Bosnia, U.S. Probes Secret Munitions Plant." *Washington Times*, 6 February 1996, A1.

"CIA: Iraq dodges U.N. monitoring." *Washington Times*, 7 October 1994, A19.

"CIA, Other Agencies are Spying in Bosnia." *Washington Times*, 19 January 1996, A13.

"CIA Unveils Intel System For Bosnia Peacekeepers." *Defense News*, 15-21 April 1996, 2.

Cohen, Roger. "C.I.A. Report Finds Serbs Guilty In Majority of Bosnia War Crimes." *New York Times*, 9 March 1995, 1.

Cooper, Pat. "Stealthy UAV Gives Instant Imagery." *Defense News*, 5 June-11 June 1995, 4.

________. "U.S. Intelligence Setup Debuts on Bosnia Stage." *Defense News*, 22-28 January 1996, 6.

Courturier, Kelly. "In Iraq, No Rescue for Those Who Also Served." *Washington Post,* 18 September 1996, 26.

Devroy, Ann. "Internal U.S. Probe Faults Policy on Bosnian Arms." *Washington Post*, 16 April 1996, A1.

Devroy, Ann and Daniel Williams. "In Foreign Policy Debate, Parties are Parting at Water's Edge." *Washington Post*, 1 May 1995, A4.

"DOD Officials Mull Sending U-2 EMTI Platform To Bosnia To Supplement JSTARS." *Inside The Air Force*, 19 January 1996, 1.

Doke, Deedee. "U.S. To Beef Up Long-Term Air Intelligence in the Balkans." *European Stars & Stripes,* 18 July 1996, 3.

Dougherty, Kevin. "Predator Spy Craft Hunts Game This Week." *European Stars and Stripes*, 12 July 1995, 4.

Farah, Douglas. "U.S.-Haitian Relations Deteriorate." *Washington Post*, 29 November 1995, A1.

Fineman, Mark. "UN Continues to Have Bad Luck in Somalia." *Los Angeles Times,* 31 August 1993, A2.

"First Picture Shows North Korea N-Plant." *Daily Yomiuri* (Tokyo) , 9 February 1990. Accessed on LEXIS-NEXIS, 10 May 1996.

Foley, Theresa. "New Satellites May Aid Nuclear Inspectors." *Space News*, 31 January-6 February 1994, 6.

Fulghum, David A. "Air Force Prepares New UAV Acquisitions, Operations." *Aviation Week and Space Technology*, 27 November 1995, 52-54.

________. "Balkans Surveillance Swap Eyed Warily." *Aviation Week and Space Technology*, 18 March 1996, 25.

________. "U.S. Pressures North Korea to Shed Nuclear Weapons." *Aviation Week and Space Technology,* 28 March 1994, 22.

________. "U.S. Reconnaissance Role Looms Large In Bosnia." *Aviation Week and Space Technology*, 4 December 1995, 22.

Fulghum, David A., and John D. Morrocco. "U.S. Readies Predator For Missions In Bosnia." *Aviation Week and Space Technology*, 5 June 1995, 22.

Gaffney, Frank. "The Deforming of Intelligence." *Washington Times*, 7 May 1996, A12.

________. "Mending the Sieve of Shared Secrets." *Washington Times,* 26 July 1995, A20.

Gertz, Bill. "Administration Plays Down Leaks of U.S. Secrets by U.N." *Washington Times*, 20 January 1995, A8.

________. "Clinton Wants Hill Off His Back." *Washington Times*, 1 November 1995, A1+.

________. "Deutch Orders Intelligence to Be 'Releasable.' " *Washington Times*, 1 May 1996, A8.

________. "Events Seen Backing CIA Report." *Washington Times*, 28 November 1995, A1+.

________. "Iranian Military, Intelligence Remain at Work in Bosnia." *Washington Times*, 19 April 1996, A15.

________. "New UN Service Cited As A Soviet Propaganda Tool." *Washington Times,* 12 March 1987, 1A.

________. "N. Korean Missile Could Reach U.S., Intelligence Warns." *Washington Times*, 29 September 1995, A3.

________. "Unattended Papers in Somalia Did Not Damage U.S. Security." *Washington Times*, 18 April 1995, A18.

Gildea, Kerry. "Lawmakers Fear UN Cannot Be Trusted With U.S. Intelligence." *Defense Daily*, 8 June 1995, 353.

Glashow, Jason. "U.S. Shops For Sniper Stopper." *Defense News*, 22-28 January 1996, 3.

Goshko, John M. "U.N. Inspectors Enter Iraq Military Installation After 11-Hour Standoff." *Washington Post*, 12 March 1996, A9.

Graham, Bradley. "Bosnia Action Helps Focus Battle Intelligence Picture." *Washington Post*, 27 September 1995, A23.

________. "Funding Proposal Altered For Bosnia Deployment." *Washington Post*, 20 January 1996, A4.

Greenhouse, Steven. "U.N. Bosnia Force to Get U.S. Spy Planes." *New York Times*, 5 June 1995, A1+.

Grier, Peter. "Gulf War Report Pushes US to Try to Find Better Ways to Assess Battlefield Damage." *Christian Science Monitor*, 18 August 1993, 1.

"Gulf War Intelligence Gets Mixed Review." *Washington Post*, 16 August 1993, A9.

Hedges, Stephen J. and Peter Cary. "Saddam's Secret Bomb." *US News and World Report*, 25 November 1991, 34-42+.

Hibbs, Mark. "Gulf War Will Shift IAEA Safeguards Priorities-By How Much?" *Nucleonics Week,* 10 February 1992, 12.

________. "IAEA Explores Iran's Intentions, Minus Evidence of Weapons Drive." *Nucleonics Week,* 13 February 1992, 12.

________ . "Special Inspections: A Transatlantic Turf War for Post-Iraq Powers. *Nucleonics Week,* 30 January 1992, 14.

Hibbs, Mark and Kathleen Hart. "IAEA, U.S. Agencies Underestimated North Korea's Refueling Capacity." *Nuclear Fuel,* 6 June 1994, 5.

Hibbs, Mark and Naoaki Usui. "Soviet Warning to North Korea Viewed As Signal to Tokyo, Seoul." *Nucleonics Week,* 18 April 1991, 8.

Hitchens, Theresa. "Data-Sharing Hampers NATO's Bosnia Plan." *Defense News*, 23 October-29 October 1995, 1-4.

Hitchens, Theresa, and Neil Munro. "Pentagon May Bolster U.N. Intelligence Capabilities." *Defense News*, 15-21 November 1993, 20.

Hoagland, Jim. "Briefing Yeltsin On Iran." *Washington Post*, 17 May 1995, A23.

Hooper, Richard. "Strengthening IAEA Safeguards In an Era of Nuclear Cooperation." *Arms Control Today*, November 1995, 14-18.

Hyde, Henry. "Secret Intelligence: The Nation's First Line of Defense." *Washington Times*, 22 January 1996, A23.

"IAEA Director Views Nuclear Policies." Berlin *Die Welt*. AU0208192593. *FBIS Daily Report—Western Europe*, 3 August 1993, 1-4.

"Intelligence Effort in Gulf Criticized." *Washington Times*, 16 August 1993, A3.

"Iraqi Arms Disclosures Not Full, U.N. Envoy Says." *Baltimore Sun*, 6 December 1995, 14.

"It's Flawed, But It's Still Needed." *Los Angeles Times*, 23 October 1993, B4.

Jensen, Ron. "GIs Keep Sharp Eye for IFOR." *European Stars and Stripes*, 3 April 1996, 1.

"Joint Stars To Leave For Bosnia Dec. 14." *Defense Daily*, 12 December 1995, 6.

Komarow, Steve, and Jack Kelley. "NATO Lays Out Mission's Limits." *USA Today*, 3 January 1996, 2.

"Kurdish Refugees arrive in Guam." *Pacific Stars & Stripes*, 19 September 1996, 1.

Landers, Jim. "Baker Warns GOP Not to Micromanage U.S. Foreign Policy." *Dallas Morning News*, 13 January 1995, A15.

Lardner, Richard. "Intelligence 'Fusion' Will Be Major Challenge For U.S. Forces In Bosnia." *Inside The Pentagon*, 30 November 1995, 1.

"Lawmakers urge return of Haiti documents." *Washington Times*, 3 December 1995, A3.

Lederer, Edith M. "Jane's: Iraq Has Nearly 300 Operational Warplanes." Associated Press, 3 September 1993.

Lewis, Paul. "Reluctant Warriors: U.N. Member States Retreat from Peacekeeping Roles." *New York Times*, 12 December 1993, A22.

________. "U.N. Experts Now Say Baghdad Was Far from Making an A-Bomb Before Gulf War." *New York Times*, 20 May 1992, A6.

________. "U.N. Is Developing Control Center to Coordinate Growing Peacekeeping Role." *New York Times*, 28 March 1993, A10.

________. "U.N.'s Inspectors To Challenge Iraq." *New York Times*, 16 February 1993, A11.

________. "United Nations Is Finding Its Plate Increasingly Full." *New York Times*, 27 September 1993, A8.

________. "U.N. Sends Atom-Detecting Copters to Iraq." *New York Times*, 19 September 1993, A14.

________. "U.N.'s Top Troop Official Sees No Need For War Room." *New York Times*, 27 December 1992, A12.

Lippman, Thomas M. "U.N. Chief Faulted in Somalia Mess." *Washington Post*, 29 April 1994, A16.

________. "U.S. Officials Say Haitians Stymied FBI." *Washington Post*, 5 January 1996, A1.

Meisler, Stanley. "Activist U.N. Leader on Firing Line." *Los Angeles Times*, 9 November 1993, C1.

Milhollin, Gary. "The Iraqi Bomb." *The New Yorker*, 1 February 1993, 47+.

"Missteps by U.N. Panel Are Cited for Iraqi Resistance to Inspection." *Washington Post*, 30 July 1992, A20+.

Myre, Greg. "After 5 Years in Iraq, Work Is Still Turbulent for U.N. Arms Inspectors." *Washington Post*, 9 April 1996, A16.

"NATO balks at sharing Bosnia intelligence." *Baltimore Sun*, 27 October 1995, 15.

O'Conner, Mike. "Indicted Bosnian Serb Slips Through U.N.'s Hands." *New York Times,* 9 November 1996, 6.

Pincus, Walter. "CIA Expands Strategic, Tactical Intelligence for Diplomats in Bosnia, Official Says." *Washington Post*, 10 February 1996, A24.

________. "CIA, Military Spy Mission Set for Bosnia." *Washington Post*, 13 January 1996, A1+.

________. "Intelligence Battleground: Reform Bill." *Washington Post*, 30 May 1996, A29.

________. "Reconnaissance of Bosnia Goes On-Line." *Washington Post*, 13 April 1996, A24.

________. "U.S. Sought Other Bosnia Arms Sources." *Washington Post*, 26 April 1996, A15.

Pine, Art, and John M. Broder. "U.S. Faults Intelligence in Failed Somalia Raid." *Los Angeles Times*, 31 August 1993, 1.

Pomfret, John. "Grim Evidence Points To Muslims' Graves." *Washington Post*, 19 January 1996, A1.

"Predator Flees Bosnia For Friendlier Skies." *Defense News*, 30 October-5 November 1995, 2.

Preston, Julia. "No Mission To Burundi, U.N. Says." *Washington Post*, 3 November 1993, A10.

Priest, Dana. "U.S. to Return Documents Seized Last Year in Haiti." *Washington Post*, 6 December 1995, A33.

Quinn-Judge, Paul. "Embarrassment of Glitches at Pentagon." *Boston Globe*, 28 September 1995, 2.

"Republicans Complain About Mishandled Documents in Somalia." *Associated Press Worldstream*, 17 March 1995.

Reuhl, Lothar. "IAEA Director Views Nuclear Policies: Interview with IAEA Director General Hans Blix." *Die Welt* (Berlin), 2 August 1993, 7.

Richburg, Keith B. "Aideed Exploited UN's Failure to Prepare." *Washington Post,* 5 December 1994, A1.

________ . "In War on Aideed, UN Battled Itself." *Washington Post,* 6 December 1993, A36.

________. "Pakistani Says UN Bungled on Aideed." *Washington Post,* 3 November 1993, A11.

________. "UN Mission in Somalia Seen Beset by Infiltrators." *Washington Post,* 7 September 1993, A1.

________. "UN Report Criticizes Military Tactics of Somali Peacekeepers." *Washington Post,* 5 August 1993, A22.

________. "U.S. Completes Pullout from Somalia." *Washington Post,* 26 March 1994, A1, A18.

Risen, James. "Bosnia Denies Former Aide's Intelligence Role," *Los Angeles Times,* 13 February 1997, 6.

Rohter, Larry. "U.S. Documents Frustrate Guatemalans." *New York Times,* 9 August 1996, A12

Risen, James. "Experts Warn U.S. Intelligence Help Has Limits." *Los Angeles Times* (Wash. Ed.), 7 June 1995, 1.

Rohter, Larry. "Haiti Accuses U.S. of Holding Data Recovered by G.I.'s." *New York Times*, 28 November 1995, 1.

Sanai, Ruth. "Why Can't they Find Aidid?" (text). *Associated Press Wire Service,* 6 October 1993.

Sanger, David E. "North Korea to Drop First Veil from Nuclear Sites." *New York Times,* 4 May 1992, 7.

Scarborough, Rowan. "Pentagon Learns by Spying on Its Spies." *Washington Times*, 22 January 1996, 1.

Schmitt, Eric. "American Soldiers Will Use Weapons Honed for Bosnia." *New York Times*, 5 December 1995, 1.

Sciolino, Elaine. "U.S. Aid to Bosnia: Secret Plan Boomerangs in Congress." *New York Times*, 26 April 1996, 1+.

Seabolt, Amee. "Reservists Bolster Mission Intelligence Effort." *European Stars and Stripes*, 6 February 1996, 5.

Serrano, Richard A. "Halt Secret-Sharing With UN, GOP Urges." *Los Angeles Times*, 18 March 1995, A8.

Sloyan, Patrick J. "A Look At...The Somalia Endgame: How the Warlord Outwitted Clinton's Spooks." *Washington Post,* 3 April 1994, C3.

Sloyan, Patrick. "Low Intelligence During Gulf War." *New York Newsday*, 16 August 1993, 16.

Smith, R. Jeffrey. "GOP Asks to End Spy Data Sharing." *Washington Post*, 17 March 1995, A6.

________. "High-Tech Cooperation In Bosnia." *Washington Post*, 19 January 1995, A30.

________. "Intelligence Documents Mishandled in Somalia." *Washington Post*, 19 April 1995, A26.

________. "Iraq Bars U.N. Inspection Team Seeking Records." *Washington Post*, 9 March 1996, A18.

________. "Iraq Is Hiding 6 to 16 Scuds, U.N. Suspects." *Washington Post*, 21 March 1996, A1.

________. "N. Korea and the Bomb: High-Tech Hide-and-Seek." *Washington Post*, 27 April 1993, A1+.

________. "Tracking Aideed Hampered by Intelligence Failures." *Washington Post*, 8 October 1993, A19.

________. "U.N. Team Comes Up Empty-Handed." *Washington Post*, 30 July 1992, A20.

Smith, R. Jeffrey and Julia Preston. "Secret U.S. Papers Left In Somalia." *Washington Post*, 12 March 1995, A1.

________. "U.S. Probes Security for Somalia Files; Secret Documents Left Unprotected by UN." *Washington Post*, 12 March 1995, A1.

Starr, Barbara. "The Jane's Interview: Robert Gallucci." *Jane's Defence Weekly*, 11 February 1995, 32.

Stogel, Stewart. "Missile Plans by Iraq May Aim at Europe." *Washington Times*, 16 February 1996, A1.

"The Struggle Against Secrecy." *New York Times*, 3 January 1996, 14.

Tignor, Brooks. "Intelligence in E. Slavonia Leans Heavily on Foot Patrols. *Army Times*, 11 March 1996, 10.

Toups, Catherine. "U.N. Bars Ex-envoy From a Hearing." *Washington Times*, 13 October 1995, A19.

"U-2s in France." *Washington Post*, 6 January 1996, A13.

"UN and American Officials Mishandled U.S. Intelligence Documents." *Wall Street Journal*, 19 April 1995, A1.

"U.N. Approves Monitoring of Iraq." *Washington Post*, 28 March 1996, A28.

"UN Breached U.S. Intelligence Four Times." *Reuters World Service*, 21 March 1995.

"A U.N. Office Looks to Prevent Wars." *New York Times*, 16 April 1989, A11.

"U.N. Search in Baghdad Proves Futile." *Washington Post*, 11 March 1996, A20.

"U.S. Delegates to the UN are Named by Reagan." *New York Times*, 19 September 1985, A10.

"U.S. Inflated Jets' Blows to Iraqi Tanks." *Chicago Tribune*, 16 August 1993, 2.

"US Intelligence on Iraq Faulted." *Boston Globe*, 16 August 1993, 4.

"U.S. Miffed Over French Behavior on Rescue Tries." *Navy Times*, 9 October 1995, 24.

"U.S. Offers Communication Systems to U.N. Forces in Bosnia." *Defense Daily*, 7 June 1995, 347.

"U.S. Offers Evidence of Serb Killings." *Washington Post*, 11 August 1995, A31.

"Upbeat White House Reports on Bosnia Comes After Grim Pentagon Assessment." *Washington Times*, 21 March 1996, A10.

Urquhart, Brian, and Michael Doyle. "Peacekeeping Up to Now: Under Fire from Friend and Foe." *International Herald Tribune*, 16-17 December 1995, 6.

Vulliamy, Ed, and Peter Beaumont. "US Spells Out Ban on Intelligence Sharing With NATO." *Sunday Observer* (United Kingdom), 13 November 1994, 16.

Waller, Douglas. "Saddam Spills Secrets." *Time*, 4 September 1995, 41.

Walsh, Mark. "DIA Warns of 'Dim' Prospects For Post-NATO Bosnia Peace." *Defense Week*, 18 March 1996, 10.

Wedgwood, Ruth. "Truth Sleuth in Iraq." *Washington Post,* 19 June 1996, A19.

Weiner, Tim. "Congress Is Denied Report on Bosnia." *New York Times*, 17 April 1996, 1.

________. "Out of the Cold: U.S. and Russian Spies Share Cloaks in Bosnia." *New York Times*, 19 January 1996, 9.

Weiser, Benjamin. "The Once and Future Spy Mission." *Washington Post,* 2 November 1991, A14.

Wolf, Jim. "U.S. Misread Iraq's Bomb Plans, Report Says." *Philadelphia Inquirer*, 16 August 1993, A3.

Yost, Mark. "Shadow Boxing Off the Bosnian 'Coast.' " *Wall Street Journal*, 3 January 1996, 1+.

Appendix B
UNITED NATIONS ON-LINE DATABASES

Marilee Cunningham
Intelligence Specialist First Class, U.S. Naval Reserve
April 1997

Official UN databases provide information on peacekeeping, on humanitarian affairs, and on refugee and human rights issues. In general, UN databases provide organizational and legal background on issues, whereas international, national and non-governmental agencies make available UN-related operational information through links to publications and news services. Research centers and universities often provide full-text articles and research products.

UNITED NATIONS HOME PAGE

The United Nations Department of Public Information (DPI) manages its World Wide Web services from its Secretariat offices in New York. This is the United Nations Home Page, and is the starting point for basic UN information. On the Home Page menu, there are choices of general and topical icons. A click on an icon will move you to a second page menu with more detailed contents. For example, "About the UN" contains historical descriptions of the principal organs, the UN Charter and the Universal Declaration of Human Rights. An on-line world map allows a researcher to click on the web sites of the UN's offices or specialized agencies worldwide.

The following list of addresses for UN-related web sites may offer a useful starting point for research on UN issues. The basic UN web sites are provided first, followed by a general list of non-UN sites that relate to UN issues. Peacekeeping, humanitarian and human rights sites are listed in detail.

United Nations Internet Sites

United Nations Home Page	http://www.un.org
About the UN	http://www.un.org/aboutun/
General Information	http://www.un.org/geninfo/
Databases	http://www.un.org/databases/
What's New	http://www.un.org/NewLinks/
UN News	http://www.un.org/News/
UN Around the World	http://www.un.org/aroundworld/
UN Departments, Offices, Programs	http://www.un.org/Depts
Department of Peacekeeping Operations	http://www.un.org/Depts/dpko/
Department of Humanitarian Affairs Web	http://www.un.org/Depts/dha/
DHA Online	http://156.106.192.130/dha_ol/
DPCSD Home Page	http://www.un.org/dpcsd
Economic and Social Development	http://www.un.org/ecosocdev/
Humanitarian	http://www.un.org/ha/
Human Rights	http://www.un.org/rights/
International Law	http://www.un.org/law/
Official Web Site Locator for the UN System of Organizations	http://www.unsystem.org/
Other UN and International Organizations and Related Links	http://www.undcp.org/unlinks.html
Peace and Security	http://www.un.org/peace/
Permanent Missions to the UN	http://www.undp.org/missions/index.html
REFWORLD	http://www.unhcr.ch

ReliefWeb	http://www.reliefweb.int/
Security Council Documents	http://www.un.org/Docs/sc.htm
UNICEF Home Page	http://www.unicef.org/
UN Demining Database	http://www.un.org.Depts/Landmine
UNDP Server	http://www.undp.org
UN Documents	http://www.undcp.org/cgi-bin/docs (keyword searches) http://www.un.org/Docs/
UN Gopher Menu	gopher://nywork1.undp.org
UN Non-Governmental Liaison Service	http://www.un.org/MoreInfo/ngolink/welcome
UN Office at Geneva	http://www.unog.ch/
UN Office at Vienna	http://www.un.or.at/
UN Volunteers	http://www.unv.org gopher://gopher.unv.ch:70/1
Web Sites in the UN System	http://www.un.org/search/map/

Non-United Nations Internet Sites

Academic Council on the UN System	http://www.brown.edu/Departments/ACUNS
Afghanistan News Service	http://www.afgnews.gnet.com
American Forces Official News Site	http://www.dtic.dla.mil/afps/
American Journal of International Law	http://nisp.ncl.ac.uk/hyp
Amnesty International	http://oneworld.org/amnesty/index.html
Appendix C, International Organizations and Groups	http://www.teachersoft.com.library/ref/atlas/append03.htm
AsiaWeek	http://www.pathfinder.com/@@s4BrbAUA5Tecv0OV/Asiaweek/current/issue/current.html
Balkan Monitor	http://users.aol.com/Balkaninst/monitor.html

Best Practices Database (Togethernet)	http://www.best practices.org/html/ index.html
Bonn ICC	http://bicc.uni-bonn.de/
Bosnia Home Page	http://www.cco.caltech.edu/~bosnia
BosniaLink	http://www.dtic.dia.mil/bosnia/
Bureau of International Organizations Affairs	http://www.state.gov/www/issues/ united.html
Canadian Institute of Strategic Studies	http://www.ciss.ca
Canadian International Demining Centre	http://eagle.uccb.ns.ca/demine/
CARE, International	http://www.care.org
Carter Center	http://www.emory.edu/CARTER_CENTER/
Catholic Relief Services	http://www.devcap.org.crs/
CDI Peacekeeping Citation List	http://www.cdi.org/issues/pkcite
Center for Defense Information	http://www.cdi.org
Christian Science Monitor	http://csmonitor.com
Conflict Resolution Resources	http://infomanage.com/ConflictResolution/
Contemporary Conflicts	http://www.cfcsc.dnd.ca/links/wars/ index.html
Commission on Global Governance	http://www.cgg.ch
Commonwealth Foundation	http://www.oneworld.org/com_fnd
Cornell Law School	http://www.Law.cornell.edu
CSIS—Center for Strategic & International Studies	http://www.csis.org
Department of State	http://www.state.gov
DIANA	http://www.law.uc.edu:81/DIANA/
Disaster Response and Resources	http://www.igc.apc.org/ ia/disaster.html

Doctors Without Borders	http://www.tiac.net/users/dwb/
Economist	http://www.economist.com/
Eldis - UN Electronic Resources List	http://www.ids.ac.uk/eldis/ un/un_lele.html
European Community Humanitarian Office	http://europa.eu.int/en/comm/echo/echo.html
Eye on Africa News	http://www.webperfect.com/ afrinet/ news.html
FAS Arms and Intelligence Information	http://www.fas.org/index.html
Food for the Hungry	http://www.fh.org
Forced Migration Projects	http://www.soros.org/migmon.html
Foreign Military Studies Office	http://leav-www.army.mil/fmso/index1.htm
Geneva International Organizations	http://www.isoft.ch/GenevaGuide/orgfil/inx/ io.html
Global Communications Network	http://www.igc.apc.org
Global Democracy Network	http://server.gdn.org/gdn/
Hoover Institution	http://www-hoover.Stanford.edu/default.htm
Humanitarian Homepage	http://www.aber.ac.uk/~inpwww/res/ dissites.htm
Human Rights/ Humanitarian Assistance	http://www.pitt.edu/~ian/ resource/ human.htm
Human Rights and International Law Page	http://www.trincoll.edu/academics/ departments/pols/guide/research/ institutions.html
Human Rights Home Pages	http://www.gdn.org/links/hrhp.html
Human Rights International	http://www.intnet.net/pub/ Human-Rights/
Human Rights Quarterly	http://muse/jhu.edu/journals/ human_rights_quarterly/toc/hrqv018.htm
Human Rights Reference	http://www.fiu.edu/~caj/file8.htm

Human Rights Watch	http://www.igc.apc.org/igc/issues/hr/
Human Rights Web	http://www.hrweb.org
HungerWeb Home Page	http://www.hunger.brown.edu/Departments/World_Hunger_Program/
HSS Abstracts of Publications	http://www.isn.ethz.ch/iiss/pr.htm
IBNET International Organizations	http://www1.usa1.com/~ibnet/intorghp.html
IFOR/SFOR: Former Yugoslavia Past and Present	gopher://marvin.nc3a.nato. int:70/11/Yugomain%09$
Immigration and Refugee Rights	ftp://igc.apc.org/pub/ igc_apc_info/immigration-and-refugees
Institute of Global Conflict and Cooperation	http://www-igcc.ucsd.edu/igcc2/about.html
International Legal Materials	http://radbruch.jura.uni-mainz.de/~baab/ematerials.html
Institute on Global Conflict and Cooperation	http://www-igcc.ucsd.edu/ igcc2/about.html
Institute for National Strategic Studies, NDU	http://198.80.36.91/cgi-bin/wais.pl
Strategic Assessment 1996	http://198.80.36.91/ndu/ inss/sa96/sa96ch11.html
INTAC Human Rights Web	http://www.intac.com/PubService/human_rights/
Interaction Disaster Response	http://www.interaction.org/ia/disaster.html
International Development Exchange	http://www.idex.org/
International Institute for Sustainable Development	http://iisd1.iisd.ca/
International Organizations	gopher://marvin.nc3a.nato.int:70/11/other_International%09$

International Federation of Red Cross and Red Crescent Societies	http://www.ifrc.org
International Peacekeeping News	http://csf.colorado.edu/dfax/ipn/ipnblrb.htm
International Rescue Committee	http://www.intrescom.org/
International Service Agencies	http://www.charity.org/disast.html
Jesuit Refugee Service	http://www.intac.com/PubService/ rwanda/ jrs.html
Journal of Humanitarian Assistance	http://131.111.106.147/jha.html
Lester B. Pearson International Peacekeeping Training Centre	http://www.cdnpeacekeeping.ns.ca
Library of Congress	http://lcweb.loc.gov/Z3950/gateway.html http://lcweb2.loc.gov/glin/
Marshall European Center for Security Studies	http://www.marshall.adsn.int/ marshall.htm/
Migration News	http://migration.ucdavis.edu/mn/mntext.htm
Military Review	http://www-cgsc.army.mil/milrev/index.htm
Multilaterals Project	http://www.tufts.edu/fletcher/ multilaterals.html
Multinational Force & Observers	http://www.iaw.on.ca/~awoolley/mfo.html
National Defense University	http://www.ndu.edu/ndu/inss/strforum/ z302.html
NGO — Department of State contact	http://americas.fiu.edu/./plan.html http://131.94.20.45/plan.html

NGOs on the Internet	http://www.igc.org/igc/members/index.html http://www.clark.net/pub/pwalker/home.html http://www.jca.or.jp/index-e.html http://www.ai.mit.edu/people/ellens/non.html
North Atlantic Treaty Organization	http://www.nato.org gopher://gopher.nato.int/
Norwegian Collection of Human Rights Information	http://www.idt.unit.no/~isfit/human.rights.html
OneWorld Online	http://www.oneworld.org
Organization for Security and Cooperation	gopher://marvin.nc3a.nato.int:70/11/ Other _ International/csce%09+application/ gopher+-menu
Organization of American States	http://www.oas.org
Oxfam	http://oneworld.org/ oxfam/index.html
Pan American Health Organization	http://www.paho.org
Partnership for Peace	gopher://marvin.nc3a.nato.int:70/11/partners%09$
Peace and Security Integrated Internet Resource Guide	http://www.cfcsc.dnd.ca/links/
Peace and Conflict	gopher://csf.Colorado. EDU:70/11/peace
Peace Brigades International	http://www.eco-ops.com/pbi/links.html
Peacekeeping 96	http://www.baxter.net:80/peacekeeping
Peacekeeping-Canadian Service	http://peacekeeper.kos.net/pk1.html
Peacekeeping Veterans Page	http://www.islandnet.com/~duke/cpva.htm
Project on Peacekeeping and the UN	http://www.clw.org/pub/clw/un/unpeace.html
Program on Peacekeeping Policy	http://ralph.gmu.edu/cfpa/peace/peace.html

Progressive Directory of the Institute for INTAC Access Corporation	http://http.intac.com/PubService
Rand Research Briefs	http://www.rand.org/ publications/RB/ #internat
Refugee and Human Rights Internet Resources	http://www.yorku.ca/research/crs/ internet.htm
Refugees International	http://www.refintl.org/
Refugee Studies Programme	http://www.geh.ox.ac.uk/rsp/
ReliefNet	http://www.reliefnet.org
ReliefWeb	http://www.reliefweb.int/
Researching Indigenous Peoples' Rights	http://www.law.uc.edu:81/Diana/ipr.html
Rice Library Section	gopher://riceinfo.rice.edu
Russia Today Home Page	http://www.russiatoday.com/
Social Issues and Services	gopher://vienna.hh.lib.umich.edu
Stimson Center	http://www.stimson.org/pub/stimson/
Stockholm International Peace Research Institute	http://www.sipri.se/
Swedish Armed Forces International Centre	http://www.mil.se/fm/arme/swedint/ compcent.htm
Texas State Electronic Library	http://link.tsl.texas.gov/
Treaties	gopher://wiretap.spies.com
UN Association in Canada	http://www.unac.org/index.html
UN Documents	http://www.umn.edu/humanrts/un-orgs.htm
UN Yale Scholars' Workstation	http://www.library.yale.edu/ un/unhome.htm
University Center for International Studies at University of North Carolina	http://sunsite.unc.edu/ucis/

University of Cincinnati College of Law's DIANA	http://www./law.uc.edu:81/DIANA/
University of Minnesota Human Rights Library	http://www.umn.edu/humanrts
U.S. Agency for International Development (USAID)	http://www.info.usaid.gov
U.S. Army	http://www.army.mil
U.S. Army War College	http://carlisle-www.army.mil/usawc/
U.S. Army War College Library	http://carlisle-www.army.mil/ library/
U.S. Army War College Library	http://carlisle-www.army.mil/ library/bibs/ peace96.htm
U.S. Army War College Quarterly, Parameters	http://carlisle-www.army.mil/usawc/ Parameters/a-Index.htm
U.S. Information Service-European Focus-Croatia	gopher://smile.srce.hr
U.S. Institute of Peacc	http://www.usip.org/
Virtual Library on International Development	http://www.ids.ac.uk
Voice of America	http://www.voa.gov
War Crimes Tribunal Home Page	http://www.cij.org/tribunal http://www.igc.apc.org/TRIBUNAL/
War Criminals	http://www.cco.caltech.edu/~bosnia/ criminal/criminals.html
Woodrow Wilson Center	http://wwics.si.edu/
World Bank	http://www.worldbank.org
World Health Organization	http://www.who.org
Yale University Law School	http://elsinore.cis.yale.edu/ dianaweb/ diana.htm

ABOUT THE PRINCIPAL AUTHOR

Perry L. Pickert holds a degree in Law from George Mason University and a PhD from the Fletcher School of Law and Diplomacy of Tufts University. He has taught at the Doshisha University in Kyoto, Japan, and at the Joint Military Intelligence College. Dr. Pickert has served on active duty in the U.S. Marine Corps, and is currently a Colonel in the Marine Corps Reserve. He has served as an intelligence analyst at the Central Intelligence Agency and Defense Intelligence Agency. His publications include papers on Japanese foreign policy, jurisprudence, the law of treaties and international law.

Index

A

B

C

D

E

F

H

I

J

M

N

O

P

R

S

T

U

V

W